*A History of the American Worker*

*1920–1933*

# THE LEAN YEARS

*Irving Bernstein*

**Introduction by Frances Fox Piven**

Haymarket Books
Chicago, Illinois

This edition published in 2010 by Haymarket Books
First published in 1969 by Houghton Mifflin
© 1969 Irving Bernstein
Introduction © 2010 Frances Fox Piven

Haymarket Books
PO Box 180296
Chicago, IL 60618
773-583-7884
www.haymarketbooks.org
info@haymarketbooks.org

Trade distribution:
In the U.S. through Consortium Book Sales and Distribution, www.cbsd.com
In Canada, Publishers Group Canada, www.pgcbooks.ca
In the UK, Turnaround Publisher Services, www.turnaround-uk.com
In Australia, Palgrave Macmillan, www.palgravemacmillan.com.au
All other countries, Publishers Group Worldwide, www.pgw.com

Cover design by Adam Bohannon.
Upper cover photo of an unemployed worker during the Depression. Lower
cover photo of a scuffle with a store-keeper attempting to scab on a strike at the
Jones and Laughlin Corporation steel plant in Pennslyvania, May 1937.

Published with the generous support of Lannan Foundation
and the Wallace Global Fund.

ISBN 978-1-608460-63-2

Library of Congress Cataloging-in-Publication data is available.

Printed in Canada

# Contents

TO THE MEMORY
OF
*Edgar L. Warren*
*1904–1956*

# Jon Kelley Wright
## Workers' Memorial Book Series

On September 22, 2007, the Chrysler Corporation murdered Jon Kelley Wright. After working over twenty years at their Kokomo, Indiana, die-casting plant, the machine he operated crushed him to death because faulty safety equipment had been disabled instead of replaced. Kelley was an outspoken critic of management's dangerous practices and an advocate for safety on the job. Months before his death, he helped organize meetings where management said that replacing the safety equipment "wouldn't be cost effective."

As the beneficiary on one of my uncle's modest life insurance policies, I endowed the Jon Kelley Wright Workers' Memorial Fund through the Center for Economic Research and Social Change. This fund allows Haymarket Books to publish a series of books about the labor movement and struggles of working people to change the world.

Thousands of people are killed on the job each year just in the United States. We invite anyone who has lost someone due to an unsafe workplace to memorialize their loved one through this book series. To read the memorials and find out more, please visit: http://WorkersMemorialFund.org.

I hope that the Jon Kelley Wright Workers' Memorial Book Series will inspire others to dedicate their lives to the struggle for a world where safety on the job is more important than profits, and that it will help keep the memory of my beloved uncle alive.

In solidarity,
Derek Wright

To contribute to this project, please send tax-deductible donations to the fund payable to "CERSC" (with "Workers' Memorial Fund" in the memo) to:CERSC, P.O. Box 258082, Chicago, IL 60625

*The Lean Years* is a book from the research program of the Institute of Industrial Relations, University of California, Los Angeles. Paul Bullock of the Institute Staff did much of the research for this book and was of inestimable value throughout its preparation.

# *Preface*

In this work I have sought to break with the tradition that has dominated the writing of American labor history. The labor economists pre-empted this field at the end of the nineteenth century and their influence — notably in the towering figure of John R. Commons — has since been supreme. Most of their energies have gone into the examination of two interrelated problems — the emergence and development of the trade union as an institution and its place in the labor market. These are important problems from many points of view, including history. I do not believe, however, that they are all of labor history.

Hence this book covers a wider field. It begins with the worker rather than with the trade union. I am, of course, concerned about the worker when he is organized and devote considerable attention to the manner in which his union bargains for him. But this is not all. I am also interested in him when he is unorganized, in his legal status, in his political behavior, in his social and cultural activities, and in how the employer and the state treat him. In other words, this book is about the worker in American society at a particular stage of its development. This approach, it seems to me, is unusually fitting for the twenties and the early years of the Great Depression, because this was a time in which unions went into decline and collective bargaining had little impact.

Those who have recently written about this period have encountered disbelief among some of their readers. The present world is so far removed from the world of the twenties and especially of the thirties that many who did not live through the earlier times or who have forgotten them refuse to believe things were so different. These authors, some conclude, have written fiction rather than history. If readers of this book react this way, I suggest that they assault the mountain of citations at the back of the volume. This is a challenge and not a recommendation.

This book is the first part of a larger work. I plan to write a second volume on the history of American labor from the inception of the New Deal to World War II.

My debt to others for help is incalculable. Most of all it is to the Institute of Industrial Relations of the University of California, Los Angeles, which provided finances, research assistance, library facilities, editorial and stenographic aid, and, most important, a climate that encouraged scholarly work. The Sidney Hillman Foundation generously made two grants to underwrite travel to archives and libraries. The following persons diligently collected materials: Gerard A. Brandmeyer, Robert I. Conhaim, Daniel S. Day, Robert L. Harper, Martin Horowitz, Wilford G. Hunter, Paul Jacobs, Ramon E. Ruiz, Mrs. Rachel R. Seldin, and Hyman Weintraub. Paul Bullock's contributions (good cheer was by no means least) must be described as massive. Mrs. Anne P. Cook edited and Mrs. Lois Hurwitz typed the manuscript, each with customary assiduity and care. Many librarians and archivists put up with unreasonable and unseasonable demands. Since they are so numerous and I should not want to discriminate, I thank them in a body. The following persons were kind enough to read the manuscript, and they offered many suggestions for its improvement: Benjamin Aaron, H. M. Douty, Herman Kahn, George E. Mowry, Melvin Rothbaum, Karl de Schweinitz, and Craig Wylie. Ultimately, I am responsible for errors and deficiencies in the book.

IRVING BERNSTEIN

Sherman Oaks, California

# *Introduction*

WITH THE ONSET of the Great Recession of 2008, many observers began to look back to the era of the Great Depression for the lessons that period could offer about our ongoing economic and social troubles. And there is no better way to begin the search for lessons than in a reading or rereading of Irving Bernstein's two-volume masterful history of the 1920s and 1930s.

Bernstein's project in these volumes is to write nothing less than a comprehensive history of American workers during the climactic decades that transformed the country. He approaches his task with a zeal for the facts that we associate with the best of investigative reporters, following each lead wherever the trail goes, and I think it is this radical empiricism that makes his work so valuable and so enduring. He wants to know everything that bears on the experience of working people, and he draws his sense of what is significant broadly from the social sciences. So we learn a lot, about the changing demography of the working class, shifting patterns of settlement as European migration slowed and internal migration from farm to city increased; about changes in wages and hours and overall employment, the new developments in production and the organization of work; about speedup and the often suffocating influence of small-town churches in league with employers; about company towns organized like plantations, and factories seeded with employer spies and goons; and about the paralysis of the unions and the voting patterns of workers. These are all relatively conventional "variables" in descriptions of the working class. However, Bernstein's zealous empiricism leads him to go beyond the usual material to provide a detailed and wide-ranging survey of worker resistance that took unconventional form in mob actions, demonstrations, self-help efforts, and strikes.

Of course, no one can simply be an empiricist, a compiler of the facts and nothing but the facts. Obviously, judgments have to be made about which evidence is to be gathered, where to search for it, how to assess its reliability, and how to order, present, and interpret it. Inevitably, the researcher, whether investigative reporter or historian, approaches his or her subject with a philosophy and at least the rudiments of a theory. Bernstein did have a philosophy and a theory. Broadly, he belonged to the school of historians we call progressives, meaning simply that he thinks there is a forward direction to our history, that we are getting better and wiser, and as we do, we improve and reform our social institutions.

In particular, Bernstein believed that with intelligence and good will, we would reform our industrial and capitalist system. He worked at the University of California's Institute of Industrial Relations and imbibed deeply the gospel of labor experts associated with the reform labor policies of the New Deal. One pillar of the faith had to do with government protection of workers from the instabilities of markets and the contingencies of biological frailty. The social policies that were advocated included unemployment benefits, old age and sickness and disability insurance, and cash assistance to those who were orphaned, or blind, or disabled. Another set of ideas had to do more directly with the governance of industrial relations, and was directed particularly to securing stability and balance in the sphere of production. Bernstein entitled chapter 1 of *The Lean Years* "The Worker in an Unbalanced Society," and by "unbalanced" he meant an imbalance of rewards, particularly as wages fell and unemployment rose after the collapse of 1929, and an imbalance of power in the workplace. The imbalance of power was the more fundamental condition, for it not only enabled employers to press down hard on wages, but it left workers with little recourse against hard and unsafe working conditions, against the speedup (or the stretch-out, as it was known in the textile industry), or simply against the capricious and arbitrary boss or foreman. The solution constituted the second pillar of the faith:

government regulation of wages, hours, and working conditions, and government protection of the right of workers to organize.

In this first volume, Bernstein carefully traces the experience of working people from 1920 to 1933, from the years of the roaring twenties through the trough of the economic collapse that began in 1929, up to the swearing in of the Roosevelt Administration. As in our own time, the market collapse was preceded by a period of boom and speculation that produced huge fortunes for a few, and a culture that celebrated fabulous riches and excess. But money, booze, jazz, and flappers notwithstanding, the decade also brought hard times to many workers. Mining, agriculture, and textiles were in a slump, and the workers in these sectors bore the hardships that resulted. The first worker protests of the era erupted out of the desperation of hard-pressed Southern textile workers who had only recently left impoverished tenant farms and mountain villages for the textile mills and found themselves ground down by exhausting work for long hours in filthy mills and for pitiful earnings. (It was of course this vulnerable labor force that drew textile manufacturers to the south, sometimes from as far away as Germany, so globalization is not really new.) The mill workers finally rose up early in 1929. But their strikes were ultimately crushed by the conditions that have always thwarted unionism in the American South: the religiosity and xenophobia of Southern communities, state and local politicians ready to ally with employers, the easy resort to violence, and the feebleness of the efforts of national unions to organize under these conditions.

Over the next four years, the poverty and unemployment that afflicted the South spread across the country as the Great Depression took its toll in rapidly rising unemployment, wage cuts, worsening working conditions, evictions and foreclosures, and even cases of actual starvation. But most observers saw little evidence of a spirit of rebellion. Bernstein quotes Louis Adamic in December 1931, when unemployment was soaring, "I have a definite feeling...that millions of them, now that they are unemployed, are licked" (435). "Workers on the way down," writes Bernstein, "were in no mood to improve, far less to reorganize, society" (436).

In other words, viewed from afar, most of the people who were suffering the hardships of the Depression were depressed and even ashamed, ready to blame themselves for their plight. But the train of developments that connects changes in social conditions to a changed consciousness is not simple. People, including ordinary people, harbor somewhere in their memories the building blocks of different and contradictory interpretations of what it is that is happening to them, of who should be blamed, and what can be done about it. Even the hangdog and ashamed unemployed worker who swings his lunch box and strides down the street so the neighbors will think he is going to a job can also have other ideas that only have to be evoked, and when they are, make it possible for him on another day to rally with others and rise up in anger at his condition.

Bernstein is too much the empiricist, too much the detail man, to ignore the growing if scattered evidence even in the early years of the Depression of defiance and protest. His historical account is distinctive for the attention it gives to the episodes of mobbing and rioting that marked the early 1930s, and it is also unusual for his effort to chronicle the efforts of radical organizers to escalate or channel this defiance, and this despite his general disapproval of those radicals, especially those who were Communists.

From time immemorial, hungry people have mobbed and looted food from local markets, and they did this again in the early years of the Depression, although no accurate accounting of these episodes exists if only because the merchants whose supplies were taken feared that calling the police would lead to the press coverage that would only encourage more episodes. Prodded by desperation, people also flocked to unemployment demonstrations, often organized by Communists, and usually (often not without reason) labeled riots by the press. Beginning in 1929 and 1930, crowds assembled, raised demands for "bread or wages," and then marched on City Hall or on such local relief offices as existed.

In the big cities, mobs of people used strong-arm tactics to resist the rising numbers of evictions. In Harlem and the Lower

East Side, crowds numbering in the thousands gathered to restore evicted families to their homes. In Chicago, small groups of Black activists marched through the streets of the ghetto to mobilize the large crowds that would reinstall evicted families. A rent riot left three people dead and three policemen injured in August 1931, but Mayor Anton Cermak ordered a moratorium on evictions, and some of the rioters got work relief. Later, in August 1932, Cermak told a House committee that if the federal government did not send $150 million for relief immediately, it should be prepared to send troops later. Even in Mississippi, Governor Theodore Bilbo told an interviewer: "Folks are restless. Communism is gaining a foothold. Right here in Mississippi, some people are about ready to lead a mob. In fact, I'm getting a little pink myself." Meanwhile, also in summer 1932, farmers across the country armed themselves with pitchforks and clubs to prevent the delivery of farm products to markets where the price paid frequently did not cover the cost of production.

Before much of this desperation was registered in the mass media or in the musings of intellectuals, it was registered in the voting booths. In the election of 1932, Americans elected Franklin Delano Roosevelt to the presidency, and a Democratic majority to the Congress. It was one of the infrequent great realignments of American electoral politics. Still, no one could be sure of its significance. After all, the Democratic platform of 1932 was not much different than the platforms of 1924 and 1928. In fact, the election did usher in a new era, although it was not the election alone. Rather it was the complex and intricate dynamic that ensued between political leaders and the aroused populace with whom they now had to contend. The New Deal that they created together is the subject of *The Turbulent Years*, the second volume of Bernstein's magisterial study.

Frances Fox Piven
February 2010

# Revolt in the Piedmont

IN THE GOLDEN SPRING of 1929 nature smiled in the Southern Appalachian Piedmont. To the west in the misted mountain mass of the Blue Ridge and the Great Smokies the redbud and the dogwood were in flower and the mountain laurel, the rhododendron, and the burning bush (called by the mountain folk "hearts-a-bustin'-with-love") were in bloom. From Virginia to Georgia the streams flowed placidly down the Ridge across the red clay of the rolling Piedmont hills out to the sea: the Roanoke, the Dan, the Broad, the Catawba, the Yadkin, the Wateree, the Pacolet, the Tiger, the Saluda, the Rocky, the Savannah. This historic southern land with its profoundly agricultural tradition seemed far removed, indeed, from the dynamic centers of American society — the great cities of the East, the Midwest, and the Far West with their agglomerations of money, workers, technology, production, and culture. Yet, here in the Piedmont, in this remote and unlikely region, events occurred in that fateful spring that were to foreshadow in the most remarkable detail the turbulent labor history of the whole nation in the decade that followed.

1

The agricultural character of the Piedmont began a slow metamorphosis after Appomattox. The ready availability of water power at the fall line of the rivers, of bituminous coal, of raw cotton, of a favorable climate, and, above all, of cheap labor proved inviting to the textile industry. The invasion by the mills stepped up markedly in the present century. By the time Herbert Hoover was inaugurated as President on the 4th of March 1929, the Southern Appalachian area had become the paramount textile-producing region of the United States. The stations on the main route of the Southern Railway through the Piedmont from Washington to Atlanta read like a directory of textile centers: Lynchburg, Danville, Greensboro, High Point, Salisbury, Charlotte, Gastonia, Gaffney, Spartanburg, Greenville, and Gainesville. The towns clustered along the railroad like beads on a string and the traveler was seldom out of sight of a mill. The local boosters, echoing in softer accents Sinclair Lewis' Babbitt in Zenith, bragged of a mill to a mile.

They knew whereof they spoke, for the textile industry formed the fulcrum of economic life and the outlook for the future of the region turned upon it. The manufacturing census of 1927, for example, revealed that the nation's cotton textile production was concentrated in the South, 67 per cent as measured by yardage and 56 per cent by value. Of some 1,100,000 workers in all branches of the industry in the late twenties, about 300,000 were in the South, with 100,000 in North Carolina, 69,000 in South Carolina, and 25,000 in Tennessee. The predominant segment, of course, was cotton, but rayon made its appearance at this time as did the hosiery mills, escaping northern unionism and high wage rates.

The community acknowledged the standing of the industry by yielding to its management the decisive voice in shaping southern affairs. "The cotton industry," George Sinclair Mitchell remarked, "reproduced for its owners the position of power held by the masters of plantations." Sinclair Lewis, after a trip to Marion, North Carolina, in 1929, put it characteristically: " . . . the mills control the banks, the banks control the loans to small businessmen, the small businessmen are the best customers of the professional men — even when the latter are professional men of God — and so the mills can back up the whole human train, down to the clerical caboose." On issues that affected their interests the millowners exercised firm control over the machinery of state and local government. Nearly all representatives and senators from the southern textile states in Washington felt it their sacred duty to protect the industry against outside encroachment in such matters as foreign competition, the child labor amendment, and federal investigation of working conditions. When an occasional critical voice was raised in protest, like that of forty-one southern churchmen in 1927 in "An Appeal to Industrial Leaders of the South," the millowners' hostility guaranteed that it would not be heard.

But, despite general prosperity in the United States, all was not well with the industry at this time. Economists muttered about the "sickness" of textiles, as they did about coal, pointing to the gnawing problem of overproduction in a shrinking market. The downturn began in 1924, preceding the onset of the Great Depression by half a decade. A leading student of the industry, Claudius T. Murchison, observed that an average of twenty-five textile shares fell from $144.50 in 1923 to $71.48 in 1930, almost all prior to the crash. Less than half the southern mills paid dividends in 1929, and there were many bankruptcies. He noted "the extraordinary instability of operations with which the industry is cursed" resulting from economic forces that "constitute a perfect carnival of violence and unrestraint." In the twenties phenomenal gyrations in the price of raw cotton caused fluctuations in output that had no relation to demand. The postwar emphasis on the "treacherous whims of fashion" was hard on an industry accustomed to staples. The flapper's newly revealed knee dimples were eyed pleasurably by all men except those in the textile business. Style even infected denims, ginghams, Osnaburgs, overalls, draperies, curtains, upholstery, sheets, and flour bags. Competition from abroad and from other fibers, notably silk and rayon, took large bites out of the domestic market for cotton. Finally, the machinery for selling mill products through the commission merchant generated continuous downward pressure on prices. An unrationalized industry, consisting primarily of small, locally owned units, was helpless against these forces.

Instability forced mill management to take a long hard look at costs, primarily labor costs. Each mill strove to capture a larger share of the shrinking market by producing more at lower unit costs. The pursuit of individual salvation ended in collective damnation. The tools with which employers turned the screws on labor were basically the stretch-out and night work. The stretch-out (known as the speed-up in other industries) was the requirement that the worker operate more machines without an increase in wages. Textile firms, North and South, introduced this system generally in the late twenties. The manner is illustrated by a story, doubtless apocryphal, that went the rounds in the South at the time.

> A man went to the plant and asked for a job. The boss said, "All right! but before we give you a job I will give you a test." . . . The boss gave him a hand brush and said: "You throw that hand brush as far as you can." The fellow had been a baseball player, and he flung the brush down to the other side of the weave shop. The boss said: "All right! the job is yours. You run all these looms."

The stretch-out, W. J. Cash wrote, "violated the whole tradition of the South." Southerners were wrenched out of their native easy-going ways and required to expend more energy than the climate permitted. The device for raising output quickly at low cost was night work, called by President Thomas F. McMahon of the Textile Workers the "blight that is in our industry." Though many employers detested it, no one was influential enough alone to lead in abolishing the practice.[1]

The South's greatest asset in its bid for industrialization was its workers, for their services were in enormous supply and could be bought at pitifully cheap rates. They came almost exclusively from two sources: the poor white tenants and the mountain people, both predominantly Anglo-Saxon and long settled in the area as subsistence farmers. There were virtually no migrants from other regions or immigrants from foreign lands. The South had many more potential workers than the mills could absorb, creating a chronic labor surplus. The tenants and the mountaineers shared a common derivation from a poverty-stricken agriculture. In 1927, for example, average annual gross agricultural income in ten southern states was only $609 as contrasted with $1611 in the rest of the nation. The mill was an attractive alternative; 500 families in Gaston County, North Carolina, studied in 1926–27, had an average income of $1313. "The factory held out a promise," in Harry M. Douty's words, "that the land had not fulfilled." That promise was more than economic; in place of the isolation of the farm, the factory offered the human contact of the community and the glamour of town life. When Ishma Waycaster, the mountain girl heroine of Fielding Burke's novel, received from her schoolteacher a subscription to a women's magazine,

It opened gates to a way of living so enticing in comfort, so engaging in form, so ravishing in color, that it seemed nothing short of celestial. . . . Those doorways, those halls, those vistas of bedrooms, those shimmering bath-rooms, those gleaming floors, those radiant nooks and corners of beauty, with the graceful beings from another world, curving, bending, smiling, always smiling. They took her breath.

When Ishma and her fellow workers came to the mills from the mountains and the farms they brought little with them except children, sometimes not even a surname. The region had a high birth rate; measured by procreation, North Carolina ranked first among the states. This was critical in the mills because the unit of employment was the family rather than the individual, a condition accepted with equal grace by both parties to the employment bargain. From the employer's standpoint, the family was more efficient. Many jobs required nimbleness of finger and keenness of eyesight; hence the employer's interest was in the young rather than the old. Children, not the mill, assumed the obligation to support those no longer employable. Finally, the employer subsidized housing and sought a maximum yield in labor from his outlay. To the worker in a rural tradition family employment seemed in the nature of things. He had little interest in and less knowledge of education as an avenue of improvement for his children. Since juvenile delinquency was common, he preferred the mill to the gang. And, most important, he was incapable of supporting his family on his own earnings. It was a condition of survival that his wife, or his children, or both should work. J. J. Rhyne found as a consequence that "relatively few children . . . were not working in the mill or else caring for younger brothers or sisters while the mother worked."

One class of family, however, was virtually barred from employment in the cotton factory: the Negro's. "The iron tradition of the South," Paul Blanshard wrote, "is that no white man will work in the same factory room with a Negro." As a result, of some 100,000 textile workers in North Carolina in 1930, fewer than 3000 were colored. The jobs they filled were the least attractive — those of firemen, coal rollers, scrubbers, and sweepers.

The southern millowner recognized that his cheap and plentiful labor supply was his primary asset and portrayed it with glowing pride. "This population," President John E. Edgerton of the National Association of Manufacturers, himself a southern textile executive, declared, " . . . is a native soil in which exotic radicalism does not thrive, for the worker of the South has a heritage of sturdy Americanism that . . . makes him a dependable factor in industry." With the prospect of persuading a northern factory to move, this reverential language gave way to the vulgate of the marketplace. "I believe," H. A. Wheeling, secretary of the Florence, South Carolina, Chamber of Commerce, wrote a potential migrant, "you will find the labor situation here unusually attractive. Our wages for female labor range from $6 to $12 per week."

These southern millhands were, in Edgerton's phrase, indeed of "native soil," displaying the characteristics of a rural people. They retained the farmer's individualism and, in the case of the mountaineer, went beyond to a militant independence of spirit. "Every tub," they would say, "must set on its own bottom." These workers were, as well, conservative, heedless alike of both change and progress. Those who had grown cotton in the lowlands were accustomed to spending six months in the year "settin' and studyin'," and the mountain folk to even more. Life's pace dragged, without hurry or bustle, reflecting the objective of "the maximum of comfort with the minimum of exertion." Their anger, slowly and rarely aroused, was passionate and violent and quickly passed. Emotion was normally soaked up by the churches, preponderantly the evangelical Protestant sects. Religion provided an intense personal experience and the church was the focus of noneconomic communal activity. Closely related was music. Here was a people constantly lifting their voices in song, unable to "smother down" their notes. Their music appealed "to the hands and feet more than to the head." Homogeneous and ingrown, they fused social isolation with sectionalism into an abiding distrust of outsiders, especially those from the North. The millhands were industrial nomads, moving constantly from job to job, seldom staying long enough to grow feet "with roots to 'em." Their only way to protest ubiquitously bad conditions was to quit. Hence the mills struggled with an abnormally high rate of labor turnover. The workers replied to complaints: "Movin's cheaper 'n' payin' rent." The price of shiftlessness was backwardness. When the Saxon Mills of Spartanburg, South Carolina, installed bathtubs in their houses, one worker used his to scald a hog and others to store wood, coal, and potatoes. For the millhands this world was without hope and time stood still.[2]

The machine that controlled this transitory labor supply was the mill village. This institution arose historically out of the need to group and house workers for a mill set down in a rural area. Since the labor was poor and so unable to house itself, and local real estate capital was not available, the burden fell upon the factory. With time, however, the purpose shifted to giving the millowner control over his labor force. Tom Tippett wrote:

He owns the community and he regulates the life that goes on there after the day's work is over in his mill. He has the power to discharge the worker at the mill, to refuse him credit at his store, to dump a worker's furniture out of a house, to have him expelled from church, to bar his children from school, and to withhold the service of a doctor or hospital.

The manager of a South Carolina mill declared disarmingly, "We govern like the Czar of Russia."

Company houses were located near the mill so that the employees would hear the factory whistle at 5 A.M. A study of North Carolina villages in 1926–27 revealed that the houses averaged 4.1 rooms, 71 per cent had running water, 70 per cent had inside toilets, 93 per cent had electricity, and virtually none had telephones. For this the millhand paid the very low rental of $4 per month, deducted from his pay. These residences were of relatively good quality. In Marion, on the other hand, Sinclair Lewis found "bonny homes" without running water or toilets, with overcrowding, with newspaper for wallpaper, and with clapboards he could pry apart with his little finger. "This packing box on stilts," he wrote, "is the way in which we teach them [the workers] that in this country the results of honest labor are a splendor unlike that of the hovels of the Old World."

Housing served as an implement of social stratification in the mill community. Workers lived in one part of the village and "uptown" (owners, supervisors, professionals, white-collar people, teachers, and independent artisans) in another. If there were a stream, it served as the geographic and social frontier. "It would be as unthinkable," wrote Liston Pope, "in most uptown homes of Gastonia to invite a 'common millhand' to dinner as it would be to invite a Negro." This cleavage carried over to the churches. Those who suffered from segregation harbored a deep resentment.

The millowners sought to brighten this drab existence with welfare work. Most important, because of the low level of education and the high incidence of illiteracy, was support for the public schools. The mills customarily provided all or part of the income of the superintendent and the teachers, thereby gaining dominance over policy and personnel. In addition, they often supplied community buildings, cafeterias, hospitals, playgrounds, and related facilities and equipment. Home economics, desperately needed to overcome diet deficiencies of animal proteins inducing pellagra and respiratory diseases, was sometimes taught to women. The mills, of course, subsidized the churches by providing land, meeting construction costs, paying the minister's salary and giving him gratuities at Christmas and at other times for trips. As a result, religion was a branch of the textile industry. "The ministers of Gastonia," one of them admitted, "never take the initiative on economic . . . questions. They are opposed only to things downright evil, such as pool rooms." A candid South Carolina executive put it this way: "We had a young fellow from an Eastern seminary down here as pastor . . . and the young fool went around saying that we helped pay the preachers' salaries in order to control them. That was a damn lie — and we got rid of him." [3]

Whatever liberality the mills may have shown in paying their ministers was not carried over to paying their workers. The story of income in the southern textile industry in the twenties is a dismal account of poverty. "Cotton Mill Colic," popular during the Danville strike, went:

> *I'm a-going to starve,*
> *Everybody will,*
> *Cause you can't make a living*
> *In a cotton mill.*

Senators who investigated southern textiles in 1929 concluded that the industry's wages were the lowest in manufacturing with the possible exception of tobacco, and that southern cotton mills paid only half as much as the all-manufacturing average. Hourly rates for twelve occupations in five southern states in 1928 averaged but 29.1 cents, and weekly earnings in four states averaged only $12.83. This appalling condition was alleviated only in small part by goods and services supplied by the mill-village system: low rents, coal at cost, cheap medical service, and other "welfare" activities. The widely held — and nurtured — notion that the cost of living was low in the southern textile towns was nonsense.

The facts with regard to hours and working conditions were, if anything, more depressing. The ten- or eleven-hour day was typical and a twelve-hour shift was not uncommon. Rhyne found the sixty-hour week prevailing in Gaston County: 6 A.M. to noon and 1 to 6 P.M. on weekdays, with a shift from 6 to 11 A.M. on Saturday. At the Loray mill the turn was twelve hours and at Marion twelve hours and twenty minutes, sometimes hitched to a twelve-hour Saturday to produce a work week in excess of seventy-two hours. As already noted, night work was normal and women and children, who constituted a large segment of the labor force, were employed after dark. Even in the best of the mills the nature of the work imposed severe strain and was carried on amid a terrible din of machinery in temperatures near 85 degrees. In the worst, like those in Marion, Sinclair Lewis discovered not only "clamorous shuttles . . . and ghastly fatigue," but also filthy floors, revolting toilets, and snuff chewers spitting into the drinking fountains. It is difficult to imagine which prospect was more disheartening for the mother of a large family: to start a long shift in such a mill or to end it, exhausted, and then begin the cooking and household chores for her family.[4]

The protective legislation of the southern textile states was a hollow shell. South Carolina, at least, had no workmen's compensation. Alabama imposed no limit on hours; North Carolina and Georgia restricted the work week to sixty, Tennessee to fifty-seven, and South Carolina to fifty-five hours. In all these states children fourteen and over and women were allowed to work at night. When, on July 1, 1929, Japan prohibited night work by women and children, China, India, and the United States shared the distinction of being the only important nations to countenance this condition. It is likely that the failings of enforcement were even more serious than the statutes themselves; if the industry had not resisted investigation so vigorously, one could speak with more authority. The only survey was made by five members of the South Carolina House of Representatives in 1929. They concluded that the record was "replete with instances of violations . . . in regard to the regulations of working conditions in the textile manufacturing corporations." The South Carolina Commissioner of Agriculture, Commerce, and Industry almost invariably dismissed complaints, prosecuting only five violators in three years and imposing a maximum fine of $50. The legislators found his department in "a state of inertia and lethargy," and himself "quite wakeful" in only one respect, "to suppress and excuse practically every violation of the labor laws." This lends credence to the common observation that children under fourteen worked in the mills.[5]

These wage and hour conditions gave rise to a notable economic issue of the period, the North-South differential. Though reasonable — and unreasonable — men disputed over its size, no one doubted its existence regardless of yardstick. A survey of hourly rates in twelve textile jobs in 1928 showed an average of 29.1 cents in five southern states as contrasted with 41.4 cents in New England. A Bureau of Labor Statistics study of weighted average hourly earnings for seventeen occupations revealed a difference of 43.6 per cent in 1928. For that year the same agency found weekly earnings in the Carolinas, Georgia, and Alabama averaging $12.83 as compared to $19.16 in New England. The census of 1927 showed that annual earnings in cotton goods in the South averaged $671 in contrast with $1012 in the remainder of the nation. The argument that cheap housing and welfare services justified this spread was discounted by a group of southern scholars who studied the problem. On the contrary, the differential, according to *Business Week*, was "the lure dangled before the noses of harassed New England mill owners." [6]

Despite these wretched conditions, southern cotton-textile workers were completely unorganized. In fact, unionism in the North was also weak and there were deep cleavages between organizations in the industry. Much the most important was the United Textile Workers, affiliated with the American Federation of Labor. In 1929, UTW reported its membership at 30,000, less than 3 per cent of the 1,100,000 workers in all branches of textiles. The whole membership lived in the North and almost half of it was concentrated in the semiautonomous and growing American Federation of Full-Fashioned Hosiery Workers. In basic cotton textiles only 10,000 of half a million workers were organized, primarily in Salem and New Bedford, Massachusetts. In fact, UTW declined in cotton in New England during the twenties with the shrinking market and the southward flight of the mills. It made only the most irresolute efforts to counter these forces by organizing the South. To retain its tiny foothold, the union shifted at this time from militancy to union-management cooperation, notably in the Naumkeag experiment at Pequot Mills in Salem, conforming thereby to the general drift of AFL policy. "The union," Robert R. R. Brooks concluded, "appeared to consist almost entirely of a suite of offices, a complement of officers, and a splendid array of filing cabinets."

In addition to internal weakness, UTW suffered from a long and bitter history of rival unionism stemming from "the distinguishing characteristic of textile unionism . . . its centrifugal tendencies." These contending organizations, Brooks wrote,

have proselyted each other's members, broken each other's strikes, disrupted each other's meetings, and exhausted the vituperative possibilities of the English language in mutual vilification. If one union has been less abusive than another, it has apparently been the result of an imperfection of imagination rather than a deficiency of sincere malevolence.

Itself a combined industrial and amalgamated craft structure, UTW was prey to raids from craft unions on the right, principally the Mulespinners and Lace Operatives, and revolutionary industrial organizations on the left, notably the Industrial Workers of the World and the National Textile Workers Union. This last, an arm of the Communist Party, sparked the tinder of rival unionism in the Piedmont revolt.

This organization grew out of textile strikes in the North and the world-wide shift in Communist trade-union policy in the late twenties. The bitter, violent, and unsuccessful Passaic silk strike of 1926 and the New Bedford cotton strike of 1928 provided the Communists with a nucleus of followers in the industry, whom UTW began to expel from its ranks in the latter year. This coincided with the decision of the fourth convention of the Red International of Labor Unions in Moscow in 1928 to move in all countries from "boring from within" to dual unionism. Hence the Communist Party of the United States in 1929 replaced its Trade Union Educational League, devoted to penetrating the American Federation of Labor, with the Trade Union Unity League, a rival federation. The New Bedford left-wingers in a convention on September 22–23, 1928, had already created the National Textile Workers Union, the first of the dual unions that were to make up TUUL.[7]

This, then, was the ore body from which the Piedmont revolt was to be fashioned. The jackhammer hole was drilled in the rock; the dynamite was in place; the fuse was laid. All that remained was for the charge to be ignited and the explosion to follow. That was not long in coming.

2

"This country," a southern millhand declared in the mid-twenties, "is mighty quiet, but there is goin' to be a flutter before long." It began gently in 1927 with the "Appeal" of church leaders, criticizing the village system, long hours, low wages, night work for women and children, and the absence of collective bargaining. No one was listening. It gathered modest force on August 4, 1927, when some 800 unorganized cotton-textile employees of Harriet Mill No. 1 in Henderson, North Carolina, struck to restore a wage cut imposed three years before. At the request of Bennett H. Perry, city attorney and lawyer for the mill, Lieutenant Governor Long ordered two companies of national guardsmen to the town on the 10th, one commanded by a relative of the owners. Since there had been no provocation, Long was denounced in the press and withdrew the troops after two days. On the 13th, Alfred Hoffman arrived on the scene. He was in his early twenties, a heavy-set, tough-minded but inexperienced organizer for the Hosiery Workers, trained at A. J. Muste's Brookwood Labor College of Katonah, New York. Hoffman succeeded in signing up some five to six hundred workers as members of UTW. On August 30, the mill evicted nine families of strikers from company houses and the walkout collapsed.

It served, however, as a stimulus to the AFL to push organization. In 1927 the North Carolina Federation of Labor sponsored the Southern Summer School for Women Workers in Industry at Burnsville. More important was the Piedmont Organizing Council, launched by the North Carolina Federation in the latter part of that year. The Council held enthusiastic public meetings in the towns of the region, sparked an effort to organize the tobacco industry, and provided a pattern for similar councils in neighboring states. In October 1928 delegates from six state federations met in Chattanooga to discuss drives in coal and textiles. The following month in New Orleans a southern caucus persuaded the AFL convention to adopt a resolution establishing machinery to map a campaign in the South.[8]

3

The flutter blew itself into a howling wind on March 12, 1929, when the first of the great strikes broke out in the tiny community of Elizabethton in the shadow of the Smokies in east Tennessee.

Here in Happy Valley the conjunction of the proper mineral content in the water, a large labor supply of Scotch-Irish mountaineers, free land, and a ten-year tax exemption persuaded German rayon interests to locate their mills. American Bemberg opened in 1926 and American Glanzstoff in 1928, both spanking-new plants with the most modern equipment under the same imported German management. A sleepy county seat of 3000 was transformed overnight into a modern industrial town. By early 1929 the plants employed, excluding the office force, over 3200 people, about 40 per cent female. Local business welcomed the German concerns with open arms and persuaded candidate Hoover to give his only southern speech at the new tabernacle in Elizabethton during the 1928 presidential campaign. He painted a glowing picture of the industrializing South and carried Tennessee in the election.

The strike was a spontaneous demonstration of unorganized workers, with those most warlike members of the human race, enraged girls, in the vanguard. Its origin is traced in the words of one of them, Margaret Bowen:

In October of last year [1928] I hired on to the Glanzstoff plant. . . . I was under the instruction department for two weeks, and after two weeks I was put in the inspection department. I had fifty-two girls who worked under me. . . . When I was hired on there I was to get sixteen dollars a week and a raise. The first check I got was for $10.08. . . . I asked the foreman what was the matter with my check. He said: "That is all we pay."

I felt I had to have more money. When you have to pay five dollars a week for a room and pay board and laundry work you haven't much left. One day the girls asked me why they couldn't have a raise. I asked Mr. Burnett, the foreman, for a raise for the girls. He said, "No indeed, I will not give them a raise." I asked him if he ever intended to give me a raise, and he said, "No, you are making enough." I said I could not live on what I was getting, and he said I ought to have a bank account. I said, "A bank account on $10.08 a week?"

The first pay in February I got a raise of one cent an hour.

That made it $10.64. On Friday before the 12th of March I
asked the foreman again for a raise for my girls and he refused.
On Tuesday morning, March 12th, while I was marking up my
time he and Miss Brown, the forelady, walked in the back of
my section, and Miss Brown said: "This one will do and that
one will do," and picked out all my girls except five. . . .

The girls decided to strike for a raise if they could not get
it any other way. My girls would not weigh any silk or work
at all. There was only ten pounds of silk weighed in my section all morning. . . .

They watched me all morning. One of the girls passed me
and said, "There are nine sections ready to go out if you will
take your girls and walk out." Then the girls they had taken
away from me were given $11.20, and another section of girls
were given $12.32. . . . They did not give me any raise. . . .

We have thirty minutes for lunch. The manager came
in and asked me and two other girls if we were planning on a
strike. Nobody said anything. He said, "I have heard that you
are going to strike at 1 o'clock." Nobody said anything. He
said, "If you will stop this we will give the section girls twenty-
two cents an hour." He did not say anything about the inspection girls who were doing the work. . . . While he was talking
to us Miss Brown was gathering up the other section girls.
When she got hold of them they decided that then was the
time to strike. Out of 550 girls only 17 were left in the mill.

By March 16, the entire Glanzstoff force was on strike and the
Bemberg workers joined them two days later. Dr. A. Mothwurf,
president of both mills, announced that he would not deal with
the employees until they returned to work. Aided by neighboring building tradesmen, the millhands launched Local 1630 of
UTW, which enjoyed a phenomenal growth. Sherwood Anderson,
who attended a union meeting at which fifty members were in-
ducted, reported that the workers "have got a realization of each
other. They have got for the moment a kind of religion of brotherhood."

The management at first dealt with the crisis in ambivalent
fashion. It sought and on March 13 obtained a sweeping injunction

that was issued without notice or hearing to the defendants. The order, in addition to the usual prohibitions, forbade the strikers to picket at all or to interfere "in any way . . . with complainants, their employees, or those seeking employment." At approximately the same time Mothwurf entered into negotiations to settle the dispute, following the intervention of federal conciliator Charles G. Wood. On the night of March 21–22, Wood arranged a meeting in a hotel in nearby Johnson City of Mothwurf and his assistant, Alfred Hoffman of UTW, Paul J. Aymon, president of the Tennessee Federation of Labor, Captain Frank Broyles of the Tennessee National Guard, and J. Moreland, sheriff of Carter County. The parties reached an agreement that provided for rehiring of strikers without discrimination for union membership, withdrawal of the injunction, recognition by the company of shop committees to settle grievances, and a wage increase for Glanzstoff employees to equalize their rates with those at Bemberg. Unfortunately, the agreement was not reduced to writing.

When the terms were published in the press, Mothwurf released a statement denying that an agreement had been made or that he had even met with the union people. Meanwhile, the strikers were gradually drifting back to work despite the company's failure to perform.[9] President Green of the AFL then sent his crack trouble-shooter, Edward F. McGrady, to Elizabethton.

McGrady, who was to play an important role in the labor events of the thirties, was born into an Irish Catholic family in 1872 in Jersey City, where he received a high school education. Moving to Boston as a youth, he studied economics and business at night at English High School and boxed on the side. In 1894 he became a pressman on the Boston *Herald* and actively entered union work, becoming head of the web pressmen in 1907. From there he moved on to key labor positions — president of both the Boston Central Labor Union and the Massachusetts Federation as well as national organizer for the Printing Pressmen. He also won election to the Boston Common Council and the Massachusetts House of Representatives. His experience in both labor and politics persuaded Gompers to name him legislative representative for the AFL in 1919, thereby projecting him onto the national scene. McGrady, *Time* wrote, "slim, dapper and energetic . . .

with a good cigar in his mouth and the double-breasted manner of a gentleman of substance . . . strides into strike conferences as Adolphe Menjou might enter a ballroom." By 1929, Ed McGrady knew the labor movement as well as the back of his hand. His intelligence and negotiating skill were among the Federation's brightest ornaments. "Year in and year out," Paul Y. Anderson wrote, " . . . I have seen Ed McGrady fight the battles of the poor and oppressed . . . and have never known a more fearless and incorruptible man." [10]

About April 1, Harry Schultz, secretary of the Elizabethton Chamber of Commerce and employment agent for the mills, told McGrady that the wage scale would be accepted and that 300 strikers would be reinstated. On April 4, however, violence displaced negotiation when the local business community, frightened by the specter of trade unionism, "determined that the strike menace be nipped in the bud." At midnight Hoffman was seized by a mob of twenty men in the Lynwood Hotel, blindfolded, shoved into a car at the point of a gun, driven over the North Carolina line, and ordered "under pain of death" not to return. He thought the leader was a realtor named Perry and the crew included several businessmen and policemen. At 2 A.M. an armed gang led by Crawford Alexander, president of the First National Bank, and consisting of the town's "best elements," hauled McGrady out of bed in his hotel room, ransacked his belongings, pushed him into a car, and drove him to Virginia. A pillar of society, McGrady said, pointed a revolver at him and said he would "fill me full of holes if I returned." At 3 A.M. a third mob, led by an elder of the Presbyterian Church, repaired to the home of J. B. Penix, a local unionist, and dragged him to the ground. When he called for help his sister, a mountain girl, appeared with a rifle. After an exchange of shots, the citizenry fled. Things were warming up.

Ignoring the threats, Hoffman and McGrady paraded on the streets of Elizabethton on the 5th, guarded by "young, soft-voiced mountaineers," and lodged themselves in a private home "whose rooms were veritable arsenals of Winchesters." On Sunday, April 7, William Green addressed a throng of 4000 at the tabernacle, pledging the Federation's support to the millhands. The rayon management, now determined on a showdown, replied by discharging unionists *en masse.*

Local 1630 countered on April 15 by calling a second strike that shut down both mills. This time it was met by military force, 800 state police and deputy sheriffs ordered out by Governor Horton and the Carter County authorities. Neither the state nor the county suffered unduly since, as Mothwurf stated publicly, the management paid the Tennessee police directly at an estimated cost of $1000 per day (hoping to be reimbursed later) and advanced $50,000 to the county. As a further complication, apparently of interest only to the union attorneys, the police arrived in National Guard uniforms carrying Guard arms and equipment in contravention of a federal statute governing the issuance of this property. The purpose of the troops, in George Fort Milton's words, was not "to preserve the peace," but rather to help "the managers of the mills in suppressing the strike." Patrol parties reported to the German superintendent of one of the plants rather than to their officers; a cafeteria fed the "soldiers" and supplied free smokes; and the mill provided an officers' club.

The strikers picketed in defiance of the injunction of March 13. As a result, some 1250 were arrested and, after a riotous trial, 43 were convicted of contempt. Many acts of violence were committed on both sides, culminating in the blasting of the town's main water line on May 16. Not averse to fishing in troubled water supplies, the Communists sent agents in from the NTW strike in Gastonia to stir up rank-and-file opposition to a settlement.

The Textile Workers, with the formidable power of public authority ranged against them, had no such aversion to an agreement. In fact, several mediation efforts were undertaken. Major George L. Berry, president of the Printing Pressmen's union and a prominent Tennesseean, intervened with, he claimed,• Governor Horton's blessing. Mothwurf, however, refused to have anything to do with him. The major, a man hardly inclined to avoid a dirty argument merely because of its irrelevance, exploited the German origin of the management to refight World War I.

More important was the AFL overture to the newly elected lieutenant governor of New York, Herbert H. Lehman. Lehman Brothers had served as bankers for the Elizabethton venture, and

Lehman himself was a director of American Bemberg until his resignation on April 18, 1929, because of the strike. On May 1, the New York Federation of Labor asked him to urge the management to deal with McGrady. Since he was persuaded that discharge for union activity was neither "wise nor proper" and that the use of armed force was unjustified, Lehman readily concurred. His appeal, he wrote later, had no effect beyond incurring "deep resentment against me. . . . Even my motives and good faith have been questioned."

Mediation proved dramatically successful on May 25 as the result of intervention by a pretty twenty-eight-year-old girl, Anna Weinstock, a former Massachusetts necktie worker now representing the Labor Department. She operated in secrecy for two weeks, shuttling between Elizabethton (Mothwurf distrusted her) and Washington (to confer with Labor Secretary Davis) and New York (to deal with "rayon mill interests" and union leaders). The company, it was reported, preferred agreement to battle because the strike was costing $40,000 a day, UTW because it had no choice. The terms were: (1) former employees shall register for employment; (2) if an employee is not reinstated, the company shall give its reason; (3) if the employee is dissatisfied with the reason, he may take the matter up with the mills' new personnel officer, E. T. Willson, who shall act as "an impartial person"; (4) Willson shall be the sole judge in such cases; (5) the mills shall not discriminate against an employee because of union affiliation provided his activities were "legitimate" and "not carried on at the plants"; and (6) management shall meet with a committee of employees to adjust grievances. The Textile Workers, to speak with some moderation, had not tasted of the fruits of victory and it was not easy to persuade the membership to accept the agreement. In fact, the union's sole hope of survival hinged upon the good faith of Willson, a New Jersey textile executive who had represented employers in the Passaic strike.

Willson, however, was determined to destroy rather than to preserve the union. On September 19, notices were posted announcing, "The management does not intend at any time to discuss any matters . . . with outside individuals or organizations." Employees who disapproved were advised "not . . . to remain in our employ." He discriminated against strikers, promoted a company union, and launched a paternalistic welfare program. Some 1000 blacklisted workers called a pathetic protest strike in March 1930, which the mills simply ignored. "The industrialists of the South," Milton concluded, "dread the appearance of the unions, and show every intention of making a last-ditch fight against them." In the first major battle they dealt the Textile Workers and the American Federation of Labor a staggering defeat.[11]

## 4

If, on April 1, 1929, the revolution according to Marx and Lenin had been proclaimed on a Seventh Avenue street corner somewhere between 24th and 31st Streets on the island of Manhattan, it would have excited a good deal of comment. When it was in fact pronounced in the remote Piedmont town of Gastonia, North Carolina, it conjured up utter astonishment. The strike of the Communist-controlled National Textile Workers Union at the Loray mill was a phenomenon without parallel in the chronicle of American labor.

"North Carolina," a Communist spokesman declared, "is the key to the South, Gaston County is the key to North Carolina, and the Loray Mill is the key to Gaston County."[12] According to a 1927 survey, Gastonia was the leading textile center of the South, with more than 570 mills and nearly 10,000,000 spindles within 100 miles. Loray, the largest mill in the area, with 3500 employees, was the cord-tire fabric division of the Manville-Jenckes Corporation of Rhode Island. This "foreign" aspect joined with the reputation of the Loray workers for immorality to set the mill and its village apart from the community. Several factors — overcapitalization of the parent corporation, the textile depression, and competition from fabric plants built by the tire companies — induced the management to retrench in the summer of 1927. A new resident agent, G. A. Johnstone, was installed with instructions to save $500,000 a year. He was remarkably successful. He introduced the stretch-out without benefit of time studies or consultation with the workers, extended piecework, replaced high-wage with low-wage labor, and effected two 10 per cent wage cuts. By early 1929 the number of employees had been reduced to 2200.

These policies aroused deep resentment among the millhands. On March 5, 1928, weave-room workers staged a brief spontaneous walkout against the stretch-out and wage cuts. When the situation worsened during that year, the presiding Methodist elder of the district, Reverend W. A. Newell, wrote to the president of Manville-Jenckes, urging action to relieve the tension. In November the corporation fired Johnstone, provoking a joyful demonstration by Loray workers, and the following month J. A. Baugh took over. He sought to check the spreading disaffection, but it was too late.

The National Textile Workers Union had determined upon a campaign to organize the South, and agents who visited Gastonia in September and December of 1928 chose the Loray mill as the target. On January 1, 1929, ill-starred Fred E. Beal arrived in North Carolina and set to work. Beal was a stocky, towheaded, cleft-chinned, trade-union radical. He had been born in New England of old but poor Yankee dirt-farmer stock and had begun work in the textile mills of Lawrence at fourteen. He had walked out with the IWW in the great Lawrence strike of 1912, swept away by the oratory of Big Bill Haywood. After World War I he moved restlessly from one left-wing organization to another — One Big Union, the Socialist Party, and various textile unions. His disillusionment over the Sacco-Vanzetti case and his leadership in the New Bedford strike brought him into the Communist Party in 1928. Logically enough, NTW picked Fred Beal to lead its southern drive.

For two months Beal worked in the Charlotte area, getting a feel of the southern situation. After being told that Loray was a keg of dynamite, he arrived in Gastonia in March and rapidly built up an underground organization at the mill. Ed Spenser, an efficient company spy who was later promoted to employment manager, warned the management of the growing union. On the 25th, Baugh fired five unionists, arousing resentment among the workers, who demanded an immediate strike. Beal, realizing that the organization was unprepared for a walkout, was helpless to stem the tide. Hence, on March 30, he brought the union into the open with a public meeting attended by more than 1000 workers. They elected a committee and voted for an immediate strike. On Monday, April 1, both shifts walked out almost to a man. As Dick Bedenfield, a night hand, put it, "It was a feary time that night."

At the outset the organization's goals were of a trade-union rather than political character and the demands submitted to the company on April 3 reflected this: (1) elimination of piecework; (2) a minimum standard wage of $20 per week; (3) a forty-hour, five-day week; (4) abolition of the stretch-out; (5) equal pay for equal work for women and children; (6) free baths and better toilets in the mill and screening in the houses; (7) 50 per cent reduction of rent and light charges; and (8) union recognition. Baugh took only three minutes to reject these demands. At this stage there was a good deal of community sentiment in favor of the strike.

With Baugh's denial, economic questions were forgotten and political issues became paramount. Conciliator Wood, looping through Gastonia on his way from Elizabethton, declared that this was "not a strike, but a revolt" and that a settlement was inconceivable until "the workers divorce themselves from their communistic leaders." The AFL denounced the strike and instructed its affiliates to refrain from any support, financial or moral. On April 4, after some picket line scuffling, Governor O. Max Gardner ordered a howitzer company of the National Guard under Battalion Commander S. B. Dolley to Loray village. The following day the Gastonia *Gazette* ran a full-page ad "paid for by citizens of Gaston County" declaring that the strike was for "the purpose of overthrowing this Government and destroying property and to kill, kill, kill. The time is at hand for every American to do his duty." The entire "uptown" community of Gastonia and the state was now aroused to destroy the Loray strike.

Clutching at an unparalleled opportunity to capture world-wide attention, the Communist Party rushed representatives of its apparatus to North Carolina: the Workers' International Relief, the International Labor Defense, the Young Communist League, the

Young Pioneers, and the *Daily Worker,* among others. Control of the strike shifted from Beal to the leaders of these party organizations. They included Alfred Wagenknecht and Amy Schechter of the relief agency, George Pershing and Clarence and Edith Miller of the YCL, party boss William Z. Foster, and Vera Bush and Albert Weisbord of the executive committee of NTW. They arranged for delegations of emaciated workers to visit New York and other northern cities and raised a good deal of money ostensibly for relief. To these functionaries the trade-union objectives of the strike were of no consequence. Weisbord told Beal, "We must prepare the workers for the coming revolution." They insisted that racial equality should be a prime issue despite the fact that the Loray mill had only two Negro employees, both of whom departed when the trouble began. Weisbord stoked the fire on April 8 by appealing to the Guard troops to mutiny and join the workers against the bosses. As Paul Blanshard wrote, these tactics "had all the ear-marks of the propaganda kindergarten of the Third International." The result they guaranteed was iron determination by the leaders of the community to smash the strike. One can only wonder what the Loray millhands — unable to distinguish between NTW and UTW, to say nothing of the Socialist and Communist Parties — made of all this.

A clue may be found in the fact that the strikers' lines began to crack by April 10. Their final paychecks had been spent, and the Workers' International Relief, though articulate, was deficient in the grocery department. When efforts by pickets on the 15th to prevent strikebreakers from entering the mill collapsed, the strike, as a strike, was over.

Force was now triumphant. During the night of April 18, a mob of armed and masked men descended upon and utterly demolished the union headquarters. They then proceeded to the commissary to wreck the furnishings and burn the food. Dolley's troops, only 500 feet away, managed to "sleep" through the holocaust. They arrived just after the vandals had left and seized a group of strikers who were turned over to the police for destroying their own property. This was too barefaced even for the Gastonia authorities and they were soon released. No effort was ever made to apprehend the culprits.

On April 20, Governor Gardner ordered the withdrawal of the National Guard, presumably because the strike was broken. The union, however, refused to admit defeat. When, on May 6, the mill evicted sixty-two families of strikers from company houses, NTW erected a tent colony on a vacant lot to serve as its headquarters and as housing for some fifty families. Morale was sustained by the cooperative endeavor of construction and by the union's minstrel, Ella May Wiggins, who each night serenaded the strikers with ballads in the mountain style about their troubles. Fearful that another wrecking crew would pay a call, they created an armed guard of their own members, soon joined by two outside Communists, George Carter and Joseph Harrison.

Trouble was not long in coming. Beal staged a demonstration at the mill at the change of shift on the night of June 7 which resulted in a nasty scuffle.[13] As tension rose, Mrs. Walter Grigg, staying with her sick sister near the tent colony, phoned the police: "If we ever need your protection, we need it now on North Loray Street." Police Chief O. F. Aderholt, officers Tom Gilbert, C. M. Ferguson, and Adam Hord, and former deputy A. J. Roach drove out. Ferguson remained with the car and the four others entered the union grounds without a warrant. Accosted by either Harrison or Carter, they placed him under arrest and took away his gun. They then walked to the union hall and were stopped by armed guards. After some shouting, apparently started over the absence of a warrant, a shot was fired, probably by striker W. M. McGinnis, followed by an exchange of fifteen or twenty more shots. Four officers lay on the ground, wounded, Aderholt mortally. The only person hit on the union side was Harrison. All the policemen were struck by either No. 4 or No. 6 shot; the only gun carried by an officer who was not hit contained buckshot. Boxes of No. 4 were found in the union headquarters. There is no evidence that Beal was armed.

Hysteria gripped Gastonia in the wake of the Aderholt murder. A mob led by the local attorney for the mill descended upon the tent colony and demolished it. The residents were either put in jail or went into hiding. Beal, aided by his personal guard, K. O. Byers, drove the wounded Harrison to the hospital, where Beal was recognized. Followed by armed men, he decided that the only alternative to lynching was flight. Beal and Byers fled first to Charlotte to the home of the union's attorney, Tom Jimison, and then to Spartanburg, South Carolina. Here they were picked up by the police and returned to Gastonia. These two and fourteen others, including three women, were charged with conspiracy leading to murder.

The attention of the entire nation and much of the rest of the world was focused on the trial of the Gastonia strikers that opened on August 26, 1929. With the martyrdom of Sacco and Vanzetti still a green memory, the Communist Party exploited the case as "a frame-up"; its legal arm, the International Labor Defense, behaved as though the defendants were more useful convicted than acquitted. The Loray mill, the Gastonia *Gazette,* and the town authorities were determined to destroy the Communists, above all, Beal. The attorneys for the defense included Leon Josephson of New Jersey for the ILD, and — volunteered by the American Civil Liberties Union — John Randolph Neal of Tennessee, who had participated in the Scopes trial, and the brilliant Arthur Garfield Hays of New York. Both Neal and Hays repudiated the "frame-up" line and the ILD refused to permit the latter to serve for the ACLU; he was called "consultant counsel." [14] The titular head of the prosecution battery was the breezy, theatrical solicitor, John G. Carpenter. Its most prominent member was Clyde R. Hoey, the suave and eloquent brother-in-law of Governor Gardner. Hoey was marked by his flowing gray locks, cutaway, and boutonniere. Another was A. L. Bulwinckle, the local attorney for Manville-Jenckes, leader of the vigilantes, and later a member of Congress. The governor chose the best-qualified jurist in the state to conduct the trial, lean, laconic, soft-spoken Judge M. V. Barnhill.

The trial opened in Gastonia on July 29 with an immediate plea by the defense to move the proceedings because a fair trial could not be held there; inflammatory *Gazette* editorials were cited. Barnhill granted a change of venue to Charlotte in neighboring Mecklenburg County, where the trial got under way on August 26. An exhaustive examination of veniremen, 408 in all, resulted in a jury of seven workers (two of them unionists), four tenant farmers, and a grocery clerk. Carpenter presented his case for conspiracy, culminating in a fantastic episode derived from the cur-

rent movie, *The Trial of Mary Dugan*. He brought into the court-
room a black-shrouded, life-sized, bloodstained dummy of Aderholt,
which he unveiled dramatically. The murdered man's widow and
daughter wept; the jurors stared transfixed; and the judge ordered
that the image be removed. One juror, Joseph C. Campbell, became terror-stricken and went mad. This led Barnhill to call a
mistrial on September 9. Several jurors told reporters that on
the basis of the case thus far presented they would have voted for
acquittal.

The indignation in Gastonia was immense and led to a ferocious
outbreak of mob violence. That night hundreds of men in automobiles roamed through Gaston and adjoining counties, destroying
NTW and ILD property and terrorizing their sympathizers. A
mob seized Morris Wells, a British Communist, and two Carolina
union organizers, Cliff Saylor and C. M. Lell. They were driven
into the woods beyond Concord, where, according to Wells,

> They brought me out of a car and immediately told me to
> pull my trousers off. Then they gave Lell and Saylor a belt
> apiece.
> They forced me to bend over and touch my toes and told
> them to start whipping me. This, of course, they refused to do,
> and immediately somebody jumped on me, threw me on the
> ground, sat on my head, and about ten of them lashed me with
> branches from trees on my naked body.

The mob fled with the approach of a car. For this act the authorities arrested eight Communists, including Lell and Saylor, for conspiring to revolt against the government of North Carolina. This
charge was dismissed. Wells identified five of his floggers, who
were tried and not convicted because his testimony was im-
peached on the ground that he did not believe in God.

The NTW called a meeting for South Gastonia on Saturday,
September 14. A truckload of unionists en route there included
Ella May Wiggins, the same Ella May whose most popular "ballet,"
"Chief Aderholt," ran,

> *They locked up our leaders, they put them in jail,*
> *They shoved them in prison, refused to give them bail.*

*The workers joined together, and this was their reply:*
*We'll never, no, we'll never let our leaders die.*

The leaders were not destined to die, but Ella May was. Vigilantes pumped shots into the truck and this twenty-nine-year-old mother of five (four others had died of whooping cough) fell into the arms of little, wizened Charlie Shope, crying, "Lord-a-mercy, they done shot and killed me!" Although the murder had been committed in broad daylight in the presence of more than fifty people, the five Loray employees charged with the crime were acquitted. Ella May's dubious reward was elevation to the Communist pantheon of illustrious martyrs and heroes.

By the time the second trial opened on September 30, the union had called off the strike and abandoned the tent colony. At the outset Carpenter announced that the state was dropping charges against nine defendants, including the three women, and was reducing the charge against the seven others from first to second-degree murder. Hays and Neal, eased out by the ILD, were no longer counsel. This time the jury consisted of nine farmers, a rural mailman, a Ford employee, and a retired businessman. Acting under party instructions, Beal and his codefendants confined their testimony to the facts and avoided propaganda. They were horrified when Edith Miller of the Young Communist League proclaimed revolution and denounced religion from the witness stand. This played into the hands of the prosecution, which, with little restraint from Barnhill, had shifted the issue of the trial from murder to heresy. Of Carpenter's summation ("The union organizers came, fiends incarnate, stripped of their hoofs and horns, bearing guns instead of pitchforks . . ."), the *New York Times* editorialized: "There have been histrionic efforts by lawyers before . . . but probably none ever rivaled in variety and gymnastics the exhibition given by this North Carolinian." The jury returned a verdict of guilty in less than an hour. The four northerners, including Beal, received sentences of seventeen to twenty years, two others of twelve to fourteen, and the last of five to seven years.[15]

Pending their appeal to the North Carolina Supreme Court, the convicted men were released on bail, $27,000 raised by the ACLU from the Garland Fund. They decided to visit the "workers' paradise," where the Soviet authorities paraded them about as proletarian martyrs of capitalist injustice. When the court denied their appeal in March 1930, the seven remained in Russia and the bail was forfeited, outraging the ACLU. Four, apparently, remained there permanently, one died, and the one with the shortest sentence returned to serve his time.

Beal stayed in the USSR until 1933, by which time he had become thoroughly disillusioned. He escaped to America and went underground. His autobiography, a hymn of hate against Bolshevism, ran in the Hearst papers and was published as a book in 1937. The following year he was captured and returned to North Carolina to prison. "I would rather be an American prisoner," he declared, "than a free man in Russia." He wrote friends from Caledonia Farm that life "is tremendously lonesome, down here in the South . . ." and he was eager to get out. Persuaded of his innocence, a committee of distinguished liberals agitated for his release in 1939. Their plea for a pardon was rejected by Governor Hoey, Beal's former prosecutor, though Hoey did cut seven years from his sentence. In 1941 the AFL convention unanimously adopted a resolution sponsored by the Hatters Union urging Governor J. Melville Broughton to grant full pardon. On December 6, President Green forwarded the resolution with a strong personal endorsement to the governor, and on January 9, 1942, Beal became a free man. He labored briefly in a knit-goods shop in New York and then spun out the remainder of his life in a struggle with illness and poverty. He died of a heart attack, embittered and forgotten, in his brother's home in Lawrence in 1954.[16]

Fred Beal was a symbolic American radical, perpetually out of joint with the times. In the twenties, when it was an act of daring to do so, he spoke out as a Communist leader. In the thirties, when there was much sympathy for Communism, he was one of the first apostates. In the revulsion against Communism following the second World War he was temperamentally unfit to achieve prominence as an informer. Beal's political career was one-dimensional; he walked a straight line to the revolution and then turned back to his starting point. In neither direction did he bother to glance to the side or above. His life was a tragic essay revealing the incompatibility between trade unionism and Communism.

## 5

While Beal was sitting in jail, another great strike erupted on July 11, 1929, at the foot of the Blue Ridge in Marion, North Carolina. "Marion," proclaimed its Kiwanis Club, "is an ideal happy home town, with a fairyland around it. . . . Labor . . . is . . . of a most intelligent, loyal, and desirable kind." In fact, the Federal Council of Churches found the working and living conditions in the Baldwin and Clinchfield mills so bad that it could describe them only as "unbelievable." Reverend William B. Spofford declared that girls worked their first thirty days without pay, followed by four months at 5 cents per hour. The shift was twelve hours and the work week sixty hours; children were worked illegally; wages of $8 to $10 a week were usual; and the stretch-out was introduced in the crudest fashion. Mary Frances Gentry, a Clinchfield employee, stated: "Everybody spits on the floor. . . . The toilets are filthy. . . . Water is put in the toilet-room in a pail carried from one of the wells in the village. . . . All the workers in one room drink from one dipper." According to Sinclair Lewis, the housing was "atrocious."

These conditions and the growing contagion of the Piedmont revolt spurred the Baldwin employees to organize. In April, Lawrence Hogan (in Lewis' words, "a huge square-shouldered Irishman with a quiet voice and a vast efficiency") and Dan Elliott ("sensationally good-looking . . . like Henry Ward Beecher with his lion's mane") launched a union. Hogan visited Alfred Hoffman in Elizabethton to ask for help, which was promised. In June the local people called a public meeting with an overflow attendance from both mills. The Baldwin management responded by discharging twenty-two unionists. On July 10, Hoffman tore himself loose from the Tennessee conflict and arrived in Marion. The next day a local committee met with R. W. Baldwin, president of the Marion Manufacturing Company, a man whose ignorance was described by Benjamin Stolberg, who interviewed him, as absolute. The union asked for a reduction in hours from twelve to ten with no loss of pay, rehiring of the twenty-two fired for union activity, and agreement to meet with an employee committee on grievances. Baldwin peremptorily rejected these demands.

Hoffman was in the impossible position of being helpless either to prevent or to conduct a strike. He pleaded with the local committee not to walk out, warning them, "There isn't a cent of money for relief." Their reply was, "Hell! We've done struck." He was beset with the added complication that he was from the Hosiery Workers and the local belonged to the Textile Workers, and neither UTW nor the AFL offered much support. His main backing came from the more militant Brookwood Labor College people — Tom Tippett, A. J. Muste, and William Ross.

To keep down relief costs, Hoffman sought to prevent the 1500 Clinchfield workers from joining the 650 Baldwin employees already on strike. The matter was taken out of his hands when the management first fired 100 union members and then locked out everyone early in August. On the 19th, Clinchfield reopened in the face of mass picketing, and the governor ordered troops into its village. On August 28, after eviction of a striker and occupancy of his house by a strikebreaker, a group of unionists moved the latter's furniture out. For this, 148 people, including Hoffman, were arrested on charges of "insurrection against the state," rioting, and resisting an officer. Early in September the soldiers took over both villages and smashed the strike.

At this point L. L. Jenkins, an Asheville banker and textile manufacturer, arranged a conference of the management of both mills and the union people in the presence of the governor's adviser, Judge Townsend. An oral agreement was reached to cut the work week to fifty-five hours with a corresponding wage reduction and to rehire the strikers without discrimination, except for twelve at the Baldwin mill. The workers grimly accepted their defeat and returned to work on September 11. The troops were immediately withdrawn.

Both mills effected the hours reduction and violated the no-discrimination provision; more than 100 strikers were blacklisted. Outraged by this bad faith, Jenkins returned to Marion on September 27 and sought in vain to see Baldwin. As tension built up in the Baldwin mill, the night shift walked out in the early morning hours of October 2, congregating on the road before the front gate. The superintendent called in Sheriff Oscar F. Adkins, who brought along eleven deputies, six of them paid by the mill. When the strikers tried to persuade the day shift not to enter, Adkins released tear gas into their ranks. What followed has been described by Sinclair Lewis:

> This is the story of Old Man Jonas.
>
> When Sheriff Adkins threw tear-gas at the strikers, Old Man Jonas, the striker nearest to Adkins, attacked him with a stick. Adkins was broad, fat, strong, about forty years old, armed, and supported by the majesty of the Carolina law, which he represented. Beside Jonas was the distinguished constable, Broad Robbins, aged perhaps fifty, but as powerful and menacing as a wolf. And Old Man Jonas was sixty-eight, and so lame with rheumatism that he had to walk with a cane — the cane with which he struck the sheriff.
>
> One would have thought that these two proud and powerful guardians of law and order would have been able to control Old Man Jonas without killing him. Indeed they made a good start. Adkins wrestled with him, and Broad clouted him in the back of the head. Jonas fell to his hands and knees. He was in that position when he was shot. . . .
>
> After the riot, Jonas, wounded fatally, was taken to the hospital with handcuffs on, was placed on the operating-table, with handcuffs still on, and straightway he died on that table . . . with his handcuffs on.

While Jonas was being handcuffed, the deputies opened fire. Three strikers were killed, three mortally wounded, and twenty-five seriously wounded. All those who died were shot in the back. One deputy suffered a scratched cheek. A reporter for the Asheville *Citizen,* the only disinterested person present, saw no shots fired by strikers. When the wounded were taken to the Marion Hospital (many workers had contributed toward its construction), they were required to pay in advance. The head nurse explained that the Duke Power Company usually took care of charity patients but would not in this case. Two companies of the National Guard arrived the following day.

A simple funeral was held on October 4, 1929, for the four already dead. No local minister would officiate, so the services were conducted by James Myers of the Federal Council of Churches and an old mountain preacher, Cicero Queens, who dropped to his knees and prayed: "O Lord Jesus Christ, here are men in their coffins, blood of my blood, bone of my bone. I trust, O God, that these friends will go to a place better than this mill village or any other place in Carolina." The Asheville banker Jenkins also spoke out: "As a millowner I feel that what I am today and all that I have I owe to people like you, to the men and women who for forty years have stood faithfully by the spindle and loom. . . . You are my people. I love you."

On November 21, Hoffman and five strikers were tried for the furniture incident. The insurrection charge was dropped and on November 30 they were convicted of rioting, Hoffman being fined $1000 and sentenced to thirty days in jail and three others to six months on the chain gang. Between them, the Baldwin and Clinchfield mills evicted eighty-nine "undesirable" families from company houses. On November 8, S. J. McAbee, pastor of the Marion Baptist Church, and A. R. Fleck, chairman of the board of deacons, both employees of the Baldwin mill, notified 100 strikers that they had been dropped from the church rolls. The trial of Adkins and his deputies for murder opened early in December in Burnsville. The officers pleaded self-defense. They were acquitted on December 22 so, in the words of a juryman, "they could go home for Christmas." The Marion strike had been liquidated.[17]

<br>

# 6

The high winds howling through Tennessee and North Carolina blew into a gentle zephyr when they crossed the South Carolina line. Here in the spring of 1929 occurred a series of spontaneous strikes directed against the recent introduction of the stretch-out and marked by the almost total absence of unions. The leading walkouts involved 1200 operatives at Ware Shoals, 1200 at Pelzer, all three mills of the Brandon Corporation in Greenville, 700 employees of the same concern at Woodruff, 750 at Central, three mills in Union, and 1000 people at Anderson. They were unusually orderly and remarkably successful in eliminating the stretch-out.

This was due in part to the attitude of the millhands toward unions. "No," a Brandon striker declared, "we don't want no organizers from outside.... We're doin' this ourselves." When two organizers showed up, "we just told 'em how much we appreciated their good feelin', an' gave 'em a drink of Coca-Cola, an' put 'em on the street car."

The only trouble took place in Ware Shoals on July 11, when three unionists — George L. Googe of the AFL, O. D. Gorman of the Railroad Telegraphers, and John A. Peel of UTW — were threatened by a mob for addressing a meeting. A detective sent by Governor Richards spirited them away before violence occurred. When President McMahon of the Textile Workers complained to the governor about the deprivation of civil liberties, Richards replied: "Your impertinent, threatening telegram ... will receive only such consideration as communications of its character deserve."

South Carolinians — workers, owners, and public officials alike — wanted no outsiders in the state. The very weakness of the leaderless strikes was their strength, since it won popular support. It is significant that South Carolina was the only state to investigate working conditions in the textile industry and that Representative Olin Johnston's committee reported strongly in favor of the millhands.[18]

## 7

The Piedmont revolt presented the AFL convention that met in Toronto on October 7, 1929, with its most dramatic challenge of the twenties. For the better part of a decade the Federation had remained becalmed as the economic currents about it swept forward. Would it seize leadership of the largely spontaneous southern uprising or would it continue to sit still?

Many within and outside its ranks devoutly prayed that the AFL bestir itself. On July 20, representatives of the Textile Workers, the Women's Trade Union League, the Workers' Education Bureau, and the Federal Council of Churches met in Rye, New York, on the estate of Mrs. Daniel O'Day, a native of Georgia, to plan a campaign. The southern state federations, conferring at Rock Hill, South Carolina, on September 29, called upon the AFL to organize the South. When the delegates gathered in Canada, they were fully aware of their historic opportunity. They could not have failed to sense as well another electric element in the atmosphere: on September 5, the great Wall Street bull market had sustained its first shock, followed by a series of minor jolts that culminated in the catastrophe of October 24. The era of the Great Depression had opened.

Observers at the convention, nevertheless, reported "a pitch of enthusiasm not seen in labor gatherings since the spring tide of the Knights of Labor." The Executive Council urged all AFL affiliates to plan a southern drive in the coming year. The Textile Workers introduced a resolution authorizing the officers of the Federation to raise funds and to call a conference of international unions to map the campaign. Speaker after speaker arose on October 15 to endorse the motion, echoing the words of J. W. Fitzpatrick of the Waterbury Central Labor Union: "We are on trial before the world." The convention adopted the resolution in a unanimous rising vote.

Shortly afterward Green issued a call to the presidents of the 105 affiliated internationals to meet in Washington on November 14. This conference agreed that each union would supply at least one organizer, a committee with headquarters in a southern city would direct the campaign, and the unions would be asked to bolster the slender treasury of the Textile Workers. President Green later named a committee consisting of Paul J. Smith, chairman (AFL organizer), Francis Gorman (UTW), and W. C. Birthright (Tennessee Federation), which opened an office in Birmingham. The surface harmony of the meeting concealed a basic disagreement over policy. The southerners advocated a militant union drive; the building and railway trades, apparently led by the Carpenters, cautioned against "spectacular campaigning."

The conservatives prevailed, as evidenced by Green's widely heralded speaking tour of the South in early 1930. He addressed himself to "uptown" rather than the millhands, attempting to sell the AFL to employers rather than workers. To the upper classes he announced, "There is no sword in our scabbard." Before audiences of politicians, financiers, manufacturers, and teachers he flayed the Communists and proclaimed the respectability and moderation of the AFL. "The policies he advocated," observed the Memphis *Commercial-Appeal*, "might have come with propriety from the president of the American Bankers' Association."

Behind Green trotted Geoffrey Brown, the Federation's consulting engineer and specialist in union-management cooperation. "We can not win the South," Green wrote Brown, "unless we ... convince the owners of the textile mills that it would be ... more profitable for them to deal with organized labor." Brown's job was to explain the cost advantages of the Naumkeag union-management cooperation plan to employers and to help them install it in their mills. Between March 1930 and September 1931 he held more than 200 conferences with southern cotton-mill managers. "The millowners," Jean Trepp wrote, "listened politely to Mr. Brown's speeches, informed him that they were perfectly well able to manage their plants without assistance, and ushered him out the door." His vigorous salesmanship was not without some effect: three tiny Columbus, Georgia, firms — a food packer, a syrup factory, and a hosiery mill — bought his plan. In each case the price Brown paid was AFL support of the company's sales. Since none was large enough to benefit from Naumkeag efficiency, the program was a failure.

A combination of ubiquitous, embattled employer opposition, mounting economic adversity, and growing AFL faintheartedness and division slowed and then destroyed the southern organizing drive. Instead of a minimum of 105 organizers, the Birmingham office actually had nine, supplemented by twelve working directly for internationals, of whom five were with UTW. By September 1930, the AFL claimed the formation of 112 locals, 31 in textiles. In the latter case, at least, the organizations had no bargaining status because the mills refused to deal with them and discharged their members. The unions were virtually powerless to strike in retaliation. The Federation's contribution to UTW as of August 31, 1930, was a paltry $41,500. This led the Textile Workers at the 1930 AFL convention to propose a special per capita tax to underwrite the campaign. The motion was defeated by parliamentary maneuver when Carpenters' delegate Feeley refused unanimous consent. The Carpenters, in fact, had opposed AFL aid to the Textile Workers from the outset.[19]

8

The southern campaign reached its doleful climax in the Danville, Virginia, strike of September 29, 1930, a conflict upon whose outcome, both sides recognized, hinged the future of textile unionism in the Piedmont. The Riverside & Dan River Mills Company, in 1930 almost half a century old, was the largest textile firm in the South, with over 4000 employees. It operated two facilities, one in the heart of Danville along the river and the other in the nearby mill village of Schoolfield which Louis Stanley called "a poultry farm with telephone booths." Management was local, notably in the person of the president, H. R. Fitzgerald, a dyspeptic elderly gentleman, sensitive about his deafness and speech imperfection. Ownership was also local, concentrated in the Fitzgerald family, J. R. Pritchett, president of Danville's largest bank, and Roger James, publisher of the town's dailies, the *Register* and the *Bee*. By southern standards Riverside & Dan River was a model employer: wages were relatively high, the work week was only fifty-five hours, welfare was liberal, and a company union had existed since 1919. This last, called Industrial Democracy, was patterned after the federal government with a senate for foremen and a house of representatives for operatives. Its presumptive function was the democratic resolution of mill problems.

These favorable employment conditions reflected prosperity; during most of the twenties the company paid a 10 per cent dividend plus extras on its common stock. The textile depression overtook Riverside & Dan River in 1929, the worst year since the war, and dividends were paid out of surplus. Fitzgerald then called in a Boston engineering firm to install the stretch-out. In January 1930 he proposed to the Industrial Democracy a 10 per cent wage cut, effective the first of February. The senate accepted the reduction; the house of representatives, despite a flood of oratorical blandishment, turned it down. Fitzgerald, tossing Industrial Democracy out the window, simply posted a notice that wages were reduced. In addition, he eliminated both time and one-half for overtime and pay for stoppages due to lack of material.

These acts precipitated a movement to unionism. The skilled loom fixers, with a tradition of organization dating back to 1919, sent a delegation to see William Green, who was speaking in Richmond. He notified the Textile Workers, and Frank Gorman, the union's vice-president, promptly appeared in Danville in early February to organize Local No. 1685. Gorman, assisted by Matilda Lindsay, a Virginian representing the Women's Trade Union League, was to dominate the Danville conflict and to give it a dynamic leadership unmatched in any other Piedmont strike.

Francis Joseph Gorman was a Yorkshireman, born in 1890 in Bradford, England, one among many British workmen destined to rise in the American labor movement. His father owned a small pub which served as headquarters for the Bradford wool workers. "As a child," Jonathan Mitchell wrote, "Gorman listened to legends of British trade unionism, its martyrs and heroes and victories." He emigrated to America at thirteen and went to work as a sweeper at $4 a week for Atlantic Mills in Providence. He joined the union in 1910, participated in his first strike in 1919, became an organizer in 1922, and vice-president of UTW in 1928. He had helped lead the Marion strike and was profoundly impressed by the massacre. Mitchell described him as

a little man, on the Napoleonic model. His most distinguishing feature is his eyebrows, placed very high above his eyes, giving him an expression of perpetual questioning, perpetual alertness. ... He manages to keep his manner of easy efficiency. As the point arrives in conference when something has to be made clear or decided upon, his whole force is thrown behind what he says. Otherwise he watches things slip by without a muscle moving. He sees everything, hears everything and there is very little he does not know.

*Time* characterized him as "affable, articulate, self-contained." By 1930 he was a mature and seasoned trade-union leader, by a wide margin the strongest in the Textile Workers. One may wonder how high Gorman's star might later have risen had he chosen some more promising industry than textiles in which to work.

Local No. 1685 held its first public meeting on February 9 and the response was enthusiastic. On March 26, the union claimed 3000 members and by the end of the summer virtually every mill worker had signed up. Gorman sustained morale with mass meetings and songs, including "Cotton Mill Colic." In addition, he won the firm backing of the Virginia Federation of Labor and wide community support in Danville, including much of the business element and the Ku Klux Klan. "The whole city throbbed with the organization campaign."

Gorman's only remaining problem was the insoluble one: to persuade Fitzgerald to bargain. The mill president's deep-seated hatred of unions was bolstered when a labor man, not from UTW, ridiculed his speech defect at a public meeting. Fitzgerald fired unionists in mounting numbers, reaching the staggering total of 2500 by the end of August. Their relief constituted a formidable drain on the local's treasury and, with their growing numbers, the rank-and-file pressure for a walkout became irresistible. Gorman, realizing that the deepening depression and UTW insolvency spelled inevitable defeat, staved off a strike for seven months. He explored every avenue of negotiation and mediation, including Geoffrey Brown's union-management cooperation, to no avail.

Early in September the national UTW convention, despite Green's plea not to strike, authorized action. In mid-month 95 per cent of the local's membership voted to strike. Now there was no turning back; on the 29th the workers walked out in perfect solidarity.

At the outset Gorman's pickets paraded peacefully before the mill gates. Fitzgerald, nevertheless, obtained injunctions on September 30, one for Danville and another for Schoolfield. They were prepared by company counsel, were issued *ex parte,* and were conventional in substance. The Schoolfield order aroused mild comment when it was revealed that the judge who signed it, J. T. Clement, owned twenty shares of the corporation's stock. On October 2, Governor Pollard offered mediation, to which UTW agreed. Fitzgerald answered, "The property of our company belongs to our stockholders . . . [and] they will have nothing to do with these outside professional trouble makers." The early phase of this otherwise quiet walkout was enlivened by the arrival of William Murdoch, secretary of the Communist textile union, who passed out dodgers attacking Gorman as the arch betrayer of the strikers. Murdoch was promptly clapped into jail and viewed the conflict from that vantage point for the next three months.

The weary autumn weeks dragged by as Fitzgerald played for time, knowing that the empty union treasury could not stand a long strike and that he could gradually recruit employees from the army of jobless textile workers in the Piedmont. He was right; Gorman's main worry was relief. As already noted, UTW got nowhere at the AFL convention and two financial appeals by Green to the labor movement produced disappointing results. The main sources of funds proved to be the Textile Workers themselves and church and liberal groups. The means, however, were totally inadequate to the task.

The first two months of the strike were almost free of violence. On November 24, Fitzgerald, having a fair labor force at his disposal, ordered the factory whistles blown. The union, disregarding the injunctions, replied with mass picketing. This was followed by physical clashes, stoning of houses, dynamite discharges, stopped trolleys, and other acts of violence. Hence, on November 26, the governor sent almost 1000 National Guard troops into the area. Thereafter the mills found it easier to recruit and by mid-December, according to UTW, 1272 were at work. At that time Fitzgerald, who was not a master of public relations, served eviction notices upon forty-seven families effective Christmas Eve. The howl of protest that arose persuaded him to offer a period of grace; the first batch of fourteen families was tossed out on December 29.

On the last day of 1930 the union made a dramatic plea for settlement. Before a crowd of 7000 in Danville, William Green made this proposal: termination of the walkout; strikers to return to work without discrimination; and referral of disputed issues to a board of arbitration consisting of two workers, two company representatives, and either Admiral Richard E. Byrd or former Governor Harry Flood Byrd. Fitzgerald, smelling victory, was adamant and declared, "I have nothing whatever to say." This brain child proved stillborn.

The strike disintegrated during January 1931, and collapsed on the 29th of that month. On the preceding day Gorman advised the union people to return to work and to contribute a dollar a week apiece to support those the company would not take back. This they voted to do. He then issued a press statement that put a good face on a bad situation by stretching the truth. Gorman argued that Fitzgerald was taking back strikers without regard to union membership, thereby honoring a "principle of labor." With the acceptance of this principle, there was no further justification for the strike. This was nonsense. Flowery language could not conceal the fact that the Textile Workers had suffered a staggering defeat and that unionism was now dead in the Piedmont.[20]

<br>

## 9

Henderson . . . Elizabethton . . . Gastonia . . . Marion . . . South Carolina . . . Danville. These were the battlefields of the Piedmont revolt, the grounds on which the southern textile worker and the American labor movement lost a war. "A stone," indeed, "came rollin' — rollin' through Dixie," but there had been no "tearin' down de kingdom ob de boss."

The causes of this defeat are to be found in the millhand, in the millowner, in the community, in the economic situation, and in the unions. The explosive that touched off the textile worker was the stretch-out rather than a yearning for organization. His rural tradition, his ingrained individualism, his ignorance, his isolation, his restless mobility, his apathy, his poverty, and his suspicions of northerners joined to impede his capacity to act collectively. Moreover, he was, as he well knew, only a replaceable part in the machine. He could see the surplus labor in southern agriculture at the borders of his own village, another ever ready to step into his job in the mill at an appallingly low wage rate.

Perhaps even more important was the millowner, the new master of the South, successor to the plantation owner. He was pathologically opposed to collective bargaining. In his mind there was no distinction between the AFL and the Communists; each represented a fundamental challenge to his conception of southern society. Through the instrumentality of the mill village he could deny the striker a job, evict him from his house, spy on him in private affairs, expel him from church, and deny him medical services. As the reward for loyalty, the millowner could offer the worker the fruits of paternalism.

To dominant "uptown" in the typical Piedmont community the union was a foreign institution that threatened to destroy cherished local values. The press and the church arrayed themselves in almost solid phalanx alongside the millowners. Civil authority, local and state, condoned, if it did not actually sponsor, the deprivation of civil liberties and the perpetration of floggings and outright murder. The record of the courts speaks for itself. Eight people were slain in strikes. No one was convicted for the death of seven strikers; the only conviction was for that of a policeman. Members of five antiunion mobs were tried with no convictions. "In every case where strikers were put on trial," Weimar Jones wrote, "strikers were convicted; in not one case where anti-unionists or officers were accused has there been a conviction." The courts issued injunctions whenever employers asked for them, all *ex parte* and some extraordinarily sweeping in their prohibitions. Similarly, governors were perfectly willing to order troops into struck communities to break strikes.

The Piedmont uprising was ill timed in relation to business conditions. The wave of walkouts in the spring of 1929 ran head-on into the textile depression. Gorman's masterful performance at Danville was hit with both barrels, the industry decline and the Great Depression. All the economic guns were in the employer's arsenal.

Finally, the American Federation of Labor failed to provide the revolt with positive leadership. It was, in effect, taken by surprise and allowed events to shape policy rather than the reverse. Its exertions, once aroused, were too little and too late. The AFL strategy, cooperation rather than militancy, exposed a flank to the criticism of liberals and radicals within and outside its ranks. One may query, however, whether it was more gratifying to be impaled on the left or the right horn of a dilemma when impalement was certain in either case.

A careful search of the wreckage reveals that not quite all was lost. There was some improvement in working conditions. The mills in Gaston County, for example, reduced the work week from sixty to fifty-five hours with the same take-home; at Marion hours were shortened by six per week, wages rose 5 per cent, and welfare was liberalized. At its 1930 convention the Cotton Textile Institute voted to abolish night work for women and minors under eighteen.[21] More important than economic change, however, was a stirring in men's minds. The decent people of the South were profoundly disturbed by the rot exposed when the stone was rolled over by the Piedmont revolt. Religious bodies began seriously to study and debate what might be done to better the lot of the millhand. The universities, notably North Carolina, undertook systematic investigation of the textile industry and the mill-village system. Finally, the strikes left nuclei of workmen, though bitter in defeat, determined to do battle again for their unions when the time was ripe.

## 10

The Piedmont on the eve of the Great Depression was a microcosm of all America in the somber decade to follow. On this beautiful and tragic land far from the centers of industrial power the mill-hands' revolt put in relief the great labor issues that were to absorb the entire nation in the thirties. Here were the problems of economic collapse — of poverty, of unemployment, of relief. Here, too, were the questions of labor standards — of low wages, of long hours, of night work for women and children, of factory sanitation and company housing, of workmen's compensation. Here, as well, were the fundamental issues of collective bargaining — of the right to organize and bargain, of discrimination for union membership or activity, of the company union, of the labor injunction, of the right to strike and conduct strikes, of the appropriate role of the government in labor disputes. Here also were the chronic problems of the American labor movement — of its weakness, internal division, and drift, of the deep-seated reluctance of craft unions to sponsor industrial organization, of rival unionism, of communism. Here was the painful issue of the stretch-out — of the employer responding to a falling market by extracting higher output from his workers by speeding them up. Here was the problem of the rigidity of the American employer — of his obsessive distaste for collective bargaining and of his frequent reluctance to share the fruits of industry with his employees. Here was violence, the extraordinary American tradition of resolving disputes with guns instead of words. And here, finally, was a central issue of a democratic society — whether the majority or merely a few of its members were to make its basic economic decisions.

# I

## THE TWENTIES

## CHAPTER 1

# The Worker in an Unbalanced Society

THE SYMBOL of the twenties is gold. This was the age of the gold standard, a time when people with money slept with confidence: their banknotes were redeemable in the precious metal. Small boys received gold watches on ceremonial occasions, and little girls were given gold pieces as birthday gifts. The noted Philadelphia banking family, the Stotesburys, equipped their bathroom with gold fixtures ("You don't have to polish them you know"). Writing in gloomy 1932, the economist Frederick C. Mills spoke of the economy of the twenties as having "the aspects of a golden age." The historians Charles and Mary Beard titled the introductory chapter on the twenties of *America in Midpassage* "The Golden Glow." To a contemporary reader the title seemed just right.

Yet hindsight finds the image unfitting. The twenties were, indeed, golden, but only for a privileged segment of the American population. For the great mass of people whose welfare is the concern of this study — workers and their families — the appropriate metallic symbol may be nickel or copper or perhaps even tin, but certainly not gold. Although on the surface American workers appeared to share in the material advantages of the time, the serious maladjustments within the economic system fell upon them with disproportionate weight. This interplay between illusion and reality is a key to the period. In fact, this was a society in imbalance and workers enjoyed few of its benefits.

1

In the twenties two population changes occurred that were to prove profoundly significant to labor: the shift from farm to city speeded up and immigration from abroad slowed down. The American farmer's venerable propensity to move to town reached a climax. During the ten years from 1920 to 1929, according to the Department of Agriculture, 19,436,000 people made the trek; in every year except 1920 and 1921 over 2 million left the land, though many returned. The farm population, despite a higher fertility rate, declined by 3.7 per cent between 1920 and 1930 (31.6 to 30.4 million), while the nonfarm population rose by 24.6 per cent (74.1 to 92.3 million). Not only did these displaced husbandmen go to town; they appear to have gone to the big towns. Communities with over 100,000 grew by 32.4 per cent from 1920 to 1930, while those with 2500 to 5000 increased by only 7.6 per cent. Never before had the United States experienced such an immense flow from farm to city.

This was, in the words of the National Resources Committee, "a migration of hope," folks moving to improve their lot. They had to reckon with the economic paradox of the time, rural depression in the midst of relative urban prosperity. Agricultural prices had collapsed in 1921 and simply failed to recover. For many farmers city employment at almost any wage represented a rise in income. Another factor was the marked increase in agricultural productivity. This was the era in which the internal combustion engine revolutionized American agriculture by displacing the horse, the mule, and, most important, the farmer, his wife, and his children. Between 1920 and 1930, the number of trucks on farms rose from 139,000 to 900,000 and tractors from 246,000 to 920,000. In contrast with a sale of only 3000 combines in 1920, the implement factories disposed of 20,000 in 1929. Finally, there was the eternal lure of the city — the opportunities, satisfactions, and glamour of urban living as compared with the drudgery and isolation of life on the land. As the boys sang at American Legion conventions: "How ya gonna keep 'em down on the farm after they've seen Paree?"

The impact of this movement upon labor can hardly be exaggerated. Employers, despite the drop in immigration from abroad, had at their disposal a great pool of workmen, particularly the unskilled and semiskilled. This large labor supply, inured to the low level of farm income, relieved an upward pressure on wage rates that might have occurred. Workers drawn from a rural background were accustomed to intermittency and so did not insist on regularity of employment. Although they adapted readily to machinery, they were without skills in the industrial sense. The fact that the price of skilled labor was high and of unskilled low induced management to substitute machines for craftsmen. The displaced farmers carried into industry the agricultural tradition of mobility, especially geographic and to a lesser extent occupational. They brought with them, as well, the conservative outlook and individualistic accent of the rural mind. Since they were predominantly of older stocks, their entry into the urban labor force had an Americanizing influence, reversing the tendency to ethnic diversity produced by the wave of immigration that preceded World War I. There was, however, one divisive element in this trend to homogeneity: the Negro's emergence on a large scale in the urban working class.

The unskilled rural Negro of the South won his foothold in northern industry during the war, particularly in the metalworking, auto, and meat industries. By 1923, for example, Ford had 5000 colored employees. In the early twenties the demand for this class of labor was brisk, but slacked off after 1924, when industry in the North achieved a labor supply equilibrium. Some 1,200,000 Negroes migrated from South to North between 1915 and 1928. At this time the Negro took a long stride in the direction of integration with the dominant urban industrial society in America. Folklorists at the end of the twenties, for example, found a Negro cook in Houston singing:

> *Niggers gittin' mo' like white folks,*
> *Mo' like white folks every day.*
> *Niggers learnin' Greek and Latin,*
> *Niggers wearin' silk and satin —*
> *Niggers gittin' mo' like white folks every day.*

To the employer the agricultural influx was a blessing. The resulting surplus of labor gave him little cause to fear turnover; money wage rates were stable; and unionism was in the doldrums. To the labor movement the migration was a short-term disaster. In the

economic and political context of the twenties this accretion to the
urban labor force was unorganizable. For the economy as a whole
the movement was, of course, both inevitable and desirable, but
it carried a danger. With a larger number of people now wholly
dependent upon wages and salaries, President Hoover's Committee
on Social Trends noted, "any considerable and sustained interruption in their money income exposes them to hardships which
they were in a better position to mitigate when they were members of an agricultural or rural community." [1]

As important to labor as the flight of the farmer to the city was
the fundamental change in immigration policy, almost shutting a
door that had remained wide open for three centuries. The turn
came in 1917 with the passage of a law over President Wilson's veto
requiring aliens over sixteen seeking admission to demonstrate
the capacity to read "the English language, or some other language
or dialect." The purpose was to discriminate against immigrants
from southern and eastern Europe, who were presumed to be less
literate than those from the northwestern part of the continent.
The end of the war in 1918 promised a flood of immigrants from
the Mediterranean and Eastern nations despite the literacy test.
Hence restrictionists pushed through an emergency statute in 1921
that limited the annual inflow from any country to 3 per cent
of its nationals resident in the United States in 1910. This national origins principle was made permanent in 1924 in a law
that reduced the rate to 2 per cent and employed the census of
1890 as the base. The restriction was to take effect in stages,
reaching full impact in fiscal 1931. The objectives were dual: to
cut the total volume sharply and to establish a national origins
distribution in favor of the British Isles, Germany, and Scandinavia.
Under the final quotas Germany, for example, was permitted 50,000
immigrants annually as contrasted with only 4000 for Italy.

The legislation achieved the aims of its sponsors. The average
annual number of immigrants entering the United States fell from
1,034,940 in the prewar years 1910–14 to 304,182 in 1925–29, a
drop of 70.6 per cent. In the case of Germany the average annual
inflow actually rose from 32,237 in 1910–14 to 47,506 in 1925–29.
For Italy, by contrast, the average fell from 220,967 in 1910–14 to
13,498 in 1925–29.

Immigration restriction had a significant impact upon labor in the twenties and a greater one in the following decade. The earlier tendency toward ethnic, social, and cultural heterogeneity was reversed. The AFL's failure in the great steel strike of 1919 was symbolized by a poster got out by United States Steel, displaying an impassioned Uncle Sam ordering:

*Go back to work!*
*Ritornate al lavoro!*
*Wracajcie do pracy!*
*Griz kite prie darbo!*
*Idite natragna posao!*
*Chodte nazad do roboty!*
*Menjenek vissza a munkaba!*

During the twenties most of the corporation's foreign-born employees learned to speak English, and the proportion of native-born rose. "With the doors almost closed," an International Labor Office report declared, "education is expected gradually to destroy the obstacles which language and illiteracy have hitherto raised ... and so to produce in time a homogeneous working population seeking the same objectives and the same standard of well-being."

During the twenties declining immigration joined a falling birth rate to slow population growth, with the obvious implication for the labor force. As significant as the gross change was its selective character; the entry of unskilled labor from abroad was virtually halted, while the inflow of skilled workmen, for whom there was a considerable demand, was little impaired. The old American custom of employing the most recent immigrants to do the heaviest and dirtiest work had produced constant upward occupational mobility. Now it would be harder for the worker to rise and, by the same token, easier for him to develop class consciousness. Further, as Sumner H. Slichter pointed out, restriction required management to reverse its policy "to adapt jobs to men rather than men to jobs." Hence employers sought to use labor more efficiently. A key solution, of course, was mechanization, helping to explain the high rate of technological advance during the decade.[2]

Immigration restriction, by making unskilled labor more scarce, tended to shore up wage rates. Equally important was the effect upon wage differentials. Low rates for untrained immigrants were in large part responsible for the very wide spread between unskilled and skilled rates. Restriction would tend in time to narrow this differential.

2

Both the flight of the farmer and the curtailment of immigration spurred the mechanization of industry. A dominant characteristic of the American economy in the twenties was the speeding up of the rate of technological change. "In the big plants visited," a British mission reported, "no man is allowed to do work which can be done by a machine." During this decade people in other parts of the world exhibited a consuming curiosity about American factories in much the same way that Americans were curious about Admiral Byrd's discoveries in the Antarctic. The foreign observers who toured United States industry in large numbers were invariably impressed with the eagerness of management to replace workers with machines, to scrap old machines for new ones. The British group, manifesting mixed admiration and disquiet over so large a dose of Progress, found something to cheer about: "It was a relief to get away from the rattle of the conveyor ... into the comparative quietude of these tool rooms, where one could hear the honest impact of hammer on chisel, the scraping of a file, and watch the fashioning of tools. . . ."

The main reason for the quickening pace of technological change was that machinery was cheaper than labor. "I think," a foreign observer declared, "the use of specialized machines is mainly the result of a great scarcity of skilled labor." Turning the coin over from labor supply to labor's price, an employer wrote in 1927:

> In spite of the fact that wages in our factory have more than doubled in the past fifteen years, our manufacturing costs are actually lower now than they were at the beginning of that period. High wages, forcibly thrust upon us by the war, and

always opposed by those in charge of our business, have lowered our manufacturing costs, by making us apply machinery and power to tasks formerly done by hand.

The conditions for mechanization were almost ideal: wages were high in relation to the price of machinery, immigration was limited, and the capital market was abundant and easy. These factors created — as the current phrase had it — the Machine Age. Eugene O'Neill wrote a play about it, *Dynamo,* as did Elmer Rice with *The Adding Machine.* The term "robot," exported from Czechoslovakia, became part of the American language.[3]

The march of machinery in the twenties affected almost every segment of the economy, and a few dramatic illustrations suggest its impact. In 1927 the introduction of continuous strip-sheet rolling opened a new era in sheet-steel and tin-plate production; a continuous mill had the capacity of forty to fifty hand mills. The Danner machine for glass tubing, first offered in 1917, completely replaced the hand process by 1925. The Ross carrier for handling lumber came into general use. The first successful machine to produce a complete cigar was patented in 1917; by 1930, 47 per cent of the 6.5 billion cigars turned out were made by machine. Mechanical coal-loading devices were widely accepted, while mine locomotives displaced the horse and the mule for haulage. Heavy construction was revolutionized by the power shovel, the belt and bucket conveyor, pneumatic tools, the concrete mixer, the dump truck, and the highway finishing machine. The street-railway industry converted to the one-man trolley. Several communication devices won general acceptance: the automatic switchboard and dial telephone, the teletype, and the market-quotation ticker. The motion picture industry entered a new phase with production of the first "talkie" in 1926. More important in the aggregate than these spectacular innovations, however, were the countless small changes which produced, for example, extraordinary increases in output in blast furnaces, in pulp and paper manufacture, in the automobile and rubber tire industries, and in beet sugar mills. Between 1919 and 1929, horsepower per wage earner in manufacturing shot up 50 per cent, in mines and quarries 60 per cent, and in steam railroads 74 per cent.[4]

Advancing technology was the principal cause of the extraordinary increase in productivity that occurred during the twenties. Between 1919 and 1929, output per man-hour rose 72 per cent in manufacturing, 33 per cent in railroads, and 41 per cent in mining. Put somewhat differently by David Weintraub, unit labor requirements (the number of man-hours required per unit of output) declined between 1920 and 1929 by 30 per cent in manufacturing, 20 per cent in railroads, 21 per cent in mining, and 14 per cent in telephone communications. Mills estimated that the physical volume of production for agriculture, raw materials, manufacturing, and construction climbed 34 per cent from 1922 to 1929, an average annual increment of 4.1 per cent. It was his impression that services, if they had been measurable, would have shown an even faster rate of growth. In fact, Americans generally were inclined to explain their economic society largely in terms of its mounting fruitfulness. When W. Wareing, an official of the British Amalgamated Engineering Union, asked John W. Lieb, vice-president of the Edison Company of New York, the secret of high wages, the reply came back promptly: "Productivity."

Rising output was the central force in the steady growth of national income during the twenties. Measured in current prices, which fluctuated narrowly, Simon Kuznets found that national income moved from $60.7 billion in 1922 to $87.2 billion in 1929, a gain of 43.7 per cent, or an average increment of 6.2 per cent per year. The share going to wages and salaries mounted from $36.4 billion to $51.5 billion, an increase of 41.5 per cent. The wage and salary proportion remained unusually constant at about 59 per cent of national income. The share of dividends rose more sharply from $3 billion in 1922 to $6.3 billion in 1929, up 110 per cent. This resulted in a relative increase in dividends from 5 per cent to 7.2 per cent of national income. Wage earners, in other words, did not enjoy as great a rise in income as did those in the higher brackets. A noted study by the Brookings Institution confirms this with respect to the wage and salary share, concluding that "since the war salaries have expanded much more rapidly than wages."[5]

❋

3

The labor force that shared this national income entered a new phase in the twenties, a slowing rate of growth accompanied by a shift from manual to nonmanual employment. Immigration restriction joined with a falling birth rate to retard population advance. In contrast to a gain of 24 per cent in the first decade of the century, between 1920 and 1930 the number of people ten years old and over rose only 19 per cent.

More dramatic than slowing over-all growth was the marked movement from blue-collar to white-collar work, from physically productive to overhead employment. The total number of gainful workers advanced from 41.6 to 48.8 million between 1920 and 1930, a gain of 17.4 per cent. Despite this, the extractive industries — agriculture, forestry and fisheries, and mining — suffered a loss of 3.4 per cent, from 12.2 to 11.9 million persons. Similarly, the manufacturing labor force remained almost stationary, rising only 0.9 per cent from 10,890,000 in 1920 to 10,990,000 in 1930. By contrast, the predominantly white-collar and service industries rose sharply. Trade, finance and real estate, education, the other professions, domestic and personal service, and government employment climbed 45.7 per cent from 11.5 to 16.7 million.

The same pattern emerges when the analysis is transferred from industry to occupation. Between 1920 and 1930, the number of manual workers in the labor force (farmers, farm laborers, skilled workers and foremen, semiskilled workers, and laborers) rose only 7.9 per cent from 28.5 to 30.7 million. Nonmanual workers (professionals, wholesale and retail dealers, other proprietors, and clerks and kindred workers) advanced 38.1 per cent from 10.5 to 14.5 million. During the twenties, that is, the American worker on an increasing scale took off his overalls and put on a white shirt and necktie.

Or, put on an elegant frock, silk stockings, and high-heeled shoes, for women entered the labor force at an accelerated pace at this time. The number of females fifteen and over gainfully occupied rose 27.4 per cent between 1920 and 1930, from 8.3 to 10.6 million. By the latter date, in fact, almost one of every four persons in the labor force was a woman. In Middletown the Lynds found that 89 per cent of the high school girls expected to work after graduation, only 3 per cent indicating they definitely would not. This female employment came as a jolt to foreigners, especially the British.

It was a remarkable sight to see rows of bobbed, gum-chewing, spruce females seated on each side of a rapidly moving conveyor and so busily engaged with their work that not one of them had time to cast a passing glance upon the group of stalwart Britishers, who had considerable difficulty in following the movements of their nimble fingers.

Even more impressive was the 28.9 per cent increase between 1920 and 1930 in the number of employed married women, a rise from 1.9 to 3.1 million. In Middletown the old rule that a girl quit her job with marriage broke down under economic necessity in the twenties. A jobless husband or a need to support a child's education forced working-class mothers into the factories, shops, and offices. The female influx was another bar to organization. Even women who intended to work permanently carried over a vestigial attitude of impermanency that made them hesitant to take out union cards.

The decade of the twenties by contrast witnessed a decline in the employment of children. While in 1910 about one fourth of the boys aged ten to fifteen and one eighth of the girls of the same ages were employed, by 1930 the proportion of boys dropped to 6 per cent and of girls to 3 per cent. The Lynds found an almost total absence of child labor in Middletown. This great social advance was accompanied by a sharp rise in school attendance. The total increase at all levels of education exceeded 6 million between 1919 and 1928. The percentage of those between 14 and 17 enrolled in high school rose from 32 per cent in 1920 to 51 per cent in 1930. "If education is oftentimes taken for granted by the business class," wrote the Lynds, "... it evokes the fervor of a religion, a means of salvation, among a large section of the working class." There were many reasons for the decline in child labor: laws in most states fixing a minimum age for employment and compelling school attendance, the pressure of reform groups and organized labor, advancing mechanization, an adequate adult labor supply, and rising personnel standards in industry.

At the other end of the age scale, older workers struggled with diminishing success to hold on to their positions in the labor force. An advancing economic society placed a premium on speed and nimbleness over experience and judgment. Management came generally to accept the view that senior employees were not as productive as younger workers and that they imposed added liabilities upon those firms that provided insurance, medical, and pension plans. As a typical Middletown employer expressed it: "I think there's less opportunity for older men in industry than there used to be. The principal change I've seen in the plant here has been the speeding up of machines and the eliminating of the human factor by machinery." This opinion crystallized in the widespread adoption of age limits for hiring. Studies of Dayton, Ohio, and the states of Maryland and California revealed that a large proportion of employers fixed these limits at ages ranging from thirty-five to fifty, particularly in utilities and transportation, where pension plans were common. The inevitable consequence was a higher incidence of unemployment among older workers; once let go, they found it extremely difficult to find new jobs. This problem so concerned the Couzens Committee, investigating unemployment for the Senate in 1929, that it urged industry, the states, and the federal government to consider a system of old age pensions.[6]

The organization of the labor market was haphazard in the extreme. Since the United States Employment Service was ineffective and collective bargaining governed hiring in only a handful of industries, the typical employer picked at will. The only restraint upon his power to hire was tightness in the labor market, and this simply did not exist during the decade except for a few months in 1923. The person seeking work in most cases was both powerless and incapable of exercising a rational choice if alternatives were available. In Middletown, for example, "most of the city's boys and girls 'stumble on' or 'fall into' the particular jobs that become literally their life work." The fetish workmen made of education was in part, at least, a yearning for rationality in an unreasoning world.

The worker was seldom afforded the opportunity to rise in the social scale. He lacked the qualifications for the professions and the capital for business. His main hope for upward mobility was within the hierarchy of the firm that employed him. Even here, however, the opportunities were limited. In twenty-one months in 1923–24, plants employing 4240 workers in Middletown had only ten vacancies for foremen — one chance in 424. A businessman, the Lynds found, looked forward to the steady improvement of his lot. But, "once established in a particular job, the limitations fixing the possible range of advancement seem to be narrower for an industrial worker." His position, of course, was more dismal if he happened to be a member of a minority group. In greater or lesser degree, the Irish, the Italians, the Jews, the Mexicans, and the Negroes suffered in the labor market. To dwell only upon the last, the ones who probably enjoyed the doubtful distinction of sustaining the most severe discrimination: Negroes were the last to be hired and the first to be fired, were seldom allowed to do skilled work and almost never given supervisory jobs, were assigned the older, dirtier, and less pleasant work places, were paid less for the same work, and were often denied membership in labor unions. A Negro song of protest went this way:

> *Trouble, trouble, had it all mah day.*
> . . . . . . . . . . . . . . . . . . . .
>
> *Can't pawn no diamonds,*
> *Can't pawn no clo'*
> *An' boss man told me,*
> *Can't use me no mo'.*
>
> *Rather get me a job, like white folks do.*
> *Rather get me a job, like white folks do.*
> *Trampin' 'round all day,*
> *Say, "Nigger, nothin' fo' you."* [7]

This complaint could have been voiced as well by white members of the labor force, since the prosperity of the twenties was accompanied by heavy unemployment. Foreign observers reported more men than jobs in each locality they visited. The absence of government statistics, disgraceful in itself, makes it impossible to report the actual volume of joblessness. Evidence that severe unemployment existed, however, is beyond dispute. The noted Brookings Institution study, *America's Capacity to Produce*, estimated that the economy in 1929 operated at only 80 per cent of its practical capacity. Weintraub calculated that the jobless constituted 13 per cent of the labor force in 1924 and 1925, 11 per cent in 1926, 12 per cent in 1927, 13 per cent in 1928, and 10 per cent in 1929. Woodlief Thomas made minimum unemployment estimates for nonagricultural industries of 7.7 per cent in 1924, 5.7 per cent in 1925, 5.2 per cent in 1926, and 6.3 per cent in 1927.

Studies of particular localities and firms reinforce this conclusion. The University of Pennsylvania's Wharton School of Finance survey of Philadelphia in April 1929 revealed that 10.4 per cent of the wage earners were idle, the great majority because of inability to find work. A study in November of the same year in Buffalo showed 10 per cent of the labor force totally unemployed and an additional 6.5 per cent on part time. Half of the men and almost two thirds of the women had been out of work more than ten weeks. In Middletown in the summer of 1924 a firm that considered 1000 workmen its "normal force" actually employed 250. In the first nine months of that year only 38 per cent of the heads of the working-class families studied worked steadily. When out-of-town firms offered to run ads for machinists in 1924, Middletown employers persuaded the local papers not to carry them in order to preserve the town's pool of skilled workmen. United States Rubber closed its New Haven plant in April 1929, throwing 729 out of work, and its Hartford plant in September 1929, making another 1105 jobless. A study of their experience in finding work revealed that average lost time in New Haven was 4.38 months and in Hartford 4.33 months. Both groups suffered disastrous losses in earnings even when they were fortunate enough to find new jobs. A similar survey of displaced cutters in the Chicago men's clothing industry in the twenties told much the same story.

So severe, in fact, was unemployment during the decade that social workers, burdened with the misery that followed in its wake, became alarmed. The International Conference of Settlements, meeting at Amsterdam in 1928, heard the Belgian economist Henri de Man claim that industrialism produced both more goods and more permanently unemployed. The National Federation of Settlements, convening in Boston that same year, found that unemployment was the prime enemy of the American family. Nor were all employers as callous as those in Middletown. It was on December 17, 1928, that President Daniel Willard of the Baltimore & Ohio made his famous statement before the Couzens Committee:

It is a dangerous thing to have a large number of unemployed men and women — dangerous to society as a whole — dangerous to the individuals who constitute society. When men who are willing and able to work and want to work are unable to obtain work, we need not be surprised if they steal before they starve. Certainly I do not approve of stealing, but if I had to make a choice between stealing and starving, I would surely not choose to starve — and in that respect I do not think I am unlike the average individual.

The least onerous form of unemployment — seasonal — worsened during the twenties. Mild government pressure to regularize production in those trades noted for intermittency — construction, garments, maritime, and entertainment — had no noticeable effect. In addition, the great new automotive industry and its suppliers contributed heavily to seasonality. "Because of the ease with which labour can be obtained and discarded," an Australian observed, "there is little necessity for the employer to stabilize his rate of production over the year."

Far more serious was technological unemployment, the price paid for progress. A paradox of the American economy in the twenties was that its glittering technical achievement gave birth to a dismal social failure. At the top of the boom in 1929 Wesley Mitchell wrote that technological unemployment "is a matter of the gravest concern in view of the millions of families affected or threatened . . . and in view of their slender resources." Weintraub estimated that between 1920 and 1929 in manufacturing, railways, and coal mining, machines displaced 3,272,000 men, of whom 2,269,000 were reabsorbed and 1,003,000 remained unemployed. There were, naturally, sharp variations in employment impact among industries. This is evident from Jerome's figures on labor time saved by particular machines: talkies saved 50 per cent, cigar machines 50 to 60 per cent, the Banbury mixer 50 per cent, the highway finishing machine 40 to 60 per cent, and various coal loaders 25 to 50 per cent. One of the coal devices was invented by a man named Joy. Union miners in Kentucky had a song about his contraption which they called "Joy Days."

> *Here is to Old Joy, a wonderful machine,*
> *That loads more coal than any we've seen.*
> . . . . . . . . . . . . . . . . . . . .
>
> *Ten men cut off with nothing to do,*
> *Their places needed for another Joy crew.*
> . . . . . . . . . . . . . . . . . . . .
>
> *We will pick out a spot with plenty of room*
> *Where Joy can rest till the day of doom.*
>
> *We will call it a holiday to dig him a nice grave,*
> *Then march in a body to lay him away.*
>
> *We will lay him away as it should be done,*
> *And pay all expenses from our burial fund.*
>
> *Monuments we will buy, inscribed nice and neat,*
> *And place one each at his head and feet:*
>
> *"Here lies Old Joy, a man we couldn't use,*
> *For the damned old hellion wouldn't pay any dues."* [8]

Mr. Joy's coal loaders and the other mechanical marvels of the time did more than displace men; they radically and continuously changed the content of jobs in American industry. Whether the net effect was to raise or lower the general level of skill is a nice question to which there is no ready answer. In the expanding New York commercial printing industry, for example, the substitution of machine-fed for hand-fed presses increased the demand for skilled operators and reduced demand for less skilled hand-feeders. Jerome found that mechanization had a differential impact in various segments of the industrial process: in material handling it displaced the unskilled; in systematizing the flow of production it reduced the skilled; in displacing manual by machine processing it usually diluted skills; in improving already mechanized operations it cut down on the semiskilled; in stimulating machine construction and repair it increased the demand for the skilled. A workman taking a job in the twenties had little way of knowing whether his skills would improve or decline; he could be reasonably certain, however, that a machine would soon change the content of his job.

The labor surplus during the decade was the principal reason for the low turnover rate, which fell to one half the prewar level. A contributory, though secondary, factor was the personnel management movement, one of whose main objectives was to stabilize the labor force within the firm. Excepting a few months in early 1923, turnover was unusually low. A study of manufacturing industries by the Metropolitan Life Insurance Company revealed that the median monthly rate of accessions fluctuated narrowly between 3.3 and 5.2 per cent and of separations between 3.1 and 4.0 per cent in the years 1924–29. Industry made few hires and workers seldom quit. This was, in W. S. Woytinsky's words, "a period of increasing labor market rigidity." [9]

The issue of unemployment, serious though it was, excited little general interest. It received no more than passing attention in the 1928 presidential campaign. In Middletown, despite severe joblessness, "unemployment as a 'problem' virtually does not exist." The business people granted that steady work was a desirable objective but considered it quite utopian. Clinch Calkins found three widely held ideas at the time: that unemployment existed only in bad times, that the only ones who suffered were those too thriftless to save, and that a man who really wanted work would find it. The fact that all were false in no way limited their currency.

The pervasiveness of the problem, however, compelled some squaring off with reality. The stirrings among social workers have already been noted. A handful of firms — notably Dennison Manufacturing, Hills Brothers, Procter & Gamble, Columbia Conserve, Packard, and Leeds & Northrup — sought to level out seasonality. The Amalgamated Clothing Workers and the International Ladies' Garment Workers set up unemployment insurance or guaranteed employment schemes in a few markets. Mr. Justice Brandeis and industrial engineer Morris Llewellyn Cooke tried to persuade President Frank Aydelotte of Swarthmore to establish an unemployment study unit at the college under the direction of Paul Douglas, a project that had barely got under way when the market crashed. Finally, the Senate Couzens Committee held hearings on unemployment in late 1928 and early 1929 and proposed this modest program: adequate statistics, reorganization of the United States Employment Service, encouragement of private unemployment insurance schemes, planning public works with an eye to stabilizing employment, and study of both the effects of industrial concentration on employment and the feasibility of a system of old age pensions. Virtually no one listened.[10]

4

Labor's burden in this period of prosperity was not limited to unemployment; workers faced as well an unequal distribution of income. There were in 1929, the Brookings Institution found, 27,474,000 families of two or more persons. Nearly 6 million families, over 21 per cent, received less than $1000 per year; about 12 million, more than 42 per cent (including those below $1000), had incomes under $1500; nearly 20 million, 71 per cent (including those under $1500), took in less than $2500. The combined incomes of 0.1 per cent of the families at the top of the scale were as great as those of the 42 per cent at the bottom. The number who received over $1 million per year rose from 65 in 1919 to 513 in 1929. The distorted distribution of savings was even more striking. The 21,546,000 families at the low end, 78.4 per cent, had no aggregate savings at all, while the 24,000 families at the high end, 0.9 per cent, provided 34 per cent of total savings. The authors of *America's Capacity to Consume* went further:

It appears . . . that . . . income was being distributed with increasing inequality, particularly in the later years of the period. While the proportion of high incomes was increasing . . . there is evidence that the income of those at the very top was increasing still more rapidly. That is to say, in the late twenties a larger percentage of the total income was received by the portion of the population having very high incomes than had been the case a decade earlier.

Inequality in distribution exerted a constant pressure upon those at the bottom of the scale to supplement the head of family's job earnings. A study of federal workers in five cities in 1928 with salaries not in excess of $2500 showed that 15 to 33 per cent of the husbands took outside work, 15 to 32 per cent of the wives got jobs, and many children contributed to family income. Only 2 to 10 per cent of the families lived within the husband's government salary.

Even in the relatively prosperous year 1929 a majority of workers' families failed to enjoy an "American standard of living." This conclusion cannot be substantiated precisely, because the government made no survey of workers' budgets between 1919 and the mid-thirties, another illustration of the sorry state of labor statistics. The most careful contemporary student of the problem, Paul Douglas, made estimates for larger cities that can be keyed in roughly with the family income distribution published in *America's Capacity to Consume*. Though Douglas' work, *Wages and the Family*, appeared in 1925 it is not inapplicable to 1929, because retail prices fluctuated fairly narrowly.

Douglas set out four standards of living: poverty, minimum subsistence, minimum health and decency, and minimum comfort ("the American standard"). At the poverty level the family would have an inadequate diet, overcrowding, and no resources for unexpected expenses. This would cost a family of five $1000 to $1100. In 1929 there were 5,899,000 families of two or more with incomes of less than $1000. The minimum subsistence level was sufficient to meet physical needs with nothing left over for emergencies or pleasures. To reach it a family of five needed $1100 to $1400. There were 11,653,000 families of two or more who received less than $1500. The minimum health and decency level supplied adequate food, housing, and clothing as well as a modest balance for recreation. It cost $1500 to $1800. There were 16,354,000 families with incomes under $2000. Since "the American standard" required an income of $2000 to $2400, it seems safe to conclude that the majority of wage earners' families failed to reach this level.

Income inequality and the relatively low standard of living of American workers, however, did not arouse social protest. There were two principal reasons for this silence. The first, doubtless the more important, was that the material well-being of the employed sector of the labor force was improving. Lincoln Steffens wrote in 1929: "Big business in America is producing what the Socialists held up as their goal: food, shelter and clothing for all." Douglas estimated that the average annual earnings of employed workers in all industries, including agriculture, advanced from $1288 in 1923 to $1405 in 1928, a gain of 9.1 per cent. Their real annual earnings improved slightly more, 10.9 per cent. The movement of wages, money and real, actually understates the impact of the rising standard of life because it fails to account for either the diversity of items on which income was spent or the benefits available free. In the twenties consumption broadened markedly to encompass goods and services that made life easier and more diverting — automobiles, telephones, radios, movies, washing machines, vacuum cleaners, and electric iceboxes, as well as improved medicine, hospitalization, and life insurance. The growth of installment buying made the consumer durables available to many with small cash resources. To a limited extent workers were able to share in this advance; ownership of a Model T, even if shared with the finance company, was more than entertaining: it inclined one to accept things as they were. In addition, all segments of the population benefited from the sharp improvement in free social services, most notably education, but including also public libraries, playgrounds and parks, and public health facilities.

The other reason for the failure of social protest to emerge was that the standard of living of American workmen, regardless of its deficiencies, was among the highest in the world, a consideration of no mean importance to urban masses who were largely immigrants themselves or the children of immigrants. Foreign observers visiting this country were, on the whole, im-

pressed with the differential in living standards between the
United States and their own nations. "Taken all in all," André
Siegfried remarked, "the American worker is in a unique position."[11]

## 5

The uniqueness of the American worker's position in the late
twenties with respect to wages, hours, and conditions of employment deserves examination. In so far as wages are concerned, it
is necessary to note again the inadequacy of the statistics. Though
they are superior to those for employment, the data leave much
to be desired. Those who doubt this statement are referred to the
preface of Douglas' *Real Wages in the United States, 1890–1926*
for an account of the extraordinary expenditure of energy demanded of the serious student of wages at that time. To this
must be added some reluctance by employers, the prime source,
to reveal how much they paid their workers.

During the prosperity of the twenties wages, money and real,
moved gently upward. Unlike the two preceding periods of good
times, the turn of the century and the first war, there was no sharp
rise. In fact, wages in the era 1923–29 were characteristically stable,
reflecting the surplus of labor and weak unions.

Average hourly earnings in all industries, according to Douglas,
advanced from 66.2¢ in 1923 to 71¢ in 1928. A survey of 1500 manufacturing plants by the National Industrial Conference Board revealed that their average hourly earnings moved from 54¢ in
1923 to 58.1¢ in 1929. Hourly earnings in bituminous coal fell
from 84.5¢ in 1923 to 68.1¢ in 1929. Railroad earnings moved from
56.5¢ in 1923 to 62.5¢ in 1929. The average hourly earnings of
common laborers in the basic steel industry were 41.7¢ in 1923 and
41.4¢ in 1929. The average daily wages without board of farm
laborers were $2.25 in both years.

Weekly earnings, according to the same sources, were cut from
a similar pattern. The Douglas figures for all industries were
$30.39 in 1923 and $33.32 in 1928. The NICB series for manufacturing advanced from $26.54 in 1923 to $28.24 in 1929. Weekly
earnings in bituminous coal were virtually unchanged, $25.60 in

1923 and $25.72 in 1929. On the railroads there was a rise from $26.65 in 1923 to $28.49 in 1929. Farm wages without board per month were $48.25 in 1923 and $51.22 in 1929.

The movement in real wages was little different since the Bureau of Labor Statistics Cost of Living Index showed virtually no change in the terminal years. Real hourly earnings in all industries, Douglas found, rose 7.2 per cent between 1923 and 1928, while real weekly earnings, reflecting some drop in hours, advanced only 2.5 per cent. The NICB, covering real earnings in manufacturing at the end of the period, found that hourly rose 2.1 per cent and weekly 0.7 per cent between the opening quarter of 1928 and final quarter of 1929.

These developments stand out in sharper relief by examining the wage experience of the quarter of a million employees of the United States Steel Corporation. Their average hourly earnings moved sharply upward from 58.3¢ in 1923 to 65¢ in 1924 and then slowly up to 68.5¢ in 1929. Their average weekly earnings rose gradually from $34.54 in 1923 to $35.70 in 1928 and then declined to $31.67 in 1929. Real hourly earnings between 1923 and 1929 advanced 17.4 per cent and real weekly earnings fell 8.3 per cent.

A striking feature of the American wage structure at the end of the twenties was the unusually wide spread that characterized differentials. A major finding of a contemporary International Labor Office study of industrial relations in the United States was that differentials were greater here than in other nations. They were more than marked; with the notable exception of the Ford Motor Company, they were ubiquitous.

Regional differentials, of course, were dramatic when they involved wage rates paid in the South. A study of hourly earnings in seventeen cotton-textile jobs in 1928, for example, revealed that the weighted average paid by mills in New England exceeded that paid in the South Atlantic area by 43.6 per cent. Another survey of twelve jobs in the same industry and year showed that the average in five New England states was 41.4¢ as contrasted with 29.1¢ in the same number of southern states. The prevailing rate for common labor by region on January 1, 1928, was as follows:

East South Central    27¢
South Atlantic        29
West South Central    31
West North Central    41
Mountain              44
New England           47
Pacific               47
East North Central    47
Middle Atlantic       49

The common labor rate in basic steel in 1929 ranged from 27.9¢ in the southern to 45.6¢ in the Great Lakes districts.

The spread in differentials based upon skill was also unusually wide. In 1929 many firms, particularly those that were not organized, paid their craftsmen approximately twice as much as their male laborers. In the steel industry, for example, average hourly earnings in blast furnaces were 91.8¢ for blowers and 37.3¢ for laborers, in puddling mills $1.374 for heaters and 38.9¢ for laborers. In foundries earnings for pattern makers were 83.3¢ and for laborers 49¢. In the furniture industry hand carvers earned 95.6¢ and laborers 37.8¢. In meat packing splitters averaged 87.9¢ (maintenance bricklayers $1.322) and laborers 46.6¢. In the cigarette industry machine fixers earned 57.3¢ and laborers 30.1¢.

At least as significant is the conclusion suggested by the available data that skill differentials widened rather than narrowed during the twenties, a further illustration of distortion in income distribution. A study by the Federal Reserve Bank of New York of twenty manufacturing industries in its reserve district showed that the common labor hiring rate advanced only 3¢ between 1923 and 1927. Douglas came up with similar results for unskilled labor nationally, which led him to observe: "The failure of the unskilled to share in the general advance which was obtained during the eight years from 1919 to 1926 . . . is indeed startling."

To a considerable though immeasurable extent these skill differentials rested upon an ethnic base. American industry historically had tended to use the most recent immigrant strains and Negroes for the heaviest, dirtiest, and lowest paid work. In the twenties unskilled jobs were filled largely by the great prewar outpouring from southern and eastern Europe supplemented by Mexicans and Negroes, and these ethnic groups bore the brunt of wage discrimination.

Differentials based upon sex were general, if one gives weight to the fragmentary statistics; the growing number of women entering the labor force could count upon unequal treatment in wage rates. The NICB survey of manufacturing, for example, found that the average hourly earnings in 1929 of male skilled and semiskilled workers were 67¢, of male unskilled 50.3¢, and of females at all levels of skill 40.1¢. In foundries in 1929 the earnings of male coremakers were 74.4¢ and female 46.9¢, male laborers 49¢ and female 38.6¢, male assemblers 65.7¢ and female 44.1¢. In meat packing in 1929 earnings of male trimmers were 52.1¢ and female 37.1¢, male blowers, graders, and inspectors 51.7¢ and female 38.4¢, male machine tenders 53.1¢ and female 35.4¢. In the furniture industry in 1929 male assemblers earned 56¢ and female 31.7¢, male craters and packers 43.5¢ and female 33.1¢, male finishers 50.5¢ and female 37.1¢. In cotton goods, earnings of male frame spinners in 1928 were 33.9¢ and female 27.6¢, male creelers 29.8¢ and female 23.9¢, male weavers 39.2¢ and female 37.1¢.

Again, the spread widened during the twenties, if the NICB survey is a guide. In 1923 the differential in manufacturing between the average hourly earnings of the male skilled and semiskilled over females of all grades of skill was 22.8¢; by 1929 the gap had broadened to 26.9¢. In 1923 the male unskilled enjoyed an advantage of 6.3¢ over females of all skills; in 1929 the spread reached 10.2¢. The rule in American industry was unequal pay for equal work based upon sex.

Another differential of note in the twenties was that between union and nonunion rates. Although it is not possible to measure this spread statistically, its existence is beyond question. Douglas, for example, calculated average hourly earnings in 1926 for the following predominantly organized industries: building trades $1.313, granite and stone $1.301, newspaper printing $1.150, book and job printing $1.037, planing mills $1.027, metal trades 96.1¢, baking 92.5¢, and bituminous coal 71.9¢. By contrast, earnings in the following mainly nonunion manufacturing industries in 1926 were: steel 63.7¢, shoes 52.8¢, meat packing 49.4¢, woolens 49.1¢, sawmills 36.1¢, and cotton 32.8¢. An Australian delegation which visited the United States in 1927 concluded that unions had a substantial effect in keeping nonunion rates from falling, since employers feared that wage cuts would lead to organization. This differential, like the others, widened during the twenties. That is, some unions, particularly in the building trades, pushed wages up more rapidly than did the employers of unorganized workers. A study by Frederick C. Mills of the annual rate of advance in nine wage series between 1922 and 1929 placed union wages in the lead. Trade unions, though on the defensive at this time, succeeded in maintaining and even improving wage differentials over unorganized workers, another illustration of the inequity of income distribution inasmuch as union membership was heavily weighted by the skilled.

A final differential was that between urban and farm wage rates. According to the Bureau of Agricultural Economics, daily farm wages without board reached a postwar peak of $3.46 in 1920 and then declined to $2.25 in 1923. There was no change during the balance of the decade, the rate closing out in 1929 at an identical $2.25. Douglas estimated that the spread between urban factory workers and farm laborers rose from $18.22 per week in 1920 to $21.12 in 1926. Once again, differentials widened and income distribution became more distorted.[12]

In conclusion, wages in American industry in the twenties were characterized primarily by very sharp differentials of all sorts and by very slow movement. That the spreads were too wide is evident from both a contemporary comparison with other nations and from the great pressure to narrow them which arose in the following decade. There can be no doubt that these differentials nourished general discontent among workmen even though little voice was given to it at the time.

"During the past decade," the authors of the NICB study wrote in 1930, "the stability of hourly and weekly earnings . . . stands out as the most significant feature." The vaunted high-wage philosophy of American industry, of which more later, appears to have activated employers' vocal chords more than their purse strings. The International Labor Office study could find few firms outside Ford that raised wages in response to this ideological appeal. Unions, bargaining for only a minor fraction of the labor force, had no more than a secondary impact upon wages. Their main effect affirmatively was to push their members' rates up somewhat more rapidly than nonunion rates and, negatively, to serve as a brake upon falling rates in both sectors. In the latter case unions contributed to general wage stability.

The stickiness of money and real wages between 1923 and 1929, at a time when productivity was rising dramatically, had an unhealthy effect upon the economy as a whole. As Douglas observed, "This failure of real wages to advance was at least one cause of the rising profits during this period, and was consequently an appreciable factor in the extraordinary increase of stock market values which occurred." Between 1923 and 1929, according to Simon Kuznets, the dividend component of national income rose 64.1 per cent while wages and salaries advanced only 20.6 per cent. The cases of U.S. Steel and Toledo-Edison are instructive. While hourly earnings in Big Steel rose modestly and weekly earnings fell, profits almost doubled between 1923 and 1929. Toledo-Edison's net earnings advanced from $2.8 million in 1925 to $4.5 million in 1929; no general wage increase was granted during this period. Noting the sharp rise in profit margins, Mills commented, "An ultimate explanation of the economic collapse which was precipitated in 1929 must give full weight to this striking fact." [13]

The stability that was so notable a feature of wages in the twenties was characteristic of hours of work as well. Douglas calculated that weekly hours in all industries were 50.4 in 1923 and 49.8 in 1926. For full-time hours in manufacturing the Census of Manufactures reported 51.1 in 1923 and 50.6 in 1929, the Bureau of Labor Statistics 51 in 1923 and 50.3 in 1926, the NICB 49.9 in 1923 and 49.6 in 1929. Actual weekly hours in manufacturing, according to BLS, were 47.3 in 1923 and 45.7 in 1929; according to NICB, 49.2 in 1923 and 48.3 in 1929. An index constructed by Lazare Teper of weekly hours in eleven industries (ten manufacturing, plus construction) revealed a decline of only 0.1 per cent between 1923 and 1928.

Although there was a good deal of talk in the twenties about shortening the work week, almost no one did anything about it. The steel industry, in the face of public condemnation of the twelve-hour day during the 1919 strike, improved hours early in the decade. Yet in 1929 average full-time weekly hours were still 54.6, and 14 per cent of steel employees customarily worked in excess of sixty hours. The AFL endorsed the five-day week in 1926 but made no effort to achieve it. In January 1928 the Clothing Workers sought the forty-hour week in the Chicago and Rochester markets without success. The railway unions, disturbed over technological unemployment, came out for the eight-hour day and the five-day week in April 1929, but accomplished nothing. The notable gains were made by the decade's most prominent anti-Semite, Henry Ford, and the Jewish Sabbath Alliance. Ford inaugurated the five-day week in his plants in 1926, and the Alliance persuaded a matzoth factory to institute this schedule shortly afterward. A survey in 1928 uncovered only 216,000 workers on five days, many of them working as many hours as they had on the six-day week. The only general improvement that occurred was the five-and-one-half-day week; the Lynds found that the Saturday half holiday prevailed in Middletown.

Unions, excepting the case of Ford, were mainly responsible for these modest gains. Further, organized workers enjoyed a marked superiority in hours of work. Douglas found that in 1926 average weekly hours in six primarily union manufacturing industries were 45.9 in contrast with 52.2 in the eight predominantly nonunion industries he studied.

The economic significance of stability of hours at a high level in the face of rising productivity is much the same as that for wages. Advancing technology permitted a sharp reduction in the work week; with spotty exceptions, no gains were made. Nor is there any evidence that American workers, as distinguished from unions, sought shorter hours. As an Australian observer remarked:

> I think that the most striking thing about labor in America is that it has become the slave of the paymaster. In Australia men value their hours of leisure too highly to sell them for any wages. In America men can be got to work . . . for almost any hours if it means extra pay.[14]

In 1929 there were very few workers who enjoyed what are now called fringe benefits. In fact, the only benefit mentioned in the 1929 *Handbook of Labor Statistics* was vacations with pay. This source indicates that virtually no production workers, excepting a handful in the unionized trades, received this benefit, providing a sharp contrast with European experience. If New York City was typical, the majority of salaried employees got paid vacations, usually two weeks. The situation with respect to holidays with pay was similar; they were virtually unknown for hourly-paid workers with the exception of a few covered by union contract, but they were generally granted to salaried people. Differentials for night shift work do not seem to have existed at all. A fair proportion of workers received a premium for overtime, usually time and one half, but this was hardly a prevailing practice.[15]

Perhaps the most serious shortcoming of industrial relations in American industry in the twenties was the inadequacy of grievance machinery outside the unionized firms. To be sure, a fair number of plants had company unions, more fully treated below, whose main accomplishment was grievance handling. Further, the personnel management movement mitigated some of the harsher aspects of shop relations by transferring the power to discharge from foremen to personnel managers. Yet in 1929 only a few American plants had personnel departments, and they were concentrated almost exclusively in the large firms. The nostalgic and comforting notion that the president's door was always open to the aggrieved worker was badly out of date. In the case of Middletown the presidents of three of the largest manufacturing firms lived in other states. When an Australian visitor checked such a claim in a Detroit plant, he discovered that the president worked in New York and had not been seen by a high official of the company for ten years. In fact, the great majority of workmen in American industry had no effective means of voicing grievances. Hence countless legitimate complaints went unheard, with the consequent embitterment of workers toward their bosses which was to manifest itself so dramatically after the crash.

The lot of the worker without recourse to a grievance procedure

is dramatized in the testimony of an Englishman who worked
for Ford:

It's worse than the Army, I tell ye — ye're badgered and vic-
timized all the time. You get wise to the Army after a while,
but at Ford's ye never know where ye're at. One day ye can go
down the aisle and the next day they'll tell ye to get the hell
out of it. In one department they'll ask ye why the hell ye haven't
got gloves on and in another why the hell ye're wearin' them.
If ye're wearin' a clean apron, they'll throw oil on it, and if a
machinist takes pride in 'is tools, they'll throw 'em on the
floor while he's out. The bosses are thick as treacle and they're
always on your neck, because the man above is on their neck,
and Sorenson's on the neck of the whole lot — he's the man that
pours the boiling oil down that only Henry makes.

This experience was certainly not typical of American industry as
a whole. Yet it does reveal what could and sometimes did happen
in the absence of due process in the shop.

Only the unionized sector of industry contained adequate grievance procedures and even here the picture was spotty. At the end
of the decade the BLS found that most agreements provided for
some machinery. The majority, however, terminated with conciliation. Only twenty-three of eighty-six international unions had
locals with contracts that required arbitration as the final step
in the grievance procedure, and these were concentrated largely
in the building and printing trades. In the railroad industry,
system boards of adjustment handled grievances but with something less than full success. In this, as in other matters, the
needle trades led the way. The ladies' garment, men's clothing,
fur, and headgear industries all had well-established permanent
arbitration systems. Several of the impartial chairmen, notably
Herbert H. Lehman, Harry A. Millis, and William M. Leiserson,
accumulated experience in the twenties that was to prove in-
valuable when they moved on to a larger stage in the following
decade. Finally, the hosiery industry adopted the needle trades
system in the first national agreement between the manufacturers
and the hosiery workers in 1929, with Dr. Paul Abelson becoming
impartial chairman.[16]

6

The urban worker without effective means of voicing his grievances within the shop began to express them haltingly by indirection in his vote. The inadequacy of the statistics measuring the economic lot of labor in the twenties is compounded in an attempt to assess political behavior, for the election results afford no precise way of separating voters who were workers from those who were not. Nor did the 1928 presidential election, the basis of the present analysis of workers' political attitudes, provide evidence of a labor vote as such.

The presidential race in which Herbert Hoover decisively defeated Alfred Smith has been conventionally regarded as a triumph for the *status quo,* an election in which the voters of the nation reaffirmed their approval of the happy marriage between the Republican Party and Coolidge prosperity. As a Hoover campaign card put it:

HARD TIMES
Always come when Democrats try to run the nation.
ASK DAD — HE KNOWS!
Take No Chances!
Vote a Straight Republican Ticket!!

To be sure, domestic bliss was ruffled by two seemingly extraneous issues: prohibition and Al Smith's Catholicism. According to the usual view of the election, the "real" issues of the day — the fragility of prosperity, the sorry plight of coal and textiles, the farm depression, and the inequities in income distribution — were largely ignored.

Reassessment of the 1928 election against the backdrop of political developments in the thirties has placed it not at the close of an old era but rather at the onset of a new one. There can be no doubt of the soundness of this approach and its relevance to the present study.

The central emerging force in American political society at this time was what Samuel Lubell has called the revolt of the city.

The 1920 census was the first to show that a majority of the people in the United States lived in urban areas. The immense movement of population to the cities came primarily from immigration and secondarily from agrarian regions, largely the Appalachian area and the South. Both streams flowed into the urban working class and contributed to its growth by a much higher birth rate than that characteristic of the older stocks that formed the backbone of the middle class and the Republican Party. Between 1920 and 1928 some 17 million potential voters reached the age of twenty-one, mainly the children of poor immigrants and migrants to the cities. To them, Lubell has observed, "the loyalties of Appomattox and the Homestead Act were details in history books"; nor did they owe allegiance to the individualistic tradition of the farm and the small town.

The 1928 presidential election was the first in which this emergent force became evident, but it was not as sharply defined as it was to become later, reflecting the crosscurrents of a transition phase. In part the conflict was between city and farm, in part between the ethnic strains of the "new" immigration pressing for status against the older Anglo-Saxon and northern European stocks, in part between Catholics and to a lesser extent Jews pushing into a dominantly Protestant society, and in part between the working and middle classes. Where the new forces joined, as in Boston, the Democrats made sweeping gains by virtue of the coincidence of urbanism, Irish Catholicism, and the working class. Where they were blurred, as in Los Angeles, the Democrats made only slight advances because urbanism was diluted by transplanted midwestern farmers who were mainly old stock Protestants and were without a working-class outlook.

The Democratic Party, entering the twenties with a predominantly Anglo-Saxon, Protestant, and rural tradition, was the first arena in which this struggle was fought out. At the Madison Square Garden convention of 1924 the older elements in the party — rural, old American, Protestant, southern, western, and middle class — rallied behind William Gibbs McAdoo, while the new forces — urban, "new" immigration, Catholic, Jewish, eastern, and working class — formed behind Al Smith. The agonizing draw these protagonists fought in the Garden marked the turning point in the transformation of the Democratic Party. By 1928 the revolt of the city was triumphant within that party and Smith won the nomination handily at Houston.

In the election the new forces coalesced behind the Smith candidacy. As Richard Hofstadter has said:

> It was . . . in the person of Al Smith that urban immigrant America first produced a national hero. Smith was a paradox, for he was a Tammanyite and yet a Progressive, a product of an urban machine whose name was synonymous with corruption, and yet a political leader whose governorship gave ample evidence of warm interest in popular welfare. A Catholic, a wet, a graduate of the city streets who had never been to college, an adroit politician with a history of genuine achievement, he became a symbol of the possibilities of urban America. With his coarse voice, and uncertain pronunciation and syntax he was a perfect victim for American snobbism, but for the same reason he was a sympathetic figure to those who were shut out from the respectabilities of American middle-class life, and above all to the immigrant stocks.

William Allen White, the Sage of Emporia, voiced the outrage of rural America in a speech at Olathe, Kansas, on July 12, 1928, in which he branded Smith the apostle of the saloon, prostitution, and gambling.

Hoover epitomized the contrasting forces. He was primarily of Anglo-Saxon stock, was a Quaker, and had been born on a farm in Iowa. The Republican candidate extolled the rural virtues, nostalgically invoking the "rugged individualism" characteristic of an earlier America. The party for which he spoke was wedded to these values by both habit and design.

Hoover's smashing victory — he polled 21,385,000 votes to Smith's 14,981,000 — was a triumph for the rural, Protestant, old American, middle-class forces. As the St. Paul *Pioneer-Press* rejoiced: "America is not yet dominated by its great cities. Control of its destinies still remains in the smaller communities and rural regions, with their traditional conservatism and solid virtues. . . . Main Street is still the principal thoroughfare of the nation." [17]

In view of the events to follow, however, the vote for the victor, Hoover, was not nearly so enlightening as that for the vanquished, Smith. The accompanying table contrasts the percentage of the major party vote garnered by the Democrats in 1928 with the percentage in 1920 in the major metropolitan areas of the United States (La Follette's powerful third-party showing in 1924 makes comparison with that election less meaningful): [18]

## DEMOCRATIC PER CENT OF MAJOR PARTY VOTE

| City | 1920 | 1928 |
|---|---|---|
| **Northeast** | | |
| Boston | 38.5% | 67.3% |
| New York | 30.5 | 62.1 |
| Jersey City | 38.1 | 60.5 |
| Providence | 36.6 | 53.1 |
| New Haven | 36.5 | 50.5 |
| Baltimore | 40.9 | 48.3 |
| Buffalo | 28.8 | 46.6 |
| Hartford | 35.9 | 46.4 |
| Pittsburgh | 22.5 | 42.7 |
| Newark | 26.1 | 41.3 |
| Philadelphia | 22.7 | 39.7 |
| **Midwest** | | |
| Milwaukee | 25.8 | 57.4 |
| St. Louis | 39.4 | 52.2 |
| Chicago | 23.7 | 46.9 |
| Cleveland | 32.1 | 46.1 |
| Kansas City | 49.0 | 43.3 |
| Cincinnati | 40.8 | 42.7 |
| Indianapolis | 43.5 | 40.1 |
| Minneapolis | 24.2 | 39.2 |
| Detroit | 19.0 | 37.1 |
| **West** | | |
| San Francisco | 25.4 | 50.2 |
| Salt Lake City | 40.9 | 49.8 |
| Portland | 38.1 | 37.4 |
| Denver | 34.4 | 35.9 |
| Oakland | 22.7 | 33.9 |
| Seattle | 22.9 | 32.6 |
| Los Angeles | 23.8 | 29.0 |

South

| City | 1920 | 1928 |
|------|------|------|
| New Orleans | 64.7% | 79.5% |
| Memphis | 65.0 | 60.1 |
| Atlanta | 66.5 | 59.8 |
| Richmond | 76.7 | 48.7 |
| Birmingham | 77.8 | 48.1 |
| Houston | 65.7 | 44.2 |
| Louisville | 45.1 | 39.7 |
| Miami | 58.2 | 39.0 |
| Dallas | 74.2 | 39.0 |

In interpretation of the table, the 1920 election was evidence of the traditional urban strength of the Republican Party; Harding carried all twenty-seven cities outside the South as well as Louisville, and in only the case of Kansas City was the outcome close. By 1928, however, a great shift had occurred. In twenty-four of the nonsouthern centers Smith made gains, usually very heavy, and he carried eight. He lost ground in only three. The result in the South was in exact reverse. Smith fell far behind the 1920 Democratic candidate, Cox, in eight of the nine southern towns; the only one in which he advanced was that most cosmopolitan and Catholic of the cities of the South — New Orleans. In fact, Hoover in 1928 carried seven of these nine communities. Regionally the urban drift to the Democrats was most dramatic in the Northeast, less so in the Midwest, and least in the West, with the Republicans gaining only in the South.

A similar pattern emerges from an examination of the nonurban counties in which coal mining was concentrated in the states of Pennsylvania, Illinois, Indiana, West Virginia, Kentucky, and Alabama. Excepting the last, all went heavily for Harding. In the ten predominantly coal counties of Pennsylvania the Democratic share of the two party vote climbed from 36.3 per cent in 1920 to 44.7 per cent in 1928, and in the five Illinois mining counties from 37.5 to 48.7 per cent. There was little change in the two coal counties of Indiana, the northern state in which the Ku Klux Klan exerted its greatest influence — 47.7 to 45.3 per cent. The same can be said of border West Virginia's sixteen leading coal counties, 43.3 per cent in 1920 and 42.8 per cent in 1928, and of border

Kentucky's ten main coal counties, 39.5 and 40.7 per cent. In Alabama's two mining counties the Democratic share dropped from 71.9 per cent in 1920 to 49.2 per cent in 1928.

In conclusion, city workers and coal miners, their numbers growing prodigiously, began in the twenties that great movement into the Democratic Party that was to become so critical a feature of American politics in the following decade. In large part this voting shift spoke with the voice of protest. But the grievances of labor in 1928 were primarily related to status, ethnic and religious minorities yearning for equality. In lesser part the complaints were economic. With the crash and the Great Depression that followed, economic protest became the cutting edge of politics; at that time American labor was simply to reaffirm in larger measure the political choice it had already made.

By way of postscript for 1928 it is necessary to chart the dismal labor showing of the Marxist parties. Norman Thomas on the Socialist ticket polled only 268,000 votes, more than a third of them in New York. He ran far behind Debs's 902,000 in 1920. The Communists, led by William Z. Foster, did much worse, winning only 48,000 adherents. American labor, obviously, showed little inclination to choose either of these parties as the vehicle of protest.[19]

# 7

Although the 1928 election was a portent for the future, its contemporary significance for labor lay in the fact that Hoover and the Republican Party scored a signal victory. This could not have occurred unless many workers had voted for Hoover, and their willingness to do so is suggestive of their social outlook at the end of the twenties.

Observers were struck with the materialism that permeated all levels of American society, including labor; workers shared with their bosses a devout reverence for the almighty dollar. In Middletown workmen derived little satisfaction from their work. "There isn't twenty-five per cent of me paying attention to the job," a bench molder stated. Since this frustration was linked to a dim prospect for advancement as workers, the more energetic strove to enter the middle class. The acquisition of money was the main objective of life, and people were measured by the externals money bought — where they lived, how they lived, the make of car they drove. In the shops, workers were more concerned with maximizing income than with learning skills or gaining leisure by shorter hours.

Inasmuch as this materialism was joined to a vestigial rural tradition of individualism as well as a heterogeneous labor force, trade unionism found the social climate forbidding. As Lewis L. Lorwin pointed out, "The desire for steady employment and higher earnings became more dominant in the minds of the workers than the feeling for industrial freedom and independence."

Among the workers who benefited economically the mood was conservative. "The American workman," a French visitor observed, "when he realizes that society assures him a comfortable income, is ready to accept the existing organization of industry. He has made an excellent place for himself . . . so he has no wish to destroy it by stirring up a revolution." From the standpoint of social outlook Douglas emphasized the direction rather than the amount of change in real wages. The fact that the lot of the workers was improving rather than deteriorating made them "more satisfied with the social and political system." "Arise ye wretched of the earth," the appeal of the "Internationale," he found "curiously unreal to the better-paid American workers who, with few exceptions, are not afflicted with starvation, and the more skilled of whom own automobiles, radio sets, small homes, and bank books, as well as chains." [20]

This comment by Douglas raises a question: Did a working "class" emerge? Manipulations of census data are not significant because the problem is in the realm of ideas rather than of statistics. The answer is two-headed and, in a sense, internally contradictory. On the one hand, a growing proportion of the labor force found itself in an employee rather than a self-employed status, a fact of immense importance in the daily lives of the people involved. On the other hand, they failed to develop class consciousness — self-realization as a proletariat — in the Marxist sense.

This dichotomy formed the central finding of *Middletown:*

It is . . . this division into working class and business class
that constitutes the outstanding cleavage in Middletown. The
mere fact of being born upon one or the other side of the watershed roughly formed by these two groups is the most significant
single cultural factor tending to influence what one does all day
long throughout one's life; whom one marries; when one gets up
in the morning; whether one belongs to the Holy Roller or
Presbyterian church; or drives a Ford or a Buick; whether or not
one's daughter makes the desirable high school Violet Club; or
one's wife meets with the Sew We Do Club or with the Art
Students' League; whether one belongs to the Odd Fellows or to
the Masonic Shrine; whether one sits about evenings with one's
necktie off; and so on indefinitely throughout the daily comings
and goings of a Middletown man, woman, or child.

Yet, search as they did, the Lynds failed to find evidence of
working-class consciousness. Radical movements had no influence; left-wing publications were virtually unknown; and even
the relatively conservative AFL struggled merely to survive.
Though the great majority of workers were destined to remain
workers for the duration of their productive lives, many were
sustained by the hope of rising to a higher class. Large majorities
of high school boys and girls, for example, could find nothing up-
setting in the fact that some people were rich. If the collectivity
of workers constituted a "class," it was an inert body with little
dynamism or direction.[21] The labor movement reflected this inertia.

## CHAPTER 2

# The Paralysis of the Labor Movement

COMING FROM A LAND with a vigorous tradition of trade unionism, H. G. Adam, an Australian visiting the United States in 1928, was appalled by the condition of the American labor movement. He referred disparagingly to "kow-towing unionists." One told him, "We do not foment strikes. . . . We get what we can by going to the employer and asking for it." He later saw this business agent at a Chamber of Commerce luncheon. "Labour organization," he observed, "exists only by the tolerance of employers. . . . It has no real part in determining industrial conditions." What struck him particularly was the absence of working-class solidarity. "Unionism in America is not a political creed or a social movement." Each trade sought only its own material advantage and lost no time worrying about others.

A favorite sport of writers at this time was to denounce the American labor movement. Magazines were full of articles with such titles as "The Collapse of Organized Labor," "Decline of Organized Labor in America," and "The Twilight of the A. F. of L." The American Federation of Labor, the repository of the bulk of union membership, bore the brunt of these attacks. On October 8, 1929, the Scripps-Howard newspapers, traditionally friendly to the Federation, published a powerful attack entitled, "Where Is the A. F. of L.?" "The truth is," the editors concluded, "that the A. F. of L. is failing miserably in its stewardship. Every year its weakness is more apparent. . . . The A. F. of L. is accurately described as the aristocracy of labor. All aristocracies are subject to dry rot." Although William Green was incensed, some within the movement were prepared to admit its accuracy. After conferring with the publishers, George Berry, president of the Printing Pressmen, wrote: "To be perfectly frank about it, I think the editorial was a 'corker' and told the directors to give us more of the same kind of 'stuff'."

These writers who attacked the AFL pointed repeatedly to the same weaknesses: the emphasis on a craft structure, the ignoring of industrial unionism, jurisdictional disputes, inertia in organizing the unorganized, weak or tyrannical or corrupt leadership, philosophic individualism, fraternization with businessmen, and political impotence. As E. W. Shimmons summed up, the AFL is "a life raft, — though now beginning to get waterlogged, — for skilled labor." [1]

Though harsh, this criticism had merit. In 1929 the United States labor movement stood still as the main stream of American society swept by.

1

Union membership, which had touched a peak of 5,047,800 in 1920, according to Leo Wolman, fell precipitously to 3,622,000 in 1923. For the six following years it showed little change, and that was downward. In 1929 there were 3,442,600 members. By 1930 union membership constituted a bare 10.2 per cent of the more than 30 million nonagricultural employees counted in the census, a marked drop from 19.4 per cent in 1920.

Equally serious was the fact that organization was heavily concentrated in a handful of industries, notably construction, coal, railroads, printing, clothing, street railways, water transportation, and music. Great segments of American industry were either totally devoid of unionization or showed only a trace. This was the case with most of manufacturing, including such important industries as steel, automobiles, electrical equipment, rubber, cement, textiles, chemicals, and food. In the extractive industries effective unions existed in neither nonferrous metals nor petroleum. Motor transportation revealed only a smattering of membership. Utilities, banking, insurance, retail and wholesale trade, the professions, and domestic and personal service were predominantly unorganized. Furthermore, the uneven prosperity of the twenties fell with a heavy hand upon unionism. Several fairly well organized industries, coal and New England textiles, were "sick," while two others, clothing and shoes, shared hardly at all in the good times.

A number of once proud and powerful organizations met with disaster. The downfall of the United Mine Workers was most important and will be recounted in detail below. The International Ladies' Garment Workers' Union, which had had 105,400 members in 1920, was torn asunder by competition from nonunion shops and a bitter conflict between right-wing and Communist forces in the mid-twenties. By 1929 the anti-Communist group was in full command — of a shadow of the former organization. It had but 32,300 members and was penniless. In fact, on June 15, 1928, banker Herbert H. Lehman loaned the ILGWU $25,000, interest free, "enabling us," in the words of President Benjamin Schlesinger, "to a substantial extent to maintain the integrity of the organization." The manager of an ILGWU local wrote in 1929: "The situation in the industry is deplorable; the situation in the union calls for nothing but gloom." The Mine, Mill and Smelter Workers, heirs to the militant tradition of the Western Federation of Miners, disintegrated. In 1926, President Charles A. Moyer and his entire executive board were forced to resign, and the 1927 convention was attended by only half a dozen delegates. "The organization," V. H. Jensen has written, "was hanging on to life by a thread when the depression struck." In March 1929, the executive board of the Brewery Workers voted to postpone the convention on financial grounds; declining membership and income made it necessary to conserve funds for the fight against prohibition. The Hotel and Restaurant Employees, once primarily a bartenders' organization, suffered from both the general decline of unionism and the impact of the Eighteenth Amendment; its membership fell from 66,000 in 1917 to 40,000 in 1925. At the 1929 convention President Edward Flore quipped: "An optimist is a bartender who pays his union dues." The Seamen's Union, which had 115,000 members and contracts on all coasts in 1920, collapsed during the decade. "The members," Hyman Weintraub wrote, "melted away, vanished, disappeared." The shipowners asserted complete control over wages and conditions on the waterfront. The union had virtually no income and had to accept a donation from the British maritime organization in 1929 to remain afloat. The 1927 "convention" consisted of nine delegates, and the pretense of holding one the following year was abandoned. This tale of union woe could be multiplied many times over.

A significant feature of labor's decline in the twenties is that it struck especially hard at organizations that were either wholly or predominantly industrial in structure. This was true of the coal miners, of Mine Mill, of the Textile Workers, of the ILGWU, and of the Brewery Workers. At the same time many craft unions either held their own or made gains. The building trades, for example, advanced from a membership of 789,500 in 1923 to 919,000 in 1929, the printing trades from 150,900 to 162,500, and the railway organizations declined modestly from 596,600 to 564,600. This shift in membership strength was reflected increasingly within the American Federation of Labor. Craft organizations, with their conservative outlook on both internal and general matters, came to dominate both the Executive Council and the conventions of the AFL, with an inevitable impact upon policy.

The differential penetration of unionism can be visualized more sharply at the local level. For this purpose C. L. Christenson's cross section of collective bargaining (exclusive of interstate transportation) in Chicago in 1929 is helpful. Of the city's 1,326,000 workers, 294,000, or 22 per cent, were organized, approximately twice the degree of unionization in the nation.

Among industry groups construction revealed the highest level of organization, 98,000 of 121,000 workers, or 81 per cent. It was followed by local transportation and communication with 65,000 of 93,000 or 70 per cent. Here the street railways were completely unionized, as was three fourths of local trucking; the telephone industry, however, had no organization. The public service, with 21,000 of 55,000, 39 per cent, came next. In fourth position was manufacturing with 64,000 of 380,000, 17 per cent. Here building materials, related to construction, led the way, followed by cigars, beverages, wearing apparel (notably men's clothing), and printing (particularly newspapers). By far the most important manufacturing industry in Chicago, metal products, showed only 8900 union members of 142,000 workers, 6 per cent. Tied for fifth at 12 per cent were domestic and personal service (21,000 of 180,000) and professional service (10,000 of 85,000). In the former, unionization was concentrated almost entirely among building service employees and barbers; in the latter, exclusively in the amusement crafts. Trade was seventh, with a slight 8 per cent (13,000 of 156,000) of its potential organized. Here unionism was concentrated in butcher shops, lumber and coal yards (again tied to construction), and oil stations; the high-employment grocery, department, and clothing stores were essentially unorganized. Last place was occupied by clerical services, with no members among 255,000 workers.

Christenson noted that union strength tended to gather in industries characterized by local product markets and small units. Here labor organizations could more readily maintain control over the supply of labor, particularly where skills were involved, as in the building, printing, and metal trades. Once firmly established in these areas, unionism tended to spread to related industries, especially to those employing the building trades and the teamsters. A further assist existed in some industries (for example, motion picture theaters and newspaper printing) from the fact that labor cost was a minor fraction of total cost. In industries organized in large units with national markets, unions had made almost no headway. Here, too, hostile employers' associations were most active in fighting the establishment of collective bargaining. In general, five groups had failed to organize: semiskilled and unskilled factory workers, professionals, clerical workers, those employed in trade, and domestic servants.[2]

The failure of union membership to advance in the twenties was a source of contemporary bafflement to labor economists. The theory of union growth to which they generally subscribed was the business cycle, that membership expanded in good times and contracted in bad. Hence they expected the labor movement to rise in the prosperity of the twenties. In fact, union growth is responsive to a complex set of forces which are only partly cyclical in origin; therefore, the stagnation of the twenties must be explained in pluralistic terms.

A basic reason for union failure was the heterogeneous labor force. There have been few periods in American history in which workers have been so sharply divided, and the labor movement — composed predominantly of older white stocks, skilled workmen in the manual trades, and males — held out little appeal to these diverse elements. This was the time when the great prewar wave of immigrants from southern and eastern Europe and their progeny were adjusting to American life, and, with a few exceptions, these ethnic groups found little that was attractive in native trade unionism. Displaced farmers who migrated to town and formed a large segment of the labor force in such industries as textiles, autos, and rubber brought with them a rural tradition of individualism. The Negro found the unwelcome mat laid out for him at the union door. The marked shift from manual to white-collar work placed a growing proportion of the labor force largely beyond organization. The related rising incidence of female employment had a similar effect.

A second factor was that the social climate was too severe for the delicate plant of unionism. "The business of America," President Coolidge observed soberly, "is business." Buttressed by Horatio Alger, the success stories in the *American Magazine*, and Bruce Barton's translation of the New Testament into the lingo of the advertising game, the businessman emerged as the hero of the age. His influence was not limited to economic affairs. "Businessmen crowded into the White House until the luncheon guest-list looked sometimes like a chart of interlocking directorates of high finance," Willam Allen White wrote. In the mansion of the dominant business philosophy there was no room for trade unionism. Those shrewd managers who conceived the "American Plan" sold the idea that collective bargaining was worse than bad, it was un-American. The mood of the times stressed individualism; one got ahead by himself and not by collective action. This notion permeated the outlook of the working class.

Third, economic expansion in several forms militated against labor organization. The major new industries that emerged, notably automobiles, utilities, chemicals, and rubber, were bitterly antiunion. A number of others, especially coal, textiles, and hosiery, migrated to the inhospitable South. The enlargement of enterprise was invariably at a cost to labor organization. The great merger movement of the twenties produced combinations in steel, baking, autos, tobacco, and glass that were without exception opposed to collective bargaining.

Craft unionism, fourth, was structurally obsolete in many parts of this new economic society. Mechanization diluted or transformed traditional skills, and labor organizations were either unwilling or unable to make structural adaptations to the changes. Further, large new segments of the labor force could not be accommodated within the existing craft system. Union leaders preferred to hold on to what they had when they could and undertook no major offensive to organize the unorganized.

Fifth, employers' policies, which will be dealt with more fully later, were antiunion either in purpose or effect. There was the panoply of belligerent tactics, of which the company union and the hostile employers' association were noted examples, which were designed to frustrate unionism. Similarly, welfare capitalism, by cementing the loyalty of the worker to the firm, weakened the appeal of labor organization.

A sixth factor was the generally unfriendly attitude of the courts in labor cases, considered in detail in Chapter 4. Perhaps most notable was the widespread willingness of judges to grant injunctions and also the blessing they gave to the yellow-dog contract. Where a court issued an injunction to enforce such a contract under the notorious Hitchman doctrine, it was literally illegal for workers to form or join a union.

Finally, the business cycle, though it swung upward, contained elements that neutralized the prospect for union growth. One was that the cost of living remained stable, and the other that, excepting a few months of 1923, there was always a substantial volume of unemployment. In addition, real wages rose somewhat and, to the extent that they were spent on automobiles, movies, and radios, tended to divert workers' interests from unionization.[3]

A further sign of union weakness in the twenties was the marked decline in the number of strikes, producing a calm seldom if ever matched in American industrial history. H. M. Douty's index of the average annual rate of work stoppages (1916–21 = 100) showed:

|         | Disputes | Workers involved |
|---------|----------|------------------|
| 1916–21 | 100      | 100              |
| 1922–25 | 34       | 43               |
| 1926–30 | 18       | 11               |

By 1929, therefore, the strike as an instrument of collective bargaining, to say nothing of social protest, had fallen into almost total disuse. Further, if we are to believe J. I. Griffin's figures, even those isolated stoppages that did occur were more likely to disappoint than please their instigators. In 1927, he reported, 41.4 per cent of strikes failed compared to 25.5 per cent that succeeded; in 1928, 39.3 to 27.9 per cent; and in 1929, 41.2 to 28.1 per cent.

The causes of this industrial quiescence are not hard to find. In part it was a reflection of union debility and the accompanying program of labor-management cooperation. There were no great organizational drives and the predominantly craft organizations, where they did bargain, were loath to strike for better conditions. On the employer side the combination of the carrot of welfare capitalism and the stick of repression dissuaded workers from joining unions and so from fashioning an instrument for strikes. Finally, the economic climate was not conducive to industrial disputes; the cost of living was stable and the real wages of those who were employed advanced modestly.[4]

In the twenties union leaders seemed bereft of ideas to deal with this decline of their movement. They were ideological prisoners of the past.

2

In 1928, James A. Duncan, president of the Granite Cutters union since 1895 and first vice-president of the AFL since 1894, died. He was the last of the Federation's original founders to pass from the scene, and his death followed by four years that of the dynamic English Jew who in the public mind *was* the American Federation of Labor for the better part of half a century. As Clifton Fadiman has rhymed:

> *Samuel Gompers*
> *Found the labor movement in rompers.*
> *After many changes and chances,*
> *He left it in long pantses.*

Gompers, as a great leader should, both shaped and mirrored the policies, structure, and administration of the AFL. Hence the legacy that he passed down to the second generation of leaders in effect constituted the Federation as it was in the late twenties.

Gompers accepted capitalism not because he considered it an ideal system for the worker but because it was here and here to stay. The job for labor was to make the best of it pragmatically. The house of Utopia would take care of itself; philosophers might debate its furnishings but busy unionists had no time for idle speculation. Conflict between the classes was endemic under capitalism, but not the class struggle in the Marxist sense. Rather it was a contest over how the economic pie would be cut. Here labor's aim was both clear and simple: "More, more, more, now."

The foundation of power was economic organization. Workers, therefore, must engage in voluntary self-organization to make sure that they got "more." For the worker the supreme loyalty must be to the union; for the union supreme loyalty must be to the economic advancement of the worker. For the organization this loyalty must be exclusive, uncontaminated — "pure and simple." Nonworkers who intervened in union affairs were meddlers; Gompers viewed with suspicion intellectuals, well-intentioned reformers, and Socialists. "Voluntarism" was the key word in his philosophy, and self-organization of the working class lay at its base. "Gompers," John R. Commons observed, "became even more class conscious than Marx himself."

The trade union's purpose was to maximize the price of labor through collective bargaining. It sought to control labor, not to control industry. The sanctions in bargaining were the strike, the picket line, and the boycott, weapons that must be protected at all costs. The consummation of bargaining was the trade agreement, whose terms were to be scrupulously observed by unions and employers alike.

The framework of self-organization was the craft; workers with the same skill shared more in common than those who worked in the same plant, industry, or locality. History had shown that craft organizations survived under pressure while the others collapsed. Patterns of craft sank deep roots. A machinist would say to a boilermaker: "Listen, pal, you don't have a trade. All you have is a habit." Though Gompers dealt with industrial organizations and ultimately favored the organization of the unskilled and semi-skilled, as well as women and Negroes, he relegated them to a secondary place in his scheme of the labor movement. Further, his personal position as president of the Federation rested upon an uneasy coalition of powerful craft organizations. Industrial unions, he felt, fouled the jurisdictional ground plan of the AFL by crossing the lines of skill. The problem with which they were designed to deal could best be handled either by voluntary merger of craft unions or by formation of trade departments, such as the building and printing trades departments.

The sovereignty of the international union derived from the charter it received from the AFL, its jurisdiction, its title to job territory in a property-conscious society. This title was inviolate; workers could not elect another representative, no other organization might trespass upon the jurisdiction, and the Federation might not withdraw a union's title without its consent. The worst of all heresies in Gompers' eschatology was dual unionism, unlawful aggression upon job territory to which title was held. G. E. Barnett has noted, "The amazing fact . . . is that American trade unions alone among all the trade unions in the world are engaged on a large scale in political jurisdictional disputes." The only solution to a conflict between unions over job territory was voluntary agreement between them, with the Federation acting merely as "honest broker." The AFL was powerless to impose a settlement upon a strong union since it would simply withdraw from the Federation, an essay in self-defeat.

Ultimate power within the labor movement resided in the international union. The local was a necessary evil, intrinsically irresponsible. If a local were allowed to bargain and strike at will, it would undermine the standards of sister locals and squander the defense fund. Hence it must be subjected to the constitutional discipline of the international. As the repository of jurisdiction and the power to bargain, the international union bore a similar relationship to the Federation. In Gomper's view, the AFL was a loose confederacy, a voluntary association of autonomous internationals. "To the International Unions," he declared, "belong all power not specifically delegated to the Federation." As a result, the AFL's most powerful organ was the Executive Council, the constituted assembly of presidents of the powerful internationals. The role of the AFL president internally was that of mediator, to cajole, advise, and reconcile differences between internationals, but never to order.

Gompers harbored a profound distrust for the state when it intervened in economic life. "The gulf between politics and industry is as wide as the seven seas and as deep." Industry, therefore, must be self-governing, with employers and workers sharing equally in an industrial democracy. The only labor legislation he genuinely favored was that to encourage and protect self-organization and vital union activities — the strike, picketing, and the boycott. He had little stomach for social legislation, laws fixing minimum wages and maximum hours, except as they affected the weak and unorganized, like women and children. Gompers opposed state-sponsored unemployment and health insurance and was unenthusiastic about old age pensions. The branch of government he feared most was the judiciary, for judges, he thought, knew least about economic society, and life tenure protected their normally antilabor prejudices. "God save Labor from the Courts," he declaimed. Gompers was against government ownership of the railroads and utilities. Employees of the state lacked freedom to organize, to bargain, and to strike; they were better off dealing with private employers. To the Socialists he announced: "Morally you are unsound; socially you are unsafe, and industrially you are an impossibility." A union that sought to create a labor party was mixing oil with water. With occasional historic exceptions, he favored limiting political activity to electing labor's friends and defeating its enemies.

Gompers was a nationalist and in his later years a bit of a superpatriot. Despite the fact that he was himself an immigrant, he vigorously espoused restriction, particularly Chinese exclusion. Nor did he object to the protective tariff where it sustained labor standards in industry. Gompers strongly opposed international Marxism, both of the Second and Third International variety, and especially after the Russian Revolution. His voice was one of the earliest and loudest to denounce the USSR and the Communist

Party. In fact, he regarded the AFL as the principal bulwark of American capitalism and democracy against Communism. To the extent that patriotism made the labor movement respectable he enjoyed respectability, but it was not a paramount consideration.[5]

3

After a prolonged illness Sam Gompers died on December 13, 1924. His choice for the succession was Matthew Woll of the Photo-Engravers, generally regarded as the "crown prince," but Woll had great enemies, notably John L. Lewis of the Mine Workers. The aged Duncan of the Granite Cutters eagerly sought the office, at least for the interregnum until the next convention, but could find no one to support his candidacy. When the Executive Council met on December 19, 1924, the stage directions were explicit: the man must be liked by all and detested by none and he must be a pallid contrast to the flamboyant Gompers. In other words, he must be willing to be led rather than determined to lead. The two most powerful organizations in the Federation, the Miners and the Carpenters, were in agreement upon their man. When the ten-member Council voted, eight cast their ballots for William Green. Green and Duncan politely refrained from voting.

The new president was both symbol and symptom of the state of the Federation in the twenties. Although the choice might be considered a historic accident in that he had hardly been heard of, it was an accident shaped by history.

The Greens — Hugh, an English coal miner, and Jane, his Welsh bride — had settled in Coshocton, a mining town in central Ohio, in 1870. Their first son, William, was born on March 3, 1872, in a miner's shack and was reared in a small house on Hardscrabble Hill. The family was large, content, deeply religious, and very poor. The boy received a brief education in a one-room schoolhouse and aspired to the Baptist ministry. Since there was no money to pay for the education, at sixteen he joined his father in the mines.

Hugh Green was a confirmed trade unionist and the boy quickly absorbed his philosophy. Naturally articulate and dedicated, William won office in his local union at eighteen and gradually advanced within the hierarchy of the United Mine Workers. By 1900 he had become president of Subdistrict 6 and in 1906 president of the Ohio district. He married at twenty-one and became a devoted husband and the father of six children. Green was a proud Elk, Odd Fellow, and Mason. Elected as a Democrat, he served two terms in the Ohio Senate from 1911 to 1915. While there he successfully sponsored several labor laws, one a mine-run statute abolishing screens at the mines and tipples and the other the basic workmen's compensation statute of Ohio. In 1911 he was appointed statistician of the international and two years later was elected its secretary-treasurer. This was probably the happiest time of his life, since he enjoyed the impersonality of facts and figures more than the turmoil of union politics. In 1913 the seventh vice-presidency of the AFL Executive Council fell vacant and was offered to UMW President John P. White, who refused it as beneath his dignity. It was then extended to the miners' second in command and Green promptly accepted. The habit of availability was yielding a good return.

Though of modest height, Green possessed a broad frame and an ample midsection, upon which he wore a heavy gold watch chain. His face formed an almost perfect circle and revealed a cherubic mouth, a turned-up nose, an expanse of forehead under thinning hair, and kindly smiling eyes behind metal-rimmed spectacles. The many years he had spent underground left indelible marks on his complexion — blue spots shot deep under the skin. In manner, Raymond Clapper said, he was in a rather dignified way "as plain, as plodding, and as undramatic as his name." He was a steady Baptist who neither smoked nor drank. He wore conservative well-tailored clothes and exuded respectability. He enjoyed addressing business and banking leaders as well as students at prominent universities. Green's platform manner was measured in tone and stentorian in volume, accompanied by loose waves of the hand. His voice lulled rather than stirred his audiences, and the ideas he conveyed were usually encased in platitudes. Westbrook Pegler in a gesture of unfriendliness branded him the "All-American mushmouth." Green was impeccably honest and did not lack personal courage. His fundamental outlook was decent and humane; he had warm sympathy for oppressed and persecuted peoples, detested prejudice in all its forms, sought to assist political prisoners with whose views he disagreed, and held firmly to the concept of free speech. He accepted the legacy of ideas handed down by Gompers without question, excepting only the pre-eminence of the craft form. As a miner, Green was a firm, though circumspect, believer in industrial unionism.

Green's weaknesses, however, were fundamental: he was an uncomplicated intellectual mediocrity and he was without the power to lead. As John Lewis was to remark in an unkind moment: "Explore the mind of Bill Green? Why, Bill and I had offices next door to each other for ten years. . . . I have done a lot of exploring in Bill's mind and I give you my word there is nothing there." Sensitive to his limitations, Green allowed his ego to be warmed in the spotlight of national prominence and he swallowed flattery in big mouthfuls. He liked people and was anxious that they should like him. More important, however, was the fact that he could not command the respect of his peers. Benjamin Stolberg caustically observed of the 1926 AFL convention:

> Detroit was William Green's convention. It showed his weakness, in which lies his strength as an incumbent of his office. He can continue to lead the American Federation of Labor as long as he follows the hard men on its Executive Council — Tobin, Duffy, Rickert, Fischer, Woll; as long as the heads of the Big Three Internationals — the miners, the carpenters, and the electrical workers — think he is safe. At Detroit they all tested his strength. They found him weak. They are for him.

During Green's incumbency, power within the Federation flowed from the president to the Executive Council. So long as the members of the Council were in essential agreement, as was the case in the late twenties, the organization could present a good face to the world. With the Great Depression and the acute issues it raised, however, division within the Council was to become inevitable and the man its members had chosen to lead them was incapable of producing unity. He viewed the AFL as "a family." It was the function of the officers, in his words, "to find a basis of accommodation, harmonize conflicting opinions, to settle differences which arise, not among enemies, if you please, but among the family . . . of organized labor." He was a man of peace who shunned conflict and failed to understand how reasonable men could engage in it. He was a master of what Lewis has called the policy of "anxious inertia." [6]

4

Under Green's gentle leadership in the twenties the Federation assumed a new posture, one that it had never taken since its inception in the eighties. It shifted from militancy to respectability. With business supreme, the AFL sought to sell itself as a necessary auxiliary of business. The Federation voiced concern not just with the welfare of the worker, as in the past, but now also with that of the employer. Further, it advertised itself both as a proponent and a bastion of the existing order of society, an enthusiastic admirer of capitalism and a stanch enemy of bolshevism. In the New Era, labor too was determined to be, if not stronger, at least new. This mood evidenced itself in a panoply of policies adopted by the AFL and its constituent unions in the latter part of the decade.

One of the most notable was union-management cooperation, that is, a joint program to make production more efficient. "More and more," Green urged in 1925, "organized labor is coming to believe that its best interests are promoted through concord rather than by conflict." Hence "unions will increasingly concern themselves to see that management policies are efficient. Unless management is efficient, labor standards cannot keep advancing." In return for this effort to improve output, the AFL hoped for more general acceptance of unionism by employers. This was evident in the noted union brief submitted in the injunction proceeding in 1928 involving the company union on the Interborough Rapid Transit system. Trade unionism was justified in large part upon the grounds that it would "increase production, eliminate waste, and maintain continuity of service."

Fine as this program sounded, it won acceptance in only a tiny fragment of even unionized industry — four or five well-publicized arrangements and a handful of others. The most substantial experiment took place on the railroads and was fathered by Otto S. Beyer, Jr., who had sponsored a cooperative scheme in the government's Rock Island arsenal during the war. After several years of his urging and the push given the unions by the collapse of the 1922 shopmen's strike, Beyer was permitted to set up an experimental scheme in the Glenwood shop of the Baltimore & Ohio in 1923. The following year it was extended to all B & O roundhouses and repair shops and was endorsed by the AFL Railway Employees' Department, which hired Beyer as its technical adviser. In 1925 cooperation was adopted by the Canadian National, the Richmond shops of the Chesapeake and Ohio, and the Chicago and North Western, and the next year by the Chicago, Milwaukee, St. Paul and Pacific. The last two plans were abandoned at the end of the decade.

The following principles were accepted in the railroad plans: recognition by the carriers of unions affiliated with the Railway Employees' Department; establishment of local joint committees meeting periodically with equal representation from each side; meetings on company time; written suggestions by committee members to improve efficiency; authorization to local management to institute suggestions not costing more than a fixed amount with appeal to higher management for more expensive changes; and creation of joint regional and system committees to deal with suggestions not disposed of at the local level. Obviously, the plans could work only if both sides participated enthusiastically.

According to Sumner H. Slichter, the results of the railway experiments were mixed. On the affirmative side, workers benefited from improved relations with management, a reduction in the number of and better handling of grievances, superior working conditions, larger union membership, somewhat higher wages, and more stable employment. The carriers benefited from some gains in output, the elimination of waste, and improved quality of work. Negatively, he pointed mainly to the fear by workers that the plans would curtail employment, the difficulties stemming from the weakness of the shop-craft unions, opposition from the lower ranks of management, and disagreement over who would get the fruits of improved efficiency. That the disadvantages seem to have outweighed the advantages is evident from the fact that the movement lost ground before the decade was out.

A second experiment in cooperation took place in the Cleveland ladies' garment industry. On December 24, 1919, as a compromise between ILGWU insistence on timework and employer efforts to retain piecework, the parties established a system of production standards in the Cleveland market. Costs were critical because of a competitive disadvantage with New York and because both sides sought to avoid subcontracting by the predominantly "inside" Cleveland shops. The plan soon ran into difficulties, for the workers were dissatisfied with earnings under the standards and distrusted the time-study engineers and the basic data with which they worked. As a result, the program experienced a series of crises during the decade.

More notable were the efforts in the cotton textile industry, north and south. The Naumkeag Steam Cotton Company of Salem, Massachusetts, manufacturer of Pequot sheets and pillow cases, had been a profitable firm that paid high wages and maintained a closed shop with the United Textile Workers. The general decline of the industry hit Naumkeag in 1926. To forestall the stretch-out, which many companies were introducing, the union proposed and management accepted cooperation in 1927. Meetings were held to improve the quantity and quality of production with modest success. When the year 1928 proved financially disastrous, however, the company in December reluctantly proposed the stretch-out along with wholesale dismissals which aroused intense worker opposition. As an alternative the union called upon Morris L. Cooke, who arranged for an engineering study which showed that the cost problem was acute. This led on March 1, 1929, to the establishment of "joint research" (a fancy name for the stretch-out) for increasing work performed by individual operatives. The program, with misgivings all around, barely got under way when the crash arrived. From the Textile Workers' experience at Naumkeag stemmed the union-management cooperation proposal that was so prominent a feature of the southern textile organizing drive in 1929, whose dismal failure has been charted in the Prologue.

A fourth venture in cooperation took place at the Rocky Mountain Fuel Company, the second largest of the Colorado producers, and stemmed from the fact that a woman of unusual vision, Josephine Roche, acquired control in 1927. As a result of observing the bloody Colorado strike of 1913–14, she was determined to establish successful collective bargaining. Miss Roche assembled a like-minded group of executives: Merle D. Vincent, a distinguished progressive attorney, John R. Lawson, a former official of the miners' union, and Edward P. Costigan, another noted liberal lawyer. On August 16, 1928, Rocky Mountain Fuel entered into a first agreement with the United Mine Workers. The men received a favorable differential in wages over the prevailing scale. In return, they pledged "co-operative effort and increased efficiency." This took the form of pushing consumption through a coal sales committee and output by a joint pit committee. Productivity rose from 5.27 tons per man per day in 1928 to 5.98 in 1929. How much of this gain was due to improved worker as contrasted with managerial efficiency is impossible to say. What is clear, however, is that the experience was unique in the coal industry and differed from all other cooperative schemes in that the initiative came from management rather than the union. So impressed was Lieutenant Governor Herbert H. Lehman of New York with the social value of this venture that he granted Miss Roche a loan in May 1929.

A scattering of other AFL unions also experimented with cooperation: the Street Railway Employees in the Philadelphia and Pittsburgh transit systems, the Hosiery Workers in its first industry-wide (or, more accurately, union-wide) agreement in 1929, and the Printing Pressmen. This, however, was the limit of actual experimentation undertaken by affiliates of the Federation.

A union outside the AFL, the Amalgamated Clothing Workers, also adopted cooperation, here to meet the competition of nonunion shops, a particularly acute problem because the Amalgamated was weakest in the growing low-quality markets. In response to a demand by Chicago manufacturers to cut wages in 1924, the union devised this policy: no strikes in union shops; organization of nonunion markets; limited concessions on wage rates; extension of piecework or standards of production; abandonment of restrictive rules that affected costs; and assistance to employers to improve garment design, reduce costs, and raise quality. In Slichter's judgment, the program produced mixed results. Both total employment and the proportion of workers organized declined from 1923 to 1929; employment in nonunion areas advanced; the wage differential between organized and unorganized markets failed to increase; the union retained a larger share of the market than it would have without the policy; and the Philadelphia shops were unionized in 1929.

Viewed as a whole, union-management cooperation must be regarded as a failure. Experiments were undertaken in only a handful of firms and were soon abandoned in some of them. No gains, excepting Rocky Mountain Fuel, were registered toward the end of the decade. When the union proposed cooperation it was as an alternative to something worse. The movement can be understood only as a facet of general union decline in the twenties and it did virtually nothing to stem that tide. It was, in other words, an answer to evident weakness — a lost strike, declining employment, the stretch-out, growing nonunion competition. In fact, cooperation was at odds with several deep-rooted convictions held by the labor movement: "more," the standard rate, organization of all competing plants in an industry, job control and employment maximization for union members, and the unilateral responsibility of the employer to worry about increasing production. That labor leaders had little faith in, and in some cases less understanding of, cooperation is evident from a conversation that occurred in Philadelphia at the end of the twenties. The International Association of Machinists had enthusiastically sponsored the movement. When the union's president, Arthur Wharton, was asked in the presence of the industrialist Morris E. Leeds what contribution the IAM could make to improve efficiency at the Leeds & Northrup plant, Wharton candidly admitted that he did not know.

Similarly, industry as a whole turned a deaf ear to Green's plea for cooperation. Most of the firms that did accept it were either confirmed in their espousal of collective bargaining, like the B & O, Naumkeag, Rocky Mountain Fuel, and Hart, Schaffner & Marx, or small employers, such as predominated in the garment industries and hosiery. For the most part, American business, like the southern textile industry, reasoned that it could push output more effectively without a union and, further, that the matter was in any case none of organized labor's business.[7]

Related to union interest in cooperation was the sharp reversal in the AFL's historic opposition to scientific management, dramatized earlier in the battle between Gompers and Frederick Taylor. The individual most responsible for the shift was Morris Llewellyn Cooke, who worked on both the unions and the engineers to effect a *rapprochement*. Gompers became interested shortly after the war as a result of a barrage of criticism of union practices restricting output. He apparently hoped to improve the Federation's public relations by emphasizing productive efficiency and the elimination of waste, and he was soon talking as though the AFL had shown industry the way in this area. At the same time the Taylorites moved in the direction of "humanizing" their system, to consider the worker as something more than a cog in the industrial machine. By the time Green took office a fine friendship was blossoming into a love affair. In December 1925 he delivered the major address at the joint meeting of the Taylor Society and the Management Division of the American Society of Mechanical Engineers, making a very favorable impression. In the spring of 1927 in Philadelphia, leaders on both sides joined in a Trade Union Conference on Elimination of Waste in Industry. In his presidential address to the Taylor Society in 1928, Cooke asked the engineers to urge workers to join unions. The 1929 AFL convention listened to a small brigade of engineers, and the Taylor Society loyally postponed its meeting scheduled for May in Charlotte, North Carolina, to demonstrate solidarity with textile workers striking against the stretch-out. And, as noted earlier on page 35, the Federation engaged the engineer Geoffrey Brown to deal with the technical side of the southern drive.[8]

What all this meant is a question. Certainly, it was a healthy intellectual exercise for both the engineers and the unions to expose themselves to the other's point of view. If the engineers hoped that the AFL would market scientific management to industry, they must have been disappointed. There is no doubt that the Federation failed to sell unions to employers by embracing scientific management, as Brown's performance in the South amply demonstrated. The labor movement was no more successful in employing a middleman than in selling direct.

Following from labor's growing interest in cooperation and scientific management was the emergence of a new AFL wage policy in 1925 — the linking of wages to productivity. The convention resolved that real wages should progress "in proportion to man's increasing power of production." The pronouncement stemmed from the anomaly of textiles: wage cutting in an era of mounting national output. This productivity theory Gompers, wedded to the notion of "more," had earlier "sarcastically scored as the abstract musing of a professor shut up within library walls." Since economists were just beginning to construct indices of man-hour output, the Federation could do little more than endorse the general principle. There is no evidence in either contemporary wage movements or collective bargaining that the policy had a significant direct effect, though it may have served a public relations purpose.[9]

These signs of growing conservatism were evident as well in the labor banking movement launched by the independent Brotherhood of Locomotive Engineers in 1920. The theory was that wage earners' financial resources would be mobilized to promote labor enterprises and to influence the labor policies of industry, though neither objective was achieved. Only a handful of unions went into it, notably the railway organizations — with the Locomotive Engineers developing a chain of twelve banks — and the Clothing Workers. The movement reached its peak in 1926, when there were thirty-five banks with resources in excess of $126 million. Decline set in rapidly so that by 1929 only eighteen were left, with resources of just under $79 million. Excepting the two Amalgamated institutions, the union banks were not distinguished for either competent or disinterested management. Most labor organizations felt that their members' roles as union men and consumers should not be diffused by developing their interests as depositors and producers.

In addition to banking, the unions moved into insurance with the establishment of the Union Labor Life Insurance Company. In 1925, Green called a conference of representatives of some fifty internationals who decided to establish the enterprise. Matthew Woll became president and the other officers were also union officials. The theory was to persuade members to buy "a policy with a union label on it, from the company owned, organized, and operated by the trade unions." The sponsors hoped to avoid special charges imposed by private carriers and to shake workers loose from employer-sponsored insurance systems. In 1927 the stock was held by the AFL, 60 internationals, 367 locals, 43 miscellaneous bodies, and 314 individual union members. The company reserved control over stock disposition to guarantee the continuance of union predominance in ownership.[10]

A further indication of labor's mounting conservatism was the position the AFL took toward the 1928 presidential election. Four years earlier the Federation, disrupting an unbroken tradition of neutrality in presidential contests, had endorsed Senator La Follette. Progressives within and without the labor movement hoped that this act would serve as a precedent for growing political participation, a hope that was soon to be dashed.

The inclination of most AFL leaders was toward Al Smith, and with good reason. As governor of New York, Smith had an excellent labor record. In his annual message of January 1928, for example, he had called for curbing the injunction by statute, the main issue of legislative interest to the Federation. Smith was warmly endorsed by the state federations of New York, New Jersey, Rhode Island, Nebraska, and Utah. Many union officials, like Green, were themselves Democrats and several were active politically, such as Tobin of the Teamsters and Major Berry of the Pressmen (there was, in fact, a boomlet for Berry for Vice-President). Nevertheless, the Federation did not come out for Smith. Three powerful union leaders were Republicans — Lewis, Hutcheson, and Woll. Lewis went on the radio to support Hoover, calling him "the foremost industrial statesman of modern times." Further, a Republican victory was generally anticipated and no one believed labor could prevent it by endorsing Smith. Under the circumstances, therefore, a reversion to neutrality was the safest course, and in 1928 the Federation could hardly be accused of being anything but safe. It decided neither to reward its "friend" nor to attack its "enemy." [11]

Another sign of growing conservatism was the AFL disenchantment with workers' education that manifested itself at the end of the decade. This movement had got under way right after the war and immediately won enthusiastic Federation backing. The leading organizations were the Workers' Education Bureau, formed by trade unionists and educators in the early twenties, and Brookwood Labor College, located in Westchester County, New York, created in 1921 under the direction of A. J. Muste, a minister with a deep interest in labor and progressive issues.

The Federation embraced the Bureau warmly. In 1923 an agreement was made to give the AFL representation on and eventual control over the Bureau's executive committee, and a vigorous program of teaching and publications for wage earners was launched. The unions were exhorted to participate and much progress was made; in the first half of 1925, for example, forty-one unions were affiliated with the Bureau, and its secretary, Spencer Miller, Jr., was invited to address the AFL convention. The mood was reflected in Green's remark at the 1925 conclave: "This department might well be regarded as an arm of our great movement, and we want to make that arm strong, we want to strengthen it through affiliation of all national and international unions, state and central bodies, in the Workers' Education Bureau." By 1926, however, the Federation began to doubt. Andrew Furuseth of the Seamen grumbled that the books issued by the Bureau, which he had read, took a viewpoint directly opposite to that held in the AFL. In 1928 the Executive Council frankly admitted that the workers' education movement posed a threat to the unions, presumably by allowing workers to question policies to which the Federation was firmly wedded. It was necessary, the Council announced, to restrict "interference with the trade union's final and absolute right to determine its own policy." Hence control over the program must be vested in the union rather than the school. A Commission on Workers' Education was created to reappraise the entire AFL policy. Even the Bureau's most noted success, a series of labor classes sponsored by the California Federation and the University of California, had trouble. A labor official active in the Bureau was critical of college participation. John Kerchen, head of the labor program at the university, replied:

The fact is . . . that there is more progressive thought in the colleges than there is in the labor movement. There are some things we teach in the University of California we wouldn't dare teach in the labor classes. We have classes in the study of social reform. That wouldn't be tolerated in the A.F. of L. Why, in the university we have a class in the history and theory of revolutions. Imagine my teaching that in the trade union classes! . . . We give the classes that the A.F. of L. desires. There is no demand for classes in Marxism, radical economics, or questions of the control of industry. The A.F. of L. accepts the present order of society. We are living in bad air, but we have to breathe it. We are not trying to change the air.

By 1929, obviously, no one on either side was happy.

Even more acidulous, however, was the controversy over Brookwood. The school offered a two-year course, mainly in the social sciences, to approximately fifty trade unionists in a "peaceful, pastoral setting . . . away from the feverish and exhausting struggle in the factories, mills and mines." Muste averred that Brookwood was concerned with instilling in workers a consciousness of class but denied that the objective was propagandistic. He personally opposed capitalism but was not a member of the Communist Party. Although the AFL itself had no direct connection with Brookwood, the Workers' Education Bureau and a number of affiliated unions participated in its program, and its staff formed a local of the Teachers union. The conservative leadership of the Federation, however, looked with suspicion upon the Brookwood experiment, and when, in 1926, several students and instructors joined John Brophy's "Save-the-Union" movement to wrest leadership of the United Mine Workers from Lewis, a break was inevitable. Matthew Woll was delegated to investigate the school and reported to the Executive Council that its curriculum was propagandistic and communistic as well as a threat to the principles of the American Federation of Labor — primarily by "dual unionism." In August 1928, the Council, basing its action upon the Woll report, publicly condemned Brookwood and instructed Federation affiliates to withhold support from it. After heated debate, the 1928 convention endorsed the decision of the Executive Council.[12]

A final symptom of the times was a deterioration in the relationship between organized labor and the Negro. In 1929, John P. Frey of the Metal Trades Department addressed an Interracial Conference in Washington and urged Negroes to join unions, for which he was taken vigorously to task by the National Association for the Advancement of Colored People. Hurt, Frey wrote the chairman of the Association: "There is nothing I know of which would be more . . . constructive than to have the leaders of the colored race in this country publicly advise the negro workmen to become trade unionists." He failed to point out the impracticality of his advice since many unions had slammed their doors shut against the Negro.

The problem, though long-standing, became acute during this decade because of the emergence of the Negro industrial worker in the North. Sterling Spero and A. L. Harris wrote:

> The essence of this change has been the shifting of the Negro's position from that of a labor reserve to a regular element in the labor force of nearly every basic industry. It has brought the Negro face to face with problems of working conditions, which, though they may contain many special elements, are essentially the same as the problems of other workers. They are consequently problems with which the Negro cannot cope successfully without the cooperation of his white fellow workers.

This cooperation was not forthcoming. Although the AFL barred racial discrimination in union membership, the policy was of no significance because power over admission resided in the internationals. The Boilermakers and Machinists, for example, got around it simply by incorporating a racial clause in their rituals, binding members to propose only white workmen for membership. By the end of the decade twenty-four internationals discriminated directly in either their constitutions or rituals, ten of them AFL affiliates, and the majority in rail or water transportation. Many other unions did so informally. As a consequence, Negro union membership was only a minor fraction of the race's employment. The Urban League estimated total Negro membership in 1926–28 at 81,658, distributed as follows: independent

Negro unions, 12,585; Longshoremen, 12,381; Hod Carriers, 10,131; Maintenance of Way Employees, 10,000; Mine Workers, 5000; Musicians, 3000; Sleeping Car Porters, 3000; and 25,561 in the balance of the labor movement.

The colored wage earner, therefore, had little alternative but to seek employment in open-shop industries, of which autos, steel, and meat packing were notable examples. More distressing still was the firm establishment of the Negro in the role of strikebreaker at this time. He was recruited for this purpose in the 1919 steel strike and was widely used in the few disputes that occurred in the late twenties, such as the coal strikes in Pennsylvania and Ohio in 1927–28 and the longshore strike in Boston in 1929. The dilemma of the Negro strikebreaker was captured in a contemporary novel, *Home to Harlem,* by Claude McKay.

> "But it ain't decent to scab," said Jake.
> "Decent mah black moon!" Shouted Zeddy, "I'll scab through hell to make mah living. Scab job or open shop or union am all the same jobs to me. White men's don't want niggers in them unions nohow. Ain't you a good carpenter? And ain't I a good blacksmith? But kain we get a lookin on our trade heah in this white man's city? Ain't white mens done scabbed niggers outa all the jobs they useter hold down heah in this city? Waiter, bootblack, and barber shop? — I got to live and I'll scab through hell to live."

The combination of union discrimination and Negro strikebreaking poisoned the relationship between organized labor and the Negro community. In 1925, for example, four colored legislators in Illinois opposed the Illinois Federation's anti-injunction bill until they had exacted a pledge from labor to permit Negro electricians to join the union and get work. In 1928, Negro leaders appeared before the Senate Judiciary Subcommittee and asked for defeat of the Shipstead anti-injunction bill. "I make the charge baldly," declared C. W. Chesnutt, "that the labor unions of the United States, broadly speaking, are unfriendly to Negro labor, and I challenge them to prove the contrary." [13]

*

## 5

This, then, was the American Federation of Labor in the twenties. But the Federation was only part of the labor movement; more important were the international unions that formed it, particularly the strong ones, and their presidents who constituted the Executive Council. The heads of two of these organizations — William L. Hutcheson of the Carpenters and John L. Lewis of the Mine Workers — were the most powerful men in organized labor and their unions wielded great influence. Moreover, Hutcheson's skilled building tradesmen and Lewis' industrially organized coal diggers were to play central roles in the labor drama that was soon to unfold.

In the twenties of the last century Ulster was impoverished and many of the poor Northern Irish migrated hopefully to the New World. Among them was William Levi Hutcheson's grandmother, Mary Campbell Hutcheson. This young widow and her small boys, Daniel Orrick and David, boarded a sailing vessel at Lough Foyle in January 1825 and sailed steerage on a dismal, wintry six-week voyage to Canada. Her husband's uncle, a successful farmer in Brighton, Ontario, had sent passage for the three of them. "If you don't come soon," he wrote, "it is likely you will starve. . . . Here you will dwell in our home and help on the farm and cook." Brighton was a frontier farm community, peopled by Scots and Scotch-Irish, and predominantly Methodist, the religion of the Hutchesons. Mary fitted herself into the rural household and raised her boys.

At fourteen Daniel Orrick, restless and detesting farming, apprenticed himself to a carpenter in nearby Coburg to learn the trade. After eight years he mastered carpentry and joined the exodus of Canadians in the forties to Michigan's burgeoning lumber industry. Daniel Orrick became a seasonal migrant worker, moving ceaselessly from timber cutting in Saginaw to ship calking in Detroit to work as a deckhand on lumber vessels on the lakes to serving as a steersman on keelboats on the rivers. Through a long life he wandered in search of a fortune he never found. When Lincoln called for volunteers in July 1861, Daniel Orrick promptly enlisted. The Civil War left an indelible scar upon him and made him a lifelong Republican, a devotion he conveyed to his children. After the war, in 1867, he married Elizabeth Culver in Bay City at the head of Saginaw Bay; he was forty-three and she was eighteen. The Culvers had migrated to the lumber country from Ohio in a covered wagon drawn by oxen.

In the sixties the great Saginaw lumber boom was under way and was to persist to the end of the century. Immense stands of pine about the Bay were cut at great speed to fill the maw of the expanding industrial economy. Lumbermen purchased virgin timberlands for $1.25 an acre from the government and made fortunes overnight. Saginaw became a boom town and the speculative fever seized the populace. Though Daniel Orrick was infected, he lacked the knack to strike it rich. But the lure of easy wealth and the power it fed left an impression upon his family.

On February 7, 1874, a neighborhood midwife delivered the third of the Hutchesons' five children in their fourteen by sixteen log house — a boy who was named William Levi. He grew rapidly, became huge and powerful, fond of fighting and good at it. William received a rudimentary education in the nearby South Williams school. At thirteen he was ready for work and apprenticed himself to his carpenter father at the Wheeler Shipyards in Bay City. He soon became dissatisfied with working conditions and fought constantly with a fellow apprentice, Collins. In the late eighties working-class disaffection was endemic in the area. Hutcheson traveled to Detroit to hear Richard Trevellick, reformer and chairman of the Eight-Hour League. The Knights of Labor invaded the Saginaw Valley, and more than 5000 lumberjacks and rivermen struck successfully for the ten-hour day despite intervention of the militia and a force of Pinkerton strikebreakers. In 1888 Gompers spoke in Saginaw, and Hutcheson eagerly received his craft-union message.

Discontented and restless, Hutcheson left home at seventeen. He tried his hand at dairy farming near Auburn, Michigan, with at least one success: he met Bessie King, daughter of a local farmer, at a Methodist Church party and married her on October 10, 1893. The time was most inauspicious because of the onset of the great depression of the nineties, and poverty was to stalk the early years of their marriage. He wandered to the wheat fields of the Dakotas and found conditions there worse than in Michigan. He journeyed to the mines of the Coeur d'Alene in Idaho in time to witness federal troops breaking a strike. This and other labor controversies of the nineties drew his interest and he was stirred by Debs's leadership of the Pullman strike. Meantime, his wife had been bearing him four children, among them the boy, Maurice, born in 1897.

In 1902 he took work in his craft at the Midland (later Dow) Chemical Company in Midland, Michigan. Conditions were bad and the men were aroused; in 1904 they formed a union under Hutcheson's leadership. The company broke the union and fired and blacklisted its mainstay. In a one-industry town Hutcheson could find no other employment, so he moved his family back to Saginaw, carrying with him a reputation as an organizer. In 1906 he became business agent for Carpenters Locals 59 and 334 and his career was launched.

Hutcheson's rise within the United Brotherhood of Carpenters and Joiners was swift. He quickly energized and expanded the locals under his control. Shortly, he ran for the general executive board in the third district and lost. On January 20, 1913, however, he won election as second general vice-president. When, on March 1, 1913, Arthur A. Quinn resigned as first vice-president because he refused to move from New Jersey to Indianapolis as the union constitution required, Hutcheson stepped in. Two years later, on October 8, 1915, President James Kirby died of food poisoning and Hutcheson, at the age of forty-one, succeeded to the highest office in the Brotherhood. He was to occupy it without interruption for thirty-six years.

In many ways the high point of Hutcheson's career was reached in the twenties. His power within the union was unchallengeable. The Brotherhood had the biggest membership of any international (322,000 in 1929), was financially secure, and operated in a prosperous, at times booming, industry. As its spokesman, Hutcheson was the decisive leader in the building trades, the group that made up the largest and most important element within the AFL. Further, as the leading Republican in the labor movement, he was not without influence in the dominant political party. Three successive Presidents — Harding, Coolidge, and Hoover — are said by his biographer to have invited him to become Secretary of Labor. In each case he refused, preferring to act as a confidential labor adviser, and, apparently, he succeeded in getting James J. Davis appointed to the secretaryship. At this time he sought the social station that befitted so important a personage. He joined the Elks and Masons and, more important, the Indiana Chamber of Commerce. In Indianapolis he lunched at the Chamber and was occasionally invited to the homes of the town's upper crust. He took to wearing custom-made clothes and a Homburg. He bought a farm in Ohio and wintered in Florida. "Big Bill" had arrived.

Hutcheson came by his sobriquet honestly: he was a mountain of a man. He possessed an enormous frame, was well over six feet in height, and weighed somewhere between 220 and 300 pounds, depending upon whether one believes friendly or unfriendly writers. His nose was prominent and bulbous, his jowls, thick; he was balding, and, above all, he had, *Fortune* said, "quick, suspicious brown eyes" that "peer . . . intently and perceive men's motives." Behind them lay a sharp mind unalloyed with self-doubt. He had great strength of will, and, once his mind was made up, was amenable neither to pressure nor persuasion. These qualities made him a natural leader who won either the respect or fear of those he led; he believed an organization needed a boss and his concept of the boss was hardly complicated. "Hutch," one of his vice-presidents remarked, "tells me what to do." He was an essentially suspicious man, inclined to believe the worst of others. Hutcheson placed his trust in his family and his devoted underlings and had few if any friends. He preferred to operate secretly; during his incumbency the union's journal and convention proceedings became remarkable for what they hid. His ways and his philosophy were fixed at an early age and he never found the slightest reason to change or even question either. His world was seen through the narrow-angle lens of the union's interests; his only concern was with what was good for the Carpenters, not with what was good for the labor movement, workers in general, or America. This was the point of view of the Saginaw lumber king.

A powerful union leader reflects the outlook and mood of his membership, and Hutcheson was no exception. As R. A. Christie has said:

There appeared in *The Carpenter* of July 1914 a picture of the carpenters who had erected the L. C. Smith Building. They stood on the roof of the completed building, a score or so of walrus-mustachioed old-time carpenters, glowering at the camera. Almost without exception, they had on under their overalls stiff collars, ties, and tie pins. They all wore white shirts, suit coats, and bowlers, derbies, or slouch felt hats. Those without overalls had gold watch chains and fobs stretched across their abundant middles. . . . The attire . . . goes a long way toward symbolizing the old-time carpenter's craft pride and character: he came to work attired like his boss. He took pride in neither wearing gloves nor getting his hands very dirty. He worked with his hat on. At the day's end he took off his overalls, folded them atop his tools in the tool shed, washed his scarcely dirty hands, straightened his tie, tipped his bowler a bit more jauntily, and sought out the nearest bar.

The key to the carpenter's outlook was his chest of tools. He owned them and he alone had the skill to use them; the Brotherhood's 1924 convention voted down a resolution that would have permitted the contractor to supply tools. This was the skilled tradesman, the "aristocrat" of labor, proud of his craft and independent of his employer. His was the strategic trade at the building site, the only one that required comprehensive knowledge. A contractor was his employer only until the job was done; he might work for a dozen during a year. He was often an itinerant, hopping not only from job to job but also from town to town with his tools and his skills. "The only responsibility most carpenters accept," Christie wrote, "is the craft responsibility that poor workmanship on good material is a sin." His loyalty was to his union which through its closed-shop hiring hall steered him to a job, through its collective bargaining agreement fixed his wages, and through its jurisdiction protected his job territory. In an industry characterized by local product and labor markets, very small units, chaotic organization, speculative financing, sensitivity to the weather, and acute responsiveness to the business cycle, the Brotherhood was his mainstay of stability.

The international union that Hutcheson took over in 1915 was a relatively loose confederation of powerful locals with a musty nineteenth-century heritage of Peter McGuire's radicalism. Big Bill soon put an end to both. The absolute supremacy of the international was established in a bitter contest with the virtually autonomous New York City locals between 1915 and 1917. The architect of Hutcheson's victory was the Canadian adventurer, Robert Brindell, who was to become czar of the New York building trades and to make a million dollars by extortion, ending his career in jail in 1921. From the standpoint of the Brotherhood, Hutcheson's alliance with a well-known thief was not nearly so important as the fact that he smashed the New York locals and their 1916 strike and reorganized them with men who were under his thumb. No local was ever to challenge him again.

Ideological unionism had been dying a natural death within the organization long before Hutcheson became president. It did, however, emit a last implausible gasp in the twenties, which he stifled in characteristic fashion. The newly born Communist Party, eager to infiltrate the big unions, launched an attack upon the Brotherhood in 1922 on the theory, seemingly rational to the party if no one else, that members of so conservative an organization must be ripe for revolution. Tiny fractions were established in several big city locals, and the quite general membership opposition to Hutcheson's combination land speculation and home for aged carpenters at Lakeland, Florida, was exploited. The results were disastrous for the aggressors. Investigating committees were sent out to purge the disaffected locals. In 1928 at Lakeland Hutcheson invited eleven leaders to present their case to a hysterically hostile convention. "Stand here beside the flag," he commanded, "the one you don't think so much of." Three were expelled from the Brotherhood and eight were either restored or placed on probation after signing non-Communist affidavits. "Hutcheson," Christie wrote, "was simply playing a game with the Red brothers, a game in which the dice were heavily loaded in his favor. When the time came, he rolled his seven [and] swept in the stakes. . . ."

The *quo* that Hutcheson returned the membership for his *quid* of personal power was protection of their job territory. No trade unionist in America has ever dedicated himself with such singleness and firmness of purpose to the preservation and extension of his organization's jurisdiction. In the local-market construction industry the conduct of collective bargaining was essentially a local function; jurisdiction, however, was the exclusive preserve of the international. Public shuddering over jurisdictional disputes left Big Bill totally indifferent.

The history of the Brotherhood is strewn with the wreckage of battles fought and invariably won over the control of work. The principle the union established at the outset was that anything made of wood was carpenter's work. "God created the forests," goes an old construction saw, "and He gave them to Bill Hutcheson." But the Good Lord had not been generous enough, for He had failed to reckon with technology, which substituted other materials for wood. During the Hutcheson era the principle was amended: anything *ever* made of wood was carpenter's work. The Carpenters fought with the Amalgamated Wood Workers over lumbering and sawmills, with the Sheet Metal Workers over metal trim, with the Machinists over heavy machinery, with the Iron Workers over piles, docks, and window frames, and with many other unions.

Immediately following World War I the building trades were in bad odor. There was a pent-up demand for construction that could not be filled quickly enough. The unions were engaged in bitter jurisdictional conflict contaminated with racketeering — Brindell's extortions found counterparts in the activities of Carpenter P. H. McCarthy in San Francisco and Carpenter William Schardt in Chicago. There was a great public hue and cry that the National Association of Manufacturers and other open-shop forces were to exploit in seeking to impose the American Plan upon the construction industry. Something, obviously, needed to be done.

On March 3, 1919, at the initiative of the American Institute of Architects, several employer associations and the AFL Building Trades Department created the National Board for Jurisdictional Awards to adjudicate jurisdictional disputes in the construction industry. President John Donlin of the Department and all the building-trades union leaders were enthusiastic with one exception — Hutcheson. Since he could not be certain that the Board would invariably rule in his favor, Hutcheson regarded it as a fundamental threat to the Carpenters' jurisdiction and set about its destruction. At the outset public opinion compelled him to assume a seeming support for the Board. In December 1920, however, the agency in a crucial decision awarded metal trim to the Sheet Metal Workers. The fight was on. The following year Hutcheson ordered his locals to seize trim work with any means at their disposal, and his union was thrown out of the Building Trades Department. By 1922, with the open-shop movement at its peak, Hutcheson saw his chance. The Institute of Architects, sympathetic to the open shop and a party to the Jurisdictional Board, was the lever. He asked whether it was fair to insist that a trade union submit so vital an issue as jurisdiction to an open-shop agency. Gompers, ever sensitive to the Carpenters' power, returned a ringing "No." In 1922–24 guerrilla warfare raged in the construction industry. The Carpenters struck to control metal trim, browbeat local building-trades councils to win their support, and, failing, established their own councils. The Department replied with a dual carpenters' union which made little headway. Meantime open-shop advocates exploited labor disunity.

The tide, however, was running to Hutcheson. At its 1924 convention the Department voted Donlin out, and the new AFL president, Green, was most conciliatory. By 1926 the Sheet Metal Workers saw no point in continuing the fight; they signed a jurisdictional agreement dictated by Hutcheson. The next year the Department, anxious to get the Carpenters' per capita tax, asked him the price of reaffiliation: the National Board for Jurisdictional Awards was dead. Big Bill had exacted the unconditional surrender of his enemies.

This study in sabotage was witnessed with interest from the inside by the recently defeated Democratic vice-presidential candidate, who during the early twenties was president of the American Construction Council, an active supporter of the Board for Jurisdictional Awards. While serving as Assistant Secretary of the Navy during the war, he had already tested Hutcheson in disputes involving the naval construction program and had found him tough as armor plate. By 1929, Franklin Delano Roosevelt knew full well that Big Bill was not to be treated lightly.

His view was hardly unique. Within the union, as Christie has noted, "Only one aspect of the United Brotherhood changed after 1920. That was Hutcheson's power, which grew in almost geometrical progression." William Green, it was said, "admires him, and fears him." Another labor leader, one who believed that the world was ruled by the fist, said of Hutcheson: "He was a strong man. He was never an inconsistent man. He met his problems head-on." This was the estimate of John Llewellyn Lewis.[14]


6


On April 19, 1832, striking miners in southern Wales posted a notice written in red in the Welsh language and addressed to blacklegs (we would call them scabs): "We hereby warn you the . . . last time. We are determined to draw the hearts out of all the men above-named, and fix two hearts upon the horns of the Bull; so that everyone may see what is the fate of every traitor. . . . So we testify with our blood." This awesome document was an indication of the squalor, repression, and desperation borne by Welsh coal diggers in the nineteenth century. Between 1853 and 1875, a severe depression settled upon their industry and the miners struck repeatedly in a hopeless effort to maintain their wages and conditions. In 1875 their organization, the Amalgamated Association of Miners, collapsed. In that same year a burly Welsh miner named Thomas Lewis decided that he had had enough; he emigrated, first to Australia and then to America.

Tom Lewis settled in tiny Lucas, Iowa, where he dug coal for the White Breast Fuel Company. Among the Welsh mining families, who predominated, were the Watkinses. In 1878 Tom Lewis married Louisa Watkins. Two years later, on February 12 — which was also Lincoln's birthday — their first child was born, christened John Llewellyn. He was later to declare: "On my father's side, my family were fighters. They roved a great deal. . . . They were tough people. My mother's side of the family was the quiet kind. They were scholars, teachers . . . retiring and shy." All told, Louisa was to bear eight children, six sons and two daughters.

They did not need to go to school in unionism, for it was bred in their bones. Tom threw himself passionately into organizing for the Knights of Labor and helped lead a bitter strike against White Breast in 1882. For this he earned an honored place on the company's blacklist with inevitable exile from Lucas. He worked as a night watchman in Colfax, as a coal digger in a nearby mine till the blacklist caught up with him, again as a watchman in Des Moines, and as custodian of that town's jail. Fifteen years after the strike — in 1897 — the blacklist was removed and Tom returned to his work and his countrymen in Lucas.

John grew into a powerful, aggressive boy, eager and capable with his fists. He changed schools often as the family moved about, and his formal education stopped with the eighth grade. Though he was inherently a good student, the classroom offered him little incentive. At fifteen, when the Lewises returned to Lucas, John went down into the mines, where he worked a ten- to eleven-hour day under hazardous conditions for $1.60. After hours he read voraciously and organized a debating and a baseball team, excelling in both activities. Restless, he tired of digging and tried his hand at running a mill, at carpentry, and at managing the local opera house.

In 1901, when Lewis was twenty-one, he decided to wander, migrating west for five years in a ceaseless search for the key to himself. He traveled by stagecoach, by cushion, and by rod. Since a miner seldom escapes from his calling, Lewis dug coal in Colorado, Wyoming, and Montana, copper in Colorado and Arizona, and silver in Utah. He talked at length to other workers, sounding out their hopes and frustrations. He joined unions and studied the ways in which strikes were conducted. In 1905 he was a member of the rescue crew that dragged the mutilated bodies of 236 miners from the charnel house of the Union Pacific Mine disaster at Hannah, Wyoming. He was never to forget the faces of the widows waiting at the surface.

The Lewis that returned to Lucas in 1906 was a young man going somewhere; he was matured, determined, and self-assured.

On June 5, 1907, he married the local doctor's daughter, Myrta Edith Bell, a gentle and devoted schoolteacher, who was to give him love, nurture his delicate ego, discipline his reading and thinking, and improve his platform style. She was also to bear him two daughters (one of whom died in youth) and a son.

He was now ready to launch a career in the United Mine Workers of America. Lucas, obviously, was a poor base because the Iowa coal field was of little consequence. He carefully chose his bigger stage, the great Montgomery field in southern Illinois, and settled in 1909 with his family in the town of Panama. His five brothers followed shortly and formed the nucleus of his machine that soon captured control of the local. In 1910 he was elected president and the following year was named the union's lobbyist in Springfield. His brilliance and force achieved legislative results and quickly caught the shrewd eye of Gompers. He became AFL legislative representative in 1911. In this job he roamed the country, pushing labor legislation in Washington and the state capitals, organizing in the steel, rubber, glass, lumber, and copper industries, and building a following within the UMW. These were the years of seasoning. Lewis broadened and deepened his already prodigious knowledge of American industry, polished his brilliant forensic style, and worked out, in close association with Gompers, a basic philosophy of unionism. "Lewis," *Fortune* wrote, "sensed the soundness of Gompers' doctrine that tactics, not ideals, make a labor movement."

When Lewis later became famous and powerful, Bunyanesque stories circulated about these early years, tales calculated to tout his strength, his courage, and his cunning. There was, for example, the yarn about Spanish Pete, the man-killing mule in a western mine. Cornered underground and facing Pete's murderous upraised hoofs, Lewis grabbed the sprag of his coal car and destroyed the enraged animal with a single blow between the eyes. He then filled the wound with clay and explained to the foreman that Pete had dropped dead of natural causes. Another concerned an early steel organizing effort and a Jones & Laughlin strong-arm man. Lewis and a friend were in a Pittsburgh bar and the company thug was seated back to them, leaning in their direction to catch their conversation. Suddenly Lewis shot his powerful arm around the spy's throat and dragged his head forward. Calmly, he observed to his friend as he tightened the headlock, "You know, Phil . . . it looks like a pretty decent place, but they sure let some incredible bastards in." Suddenly glancing down, he said, "My God, look what I've found! . . . a J. and L. stool pigeon. It looks like the Kaiser of the company dicks." Lewis then released his grip and warned the agent to "get the devil out of here before I break every bone in your body."

Though employed by the Federation, Lewis never permitted his eye to wander from the main objective — the miners' union. In his travels he went out of his way to meet UMW officials throughout the nation, entertaining them on his AFL expense account. In 1916 he served on the interstate wage scale committee and, more important, as temporary chairman of the convention, from which vantage point his voice carried to a large and impressed audience. Soon after, he accepted President John P. White's offer to become chief statistician of the international, moving his family to Indianapolis. The post afforded him the opportunity to become the nation's leading authority on the economics of coal and to make more friends within the organization. When White resigned in 1918, he was succeeded by Frank Hayes, an ineffectual alcoholic, who named Lewis vice-president. Since Hayes was neither well nor sober enough to serve, Lewis became the actual head of the UMW. The 1919 convention elected him acting president and two years later, at the age of forty, he won full title to this office, a prize from which no enemy but age would succeed in prying him loose.

In the twenties Lewis was in the prime of life. Physically he conveyed an impression of great power, which inclined weaker men to cower before him. Almost six feet tall, his 230 pounds were distributed over an unusually broad and thick frame. C. L. Sulzberger wrote: "His arms are short and powerful. . . . His hands are heavy but quick, with gnarled, strong fingers. His legs are squat, supple. He is remarkably light on his feet, walks with the speed and agility of a cat." But these features were minor; the focal point of the man was his face. Attention was drawn to the eyes: deep-set, probing, blue, and surmounted by enormous "shaggy red eyebrows either one of which a French gendarme would be proud to wear on his lip." His wide determined mouth was flexible and in constant motion, mounted on a huge jutting jaw. The skin was dull with a miner's pallor and was flecked with freckles. His auburn hair, worn long and loose, was parted but slightly to the left of center. The conventional facial expression displayed in public was a forbidding scowl.

Lewis dressed well in a rather formal, old-fashioned, senatorial manner. He affected well-cut dark suits, stiff collars, a straggling string tie, and a soft felt hat, usually tilted forward almost to the eyes.

Behind those eyes lay as supple and powerful a mind as has turned up in the American labor movement. This intelligence was seldom, if ever, clouded by uncertainty or self-doubt. To it he joined absolute fearlessness. He ordered a potent UMW rival, Ray Edmundson, at a union meeting: "Take that gun out of your pocket or I'll shove it down your throat." The prestige that usually went with position or wealth or high office left him totally indifferent. "The key to the understanding of Lewis's personality is to be found in his extraordinary tenacity of purpose," Saul Alinsky has noted. Once Lewis fixed upon a course of action, nothing would move him from it.

Equally impressive was his voice, an instrument calculatingly developed in the era that preceded electronic devices. "He can use his voice like a policeman's billy or like a monk at orisons," Sulzberger observed. "He can talk an assemblage into a state of eruption. He can translate a group of people into a pageant of misery, and back again." Native Welsh eloquence, fertilized with the King James Version and Shakespeare, flowered in his language. It was picturesque, flamboyant, ponderous, orotund, and almost invariably different. His words were weapons of warfare, not tools of analysis or communication. As weapons they were supremely adapted to the attack — to the epithet, the insult, the defamatory adjective. At a UMW convention he once dismissed the protest of an Irish miner with the remark, "I mined coal in Illinois when delegate Ansbury was herding sheep in Bulgaria." Later, when the irate Ansbury demanded an apology for the inference that he was a Bulgarian, Lewis replied that he, indeed, wished to apologize, not to Ansbury but "to the committee of twelve Bulgarians who . . . protested this insinuation . . . for having even suggested that such a person as Pat Ansbury could be associated with them." The list of prominent citizens who winced under his verbal lashings made up a tidy *Who's Who*. Yet Lewis, as fascinated by the sound as by the sense of words, would commit grievous errors. He could mix metaphors with the masters (his weather vanes pointed and drums beat in the same sentence). He once told a reporter, "This decision requires great circumcision." Lewis then glowered so forbiddingly that the cowed newsman did not dare to laugh.

This splendiferous Lewis was only part of the man, the half he turned to the glare of public scrutiny. The private half was warm, generous, sympathetic, and charming. He was a devoted husband and a doting father, particularly concerned to shield his daughter Kathryn against the embarrassments of her obesity. "In surroundings where he does not have to orate," *Fortune* said, "his erudition becomes wisdom and his sarcasm becomes wit."

From the outset of his career Lewis viewed himself as the protagonist in labor's unfolding drama. Modesty seldom deterred him from stalking to the center of the stage. At the 1921 AFL convention, when his position within the UMW was still shaky, Lewis had the effrontery to challenge his old mentor, Gompers, for the presidency and went down to ignominious defeat. "He who tooteth not his own horn," he advised, "the same shall not be tooted." He signed his name on a scale and with a flourish that put John Hancock to shame. Endowed himself with marvelous gifts of mind and body, he measured others by his own yardstick and found them wanting. Lewis had an eye for the fault rather than for the virtue and his view of human nature in the large — miners included — was hardly generous. He was equally contemptuous of friend and foe and sometimes to his sorrow underestimated an adversary.

Both his character and the logic of his situation drove him to the acquisition and augmentation of power. The world, he believed, was not amenable to persuasion. His prime purpose was to forge the apparatus and membership of the miners' union into a hammer capable of striking a single massive blow at his bidding. His concern with power was exclusive; he was interested in its accumulation and not in its sale. He could not be bought as could some of his predecessors and contemporaries. Nor would he exchange power for position. Lewis did not hesitate to turn down Coolidge's offer to become Secretary of Labor when the President at the instigation of Treasury Secretary Mellon (a large coal operator who perhaps wanted Lewis out of the way) invited him to join the Cabinet.

A man whose goal is power must dedicate himself to the mastery of events rather than subject himself to the dictates of theory. Lewis' realism was pure and his imagination was uncontaminated with the impractical. He operated opportunistically, compromising only with reality. "I don't give a hang what happened yesterday," he declared. "I live for today and tomorrow." In his public life he was entirely devoid of sentiment, abandoning loyal followers with no more than a shrug. He was always in perfect control of himself; his dramatic displays of emotion were designed.

Such a man can have no intimate friends; the austere and lonely Lewis confined himself to acquaintances and associates. Within the hierarchy of the union, in J. A. Wechsler's phrase, the relationship was that of Superman to John Doe. He believed that men could be bought, corrupted, or bullied into submission. In his book humility was a synonym for weakness and idealism simply did not exist. This lack of perception led him grossly to misunderstand men like Powers Hapgood and John Brophy; when they fought him because they believed him morally wrong he thought they were feathering their own nests. Lewis was a massive but selective hater, implacable in the case of a genuine rival like Roosevelt. With inferiors he contained his will-to-hate within his realism. "He who seeks vengeance," Lewis said, "ultimately destroys himself." He showed no hesitancy about calling home men he had defamed and exiled when it suited his purpose. Nor did he hesitate to embrace the devil if Satan agreed to work with him. Of subordinates his only demand was absolute and unswerving loyalty; competence was a matter of indifference. To those who bent the knee he returned loyalty in exact measure, never blaming them for their failures. As a consequence the union staff was overloaded with mediocrities, yes-men, alcoholics, sycophants, and relatives.

Lewis' manner of living was in no way unusual. Though he had been given a religious upbringing, he turned agnostic and attended no church. His only vice was fine cigars, which he smoked or chewed constantly. He drank merely for social purposes and did not gamble. His pet, symbolically, was a great white bulldog. Lewis built up a substantial private library, reading assiduously in the classics, military history, and detective stories. He even wrote a book ("Would that mine enemy had written a book"). When the times were propitious, he lived exceedingly well: a fine house, a big black Cadillac with liveried chauffeur, and excellent food. Yet, before carving the roast, he hitched up his coat sleeves in the miner's fashion.

For the key to Lewis was his vision of himself — "Think of me as a coal miner, and you won't make any mistakes." He declared:

> The thing that gives me strength is the fact that I am able correctly to interpret the aims of my people. I know the psychology of the coal miner. I know about his dreams and his ideals and trials and tribulations. I have lived with coal miners. I am one of them. My family has been associated with the mining industry for a century and a half and an understanding of the miners' problems is inbred in me. . . .
>
> I have laid down in a mine tunnel with my face in a half inch of water, and pulled my shirt up over my head, expecting to die the next minute in an explosion I heard coming toward me. And when God performed a miracle and stopped that explosion before I died, I think it gave me some understanding of what men think about and how they suffer when they are waiting to die in a coal mine explosion.
>
> . . . when I speak, I speak the thoughts of the membership of the United Mine Workers of America, because I understand them. I remain true to them and they remain true to me. . . .
>
> As an individual, my opinions and my voice are of no more consequence in our world of affairs, or in the coal industry of the country, than the voice or the opinions of any passerby on the street. It is only when I am able to translate your dreams and aspirations into words that others may understand, that my tongue possesses any strength or my hand has any force.
>
> I have never faltered or failed to present the cause or plead

the case of the mine workers of this country. I have pleaded your case from the pulpit and the public platform; in joint conference with the operators of this country; before the bar of state legislatures; in the councils of the President's cabinet; and in the public press of this nation — not in the quavering tones of a feeble mendicant asking alms, but in the thundering voice of the captain of a mighty host, demanding the rights to which free men are entitled.

This miner was convinced that coal was the essential element in America's industrial civilization. "When we control the production of coal," he declared, "we hold the vitals of our society right in our hands." Although competitive fuels might chip off pieces of the market, they could not replace coal, since their threat was primarily to household rather than to industrial consumption. What disturbed Lewis far more was the quality of coal management, which he never tired of pointing out to the operators. He found them incompetent, inefficient, backward, lazy, and disunited.

The most significant result of mismanagement was the failure to mechanize, since advancing technology was the basis for both low costs and high wages. Lewis wrote in 1925, "Fifty years have passed . . . since the first undercutting machine was introduced; yet coal mines continue to be opened, the owners of which have neither the capital nor intention to provide this essential machine." Machines and men are interchangeable; the operator chooses whichever is cheaper. "We decided it is better to have a half million men working in the industry at good wages . . . than it is to have a million working in the industry in poverty. . . ." The union's wage policy, therefore, was to make labor dear in relation to machinery, to push rates up in good times and to hold them up in bad. Operators would be forced to mechanize and the miners would then take a share of the resultant rise in productivity. "I am among those who do not believe that God ever put an idea in the mind of an inventor for the sole advantage of an employer."

To effectuate this policy in an industry with a national market it was necessary for the UMW to bargain for all coal miners under a nation-wide agreement. Industrial unionism was an indispensable

precondition and this was the historic structural base of the miners'
union. The UMW, like the Brewery Workers, had always been
exceptional in the predominantly craft-minded AFL. Further,
effective national bargaining required that the union speak for
all miners without regard to race, color, national origin, or creed.
The gospel Johnny Mitchell had preached was this: "The coal
you dig is not Slavish coal, or Polish coal, or Irish coal. It
is coal." Despite the widespread employment of Negroes as nonunion miners and strikebreakers during the twenties, the UMW
adhered to its traditional policy of no discrimination. Whites and
blacks were organized in the same locals and members of both
races were eligible for union office.

Lewis had no faith in arbitration. "I do not yield to any man
. . . the right to say how much my wages shall be, what my working conditions shall be, and what kind of education I give my
children through his fixation of my income. That is just too damned
much power to give to somebody else!" The inevitable alternative
to arbitration was the strike. For Lewis it was far more than a
bargaining sanction. He believed in conflict as the source of free
institutions and the strike as an essential element of a capitalist
society.

For Lewis was a warm if occasionally inconsistent proponent
of economic orthodoxy. He spoke out enthusiastically for free enterprise and the profit motive. Capitalism, Lewis argued, had
spawned two correlative institutions, the corporation and the trade
union. Each was a device for pooling sales, in the one case goods
and in the other labor. "The economic aims of both are identical
— gain." He considered radical ideas "the daydreams of visionaries"
and their sponsors enemies of the labor movement. In the
twenties he was one of the nation's most distinguished anti-Com-
munists, and the UMW in 1927 amended its constitution to bar
membership to Communists. He opposed state intervention in
economic life, at least when he did not need the government's
help.[15]

This, then, was the chief of the United Mine Workers at the end
of the twenties, potentially the most effective officer in the labor
movement. But, unlike Hutcheson, who was at the zenith of his
career, Lewis was at the nadir. For the coal union was a shambles.

## 7

The union whose president Lewis became in 1920 was the largest and most powerful in America. More than half a million miners were members and they were covered by contracts in almost all fields. In that year bituminous output reached an all-time peak of 568,000,000 tons; the price per ton paid by railways touched an astronomical $4.20; the number of men employed mounted to 640,000; and the UMW established a basic daily wage of $7.50. The industry radiated economic good health. In fact, the only immediate problem Lewis faced was the consolidation of his internal authority. He was not yet able to reverse the centrifugal flow of power from the international to the district organizations and he watched jealously the rising stars of potential rivals like Frank Farrington in Illinois and Alex Howat in Kansas.

At the end of the decade, however, the union lay in ruins. The cause of this extraordinary turn of fortune was the economic decline of bituminous induced by overcapacity. Even though potential output was normally excessive, high wartime prices had led to the opening of many new mines, particularly in the South. These new producers, with the advantages of more accessible and higher grade bituminous, more efficient equipment, cheap labor (often Negro), and favorable freight differentials, quickly seized the markets. By 1929 almost half the coal sold in the United States was mined in the Southern Appalachian field. Nor was needless expansion the only problem. Another was the rising competition of other fuels: oil, gas, and hydroelectricity. "Next to a scab," said a UMW organizer, "the lowest form of human life is an oilburner salesman. . . ." Still another difficulty was the increase in the efficiency of coal utilization. By 1929, for example, the railroads moved 16,007 gross tons of freight per ton of coal burned compared to only 11,628 in 1920. Finally, man-day output rose from 4 to 4.85 tons between 1920 and 1929. By 1926, according to the Brookings Institution, the bituminous industry's annual capacity exceeded one billion tons in face of a demand for half that amount. If the men had worked full time, only 150,000 to 250,000 of the 700,000 attached to the industry would have been needed to get the coal out of the ground.

The impact of this excess capacity was devastating. The price of coal plunged downward. Railways, for example, which had paid $4.20 a ton in 1920, paid only $2.40 in 1929. Equally significant was the fact that the decline began first and went furthest in the South. Between 1920 and 1930, the average mine realization price in Kentucky fell 74 per cent in contrast with a drop of 43 per cent in Illinois.

In this falling market fiercely competing operators cut costs, particularly labor costs, which were two thirds of the total. Between 1922 and 1929, according to the Bureau of Labor Statistics, average hourly earnings in bituminous fell 23 per cent, from 85.3 to 65.9 cents. Similarly, the eight-hour day, which had been universal after the war, gave way in the early twenties and the proportion of miners working nine and ten hours inched upward. Safety standards deteriorated. The half decade 1925–29 was the only such period between 1910 and 1940 in which the number of mine fatalities rose.

The United Mine Workers confronted the gravest crisis in its history. The policy Lewis enunciated was "No Backward Step!" and the form it took was the Jacksonville agreement. The union and its $7.50 base rate had collapsed in the South between 1922 and 1924, wages falling 30 to 50 per cent. Northern operators at once brought pressure for a commensurate reduction. In early 1924, after tortured negotiations at Jacksonville, Florida, Lewis persuaded the operators in the Central Competitive Field (western Pennsylvania, Ohio, Indiana, and Illinois) to preserve the $7.50 rate till March 31, 1927. Commerce Secretary Hoover, who helped mediate the controversy, hailed Jacksonville as "the most constructive development in the bituminous industry for years."

From the operators' point of view Hoover could not have been more wrong, for their economic position continued to deteriorate. Before 1924 was out they asked the UMW for a wage cut, which was refused. The positions are pointed up in the following interchange before the Senate Interstate Commerce Committee in 1928 between Charles M. Schwab, chairman of Bethlehem Steel, which had large mining properties, and Lewis:

Mr. Schwab: If I had been Mr. Lewis, for the good of the workingmen and the industry, I would not have kept wages at these high levels with the mines running as they are. Most of the miners would have been glad to have taken wages less than nonunion mines. . . .

Mr. Lewis: Suppose the mine workers had agreed to reduce wages in the organized coal territory, and then suppose, as has been done, the operators of the southern fields and your own company . . . in order to maintain their markets and keep their mines operating, would then reduce wages, would you say then that another reduction of wages would be called for?

Mr. Schwab: No; I do not, but that is an extreme.

Mr. Lewis: That is precisely the situation.

Mr. Schwab: You must know that nobody can run a mine, let us say, at $7.50 or $8 a day when every day there are many more mines running at $5.

Mr. Lewis: You admit that the industry is overdeveloped at least two-fifths?

Mr. Schwab: That is true.

Mr. Lewis: And the country will only consume a certain amount of coal mined. Suppose it reduces to $1 a day, would there be any more coal consumed?

Mr. Schwab: No; but you have to meet conditions. . . . If you persist in the high rate of wages there will not be any union mines. . . .

Mr. Lewis: Do you know we have evidence before this committee to show that wages have been reduced in some instances as low as $2.50 and $3 in certain mines in West Virginia? Where is the bottom?

Mr. Schwab: You will not prevent the bottom being reached by keeping wages so high that the man cannot work.

Mr. Lewis: Do you approve of a wage policy that will permit the most unfortunate, the most isolated, the most dependent foreign miner in West Virginia to become the yardstick that would measure the wages of organized labor in America?

Mr. Schwab: I do not want to get into a discussion of this.

In light of Lewis' refusal to revise the Jacksonville agreement, the operators set about the systematic destruction of the union. The focal point of UMW power was the Central Competitive Field and the key firm was the Pittsburgh Coal Company of western Pennsylvania, the largest producer in the nation. This company, which had had a contract with the miners for thirty-five years, had recently passed into the hands of the Mellon banking interests. Treasury Secretary Andrew Mellon and his brother Richard owned 25 per cent of the stock; Governor John S. Fisher of Pennsylvania was himself a coal operator and was known as the Mellons' candidate. The management of the company, formerly sympathetic with collective bargaining and among the prominent signatories of Jacksonville, was replaced by hostile men.

In late 1924 Pittsburgh Coal shut down and remained down until August 10, 1925, when, in violation of its agreement, the company reopened nonunion with a $6 rate. The UMW struck to enforce the contract. The company then evicted the miners and their families from company houses and brought in strikebreakers — Negroes from the South and floaters from northern cities. For their protection the company employed large contingents of armed guards, many of whom were commissioned by Governor Fisher. War broke out in western Pennsylvania, a war that became a national scandal and the subject of a Senate investigation.

Lowell Limpus, a reporter with the New York *Daily News*, wrote:

> I have just returned from a visit to "Hell-in-Pennsylvania." I have seen horrible things there; things which I almost hesitate to enumerate and describe. I can scarcely expect my story to be believed. I did not believe it myself when the situation was first outlined to me. Then I went into the coal camps of western and central Pennsylvania and saw for myself.
>
> . . . Many times it seemed impossible to think that we were in modern, civilized America.
>
> We saw thousands of women and children, literally starving to death. We found hundreds of destitute families living in crudely constructed bare-board shacks. They had been evicted from their homes by the coal companies. We unearthed a system of despotic tyranny reminiscent of Czar-ridden Siberia at its worst. We found police brutality and industrial slavery. We discovered the weirdest flock of injunctions that ever emanated from American temples of justice.

We unearthed evidence of terrorism and counterterrorism; of mob beatings and near lynchings; of dishonesty, graft, and heartlessness. . . .

The mine fields are a bubbling caldron of trouble. If it boils over — and it threatens to do so — blood must flow freely and many lives pay the forfeit.

The combination of armed power and starvation destroyed the union. How many people, largely women and children, lost their lives will never be known. The conditions of poverty, filth, and disease under which strikers and scabs alike lived were almost beyond belief. According to H. T. Brundidge, a reporter for the St. Louis *Star*, prostitutes and liquor were available on company property. Crimes of violence were a common occurrence. A colored strikebreaker, for example, told the Senate committee that the company paid him and a buddy each $25 to fire guns into the homes of strikers.

Although Pittsburgh Coal hardly achieved high output under these conditions, it did gain its main objective, smashing the UMW. Most of the smaller companies in Pennsylvania followed this pattern, and the operators in other states were not far behind. In West Virginia the open shop was encased in a legal strait jacket. Miners were required as a condition of employment to sign yellow-dog contracts. "I am not now a member of the United Mine Workers . . . and I enter this employment with the understanding that the policy of the company is to operate a nonunion mine . . . and would not give me employment under any other conditions." Thus read the notorious Red Jacket yellow dog, the employment agreement that the federal courts under the Hitchman doctrine held a valid contract, enforceable by injunction in perpetuity. Lewis declared, "I can not legally say to any one of those 40,000 men . . . 'Come and join our union; it will better your condition'; because I would be in contempt. . . ." Between 1924 and 1928, the UMW expended more than $8 million on fruitless litigation on the Red Jacket and related cases.

By the end of the decade the magic $7.50 of Jacksonville was an antediluvian memory. Pittsburgh Coal had cut wages three times. The nonunion maximum was $4.50 and some operators were down to $1.50. In 1927, at the expiration of the Jacksonville agreement, the miners and the unionized operators had sparred at Miami without result. By 1928 even Lewis no longer sought to hold the line. The UMW gave up a centralized wage policy and instructed each district to make the best deal it could. Ohio accepted a one-third reduction; Illinois and Indiana took 18.7 per cent less; the Iowa rate dropped to $5.80. But these were union scales and in 1928 the UMW bargained for only 20 per cent of the nation's bituminous miners. So desperate was Lewis that he turned to the federal government for help. On his initiative Senator James E. Watson of Indiana introduced a bill in 1928 that would have encouraged mergers and pooled sales by the industry along with a guarantee to workers of the right to organize and bargain collectively. The Watson bill got nowhere, but its reciprocal formula was to recur later.[16]

In this wreckage there were but three remnants of strength: Illinois, anthracite, and the Rocky Mountain Fuel Company. Somehow, District 12, Illinois, held its own through the storm and in 1929 retained 50,000 members, whose loyalty to the international, as will be recounted in Chapter 10, was something less than absolute. Anthracite, though a declining industry, was located entirely in Pennsylvania and had no southern competitors. Its price structure remained stable and there was little pressure on wages. The hard-coal districts held their membership and by 1929 constituted the largest element within the union, the tail wagging the dog. In August 1928, in the exception that proved the rule, the UMW negotiated a first agreement with the Rocky Mountain Fuel Company, already dealt with on page 100.

The collapse of bituminous and the disintegration of the UMW during the twenties opened the door wide to factionalism and dual unionism. Here was the real test of Lewis' mastery of the art of power, of destroying enemies within and without and of building a monolithic machine.

The first of the rebels was that bull from Kansas — Alex Howat, president of District 14. He ran for vice-president of the UMW against Lewis' man, Phil Murray, in 1920 and was defeated. Howat then provided Lewis with the lever he sought by calling a strike in violation of contract. On October 21, 1921, Lewis revoked the charter of District 14 and expelled Howat from the union. The Kansan appealed through both the UMW judicial machinery and the courts and received his answer at the 1924 convention when he was thrown bodily off the platform.

A more serious threat was posed by the fox, Frank Farrington, the president of District 12, who was covetous of Lewis' job and spoke for a major mine field. He fought every effort to centralize authority and bargaining, and made district autonomy a popular issue. Too shrewd to attack Lewis frontally (Lewis spoke of his "surreptitious and nocturnal activities"), Farrington supported those, like Howat, who were willing to run the risk. Corruption proved Farrington's undoing. On August 25, 1926, Lewis with fanfare revealed to the executive board of District 12 a secret contract between Farrington and the Peabody Coal Company under which the former was to be paid $25,000 a year for three years as the latter's "labor relations expert" while serving as an officer of the district. The board promptly suspended him. Lewis refused any explanation of how he came into possession of the contract, a fact that has encouraged nasty rumors.

John Brophy, president of District 2, central Pennsylvania, was an unassuming, cheerful, idealistic little man, as faithful in his devotion to trade unionism as he was to his Catholicism. Genuinely convinced that Lewis' policies were disastrous, Brophy launched the "Save-the-Union" movement in 1926. He advocated a militant organizing drive, a labor party, nationalization of the mines, close cooperation between bituminous and anthracite districts, and reinstatement of those expelled. He ran for president in 1926, rallying about him all those who hated Lewis: followers of Howat, the Communists, and trade-union radicals like Powers Hapgood and the Musteites. Brophy was defeated overwhelmingly and, though he charged fraud, would probably have lost even if the votes had been counted honestly.

By December 1926, Lewis had deposed the three men within the UMW who were likely to cause him the most trouble. He now faced the threat of dual unionism in the form of the Communist National Miners' Union. The UMW had for years had a Communist nucleus with its major strength in Nova Scotia, leading Lewis in 1923 to revoke that district's charter. The left-wingers had then turned unavailingly to Brophy's movement. The collapse of the UMW in the Central Competitive Field afforded them a new opportunity. As the novelist Fannie Hurst told the Senate committee after visiting the camps: "Here is a happy hunting ground for sowing the seeds of dissension and hate and rebellion, particularly in a country where contrasts are so cruelly wide apart." To exploit this discontent, the Communists organized a Pennsylvania-Ohio Relief Committee, giving Lewis an excuse to expel the leaders. Shortly after, the Red International ordered the formation of dual unions and these men met in Pittsburgh September 9–16, 1928, to form the National Miners' Union. This organization was active in Pennsylvania, northern West Virginia, Ohio, and Illinois and made a special and unsuccessful appeal to Negroes. The NMU, Lewis snorted, enrolled only 4000 to 5000 miners at this time and was "a ragtag bobtail membership of renegades." More was to be heard from it later on.

The critical struggle was with District 12. The ousting of Farrington had merely removed a leader without excising the issue: district autonomy. UMW decline in the twenties simply aggravated the conflict; Illinois provided a disproportionately large share of the international's income and in return received no protection against nonunion competition. For the district leaders the Brophy movement proved the futility of a direct challenge to Lewis, and the NMU was no real alternative to trade unionists. For Lewis, obviously, control over the Illinois membership and income was indispensable. Since there was no basis for compromise, war was inevitable, a war which was to drag on in one form or another for decades.

The opening shot was fired by one Joe P. Goett of Peoria, who wrote a circular urging the miners to reject the wage reduction negotiated by District 12 officers in 1928. On October 8 of that year the district executive board expelled him and four others, leading to a strike in the Peoria subdistrict. Goett and his followers immediately appealed to Lewis, who restored their membership. If he had not theretofore been a Lewis agent, Goett now became one. He then won election to the presidency of the subdistrict in January 1929, and launched an attack upon the district officers for the "sellout" wage agreement and for juggling the votes in the ratification referendum. He carried these charges to the floor of the district convention held in Peoria in the spring but made no headway against the anti-Lewis majority.

This convention, however, turned up fraudulent real estate transactions among the subdistrict officers in Franklin County, thereby giving Lewis an excuse to intervene allegedly to clean up corruption. On June 8, 1929, he revoked the charter of this Subdistrict 9 and vacated its offices. Under UMW law, the property of a dissolved subordinate body became the property of the international. A complicated series of legal maneuvers resulted in the failure of the ousted officers to obtain a permanent injunction restraining Lewis from seizing the property. In the course of the controversy two of these men, D. B. Cobb and Ed Loden, "confessed" that money for groceries for striking miners had been embezzled, that votes had been bought in an election in December 1928, and that District 12 had allocated $10,000 to fight the international.

On October 15, Lewis, grounding his action upon these charges, revoked the charter of District 12. Goett popped up again as provisional vice-president of the new body. The bitter fight that followed, leading to formation of a dual United Mine Workers in 1930 and the Progressive Mine Workers in 1932, is a story told later in Chapter 10. Suffice it to say here that this was the fifth time Lewis had lifted a district's charter: northwestern Canada in 1919, Kansas in 1921, Nova Scotia in 1923, West Virginia in 1924, and Illinois in 1929. He was willing to run the risk that his acts would be found illegal under the UMW constitution in order to undermine district autonomy. The opportunity to remove legal doubt occurred in 1930 when the Illinois rebels set up their dual union at Springfield. Lewis took advantage of his enemies' absence from his own convention to amend the UMW constitution: "Charters of districts, sub-districts and local unions may be revoked by the International President, who shall have authority to create a provisional government for the subordinate branch. . . ." Under this language he would have need neither to show cause nor to obtain the approval of the executive board, the convention, or the membership. To this must be added the fact that many districts by the end of the twenties were ghost organizations without membership or income, whose officers were named by Lewis and depended upon him for funds. From the wreckage of coal and the union, therefore, Lewis had salvaged something: absolute control over the UMW machinery. He was never again to be seriously challenged from within.[17]

## 8

The weakness of the American Federation of Labor and its constituent unions in the twenties invited competition from the left. It came from two sources — the youthful Communist Party and the aged Industrial Workers of the World.

After World War I the Third International faced a dilemma in the Western nations: to penetrate the existing labor movements or to create dual Communist unions. In an essay entitled *"Left-Wing" Communism: An Infantile Disorder*, Lenin laid down the line. The first (present) stage of worker organization is the trade union, which in time will reach the second stage of the revolutionary soviet. "The Party must work with the masses wherever they are to be found, however ultra-reactionary their institutions may be." Rather than fence themselves off with childish slogans, Communists must "resort to all sorts of devices, manoeuvres, and illegal methods, to evasion and subterfuge in order to penetrate into the trade unions, to remain in them, and to carry on Communist work in them at all costs." In 1921 the Comintern, meeting in Moscow, officially adopted the Leninist policy of "boring from within."

The American Communist leader William Z. Foster was quick to call the turn: in November 1920 he launched the Trade Union Educational League. TUEL emphasized that it was not a union and neither issued charters nor collected dues. Its job was to coordinate CP penetration of the American labor movement during most of the twenties. According to Benjamin Stolberg, TUEL's finances and directives emanated from Moscow and its real bosses were Carl E. Johnson (Scott), Boris Reinstein, Joseph Pogany (John Pepper), and Gussev (P. Green).

Communist nuclei established themselves in a number of organizations without seriously threatening the trade-union leadership.

This was the case with the Machinists, Carpenters, Mine Workers, Textile Workers, Boot and Shoe Workers, Pullman Porters, and Seamen. The main TUEL drive was in the needle trades, where the labor force was concentrated in New York City and consisted largely of immigrants from eastern and southern Europe, many with a Marxist background. The CP goal was amalgamation of the four garment organizations into a single union under its domination. In 1922, TUEL established Needle Trades and Furriers Sections, and a Yiddish newspaper, *Freiheit*, to combat the anti-Communist *Forward*.

TUEL made only slight headway in the Amalgamated Clothing Workers. Coatmakers' Local 5 in New York was penetrated in 1924, followed by an unauthorized strike. For this three leaders of the local were suspended in January 1925. Mass meetings called by TUEL in protest were captured by right-wingers, and the New York revolt soon died down. In 1926–27, there were sporadic disturbances in Montreal, Toronto, and Rochester. President Sidney Hillman's policy was to permit the Communists to talk themselves out, to outnumber them at meetings, and to subvert their leaders. "I said to one of their high priests: 'Any time you can take the Amalgamated you are entitled to it, but don't expect us to deliver it to you.'"

TUEL inroads into the Millinery Workers were deeper but no more enduring. The Communists established themselves in locals in Boston, the Twin Cities, Los Angeles, Toronto, Montreal, and, most important, Local 24 in New York. A spirited fight took place for control of 24 which ended in victory for the right-wingers in 1924 under Alex Rose. TUEL then won over the girls in New York trimmers' Local 43. The international countered by amalgamating 43 with 24 in 1928, an act which led to warfare in the millinery district, climaxed by a bloody street brawl outside the Princeton Hat Company on April 19, 1929. At the convention that year the international won a handsome victory on the amalgamation issue, expelled the leaders of Local 43, and amended the constitution to ban membership in a dual organization and to authorize suspension of a local that refused to obey decisions of the executive board. The lesser markets were soon cleaned up.

The conflict in the ILGWU became a devastating civil war following the election of the determined anti-Communist, Morris Sigman, as president of the international in 1923. On August 16, the executive board ordered TUEL cells to disband and suspended nineteen officers of Local 22 in New York and thirteen officials in Chicago, reorganized two Philadelphia locals, and took similar action in Boston and other small markets. In 1924, Sigman required candidates for office to take non-Communist oaths, which all the TUEL leaders cheerfully signed. They promptly won elections in New York Locals 2, 9, and 22, consisting of the mass of workers in the cloak and dress industries and thus the heart of the union. By the following year TUEL had captured the New York Joint Board. At the stormy Philadelphia convention in late 1925, Sigman retained control of the international by a narrow majority consisting of the out-of-town locals, the Italian unions in New York, and David Dubinsky's skilled cutters in Local 10.

The main battleground was the New York cloak industry, which was disorganized and for which a commission appointed by Governor Smith in 1924 had recommended reorganization, including the employer's right to discharge surplus workmen. Sigman backed the plan and the Communists opposed it. On July 1, 1926, the latter under CP orders called a hopeless strike of 30,000 cloakmakers that was to last for twenty-eight tortured weeks. "Seldom in the history of American labor," Stolberg wrote, "has a strike been so incompetently, wastefully and irresponsibly conducted." Its cost was about $3,500,000, $800,000 of which the Joint Board with revolutionary fervor misappropriated from employer funds deposited as security for contracts. For its strong-arm work the industry engaged the services of the Legs Diamond gang, and the Communists countered by hiring Little Augie's mob. Both, in fact, were controlled by Arnold Rothstein, the mastermind of the 1919 Black Sox scandal and czar of the New York underworld. In November the strike and the Joint Board collapsed. Sigman took over the wreckage on December 13, including the debt of $800,000. His victory in New York proved decisive, and within a year or two the Communists were ejected from their bridgeheads in Chicago, Montreal, Boston, Baltimore, Los Angeles, and San Francisco. The trade unionists were in possession of a clean but bankrupt union.

TUEL's sole continuing success was with the Fur Workers. The Communists won a toehold in New York Locals 1, 5, 10, and 15 as well as the Joint Board in 1920, following a disastrous strike. This they converted into firm control by victory in the elections of May 23, 1925, the vote reflecting worker discontent with the economic situation in the fur industry. Under Ben Gold's vigorous leadership they almost captured the international at the November 1925 convention. Failing there, the Communists led a general strike in the New York market on February 16, 1926. The settlement of June 11 was a great left-wing victory, providing most notably for the forty-hour week, and led to the communization of the Philadelphia, Boston, Newark, and Chicago locals. Gold was firmly in the saddle and would almost certainly have seized the international at its 1927 convention.

Hence on July 19, 1926, the AFL stepped in; Green appointed a committee of Federation bigwigs to investigate the internal affairs of the Fur Workers. The report charged Communist leadership of the strike, TUEL control of the Joint Board, beatings of non-Communists, misuse of funds, and bribing of the police. The Executive Council on January 13, 1927, instructed the international to expel left-wing officers and revoke the charters of the board and the locals. Since the international had neither money nor rank-and-file support, Green named an AFL committee that in effect served as a receivership. On March 2, it expelled thirty-seven officers, dissolved the New York board and locals, ordered property turned over to itself, and set up a new joint council. Chaos resulted in the fur market. Gold replied with a strike on June 3 that showed both the manufacturers and the AFL his membership strength. The former had no alternative but to deal with him, and the latter none but to withdraw ingloriously from the fur industry.

In 1928 the Communists decided to destroy the remnants of the international, and their locals ceased per capita payments. At the end of December 1928, conventions of furriers as well as dissident cloak and dressmakers amalgamated into a new Needle Trades Industrial Union. Moscow had reversed itself; TUEL was dead and the day of the Communist dual union had dawned.

By 1928 it was clear to everyone that TUEL "boring," excepting the furriers, had failed dismally because too few Communists had got "within" the trade unions. This became apparent at the very moment when Stalin was consolidating his control over the party apparatus in the Soviet Union and so over international Communism. He had already destroyed Trotsky on the left and was about to attack Bukharin on the right. The latter advocated a slower pace for the revolution within the USSR and greater consideration for the institutions of each nation abroad. In assaulting Bukharin, Stalin adopted Trotsky's arguments; the Comintern and the Red International of Labor Unions veered sharply leftward to attack democratic institutions frontally, notably the trade unions. Lozofsky, RILU's boss, denounced the American party for "dancing quadrilles around the AFL," and the Comintern in the summer of 1928 ordered TUEL to become a dual labor movement. The "infantile disorder" at which Lenin had snorted was now the official policy of world Communism. Many American functionaries, unlike Foster, were unable to shift gears abruptly. This was the case with the party secretary, Jay Lovestone, who formed a splinter anti-Stalinist Communist Party, usually identified as the Lovestoneites, that was to have something of a labor history in the thirties.

The Comintern had named the enemy: "Taking its main gospel from the tablets of imperialist politics . . . the deliberately anti-socialist and openly counter-revolutionary American Federation of Labor . . . a force directed against the proletariat and revolution." American Communists were now enjoined to destroy the AFL from without.

In September 1929, at a convention in Cleveland otherwise notable for the *coup de grâce* administered to Lovestone, the Stalinists interred TUEL and gave birth to the Trade Union Unity League. The masses, according to Foster, were in a rebellious mood and TUUL was "a dramatic demonstration of the growing radicalization of the American working class." Its objective was to organize the unorganized in industrial unions, that is, the unskilled and semi-skilled workers largely overlooked by the AFL. Its method was to be openly revolutionary, to array class against class, to conduct mass violations of labor injunctions, to arouse Negroes, to have no traffic with "social reformism." TUUL spawned a series of new unions dual to AFL affiliates: National Miners' Union, National

Textile Workers, Needle Trades Workers, Marine Workers, Auto Workers, Steel and Metal Workers, and others. Excepting the furrier element in the Needle Trades organization, their membership was either insignificant or evanescent; most of them proved to be little more than paper formations. Foster, a man seldom given to understatement, told the Fish Committee more than a year after the crash that TUUL unions had 25,000 members.

The failure of the Communist Party to take over or replace the AFL had one unlooked-for result: entrenchment of the Federation's conservative leadership. The First Commandment became opposition to Communism. "It is no secret," Woll declaimed, "that the American Federation of Labor is the first object of attack by the Communist movement. Consequently the American Federation of Labor is the first line of defense." Progressives within the Federation either needed conservative help to fight the left or became reluctant to propose reforms for fear of being branded Communists themselves. A favorite AFL policy became opposition to the recognition of the USSR. At a time when few Americans took domestic Communism seriously, the Federation executives fought it bitterly, and that struggle was to leave an enduring mark upon their thought.[18]

9

The AFL and TUUL shared at least one thing: the enmity of the Industrial Workers of the World. Neither, however, had much to fear, because the IWW was barely alive. The organization had attained peak strength in 1917 and suffered a disastrous decline after the war. Always plagued by the centrifugal forces generated by its anarcho-syndicalist philosophy, the IWW split apart at its 1924 convention. The dissident group was doctrinaire, for example, opposing clemency for Wobblies jailed under the criminal syndicalism laws, ownership of property (a headquarters building), and moderately high initiation fees and dues. These purists formed a rival union that soon passed out of existence, leaving the demoralized main body in the hands of the more practical group.

This IWW lost ground steadily in the industries where it had once been strong — lumber, metal mining, agriculture, and marine transportation. Its only significant activity, in fact, was in a new area — bituminous coal, where the collapse of the United Mine Workers invited radicals of all stripes. On August 21, 1927, IWW called a national one-day protest strike against the execution of Sacco and Vanzetti. The only workers to respond in substantial number were the coal miners of southern Colorado. This led to a stoppage over economic issues that began on October 18 and lasted four months, accompanied by much bloodshed and police terrorism. It was, in fact, the killing of six miners and the wounding of many others on November 21 at the Columbine Mine of the Rocky Mountain Fuel Company that led Miss Roche to overhaul that firm's labor policy. Significantly, the agreement she made was with the UMW rather than with the IWW.

This short-lived success in coal was to stimulate the Wobblies to later adventures in that industry. In 1929, however, they had little strength there or anywhere else. How many workers the IWW enrolled is difficult to say. An indication may be derived from the fact that only 719 ballots were cast in a nation-wide referendum early in 1929. Clearly, the IWW had failed to interest workers in its program. "This inability," J. S. Gambs has concluded, "is not to be explained only by the poor quality of leadership and membership . . . but also by the fact that, in America, the seeds of revolution fall on stony ground." [19]

10

"What the labor movement . . . needs now," wrote William M. Leiserson in the spring of 1929, "is a lot of strong criticism showing up their weaknesses and their stupidity. That is the only way . . . in which they can be awakened and stimulated to perform the functions . . . which they ought to be performing." During the twenties, in effect, the unions stood aside as American industry raced ahead. The internal shortcomings of the AFL, to say nothing of the radical organizations, were self-destructive. Wage earners showed little interest in the movement. As Green, in a melancholy mood, wrote the organizer who sought to unionize the Nash automobile plant, "The appalling indifference of the workers themselves is a difficulty that seems to be insurmountable." [20] Equally if not more discouraging was the hostility of employers.

CHAPTER 3

# The Employer: Concord or Discord?

"AMERICA is an employer's paradise," the sharp-eyed Australian
H. G. Adam observed in 1928. He was most certainly right. At
no other period in the twentieth century, at least, were employers as a class so free of the countervailing restraints of a pluralistic society as during the twenties. Labor organizations were de-
plorably weak and government was dedicated to fostering the
employer's freedom. The businessman rode high, his voice the
decisive one in a business society dominated by business interests.
"Just as in Rome one goes to the Vatican and endeavors to get
audience of the Pope," wrote English traveler J. A. Spender in
1928, "so in Detroit one goes to the Ford works and endeavors
to see Henry Ford."

Yet it cannot be said that employers in their dealings with
their employees were content or even at ease in this paradise
they allegedly enjoyed. Their outlook was marred by internal
disharmony, uncertainty, and negligence. Cyrus Ching, then industrial relations manager for United States Rubber, recalls a meeting of the National Metal Trades Association in New York in
1920 at which he and his counterpart at International Harvester,
Arthur H. Young, spoke. Both talked in a general way about bettering communication with employees and, of course, shied away
from anything so "radical" as unionization. When they were
through, the prominent industrialist who served as chairman announced with deadly seriousness: "Gentlemen, you have just heard
two talks on Bolshevism." [1]

✿

1

This decade constituted a transitional stage in the development of American industry, one in which enterprises were growing rapidly in size, in which improved technology and rational methods were being applied to production and distribution, in which management was separating from ownership and becoming both professionalized and "scientific," and in which employers groped uncertainly in dealing with the serious labor problems their productive endeavors were largely instrumental in creating. Businessmen were far more comfortable handling units of production and dollars of profit than they were dealing with the people who were their employees. As a consequence, labor was a question to which they seldom addressed themselves. "The real difficulty of labor relations," industrialist Sam A. Lewisohn wrote, "has been one of neglect." A common observation of the time was that top executives, generally speaking, showed no interest in industrial relations, and their negativism permeated the ranks of supervision. Another was that management had failed to employ the boldness and imagination with labor that it had applied to production. When the superintendent of an iron mine on the Mesabi was asked what he wanted to do more than anything else, he replied instantly: "Cut a dollar a ton off the cost of ore." He would not hesitate to reduce wages to achieve this end. "You have to be tough when you're handling iron."

At bottom, this negligence stemmed from a fundamental uncertainty over the place of labor in the business system. Employers did not know whether to clutch workers to their breasts as partners in a great cooperative adventure in production or to keep them at arm's length as potential, if not present, enemies of capitalism. They would refer patronizingly to the worker as a pillar of society ("There is no better American citizen . . . than the average American worker," Charles M. Schwab declared) and proceed promptly to truss him up. Employers could not decide whether their interests were better served simply by keeping labor disorganized or by putting it into organizations under their control. A general theme at management meetings was "the harmony of interests" between employers and employees. By this phrase the speakers meant that workers were to harmonize themselves with the goals and methods of management, and, failing that, employers had the obligation to use harmonious coercion. At a time when autocratic statements had become taboo, autocratic methods were widespread. Employers were unsure whether to regard the worker as a displaceable cog in the productive machine or as an indispensable consumer of industry's rising output, his wage as a cost item to be kept low or as an income factor to be pushed high. Finally, there was a general tendency within management to consider labor as an exclusively intra-firm problem at the very moment when industry-wide and interindustry forces were becoming decisive.

This ambivalence manifested itself most dramatically in the extraordinary shift in the labor policy of employers that occurred during the decade. At the outset management launched the so-called American Plan, a full-scale direct attack on trade unionism with the panoply of hostile techniques. In the latter part of the twenties employers veered sharply to the gentler methods of paternalistic welfare capitalism.

This schizophrenia contributed to those "astonishing contrasts in organization and disorganization" that President Hoover's Committee on Social Trends found so marked a feature of American society. "Not all parts of our organization are changing at the same speed or at the same time. . . . These unequal rates of change . . . make zones of danger and points of tension." In the twenties, employers, when they were aware of them at all, were inclined to sweep these dangers and tensions under the rug.[2]

2

On September 17, 1919, the eve of both the steel strike and President Wilson's conference on industrial relations, John D. Rockefeller, Jr., called upon Henry Clay Frick and Judge Elbert Gary, the two men who more than any others shaped the policies of America's largest industrial corporation, United States Steel. He urged them to consider either collective bargaining or employee representation (now known as company unionism). The following day Rockefeller wrote his good friend W. L. Mackenzie King that he found Frick "utterly opposed . . . and ready to close up every mill if a strike occurred." Gary objected to "representation of any kind, believing that it is only the entering wedge to the closed shop, which he feels is fatal to business." The following year Herbert Hoover, disturbed over the contemporary strike wave and the world-wide rise of radicalism, called a meeting of key industrialists who held "advanced views toward employee relations" at the Metropolitan Club in New York. Among those present were A. C. Bedford, president of Standard Oil of New Jersey, C. B. Seger, president of U.S. Rubber, and C. A. Coffin, chairman of General Electric. Hoover, as one of those present later wrote, proposed that they "establish liaison" with Gompers and the AFL. "The idea got a very cold reception." Each of these well-intended overtures was doomed to failure because industry had elected to fight labor organization with all the weapons in that well-stocked arsenal that came to be called, amazingly enough, the "American Plan."

The message of this antiunion drive was as simple and direct as a soap ad: the closed shop is bad; the open shop is good. In the backwash of a great war, when patriotism was a readily marketable commodity, it was a simple matter to package this message as "Americanism." Dr. Gus W. Dyer, idealogue of the National Association of Manufacturers, declaimed in 1920: "You can hardly conceive of a more un-American, a more anti-American institution than the closed shop. It is really very remarkable that it is allowed to exist . . . under the American flag." In 1923 the NAM president, John Edgerton, declared: "I can't conceive of any principle that is more purely American, that comes nearer representing the very essence of all those traditions and institutions that are dearest to us than the open shop principle." Old Glory had been draped over the gun barrel.

Allegedly, the "open" shop was one "with equal opportunity for all and special privileges for none," where nonunion and union man alike received nondiscriminatory treatment. In the great majority of cases, however, this was nothing more than fraudulent propaganda. In fact, open shops were normally closed nonunion shops, where a trade-union member who wore his affiliation honestly was either denied employment or fired. "Some employers deny this but most of them frankly admit it."

The steel industry's success in smashing the 1919 strike gave the antiunion drive a running start and helped fix its tone. As was said of one of the architects of that victory, Tom Girdler, boss of Jones & Laughlin's Aliquippa works: "His labor policies were such that Aliquippa was known to steel men as 'the perfect company town' and to radicals as 'the Siberia of the industry.' " By the fall of 1920 a network of open-shop organizations covered the nation. New York State had over 50, Massachusetts 18, Connecticut 20, Illinois 46, Ohio 17, Michigan 23, and so on. Notable local bodies were the Detroit Associated Industries, the Minneapolis Citizens' Alliance, Associated Industries of Cleveland, the Chicago Citizens' Committee to Enforce the Landis Award, the San Francisco Industrial Association, and the Los Angeles Merchants and Manufacturers. A meeting of twenty-two state associations in Chicago in January 1921 drew the local groups together and officially adopted the name "American Plan." The campaign was a remarkable success. In traditionally open-shop towns like Detroit and Los Angeles, labor's wartime gains were wiped away. Even in historically unionized San Francisco the organizations suffered crippling blows. Belligerent employers' associations undermined the Seamen's Union in its 1921 strike, destroyed the Meat Cutters and Butcher Workmen's organization in the packing industry, nipped incipient textile unions in the bud, and even made inroads on the building trades, notably in Chicago and San Francisco. By October 1921, Schwab was able to reassure employers at a meeting of the Illinois Chamber of Commerce: "Go to your golf this afternoon and to your offices on Monday with a feeling of optimism in your hearts."

The primary significance of the American Plan movement in the present context is that it represented a full-blown development of the techniques of hostility to trade unionism. This articulated system of belligerency was to reappear in the thirties in the same form. Hence it is necessary here to describe it with some detail. At this point it should be noted that all but three of these methods were lawful, and only occasional state statutes — which were easily evaded — restricted industrial espionage, strikebreaking, and industrial munitioning. The law of labor relations is considered in the next chapter.

The simplest devices of the employer to prevent or destroy a union in his plant were discrimination against and discharge of members. In more highly developed form a group of firms, usually through an employers' association, maintained a blacklist of workers whom they would fire or refuse to hire. In the steel industry in the twenties, for example, rosters of union "agitators" were exchanged and no mill would hire a union man. The practices were probably employed by a majority of American corporations. Their effectiveness "in hindering successful organization is hardly open to dispute."

These rudimentary devices were institutionalized in what employers called the "individual" and unionists branded the "yellow-dog" contract. Here the employee entered into a written agreement in which he accepted as a condition of employment that he would not become a member of a union or attempt to organize his fellow employees. Yellow dogs first became prominent in the New England textile industry in the 1870's, and in the twenties of the present century were widely used in the coal, hosiery, street railway, and shoe industries.

The labor injunction, which had first appeared in the 1880's, achieved its widest use during the twenties. Perhaps the most notable injunction was that issued by Judge James Wilkerson at the request of Attorney General Harry Daugherty on September 1, 1921, during the railway shop-crafts strike. In effect, Wilkerson forbade the unions, their officers, attorneys, or members to have anything to do with the strike.

Industrial espionage, developed shortly after the Civil War, was one of the blackest chapters in the volume of employer practices. Loyal union members assembled in a meeting could usually be certain that someone in their midst was an employer agent. An executive who was active in industrial relations at the time has declared that espionage was general during the twenties. A leading AFL official estimated that there were 200,000 spies at work in 1928 and referred a foreign visitor to two pages of private detective agencies listed in the Chicago telephone book. The annual income of three of these agencies during the decade was estimated at $65 million. The people engaged in industrial espionage, according to the nation's leading private detective, William J. Burns, "are the biggest lot of blackmailing thieves that ever went unwhipped of justice." Espionage was supplied by these so-called detective agencies, by employers' associations, and sometimes by corporations themselves. The La Follette Committee, after an exhaustive investigation, concluded that espionage was the most efficient system to prevent unions from forming, to weaken them once they gained a foothold, and to wreck them when they tried to test their strength.

The experience of Carl Holderman, vice-president of the Hosiery Workers, in the fall of 1929 is illustrative. He was approached by an impressive-looking gentleman who represented himself with credentials as an agent of the American Bankers Association. He offered Holderman $150 per month to supply information on prospective strikes in the hosiery industry. The bankers, he said, did not want to loan money to firms that might soon be engaged in disputes. After checking with the union's officers, Holderman decided to lead him on and tentatively accepted the offer. The agent instructed Holderman to bring sharp pressure on the Gotham Hosiery Company for higher wages. The union then found that the detective agency for which this man worked had approached the management to tell them trouble was brewing in their plants and that the agency could handle it for them. At the next meeting in Paterson, Holderman had the agent arrested under a New Jersey law that made it a crime to bribe a union official. The man's name and address proved fictitious and he refused to divulge any information about himself. Bail was paid in cash by the Philadelphia manager of the Railway Audit and Inspection Bureau, a notorious detective agency. The Bureau then employed expensive and politically potent legal talent to have the case quashed, without success. The agent was fined $500.

The more usual technique called for placing spies and *agents provocateurs* in the plant and in the union (particularly in the office of secretary). Key objectives were the names of employees who were members of the union, advance strike plans for alerting the employer, the precipitation of a strike before the union was prepared, and the discrediting of union leadership with the membership. Spy reports were used throughout the campaign against the union: in forming the blacklist, in discrimination and discharge for union activity, in instilling fear among the employees, in breaking strikes, in initiating the company union, and in supplying affidavits for the labor injunction.

Strikebreaking and espionage were linked policies and were supplied by the same sources — private detective agencies and employer associations. The employment of private armies to suppress unions existed only in the United States, where they grew out of a history of employer refusal to accept collective bargaining and of turbulence in industrial relations. Public investigations revealed and condemned the use of strikebreaking in virtually every major dispute after 1882. Prior to 1900 employers usually recruited strikebreakers and guards themselves, but thereafter, as unions became stronger, detective agencies and employer associations supplied this service.

By 1910 distinct occupational types developed. The labor supply consisted at first of immigrants, recruited for their ignorance and gullibility, but later of "strikebreakers by calling," that is, the socially maladjusted and denizens of the underworld, many of whom had criminal records or were professional criminals. Certain street corners became known as "open markets" where the agencies could on short notice collect hundreds of men via the "grapevine." The lowest echelon occupationally consisted of strikebreakers, or "finks," who replaced the strikers. Above them were the strike guards, or "nobles," who carried arms and "protected" the loyal workers and property. They were often deputized as police officers in order to legalize their activities. Another type sometimes used was the propagandist, or "missionary." He posed as a neutral, usually a salesman, and moved among the strikers spreading defeatism. At the top were the strike lieutenants, who organized and executed the operation. All looked with contempt upon "scabs," workers who permanently replaced strikers. The strikebreaker was unqualified by character and training to perform work, his function being to shock the morale of the strikers and intimidate them into returning to work.

Violence was an inevitable consequence of strikebreaking.

Strikers universally detested the intruders and a little powder would set off the charged atmosphere. Strike guards were not reluctant to use their arms, and it was, in fact, in the financial interest of the agency to promote violence in order to prolong the strike. Employers who hired such services were aware of the character of the guards and often asked that they come armed. Sometimes the employer would purchase industrial munitions on his own initiative.

The strikebreaking agencies did a land-office business during the American Plan period. Pearl Bergoff, operator of the leading Bergoff Service, for example, charged the Erie Railroad a record $2 million to smash the 1920 switchmen's walkout. Between 1924 and 1929, however, this "industry" withered under the combined effects of union weakness and industrial calm. Bergoff described his business at that time as "atrocious."

Very large employers, particularly in steel, and those whose operations were located in isolated communities, as in coal and metal mining, developed the private police system. These police originated with the railroads in pioneering days to protect property because public forces of order were inadequate. Even at the start they defended the interests of the employer and only incidentally exercised the nonpartisan function of guardian of the law. There was no final accountability to the public, nor corrective for antisocial action. "The use of private police as an agency of labor policy," the La Follette Committee concluded, "must be viewed . . . primarily as an attempt to impose upon labor a selfish, private interest by means of private armies." Like espionage and strikebreaking, with which it was closely linked, this system tended to create violence and was marked by "a long and bloodstained history." Three states — Pennsylvania, Maryland, and South Carolina — enacted statutes in the nineteenth century which specifically legalized company police and made it possible to deputize officers and thereby lend them the authority of the law. Of these, the Pennsylvania Coal and Iron Police were the most important and notorious. Their conduct during strikes became a national scandal. In a 1928 coal walkout, for example, a striker declared that the only civil right he retained was "peaceful breathing." Another, who was badly beaten by four policemen on the main street of Bentleyville, brought criminal action. Although he produced before the grand jury five eyewitnesses and two ends of a mace which had been broken on his head, the case was dismissed and he was confined to jail.

When private police operated within the confines of a company town, a system of virtual industrial peonage was created. The United States Steel Corporation, for example, in the communities it dominated, sought to insulate immigrant workers against outside influence. The employees lived in company houses, were supplied with utilities provided by the corporation, and were subject to constant surveillance in their family and social activities. Housing, gas, electricity, and water became instruments of labor policy. A union organizer entering such a town was spotted, and he and the employees to whom he spoke were submitted to "rough shadowing."

The use of force ultimately involved in many of these practices led to industrial munitioning. Its origins go back at least to 1890, and thereafter it became a large and lucrative business. Sales of munitions were correlated with the labor policies of employers and the incidence of organizational strikes; the steel industry, for example, provided the largest market. Strikes in which the employer refused to recognize the union could not be settled; they could only be broken. The offensive purpose of industrial munitions was revealed by the weapons involved — tear and sickening gas, shells and guns to discharge them, and, to a lesser extent, machine guns. They were usually purchased in anticipation of a strike. The munitions companies followed labor difficulties in their sales campaigns, and the detective agencies often acted as commission agents. Frequently private purchasers would supply public law enforcement officers with weapons in anticipation of a dispute.

Opposition to trade unionism was the main purpose of some employer associations, that is, collective action to prevent or destroy collective bargaining. These belligerent associations attained peak activity during the American Plan period, and the momentum of their success carried them through the balance of the decade and on into the thirties. C. E. Bonnett wrote of them:

> The belligerent associations may fight the union in actual battles with machine guns; it may oppose the union in legislative and political matters; it may combat all union strikes; it

may carry on a continual propaganda against the union in every particular or only against certain practices ... it may effectively blacklist all union members by means of a card-index system; it may attempt to destroy all the sentimental appeal in the betterment activities of the union by doing welfare work; or it may combine a few or all of these activities in its general campaign against the union. The secret service system ... is characteristic. ...

Their organization might be on a locality basis, for example, the Industrial Association of San Francisco and the Merchants and Manufacturers Association of Los Angeles; on an industry basis, as was the case with the National Metal Trades Association; or a federation, as with the National Association of Manufacturers. A brief examination of the activities of these representative groups suggests the nature of belligerent associations during the twenties.

The Industrial Association of San Francisco, formed on November 8, 1921, was a local expression of the nation-wide open-shop drive, primarily directed at the construction industry. Large employers in the city in the building materials, manufacturing, retailing, railroad, banking, and insurance industries, as well as the Chamber of Commerce, determined to destroy the powerful building trades, the decisive element in the local labor movement. Since they considered the contractors unreliable on the open shop, they established a permit system administered by the Association. The builder was required to sign a pledge to operate open shop in order to get a permit to obtain materials. It was enforced by daily inspections, by fines and expulsions from the Builders Exchange, by the establishment of a hiring hall for nonunion mechanics, by an espionage service, and by the unwillingness of banks to lend to noncomplying contractors. The Association fixed wages, revamped trade rules, and broke strikes. To maintain the nonunion labor supply, it imported craftsmen and encouraged an increase in the number of apprentices. Its income from 1921 to 1925 was estimated at just under $1,800,000. The Industrial Association was affiliated nationally through the NAM and the American Plan Open Shop Conference.

Its Los Angeles counterpart was the Merchants and Manufacturers Association, which had been founded in 1896 and had fought unions with the support of the city's leading newspaper, the *Times*, since 1900. The labor movement, historically weak in the community, made modest gains during and immediately following World War I. The M and M responded quickly. In June 1921 it launched an open-shop "Labor Temple" in its industrial relations department, a free hiring hall for nonunion workmen. Registrants had to sign this statement: "I pledge myself to conform to the American Plan of Open Shop." The operation was a success; several unionized crafts were converted to a nonunion basis and strikebreakers were provided employers in other communities. In 1922 the M and M helped form the American Plan Open Shop Conference in Salt Lake City. In mid-decade it established a legislative department in Sacramento to oppose more liberal labor laws. By 1929, *Southern California Business,* publication of the Chamber of Commerce, boasted correctly that Los Angeles "has become known as one of the greatest open-shop centers in the world."

The National Metal Trades Association was organized in 1899 and came to represent many hundreds of employers in the metal-fabricating industries in the East and Midwest, including some very large corporations. The declaration of principles, which all members were required to sign, affirmed management's sole right to conduct a business, refusal to deal with striking employees, absolute freedom to discharge, unilateral determination of wages, and establishment of apprenticeship rules exclusively by the employer. To effectuate these policies the Association pooled the resources of its members in espionage, strikebreaking, and blacklisting. Its spy net was in operation by 1906; it maintained a staff of professional strikebreakers; and by 1909 it had a blacklist with over 200,000 names. Certificates of merit were awarded employees who continued to work during a strike. In 1913 it adopted rules which required that members obtain the approval of the Association for agreements with their employees and prohibited their resignation during a stoppage. Severe penalties were imposed for violations. If a member had a strike in his plant, NMTA experts assumed complete control over the strikebreaking operation.

The American Plan period constituted the all-time peak of NMTA activity. Income from dues and initiation fees skyrocketed from $127,696 in 1918 to $541,236 in 1921. Its most notable success was the smashing of a general strike called by the Machinists on April 29, 1920, against 100 metal trades firms in Cincinnati. The fact that this union's membership declined from 330,800 in 1920 to 77,900 in 1924 was not unrelated to NMTA effectiveness. The latter half of the decade was quiet; Association members experienced only five strikes from 1924 to 1929.

The National Association of Manufacturers operated at the opinion-forming and legislative levels and was the largest and most influential of these bodies. Though formed in 1893, the NAM did not become primarily concerned with labor policy till the turn-of-the-century rise in union strength. In 1903 it adopted a declaration of labor principles closely resembling those of NMTA.

In 1920 the NAM established an Open Shop Department charged with the collection and dissemination of information, the fostering of local groups to "spread . . . open shop principles," and the coordination of local and national associations in this field. The zeal with which the work was undertaken is evident from the fact that John E. Edgerton, who had been a director, was elected president of NAM in 1922 and held that post for a decade. Edgerton took a back seat to no one in declaring, "I am unalterably opposed to the present form in which so-called labor is organized." A major function of NAM was to serve as spokesman for industry on labor legislation, and its urbane and articulate general counsel, James A. Emery, made frequent appearances before congressional committees. The representatives and senators who listened to him could hardly have been surprised by what he said since Emery invariably opposed whatever was proposed. In 1924, for example, he attacked the child labor amendment, in 1926 the Railway Labor Act (which, incidentally, the carriers themselves joined in sponsoring), and in 1928 a bill to limit federal courts in the issuance of labor injunctions.

The final and in some ways the most important device employers used to prevent or undermine labor organization was the company union. Here, however, the motive was not exclusively belligerent, since some employers genuinely sought an improvement in personnel relations through machinery for the airing of employee grievances in an era of little direct contact between top management and workers. This affirmative purpose and the nature of the company-union movement will be discussed presently.

Suffice it to say here that most of the firms that introduced plans were spurred to do so by fear of trade unionism rather than by devotion to company unionism. This is quite evident from the statistics of the National Industrial Conference Board: the Board found 490 firms that established plans during the turbulent years 1919–24 and only 73 that did so in the calm period 1924–28. Many, in fact, were set up to counter an organizing drive or a strike. The experience of the Pennsylvania Railroad was typical; as one of the means of breaking the 1922 shop-crafts strike, President W. W. Atterbury introduced an employee-representation plan. "The great majority . . . were set up entirely by management," the Bureau of Labor Statistics found. "Management conceived the idea, developed the plan, and initiated the organization." [3]

### 3

The link between belligerency and welfare capitalism was supplied by John D. Rockefeller, Jr., and the policies and programs he sponsored. To understand them, it is necessary to go back in time to an incident involving, as does so much else in American labor history, the men who go down into the pits to dig coal.

In 1902 the elder Rockefeller acquired about 40 per cent of the common and preferred stock of the Colorado Fuel & Iron Company, much the largest coal producer in the Rocky Mountain area, with extensive properties on both slopes. The investment proved disappointing, no dividends being paid on the common for many years. The management of CF & I — L. M. Bowers, chairman, J. F. Welborn, president, and E. H. Weitzel, manager of the fuel department — was bitterly antiunion and determined to resist organization by any means. With his father's retirement from active business, young Rockefeller succeeded to a seat on the board. Although a sincere, upright, deeply religious, and fair-minded man, he was almost totally ignorant of the company's affairs and of labor problems.

In 1913 the United Mine Workers launched an organizational drive under the leadership of John R. Lawson in the southern

Colorado field which was highly successful. Demands were presented to the companies, including CF & I, for a 10 per cent wage increase, observance of state mining laws, discharge of armed guards, free choice of boardinghouse and doctor, and, critically, union recognition. The operators refused to talk with UMW representatives and in August the great bloody Colorado strike began. The men, obviously aggrieved over conditions, heeded the call enthusiastically. The companies evicted them and their families from their homes, and the union set up tent colonies nearby. The operators imported several hundred armed guards through the Baldwin-Felts detective agency, and the miners armed themselves. Violence was in the wind and the overt act, the murder of a union organizer by a detective, occurred on August 16. From that point on, as participants later stated, "the 1913 strike wasn't a strike at all. It was a civil war." On October 26, Governor E. M. Ammons ordered the entire Colorado National Guard to Las Animas and Huerfano Counties, and it was soon behaving as though it were an agent of the operators. On January 4, 1914, Mother Jones ("Pray for the dead, but fight like hell for the living!") arrived in Trinidad to help the miners and was promptly clapped into jail for disorderly conduct. The following April 20, a pitched battle between the Guard and the miners occurred at the Ludlow tent colony. The militia captured the settlement, raked it with machine guns, and set it on fire. Eleven children and two women, who had fled to a cave to escape the gunfire, were smothered to death. This was the infamous "Ludlow massacre" that spread horror through the nation and heaped fuel on the conflict in the mine country. By April 25 the governor notified President Wilson that he could no longer maintain order in Colorado. The President on the 29th directed federal troops to enter the state to restore peace.

The impact of this calamity upon Rockefeller was immense. At the outset his information had come entirely from Bowers and Welborn, who told him that the employees were content, that the strike had been thrust upon them by outside agitators, and that the union must be destroyed. He gave them his unqualified support, declaring to the House Committee on Mines in March 1914, "We expect to stand by the officers at any cost." Condemned when it was taken, this position became ludicrous a few weeks later when the massacre occurred, leading to public revulsion against the Rockefeller family and their enterprises, both business and philanthropic. The outcry was in no way dampened by the fact that Standard Oil had recently been a prime target of the muckrakers. Mass meetings, hostile parades, and the picketing of the office of John D. Rockefeller, Jr., at 26 Broadway and his house on 54th Street followed. The pressure mounted still further when President Wilson, after a careful canvass by his agents, proposed on September 5 a settlement providing for enforcement of the mining laws, nondiscriminatory re-employment of strikers, establishment of a grievance committee at each mine consisting of employees only, waiver of union recognition, and discharge of mine guards. Since the strike was by that time lost, the UMW accepted; the operators, however, rejected even this pittance.

The shock of the experience produced a dramatic awakening within Rockefeller. The strike's "many distressing features," he informed the Commission on Industrial Relations early in 1915, "have given me the deepest concern. I frankly confess that I felt there was something fundamentally wrong in a condition of affairs which rendered possible the loss of human lives, engendered hatred and bitterness, and brought suffering and privation upon hundreds of human beings." Something, obviously, had to be done. "I determined that in so far as lay within my power, I would seek means of avoiding the possibility of similar conflicts arising . . . in the future."

The Rockefeller Foundation, of which he was president, had recently created a division of economic research, and the Colorado strike was selected as its first topic for study. Upon the recommendation of President Charles W. Eliot of Harvard, the Canadian W. L. Mackenzie King, an eminently qualified man, was chosen to head the project. King had studied labor problems at Toronto, Chicago, and Harvard; had resided at Hull House; had organized the Canadian Ministry of Labour and had served as minister; and had been the author of the Industrial Disputes Investigation and Combines Investigation Acts. Further, he instantly won Rockefeller's complete confidence and they were to become the closest of friends.

King's thinking moved in the direction of company unionism, which was understandable since it was much in the air. A notable plan had been introduced at the Philadelphia Rapid Transit Company in 1911, and John Leitch's "Industrial Democracy" had made its bow at Packard Piano Company in 1912. Even before the strike was over, King recommended establishment of a board representing both employer and employees to discuss conditions and grievances. Welborn was unenthusiastic; Bowers was strongly opposed, leading Rockefeller to fire him. King spent two months in Colorado studying the situation and persuading Welborn to go along.[4]

In September 1915, King's proposal — variously to be known as the "Colorado Industrial Plan" or the "Rockefeller Plan" — was launched in a blaze of publicity that suggested the fine hand of the Rockefellers' public relations expert, Ivy Lee. On the 20th, Rockefeller began a two-week inspection tour of the CF & I mines — talking to superintendents, miners, wives and children, visiting the pits, homes, schools, and washhouses. At a social function at the Cameron camp he danced with virtually every woman on the floor, to the delight of newspaper readers all over the nation. He met William Hood, a colored miner:

"Is you Mistah Rockyfeller. . . . Now is dat so! An' you-all heah shakin' hands wid a black boy like me! . . . I'se a most faithful employee for you-all, suh. An' I wants to know, suh, when I'se goin' tuh git in on de pension-list? . . ."
"Well, I'm not on the pension-list myself, yet, William."
"Yes, but you-all ain't doin' no laborious labor."

On October 2, Rockefeller appeared before a joint meeting of the officers and employees at Pueblo to sell them the plan. He did the same for "the people of Colorado" in an address to the Denver Chamber of Commerce six days later. An article, ostensibly from his pen, entitled "Labor and Capital — Partners," appeared in the January 1916 issue of the *Atlantic Monthly*. Seldom has an industrial relations program been launched with such impressive staging and with such striking initial success. In October 1915 the directors accepted the plan, and 2404 of 2846 voting employees (4411 were eligible) cast ballots in its favor.

The plan fell into two parts, "The Industrial Constitution" and a "Memorandum of Agreement" covering working conditions. The former provided for annual meetings of employees to elect representatives "from among their number," one spokesman for each 150 workers. The representatives were to meet with management in a district conference — there were five districts — each of which had joint committees on industrial cooperation and conciliation, safety, sanitation, and education. At least once a year a company-wide conference was to be called of all employee representatives and the top management. CF & I agreed to observe the mining laws and to post the wage scales and working rules. "There shall be no discrimination by the company or by any of its employees on account of membership or non-membership in any . . . union." Management reserved the right to hire, fire, and direct the work force. A list of dischargeable offenses was to be posted at each property. Employees were granted the right to make purchases at both company and noncompany stores and to engage checkweighmen (provided by law). The grievance procedure allowed an employee to appeal an order to his mine superintendent, to the president's industrial representative, to the division superintendent, to the assistant manager or manager, and ultimately to the president. An employee representative with the president's approval might bring a dispute before the committee on industrial cooperation and conciliation with final recourse to a tripartite board of arbitration, the neutral member to be selected by the Colorado Industrial Commission. The company assumed the entire cost of the plan.

The second part consisted of the agreement executed on October 2, 1915, between CF & I and the employees' representatives to run until January 1, 1918. It fixed the rental on dwellings, set the rates for electricity, water, and fuel, established the eight-hour day underground and for coke-oven employees, with nine hours for outside labor, and continued the existing wage scale. It also provided that "if, prior to January 1, 1918, a general increase shall be granted in competitive districts . . . a proportional increase shall be made."

The announcement of this plan was, on the whole, well received by the press and the public. There were, of course, grumblings in

Wall Street and denunciations by the United Mine Workers. A contemporary analysis by John A. Fitch went to the nub. "It is not democracy . . . it is not . . . collective bargaining, though it may be a step in the direction of both." The establishment of democracy and bargaining is "the business of the employees. No one can attend to that for them, however good his intentions." Yet, for its time the plan "stood out like a mountain peak."

Since the plan had been unilaterally conceived and introduced by the employer (in fact, by the principal stockholder over the covert opposition of management), the quality of its administration was critical to its success. King had foreseen this and his solution was the appointment of Clarence J. Hicks as Welborn's industrial representative. Hicks had been active in railroad YMCA work and in charge of industrial relations at International Harvester. He did his best to whip up enthusiasm among the supervisors and miners, improve housing, build churches and Y's, and develop schools. Hicks's talents, however, were too substantial to waste on so small an operation as CF & I; in 1917, Rockefeller transferred him to Jersey Standard.

With his departure, the inherent defects in the Rockefeller Plan manifested themselves, notably in regard to wages. CF & I, operating in a minor coal field, had historically followed the wage movements in the major unionized fields and this had been recognized in ambiguous language in the 1915 agreement. Between September 1916 and the summer of 1920, the UMW either negotiated or the government imposed six wage increases in the Central Competitive Field, all of which were put into effect in the Colorado mines. As a CF & I employee representative said of the UMW: "They fight our battles. They make the sacrifices and we reap the harvest." That this feeling was widespread was evident from the fact that a very large majority of CF & I's employees joined the national coal strike of November 1, 1919. During the depression of 1921 the company determined to wipe out the last three increases by a wage cut of 30 per cent, thereby breaking with the national pattern. With only one day's notice, management on September 1 reimposed the 1917–19 scale and the men immediately struck. The Colorado Industrial Commission held the wage reduction procedurally illegal for failure to give thirty days' notice. The company then met this requirement by announcing an effective date of November 17, making a second strike inevitable. On the 16th the governor declared Huerfano County "in a state of insurrection and rebellion," although no stoppage had yet occurred, and dispatched troops to the mines, thereby providing the means to break the strike that followed. In 1922, following a prolonged walkout in the Central Competitive Field, which the CF & I miners joined, the company restored the 1920 scale. If this wage experience did not expose the plan's bankruptcy, it amply demonstrated how slight was its hold over the men in the crucial area of wage determination.

The management, in fact, needed no convincing. In 1916, Rockefeller, interpreting "The Industrial Consititution" literally, had given a UMW organizer permission to visit the camps. Weitzel protested bitterly. "[I] believe it our duty to use all the means we can to protect our employees against exploitation whether by labor unions or other fakirs. . . . With a free hand these people could in a few months enroll practically all our foreigners." During the 1919 dispute Weitzel urged a form of yellow-dog contract. Despite King's vigorous opposition, Rockefeller did not stand in the way. Each miner was required as a condition of employment to sign a statement that CF & I "is operated as an open shop" and "I will co-operate in maintaining the rules and agreements relating to my service." Obviously, neither the management nor Rockefeller was prepared to abide by the nondiscrimination clause in "The Industrial Constitution" when faced with the ultimate test.

In 1924 the Russell Sage Foundation published an exhaustive investigation of the plan. Failings in the wage area, of course, received emphasis. The responsibility of employee representatives for grievances was found to be "uncertain and variable." Representatives, fearing discharge, seldom pressed complaints. "Many of the miners' representatives were timid, untrained, and ill-prepared to argue the grievances of the miners. . . ." Interest in the plan among the men, never great, declined over the years and the company had to resort to pressure to get even half of them to vote in elections. The tangible gains made were in welfare: medical care, housing, schools, churches, and recreation facilities. But this

was entirely due to the initiative of management. "Neither in the
written plan nor in practice do the employes' representatives have
responsibility for decisions." As the study concluded, "The experiment which Mr. King planned and which Mr. Rockefeller has . . .
so effectively interpreted . . . is as yet incomplete. . . . An 'industrial constitution' . . . it has not yet become."

The Rockefeller Plan at CF & I, launched with such good
intentions, was destined never to become anything more than a
halfway house. It limped through the twenties. In 1933, in one of
the first free elections conducted by the National Labor Board
under Section 7(a), the miners voted 877 to 273 for the UMW
over the representation plan. Late that year CF & I abandoned the
Rockefeller Plan and negotiated its first genuine collective bargaining agreement with the United Mine Workers of America.[5]

Although the employee-representation plan had little success
with the coal miners in Colorado, its sponsor's philosophy and
policies were to have a great impact upon management thinking
in the twenties. Rockefeller, at the expense of a personal aversion
to public appearances, conscientiously broadcast his ideas, speaking
to audiences of the YMCA, the universities, the Chamber of
Commerce, as well as to congressional committees and President
Wilson's industrial conference. In his own mind he was merely
applying his deep-seated Christian principles to the employer-
employee relation. Rockefeller urged that "every man is his
brother's keeper," that there exists in industry as elsewhere a "kin-
ship of humanity," that "right principles . . . effect right relations,"
that "the letter killeth but the spirit giveth life." Employer
spokesmen in the twenties followed him in laying stress upon the
Christian ethic.

The heart of the Rockefeller philosophy was what he labeled
"human relations," understanding by managers that their employees
were "human beings" and by workmen that managers and investors
were "also human beings." Conflict, as he saw it, was both undesirable and wicked. He found it "wantonly wasteful"; both parties
and the innocent public were losers. "To say that there is no way
out except through constant warfare between Labor and Capital
is an unthinkable counsel of despair."

The alternative in his view was a "harmony of interests," that employer and employee must "join hands and recognize that their interest is a common interest." Each was indispensable to the other in the development and sharing of the earth's riches. "Co-operation of Labor and Capital may well be regarded . . . as the most vital problem of modern civilization."

Since he assumed "the fundamental fairness of men's purposes," the major impediment to achieving harmony was poor communication. "When men get together and talk over their differences candidly, much of the ground for dispute vanishes." In an earlier era enterprise was so small that direct contact between employer and employee was inescapable. Large industry, however, "has of necessity erected barriers . . . thus making it more difficult for them to understand each other." Since human needs had not changed with advancing technology, it was necessary to devise machinery to improve communication. The means lay in the more perfect organization of capital and labor. The former organized itself in the corporation; the latter was to be organized in employee representation, the company union. Whether the trade union could serve the same purpose was uncertain. Although Rockefeller never spoke in derogation of organized labor, he carefully omitted it from his scheme of a better industrial society.

These ideas gradually seeped through the hard crust of employer thought and by the late twenties, if not in the ascendant, were certainly an important influence in corporate labor policy. The harmony-of-interests doctrine was almost universally accepted by businessmen, although for many, if not most, the "interests" were their own. The human relations concept won wide approval. In the mid-twenties, for example, executives of ten of the largest American firms issued a manifesto declaring, "The human element in industry is the factor of greatest importance. . . . Employer and employee . . . must seek to understand each other's problems, respect each other's opinions, and maintain that unity of purpose and effort upon which the very existence of the community . . . and the whole future of democratic civilization depend." This reflected, in part, a recognition of the relationship between the morale of the work force and its productive efficiency. An enlightened manufacturer, Henry S. Dennison, commented in 1929 upon emergent social responsibility in business. He pointed to the rash of codes and books on business ethics. "A growing number of business men," Dennison wrote, "care a great deal for something more than what they get out of business for themselves." He was particularly impressed with their sense of obligation to the enterprise itself, to its investors, and to its customers. "Toward employees there is less feeling of responsibility; but there is some."

The Rockefeller influence in the area of policy was at least as important as in the realm of ideas and it began, of course, with those firms in which the Rockefeller family held a financial interest. In 1918–19, Mackenzie King was sent to the various Standard Oil companies and the Consolidation Coal Company, among others, to study industrial relations practices and make recommendations for their improvement. In general, his reports followed the pattern he had laid down at CF & I.

An example was Standard of Indiana. King's report of February 14, 1919, became, in the words of the firm's historian, "the Magna Carta in guiding the company in its labor relations program," and his suggestions were gradually effectuated over the decade that followed. An employee representation plan closely resembling that at CF & I was introduced on June 5, 1919, and an industrial relations department was created to administer it. In the spring of 1920 this department began an intensive safety program. The following year the company launched an employee stock-purchase plan, with a second offering to follow in 1926. Standard financed a community house in Whiting, Indiana, dedicated as a war memorial in 1923. An employee death benefit plan was established in 1924, paying dependents amounts ranging from $500 to $2000 in accordance with the deceased's length of service. Wood River, Illinois, received a recreational center and swimming pool in 1926.

This endeavor, however, paled beside the industrial relations program at the greatest of the Rockefeller properties, Jersey Standard, which was to prove the most ambitious and enduring monument of the welfare capitalism of the twenties. In 1915–16 there had been a bitter and violent strike at the Bayonne refinery. At Rockefeller's insistence, Hicks was brought in from Colorado in 1917 to repair the damage and to devise a new labor policy. His opportunity exceeded that at CF & I in every respect: the company was much larger; its financial resources were immense, making possible costly undertakings that could not have been considered in Colorado; it provided steady rather than intermittent employment; the president, A. C. Bedford, as well as the principal stockholder, supported Hicks; and he dealt with relatively docile oil workers with little exposure to unionism, rather than militant coal miners with a deep attachment to the labor movement.

The Hicks program was impressively launched in 1918. Its heart, of course, was the company union, which was first introduced at the Bayonne refinery and later extended to other facilities. A personnel and training division was created to deal in orderly fashion with hiring, placement, and training. A company-financed annuity plan provided for retirement of men at sixty-five and of women at fifty-five. Survivors' benefits and sickness benefits were provided in 1918, and accident benefits the next year. To keep the costs of these programs at the minimum, a medical division was created which employed full-time physicians and nurses at the company's plants. Paid vacations, virtually unknown in American industry at the time, were granted to salaried employees in 1918 and to hourly-rated people in 1922. A stock-acquisition program was undertaken in 1921. The work week of refinery personnel which had been fifty-four hours in 1918, was reduced to forty-eight in 1920 and to forty in 1930. In 1922, Jersey published a statement of policy providing, in addition to the matters mentioned, that the company would meet the prevailing wage rates in the communities in which it operated, would create sanitary working conditions, would encourage plant safety, and would promote employees on the basis of ability and length of service.

Hicks, with his "interesting combination of persuasiveness, piety, and shrewdness," dealt masterfully with his problem. He wanted "to achieve security for the Jersey wage earner," but he was also "directly concerned with insulating that worker against the temptations of trade unionism." With his arrangements there was no need for Baldwin-Felts, the National Guard, or labor injunctions. *Fortune* said, "Hicks was one of the shrewdest oppositionists organized labor found in the twenties, because he never met the trade unions head on."

The Rockefeller policies, particularly the example of Jersey

Standard, exerted a profound influence upon American industry as a whole in the twenties. In 1919, Mackenzie King made several more of his now famous studies with recommendations at non-Rockefeller properties, notably General Electric and Bethlehem Steel. That same year, at the suggestion of Bedford and Owen D. Young of GE, a special conference committee of corporate presidents and industrial relations executives of ten (later twelve) very large firms was formed under Hicks's chairmanship to pool information and develop policy. The companies represented included such giants as Jersey, American Telephone and Telegraph, General Motors, and United States Steel. In the twenties, as Hicks has pointed out, "employee representation plans and works councils developed in nearly all important branches of American industry." Those corporations that were successful in destroying trade unions in American Plan days took the lead in replacing them with company unions of the Rockefeller type. Important illustrations were Bethlehem Steel, International Harvester, Procter & Gamble, and the Pennsylvania Railroad. Following the model developed by Hicks, welfare capitalism — described in the next section of this chapter — became the order of the day.

The formation of Industrial Relations Counselors, Inc., provided another mechanism for the spread of these policies. In the summer of 1921, Rockefeller, King, and Raymond B. Fosdick, the Rockefellers' attorney, decided that the time was ripe to institutionalize the King procedure with a permanent corps of industrial relations specialists. They engaged George J. Anderson, formerly with the New York Employing Printers, and a small staff, which was quartered at Fosdick's office. Anderson conducted surveys of a number of firms in which Rockefeller was interested: Consolidation Coal Company, Davis Coal & Coke Company, the Western Maryland Railway, and several oil companies. These studies were instrumental in establishing the Rockefeller policies. In 1924, Anderson became vice-president of Consolidation Coal and was replaced by Arthur H. Young, formerly manager of industrial relations at International Harvester. Under Young's vigorous leadership, the work was expanded to firms outside the Rockefeller group. In 1926 the staff was incorporated as IRC and took up its own offices. This firm was the pioneer consulting group in the field of industrial relations research and application. Reliance upon Rockefeller financing, at first heavy, diminished with Young's success in getting outside business.

Another area in which the Rockefeller circle led the way was in launching the university industrial relations institute movement. Here, Hicks was the instigator. A graduate of the University of Wisconsin himself, Hicks was disturbed by the emphasis which John R. Commons and his followers at that institution placed upon trade unionism and collective bargaining, as well as by a similar stress apparent at other schools. In 1922, therefore, he persuaded Princeton University to establish an industrial relations section as a subdivision of the Department of Economics. Its purposes were to gather a specialized library in labor relations and labor law, to give "unbiased instruction based on facts thus gathered," to conduct research, to make information available to businessmen and union leaders as well as university people, and, somewhat later, to conduct an annual conference for executives in industrial relations. Rockefeller was persuaded to underwrite the cost of this venture.

Rockefeller's program, in the words of his biographer, "profoundly affected the industrial picture of his generation." One might add, "And of later generations as well." The "human relations" philosophy was carried forward by Elton Mayo and his followers at the Harvard Business School in the thirties and forties and by the various human relations groups at the universities and in industry following World War II. The essential ideas, as well as the very name of the movement, were those Rockefeller had laid out in 1915: human understanding, the undesirability and eradicability of conflict, harmony of interests in the shop community, and improved communication. The only basic change was the gradual replacement of Christ by Freud, the sloughing off of the Christian ethic and the substitution for it of a sort of group psychoanalysis. The Rockefeller policies, as they took root in industry, formed a bridge between the warfare of the American Plan and the paternalism of the welfare capitalism that became the dominant feature of employer policy in the late twenties.[6]

*

4

Welfare capitalism embraced numerous features in the areas of employee organization, management structure in dealing with labor, wage determination, hours of work, and welfare. The critical element was the first, finding expression in the company union, since it represented a basic shift in the attitude of some employers toward the problem of government in the shop. "Employee Representation," William M. Leiserson wrote in 1928, "means that management has substituted constitutional for autocratic government in industry." Employers, under the very nose of the labor movement, expropriated the forms of collective bargaining: shop chairmen, joint committees, grievance procedure, negotiations, arbitration, and the closed shop. Equally important, they appropriated the unions' slogan, "industrial democracy." In the old system of shop government the wage earner was "an outsider, an alien." He was considered "a commodity, or a machine," guaranteed "no rights, privileges, or immunities . . . which management was bound to respect." With the company union, Leiserson pointed out, employers came to recognize the trade-union concept of shop government, "the citizenship theory of labor relations."

But the employer's acceptance of this theory was conditioned upon the employees' acceptance of the idea that the firm was an island, cut off from contact with other companies in the same labor market or the same industry. Rockefeller and his followers preached that "the fundamental idea of Welfare Capitalism [is] that the only solidarity natural in industry is the solidarity which unites all those in the same business establishment." The great goal of industrial harmony could be achieved only within the insulated system of the firm. "The old, strong, high barrier between employer and employe," Arthur Young declared in 1924, "shall be leveled to the ground — shall become . . . an imaginary dividing line that a man can step across and not know he has passed from one camp to the other." He envisioned the time when a strike would become "a public shame," when wages and hours would be determined by "the full and free consent of both employer and employed" as "the conditions of the business warrant." Young anticipated the not distant day when employee representation would be universal, creating islands of self-government throughout industrial society. "It will make its own laws and do its own enforcing, and the essence of those laws will be a compound of reason, common sense, fairness and frankness."

Several types of contemporary evidence demonstrated the unreality of this assumption, not least among them being the considerations that led to the initiation of plans. They did not include spontaneous generation by employer and employed within the isolated plant. Rather, the management alone set up the program, usually in response to trade-union pressure from without. Further, many companies, facing the threat of organization or a strike, hurriedly imposed a plan that was simply copied from another. Finally, the NAM, the National Industrial Conference Board, and the American Management Association encouraged the company union on a national basis during the decade.

Inasmuch as most employers launched a company union to counter a trade union, the firms in which the former appeared were unorganized, often after defeating an outside organization. The total number of companies that introduced plans was relatively low. The NICB, which made surveys at two-year intervals between 1922 and 1928, found only 385 in the former year and 399 in the latter, with a peak of 432 in 1926. As measured by employees covered, however, the growth was steady from 690,000 in 1922 to 1,547,766 in 1928. This reflected a rising incidence among large firms. Many small plants that adopted employee representation in American Plan days discarded it as the decade wore on, while big companies either grew in size or entered the field. By 1928 over 63 per cent of the workers covered were in concerns with more than 15,000 employees. The industries that embraced company unionism on a substantial scale were oil, railways (for nonoperating crafts), farm machinery, electrical equipment, textiles, utilities (especially telephones), meat packing, and, to a lesser extent, steel.

Although there were structural differences between plans, they shared many characteristics in common. Participation was restricted to employees. In some cases membership followed automatically from employment (in effect, the closed shop) and in others the worker made the choice himself. Management was almost invariably a party to the functioning of the organization and in some cases might veto amendments to its constitution or even disband it. The employer assumed the entire cost. Employee participation was limited to the election of representatives, and most plans made no provision for membership meetings. Time spent by representatives in company union activities was usually compensated for by the employer at the employee's regular rate of pay. Representatives met with management at stated intervals, usually to discuss individual grievances, plant safety, and productive efficiency. Occasionally, permissive arbitration might be invoked in case of a deadlock. The employee representatives had no contact with other company or trade unions in the industry. Management reserved the right to hire and fire, strikes were prohibited, and representatives were allowed no voice in determining basic wages and hours.

From the employer's standpoint, the company union afforded several advantages, most important as an alternative to the trade union subject to his control. There is no recorded case of an employee-representation plan that grew into a genuine union during the twenties. On the matter of who ran the company unions, a caustic Australian traveler was reminded of the story of the Tiger and the Young Lady from Riga: "The Young Lady . . . was inside the Tiger." A second advantage to the employer was opening a channel of communication to the men. Wage earners were better informed about company policies and their resulting morale, presumably, was higher. Stemming from this, third, was an improvement in productive efficiency. At Procter & Gamble, for example, the monthly meetings were devoted almost entirely to suggestions for bettering plant operations. Finally, to the extent that the plans disposed of grievances — and they varied greatly in effectiveness — management benefited from more harmonious relations in the shop. The principal danger was that the educational experience for employees in an imposed organization might lead them later on to demand self-organization.

For the employees company unionism provided a number of gains. Most notable, perhaps, were those in the area of safety and health, where employers responded quite readily to complaints. In firms with effective grievance procedures the number of grievances declined and a machinery existed to dispose of the remainder. Many workers beyond the pale of the labor movement — the unskilled and semiskilled, clericals, recent immigrants, and Negroes — regarded the company union with all its inadequacies as preferable to nothing.

The weaknesses of employee representation were self-evident, critically the absence of bargaining power. The company union lacked authorization to strike, had no funds to finance a stoppage, and was incapable of coordinating its acts with organizations at other firms in the industry. Its only sanction, if it may be called that, was persuasion. A second shortcoming was inability to bargain over the basic employment issues, wages and hours. At Jersey Standard, for example, the representation meetings during the twenties largely degenerated into repeated employee requests for a wage increase, with continued management promises that they "would be looked into." The company union was ineffective with respect to wages and hours because, among other reasons, its spokesmen knew nothing about conditions in other plants and were not experts in bargaining. Even grievance handling revealed serious inadequacies. Representatives tended to curry favor with management by not pressing a legitimate complaint, or simply accepted a first-step rejection without appeal. At Procter & Gamble no grievance was filed over a discharge during the first decade of the plan's life. Workers sometimes called these organizations "Kiss Me Clubs." A grievance procedure worked only when management determined to make it work.

The long-term significance of the company-union movement lay not in what was achieved in the twenties — actually little was gained — but in the door it opened to education in industrial democracy. Employers and workers alike became accustomed to the need for organization in shop relations. Foreign observers inclined to regard the employee-representation plan as "a transitional stage" in the development of collective dealing. Young, a leading salesman for company unionism, pointed out that workers shared with other Americans "an inborn and instinctive hostility against any sort of government without the consent of the governed." "Human organizations," Leiserson philosophized, "have a way of evolving according to laws of their own. . . . The management has started a movement in the direction of democracy in industry which is bound to grow." [7]

Almost as important as company unionism contemporaneously and more so in the long run was the personnel management movement. In fact, the congeries of policies labeled "welfare capitalism" was as often called "personnel management."

This movement emerged in the twenties because of the pressing need in large enterprises to substitute rational for opportunistic methods in the management of labor. In industry the organization was replacing the individual. The traditional American all-purpose, all-weather executive in the family-owned firm was not competent to direct the modern corporation, least of all its labor force. David Harum could not become president of General Motors and the fact that he was head of Ford simply demonstrated that every rule had its exception. This was the period of the professionalization of management and its divorcement from ownership. Yet these professionals, increasingly the engineers, were as unprepared to deal with personnel as the old owner-manager. Despite "the overwhelming importance of a proper administration" of labor relations, Lewisohn observed, engineer executives were marked by a "lack of preparedness ... to handle these matters properly." Neither the engineering nor the new business schools provided this training.

But it was the intellectual stimulus of the engineers through the Taylor movement that led to personnel management. Frederick W. Taylor, the founder of scientific management, sought to quantify, systematize, and coordinate the productive process in order to maximize output and minimize cost. He introduced schemes to analyze jobs, to apply time and motion study to work, and to pay by the piece rather than the hour. The next step was to extend Taylor's "scientific" method to the entire personnel relationship.

The timing could not have been better arranged, since the Taylor movement won acceptance just as World War I overturned the American labor market. The prewar market had been characterized by an oversupply of cheap immigrant labor; its consequent personnel policies were adapting jobs to men and getting output by driving workers. Between 1915 and 1920, the market was turned upside down: immigration halted, turnover skyrocketed, and wages leapt upward. Employers were compelled by economic circumstance to re-examine their personnel practices.

The interest that developed during the twenties was extraordinary. Adam wrote: "More is written and talked about labour — how to handle it, nurse it, feed it, amuse it, bury it — than in any other country." Much of this discussion was hokum. A widely held notion, for example, was that personnel management was a branch of philanthropy, leading a British mission to point out soberly that the employer who removed stools and installed chairs with backs was more concerned with raising the worker's output than with the well-being of the seat of his pants. The American employer's propensity for "science," his susceptibility to fads, and his unquestioned ability to pay induced charlatans to invest personnel management with a salable aura of pseudo-science complete with jargon. Personnel management was commonly called "The Science of Industrial Relations." "If the fact that a man works better standing on his feet than on his head were to strike an American industrial expert as interesting," Adam noted sourly, "he would write a book with diagrams, graphs of blood pressure, and the tabulated results of numerous practical experiments to prove it." In fact, as Leiserson pointed out, personnel management was not a science at all, but rather "a method by which employers manage their employees." Its purpose was to improve the efficiency of the enterprise rather than to pursue knowledge. If these objectives were confused, the attitude of one of the parties in labor relations was "unconsciously . . . assumed to be that of disinterested science." Finally, the "vision" of personnel management tended to overstimulate the poetic fancy in an area that was wholly mundane. This movement had been built, *Fortune* declaimed, "as the cathedrals of the twelfth century were built; stone by stone; anonymously."

Stripped of this nonsense, personnel management dealt with real problems, on the whole, in a sensible and enduring fashion. The agency through which it worked was the personnel department, a new division of management comparable to finance, manufacturing, and sales. Its purpose was to handle those labor problems top executives had earlier ignored by delegating them to foremen.

The department performed a staff function — collecting information, rendering services to line supervision, and helping to shape and administer labor policies. It was not expected to manage labor directly. In larger corporations the department was often divided into two sections: one, employment management, with responsibility over recruiting, testing, placement, training, promotion and demotion, discipline, grievances, absence and tardiness, quitting, and discharge; and the second, employment service, with responsibility for safety and sanitation, health, feeding, rest periods, recreation and vacations, and provisions for illness, accidents, disability, unemployment, old age, and death. In some cases the latter was concerned, as well, with housing, schooling, transportation, legal aid, and credit.

Staffing proved difficult during the war because almost no one was trained in personnel work. Some who entered at the outset oversold the importance of their jobs and intruded upon line functions with unhappy results. Fluidity was apparent in the range of titles they adopted: employment manager, personnel manager, industrial relations secretary, employees' service director, labor manager, and welfare manager. The depression of 1921-22 gave the movement a good shaking out, and by the late twenties professionalization was under way. The University of Rochester launched the first training course in 1917 and other colleges soon followed the example. The National Association of Employment Managers was founded in 1916 and was succeeded by the Industrial Relations Association of America in 1919. The latter, in turn, was part of the merger in 1923 that became the American Management Association. Though it had wider interests, AMA created a personnel division in 1929. This association in 1930 had over 4300 members. The Personnel Research Federation was launched in 1921 and published a journal. This activity stimulated a great deal of research which the new personnel managers eagerly read.

Despite these advances, personnel departments at the end of the decade existed in only a small number of firms; a mere 12 per cent of wage earners in manufacturing were estimated to be employed in such establishments. Again, as in the case of company unionism, the development was confined primarily to large companies. A National Industrial Conference Board survey in 1929 showed that 34 per cent of companies with 250 or more employees had departments, as contrasted with only 2.5 per cent of those with fewer than 250 workers.[8]

A notable achievement of personnel management was the introduction of order into the process of hiring, firing, promoting, and transferring employees. This necessitated a revolution in the power of the foreman to deal with these matters. Earlier, hiring had been by "the crook of the finger." At the start of the shift the foreman, after deciding how many men he needed, proceeded to the "line-up" at the gate, where he chose those he wanted. Even when he was honest, the system was absurdly inefficient, since his criteria of selection were at best arbitrary and capricious. One foreman, for example, tossed an apple into the crowd and hired the man who caught it. There was only a fair chance the worker would be fitted to the work; supervision knew little or nothing about his past, sometimes not even his name; records were not kept; and turnover was certain to be high. Moreover, the system was an invitation to dishonesty. Job selling, kickbacks, and nepotism were rife in American industry. United States Steel, whose hiring practices constituted a "chamber of administrative horrors," in *Fortune*'s words, had a single department in the Gary works with fourteen members of one family on its supervisory force. Since dismissal, promotion, and transfer were handled by foremen in similar fashion, they led to the same abuses and inefficiencies. At International Harvester, for example, the same incompetent individual was hired and fired twenty-six times at one plant in one year.

The critical task was to break the power of the foreman. This was a first order of business in those firms which established personnel management. His place was taken by the employment office, which, ideally, worked in the following manner: Job analysis broke down the elements of each occupation in the plant. Prospective employees filled out application forms which were filed. Applicants were interviewed, tested, and examined medically. The foreman then requisitioned a man to fill the specifications of a particular job, and the office supplied him from its file. Similar procedures were followed in promotions and transfers, with a resulting emphasis upon merit and length of service rather than favoritism

in selection. The foreman was stripped of his authority to discharge. He could only recommend to personnel, which either sustained him or transferred the employee to another department.
Progressive companies instituted exit interviews to determine why
people quit or were dismissed as a means of discovering sources
of discontent.

In the twenties this ideal system was seldom realized. Only
a minority of firms tried it at all and their personnel departments
suffered from a shortage of trained people as well as of funds.
Foremen resisted the attrition of their power and frequently gained
top-management support by playing upon the fear of a breakdown
in discipline. Multiplant companies, like Jersey Standard and
Procter & Gamble, only slowly extended these practices to outlying
operations. But a start was made in establishing modern policies.
Many firms conducted classes in foremanship, over 900 doing so
in 1927, while some companies got out handbooks for these supervisors. "Restricting the freedom of the foreman to discharge," Sumner H. Slichter observed, "has profoundly affected his methods of
handling men because it has deprived him of his chief disciplinary device." To get output, he was compelled to replace the
threat with the pat on the back. Advancement based on merit
and seniority opened an avenue of opportunity for competent and
steady employees.

A noted achievement of personnel management was the improvement of physical working conditions. In the twenties the
factory, especially the large one, became a safer, cleaner, more
spacious, and better lighted, heated, and ventilated place in which
to work. Travelers from abroad were impressed and pointed out the
contrast with establishments in their own countries. The personnel argument for this development was that it raised productivity,
was socially desirable, and reduced the number of grievances and
hence removed one excuse for unions. Perhaps the most dramatic
gains were in the area of safety. Machines and equipment were
engineered for safe use; plants were laid out to avoid hazards;
governmental, insurance, and civic bodies collected and published
accident statistics; and many employers conducted shop educational programs. "Safety is the greatest non-controversial factor
in all industrial relationship . . . it has absolutely no negative values;

and . . . owners, managers, employes, the public and every part of society is affected in a beneficial way by safety activities," Young said.

The job analysis undertaken in connection with hiring led to the rudimentary beginning of systematic wage determination within the plant. By breaking down the individual job into its functions, personnel people were able to rank it in relation to other jobs in the shop and thereby to fix meaningful wage rates. A few companies, such as International Harvester, attacked this problem seriously, but they were exceptional. Top management, apparently, resisted changes in wage policy, where the cost impact was direct. The American wage structure in the twenties, as has already been pointed out, was basically irrational, riddled with personal rates, accidental rates, and a great variety of unreasonable differentials.[9]

A basic element of welfare capitalism was the Doctrine of High Wages. Prior to the twenties American employers, generally speaking, adhered to the philosophy that wages should be fixed at the lowest level necessary to recruit a labor supply. When Ford, for example, announced the Five-Dollar Day in 1914, he was denounced by other captains of industry as "a Utopian," "a Socialist," and "a traitor to his class." During the depression of 1921 the NAM pronounced its faith in "the operation of economic law" at a time of "drastic economic adjustment." Wages could not be maintained at "an artificial economic level." By 1926, however, the leaders of industry had drastically overhauled their philosophy of wages. "It is now widely believed," a thoughtful employer wrote, "that, where an appropriate increase in productivity can go along with an increase in wages, the consequent increase in purchasing power results . . . in increases in the quantities and varieties of goods which can be sold." Employers, apparently, had come to accept the mass-market purchasing-power theory. In exalted form, this wage creed became a pillar of the New Era. "To the new capitalism," *Fortune* intoned, "the wage-earner . . . is a purchaser, a partner, and the key to production. . . . His wages are dictated . . . by ambition for a market and a desire for willing cooperation. . . . The new capitalism . . . is a social conception as radical as Stalinism in its ultimate purpose."

The Doctrine of High Wages as enunciated by employers in the twenties was largely an exercise in verbal gymnastics. The contemporary rise in real wages occurred primarily at the start of the decade because of falling prices rather than rising wages. Adherence to "the economy of high wages," George Soule has pointed out, was "a rationalization after the event." Between 1925 and 1929, when employers were most vocal in lip service to the creed, they lifted wages hardly at all, permitting productivity to forge ahead, with resulting economic maladjustment. Further, they allowed a great variety of unreasonable differentials to exist and even widened many of them. In fact, the only concrete achievement of the new philosophy was an assist in preventing a decline of wages. In the labor market in most industries in the late twenties — characterized by a surplus of labor and weak unions — there was little to stop employers from cutting wages except self-restraint. They justified its exercise with this new philosophy.

The case of Ford was typical. Except for his manufacture of the Model T, the public knew Ford mainly as the high priest of high wages. In 1926 he published a book, *Today and Tomorrow*, that set forth the Doctrine of High Wages in detail. Yet, Ford granted no general increase between 1919 and the crash. Moreover, in changing over to the Model A in 1927–28, he laid off 60,000 men for more than a year in Detroit alone. For many of these workers, according to Keith Sward, the price of re-employment was a lower wage rate.[10]

The case of hours of work proved much the same. Following Taylor, the personnel management movement addressed itself in the twenties to the problem of fatigue, thereby adding a new dimension to hours. A series of careful studies in Britain and the United States revealed that long hours and maximum production were not directly related, that excessive working time reduced output per hour and increased the rates of turnover, absenteeism, illness, accidents, and unrest. The employer, therefore, might actually lower his unit costs by cutting hours of work. With a handful of exceptions, notably Ford ("A six-day week is all right for machines but a five-day week is enough for men"), this argument fell on deaf ears. The prevailing workday and work week declined insignificantly during the decade because of employers' objections.

The NAM and the Chamber of Commerce vigorously opposed shorter hours. Their representatives argued that leisure and idleness were synonymous. The latter was unnatural, led to a taste for improper amusement and luxury, increased criminality and drunkenness, gave rise to radicalism, and decayed man's inherent capacities. Hence the employer was under a moral obligation to the worker to keep him in the shop for long hours. Even so progressive a spokesman as Young expressed misgivings over the five-day week, though on different grounds. "To persuade ourselves," he declared in 1927, "that we can add to wealth by subtracting from it is a form of self-deception." Personnel management barely opened the door for a more sophisticated view of hours, but hardly wide enough for passage.[11]

A more productive area for personnel management was welfare, the improvement of the material lot of the worker off the job. Here employers were primarily motivated by two related considerations: to reduce turnover and to cement loyalty to the firm, thereby weakening the worker's propensity to unionize. To a lesser extent they sought to remove the causes of grievances. A few large companies, such as Jersey Standard, Procter & Gamble, and Eastman Kodak, gained a good deal of public acclaim for their welfare plans.

By far the most popular scheme was group life insurance. It was estimated in October 1928 that 5,800,000 workers were covered by $7.5 billion of this insurance. Procter & Gamble, for example, paid the beneficiaries of a male employee $1000 and of a female $500. These group life schemes were of value only to those employed, since they terminated with loss of job and had no cash surrender value. A much smaller number of companies provided wage-loss insurance against the costs of illness, often paying $10 a week up to a maximum of thirteen or twenty-six weeks. These plans were adequate only in isolated cases.

Some 364 firms operated old age pension plans in 1929, the great majority having been established prior to 1920. These programs were highly concentrated in large firms in the railroad (especially), street railway, public utility, steel, petroleum, and electrical industries. They covered approximately 3,750,000 employees, many of whom, however, were in the managerial group.

Most of the schemes, in Murray Latimer's words, "are insecure
. . . because of inadequate financing . . . lack of actuarial soundness
. . . failure to provide proper legal safeguards . . . and . . . the
absence of definite administrative procedure for carrying out the
terms of the plans."

Some firms offered assistance with housing: United States Steel
rented houses at low cost; Kodak built and sold them cheaply;
Bethlehem Steel guaranteed second mortgages and provided free
architectural, financial, and legal advice; and Milwaukee Electric
Railway established a building and loan association for employees.
Finally, some concerns made odds and ends of welfare available:
American Locomotive sold gasoline one third off and repainted
cars at cost; Crompton & Knowles and General Electric had savings
plans; Bausch & Lomb provided inexpensive dental care.

Policy in this area more than any other led critics to brand welfare capitalism as "paternalism." The interest of some employers
in the private lives of their employees induced them to overstep
the bounds of good sense. The "sociological" department of the
Ford Motor Company, headed during the twenties by Dean S. S.
Marquis of the Detroit Episcopal cathedral, which the Ford family
attended, was severely criticized. Phelps Dodge, which *Fortune*
labeled "Presbyterian Copper," posted a sign in the social hall of
its mine in Bisbee, Arizona, that read:

Kindly Observe
following Regulations

DO NOT SHIMMY

Do Not Dance
CHEEK TO CHEEK

These welfare schemes, obviously, protected only a small fraction of the labor force against the risks of an industrial society,
and in many cases inadequately. How successful they were in
realizing their instigators' objectives is difficult to say. Large,
profitable companies with generous plans, like Jersey Standard,
Kodak, and Procter & Gamble, undoubtedly cut down on turnover
and won a goodly measure of loyalty. Firms with more modest

programs — the great majority — made less progress. A survey published in 1927 concluded that employees showed little "appreciation" for what was done for them, suspecting the employer's motives. Adam, in commenting on this "thanks-offering to success," reflected:

It should, and no doubt does, make for amiability, but such is the situation in America to-day that a man would do the work he was told to do in the way he was told to do it and for the money given, not because his employer was like a father and a mother and a cousin and an aunt to him, but because he had to do it or starve.

A phase of welfare capitalism that attracted wide attention was employee stock ownership. Possession of shares in a corporation, a spokesman for Industrial Relations Counselors hopefully declared, "makes the worker a capitalist in viewpoint and this renders him a conservative and immune from radical ideas." In addition to this ideological purpose, employers sought the conventional objectives of securing loyalty to the firm and lowering turnover.

Though individual plans varied, they had several common ingredients. The price charged the employee was usually below that prevailing on the exchange. He could make his purchase on the installment plan by a checkoff of wages, often $1 per week. There was frequently a limit on the number of shares an employee could buy, presumably to prevent worker control, though there is no evidence under any of the plans that employees sought it or even appeared at annual meetings.

These stock-purchase plans became popular after 1922, but almost exclusively with large firms. By 1927 some 800,000 employee stockholders in 315 corporations owned in excess of $1 billion in securities, approximately 4.5 per cent of the current market value of the outstanding stock in those companies. This figure was deceptive, however, because it included purchases by high-salaried people, who were certainly in the majority.

In the judgment of a perceptive contemporary observer, stock purchasing was "among the least significant of the new labor policies." Slichter found no evidence that "a few shares in a huge corporation affect the fundamental economic views of the workers." The connection between ownership and employment was so tenuous that there could be little impact upon turnover and loyalty. Further, there was the risk, perhaps remote but nevertheless present, that the prices of common stocks might fall. If they did and workers were wiped out, the results might be the opposite from those hoped for. It was very well to democratize the opportunity to pray on the floor of the national shrine in Wall Street, but what would happen if the roof caved in? When John J. Raskob, a prominent financier, declared, "Everybody can get rich," the *Arkansas Gazette* shot back, "That's rich!" [12]

The final aspect of welfare capitalism — the one that received the least attention — was stabilization of employment, a few groping experiments by industry to persuade the distressingly large lump of unemployment to go away. The characteristic view was that expressed by Samuel Insull, the utilities tycoon: "My experience is that the greatest aid to the efficiency of labor is a long line of men waiting at the gate." Only a few businessmen were prepared to admit that the problem existed at all, but they were disturbed. Owen D. Young, for example, declared that "unemployment is the greatest economic blot on our capitalistic system." Yet the efforts of nonunion industry to deal with it consisted of but thirteen schemes. In 1928 these firms employed a total of 10,920 workers, of whom 78 per cent were eligible for benefits. "The movement is young, the number of plans is small, and their coverage is relatively insignificant." The Procter & Gamble, Dennison Manufacturing, Hills Brothers, Columbia Conserve, and Delaware & Hudson Railroad plans attracted the most notice. In addition, two firms with relatively stable employment — Commonwealth Edison and Standard Oil of California — adopted the policy of transferring an employee with a year of service from the hourly to the monthly payroll, but here the objective was to reduce turnover rather than to stabilize jobs.

The largest and most noteworthy plan was that adopted in 1923 by Procter & Gamble. An employee with six months of seniority was guaranteed forty-eight weeks of employment or forty-eight weeks of pay — in effect, a guaranteed annual wage. Since the demand for soap products was relatively stable, the company was able to flatten out production over the year to eliminate seasonal unemployment. The plan was put into operation only at the northern plants; employees in the Macon and Dallas facilities, producing edible oils for a highly competitive market, as well as the cottonseed oil plants, did not share in the guarantee. In other words, those who already enjoyed a good measure of regularity were covered, while those who suffered greater intermittency were not.

To describe as negative the employer reaction to the foreign and trade-union experience with unemployment insurance would understate the case. The sponsors of the progressive private plans, in testimony before the Senate's Couzens Committee in 1928, expressed opposition to any government intervention in this area. Arthur Young in an address in the spring of 1929 to the Philadelphia Chamber of Commerce, the main burden of which was to urge a private city-wide employment exchange, warned against similar private pooling by employers for unemployment insurance. Even that tiny segment of business which recognized the problem at all, therefore, insisted upon the exclusive responsibility of the individual employer. This view was reflected in the recommendations of the Couzens Committee, which, though it brought out a comprehensive report on unemployment, confined its recommendation on insurance to private systems.

In fact, of the three basic forms of unemployment — seasonal, technological, and cyclical — two got worse during the decade. Seasonality in industries like automobiles became critical. The impact of mechanization upon jobs led *Fortune* to observe, "From the purely productive point of view, a part of the human race is already obsolete and a further part is obsolescent." The effect of the cycle upon joblessness was soon to become painfully evident.[13]

The battery of policies that constituted welfare capitalism marked a significant shift in management's outlook and had an impact upon the condition of labor. As far as employers were concerned, the Conference Board said, this movement was a phase of "the general evolution going on within industry . . . the tendency away from the haphazard, and toward the organized way of doing things." The effects upon workers were exaggerated by the prophets of the New Era. They were dampened both by the ambivalence in management's outlook and the fact that the policies were confined to large, profitable firms, which were in the minority. Small companies had less need for them and found their costs prohibitive.

Yet in the big corporations that seriously undertook the new programs the impact upon labor was considerable. The material conditions of work improved; some of the risks of an industrial society were lessened; work for regular employees was steadier; workers, particularly those shunned by the AFL (the unskilled, semiskilled, and clericals), developed a closer attachment to the employer; and the propensity to unionize was weakened. Perhaps most important, the enormous publicity these policies received, both in the United States and abroad, awakened an awareness of the plight of labor that was significant for the future. These programs represented, Ordway Tead concluded, "the setting at work of a number of educational forces the like of which have never been seen before." Employers who might later seek to turn the clock back would meet resistance not just from the labor movement but also from an enlightened public opinion. That is, the long-run bargaining position of labor was enhanced.

Welfare capitalism, stripped of the verbiage of industrial democracy, was precisely what its critics called it: paternalism. At best it could be no more than an unstable system for both employer and employee, a "transitional stage," as the foreign travelers were wont to note. As for the worker, in Slichter's words, paternalism

encourages him to form the habit of relying, not upon himself, but upon the employer, for help in the ordinary problems and even in some of the great crises of life. If the worker has a toothache the company dentist will cure it; if he has a headache or a cold, he can get treatment from the company doctor; if he or a member of his household needs an operation, the company doctor will help him find a competent surgeon; in some cases the company optometrist will measure him for glasses, and the company chiropodist will treat his corns; if he has legal difficulties, he can obtain free advice from the company's lawyer; if his wife or children are sick, a nurse from the company will visit his home to render such assistance as she can; if he wishes to save money, the company will act as agent for a bank, deduct the money from his pay check, deposit it in the bank, and do the bookkeeping for him; if he needs to borrow money, the company will lend it to him at a low rate of interest; if he wishes to own his house, the company will build one for him and sell it to him on easy terms, or help him to borrow the money to build it himself.

Would it not be better, Slichter wondered in 1929, if the worker were encouraged to do some of these things for himself?

To the employer, *Fortune* pointed out, paternalism is the most desirable relationship "*while* it works." The management "earns for itself the satisfaction of good deeds." Higher output pleases stockholders; the speed-up is taken more gracefully by labor; and union organizers must work in a hostile atmosphere. But paternalism "fails more often than it succeeds." Its tendency was to produce an unstable equilibrium, falling off either into excessive benevolence or excessive stringency. An economic disturbance might easily destroy this precarious balance and open the door to the union. The cornerstone of the structure, the company union, had an inherent propensity to disintegrate.

The central purpose of welfare capitalism — avoidance of trade unionism — could be achieved only temporarily because paternalism failed to come to grips with the main issue: a system of shop government placed in the climate of political democracy and universal suffrage. Management, Leiserson argued in 1928, was not devoting to labor problems "the same spirit of bold exploration" that it applied to production. This was evident in the failure to recognize the "distinct set of . . . governmental problems involved in the management of labor." Wages, hours, and day-to-day shop relations involved "political" considerations: "self-determination, the consent of the governed, and a voice for the wage earner." Issues of sanitation and safety were susceptible of expert solution. "But when we come to the problems of economic bargaining and government of the working forces in industry, then we enter the realm of politics and democracy." Here the expert might be better informed than the worker or stockholder, but there was no more reason to allow him to fix wages than to determine national policy. In the twenties only the rare American employer conceived of his shop as a problem in government set within the frame of a democratic society. The others were due for a rude awakening.[14]

5

From the bleak perspective of the thirties it was commonplace to look longingly back at the twenties as an era of contentment, a time when Americans shared common values and worked busily and happily together. This was hardly the case.

In 1929, Henry Ford staged at Dearborn a well-publicized celebration for his friend Thomas Alva Edison. Its purpose was to commemorate Edison's eighty-second birthday and the fiftieth anniversary of the invention of the incandescent lamp. So important was the occasion that Ford persuaded President Hoover to attend. It proved to be a memorable day. But when reporters asked the man who gave electric light to the world for an observation on his life and times, he declared: "I am not acquainted with anyone who is happy." Henry F. May has characterized this decade as a time of disintegration and fragmentation. "The twenties were a period in which common values and common beliefs were replaced by separate and conflicting loyalties."[15]

This fragmented outlook was characteristic of the American employer in his relations with the worker. He was not sure whether to crush organized labor under the American Plan or to woo the worker with welfare capitalism. He did not know whether it was better to seek discord or concord. More than anything else, he preferred not to think about the worker at all. The outward calm characteristic of the era — the apparent peace and prosperity — encouraged him to ignore the large and critical labor problems that bubbled beneath the surface. This left him unprepared to face these issues when they emerged into full view, and made it certain that they would erupt rather than come up in a smooth and orderly fashion.

But the employer, at least, in the twenties began to grope for solutions to some of these labor problems. This was in sharp contrast with the law, where the dead hand of the past reigned supreme.

CHAPTER 4

# Labor v. the Law

BY THE END of the twenties the gulf between labor and the law had become perilously wide. "Organized labor," wrote Felix Frankfurter and Nathan Greene, in 1930, "views all law with resentment...." "It would be difficult to conceive of a real advance toward 'social justice' in the United States," Donald Richberg observed in the same year, "that... would not leave a vast wreckage of judge-made law in its pathway." While the grievances of both unions and workers were manifold, the issue which transcended all others was the power of legislatures, state and federal, to meet labor's needs under the Constitution of the United States. Since the Constitution, in Charles Evans Hughes' phrase, meant what the judges said, or, more accurately, what at least five members of the ultimate tribunal said, the critical issue of labor law was the composition of the Supreme Court.

William Howard Taft had become Chief Justice on June 30, 1921, and resigned on February 3, 1930, a month before his death, his tenure spanning this critical decade. Taft's deep-seated convictions joined with his decisive position to make him the labor law architect of the era. As a federal district judge in Ohio in 1893, he had issued a pioneer injunction against a strike of the Brotherhood of Locomotive Engineers because, he reasoned, a carrier was obliged under the Interstate Commerce Act to accept the freight of a connecting road. When next year the newspapers reported that federal troops had killed thirty Pullman strikers, he wrote cheerfully, "Everybody hopes that it is true." His ambition following his retirement from the presidency in 1913 was to become Chief Justice of the United States, a dream that was to be fulfilled when the first Republican after himself entered the White House. Harding did more than name a chief; he also appointed George Sutherland, Pierce Butler, and Edward T. Sanford. With Willis Van Devanter, James Clark McReynolds, and Joseph McKenna, they formed a conservative majority that Taft could "mass" to his ends. At a conference of the court shortly after taking office, he announced that he had been chosen "to reverse a few decisions," and, chuckling, "I looked right at old man Holmes when I said it." Of labor, he wrote in 1922, "That faction we have to hit every little while." [1]

1

The law of labor relations in 1929 was found primarily in the decisions of the courts, since there were few statutes and some of the most important of those — the antitrust laws — had been interpreted essentially as restatements of the common law. The trade union as such was considered a lawful association provided that its purpose was not criminal syndicalism. The Supreme Court, speaking through Chief Justice Taft in *American Steel Foundries* v. *Tri-City Central Trades Council* in 1921, had held:

> Labor unions are recognized by the Clayton Act as legal when instituted for mutual help and lawfully carrying out their legitimate objects. They have long thus been recognized by the courts. They were organized out of the necessities of the situation. A single employee was helpless in dealing with an employer.... Union was essential to give laborers an opportunity to deal on equality with their employer.

The fundamental objective of the union, bargaining culminating in the collective agreement, was similarly lawful, although there was some disparity in the decisions over whether the resulting agreement was an enforceable contract.

The courts sapped the approbation they granted these ultimate goals of unions by imposing severe restrictions upon their short-run objectives. In 1926, in *Dorchy* v. *Kansas,* for example, the Supreme Court, speaking through Justice Louis D. Brandeis, held, "a strike may be illegal because of its purpose.... Neither the common law nor the Fourteenth Amendment confers the absolute right to strike." This rule was applied by the courts of all but one state: the legality of a strike hinged upon the purpose for which it was conducted. In California strikes were lawful without regard to purpose.

A concerted quitting of work by sailors while a vessel was at sea was mutiny, and the abandonment of a train by its crew so as to endanger human life was a crime. Workmen who quit prior to the expiration of their employment contracts were liable for the resulting damages. Many stoppages to obtain additional work were illegal, for example, to prevent an employer from working on the job, to compel him to continue operations, or to require him to hire more men than he wished. A strike to compel an employer to violate a yellow-dog contract was unlawful. Strikes to raise wages or shorten hours, however, were lawful.

The legality of a strike for the closed shop, usually arising out of a union demand to discharge workers who refused to join, was clouded. The United States Supreme Court had not ruled on the point, and the two leading lines of state decisions, in the Massachusetts and New York courts, were at loggerheads. The former held that the union must show just cause for the demand that a worker be fired and that strengthening the organization was insufficient. In some cases they even ruled strikes for recognition illegal. The New York courts, on the other hand, held strikes for the closed shop lawful even when this necessitated the discharge of nonunionists, and the Court of Appeals explicitly asserted the legitimacy of strengthening the union. Most other states had no settled law upon the question and the few that did divided almost evenly along the lines of Massachusetts and New York.

Strikes by employees of one employer or in one craft to aid workmen of another — sympathetic strikes — were often unlawful. The courts invariably condemned the extreme form: the general strike. Far more common were cases involving a refusal to work on nonunion materials, a variety of the secondary boycott, usually for an organizational purpose. There were two basic Supreme Court decisions. *Duplex Printing Press Co.* v. *Deering* involved a nationwide boycott imposed by the Machinists upon the handling and installation of printing presses manufactured in an unorganized

Michigan factory, for the purpose of unionizing its employees. The court in 1921 held the boycott violative of the Sherman and Clayton Acts and enjoinable. Justice Mahlon Pitney declared that a sympathetic strike against Duplex customers could not be regarded as peaceful persuasion. Rather, it was "a threat to inflict damage upon the immediate employer, between whom and his employees no dispute exists, in order to bring him against his will into a concerted plan to inflict damage upon another employer who is in dispute with his employees." *Bedford Cut Stone Co. v. Journeymen Stone Cutters* involved a national order by a union to its members to refuse to handle limestone produced by Indiana quarries that had gone nonunion in 1921. The objective was to reorganize their employees. The court, following the Duplex decision, in 1927 ruled the strike in violation of the Sherman Act and the quarries entitled to injunctive relief. Justice Sutherland held the legality of both the union and its purpose "beside the point." "Where the means adopted are unlawful, the innocent general character of the organizations ... or the lawfulness of the ultimate end ... cannot serve as a justification." The courts of Florida, Massachusetts, New Jersey, Pennsylvania, and Ohio adhered to the same view.

As significant as the restrictions the courts imposed upon the purposes of strikes were the limits they fixed upon the conduct of strikers. Threats, coercion, and intimidation were, of course, unlawful and were by no means limited to acts or threats of physical violence. The courts intervened if, in their judgment, the conduct provoked fear in the worker's mind. Peaceful persuasion was legal provided the objective of the strike was lawful and did not induce breach of contract, including the yellow dog. The rule for payment of strike benefits was the same: lawful on condition that the purpose of the strike was not illegal.

The critical development in the twenties occurred in the law of picketing. While all courts held nonpeaceful conduct illegal, the Supreme Court in 1921 in the Tri-City case imposed severe restrictions upon peaceful picketing. On April 22, 1914, the Tri-City Central Trades Council had struck the American Steel Foundries at Granite City, Illinois, for recognition. The unions displayed a printed notice of the strike at the entrance and posted three or four groups of pickets with four to twelve persons in each group. There were no acts of violence. Nevertheless, Chief Justice Taft ruled that these were "methods which however lawful in their announced purpose inevitably lead to intimidation and violence." Under the circumstances "it is idle to talk of peaceful communication." The very word "picket" is "sinister" and suggests "a militant purpose." Hence such picketing "is unlawful and cannot be peaceable and may be properly enjoined." The court then limited the number of pickets to one at each gate. The Tri-City decision determined the federal law of picketing, and virtually all the state courts followed the precedent. Henceforth it was virtually impossible for a union legally to man an effective picket line.

As if to drive nails in the coffin, the court a few weeks later in *Truax* v. *Corrigan* struck down an Arizona statute which forbade the issuance of an injunction to prohibit peaceful picketing. Taft held that the law "contravened the Fourteenth Amendment by depriving plaintiffs of their property without due process ... and by denying to plaintiffs the equal protection of the laws." "There is nothing I more deprecate," Oliver Wendell Holmes, Jr., observed in a famous dissent, "than the use of the Fourteenth Amendment beyond the absolute compulsion of its words to prevent the making of social experiments that an important part of the community desires in the insulated chambers afforded by the several States." This in spite of the fact that "the experiments may seem futile or even noxious to me."

The remaining union sanction, the boycott, was already legally dead in most jurisdictions. In 1908 the Supreme Court in the Danbury hatters case, *Loewe* v. *Lawlor,* had awarded a manufacturer treble damages under the Sherman Act for losses suffered from an interstate boycott of his products. In *Gompers* v. *Bucks Stove & Range Co.* in 1911 the same court approved an injunction restraining the AFL from publishing the company's name on its "unfair" list. The Federation gave up this list, and the use of the boycott atrophied.[2]

2

The discussion thus far has been of the substantive law, of the rights — or, more appropriately, restrictions upon the rights — of unions to conduct their affairs. It is necessary now to turn to procedural law, the means of enforcement, finding expression in the injunction, damage suits, and criminal actions. Of these, the labor injunction was much the most important because it cut a swath across the whole field of labor relations law and was the leading issue of labor policy in the twenties.

The injunction was an invention of the English equity courts, long before labor organizations existed, to prevent physical damage to property during the pendency of a suit. In the late nineteenth century American courts adopted the device and extended its use to several new areas, including labor. The Debs injunction, obtained by the federal government in the Pullman strike of 1894, gave the technique both notoriety and popularity. In equity theory the injunction was viewed as an extraordinary remedy to be invoked only in an emergency characterized by immediate danger of irreparable damage to physical property. In such a situation, however, the injunction was not available if there was recourse to a court of law. Nor was it intended to restrain criminal acts unless they were calculated to cause immediate irreparable damage to physical property. By the late twenties the American courts in labor cases had made a shambles of this theory, largely by embracing intangible property. "The extraordinary remedy of injunction," Frankfurter and Greene wrote, "has become the ordinary legal remedy, almost the sole remedy."

An injunction was sought by the employer (rarely the federal government) for the most part while a strike was in progress. His attorney filed a bill of equity in a trial court having jurisdiction, usually seeking out an "injunction judge." The bill described the property, alleged the union's intent to commit irreparable damage, and pleaded relief — spelled out in a draft order. At this stage the union was afforded neither notice nor hearing. The judge simply issued an *ex parte* temporary restraining order by affixing his signature to the draft submitted by the company attorney. The order invariably applied to the union, its agents and attorneys, and "all persons acting in aid of or in connection with them"; often it covered "all persons whomsoever." It commonly prohibited the use of force, coercion, and intimidation, prevented or regulated picketing, and barred boycotts, trespass, the use of the appellation "scab," and the payment of strike benefits. Sometimes the order forbade the workmen to strike or the union to hold meetings. Occasionally it committed an absurdity, as in the International Tailoring case in 1925 wherein Justice Churchill prohibited officers and members of the Amalgamated Clothing Workers from "standing in the street within ten blocks ... of the plaintiff's business." This area constituted the center of the New York City men's clothing industry and embraced the union's headquarters!

The restraining order was often sufficient to break the strike. "The tentative truth results in making ultimate truth irrelevant," wrote Frankfurter and Greene. Since it was virtually impossible to revive a strike once lost, the employer's interest in the legal process usually ended here. The judge, however, might hold a preliminary hearing, usually without examination of witnesses, to decide whether to issue a temporary (interlocutory) injunction, continuing or modifying the restraining order. A strike that had somehow survived the first step was almost certain to expire at this point. The remaining handful moved to the third stage, a full court trial with oral examination of witnesses. Here the court determined whether to issue a permanent injunction. This might occur months or even years after inception of the proceedings. Either party, of course, could carry an appeal to the higher courts, with consequent further delay.

At the end of the twenties the leading students of labor law were in accord that the marriage of the labor injunction with the yellow-dog contract was a peril to the survival of trade unionism in the United States. The Supreme Court had officiated at the wedding in 1917 in the famous and transcendently important case of *Hitchman Coal & Coke Co.* v. *Mitchell.*

In 1898 the bituminous operators in the Central Competitive Field had granted the eight-hour day, in return for which they exacted a pledge from the United Mine Workers to unionize the competitive but then minor West Virginia and Kentucky fields. A group of organized Ohio operators opened the Hitchman mine in the panhandle of West Virginia along the Ohio River and, after a strike over the wage scale, signed a union contract in 1903. The following year another stoppage occurred over the same issue. In 1906 the Hitchman miners joined a nation-wide coal strike over wages and conditions and were out for fifty-six days. During the shutdown, the board of directors fixed a new policy of employing "none but nonunion laborers." The Hitchman case was launched. At this time the mine produced about 300,000 tons annually which were sold to the Baltimore & Ohio Railroad and, increasingly, in the Great Lakes market in competition with northern bituminous. Hitchman employed between 200 and 300 miners at the main pit, and considerably fewer were engaged at two nearby mines, Glendale and Richmond.

The mines reopened on June 12, 1906. Each man who applied for employment was orally notified that he could work for Hitchman only if he promised not to join the UMW. In January 1908 this yellow-dog pledge was put in writing:

> I am employed by and work for the Hitchman Coal & Coke Co. with the express understanding that I am not a member of the United Mine Workers of America and will not become so while an employe ... and that the Hitchman ... is run nonunion and agrees with me that it will run nonunion while I am in its employ. If at any time while I am employed by the Hitchman ... I want to become connected with the United Mine Workers ... or any affiliated organization, I agree to withdraw from the employment of said company, and agree that while I am in the employ of that company I will not make any effort amongst its employes to bring about the unionizing of that mine against the company's wish.

At the 1907 UMW convention major attention was focused upon the growing competition from southern mines and the mounting pressure of northern operators. William Green, president of District 6, observed of his Ohio members during a recent strike: "They saw West Virginia coal go by, train-load after train-load. ... This coal supplied the markets that they should have had." The convention determined upon an organizational drive.

In September and October 1907, Thomas Hughes, a UMW organizer, passed among the employees of the Hitchman, Glendale, and Richmond mines. The names of those interested in organization

— and there were a good many — he entered in a little book. Hughes did not, however, sign anyone to membership; he merely persuaded them to agree to join at an unspecified future date when those so agreeing would constitute the majority. His methods were peaceful and orderly; he used neither intimidation nor force upon those he sought to persuade.

On January 14, 1908, Judge Alston G. Dayton of the federal district court granted Hitchman a temporary restraining order, which he converted to a temporary injunction on May 26, 1908, and to a "perpetual" injunction on December 23, 1912. This document was remarkable for its sweep. It applied to ten officers of the union (three were never served process and five others no longer held office by the time the case reached the Supreme Court) as well as to "all persons now members . . . and all persons who though not now members do become members of said United Mine Workers of America." They were enjoined from persuading Hitchman employees, present or future, to unionize the mine "without plaintiff's consent," from inducing breach of the yellow-dog contracts, from enticing employees, present or future, to leave employment without Hitchman's consent, from trespassing upon the premises, from inducing employees, present or future, by intimidation or abusive language to leave service or refuse to perform their duties, from picketing, or from engaging in acts of physical violence.

Judge Dayton consumed nearly five years in disposing of this case, and with some cause: he received almost 8000 pages of testimony and 800 pages of briefs. No one failed to recognize the crucial issue at stake and Dayton's opinion, by its length if not its perception, gave weighty evidence of this. In essence, he held that the UMW was a common-law conspiracy to subvert the coal industry of West Virginia, had violated the Sherman antitrust law, and had induced breach of contract. Hitchman, the judge concluded, was suffering "irremediable" damage, presumably from a strike which the UMW — this "foul and injurious" conspiracy "so glaringly designed to injure and destroy" — had not called. The circuit court reversed Dayton on the grounds that the miners under the yellow-dog contract were free to join the union (at the cost of their jobs) and the UMW's methods had been lawful. Meantime, this court stripped away the conspiracy and Sherman Act charges so as to place breach of contract squarely before the highest court in the land.

The Supreme Court, on December 10, 1917, sustained Dayton's injunction enforcing the Hitchman yellow-dog contract. The logic of Justice Pitney's opinion, if one accepted his premises, was impeccable. "The same liberty which enables men to form unions ... entitles other men to remain independent of the union and other employers to agree with them to employ no man who owes any allegiance . . . to the union." In *Adair* v. *United States* and *Coppage* v. *Kansas* the court had held federal and state legislation prohibiting yellow-dog contracts unconstitutional restraints upon personal liberty and private property. Hence the employer and the nonunion employee "are entitled to be protected by the law in the enjoyment of the benefits of any lawful agreement they may make." Each Hitchman miner who allowed his name to be entered in Hughes's book was "guilty of a breach of his contract of employment." Hughes's methods — inducing employees to subvert the system of employment "by concerted breaches of the contracts" — were "unlawful and malicious." Pitney could find no difference between agreeing to join and actually joining: "to induce men to *agree* to join is but a mode of inducing them to join."

Justice Brandeis, in a dissent with which Holmes and John H. Clarke concurred, pointed out that the heart of the injunction was the prohibition against acts undertaken "for the purpose of unionizing plaintiff's mine without plaintiff's consent." Since collective bargaining — the end — was lawful, "defendants' efforts to unionize the mine can be illegal, only if the methods . . . pursued were unlawful." Both by inducing employees merely to agree to join and by conducting himself in an orderly and peaceable manner, Hughes had adopted lawful methods. If Hughes had induced a sufficient number of miners to agree to join and had then asked Hitchman for a contract, he would have exerted pressure rather than coercion; the employer would be free to accept the agreement or the disadvantage. "Indeed, the plaintiff's whole case is rested upon agreements secured under similar pressure of economic necessity or disadvantage." By exerting its superior bargaining power over the individual miner, Hitchman had forced a closed nonunion shop upon its employees collectively. "Equality of position between the parties," Holmes had observed in the Coppage dissent, is the point at which "liberty of contract begins."

Prior to the Hitchman case the yellow-dog device had been a relatively little-used annoyance to unions. Innocent workers might be frightened by the vague consequences of the antiunion promises they signed. Aside from discharge, there were none, since the yellow dogs were unenforceable and there is no record of a case brought by an employer against a signatory employee to compel performance or to recover damages. The Hitchman case revolutionized the legal situation. For one thing, in the words of Walter Wheeler Cook, "the court is holding that almost any acts of labor unions done for the purpose of unionizing an employer's business without his consent, are illegal." For another, if the employer, as part of withholding his consent, persuaded or constrained his employees to sign antiunion pledges, he could now invoke the full power of the law through the injunctive process against — not the employees — but the union. Even tough coal miners, who had derisively hung the name "yellow dog" upon these agreements and who were normally inclined to jeer at them, were without recourse.

The impact was enormous. The miners at Hitchman, of course, lost the union that most of them probably wanted to join. In fact, even if Brandeis had spoken for a majority of the court, the decade that elapsed between Hughes's organizing and the decision would have compelled him to breathe life into a dead carcass. Far more important was the encouragement the Hitchman doctrine gave antiunion employers to adopt the yellow-dog device. By the end of the twenties, it was estimated that 1,250,000 workers had signed these contracts. Edwin E. Witte uncovered more than sixty injunctions issued to enforce them. Some of the individual orders covered large segments of an industry, like the notorious Red Jacket injunction granted by Judge John J. Parker in 1927, which effectively barred the UMW from organizing in virtually the entire West Virginia coal industry.

The labor injunction achieved its greatest popularity during the twenties. Witte found 1845 orders issued by federal and state courts in the half century 1880–1930, half of them — 921 — in the decade 1920–30. This figure takes on added meaning when viewed against the fact that employers faced very few strikes at this time. The number of injunctions issued in the New York City garment trades also concentrated in the twenties, especially in the relatively high strike years of 1921 and 1926. By the end of the decade a union calculating a strike call contended with the strong possibility, if not probability, that a restraining order would issue.

Hence some labor leaders were driven to defy the courts and constructed reputations on the number of injunctions they had ignored. Those who complied were attacked by militant unionists. John L. Lewis, who both in 1919 and during World War II achieved some notoriety for his defiance of court orders, was at this time condemned for meek submission.

The injunctive remedy, in fact, was somewhat less effective than would appear. Acts of violence, already punishable under the criminal law, were seldom affected by the prospect of a lesser penalty arising from contempt of court. In a few cases, including the Coronado Coal strike of 1914, violence was actually encouraged by the injunction. Court orders aimed at the strike itself or at picketing were more effective, though even here defiance was not uncommon. Injunctions enforcing yellow-dog contracts, by contrast, left the union helpless. Witte concluded that orders had relatively little effect upon strikes of powerful unions and great impact upon those of weak ones.

During the twenties opposition to court abuse of the injunction presaged legislative relief. Even conservative Senator George Wharton Pepper of Pennsylvania in 1924 warned the American Bar Association that "the growing bitterness of organized labor toward the federal courts" was creating a sentiment which, if unchecked, would become "revolutionary." "Must we not," he queried, "confine the courts to the sphere in which the creators of our constitutional system intended them to live . . .?"

The charges were: the *ex parte* character of the temporary order and the inability to confront witnesses at the critical procedural stages effectively denied the defendants an opportunity to present their case. Hence judges rendered decisions upon the manifestly partisan evidence submitted by affidavits, as the unusually high incidence of reversals on appeal demonstrated. "A comparison of the picture produced by . . . testimony [of witnesses] with that produced by their affidavits," Judge Charles F. Amidon observed, "has proven the utter untrustworthiness of affidavits. Such documents are packed with falsehoods, or with half-truths, which in such a matter are more deceptive than deliberate falsehoods." The orders suffered from extreme vagueness. "The injunction," wrote Frankfurter and Greene, "includes more than the lawless ... it leaves the lawless undefined and thus terrorizes innocent conduct." The very language was stereotyped, overloaded with legal mumbo-jumbo, and frequently incomprehensible to the persons whose behavior it purported to regulate. As fundamental as these procedural defects was the fact that the courts, by making social policy, absorbed legislative and executive (including police) powers — "government by injunction." Indifference to separation of powers, indefensible in itself, became intolerable in an area of bitter conflict. Francis B. Sayre wrote: "A legal machinery which casts upon a single judge the duty of awarding victory and deciding issues of tremendous social import, not as a result of a painstaking examination ... is not a procedure altogether fitted to achieve social justice." The injunction, by breaking the strike, invited disrespect for judges and for law, a dangerous state of affairs in a democratic society.[3]

The law of damage suits against labor unions, the second means of enforcement, was markedly broadened during the twenties. It was generally held at common law that an unincorporated association (the case with virtually all unions) was not of itself a legal entity and so could neither sue nor be sued. Its members individually, however, were liable for acts they perpetrated in its behalf. Union funds, held in trust for its members, were exempt from suit unless it could be shown — a practically impossible undertaking — that all the members had engaged in unlawful conduct.

The Sherman Act, by providing that a person injured in violation of the statute "shall recover threefold damages ... and the cost of suit, including a reasonable attorney's fee," opened a route for further exploration. In the Danbury hatters case a manufacturer had demonstrated to the Supreme Court's satisfaction in 1908 that a boycott against his hats was a conspiracy in restraint of trade and had been awarded treble damages of $240,000 assessed against

197 union members, almost none of whom had participated in the boycott. This decision, while deeply disturbing to the labor movement, adhered to the common-law rule in imposing liability only upon members.

In 1922, however, the Supreme Court in the first Coronado case tossed precedent aside by holding an unincorporated labor organization financially liable for its acts. The controversy arose out of the abrogation by eight coal-mining companies in western Arkansas of an agreement with District 21 of the United Mine Workers. The union struck and the operators imported strikebreakers and armed guards, with consequent destruction of property by miners. The receiver for the companies (which had gone bankrupt during the troubles) sued the international union, District 21, and several individual members for $2,200,000. Chief Justice Taft argued for the court that it was time, despite the common-law rule, to face the fact that a union was an entity rather than a mere collection of individual members. "The growth and necessities of these great labor organizations have brought affirmative legal recognition of their existence and usefulness. . . ." The law granted rights and imposed duties of many sorts upon them. It was absurd to allow an organization like the UMW with 450,000 members and ample funds unlawfully to injure private rights with financial impunity. The precedent of the House of Lords in 1901 in the Taff-Vale case, holding that unions might be sued, was cited in support. "We think," Taft concluded, "that such organizations are suable in the federal courts for their acts. . . ." After considerable further litigation, including a second Supreme Court decision, District 21 settled with the disappointed receiver in 1927 for a mere $27,500, each side paying its own costs.

Indeed, the profound concern which Gompers had expressed over the first Coronado ruling was realized only in small part. A fair number of employers brought suit (the National Erectors Association and the Iron League set a record in 1924 by asking $5,000,000 in damages from the Structural Iron Workers) but very few won favorable court action or settlement. In fact, a large number of suits were not even brought to trial, apparently serving as a form of bargaining bluff. Two considerations, according to Witte, stood in the way: procedural difficulties and inability under the principles of agency law to connect unions with alleged unlawful acts. The Coronado decision, therefore, was a big howitzer that somehow could not be made to go off.[4]

Far more important was the final means of enforcement, criminal prosecutions. Criminal law, of course, is not labor law at all, and it is a commentary on the state of labor relations in the late twenties to note the appallingly large number of arrests for felonies (murder, dynamiting, kidnaping, extortion, criminal libel, riot, inciting to riot, assault, malicious mischief, unlawful assembly, sedition, even treason) as well as for misdemeanors (disorderly conduct, obstructing traffic, disturbing the peace, trespass, loitering, assembling without a permit, even selling insurance without a license). In the New York garment strike of 1926, there were 7500 arrests in the first fifteen weeks; in the New York fur strike of that year, 884 arrests and 477 convictions; in the New Bedford textile strike of 1928, 2000 arrests; in the Elizabethton textile strike of 1929, 300 arrests in a single day; and so on and on. Labor, living so close to the criminal law, could hardly divorce itself from the great cases of the preceding forty years: the Haymarket Riot, the Haywood-Moyer-Pettibone trial, the McNamara case, the Mooney case, the Herrin massacre, and the Sacco-Vanzetti case. In 1929 Clarence Darrow, with his Lincolnesque frame and beetle-browed scowl, still practiced law in Chicago; Jim McNamara and Matt Schmidt were still in jail in California for dynamiting the Los Angeles *Times* building; Tom Mooney and Warren Billings, their shoddy trial an international *cause célèbre*, still sat in San Quentin; and the execution of Sacco and Vanzetti had occurred only two short years before.

When the very existence of trade unionism was challenged, violence was inevitable. Even the techniques of strike conduct — mass picketing, strikebreaking, and strike guards — were a hazard to the preservation of peace. No other advanced nation in the world conducted its industrial relations with such defiance of the criminal law. In 1926, for example, the lowest strike year of record in the United States and the highest for Britain, culminating in the general strike, the American display of violence far exceeded the British. Almost as serious was the growth of racketeering during the twenties as a result of the Eighteenth Amendment. In the big cities, especially Chicago and New York, the mobs moved in on the unions to engage in extortion against both employers and members.

An important reason for violence was the fact that virtually all the hostile acts of employers set forth in the preceding chapter were lawful. The courts protected the right of an employer to refuse to hire and to discharge at will for union membership on the ground that it was repugnant to compel him unwillingly to enter into a personal relationship with an employee. As a result, federal and state legislation designed to protect the worker against discrimination based upon union membership was held invalid. There were no effective legal safeguards against industrial espionage. Federal legislation did not exist. Several states had statutes which made the filing of a false report by a private detective a crime, but it was almost impossible to produce proof. The legal situation of strikebreaking was similar. There was no federal legislation and the courts defended the strikebreaker's "right to work." A number of states had "Pinkerton" laws which prohibited the importation of armed guards from other states. They were easily evaded by shipping guards and arms separately or by recruiting within the state. Private police were lawful everywhere; in fact, Pennsylvania, Maryland, and South Carolina had statutes which specifically legalized company police and made it possible to deputize officers, thereby lending them the authority of the law. Company towns were not only within the law but the public officials were usually controlled by the employer. The purchase of industrial munitions was not federally regulated; several states required licenses to buy gas or machine guns but they were easy to obtain because the statutes set no standards for issuance. The legal status of the company union was fully protected everywhere except on the railroads, where it was in doubt. The hostile acts of belligerent employer associations were, of course, lawful.

In theory the law treated both sides equally: workers might lawfully organize and bargain collectively, while employers with the same legality might frustrate freedom of association and refuse to bargain. In the realities of the market place in most industries this hypothetical balance gave the employer the best of it. And if his economic power proved insufficient, there was nothing to stop him from using a club. As William M. Leiserson has observed:

The law recognized the equal freedom of the employers to destroy labor organizations and to deny the right of employees to join trade unions. An employer could coerce or threaten his employees to keep them from organizing. He could discharge them if they joined a union, and he could refuse to hire anyone who was a member. He could decline to deal with any union of his employees or to recognize the organization or any of its officers or agents as representatives of the employees. He was free to organize a company union of his own and force his employees to join it. It was not illegal for him to employ detectives to spy on his employees in order to find out whether they talked unionism among themselves, and he could send his spies into the labor organization to become members and officers so that they might be in a better position to report union activities to him and recommend effective disciplinary action designed to stop such activities. Under such circumstances, to speak of labor's right to organize was clearly a misuse of terms. All that the employees had was a right to try to organize if they could get away with it; and whether they could or not depended on the relative economic strength of the employers' and employees' organizations.[5]

## 3

In their impact the antitrust laws were much the most important labor relations statutes on the books. The manipulation of the Sherman and Clayton Acts to restrict union activities, emerging slowly for thirty years, reached a climax in the Supreme Court in the twenties.

The Sherman law of 1890 gave statutory force to the old common-law concept of conspiracy: "Every contract, combination ... or conspiracy, in restraint of trade or commerce among the several States, or with foreign nations, is hereby declared to be illegal." A great debate was to rage for many years over whether Congress intended this language to cover trade unions. Employers argued for inclusion and the labor movement for exemption. Disinterested scholars were as hopelessly divided. This contest was for the mind of the public; the courts, with whom the interpretation of the statute ultimately rested, had no doubt.

The first Supreme Court decision to hold a business combination in restraint of trade came down in 1897; in those same seven years following passage in 1890 the federal courts held against unions in twelve cases. Any straw that the labor movement might still have clutched at vanished with the decision in the Danbury hatters case in 1908. The Supreme Court held that the law made "no distinction between classes." All conspiracies in restraint of trade, regardless of source, were unlawful. Attempts during the legislative history to exempt organizations of farmers and laborers had failed of passage; hence, the court concluded, "the act remained as we have it before us."

Relief could come only by the enactment of amendatory legislation, and to this object the AFL addressed itself in a mood of gathering concern. Between 1908 and 1914, fifteen to twenty cases arose in inferior federal courts in which the Sherman Act was invoked against labor. In one, involving coal-wheelers in New Orleans, the judge held that any strike affecting interstate commerce was unlawful; five longshoremen in Jacksonville were sent to prison for conspiring to violate the antitrust law; and Judge Dayton, as already noted, ruled that the UMW was an unlawful combination under the Sherman Act in the Hitchman case. There is little wonder that AFL pressure mounted feverishly.

In 1914 the Democratic Congress, after a tortured legislative history, enacted and President Wilson signed the Clayton Act. Its labor provisions read:

Section 6. That the labor of a human being is not a commodity or article of commerce. Nothing contained in the antitrust laws shall be construed to forbid the existence and operation of labor, agricultural, or horticultural organizations, instituted for the purpose of mutual help, and not having capital stock or conducted for profit, or to forbid or restrain individual members of such organizations from lawfully carrying out the legitimate objects thereof; nor shall such organizations, or the members thereof be held or construed to be illegal combinations or conspiracies in restraint of trade under the antitrust laws.

Section 20. That no restraining order or injunction shall be granted by any court of the United States ... in any case between an employer and employees, or between employers and employees, or between employees, or between persons employed and persons seeking employment, involving, or growing out of, a dispute concerning terms or conditions of employment, unless necessary to prevent irreparable injury to property, or to a property right, of the party making the application, for which injury there is no adequate remedy at law. . . .

And no such restraining order or injunction shall prohibit any person or persons, whether singly or in concert, from terminating any relation of employment, or from ceasing to perform any work or labor, or from recommending, advising, or persuading others by peaceful means so to do; or from attending at any place where any such person or persons may lawfully be, for the purpose of obtaining or communicating information, or from peacefully persuading any person to work or to abstain from working; or from ceasing to patronize or to employ any party to such dispute, or from recommending, advising, or persuading others by peaceful and lawful means so to do; or from paying or giving to, or withholding from, any person engaged in such dispute, any strike benefits or other moneys or things of value; or from peaceably assembling in a lawful manner, and for lawful purposes; or from doing any act or thing which might lawfully be done in the absence of such dispute by any party thereto; nor shall any of the acts specified in this paragraph be considered or held to be violations of any law of the United States.

Precisely what this verbiage meant was a matter of eager conjecture and extraordinary disagreement. Gompers hailed the Clayton Act upon its passage as "the Magna Carta upon which the working people will rear their structure of industrial freedom." In his mind it constituted "emancipation from legalism." To William Howard Taft, in his presidential address to the American Bar Association in October 1914, however, Sections 6 and 20 "are declaratory merely of what would be law without the statute." The common-law conspiracy doctrine, in Taft's view, was simply reinforced in statutory form. "The Supreme Court," Frankfurter and Greene were later to write, "had to find meaning where Congress had done its best to conceal meaning." And the Chief Justice of the court that was to decide exactly what the Clayton Act meant, if not what Congress intended, was not Gompers but Taft.

The use of the antitrust laws against labor reached a climax in the decade 1919–29. During this period there were, according to Edward Berman's count, seventy-two recorded cases in which unions, their officers, or members were defendants under the Sherman Act, far more than in the thirty preceding years. The twenties witnessed eight major Supreme Court decisions involving unions under this statute, in contrast with only two or three altogether in the earlier decades. A minimum of twenty-three criminal prosecutions, six damage suits, and forty suits for injunction were instituted. Convictions resulted in more than half the criminal cases, some with long prison sentences; two damage actions led to settlements; and the great majority of the injunction petitions were granted. Labor's defeat could hardly have been more complete. Instead of taking Gompers' view of union exemption from the antitrust laws, the courts shaped the statutes into a powerful weapon against labor.

In the Duplex case, whose facts have already been summarized, the Supreme Court conclusively established antitrust jurisdiction over trade-union activities. A federal district judge in 1917 had denied Duplex an injunction on the ground that the Clayton Act had removed the Machinists' secondary boycott from the ambit of the Sherman Act. The following year the second circuit court by a vote of two to one held that the union activity, while unlawful under the Sherman Act, was protected by the Clayton Act. In 1921 the Supreme Court, with three dissenters, overruled the lower courts. Justice Pitney for the majority held that Section 6 merely declared that a labor union "in itself" was not a conspiracy. "But there is nothing in the section to exempt such an organization or its members from accountability where it or they ... engage in an actual combination or conspiracy in restraint of trade." Section 20 had no more effect. It required that the controversy arise out of the proximate relationship of employer and employee; here there was no dispute between Duplex and its own workmen. Further, the activity complained of — a secondary boycott — was calculated to impose "extreme and harmful consequences" upon innocent third parties. The general purpose of Congress in enacting the antitrust laws was to prevent such impediments to the public's "vital interest in unobstructed commerce." Hence Duplex, despite the Clayton Act, had a right to an injunction restraining the Machinists' conduct under the Sherman law.

The door was now wide open and the traffic rushed through. A few weeks later in the Tri-City case Chief Justice Taft read picketing out from under the protective cover of Section 20. The statute "introduces no new principle ... is merely declaratory of what was the best practice always." Although laborers have the right to engage in peaceful persuasion, their methods as pickets "inevitably lead to intimidation and obstruction." Hence "it is the court's duty which the terms of Section 20 do not modify, so to limit what the propagandists do as to time, manner and place as shall prevent infractions of the law. ..."

The Coronado cases presented the court with a barrier of its own making, the precedent that mining was a local industry, not in interstate commerce, and so beyond the purview of the antitrust laws. Even this hurdle was not too high for the Chief Justice, though it took him two leaps to make it. In the first case, in 1922, Taft granted that "obstruction to coal mining is not a direct obstruction to interstate commerce," but added presciently that interference with mining "may affect it by reducing the amount of coal to be carried in that commerce." The evidence of intent to restrain commerce under the antitrust laws, however, must be direct and conclusive. Though the effect of the miners' strike upon that commerce was clear enough, the evidence before the court was insufficient to demonstrate that interference with commerce was among their primary purposes. The receivers of the Coronado Coal Company could take a hint; they asked for a new trial in order to introduce further evidence relating to intent. In the second case, in 1925, Taft was persuaded that "there was substantial evidence ... tending to show that the purpose of the destruction of the mines was to stop the production of non-union coal and prevent its shipment to markets of other States than Arkansas...." Hence the union had intended to affect commerce and so its acts came within the prohibitions of the antitrust laws. The significance of the second Coronado decision, in Berman's words, "can hardly be overestimated." Unions, like the miners, the textile workers, the shoe workers, or the clothing workers, that struck for the purpose of organizing the unorganized segment of an industry would, by obstructing production, violate the Sherman Act.

The courts so held in many cases during the twenties; among them *United Mine Workers v. Red Jacket* was notorious. On September 30, 1920, the Red Jacket Consolidated Coal & Coke Company filed a complaint against the officers of the UMW, charging them with conspiracy under the Sherman Act by seeking to organize the employees of its West Virginia mine. This case and several others that involved the same issue, embracing 316 mines with the bulk of the state's output, were consolidated in 1923. Two years later the district court ruled that the union officers had contravened the antitrust law and granted restraining orders. In a famous decision in 1927, Judge John J. Parker for the fourth circuit, resting his argument squarely upon the second Coronado case, sustained the injunctions. The union's officers, he held, "had combined and conspired to interfere with the production and shipment of coal by the non-union operators of West Virginia, in order to force the unionization of the West Virginia mines." This conspiracy was clearly in contravention of the Sherman Act. The Supreme Court, pleased with the chick that had hatched from the egg it had laid, denied a UMW plea for *certiorari* on October 17, 1927.

The greatest strike of the decade, that of the railway shopmen in protest against a wage reduction in 1922, had a significant antitrust aspect. Harding's attorney general, Harry Daugherty, convinced that this was a Communist attempt to seize the United States, proposed to the Cabinet that the government seek a sweeping injunction. The President, over the vigorous opposition of Secretary of State Charles Evans Hughes and Secretary of Commerce Herbert Hoover, authorized Daugherty to proceed. On September 1, District Judge James H. Wilkerson granted his plea by issuing a restraining order which, for the dazzling number and variety of prohibited acts, can only be described as majestic. Briefly, anyone in any way connected with the shop crafts was forbidden to do or say anything whatever in furtherance of the strike. Since many of these activities were of themselves harmless, Wilkerson found a legal basis for his decision by finding that the unions had violated the Sherman Act. Here the conspiracy doctrine was carried, in Berman's words, "to the farthest possible extreme." By this means, Wilkerson enjoined such conduct as making entreaties, holding interviews, and calling on the telephone. The Sherman Act gave him an "'omnium gatherum' in which to put every sort of act which was part of an alleged unlawful conspiracy to restrain interstate commerce."

In *United States* v. *Brims* the Supreme Court for the first time held a collective-bargaining agreement illegal under the Sherman Act. Chicago manufacturers of millwork, contractors who purchased it, and the Carpenters were parties to a contract that called for employment of union men in the mills as well as refusal to install nonunion millwork. The purpose was to prevent competition within the Chicago market of cheaper materials produced primarily in the South and Wisconsin, and to a lesser extent elsewhere in Illinois. The court held the agreement a collusive combination in restraint of trade, dismissing as of no consequence the fact that part of the commerce was intrastate.

The same court, however, in *Industrial Assn. of San Francisco* v. *United States* held lawful an attempt by San Francisco employers to protect an antiunion arrangement. Contractors were required to obtain permits from the Builders Exchange in order to purchase materials. The condition for getting a permit was adherence to the American Plan. In response to a government suit, the district court held this arrangement a conspiracy in restraint of interstate commerce in building materials under the Sherman Act. The Supreme Court reversed, ruling, in effect, that there had been no interstate commerce to restrain. To reach this astounding conclusion, Justice Sutherland found it necessary to sweep under the rug a large pile of building materials produced in states other than California. Since no plaster was made anywhere in the state, all of it obviously had to come from other jurisdictions. He disposed of this annoying fact by finding that the plaster was "commingled with the common mass of local property" after its interstate movement had ended. Plumbing supplies, also produced elsewhere, were dismissed as "incidental, indirect and remote" from commerce. The good old maxim of *de minimis* took care of the fact that producers in other states were prevented or discouraged from shipping materials into California. In the eyes of the court, interstate commerce was an India-rubber concept, one that would stretch to prohibit activities by unions and relax to permit similar activities by employers.

The flow of the antitrust tide reached its high-water mark in 1927 in the Bedford Stone case, but, as the inner workings of the court demonstrated, the ebb was not far off. Both the district and circuit courts had held that the refusal of members of the Journeymen Stone Cutters to handle nonunion limestone produced by the Indiana quarries was not in contravention of the Sherman Act and had denied an injunction. Further, when the Supreme Court met in conference after hearing argument, the Chief Justice — disturbed over mounting public criticism and committed to a policy of "massing" the court — was dismayed to discover that he probably had a five to four decision on his hands. Brandeis and Holmes were opposed and it seemed that Sanford would join them. But to Taft's surprise came the news that Harlan Fiske Stone, recently appointed by Coolidge and an apparent stanch conservative, intended to go with the minority. So close a vote in so critical a case would certainly rub sandpaper on the raw wound the court had opened with the line of decisions beginning with Duplex. Hence Taft, aided by McReynolds, brought heavy pressure upon Sanford and Stone to shift sides. The result was pleasing to no one. Sutherland wrote the opinion for the court. Brandeis, in Taft's words, dissented in "one of his meanest opinions," Holmes concurring. Stone and Sanford voted with the majority "grudgingly, Stone with a kind of kickback that will make no one happy." The fissures within the court on labor cases were now so deep that Taft could only view the future with alarm.

Sutherland argued that the union members' strike against the installation of "unfair" stone "threatened to destroy or narrow petitioners' interstate trade." Although the object was to organize the men at the quarries, itself lawful, this was of no consequence since the result was to restrain commerce. "It is this result ... which gives character to the conspiracy." The fact that the stone had come to rest locally before the men refused to work it (the ghost of the Industrial Association case) was disposed of by creating a geography of motive: the intent to restrain was interstate rather than intrastate in nature. Sanford's concurrence was painfully brief: "the controlling authority of Duplex." Stone, obviously, had no stomach for Sutherland's reasoning. The Sherman Act, he declared, did not prohibit union members from peaceably refusing to work on nonunion material. Under the "rule of reason" enunciated by the court in the nonlabor Standard Oil and American Tobacco cases, only "unreasonable" restraints of trade were unlawful. The Stone Cutters, he argued, had not conducted themselves "unreasonably." But the court had rejected these arguments in the Duplex case. "For that reason alone, I concur with the majority."

Brandeis' dissent was, indeed, "mean," for it was an attack at the foundation of the edifice the court had erected upon the antitrust laws. Whether the restraint, applied locally by stone cutters, had an effect upon interstate commerce was beside the point, since the rule of reason excluded reasonable restraints from the prohibitions of the Sherman Act. "The propriety of the union's conduct can hardly be doubted by anyone who believes in the organization of labor." Each member, upon joining the union, pledged that he would not work on stone cut by workmen who opposed the organization. Since the Indiana companies sought openly to destroy the union, the men were duty-bound to abide by their promise. The bargaining power of the employers, banded together in both local and national associations, much exceeded that of this small union. The manner in which the men conducted their strike was plainly lawful, without violence, intimidation, fraud, or even picketing. "If, on the undisputed facts of this case, refusal to work can be enjoined, Congress created by the Sherman Law and the Clayton Act an instrument for imposing restraints upon labor which reminds of involuntary servitude." The court, Brandeis ironically wrote, had found protection under the Sherman Act for a combination that embraced half the nation's steel business and another that comprised virtually the entire shoe machinery industry. "It would, indeed, be strange if Congress had by the same Act willed to deny to members of a small craft of workingmen the right to co-operate in simply refraining from work, when that course was the only means of self-protection against a combination of militant and powerful employers."

The inequity to which Brandeis drew attention could not have been pointed out at a more timely moment. In the twenties business combinations grew very large, mergers were consummated at a rapid rate, and centralized control of industry and banking was a matter of grave public concern; at the same time unions disintegrated or were weakened. The Sherman Act, clearly, had little effect upon corporate concentration and was a powerful force against labor organizations. For the latter, Frankfurter and Greene wrote, "common law doctrines of conspiracy and restraint of trade ... hold sway; activities widely cherished as indispensable assertions of trade union life continue to be outlawed." "Conspiracy" and "restraint of trade" were words without exact meaning. They wrapped the whole area of union conduct in a blanket of uncertainty. Lawful acts — like talking on the telephone — became unlawful as part of a "conspiracy." Behavior that was protected in one case was prohibited in the next. "It is impossible," George Terborgh wrote, "to draw up a catalogue of acts which alone and in themselves constitute an illegal restraint of interstate commerce." Pointing to the court's inconsistency in its definition of commerce between the Bedford Stone and Industrial Association cases, Sayre concluded that the decisions "have come to depend very largely upon the underlying philosophies and social beliefs of individual judges." Most federal judges in the twenties shared the prejudices toward organized labor that were so evident in the Supreme Court majority. As a result, Witte observed, "the federal antitrust laws constitute a vague and undefined danger to labor, which is ever becoming more menacing." It was hardly surprising that a frustrated AFL called for the repeal of the Sherman Act in 1925.[6]

4

In contrast with the experience under the antitrust laws, the twenties saw marked progress in railway labor legislation. The

Railway Labor Act of 1926, in fact, was the only federal labor statute of significance passed during the decade. It grew out of a breakdown in Title III of the Transportation Act of 1920 as well as of its administrative agency, the Railroad Labor Board. Critical decisions of the Board were repudiated by the unions in the shop-crafts strike of 1922 and by the Pennsylvania Railroad in a harrowing dispute in 1921–23. The Secretary of Labor and both Presidents Harding and Coolidge asked for changes in Title III in 1923–24. The platforms of the Republican, Democratic, and Progressive Parties all commented upon its failure in 1924. Each session of Congress witnessed the introduction of legislation, the most important being the Howell-Barkley bill of 1924. This proposal had the support of the railway labor organizations and had, indeed, been drafted by their attorney, Donald R. Richberg, with the aid of his assistant, David E. Lilienthal. Gompers and the AFL strongly backed the bill. It was, however, opposed by the carriers, who asked for more time to permit the Board to prove itself. Hence the first session of the 68th Congress adjourned without taking action.

On December 3, 1924, President Coolidge urged the carriers and unions to work out a bill upon which they could agree. The following March the Association of Railway Executives appointed a committee to study the problem, which, in turn, designated a subcommittee to deal with the union representatives. Conferences were held and a bill, much like Howell-Barkley, was agreed upon. In December 1925 the Executives voted for it 52 to 20, the majority representing some 80 per cent of the nation's railroad mileage. A joint committee then presented the bill to the President on January 7, 1926, and had it introduced the following day under the sponsorship of Senator James E. Watson of Indiana and Representative James S. Parker of New York, both stanch Republicans who had opposed the Howell-Barkley bill. Buttressed by joint support (the only opposition came from the NAM), the Watson-Parker bill sped through Congress without change. The House on March 1 passed it 381 to 13, and the Senate 69 to 13 on May 11. Coolidge, more concerned than Congress with NAM objections, sought unsuccessfully to persuade the carriers and unions to accept amendments. When they refused, he reluctantly signed the Railway Labor Act on May 20, 1926.

The statute was an artfully drawn composite of workable features of railroad labor laws going back to 1888. Its virtue was not originality but acceptability, and it could not possibly have been enacted in the twenties without joint support. In the case of several key provisions the carriers and unions confined their agreement to the language itself rather than to its meaning. Words lost substance under the pressure of achieving acceptance. The Act dealt with three problems of great importance: representation, disputes over new agreements, and grievances arising under existing contracts.

Section 2 imposed "the duty" upon carriers and their employees "to exert every reasonable effort to make and maintain agreements" and settle disputes "to avoid any interruption to commerce or to the operation of any carrier." Disputes were, if possible, to be decided "in conference between representatives designated and authorized ... to confer, respectively by the carriers and by the employees." These representatives were to be chosen by the parties in accordance with the rules of their corporations or associations "without interference, influence, or coercion exercised by either party over the self-organization, or designation of representatives, by the other."

In the context of 1926, this last sentence was the most important in the statute. Exploiting the Wilkerson injunction and their defeat of the shop crafts, most of the nation's roads, including such giants as the Pennsylvania and the Southern Pacific (as well as its subsidiary the Texas & New Orleans), had imposed company unions upon their shop and roundhouse employees and to a lesser extent upon their clerks, maintenance-of-way men, and telegraphers. The Pennsylvania, in fact, had defied the Railroad Labor Board over the very issue of disestablishment of its dominated organization. If Section 2 meant what it said, the company unions were now unlawful. The antiunion carriers, however, had no intention of dismembering these organizations, apparently hoping that the courts would find a way to accommodate company unionism within Section 2. The Supreme Court's construction of the antitrust laws must have given them heart. Further, the fact that the statute neither created an enforcement procedure nor imposed penalties in no way diminished their resolve.

A test was not long in the making. The Railway Clerks in May 1927 presented the Texas & New Orleans Railroad with wage demands that the carrier, despite a bargaining history going back to 1918, determined to avoid by destroying the union. The methods were flagrant: discharge of union members and creation of a company union called Association of Clerical Employees Southern Pacific Lines. The Clerks asked the federal district court in Houston for an injunction restraining the railway from infringing Section 2; T & NO responded that it had not violated this provision and that the Railway Labor Act was unconstitutional. Judge Joseph C. Hutcheson, Jr., granted both a temporary and permanent injunction and ordered the disestablishment of the Association. The record, he found, "teems with evidence" that the Association was "sponsored, promoted, and maintained" by the employer. This was in defiance of Section 2 because "the railroad would be in a position of surely having a vote on both sides of the table." He set aside the constitutional argument on the ground that the Supreme Court had repeatedly sustained the power of Congress to regulate interstate railways. The fifth circuit, on June 10, 1929, upheld Hutcheson's decision by a vote of two to one. The dissenter, while granting that the Association was dominated in defiance of Section 2, argued that the Act contained no means of enforcement. The carriers and the railway unions waited impatiently for the Supreme Court's disposition of the T & NO case, but it was not to come down until after the stock market crash.

The major part of the Act set forth a procedure for settling new contract disputes. It created a Board of Mediation of five members to be designated by the President and confirmed by the Senate. Carriers and employee representatives were required to give at least thirty days' written notice of an intent to change a contract. Failing agreement, the Board was to mediate, including an attempt to induce the parties to submit to voluntary arbitration. If they accepted, each side was to appoint either one or two members of an arbitration board who, in turn, were to choose one or two neutrals. In case they could not agree, the Board of Mediation would name the neutrals. The statute prescribed detailed procedures for the conduct of arbitration. Far more important was the culminating step in case of a breakdown of mediation and an unwillingness to arbitrate. In a dispute which would, in the judgment of the Board of Mediation, "threaten substantially to interrupt interstate commerce" the Board was to notify the President and he might, "in his discretion," create an *ad hoc* emergency board "to investigate and report respecting such dispute" within thirty days. During this period the carrier was to refrain from changing the conditions of employment, and for sixty days the employees were prohibited from striking.

This last was the main price the unions paid for employer support of the statute. Theretofore they had firmly resisted any tampering with the right to strike. Attorney General Daugherty, however, had taught them a lesson: the government would not stand by while the unions shut down the nation's railroads. In fact, if not in law, they had already lost the unqualified right to strike. Hence, by accepting this limitation, they surrendered something they did not really have.

Coolidge's appointees to the Board of Mediation, heavy on the side of undistinguished lame-duck politicians, were nevertheless men of some experience. The Board, whatever its inadequacies, enjoyed remarkable surface success in resolving disputes over new contracts in the late twenties; there was, in fact, only one inconsequential rail strike. The reputation of the Railway Labor Act as "a model labor law" began to emerge. This was as much shadow as substance. At this time, since the unions were weak, there were no major wage movements and so no issues upon which to stage a great dispute.

By contrast, the machinery created by the Act to dispose of grievances arising out of the interpretation and application of contracts proved an almost total failure. The language of the statute concealed without resolving a fundamental disagreement between the unions and the carriers. The former sought to restore the national boards of adjustment that the government had imposed during the war; the latter were determined to maintain system boards. The real issue was the role company unions would be permitted to play in the disposition of grievances. With national adjustment boards the trade unions would win statutory recognition of their status and thereby freeze out the dominated organizations; with system boards the antiunion railroads would preserve a function for their company unions.

Section 3 declared that the adjustment boards "shall be created by agreement between any carrier or carriers as a whole, and its or their employees." With this permissive language the road might simply refrain from reaching agreement on national boards. If the parties did agree, they were to refer grievances that remained unsettled locally to a bipartisan adjustment board, which would hear and decide the matter, its award to be final and binding. The capstone of the carriers' victory was the last paragraph of Section 3: "Nothing in this Act shall be construed to prohibit an individual carrier and its employees from agreeing upon the settlement of disputes through such machinery of contract and adjustment as they may mutually establish." Under this language it was lawful for a railroad to create a grievance machinery with its company union, leaving the trade union out in the cold.

The Railway Labor Act represented no advance in the handling of grievances. No national boards of adjustment were created; some roads refused even to establish system boards; and those local boards that were activated worked out poorly. As a consequence, thousands of individual grievances remained unsettled in the late twenties, festering sources of employee dissatisfaction.[7] In the spring of 1929, the frustrated unions launched a legislative program to amend the statute.

5

Despite its deficiencies with respect to representation and grievances, the Railway Labor Act provided a carefully articulated arrangement for dealing with contract disputes in an important industry. The contrast with the statutory machinery for the remainder of the economy was dramatic. The only other federal legislation was a sentence in the Act of 1913 establishing the Department of Labor: "The Secretary of Labor shall have power to act as mediator and to appoint commissioners of conciliation in labor disputes whenever in his judgment the interests of industrial peace may require it to be done." At first, the Secretary had asked Labor Department personnel to conciliate as an incident to their main duties. The mounting pressure of disputes during the war led to the creation of the United States Conciliation Service in 1917 under the direction of Hugh L. Kerwin, who was still director in

1929. The volume of work tapered off during the twenties. From a peak of 1780 cases in 1919, it fell to 370 in 1922 and never exceeded 559 during the balance of the decade. Kerwin's staff in 1927 consisted of only thirty-eight commissioners.

The Conciliation Service operated in a purely voluntary capacity; it entered a dispute only with the agreement of both parties and could bring no legal pressures to bear in producing a settlement. A major problem in the twenties was the failure of employers to accept the Service. In addition to a general antipathy toward collective bargaining, many employers were suspicious of the Service. This was, in part, due to its location in the Labor Department, which was legally responsible for promoting the welfare of wage earners, and, for the rest, to the fact that many conciliators were former trade-union officials.

Thirty-two states and three territories had statutes providing in one fashion or another for mediation, compulsory investigation, and arbitration, most enacted prior to 1900. In the late twenties, except in three states, these laws were of no consequence. They were seldom invoked and the boards they created did not function. In fact, in 1927 the states expended only one third as much money on conciliation and arbitration as they had in 1899, without discounting for inflation. Only New York, Massachusetts, and Pennsylvania made any pretense of activity, and New York's budget, much the largest, was but $23,000 in 1928. These states alone employed full-time mediators. Further, the Massachusetts board was mainly an arbitration agency under agreements in the boot and shoe industry. Colorado's machinery, if not active, was at least unique. As an outgrowth of the coal war of 1913–14 and Mackenzie King's influence, the state enacted a statute in 1915 patterned after the Canadian Industrial Disputes Investigation Act. Briefly, it prohibited strikes in public-interest industries pending investigation and report by the Industrial Commission, with criminal penalties for violations. The statute was invoked frequently during and after World War I in face of bitter labor opposition, but saw little use in the twenties. It was, in fact, more valuable to politicians seeking campaign issues than to the cause of industrial peace. "All told," Witte concluded, "the work of the state adjustment agencies must be put down as negligible."[8]

# 6

The state criminal syndicalism laws, the last of the labor relations statutes to be considered, were no more important as the decade drew to a close. Twenty states, mainly in the West, as well as Alaska and Hawaii, enacted these laws between 1917 and 1920. They aimed squarely at the IWW (though used somewhat against the Communists) since the pressure came from those industries into which the Wobblies had penetrated. Although the AFL neither introduced nor endorsed them, it is significant that Federation affiliates in nine states and the two territories expressed no opposition. The definition of criminal syndicalism was the key and that in the Idaho statute, the first to be passed, was typical: "Criminal syndicalism is the doctrine which advocates crime, sabotage, violence, or unlawful methods of terrorism as a means of accomplishing industrial or political reform. The advocacy of such doctrine, whether by word of mouth or writing, is a felony. . . ." The purpose of the laws was not to prevent acts of violence or the overthrow of the government; existing legislation adequately disposed of these matters. Rather, they made advocacy alone a crime and made it easy to obtain a conviction. Despite this loose and ambiguous language, the statutes were universally upheld in the state courts, and the Supreme Court of the United States in *Whitney v. California* ruled that the California statute did not contravene the Fourteenth Amendment. The criminal syndicalism statutes undoubtedly contributed to the collapse of the IWW during the twenties; there is no evidence that they had any impact upon the trade unions.[9]

# 7

The frustrations that unions faced with the law of labor relations in the late twenties were shared by workers, organized and unorganized, with respect to social legislation. This was the case with laws regulating hours of work, minimum wages, and child labor, with insurance against such hazards of an industrial society as old age and unemployment, with the organization of the labor market, and with the administration of relief.[10]

Legislation limiting the hours women might work originated in New Hampshire in 1847, and several other states followed her example in the next sixty years. In 1903, Oregon enacted a statute providing that "no female [shall] be employed in any mechanical establishment, or factory, or laundry in this State more than ten hours during any one day." Joe Haselbock, overseer of Curt Muller's Grand Laundry in Portland, caused Mrs. E. Gotcher to work in excess of ten hours on September 4, 1905. Haselbock was fined $10 for violating the maximum-hours law, and the conviction was upheld by the state Supreme Court. An appeal was taken to the Supreme Court of the United States in *Muller* v. *Oregon,* which came down in 1908. The case was remarkable both for its method and its result. Muller contended that the law was an unconstitutional deprivation of liberty of contract under the Fourteenth Amendment. Brandeis, retained as counsel by Oregon, hinged his argument upon the police power and supported it with the first of his revolutionary social and economic briefs. He devoted only two pages to constitutional reasoning and more than a hundred to a factual demonstration that long hours impaired the health, safety, and morals of working women. Of the latter, Justice David J. Brewer observed for a unanimous court, "we take judicial cognizance." Liberty of contract was a right protected by the Fourteenth Amendment, but it was not an absolute right. The state under its police power might restrict freedom of contract in order to protect citizens unable to look after themselves. Woman's "physical structure and a proper discharge of her maternal functions — having in view not merely her own health but the well-being of the race — justify legislation to protect her from the greed as well as the passion of man."

Within the next five years, thirty-nine states either enacted new legislation or bettered laws already on the books. California, for example, with no prior regulation, in 1911 established the eight-hour day and forty-eight-hour week for women, a radical innovation for the time. The movement, however, came to a virtual halt during the twenties. No new state entered the field after 1921 and the only significant improvement came in New York. Governor

Smith, after a fierce struggle for the eight-hour day, reluctantly signed a compromise bill in 1927 providing for maximums of nine daily, forty-nine and one half weekly, and seventy-eight hours of overtime annually. There was, of course, no federal regulation.

Legislation restricting the hours men might work — given the hostility of the AFL and the constitutional impediments — was a crazy quilt. A few states had general laws stating the number of hours in a day's work, but they seldom provided penalties and, even then, were rarely enforced. The only significant limitations were those aimed at specific occupational groups. An act of Congress of 1912 required the insertion of an eight-hour restriction in all contracts of employment to which the federal government was a party, excepting emergencies, transportation, and the purchase of supplies in the open market. By 1929 more than half the states and many municipalities had similar eight-hour limits for their public works contracts. The constitutionality of this legislation had been upheld by the Supreme Court in 1903 in *Atkin* v. *Kansas* on the ground that there could be no freedom of contract where the government was a party. "The work being of a public character, absolutely under the control of the State and its municipal agents acting by its authority, it is for the State to prescribe the conditions under which it will permit work of that kind to be done."

Regulation of men's hours in private employment was confined to transportation and hazardous occupations. About half the states for reasons of safety fixed a maximum of sixteen hours daily for operating employees on trains, street railways, and elevated lines. More important was the Adamson Act of 1916, by which Congress established the basic eight-hour day on interstate railroads, with overtime at time and one half following in 1919. The La Follette Seamen's Act of 1915 in a limited way regulated hours: while a vessel was in port nine hours was to be a day's work and seamen could not be required to perform unnecessary work on Sundays and holidays. During the twenties, due to the collapse of the sailors' union, enforcement virtually ceased. The courts sustained the state statutes as a proper exercise of the police power and the federal laws under the commerce clause.

Fifteen states and Alaska passed laws prior to 1922 imposing the eight-hour day in mining. Although these jurisdictions contained coal and metal mines, such leading bituminous states as Pennsylvania, West Virginia, Kentucky, Illinois, Alabama, and Ohio enacted no protective legislation. In some this was because dominant antiunion employers prevented its passage and in others because the UMW was able to maintain the eight-hour day by economic strength without governmental assistance. Constitutionality had been settled in *Holden* v. *Hardy* in 1898. "It is as much for the interest of the state," the court declared in sustaining the Utah statute, "that public health should be preserved as that life should be made secure." Underground miners, deprived of fresh air and sunlight and exposed to noxious gases and high temperatures, deserved state protection by virtue of the hazard of their employment.

The constitutionality of legislation regulating hours of men in industries other than transportation and mining, however, was in the gravest doubt. In 1905 the court by a vote of five to four in *Lochner* v. *New York* had nullified a New York law limiting men's hours in bakeries to ten as repugnant to the Fourteenth Amendment. Oregon, nevertheless, enacted a general ten-hour statute in 1913. Four years later in *Bunting* v. *Oregon* the court, five to three (Brandeis abstaining), surprisingly sustained the law under the police power without, however, explicitly overruling Lochner. While some authorities argued that Bunting was now the law (Lochner, in Holmes's phrase, was enjoying "a deserved repose"), others contended that it was not. Since no state followed Oregon with a general limitation on men's hours, the twenties closed without a test of this constitutional issue.[11]

## 8

The minimum-wage movement had its origins in the Progressive Era. The impetus came, in part, from a series of governmental and private investigations which revealed shockingly low wages for women ("the poor working girl") and minors and, for the rest, from the legislative example of Australia (1896) and Great Britain (1909). The campaign, which began in 1910, was led by middle-class reformist groups determined to extirpate a social evil: the National Consumers' League, the American Association for Labor Legislation, Father John A. Ryan's Catholic welfare group, the Women's Bureau, and the women's clubs. Excepting mainly the Women's Trade Union League, which was hardly a union, organized labor was either indifferent or hostile.

The movement won immediate and quite spectacular success. Between 1912 and 1917, twelve states (Massachusetts, California, Colorado, Minnesota, Nebraska, Oregon, Utah, Washington, Wisconsin, Arkansas, Kansas, and Arizona) enacted statutes. Their constitutionality, a critical question, was upheld by a delicate equilibrium in 1917. The Supreme Court, by a vote of four to four, failed to overrule a favorable decision of the Oregon Supreme Court; Brandeis did not participate because he had earlier served as counsel for the state. With this mixed blessing, five additional jurisdictions passed laws: the District of Columbia, North Dakota, Texas, Puerto Rico, and South Dakota. Excepting the last, all these enactments antedated 1920. By this date, the movement had spent itself, as the decisive defeat it suffered in Ohio in the early twenties amply demonstrated.

The fundamental purpose of this legislation was to invoke the power of the state to guarantee "a living wage" to sweated female wage earners. The rates of adult males were excluded from regulation — a departure from the Australian and British experience — because of the objection of the AFL to government intervention in the area which it sought to pre-empt and because of fear that the courts would nullify such legislation covering private employment as an interference with the liberty guaranteed by the Fourteenth Amendment. The sponsors hoped that regulation limited to females would be sustained as a proper exercise of the police power on the grounds that women had little bargaining power and that their health as future mothers, in effect, made them wards of the state. The fact that this argument had proved persuasive to the Supreme Court in the Muller case was a source of encouragement.

Despite a common aim, the minimum-wage laws differed markedly in method. Most of the states adopted the tripartite commission plan for fixing rates; the commission, acting either upon its own motion or upon the recommendation of a subsidiary tripartite industry wage board, set the minimums. In Utah, Arkansas, Arizona, South Dakota, and Puerto Rico, however, the legislature fixed the rates in the statute. This so-called flat-rate form failed to provide for changes in the cost of living, was generally accompanied by ineffective administration, and made no provision for apprentices and substandard workers. All the commission laws defined the living wage in only the most generalized terms; the District of Columbia commission, for example, was enjoined by Congress to fix a wage sufficient to maintain women in good health and to protect their morals. In practice, the labor and employer members submitted alternative standard-of-living budgets for a single working female and proposed rates to fulfill them; the commission then bargained out a compromise. In Massachusetts, Nebraska, and Colorado, the commissions were required to take account of the financial condition of the industry as well as the living wage. The resulting minimums were never generous, "just enough," Walter Lippmann wrote in 1915, "to secure existence amid drudgery in gray boarding houses and cheap restaurants." Moreover, in the race with the 1915–20 inflation the commissions, to say nothing of the flat rates, came out a bad second. With the exception of Massachusetts, the laws made failure by the employer to comply a misdemeanor punishable by fine or imprisonment.

This legislation, despite its shortcomings, was a bold forward step, but one that was brought to a jolting halt by the Supreme Court's ruling in *Adkins* v. *Children's Hospital* in 1923. This decision, perhaps the most important handed down in a labor case in the decade, can conservatively be characterized as extraordinary — extraordinary in the fortuitous succession of events that led to the result, in the reasoning of the court, in the opinion of the Chief Justice, and in the shock it produced.

The court by a vote of five to three declared the District of Columbia minimum-wage law for women unconstitutional, Brandeis once again abstaining. According to Thomas Reed Powell, if the case had come up in the preceding term, as it should have, the law would have been upheld five to three. The illness of a lower-court judge caused the delay. Meantime, Harding made three appointments to the Supreme Court, including Sutherland, the author of the Adkins opinion. It is a remarkable fact that of the judges at all levels of the federal judiciary who ruled on the constitutionality of minimum-wage legislation, thirty-two voted to sustain and only nine to void. Five of those nine constituted the decisive majority in the Adkins case. "Only because in the final vote some heads rather than others are the ones to be counted," Powell wrote, "is minimum-wage legislation invalid." No better demonstration could be found of the proposition that the Constitution was what the judges said it was. And what they said reflected their basic social outlook.

George Sutherland, a legal craftsman of a very high order, had drunk deeply at the fountain of Herbert Spencer's individualism. He stood apart from his conservative colleagues, J. F. Paschal has said, in that he was "a man of ideas . . . a man with a theory," to which he adhered rigorously. He exhibited no interest in competing theories of society and none in the economic and social facts of the times. "The idea of government which was the moving influence in Sutherland's life was based on his conviction that the individual is, in a sense, the only political reality." The enhancement of individual freedom was good, its limitation bad. Freedom was to be achieved simply by "reducing governmental restraint to an absolute minimum." The ultimate arbiter was the judiciary. Hence the duty of the judge was to preserve the liberties of the individual by confining the activities of the state as, in his reading of it, the Constitution dictated.

Sutherland could find no arbitrary grounds for discriminating between individuals as to the liberties they were to enjoy. As a senator from Utah in 1916, he had spoken vigorously for women's suffrage. The female half of society should share equally with the male in the right to contract, to hold property, to receive an education, and to vote.

The Adkins case presented Sutherland with an unchallenged opportunity to set forth his philosophy at the very outset of his judicial career. The facts were of the plainest sort. The Minimum Wage Commission of the District of Columbia sought to enforce the act of Congress of 1918 against the Children's Hospital, which employed a large number of women, some at less than the lawful rate. The hospital responded that the statute was an unconstitutional deprivation of its "liberty" without "due process of law" in contravention of the Fifth Amendment. Since the Fourteenth Amendment contained identical language with respect to the states, a finding of unconstitutionality of federal regulation under the Fifth Amendment would lead to the nullification of the state laws under the Fourteenth. The stakes, indeed, were high.

Sutherland began by doffing his hat to Congress, the constitutionality of whose acts was a matter of "great gravity and delicacy." Legislation must receive "every possible presumption" of validity until "overcome beyond rational doubt." Since the justice had no doubt whatever, he did not tarry to draw the line between rationality and irrationality. The "liberty" guaranteed by the Fifth Amendment was the blade edge of his guillotine. It was "no longer open to question" that the right to contract was part of "the liberty of the individual protected by this clause." This right embraced contracts of employment. In making employment contracts, "the parties have an equal right to obtain from each other the best terms they can as the result of private bargaining." The Children's Hospital, therefore, was free to engage a female at a wage rate which, in the judgment of Congress, was deleterious to her health and morals and she was equally free to seek employment at that rate.

The statute, Sutherland argued, was nothing more than a price-fixing device, setting a price upon the labor of wage earners who were capable of doing so themselves. To the extent that the sum exceeded "the fair value of the services rendered," it was an exaction upon an innocent employer to support "a partially indigent person" for whose condition he bore "no peculiar responsibility." This arbitrary payment had "no causal connection with his business." The requirement of a contract of employment was that "the amount to be paid and the service to be rendered shall bear to each other some relation of just equivalence." This, the statute "completely ignored" and in so doing was "a naked, arbitrary exercise of power." In his mind there was "no difference between the case of selling labor and the case of selling goods."

Thus far Sutherland felt himself on solid ground. He could not, however, ignore the uncomfortable fact that the court in the Muller case had sustained the Oregon law regulating the maximum number of hours women worked. If that statute had been before him, he would, presumably, have found it in contravention of the Fourteenth Amendment. Unfortunately, it was not and he bore the burden of explaining it away. Sutherland's argument was both novel and ingenious. The "ancient inequality" between the sexes had diminished with growing speed. Since 1908, "revolutionary changes" had occurred, culminating in the adoption of the Nineteenth Amendment. By 1923 the differences had almost reached "the vanishing point." Hence women no longer needed "restrictions upon their liberty of contract which could not lawfully be imposed in the case of men."

Finally, to the argument that social justice demanded this legislation, Sutherland responded that the common good would be exalted rather than struck down by sustaining "the individual freedom of action contemplated by the Constitution." The welfare of society as a whole could not be better served than by preserving "against arbitrary restraint . . . the liberties of its constituent members."

This was too much for Taft. Despite his deep-seated objection to dissenting opinions ("I regret much to differ from the Court"), the Chief Justice was constrained to write one in which Sanford joined. He could not see how regulation of wages could be unconstitutional when regulation of hours was valid. "One is the multiplier and the other the multiplicand." That is, "*Muller* v. *Oregon* . . . controls this case."

To Holmes fell the task of meeting Sutherland head on, and his dissent in the Adkins case must surely be placed among the masterpieces of his opinions. Grounds for "rational doubt" were abundant. Legislators in Australia, Britain, and the federal and state governments of the United States had seen fit to enact minimum-wage laws. "When so many intelligent persons, who have studied the matter more than any of us can, have thought that the means are effective and are worth the price, it seems to me impossible to deny that the belief reasonably may be held by reasonable men."

The sole basis for the court's decision had been found by Sutherland within "the vague contours of the Fifth Amendment," in fact, in the word "liberty." "That innocuous generality was expanded into the dogma, Liberty of Contract." Yet the word "contract" could nowhere be found in either the Fifth or the Fourteenth Amendment, but had been read into them by the courts. Liberty of contract, clearly, was not an absolute right. "Pretty much all law consists in forbidding men to do some things that they want to do, and contract is no more exempt from law than other acts." Holmes proceeded to list a long series of restrictions upon freedom of contract that the court itself had approved, including Sunday laws that "prohibit practically all contracts during one-seventh of our whole life" as well as statutes fixing "the size of a loaf of bread."

Holmes, like Taft, disinterred the body of the Muller decision that Sutherland had so carefully buried. Regulation of hours was as much an infringement of liberty of contract as regulation of wages. "The bargain is equally affected whichever half you regulate." As to the argument that the differential between the sexes had been wiped out between 1908 and 1923: "It will need more than the Nineteenth Amendment to convince me that there are no differences between men and women." (One might add, as he did not, that females resident in the District of Columbia did not even enjoy the suffrage conferred upon their sex by that amendment.)

Holmes was no more persuaded that the statute, by fixing a price for labor above its "fair value," was an arbitrary exaction. The law compelled no employer to pay anything. He had several alternatives. If he chose the one of employing females, he was only then required to pay them wages at a level of health and morality.

Holmes, whose economic predilections differed little from Sutherland's, had "my doubts" about whether the law would work. That, however, "is not for me to decide."

The Adkins decision, Powell wrote, "has evoked a more nearly unanimous chorus of disapproval than any other decision in years." Mary Anderson of the Labor Department called it a "calamity." Gompers declared that "to buy the labor of a woman is now like buying pig's feet in a butcher shop." The law reviews were filled with articles attacking the decision. Powell, whose views were typical, observed that under slavery the master had to support the slave. This system ended with the Thirteenth Amendment. Now the Fourteenth Amendment protected the employer "in getting labor for less than the cost of producing it." Amid this clangor of dissent, Sutherland heard at least one sweet note. Old seafarer Andy Furuseth, the purest and simplest of the trade unionists, wrote, "Those who have enjoyed freedom ... can not understand the real meaning of bondage, and are likely to hold out their hands for shackles."

The collapse of the edifice raised by the minimum-wage movement followed inexorably. The Supreme Court held the Arizona law unconstitutional in 1925; the same year the Kansas Supreme Court ruled that state's statute invalid; in 1927 the Supreme Court of the United States nullified the Arkansas law. Numerous lower courts, following the Adkins case, voided much of the remainder of the legislation. The legislature of Utah in 1929 repealed its law. Though a few of the statutes remained on the books, they were dead letters.[12] The sole survivor amidst the wreckage was the Massachusetts law, and no more eloquent testimonial to its ineffectiveness could be provided than the case of the Harvard charwomen.

9

Mrs. Emma Trafton, Mrs. Katherine Donahue, Mrs. Annie McIntyre, Mrs. Hannah Hogan, Mrs. H. Sullivan, Miss Catherine Donlon, Mrs. H. Malloy, and thirteen others, all scrubwomen in the Widener Library, were fired without notice by Harvard University a few days before Christmas, 1929. Their seniority ranged from two to thirty-three years. The Reverend W. M. Duvall of the Trinity Community Methodist Episcopal Church in the slums of East Cambridge, where Mrs. Trafton lived, wrote in protest to America's richest university. He pointed out that Mrs. Trafton was the sole support for her five children. President A. Lawrence Lowell replied that the cause of the action was a complaint by the Massachusetts Minimum Wage Commission that Harvard had failed to pay the lawful minimum of 37 cents per hour for female building cleaners. Mrs. Trafton and her fellow scrubwomen received 35 cents. Rather than pay the added 2 cents, Harvard discharged the ladies and replaced them with men, whose wages were not subject to state regulation. Three or four of the women received jobs as dormitory chambermaids, also excluded from coverage under the wage orders. One university building, however, did meet the legal minimum. The Fogg Art Museum paid its scrubwomen 37 cents: 35 cents contributed by Harvard and 2 cents by an anonymous alumnus.

A group of fifty-two alumni on March 16, 1930, denounced the university as "harsh, stingy, socially insensitive, and considerably short of the highest ethical standards of the time." Heywood Broun, who had spent four years at Harvard, though his scholarship failed to qualify him as an alumnus, was stirred by memories of the Old Crimson football song. "Well, Mrs. Katherine Donahue has had thirty-three years of sweeping. One might suppose at the end of that time she would have passed the last chalk line and landed in some haven of honor or security." In May 1930 the Harvard Square Deal Association announced a fund-raising ball to pay back wages to the scrubwomen. Only forty attended because, so the Association claimed, the business houses in Harvard Square refused to accept advertising. Nevertheless, a group of 268 students and alumni, headed by Corliss Lamont, son of a Morgan partner and an instructor of philosophy at Columbia, raised $3880. On the day before Christmas 1930, each of the ex-scrubwomen received a savings bank account book with the amount due her under the law. Lamont took especial care to impress upon the ladies that this was money earned and not charity.

Thus ended the affair of the Harvard scrubwomen. Its significance, aside from the women and Harvard's public relations, lay in what was revealed about the nature and enforcement of regulatory labor legislation in the twenties.

Massachusetts had been the proud pioneer in minimum-wage legislation for women and children, enacting her law in 1912. This statute was unique in that the wage decrees were merely recommendatory, depending for enforcement upon a public opinion aroused by publication of the violator's name in the newspapers. "Sentiments of decency or of vanity," Powell wrote, "may move the niggardly to mend their ways, but the recalcitrant are left free to bargain as they can and will."

Harvard's case was illustrative of both the procedure and its effectiveness. In 1920 the Minimum Wage Commission had held hearings at the State House on a proposed raise in the rate for female office and building cleaners from 30 to 37 cents. The only opposition came from a representative of the university, who claimed that the increase could not be managed within the already determined budget for the next half year. The Commission, nevertheless, ordered the 37-cent rate effective February 1, 1921. Harvard's half year, apparently, was of indefinite duration, for at no time during the decade did it meet the legal requirement. The Commission showed little more regard for its own decree, for it did nothing for seven years. In 1928 the agency at last urged the university to comply. Harvard responded that the scrubwomen received a twenty-minute daily rest period that was the equivalent of at least 2 cents per hour, an argument that could hardly be accepted. Finally, on December 18, 1929, the Commission notified Harvard that it would be publicly branded as a violator on December 26 unless its rates were raised to the lawful minimum. This led to the mass discharge.

Actually, the Massachusetts law was a joke. The National Industrial Conference Board, hardly a prolabor organization, in 1927 published an exhaustive study of its operation with devastating conclusions. Complying employers suffered competitively alongside those who defied. The machinery of administration was so cumbersome that it took twelve years to fix the wages of 85,000 females, leaving double that number uncovered. The Commission was so understaffed and inadequately financed that it was hopelessly behind in the inspections needed for enforcement. The law "has not provided incomes sufficient to maintain an adequate standard of living for the bulk of gainfully employed women. . . ." There was little evidence that the orders had raised wages in the covered occupations; decrees followed rather than preceded wage movements. Employers met the minimums when they were below going rates, the usual situation, and simply refused to comply when they were higher. "The fact remains," the Conference Board study concluded, "that . . . since 1914 . . . the general level of wages in these occupations is just about where it would have been had there been no wage law." [13]

●

10

The phase of social legislation that evoked the greatest public sympathy as well as the greatest frustration was child labor. Virtually everyone paid lip service to the demonstrable facts that the employment of children deprived them of education at incalculable social cost, disrupted family life, encouraged vice and crime, lifted the incidence of accidents and illness, induced adult unemployment, and undermined the wage structure. Yet, as President Hoover's White House Conference on Child Labor pointed out in 1930, a century of regulatory activity had produced seriously defective state laws whose enforcement, especially in the areas of greatest need, was appalling. More than one million children between the ages of ten and fifteen were counted as gainfully employed in the census of 1920. They concentrated particularly in agriculture, manufacturing (especially textiles and glass), the street trades, and industrial homework.

Regulation was a complicated task, necessitating the establishment of a minimum age for employment, a compulsory period of education to precede entry into the labor market, a maximum number of hours of work, as well as protection against hazardous and unhealthful occupations. All the states had laws that dealt with one or more of these factors. The National Child Labor Committee, founded in 1904, had been responsible for much of this legislation.

Because of the diversity in standards and the inadequacy of the state laws, the Committee in 1914 began a campaign for federal regulation. Success came almost at once. In 1916 Congress, over the opposition of only southern textile mills and the NAM, enacted the first child labor law by overwhelming majorities. It forbade the shipment in interstate commerce of goods produced in factories or canneries that employed youngsters under fourteen, employed children between fourteen and sixteen more than eight hours daily or six days weekly, or employed them between 7 P.M. and 6 A.M. The law also prohibited interstate commerce in the products of mines employing children under sixteen.

The child labor law had a brief career. Nine months after it took

effect, the Supreme Court by five to four in *Hammer* v. *Dagenhart*
held it unconstitutional. The only matter was whether the statute
was an appropriate exercise of congressional power under the
commerce clause. The Child Labor Committee had hinged constitutionality upon commerce because the court had recently sustained regulation of lotteries, impure foods and drugs, and the
white slave traffic with this authority. Justice William R. Day, in
his opinion for the court, distinguished these cases on "the character of the particular subjects dealt with." Gambling tickets,
poisoned foods, and prostitutes were inherently evil; the goods produced by children in factories and mines were "of themselves
harmless." The object of Congress was not to control the movement
of interstate commerce but "to regulate the hours of labor of
children . . . within the States, a purely state authority." If Congress under the commerce power could forbid the employment of
children, as Day saw it, "our system of government [would] be
practically destroyed."

Holmes, in dissent (speaking also for McKenna, Brandeis, and
Clarke), argued that the Act simply prohibited the movement of
certain goods in interstate commerce. "Congress is given power to
regulate such commerce in unqualified terms." Hence whether the
articles conveyed were good or evil was immaterial. "But if there
is any matter upon which civilized countries have agreed . . . it is
the evil of premature and excessive child labor." Extraneous
matters aside, the statute "does not meddle with anything be-
longing to the States," concerning itself exclusively with articles
that cross state lines. "Under the Constitution such commerce
belongs not to the States but to Congress to regulate."

The friends of child labor legislation devoted the following
decade to a strenuous effort to circumvent *Hammer* v. *Dagenhart*, an endeavor that was to end in total failure. In 1918, with
similarly big majorities, Congress re-enacted the substantive provisions of the first law, but hitched to them a 10 per cent tax on the
net profits of a mining or manufacturing establishment which
failed to comply. The court, with only Clarke dissenting, held this
statute invalid in *Bailey* v. *Drexel Furniture Co.* in 1922 as an
unconstitutional exercise of the taxing power. Congress might enact
a tax with the combined purposes of raising revenue and restrain-

ing unwanted activities; it had no authority, in Taft's words, "to give such magic to the word 'tax'" as to impose a levy whose exclusive object was to penalize.

It was now certain, given the composition of the court, that no federal regulation could clear the constitutional barrier. Hence the proponents turned reluctantly to their last recourse, constitutional amendment. In 1924 they persuaded both houses of Congress to adopt the child labor amendment by more than the needed two-thirds majority. It provided that "Congress shall have power to limit, regulate, and prohibit the labor of persons under 18 years of age." State legislation was to remain unimpaired "except that the operation of State laws shall be suspended to the extent necessary to give effect to legislation enacted by the Congress." The legislative history of the amendment ominously foreshadowed its fate. A new voice had been heard in opposition at the hearings: the American Farm Bureau Federation. The attack took on vicious overtones. Opponents, gathered into something called the Sentinels of the Republic, denounced the amendment as a subversive scheme by Socialists and Communists to destroy states' rights and to make the American child the property of the federal government. Such prominent citizens as Cardinal O'Connell of Boston, who spoke with the decisive weight of the Church in a predominantly Catholic community, President Lowell of Harvard, and President Butler of Columbia joined the enemies of ratification. In the frigid climate of the late twenties the campaign got hopelessly stuck in the ice. By 1929 only Arkansas, Arizona, California, Wisconsin, and Montana had ratified; thirty-five states, as of the end of 1932, had rejected the amendment. Except in a handful of states with adequate laws and honest enforcement, children at this time enjoyed little protection in the labor market.[14]

11

Persons at the other end of the age scale made only slight gains. For old age pensions this was a period of gestation. The first law to survive, interestingly enough, had been enacted in Alaska in 1915. In the early twenties the Fraternal Order of Eagles joined forces with the American Association for Labor Legislation to draft a model state bill providing a pension of not over one dollar a day for persons of age seventy the value of whose property did not exceed $3000. Administration, following the historic basis of care for the indigent aged, was to be lodged with the counties. The Eagles undertook an aggressive legislative campaign which achieved results in 1923, when Nevada, Pennsylvania, and Montana passed county-option laws. Nevada's system, however, remained inoperative and Pennsylvania's statute was held unconstitutional. In Montana the counties gradually entered the program. Shortly thereafter several states appointed study commissions, and still other legislatures passed pension bills which governors vetoed. The Wisconsin law of 1925 induced counties to participate by offering state reimbursement for one third of the cost. The following year Kentucky joined the pension states, but her system did not become operative. In 1927 Colorado and Maryland entered the field, the former sharing Kentucky's difficulty.

The year 1929 was a turning point. By this date a new organization, the American Association for Old Age Security, had been added to those bringing pressure to bear. At its Toronto convention the AFL for the first time endorsed old age pension legislation, a sharp deviation from Gompers' voluntarism, led, to the amazement of his detractors, by Matthew Woll. Bills were introduced in twenty-eight legislatures; California, Utah, Wyoming, and Minnesota passed them. Even more important was the fact that the first three of these states made their systems mandatory upon the counties. Finally, Governor Roosevelt of New York placed his full weight behind the demand for legislation.

Despite this progress, the old age pension movement was hardly more than incipient. In 1928, for example, only 1221 persons in the United States received pensions and their aggregate benefits came to a mere $222,559. Perhaps the most important lessons that had been learned were that pensions were cheaper than almshouses and that county option made no sense administratively.

The experience with unemployment compensation was even more discouraging. At the time of the crash neither the federal government nor the states had a program and, in fact, Wisconsin was the only jurisdiction in which the issue had been seriously debated. During the hard times of 1921, Professor John R. Commons of the state university had drafted a bill which received the support of the Wisconsin Federation of Labor and the Progressives in the legislature. Though it was introduced at every session, opposition by employers assured its defeat. America's workers, unlike those in other western nations, faced the Great Depression with no public protection whatever against the hazards of unemployment.

12

The legal status of employment exchanges was almost as bad. To the extent that the disorganization that characterized the American labor market in the twenties could be called a system, it was dominated by private, fee-collecting exchanges. In 1930 there were 1036 in New York City, 315 in Chicago, and 191 in Philadelphia. All impartial students of the problem agreed that private agencies must be subjected to the most rigid regulation, a view shared by the International Labor Office. Frequently run by crooks, these exchanges were distinguished for such practices as misrepresentation of wages, extortionate fees, kickbacks to foremen, inducement of discharges to increase business, white slavery, and blacklisting of union members. Most of the states had imposed regulation to remove some of these abuses, but it ran onto constitutional shoals. In 1917 the Supreme Court, five to four, had held a Washington statute that prohibited the collection of fees from a worker a deprivation of the liberty guaranteed by the Fourteenth Amendment. More serious, in 1928, despite a ringing dissent by Stone for himself, Holmes, and Brandeis, the court on the same grounds invalidated a New Jersey law which merely regulated the fees charged by private agencies.

The public side was equally deplorable. To meet the wartime demand for labor, the United States Employment Service had been greatly expanded in 1917–18 under the constitutional shelter of the President's war powers. It operated 773 offices in all the states and the District of Columbia. In the fiscal year 1918–19, it received more than 10 million job openings, registered over 6 million workers, and placed about 5 million of them. Despite this impressive record, the collapse of USES was as rapid as its growth. The upheaval in the labor market and merciless attacks by the NAM combined to reduce the agency to a shadow by 1921. During the twenties it served largely as an asylum for fifth-rate Republican job-seekers. Its statistical reports were a scandal. Its constructive functions consisted of running a farm labor bureau in Kansas City and disbursing modest subsidies to the states for their exchanges. In each Congress beginning with 1919 a bill was presented to reorganize USES on an effective basis, a proposal that never came close to passage. In June 1929, Frances Perkins, the New York Industrial Commissioner, designated an advisory committee of prominent citizens, headed by Arthur Young of Industrial Relations Counselors, Inc., to help devise a policy for a public employment service for the state.[15]

## 13

The final aspect of social legislation was that covering relief for the victims of unemployment. The state of the law in 1929 could well be described as archaic; its origins lay in the English Poor Law of 1601, transplanted shortly thereafter to the American colonies. The theory was that poverty was a disgraceful condition because it was rooted in shiftlessness. Many communities required persons on relief to take a pauper's oath; as late as 1934, the constitutions of fourteen states deprived them of the right to vote or hold office; a generally held view was that relief should be disagreeable in order to induce recipients to get jobs.

The responsibility for administration was lodged with local governments, a notion embedded in the common law and supported by state statutes and constitutions. The Illinois poor law was typical:

> The overseers of the poor shall have the care and oversight of such persons in their town or precinct as are unable to earn a livelihood in consequence of any bodily infirmity, idiocy, lunacy, or other unavoidable cause and are not supported by their

relatives or at the county poorhouse, subject to such restrictions and regulations as may be prescribed by the county board or by the town.

It was a virtual certainty that the officials in charge were not trained social workers. In six states administration was in the hands of the police and the courts; in rural areas it was usually a side issue for busy public officers; in cities dominated by political machines it was a means of buying votes. Local administrators, naturally enough, were concerned only with the welfare of residents of their own towns; indigent transients had no right to relief.

The federal government was presumed to bear no obligation, legal or moral, for unemployment relief. The prevailing constitutional interpretation had been expressed by President Franklin Pierce in 1854, when he vetoed a bill granting federal public lands to the states in order to assist the insane. Pierce argued that care for the indigent of all classes was an exclusive local responsibility and that the general welfare clause gave Congress no authority to invade this pre-empted area. Though occasional appropriations were made for disasters, efforts to get federal unemployment relief in 1893–94, 1914, and 1921–22 met with failure. In September 1921, for example, President Harding had called a conference on unemployment staged by Commerce Secretary Hoover which, though it urged compensatory public works, on relief simply reaffirmed the principle of local responsibility and called upon the mayors for action.

The persistent joblessness of the twenties, nonetheless, caused a new tendency whose significance was missed by most contemporary observers. Particularly in larger communities, a rising proportion of expenditures for unemployment relief was made by public rather than private agencies. Since some cities by the end of the decade were expending substantial sums for this purpose, they began to establish welfare departments and to staff them with social workers. Moreover, on April 12, 1929, at the insistence of Governor Roosevelt, New York took the lead in creating the first modern statewide system of relief for the poor. The law divided New York into county and city welfare districts. Officials were charged with the duty of restoring persons unable to maintain themselves to a condition of self-support. In so far as possible, families were to be kept together and relief was to be administered in the home.[16]

## 14

The Supreme Court over which William Howard Taft presided had compiled an impressive record. The "labor faction" was, indeed, "hit every little while." In fact, no prior era in the history of the court approached the twenties in the number of statutes invalidated, most of them labor laws.

Reaction reached its peak in the first half of the decade, when the court faced a heavy docket of cases testing the products of the Progressive and war periods. The year 1925 was a watershed, with Stone's appointment to replace McKenna marking the point at which conservatism began its decline. Thereafter great issues were few and the balance of the court, though still conservative, was more evenly drawn.

Taft's last years, as the mechanics of the Bedford Cut Stone case demonstrated, were bitter. He detested Brandeis and, incredibly, believed Brandeis controlled Holmes's vote. Stone was a traitor; Hoover, interestingly enough, he distrusted as an impossible "Progressive." In the fall of 1929 he wrote Butler that his main hope "is continued life by enough of our present membership . . . to prevent disastrous reversals of our present attitude." His objective, as he remarked to his brother Horace shortly afterward, was "to prevent the Bolsheviki from getting control."

The court in the twenties planted the seed of a great constitutional crisis, surely the greatest since Dred Scott. The central issue would be the challenge of labor's problems to archaic interpretations of the Constitution. Rumblings were already heard: La Follette made a major campaign issue of judicial review in 1924; Senator William E. Borah of Idaho proposed that the vote of seven justices be required to declare a law unconstitutional; disaffection was general and growing in the law schools.

In 1929 the timing of this crisis was uncertain and would hinge upon the outlook for the nation's economy. Continued prosperity would cause delay; economic collapse would hasten its arrival.

President Coolidge sensed trouble. "Poppa," declared his wife, "says there's a depression coming." On Coolidge's last day in the White House in March of 1929, he was visited by his old Amherst friend, Harlan Fiske Stone. They conversed for an unusually long time. As the justice rose to leave, he remarked that Coolidge had been wise not to run again for President because "during the next administration the country would undergo the most serious economic and financial convulsion since 1873." [17] Both Coolidge and Stone were right. That "convulsion," to be known to history as the Great Depression, was shortly to impose monumental burdens upon American labor which, in time, were to lead to a fundamental transformation in labor's status.

# II

## THE GREAT
## DEPRESSION

## CHAPTER 5

# The Country Is Fundamentally Sound

THE REPUBLICAN PARTY nominated Herbert Clark Hoover for President in the summer of 1928. The conditions could not have been more auspicious: peace abroad and prosperity at home. Hoover basked in the sunshine of a friendly press and his candidacy was promoted by experts drawn from the new science of advertising. Variously known as the Great Engineer and the Great Humanitarian, he had the backing of both the Republican organization and voters who admired him because he was "above" politics. His election was a foregone conclusion and the success of his presidency seemed assured.

If a wisp of cloud remained in the sky, Hoover dispelled it in his speech of acceptance of August 11, 1928. The wise policies of his Republican predecessors, he declared, had brought the nation to its present happy state. But the job was not done. Hoover asked the American people under his leadership to essay an even greater task. "One of the oldest and perhaps the noblest of human aspirations has been the abolition of poverty." Undernourishment, cold, and fear of old age could no longer be tolerated. "We in America today are nearer to the final triumph over poverty than ever before in the history of any land. The poorhouse is vanishing from among us. . . . We shall soon . . . be in sight of the day when poverty will be banished from this nation." [1]

1

Hoover's career was an epic of the self-made Horatio Alger hero: from poor orphaned farm boy to millionaire and President. Born in West Branch, Iowa, in 1874, he was exposed in his first years to the burdens and virtues of rural life. At eight, with both parents dead, he was taken into the household of an uncle in Newberg, Oregon. "Here," he later said, "I roamed the primitive forests with their carpets of flowers, their ferns, their never forgettable fragrance. There were no legal limits on the fish you could catch." Bright, vigorous, and ambitious, Hoover chose engineering as his profession and studied at the new Leland Stanford Junior University in Palo Alto. After graduation in 1895, he became a mining engineer and an instant international success. In the years following he surveyed properties and organized companies and syndicates in China, Malaya, Australia, Russia, the Middle East, South Africa, and South America. By 1914 he had accumulated a large fortune and a reputation among the knowledgeable for driving administrative ability. The war made his name a household word, first by his organization of Belgian relief and later by his service as War Food Administrator in the Wilson Administration. A respected and, in some quarters, revered figure, Hoover's qualities stimulated talk in both parties of his availability for the presidency in 1920. Though theretofore politically uncommitted, he declared himself a Republican and spoke out for Harding. His reward was appointment as Secretary of Commerce, an office he held in both the Harding and Coolidge Cabinets. His achievements, which he advertised with extraordinary effectiveness, stood out like a mountain beside the at best pedestrian and at worst malodorous records of his colleagues, excepting, of course, Secretary of State Charles Evans Hughes. His nomination for President by the Kansas City Republican convention of 1928 seemed the inevitable opening of another chapter in the success story of Herbert Hoover and the promise of American life.

The picture the public got of Hoover was of a broad sober face pushing out of a high, stiff white collar. This collar, Thomas L. Stokes remarked, "stood for the sound respectable citizen, the solid businessman, the man who busied himself about community affairs, the orthodox, the conservative." His virtues were obvious: an intellectual capacity to grapple with tough concrete problems, high energy, a tidy sense of organization, probity, an ability to inspire loyalty in subordinates, and an experience of dealing with

large affairs. His defects from a political point of view were disastrous. An essentially shy person, Hoover was formal, reserved,
and solemn in manner. "I must confess," Donald Richberg wrote,
"that I was deeply worried in my early meetings with him, and
often later, by his persistent habit of not looking at one squarely
when in conversation, and of doodling steadily the while." Hoover
was devoid of personal charm, of the beguiling tricks for ingratiat-
ing one's self with another. "He can calculate wave lengths,"
Willmott Lewis commented, "but cannot see color . . . he can
understand vibrations but cannot hear tone." Although not without humor, he gave no sign that he possessed what little he had.
Temperamentally, Hoover was a worrier and had the ability to
confuse his concern over a problem with its solution. In the face
of difficulty, which he had seldom met in his personal life, Hoover's
worrying degenerated into gloom, which he quickly communicated
to others. His skin, for a politician, was unusually thin. His prose
style, in Richard Hofstadter's words, was "suggestive of a light fog
moving over a bleak landscape" ("to unfetter the rehabilitation of
industry, agriculture and unemployment"). Yet he insisted upon
writing his own speeches. This manifested an underlying arro-
gance, an assurance that he could tackle any job no matter how
remote from his talents and knowledge. Hoover was at the same
time doctrinaire; once persuaded that he was right — and he
needed little persuasion — he refused to be shaken. When his ideas
proved wrong in practice, his mind took easy flight to a private
world inhabited by comforting myths. Most serious of all was the
fact that Hoover had neither experience in nor appetite for the
political arts of a democracy. He distrusted the press corps that
followed him about, detested campaigning, feared the crowds that
went with it, and could not mollify an outraged senator.

"In no other land," Hoover declared, "could a boy from a country village without inheritance or influential friends look forward
with unbounded hope. . . . I am indebted to my country beyond
any human power to say." The land he envisioned as his creditor
was governed by the values of nineteenth-century liberalism:
opportunity, hard work, materialism, personal achievement,
and laissez faire. The fulcrum of his system was individualism. "I
emerge . . . an unashamed individualist," he wrote in 1923. Eco-

nomic and political freedom were joined indissolubly: to destroy one was to destroy the other. Hence the main function of government was to safeguard individual liberty, to assure equality of opportunity to the citizen so that he might on his own initiative generate progress. "Even if governmental conduct of business could give us more efficiency instead of less efficiency," Hoover stated in 1928, "the fundamental objection to it would remain unaltered and unabated."

In Hoover's political theory the presidency was an office with severely restricted powers. Article II of the Constitution is what a man in relation to his time makes of it. He may assert executive responsibility and lead or he may allow power to slip through his fingers to Congress, to the states, and to private organizations. Hoover conceived of the President as a kind of cheerleader whose job was to whoop up the fans rather than lead the team on the field. Decisions he would not have hesitated to make as a private citizen or as a lesser public official, he felt he could not make in the White House because they exceeded presidential authority. His political theory was a charter of political inaction.

Hoover's view of labor was that of the conventional progressive businessman in the New Era. For the worker America was a classless land of golden opportunity. Hoover was an enthusiastic trumpeter of the Doctrine of High Wages, the means of achieving high-level consumption and so prosperity. The way to raise wages, he argued, was by increased efficiency resulting from the application of technology to production. For labor unions he held more sympathy than most of his business contemporaries. As early as 1909, he had written that unions are "normal and proper antidotes for unlimited capitalistic organization." In the twenties he welcomed the AFL's emphasis upon scientific management and union-management cooperation to improve efficiency. Further, he found men like John L. Lewis and William L. Hutcheson both personally and philosophically congenial. Though hardly a warm friend of organized labor, Hoover was certainly not its enemy.[2]

## 2

The American economy, considered as a producer of goods, reached the high point for the era in the late spring and early summer of

1929. The month of June may be considered the turning point, since it was then that the seasonally adjusted Federal Reserve Board Index of Industrial Production reached a peak at 126. The next four months witnessed an uninterrupted though unspectacular decline; by October the index had lost eight points and stood at 118. Industries, of course, fluctuated about this general pattern. May, for example, was the best month for steel with an output of 5,286,000 tons; by October tonnage slipped to 4,534,000. Auto production, climaxed in the assembly of 621,910 units in April, dropped precipitously to 380,017 in October.

By the early fall it was evident to anyone watching the indexes that the economy of the United States was in trouble. This intelligence must have been a factor in precipitating the stock market crash. This is hardly the place to recount in detail once again that catastrophic and terrifying experience. It is sufficient only to fix the dates. By Labor Day a dizzy climb by the market (the product, in William Z. Ripley's phrase, of "prestigitation, double-shuffling, honey-fugling, hornswaggling and skulduggery") reached heights never before dreamed of: the *New York Times* industrial average on September 3 was at an astronomical 452. Two days later there was a short, sharp break, the effect of which was not so much to depress prices as to prick the bubble of anticipated price rises. In the next six weeks the market was ragged. The trading week that opened on October 21 was disastrous, culminating in the panic of Black Thursday. The first two days of the following week were even more terrible. Tuesday, October 29, was the most appalling day in the history of the New York Stock Exchange; sales incredibly totaled 16,410,030 shares and the *Times* average fell 43 points. A slow slide continued during the next fortnight. On November 13, when panic ended and gloom began, the average stood at 224, down by one half in a little over two months. An era had closed. But, more important, a new one had opened with a disturbance of the utmost gravity.

President Hoover had been concerned with the economic slide during the summer but had said nothing and done little for fear of undermining the business confidence so necessary to the speculative boom. The crash removed this restraint and did far more: economic leadership shifted from Wall Street to the White House. What would the President do?

Hoover, who viewed the price-wage structure as decisive in economic policy, faced alternatives: deflation or price maintenance. Secretary Mellon and many prominent bankers were for deflation. They urged that prices and wages be allowed to sink to their natural bottoms from which, as the history of business cycles demonstrated, they would once again rise. Hoover, as a humanitarian and sincere spokesman for the New Era's Doctrine of High Wages, had no stomach for such liquidation. He stated his position confidentially at a White House conference of the nation's top industrialists in late November. The crisis, a worried Hoover told them, was far more serious than the stock market debacle; he anticipated a severe general depression that would last a long time. His aims were to minimize the human cost of unemployment, to maintain social order, and to prevent panic. A cut in wages, the President argued, would defeat these goals. Hence he urged industry to maintain the existing level of wage rates. If it proved necessary to cut rates later on, the inevitable fall in the cost of living would make it possible to do so without impairing real wages.

Hoover wanted an industry-labor agreement on wage maintenance. Since collective bargaining did not even exist in many industries, to say nothing of nation-wide bargaining, the best he could do was to get a few influential leaders on each side to express concurrence with his opinion. He did not, in fact, even get them to meet at the same time. Hence he invited Henry Ford, Walter Teagle, Owen D. Young, Myron Taylor, Alfred P. Sloan, Jr., Pierre du Pont, Walter Gifford, and a brigade of other prominent businessmen to the White House on the morning of November 21. At the conclusion of this conference, the President announced, the employers present "on their individual behalf" pledged that they would not initiate any "movement for wage reduction" and they strongly recommended that other employers follow their example. Ford, seizing an opportunity for publicity, announced a wage increase for his employees as he emerged from the conference. That afternoon Hoover met with the labor people, including Green, Lewis, Hutcheson, Frey, Woll, and A. F. Whitney. It took little persuading on the President's part to convince them to oppose wage cuts. Their only concession, if such it could be called, was to recommend that "no movement beyond those already in negotiation should be initiated for the increase of wages."

Green on November 27 wrote the affiliated unions to explain the President's policy. He emphasized its recommendatory character, since those present had no authority to bind the organizations. Green assured them that they were free to conclude negotiations for higher wages already under way and that the policy would not affect the southern organizing drive then in progress. "I feel sure that the conferences held by the President have been very helpful in stabilizing the economic and industrial situation."

The labor leaders, in fact, were pleased, if not elated, by these events. They were far more cheerful about the economic outlook than the President; he, obviously, had not communicated his private forebodings to them. "I entertain the hope," Green wrote on November 27, "that industry and business will very soon reach a normal point and that the unfavorable situation growing out of the stock market crash will be overcome." Frey on December 2 assured his British trade-union friend, W. A. Appleton, that "the worst features of an industrial depression will be avoided." As late as January 3, 1930, Green predicted a great year for the construction industry. The unionists seemed to have concluded a good bargain, giving up nothing and receiving an assurance, vague though it was, that wage levels would not fall. Finally, they must have been flattered to be welcomed at the White House in a fanfare of publicity, an experience they had not enjoyed since the Wilson Administration.

Hoover, in addition to working for wage stability, strove to shore up construction. He urged industry, the railways, and the utilities to proceed with their planned programs and, if possible, to increase building expenditures. He argued that the crash would free funds for this purpose that earlier had been diverted into the securities markets. He pledged that the federal government would not curtail its construction program. On November 23, Hoover wired the governors to stimulate their states and counties to the "energetic yet prudent pursuit of public works."

The Hoover economic policy required no direct federal action; he proposed no legislation to Congress. It was, in fact, a policy of exhortation which depended entirely upon voluntary acceptance. "This is not dictation or interference by the Government with business," Hoover on December 5 proudly told the Chamber of Commerce. "It is a request from the Government that you cooperate in prudent measures to solve a national problem." What would happen, one might inquire, if this cooperation were not forthcoming? But the simple fact was that virtually no one asked the question. Hoover was almost universally applauded for his bold, vigorous activity in preventing the crash from becoming a depression. "President Hoover," Frey wrote approvingly, "took a firm and immediate interest in the situation."[3] A current hit song caught the national mood in its title: "Happy Days Are Here Again." Significantly enough, it was from a show called *Chasing Rainbows*.

## 3

History confirmed Hoover's private fears rather than his public optimism. The crash had an immediate and disastrous effect upon the volume of employment. "When more and more people are thrown out of work," Coolidge remarked, "unemployment results." President Roosevelt's Committee on Economic Security later estimated that the number of jobless shot upward from 492,000 in October 1929 to 4,065,000 in January 1930. "A high official of our government told me at the time the stock market crashed last fall," Senator Couzens informed the Michigan Manufacturers Association at Christmas time, "unemployment jumped in two weeks from 700,000 to 3,100,000."

There was, of course, a varying amount of joblessness among industries and so among the communities in which they concentrated. The auto business virtually collapsed. Willys-Overland, which dominated the economy of Toledo, employed 28,000 persons in March 1929. At that time the company turned out 42,000 cars a month. They could not be sold; by November the payroll had plummeted to 4000. On the first of January 1930, according to the local Merchants and Manufacturers Association, 30 to 40 per cent of Toledo's male labor force of 75,000 was out of work. At that time Beulah Amidon made a tour of the Willys plant, which she described in this fashion:

> When I was taken through some of the eighty-seven buildings that make up the plant I was reminded of the old desert towns left in the wake of a mining rush. There was the same sense of suspended life, as I moved among silent, untended machines

or walked through departments where hundreds of half-finished automobile bodies gathered dust while they waited for the next cleaning or finishing process. The effect of a sudden paralysis was intensified by the infrequent groups of workers, almost lost in the vast, dim spaces, going about tasks that seemed very small and futile in the midst of the elaborate equipment for mass production, for an unending stream of assembled, tested, finished cars rolling out of the factory doors.

Detroit was little different. Its dominant firm was the Ford Motor Company, which in March 1929 employed 128,142 persons. By December the payroll tumbled to 100,500, and the worst was still to come. In April 1931, Ford employed 84,000, and half of these were working only three days a week. In August of that year the payroll dropped to an appalling 37,000. Ford's vaunted five-day week was soon forgotten. Work staggering was instituted at the outset of the depression and became general. Further, tool room men were often required to work six and even seven days. The relief obligation for the jobless workers fell on the city of Detroit, to which Ford made almost no tax contribution by virtue of the fact that all his operations except the inconsequential Lincoln plant were outside the city limits. In nearby Pontiac employment declined from 29,000 in the spring of 1929 to 14,000 in the fall. Flint was equally bad. A personal loan company there discovered in March 1930 that 50 per cent of its commitments were to jobless auto workers. This enterprising concern set about securing its loans by finding jobs for the workers; by August only 5 per cent were still out of work. Apparently, the way to find work in the auto industry was to go into hock to a loan company.

Even more distressing was unemployment in the textile industry and the towns that depended heavily upon it. The crash had compounded the depression that set in during the mid-twenties. By the end of 1930, 120,000 of New England's 280,000 millhands were totally jobless and many others worked part time, frequently for less than $10 a week. "There is, perhaps," President McMahon of the Textile Workers declared in 1930, "more destitution and misery and degradation in the mill towns of New England today . . . than anywhere else in the United States." Lowell was economically dead. At this time two thirds of the labor force was idle; every third store was vacant; doctors could not collect bills; charity was the biggest industry in town. Lawrence was as bad. A textile worker who had not worked in years told Louis Adamic: "I wish there would be a war again." New Bedford was bankrupt, and the governor of Massachusetts had to step in to reorganize its finances. In both New Bedford and Fall River local boosters persuaded runaway shirt, overalls, and underwear factories from New York to replace the textile mills. The bait was cheap female labor. The Sally Middy Company of Fall River, for example, employed 107 girls in August 1930, sixty of them for less than $8 a week. In Lawrence the Lions, Kiwanis, and Rotary joined with the Boston & Maine Railroad to form an Industrial Bureau to persuade new industries to move in. On January 5, 1930, the Bureau ran an ad in the *New York Times* offering manufacturers a saving of "15 per cent to 25 per cent on direct labor." Isidor Goldberg of the Pilot Radio & Tube Corporation of Brooklyn moved in. He paid female labor $7.20 a week, far below the statutory minimum of $12 for the electrical industry. The Minimum Wage Commission had assured him of at least two years of peace. When the labor unions protested, the Lawrence *Sun* replied, "The future of Lawrence is more vital than a technical point of law."

Autos and textiles were hit especially hard in the first phase of the depression and, since they clustered in one-industry towns, the communities they supported were among the worst sufferers. But even cities with diversified industry sustained a sharp shrinkage in employment. Philadelphia, for example, according to a careful sampling by the University of Pennsylvania, in April 1930, had 133,475 entirely out of work and 46,271 on part time in a labor force of 889,837. The Metropolitan Life Insurance Company reported that 23.8 per cent of its 355,759 industrial policyholders in forty-six larger cities were unemployed in early December 1930. In 1931 in Buffalo 26 per cent of the labor force was jobless and 21 per cent was on part time. In Cincinnati in the same year the corresponding percentages were 18 and 19. The estimates of the Committee on Economic Security, probably the best monthly figures for the nation as a whole, reveal an uninterrupted rise in unemployment to the fall of 1931. The 4-million mark was reached in January 1930; in September unemployment passed 5 million; in November it mounted to 6 million; in January 1931 to 8 million; in October it passed 9 million.

The unemployed were distributed unevenly. The numbers increased as one descended the scales of skill, income, and ethnic origin. Managerial employees suffered least, followed in order by the clerical and manual groups, with the unskilled at the bottom. Those with higher incomes were more likely to hold on to their jobs than those with low incomes. Whites made out much better than Negroes. Since manual workers with low incomes, many of them Negroes, concentrated in the metropolitan areas, large cities were worse off than small.[4]

Despite the fact of great and growing joblessness, many, if not most, Americans were hardly aware of the problem in the first year or two of the depression. In smaller communities and in parts of large cities, unemployment could not be seen. The fact that no one really knew how many were out of work left a wide field for statistical juggling. The Hoover Administration exploited the whole mechanism of opinion-molding to minimize the gravity of the situation and to raise public hopes of speedy improvement. The country, according to the official stereotype, was fundamentally sound. The President himself issued a steady stream of what Senator La Follette called "optimistic ballyhoo statements" which Hoover could hardly have believed. Secretary of Commerce Robert P. Lamont declared in February 1930: "There is nothing in the business situation to be disturbed about. Employment is picking up." Secretary of Labor James J. Davis regularly read public obituaries over the allegedly dead body of the depression. To the Kiwanis of Harrisburg, for example, he observed in early 1930 that the country had recovered quickly from the shock of the crash. Davis informed the Kiwanians confidentially that only the previous week he had notified Hoover of a marked upturn in employment. "Puddler Jim" was somewhat more somber in private. On March 28, 1930, he wrote a friend that "one doesn't improve the condition of a sick man by constantly telling him how ill he is."

These pronouncements led Elmer Davis to write the following letter to the editor of the *New York Times:*

Many of your readers will regret that you waste so much valuable front-page space on the President's statement on unemployment and the business depression. Experience teaches us that the dealings of any administration with these painful topics follow a well recognized pattern:

1. There is no depression.
2. There was a depression, but it is passing.
3. The depression, which was caused by the obstructionist tactics of the Democrats, would have ruined the country but for the protective tariff and the policies of the Republican Administration.

Your music critics do not review in detail every repetition of a familiar opera or orchestral program. Why not save space by some such notice as this: "The second music drama of the Depression Cycle was sung at the White House last night, with the usual cast."?

The gentle fog of good cheer emitted by Washington, nevertheless, had an effect in some rather startling places. Governor Roosevelt of New York, a man no one would accuse of political insensitivity, paid little attention to unemployment during the first year of depression and, despite the advice of Felix Frankfurter, barely mentioned it in his re-election campaign of 1930. Lincoln Steffens, the radical journalist, wrote a friend as late as December 18, 1930, that business "isn't as bad as Wall Street and these blooming business leaders think." He advised her to buy stocks, which he thought "swell for profits."

Others, however, were more perceptive. Governor O. Max Gardner of textile-dominated North Carolina wrote a friend on February 1, 1930: "I am facing the gravest situation that has confronted North Carolina since the Civil War. Many of our people . . . have accepted the psychology of defeat." On March 6, a young New Yorker by the name of Victor Riesel, after observing a demonstration in Union Square, went to the day room of his father's embroidery union. "There was a grown man weeping. He had no job. His family had nothing to eat." Riesel determined to devote his life to serving the wage earner. The economist Stuart Chase, returning to New York City early in April from a visit to Mexico, was appalled by the increase in unemployment while he was away. Even cheerful William Green was by August reluctantly prepared to admit that the suffering from joblessness was acute. "We can all fervently hope," Morris L. Cooke wrote on October 3, "that the prophecies that are now being made by those who should be the best informed will not be upset, but as the result of many, many interviews my feeling is very strongly that we are going to have to cope with a situation worse possibly than anything we have had since 1893." [5]

The stock market crash had little immediate impact upon wages. Rates, as distinguished from earnings, held firmly in the first year of the depression. A survey of union scales for May 1930 actually showed a rise over the spring of 1929. The average common labor entrance rates for thirteen industries, standing at 43.7 cents in July 1929, fell only to 43.1 cents in July 1930. Average money earnings per hour in manufacturing, according to the National Industrial Conference Board, declined modestly from 59 cents in the third quarter of 1929 to 58.2 cents in the last quarter of 1930.

On the anniversary of the crash Hoover could view the first year's performance under his wage-maintenance policy with a good deal of satisfaction. But the crushing weight of unemployment began to take its toll in wage rates in the latter part of 1930 and accelerated the next year. On October 31, 1930, Edward Eyre Hunt, a Hoover intimate, wrote: "My own feeling — which I think is shared by the President — is that industry has not carried through on its promise." The evidence was abundant. For the month ending December 15, 1929, the Bureau of Labor Statistics reported only 23 wage cuts; in the month ending August 15, 1931, it reported 221. By July 1931 the average common labor rate had declined to 41.2 cents while the Conference Board manufacturing average dropped to 56.5 cents by the third quarter of 1931. For the most part these decreases were made in small firms, especially in competitive industries. But the number of large employers who cut rates in 1930 and early 1931 grew ominously: Riverside & Dan River Mills, International Harvester, Fisher Body, Chrysler, National Cash Register, Firestone, Goodyear, U.S. Rubber, Westinghouse, and the entire copper industry. Further, many companies downgraded their employees or consolidated jobs. Others cut piece rates or speeded the pace of production. Even in the unionized trades, notably construction, side agreements below the contract scales became widespread. By the summer of 1931 wage maintenance was little more than a holding action and members of the Administration had begun to discuss a general retreat.

The fatal weakness of this policy was that it was addressed exclusively to wage rates. No effort was made to maintain hours; in fact, the Administration's work-spreading policy — to be developed later — had precisely the opposite effect. The work week of those employed declined sharply — in manufacturing from 44.2 hours in 1929 to 40.5 in 1931, on the railroads from 44.8 to 41.1, and in bituminous coal from 38.4 to 28.3. Hence weekly and annual earnings fell rapidly in the first two years of the depression. Since a worker supported his family on his earnings, it was small comfort to see the rate remain firm while hours fell off.

Average weekly earnings in manufacturing, according to the Conference Board, declined steadily from $28.63 in the third quarter of 1929 to $22.23 in the same quarter of 1931. The average earnings of a pick miner in the Allegheny bituminous district dropped from $52.91 in a typical half month of 1929 to $34.89 in the last half of May 1931. Average earnings per week in foundries fell from $30.39 in 1929 to $20.06 in 1931, in furniture factories from $24.52 to $16.88, in machine shops from $32.06 to $24.22. The decline in annual earnings was also severe. The national average in manufacturing dropped from $1315 in 1929 to $1110 in 1931. In Ohio the manufacturing average fell from $1499 to $1185.

This fall-off in earnings must be partly discounted by the decline in the cost of living; that is, real wages did not fall as rapidly as money wages. The BLS Cost of Living Index ( 1913 = 100) stood at 173.3 in September 1929 and was down to 152.1 by August 1931, a drop of 13.9 per cent. Real weekly earnings in manufacturing, using the Conference Board data, fell only 13.1 per cent in contrast with a decline of 28.8 per cent in money earnings.

The impact of falling earnings varied sharply among industries and industry groups. Wolman calculated the year-to-year percentage change in per capita weekly earnings for the first two years of the depression as follows:

|  | 1929–30 | 1930–31 |
|---|---|---|
| Bituminous coal | − 12.3 | − 19.1 |
| Metaliferous mining | − 6.6 | − 18.3 |
| Manufacturing | − 7.2 | − 11.3 |
| Anthracite coal | + 1.8 | − 14.4 |
| Railroads | − 1.9 | − 3.5 |
| Trade | + 1.3 | − 2.8 |
| Public utilities | + 2.2 | + 1.0 |

These differences were attributable mainly to differentials in falling demand and the strength of unionism. The consumption of copper, for example, declined more rapidly than that of electric power. The United Mine Workers union was less effective in maintaining wage standards than were the railway organizations.[6]

### 4

"This country is not in good condition," Coolidge remarked early in 1931. American wage earners could have found no reason to disagree with the former President. Increasingly their preoccupation was with the shortage of jobs. Here, again, the sage of Northampton went to the nub of the matter. "The final solution of unemployment," Coolidge observed in 1931, "is work." As the depression deepened and the lines of the jobless lengthened, there seemed a diminishing likelihood that President Hoover would provide this solution. Hence the nation listened with mounting interest to the voices raised in Congress, and especially to that of the junior senator from New York, who spoke with authority about the problem of unemployment.

CHAPTER 6

# The Ordeal of a Modest Program

MAN IS A CAPTIVE of his past. His ideas, economic and otherwise, grow out of his experience. When one stage of society meshes smoothly into the next, his ideas are reshaped in a gradual and orderly fashion. In the case of a cataclysmic historical change, such as in 1929, events leap ahead and ideas lag behind. In the first phase of the Great Depression — from the fall of 1929 to the autumn of 1931 — social forces outdistanced man's capacity to deal with them.

Hoover was an ideological prisoner of the twenties. Even Senator Wagner, who had studied the problem of unemployment with great seriousness, failed to scale the walls of his intellectual past. The program that Wagner brought forth in January 1930 was an old program. The youngest idea had been around for more than a decade and the others for much longer. It would take a leap of the imagination to describe any as radical. Every one, in fact, had either been advanced earlier by Hoover himself or by commissions appointed or presided over by him. Nor would they, even if enacted, have done much to stem the wave of joblessness. Wagner, like Hoover, had had no experience that prepared him for this disaster. He knew firsthand only such comparatively modest economic downturns as 1915, 1920–22, 1924, and 1927. Hence the senator sought to deal primarily with the milder forms of unemployment — frictional, technological, and seasonal; his program was hardly calculated to cope with the most serious type — massive joblessness stemming from a deep cyclical downswing.

But Wagner, unlike Hoover, was to demonstrate a capacity to adapt himself to the times that was in due course to make him the decisive congressional figure in the formulation of labor policy. Hence it is necessary to know something about this New Yorker.

1

Robert Ferdinand Wagner was born in Nastätten, Germany, on June 8, 1878. His older brother Gus, a cook, and two sisters emigrated to the United States before him. Robert and his parents arrived at Castle Garden in 1886, their passage having been provided by Gus. The family at first lived in a tenement on lower Avenue A and later moved to another in East Harlem. Robert's father got a job as a janitor in a tenement. This childhood experience — as a poor immigrant boy raised in the slums of New York City — decisively shaped Wagner's outlook. "I lived," he later declared, "among the people of the tenements. Unless you have lived among these people, you cannot know the haunting sense of insecurity which hangs over the home of the worker."

Wagner attended the New York public schools. It was always necessary to work: selling newspapers, running errands for a grocery store, clerking, tutoring, selling scented candies to drunks in saloons who needed to face irate wives. He went on to City College, where he made Phi Beta Kappa, played quarterback on the football team, engaged in debating, and was president of his class. After graduation in 1898, he studied at New York Law School and was admitted to the bar in 1900. Gus, by now a chef at the New York Athletic Club, was the financial angel of Bob's higher education.

Wagner, with an appetite for politics as well as for wiener schnitzel, entered political life at once. He walked into the old brownstone building of Tammany's Algonquin Democratic Club in Yorkville and demanded permission to make a speech. He got it and proved a success. His early experience was the hack work of street-corner campaign speaking. The chieftains at the Hall, ever watchful for new talent, pushed him ahead. In 1904, Wagner was elected to the Assembly; in 1908 he moved up to the state Senate where he remained for a decade, becoming his party's floor leader in 1913. In Albany he became acquainted with two other rising stars in the New York Democratic firmament: Al Smith and Franklin Roosevelt.

But more important, it was as a state senator that Wagner's name became identified with social legislation. In the spring of 1911 a fire broke out in the sweatshop Triangle Shirtwaist Factory in New York City. Since there were no fire escapes, 145 workers, mainly young girls, were trapped in the building and died. There was a great public outcry which led to the formation of a citizens' committee on safety, whose secretary was an earnest social worker named Frances Perkins. The legislature promptly created a Factory Investigating Commission with Wagner as chairman and Smith as vice-chairman. This body made an exhaustive study of factory conditions in the state. "We made sure," Miss Perkins wrote, "that Robert Wagner personally crawled through the tiny hole in the wall that gave egress to a steep iron ladder covered with ice and ending twelve feet from the ground, which was euphemistically labeled 'Fire Escape' in many factories." She also demonstrated to him the appalling washrooms as well as the exploitation of women and children. The Commission concluded that the state's inspection system was "totally inadequate." Between 1912 and 1914, the legislature completely rewrote the factory code by passing thirty-six bills regulating safety and health, reducing the hours of women from sixty to fifty-four, prohibiting female night work, and restricting child labor. Wagner's part in rewriting the New York factory code gave him a national reputation.

In 1918 he was elevated to the New York Supreme Court. His judicial career was distinguished by the decision in *Schlesinger v. Quinto*. The Cloak and Suit Manufacturers' Protective Association and the International Ladies' Garment Workers had on May 29, 1919, executed an agreement effective until June 1, 1922. It was notable for the replacement of piecework by week-work. In 1921 the Association announced that effective November 14 its members would revert to piecework. The union petitioned Justice Wagner for an injunction, which he granted on January 16, 1922, restraining the return to piecework as a breach of contract. His opinion was an interesting commentary on the issue of equality of bargaining power in an industrial society:

> While this application is novel, it is novel only in the respect that for the first time an employees' organization is seeking to restrain their employers' organization from violating a contractual obligation.

It is elementary, and yet sometimes requires emphasis, that the door of a court of equity is open to employer and employee alike. It is no respecter of persons — it is keen to protect the legal rights of all. Heretofore the employer alone has prayed the protection of a court of equity against threatened irreparable illegal acts of the employee. But mutuality of obligation compels a mutuality of remedy. The fact that the employees have entered equity's threshold by a hitherto untraveled path does not lessen their right to the law's decree.

Wagner, becalmed on the bench, itched to re-enter active political life. His opportunity came in 1926 when the Democrats nominated him for the Senate seat occupied by Republican James Wadsworth. The year was bad for the Democrats, but Wagner was lucky in that the Republicans split over Prohibition. Wagner, of course, was a wringing wet (he and Al Smith would spend a summer weekend on the porch at Far Rockaway talking politics before a neat and rapidly lengthening line of empty beer bottles) and Wadsworth was a plain wet. The drys, having no other place to go, nominated Franklin Cristman, who polled 223,000 votes, almost all drawn from Wadsworth, whom Wagner beat by a scant 121,000 ballots. The supporters of the Eighteenth Amendment, therefore, helped mightily to put Bob Wagner in the Senate.

In his three years in that august body prior to the crash, Wagner became increasingly absorbed with the problem of unemployment. He was both astounded and disturbed to learn of its incidence during the "Coolidge prosperity." It would, clearly, be necessary to devise a way to count the number of people out of work. At least part of the answer to swings in employment, he wrote in 1928, lay in "utilization of the tremendous spending power of government as a great balance wheel to stabilize the vibration of the entire industrial machinery." The disorganization of the labor market could be met by the creation of a national system of employment exchanges. Technological unemployment, though not a problem for legislation, could, he felt, be dealt with by shorter hours accompanied by higher wages.

In 1930 the senator was in the prime of life, in his early fifties and full of zest. His figure was short and stocky, his features rather thickly Germanic. His manner was deliberate, unassuming, good-humored, and friendly. Wagner was a prodigious and thorough worker. "Bobby," he would tell his son, "work is the only thing that matters." The senator's tastes were hardly proletarian. He was a snappy dresser and enjoyed being driven in a long black Cadillac. Nothing pleased him more than a monumental German dinner at Lüchow's or Hans Jager's, where he doted upon the tartar sandwiches with anchovies and raw egg, the pigs' knuckles, and the schnitzels. Wagner's mental powers were superior but not brilliant; he avoided debate, preferring to read his speeches on the floor. They were meaty and authoritative, attentively heard by large audiences. He was popular with newsmen and liked and respected by senators on both sides of the aisle.

In his youth Wagner fell passionately in love with politics and never recovered. He would talk politics far into the night or through a weekend. His son Robert, Jr., to whom he was deeply devoted — in part because of the early death of his wife and other child — was groomed for a political career. "Don't honk, Bobby," the senator once admonished him, distressed with a nearby driver on a crowded highway, "the man is a voter." Wagner was a political regular, completely loyal to Tammany Hall. Though not associated with its corrupt side, he never denounced it. Rather, he liked to describe the Hall as "the Cradle of American Liberalism."

There was an element of truth in the statement and his own career was its demonstration. The Senate that Wagner entered in the late twenties was dominated by conservatives of both parties. The handful of liberals in its midst consisted mainly of Republicans from the West, largely from rural constituencies, whose ideas had originated in the Populist and Progressive movements: Norris of Nebraska, La Follette and Blaine of Wisconsin, Brookhart of Iowa, Shipstead of Minnesota, Nye and Frazier of North Dakota, Borah of Idaho, Cutting of New Mexico, and Hiram Johnson of California. In this group Wagner was unique in being a Democrat and representing the newer immigrant working masses of the great eastern cities. The senator was a New Yorker to the bone (he became nervous when a tie-up caused the rumble of the elevated trains near his apartment to stop) and found comfort in the town's ethnic cacophony. "Senator Wagner," Oswald Garrison Villard wrote, "could speak for them — all those striving, teeming, backward hordes in our large cities, jammed into overcrowded slums as soon as they came through Castle Garden, and left to shift for themselves — for he was one of them." [1]

2

With unemployment mounting sharply after the crash, Senator Wagner announced on January 8, 1930, that he would introduce three bills to deal with the problem. The first would direct the Secretary of Labor to prepare and publish a monthly index of employment in the United States. The second would create a Federal Employment Stabilization Board to advise the President on the state of business and employment and to make advance plans for public works up to a value of $150 million per year to counteract business depression and unemployment. The final bill would establish a federal-state system of employment exchanges with administration and coordination placed in a new United States Employment Service in the Labor Department and actual operations under the states. For this purpose Congress would appropriate $4 million a year, three fourths of which would be used to underwrite the state systems. Together these proposals came to be known as the Wagner bills. They represented the most thoughtful practical effort to cope with unemployment advanced either by the Administration or in Congress in the first phase of the depression. Each was the product of careful work going back over a period of years.

The fact that the United States, the world's most advanced industrial nation, did not know how many of its citizens were out of work had long been a sore point, particularly with economists and statisticians. In fact, the American Statistical Association had designated a Committee on Governmental Labor Statistics, under the chairmanship of Mary Van Kleeck of the Russell Sage Foundation, to look into the matter. The Committee in December 1928 voted to urge the government to include a question on unemployment in the decennial census of 1930. While this would yield a figure for only one day, the Bureau of Labor Statistics, its Commissioner assured the Committee, could use the number as a base in computing monthly estimates of unemployment from the Bureau's sample of industries. Miss Van Kleeck enlisted Wagner's enthusiastic support. The Director of the Census, however, was cold to the proposal, claiming that a question on unemployment would divert his agency from its main task of enumerating population. On January 9, 1929, Wagner introduced an amendment to the census bill to require that unemployment be included. Reluctantly, the Bureau of the Census agreed to count the jobless.

On January 21, 1930, Miss Perkins, now Industrial Commissioner of New York, entered the statistical fray. That morning she had read a statement by Hoover that employment had picked up. Knowing that this was untrue of New York and that false optimism would dishearten the jobless, she worked up a reply based upon New York and such national figures as BLS was able to supply. Miss Perkins challenged the President's statistics and implied that the BLS had had nothing to do with their preparation. She was astonished to find that so dull a topic made headlines across the nation.

On April 30, the Bureau of the Census enumerated the unemployed and soon afterward reported that 2,429,069 were out of work and 758,885 were on layoff, a total of 3,187,947. Even this relatively modest figure was not low enough for Hoover. He asserted that between 500,000 and 1,000,000 of these persons were not "unemployed" because they had no intention of seeking work, and another 500,000 to 1,000,000 were between jobs, mainly in the seasonal trades. Hence the President "corrected" the Census figure to 1,900,000, which, he declared, was not out of line with unemployment in the twenties. While this is no place to examine the technical deficiencies in the Census procedure or the failure of its results to jibe with other data, there can be no doubt that the enumeration seriously understated the volume of unemployment and that Hoover's total was absurd. In fact, a prominent Census official, Charles E. Persons, resigned in protest against the methods adopted. Two careful studies, one by Robert R. Nathan and the other by Paul A. Samuelson and Russell A. Nixon, later estimated that the enumeration was off by over 1,000,000, that the actual number of jobless on April 30, 1930, was in the neighborhood of 4,400,000.

The catcalls with which the Census results were greeted, particularly in expert quarters, speeded the movement of the statistical bill through Congress. In fact, no one in either the Senate or House hearings voiced opposition to the measure. On April 29, it passed the Senate without a dissenting vote. The bill was referred to the House Labor Committee on May 5, which reported it favorably on May 19. On July 1, the House passed the statistical bill with only one opposing vote, and the President signed it on July 7, 1930.

The law provided that the Bureau of Labor Statistics should collect and publish at least once a month complete figures on the volume of and changes in employment, wages paid, and hours worked in manufacturing, mining, construction, agriculture, lumbering, transportation, communication, public utilities, retail and wholesale trade, and government service. The Bureau, however, received no appropriation for this formidable task. On August 12, Hoover named an Advisory Committee on Employment Statistics with a subcommittee on measurement under the chairmanship of Leo Wolman. Its recommendations, handed down in early 1931, included the compilation of employment statistics for construction and the services as well as figures on part-time employment in manufacturing and railroad transportation, a study of the desirability of a quinquennial census of employment, and an appropriation to the Bureau of $200,000, one fourth to be made available immediately. These urgings fell on deaf ears. The Hoover Administration made no serious effort to implement either the Wagner bill or the recommendations of its advisory committee. As unemployment mounted, it became a commonplace to observe that the statistics of the pig population were superior to those of the unemployed. "No administration . . . is quite willing to have the actual picture known," Wagner declared, "so that pretense at least may utter that prosperity exists when, as a matter of fact, we may be submerged in a very serious depression." [2]

3

The idea of adjusting the volume of public works to counterbalance fluctuations in business and employment was not new in

1930. In fact, Senator William S. Kenyon of Iowa had introduced a bill in 1919 with an appropriation of $100 million to create a United States Emergency Public Works Board to stimulate such activity in time of depression. President Harding's Conference on Unemployment, of which Hoover was the guiding genius, in 1921 endorsed planned public works. In the mid-twenties several bills incorporating this notion were dropped into the congressional hopper. In January 1928, Senator Wesley L. Jones of Washington proposed his "prosperity reserve" bill with an appropriation of $150 million, and in May Wagner advanced a similar measure. In 1929, President Hoover's Committee on Recent Economic Changes gave serious consideration to the idea and initiated an exhaustive study by the National Bureau of Economic Research. Nothing, however, was done in the unfavorable political climate of the twenties.

The theory was simple and appealing: regulate the flow of public works up or down to compensate for shifts in business activity and employment by private industry. A public-construction project would require not only direct labor in building but also indirect labor for materials, transportation, and so on. There were two major practical difficulties. The first was that public construction in the twenties constituted only one fourth of total construction, and within this minor fraction the outlays of state and local governments exceeded those of the federal government in a ratio of 13 to 1. Hence federal public works would have to be enormously expanded if they were to counter a sharp cyclical decline. The second difficulty was time. It took months and even years to get an appropriation, select and purchase a site, draw plans, and let contracts before building could get under way. Legislation, therefore, would have to provide for the advance planning of public works.

The bill that Wagner proposed in January 1930 was modest as to amount but did seek to deal constructively with advance planning. It would create a Federal Employment Stabilization Board composed of the Secretaries of the Treasury, Commerce, Agriculture, and Labor to advise the President as to the trend of business and employment. The Board would base its counsel upon the volume of construction contracts awarded in the preceding three months contrasted with the same period of the two previous years, as well as upon the BLS index of employment to be developed under the statistical bill. Upon the recommendation of the Stabilization Board the President would forward a special message to Congress requesting appropriations for emergency construction of highways, river and harbor improvements, flood control, and public buildings. The heart of the measure was Section 10, a declaration of policy "to arrange the construction of public works, so far as practicable, in such manner as will assist in the stabilization of industry and employment through the proper timing of such construction, and that to further this object there shall be advance planning of public works." The bill would authorize the appropriation of $150 million a year.

The measure encountered no difficulty in the Senate. At the hearings before the Committee on Commerce in March and April all the witnesses spoke in its favor, and the bill was reported out affirmatively. When it reached the floor on April 28, Wagner confidently urged its passage, although he expressed concern over White House silence in light of Hoover's earlier enthusiasm for the idea. Republican Senator Arthur H. Vandenberg of Michigan warmly endorsed the bill. The Senate then passed it with no recorded opposition.

Its fate in the House was quite different. The hearings went smoothly enough; the witnesses were either favorable or, in the case of James A. Emery of the National Association of Manufacturers, expressed no opposition. The problem lay in the fact that the body that conducted the hearings was, implausibly, the Judiciary Committee, whose chairman, Pennsylvania Republican George S. Graham, was determined to emasculate the bill. If Graham did not in fact act under White House instructions, the President certainly did nothing to restrain him. Under Graham's leadership, the Committee in its report of June 18 removed all the major provisions of the measure, including the critical Section 10. What had been an advance planning bill, according to John B. Andrews of the American Association for Labor Legislation, was now no more than a gesture. Or, as Wagner put it, what remained was "an empty shell." "The President," he charged, "could not have more completely destroyed the bill if he had vetoed it." Representatives

Fiorello H. La Guardia and Emanuel Celler, in a stinging minority report of the Judiciary Committee, restated these views. Graham, however, was in the saddle and on July 1 the House adopted his version, his opponents voting for it in the hope of an improvement in conference. The Senate conferees, under Wagner's urging, refused to accept the House amendments, and Congress adjourned without passing the advance planning bill.

As the gloomy winter of 1930–31 approached, the pressure for a big federal public works program mounted. The volume of private construction was falling precipitously, and local governments, faced with growing financial stringency, were deferring or eliminating building projects. It became increasingly evident that a revival of construction would have to be initiated by the federal government. The National Unemployment League, for example, asked the President to support a $2 to $3 billion works appropriation. Harold S. Buttenheim, editor of the *American City*, formed an Emergency Committee for Federal Public Works which demanded a $1 billion program, a plan that had the backing of ninety-three prominent economists. The building-trades unions in October 1930 denounced Hoover for doing nothing to overcome the construction slump. "Rumblings in Congress," in the phrase of Otto Mallery, authority on public works and warm friend of the Hoover Administration, became increasingly audible. The President's own Emergency Committee for Employment on November 21, 1930, strongly urged Hoover to ask the new Congress for a comprehensive program that would have provided more than half a billion dollars in federal funds as well as a good deal more in matching state funds for public works. The President in his State of the Union message of December 2 bent slightly before the winds of pressure: he asked Congress for an appropriation of $100 to $150 million for emergency construction, underlining the emergency character of the request. "The volume of construction work in the Government," Hoover hastened to explain, "is already at the maximum limit warranted by financial prudence as a continuing policy."

By early 1931, therefore, it was no longer possible for the Hoover Administration to dispose of the Wagner bill with tactics of the sort Graham had employed the preceding summer. The new Congress, Hoover's friend Edward Eyre Hunt pointed out, would almost certainly enact the measure. If the President vetoed, he would bear the onus of defeating advance planning, and the fact that he had proposed no substitute would do his case no good. "This leaves the Administration in a weak position." The only politically practical course was to make the bill more acceptable by amendment. This, in fact, was done and a new bill emerged that gained the approval of the Administration, Wagner, and the conference committee. The Senate passed it on January 21 and the House on February 2, with no opposition in either chamber, and the President signed it on February 9, 1931.

The Employment Stabilization Act created the same board Wagner had proposed in the original bill and did not change its functions. The essentials of Section 10 remained; the principle of advance planning was enunciated. Heads of federal agencies which did construction were to submit each year to the Board an advance plan for the next six years of projects to be undertaken and their estimated cost. In case of an economic emergency the President upon the recommendation of the Board might ask Congress for a special public works appropriation. Aside from this, the statute provided for no funds, the most important change from the original bill. Finally, the Board was directed to collect statistics on the volume of state and local public works construction.

The Act was so loosely drawn that its effectiveness would depend entirely upon the quality of its administration. Hoover himself indicated what this would be at the time he signed the bill, referring to the Board as "a small statistical body." Ogden Mills, then emerging as the strongest figure in the Administration and soon to become a member of the Board as Secretary of the Treasury, considered federal public works "destructive to the public credit, ineffective in reviving business and wasteful to the national resources." The man Hoover chose as director of the Federal Employment Stabilization Board, D. H. Sawyer, had shown no sympathy for the program. In fact, he argued publicly that the real burden of public works rested upon the cities. In addition, Sawyer was an incomparably inept economic prophet. In July 1931 he opposed a large appropriation for federal works on the ground that the employment effect would not become fully evident until 1933; by that time business would be normal and the government would be competing harmfully with private industry for scarce labor and materials. The chief of his Division of Public Construction, J. S. Taylor, opposed federal public works on principle because they "tend to weaken rather than strengthen the sense of individual and local responsibility." It is hardly surprising, therefore, that FESB was a failure. Beyond gathering statistics, it did nothing to stimulate federal construction activity and employment.[3]

4

The unemployment that followed the crash made the disorganization of the labor market a pressing national issue. The United States Employment Service, as pointed out in Chapter 4, was a grossly ineffective agency; among its lesser defects was the inaccuracy of its employment reports which served as the basis for much of the Hoover Administration's false optimism. The director of USES, Francis I. Jones, was, according to John B. Andrews, a political appointee of no competence. In 1920 he had been promised a $2400 job for making speeches for Harding. After the election he came to Washington for the payoff. The Republicans could not find him a $2400 job, so offered him the service directorship at $5000 instead. Only two states, Wisconsin and Ohio, possessed adequate employment services; even the New York agency had serious deficiencies that Miss Perkins was seeking to remedy. Three municipal demonstration centers — the Tri-City Employment Stabilization Committee (Minneapolis, St. Paul, and Duluth), the Rochester Public Employment Center, and the Philadelphia Employment Office — were established, partly with private foundation grants, to fill this near-void. The contrast between the United States and other industrial nations was stark: they had national employment services linked to unemployment compensation systems.

Legislation, obviously, was needed to bring order into the American labor market. The experts had long since worked out the principles: since both employment and unemployment were national problems, the employment service must be nation-wide; inasmuch as twenty-four states already had systems and all were jealous of their prerogatives, the states should operate the offices; the role of the federal government should be limited to grants-in-aid and to the establishment and maintenance of minimum standards of performance. President Harding's Conference on Unemployment, with Hoover presiding, had made essentially these recommendations in 1921. They were embodied in the Kenyon-Nolan bill, which was introduced at each session of Congress in the twenties without effect.

Wagner brought in an amended version of this measure in April 1928, and reintroduced it as part of his general program in January 1930. This bill provided for the creation of a United States Employment Service in the Department of Labor, headed by a presidentially appointed director general with a salary of $10,000. The existing USES would be abolished. The new agency's employees would be under Civil Service. Its purposes would be to establish and maintain a national system of employment offices and to coordinate these offices by means of publishing information on employment opportunities, setting up a clearing arrangement for labor, imposing uniform standards, and aiding in the transportation of workers to jobs. The service was to be "neutral in labor disputes, and free from political influence." The state legislatures would be invited to create employment agencies in conformity with the act in order to qualify for grants-in-aid. A state that elected to enter the system was required to match the federal grant. Congress would appropriate $4 million per annum, $3 million to be apportioned among the states in accordance with their population and the remainder to support the federal agency. The states would submit their legislation to the USES for approval, and the director general, upon a demonstration of qualification under the federal law, would issue certificates to the Treasury for payment of the grants. The state agencies would file regular reports on their activities, and the director general was empowered to revoke certificates for failure to observe standards. A federal advisory council, composed equally of employers and employees, would assist the director general in carrying out his duties, and he would require the states to create similar councils.

The bill went to hearings before the Senate Commerce Committee in March 1930, and received the endorsement of the AFL, the

American Association for Labor Legislation, the National Federation of Settlements, and a number of individual authorities. As the Committee was about to file its report, the National Association of Manufacturers submitted a brief attacking the measure on constitutional grounds. In essence, Emery argued that the bill was "an unauthorized use of the power of appropriation to control and regulate the internal police policy of the individual states." The Committee was not impressed: on April 10, it unanimously reported the employment-service bill. On May 12, the Senate, after a perfunctory discussion in which Wagner explained the bill and Senator Hiram Bingham of Connecticut restated the NAM brief, passed the measure by a vote of 34 to 27.

The main battle was to be fought in the House, where the opposition was concentrated. The hearings before the Judiciary Committee in June found increasing opposition. Wagner was able to marshal only the same supporting group that had appeared before the Senate Committee. This time Emery appeared in person to deliver a constitutional attack upon the bill. Professor Paul Douglas pointed out that this was a façade, that the real reason for NAM objection was the fear that "the employment services would be used to colonize manufacturing plants with union organizers." Since the bill required the service to be neutral in labor disputes and put watchful employer representatives on the advisory councils, Douglas could find no substance in this concern. Finally, the National Employment Board, representing the fee-charging employment agencies, opposed S. 3060 as unfair government competition with private enterprise and unconstitutional federal regulation over an area reserved to the states.

Graham, arguing infringement of the police power, had the bill referred to a subcommittee in the hope of killing it. When his fellow Philadelphian Morris L. Cooke inquired if he wished a legal opinion, Graham replied: "Oh no! we have twenty-three lawyers on the Committee." The maneuver failed. A canvass of the members of the subcommittee revealed that a few minor amendments would induce them to accept the measure and report it back to the full committee for immediate action. John B. Andrews drafted the changes and they were accepted. Graham, however, exacted a price: he insisted upon cutting the salary of the director general from $10,000 to $8500. On June 28, the Judiciary Committee reported the employment-service bill favorably. The Committee argued that the legislation was constitutional, citing the Supreme Court's affirmation of the grant-in-aid principle in the Maternity Act cases, and emphasized the fact that Hoover had repeatedly gone on record in favor of a federal-state employment service. The bill, however, did not reach the floor of the House before the session closed.[4]

Since the 71st Congress was to meet in short session in December, a showdown on the Wagner bill was inevitable. The Administration, until now not publicly identified with the fight, could no longer avoid taking a position. On October 21, as will be developed in the next chapter, Hoover created the President's Emergency Committee for Employment and named Colonel Arthur Woods chairman. PECE at once addressed itself to the employment-service issue. Woods himself, having served on the 1921 Conference on Unemployment, was sympathetic to the bill, and several of his committee members, notably Professor Joseph Willits of the University of Pennsylvania's Wharton School of Finance and Bryce M. Stewart of Industrial Relations Counselors, Inc., perhaps the nation's leading authority on the problem, were enthusiastic supporters. On November 21, Woods submitted to the President a draft for his State of the Union message to be delivered at the assembling of Congress, which, in addition to the public works proposals already noted, dealt with the employment service. "In the forefront of any measures for dealing with unemployment more effectively must be placed the establishment of a nation-wide system of public employment offices." The draft continued: "A bill before the House of Representatives in the last session attempted to meet this need and in its main principles that measure should be accepted." The only changes proposed in the Wagner bill were to make the federal and state advisory councils tripartite rather than bipartite and to give the federal council authority to approve the personnel and organization of the state offices before certificates were issued. The President, however, rejected this recommendation and his message contained no reference to the employment service.

PECE did not accept this defeat as final. On December 17,

Willits, Stewart, Hunt, and Fred C. Croxton for the Committee, B. C. Seiple, secretary of the Association of Public Employment Services, and Professor D. D. Lescohier of the University of Wisconsin, a labor market expert, agreed that S. 3060 was acceptable with a few secondary amendments. The following day Willits and Stewart met with the officials of the Labor Department — Secretary William N. Doak, Assistant Secretary R. C. White, Commissioner of Labor Statistics Ethelbert Stewart, and USES chief Jones. They were in accord that the Administration should back the Wagner bill. Their only disagreement involved the federal advisory council, the PECE taking the position noted above and the Labor Department the view that the council should be bipartite and merely advisory, that is, Wagner's position. On December 18, 1930, therefore, all the responsible people in the Hoover Administration concerned with employment matters were in full agreement that the Wagner bill should be supported, with minor amendments.

Either that afternoon or the morning of the following day the Administration position was completely reversed, and for this the President was entirely responsible. Hoover informed Doak that he would not accept the grant-in-aid principle, the heart of S. 3060, and instructed the Secretary to draw up a new bill without it. When this decision was communicated to PECE, Bryce Stewart, Willits, and Croxton reaffirmed their advocacy of federal aid and declared that Doak would have to assume full responsibility for the substitute, Stewart going so far as to say that he would not permit his name to be associated with it in any way. Doak's position was remarkably flexible. He had been the legislative representative of the Brotherhood of Railroad Trainmen and a vice-president of the American Association for Labor Legislation; both the BRT and the AALL were firmly committed to the Wagner bill. Nevertheless, Doak exhibited no qualms about reversing himself and immediately accepted responsibility for repudiating the grant-in-aid feature. Yet, he could at the same time remark to John B. Andrews, "Don't blame me ... if the bill is vetoed."

The Doak bill provided for no significant change in the existing USES. Beyond an innocuous affirmation of federal-state-municipal "cooperation," it merely proposed that the head of the agency should be made an Assistant Secretary of Labor at a salary of $9000.

Early in February 1931, the Secretary wrote Wagner to urge his support for the measure. The senator replied on February 6 that he could not give it. "My objections are not addressed to detail; they are concerned with the fundamentals. Very frankly I am convinced that your proposal does not change my bill, but destroys it." Wagner observed that the substitute made no material change in an establishment that was "universally recognized" to be "unsatisfactory and inadequate." Instead of encouraging local responsibility, Doak proposed "a system whereby the Federal Government directly enters into the domain of the states and operates placement offices on its own account and perhaps even in competition with the state." While the bill used the word "cooperation," "it provides neither the means nor the incentives to its attainment." Wagner objected to the elimination of the advisory councils, since they provided a way of gaining public confidence; keeping the employees out of Civil Service, he observed, would open the door to "political appointees." Willits, despite his own marked preference for S. 3060, was sent to remonstrate with the senator. On February 11, Willits reported, "I have been unable to find any basis of compromise with Senator Wagner which did not involve the principle of Federal aid to the States." Wagner offered a number of concessions short of this: an appropriation to develop the existing service, a deferral of federal aid until July 1, 1932, and the appointment of a study commission to report not later than December 1, 1931.

Since Wagner insisted upon federal aid and the President adamantly opposed it, a test of political strength was unavoidable, and the House provided the arena. On February 19, Doak sent his bill to the Judiciary Committee. The Committee, despite the vigorous objections of Wagner and the state industrial commissioners, reversed itself on the following day and reported the Doak bill favorably. Graham brought the substitute onto the floor on February 23. He attacked the Wagner bill on the grounds that the establishment of offices in states presently without them would be federal coercion and that it provided for an unconstitutional "dole." The main burden of reply fell upon La Guardia. He pointed to the reversals of position by Hoover, Doak, and the Judiciary Committee as well as the endorsement of the Wagner bill in 1930 by former Labor Secretary Davis. The federal government, La Guardia observed, could under the Doak bill set up offices over the objection of the states, while the Wagner bill would preserve local responsibility with federal cooperation. Representative Charles O'Connor of Oklahoma concluded the debate with this remark: "We are going to have either a wake or a wedding. I am in favor of a wedding and trust that the Doak amendment will be voted down." It was, by the large margin of 182 to 84. The House then passed the Wagner bill by voice vote with certain minor amendments agreeable to its sponsors.

On February 24, 1931, the Senate, with Wagner's urging, passed the House version of the employment-service bill. A few days later Congress adjourned, thereby placing the full responsibility for decision upon the President's shoulders.

Pressure built up quickly. A flood of letters and telegrams urging Hoover to sign descended upon the White House, many from influential persons, such as industrialists Morris E. Leeds and Ernest G. Draper, President Frank Aydelotte of Swarthmore, and Professor Herman Feldman of Dartmouth. Industrial engineer Lillian M. Gilbreth wired that she found great interest in and demand for the Wagner bill in industry. Wagner himself sent a telegram to the President, pleading with him to sign. Most important was a memorandum drawn by Hoover's Emergency Committee for Employment on March 5, which was "placed personally in the President's hands" on March 7. Colonel Woods strongly urged Hoover to affix his signature to the measure and gave him a closely reasoned argument for doing so.[5]

Nevertheless, Hoover vetoed the employment-service bill on March 7, 1931. His message, certainly one of the most remarkable in the history of the presidency, deserves quotation at length:

I have given earnest study to the so-called Wagner bill for improvement of public employment agencies, in an effort to find a method to make it of use in the present employment situation. I find upon study, however, that if I would prevent a serious blow to labor during this crisis, I should not approve the bill. I have repeatedly urged a proper extension of public employment agencies, but this bill, unfortunately, abolishes the whole of the present well-developed Federal Employment Service, and proposes after certain requirements are complied with, to set up an entirely new plan by subsidies to the states from the Federal Treasury. And even were there no other objections to the plan, it cannot be made effective for many months or even years. It is not only changing horses while crossing a stream but the other horse would not arrive for many months. This situation alone required that legislation be deferred, as it will not help in emergency but will do great damage.

The fundamental questions involved also require more consideration. This bill proposes, as I have said, to destroy the Federal Employment Service in the Department of Labor, which has developed out of many years of experience, and to substitute for it 48 practically independent agencies, each under state control, the Federal Government paying for them as to 50% and based not upon economic need of the particular state but upon mathematical ratio to population. On the other hand, the existing Federal Employment Service is today finding places of employment for men and women at the rate of 1,300,000 per annum. It cooperates and coordinates with the service already established by some 30 states. It applies its energies to interstate movements and, being a mobile service, it concentrates upon the areas in need. Beyond this, however, the present Federal Service has special divisions devoted to the planting and harvest movement in agriculture and a special organization for veterans. There is no provision for the continuation of these two very important special services under the new plan, and the interstate quality of the Federal Service is destroyed. In any event, the bill required effective action by the legislatures and governors of the various states at a minimum time requiring so long a period for its establishment as to be of no purpose in this emergency. And there is, therefore, ample time to consider the whole of the questions involved. There is no financial loss to labor in allowing this bill to lapse. While the bill provides for $1,500,000 expenditure over the next 15 or 16 months, one-half of it would be absorbed in relieving one-half the present expenditure of the states without any additional service on their part. On the other hand, the present Federal Service has available over the next 15 or 16 months nearly $1,000,000 for the conduct of its agencies, which are being rapidly expanded through the emergency appropriations.

"It is not likely," Lescohier wrote, "that any veto message of an American president ever exceeded this one in misstatements of fact." Professor Sumner H. Slichter concurred: "The veto message itself was one of the most dishonest documents I have ever read."

Beyond Hoover's assertion that he had given the matter "earnest study," there is nothing true in the message. The claim that he was preventing "a serious blow to labor" was baseless; William Green, who had a better right to speak for workers, had warmly endorsed the bill. The President's statement that he had repeatedly urged the extension of employment agencies was absurd, since he was now vetoing the measure he had previously supported in principle. The argument that the bill would not take effect "for many months or even years" was at best a half-truth; the federal part of the system would have gone into effect at once. The assertion that S. 3060 "will do great damage" in emergency was an exercise in fantasy. The bill would not have established "48 practically independent agencies, each under state control"; it would have abolished the twenty-four independent offices and have substituted for them a system conforming to minimum federal standards. The existing USES was not making placements "at the rate of 1,300,000 per annum"; this was the total for all public employment agencies, and state activity exceeded federal in a ratio of 25 to 1. The assertion that USES "cooperates and coordinates with the service already established by some 30 states" was untrue. The claim that S. 3060 "destroyed" the migratory farm-labor division had no merit; the bill explicitly provided for its continuation and, furthermore, migration had so diminished that a special division was no longer needed. The measure permitted a separate placement division for veterans. The contention that the federal appropriation "would be absorbed in relieving one half of the present expenditure of the states without any additional service on their part" was false. To qualify for federal grants, they would have to match the amount offered and the director general would make this determination. Further, New York, Pennsylvania, Illinois, Minnesota, and Wisconsin were at that moment planning expansions which they would more than double with United States aid; the Canadian dominions under a similar arrangement had enlarged their facilities sixfold.

The veto message was of such great contemporary importance and so damaged the President's reputation with persons interested in labor problems that some speculation as to his motives is in order. It must be mere speculation: the Hoover archives are not open. Lescohier's contention that Doak and Attorney General Mitchell put him up to it (though assigning ultimate responsibility to the President) makes little sense. Doak, we know, favored the bill till Hoover spoke against it; moreover, the Secretary had so little influence on anyone that it is difficult to see how he could have persuaded so stubborn a man as Hoover. Mitchell's advice, presumably, would have gone to the matter of constitutionality, the NAM argument. But the veto message did not raise this point, and the case for the constitutionality of the grant-in-aid principle was very strong. It seems clear, therefore, that the President himself made the decision, a conclusion supported by the events of December 1930, as well as by the fact that the message was written in unmistakable Hooverian prose.

Why, then, did Hoover fly in the face of his own earlier pronouncements and the advice of his experts, with the consequent alienation of public opinion (even such stalwart Republican organs as the New York *Herald Tribune* and the Buffalo *Evening News* denounced the veto) and embarrassment of his supporters in Congress? In his *Memoirs,* published in 1952, Hoover declared that he vetoed to prevent putting jobs "in control of political machines, such as Tammany in New York, or the Hague gang in Jersey City." This is patently false. The veto message itself did not refer to politics. Further, both examples cited were municipal machines and S. 3060 operated through the states rather than the cities. Finally, in New York Governor Roosevelt was then locked in conflict with Tammany, and the New Jersey state government was in Republican hands. Another possible explanation is that Hoover, by killing the employment-service bill, was really forestalling unemployment insurance. Interest in the latter mushroomed in early 1931; the American Association for Labor Legislation had launched a campaign for unemployment compensation in December 1930; Wagner's long-term goal was a combined system of employment exchanges and unemployment insurance on the European model. Hoover, given his distaste for unemployment insurance, would have had good reason to prevent "the entering wedge." Yet, the fact is that the veto message failed to mention insurance and there was no discussion of it in Congress or by PECE. Nor can stock be placed in the charge that Hoover did not want Wagner to get the credit; he had already signed two Wagner bills. In the final analysis we are left with the budget argument. S. 3060 would have required a substantial increase in federal outlays for the employment service. Hoover, we know, objected fundamentally to the grant-in-aid feature. In 1931 he was increasingly preoccupied with balancing the budget in the face of shrinking income and growing expenditures. He both believed in a balanced budget as sound fiscal policy and regarded it as a means of inhibiting new and undesirable federal programs. In the case of the statistical and public works bills he had kept a tight grip on the purse strings. The veto message contains three remarks about costs, notably the nose-holding reference to "subsidies to the states from the Federal Treasury." Hence it would seem that the motive most consistent with Hoover's character and outlook that inspired him to reject S. 3060 was the desire to avoid an increase in federal expenditures.[6]

But the effect of the veto of March 7 was to leave the unsatisfactory employment-service situation unchanged. The debate over the Wagner bill had so aroused public opinion that the President was impelled to take administrative action as a substitute for legislation. On March 12 he announced the appointment of John R. Alpine, an official of the Grinnell Company and former president of the Plumbers union, as Special Assistant to the Secretary of Labor in charge of USES. Alpine was responsible for what came to be called the "Doak reorganization." Under this plan USES opened a large number of offices in communities which it had not earlier served.

The reorganization failed either to improve the employment service or to stem the criticism. Jones, who was superseded by Alpine, resigned on August 31, 1931, with a bitter public denunciation of Doak. Alpine replied in kind the following day. The expansion, according to Gladys Palmer, was completely uncoordinated. The veterans' and farm-labor divisions were not tied in with general activities. More serious, USES opened many offices in direct competition with the states and municipalities; in fifty-three of the ninety-six cities in which it operated in 1932, USES duplicated existing offices. The state agencies were outraged by this invasion of their territory. In Virginia, for example, a friendly relationship of many years' standing was wiped out. The state's Commissioner of Labor, John Hopkins Hall, Jr., wrote Doak on May 2, 1931, that the reorganization had taken place "without in any way advising, consulting, or cooperating with this Department, all . . . sub rosa." Officials in Arkansas, Wisconsin, Pennsylvania, Illinois, New Hampshire, Massachusetts, and Minnesota recounted similar tales. W. A. Rooksbery, Arkansas' Commissioner of Labor, observed that the reorganization did not "add to the efficiency of the Employment Service, in fact we have a suspicion that the principal object . . . was . . . taking care of political friends." According to Andrews, Doak gave his pals the new jobs at his disposal, as of July 30, 1931, some fifteen being former associates in the Railroad Trainmen. The reorganization, Miss Palmer wrote, "promptly fell into disrepute."

The Hoover Administration's mismanagement of the employment-service problem was signified in an incident that occurred at an American Legion conference on unemployment in the fall of 1931. Alpine pledged that USES would help get work for veterans, concluding triumphantly, "I found two of your men jobs this morning in one hour, just using the telephone!" To this a Legion official replied: "Fine, I'll give you a list of 750,000 names to place." [7]

5

Senator Wagner, despite the modesty of his program, could derive little comfort from the fourteen arduous months of legislative activity between January 1930 and March 1931. While two of the three bills that bore his name had been enacted, there were no concrete results: neither the senator nor anyone else knew or could know how many people were out of work, and the nation was without an effective program for the advance planning of public works. Wagner's employment-service bill had been vetoed and the agency he sought to rehabilitate was a shambles. His achievements were almost entirely in the area of public education. The senator had not lost heart; he had failed to win control. President Hoover in these early years of the depression was still the ultimate source of political power. It was Hoover who had dictated the emasculation of the statistical and public works programs and who had prevented the enactment of the employment-service measure. And it was Hoover who countered Wagner with his own program for dealing with unemployment.

CHAPTER 7

# The Breakdown of Local Resources

ON RELIEF President Hoover spoke with authority. Few Americans — certainly no one in public life — had had his range of experience both at home and abroad. His reputation was universally acknowledged. The philosophy he voiced was clear, firm, and consistent. It enjoyed a wide acceptance among both the experts and the public at large.

The relief of distressed Americans, Hoover believed, was a local responsibility. The primary obligation rested upon the family, the neighbor, the landlord, and the employer. Their recognition of need was immediate and personal; their combined resources exceeded all others. The second line was the local community — the established private relief organizations affiliated in most cities with the Community Chest or the new public agencies financed out of tax revenues in some municipalities. In a grave emergency the state might offer its assistance. Federal intervention, however, was to be avoided at virtually any cost. In part, this was because it would be remote and impersonal. But more important, Hoover declared on December 13, 1930, the transfer of this local obligation to the national government would undermine that "spirit of responsibility of states, of municipalities, of industry and the community at large, [which] is the one safeguard against overwhelming centralization and degeneration of that independence and initiative which are the very foundations of democracy." Federal relief, he announced on February 3, 1931, would destroy "character" and strike at "the roots of self-government."[1]

✻

287

1

Hoover was right in pointing to private social institutions in the local community as the front line of defense, but he overestimated their resources. The family, of course, sustained the main blow, but its capabilities were severely limited. While the joblessness of the breadwinner put pressure upon his wife and older children to seek work, ubiquitous unemployment made it extremely difficult for them to find it. A study of 8722 out-of-work persons in Philadelphia in 1931 by Ewan Clague and Webster Powell revealed that their families averaged only 1.3 wage earners in contrast to 1.9 for the city's general population. Existing reserves proved both inappropriate and inadequate to tide these families over a prolonged period of lost income. The principal forms that savings took were home ownership, life insurance, and bank accounts. Unemployed workers who owned homes had trouble maintaining payments on existing mortgages and in negotiating larger ones. Most of the life insurance was of the "industrial" type, which was useless in an emergency. The only effective form of savings was cash in a bank account. Over one half the families had none. Among the whites, 46 per cent had accounts, but they averaged only $339. About the same proportion of Negro families had accounts; however, their average was but $150. The rising number of bank failures threatened even these meager resources. "It is difficult to see," Clague and Powell concluded, "how the average family with savings and other reserves could possibly have held out much over two months."

In the early years of the depression millions of neighbors performed acts of kindness to destitute families: gifts of food, sharing of warmth, shelter for the homeless, small loans, encouragement. But this was relief delivered in a wholly disorganized way. It depended not upon need but upon the whim and capacity of the giver. The fact that most of the jobless lived in working-class neighborhoods meant that the resources of those next door were little greater than their own.

Perhaps the most important form of private relief was rent forgiveness. Despite the stereotype of the greedy landlord, it is probable that property owners as a class made a greater contribution to assisting the unemployed than any other private group. Whether the motive was charity or frank recognition that rent simply could not be collected is not the point; by and large, families without income were permitted to remain in flats for which they paid little or nothing. In Philadelphia, for example, Clague and Powell found that 63 per cent of the white families and 66 per cent of the colored were in arrears. The number of evictions — notwithstanding Communist efforts to capitalize on them politically — was very low. The conviction grew among the unemployed that rent was the last item which they would pay. More important, relief agencies in some communities would assume little or no financial responsibility for rent. Philadelphia's Committee for Unemployment Relief paid no rent; this was the case intermittently in Chicago; in Cleveland the relief authorities paid half a month's rent for a family that received an eviction notice; in Toledo a family on relief got one month's rent upon notice of eviction; in Pittsburgh the agencies differed in policy — regular payment, every other month, and only to prevent eviction.

The employer, except in so far as his firm made charitable contributions or paid taxes used to support relief agencies, did little directly to assist with unemployment relief. His function, which the depression seriously complicated, was to make money rather than to give it away. Some employers were callous. In April 1931, for example, the Department of Public Welfare of the City of Detroit was supporting 5061 families of former employees of the Ford Motor Company, constituting 20 per cent of the relief load. Since, as already noted, the main Ford plants were outside the city limits, the company was obliged to pay only nominal taxes in Detroit. Further, Henry Ford opposed philanthropy. "Endowment," he said, "is an opiate of the imagination, a drug to initiative."

Some employers were more responsible and experimented with several relief policies, of which work-sharing was by far the most common. One might argue with a good deal of cogency that when an employed worker shares his employment with a jobless worker, the former rather than the employer is contributing to unemployment relief. Since the program was initiated by management and was generally regarded at the time as an employer policy, it is so characterized here. It will be discussed at length later on.

A few companies established loan funds for laid-off workmen. General Electric in 1930 set up such a plan to which employees and the company contributed equally. Persons out of work or on part time could borrow from the fund without interest (the company preferred to charge interest but acceded to the wishes of the employee representatives). This arrangement, strangely enough, was described by the president of GE as "unemployment insurance." Bethlehem Steel extended credit for rent, fuel, and purchases at company stores on an informal basis. Du Pont made personal loans to employees in need, but not after they were laid off. Goodyear operated three loan funds, helped workmen refinance homes, and cut prices in its cafeterias. International Harvester and Standard Oil of New Jersey made loans to unemployed workers. Westinghouse lent money to workers on less than half time. This company's East Pittsburgh plant was unusual in providing for direct relief. Up to June 1, 1931, employees contributed $27,000, which Westinghouse matched, and thereafter employee contributions were suspended and the company appropriated $7000 a month. This money was given directly to unemployed workers.

A handful of companies, of which Dennison Manufacturing was notable, had genuine unemployment insurance systems which antedated 1929. In the unfavorable climate of the depression, practically no others experimented with this device. The exception was a group of fourteen companies in Rochester of which Eastman Kodak was the largest. In 1931 each agreed to make an annual appropriation not in excess of 2 per cent of payroll in order to create an insurance fund. If, after January 1, 1933, there was "a prolonged period of unemployment," employed workers would contribute 1 per cent of their earnings and the companies would match the amounts. Those who made less than $50 a week would be entitled to benefits of 60 per cent of weekly earnings but not to exceed $22.50 a week. Those with over five years of service would receive the maximum of thirteen weeks of unemployment compensation. The benefits, however, were not put into effect at the time, so that the plan was only a token of good intentions.

2

The sheer magnitude of distress exposed the inadequacy of un-organized private relief at the outset of the depression. The family, the neighbor, the landlord, and the employer, even when they so wished, were incapable of grappling with unemployment relief on this scale. Hence the load shifted almost at once to the cities, to their private and public welfare agencies. *Fortune* posed the problem of the jobless urban worker: "What do you do?"

You are a carpenter. Your last cent is gone. They have cut off the gas. The kid is white and stupid looking. You have al-ways earned your own way before but you can't get a job now for love or money. What do you do?

In some, but by no means all, cities you can get a meal at the Salvation Army or the Municipal Lodging House merely by waiting a few hours in a breadline. But that's no use now. So you go to the cop. He pulls out his directory and sends you to one of the listed charitable societies. The society takes your name and gives you emergency aid if you need it. It then asks you a list of questions about your age, your nationality, your religion, and your need. Your answers to these questions will determine to which of the charities specializing in Jews, Cath-olics, Protestants, abandoned babies, homeless boys, sickly chil-dren, pregnant women, disabled veterans, and the like you should be sent. You draw the Episcopal Family Relief Society. The Relief Society clears your name through the central agency to see that you are not receiving help elsewhere and sends around within the next few days to visit your family, prepare a budget, detail a nurse (if there is one), and eventually to allot you $2 to $8 a week, depending on the locality and the funds available. If its funds are exhausted it asks you to wait. Meanwhile you register for work. You wait anyway.[2]

New York, of course, presented the biggest problem. On the other hand, it was the best equipped of the great cities to handle unemployment relief: it had many established welfare agencies run by competent social workers; it was highly organized in ethnic, religious, and economic groupings; many of its leading citizens and newspapers were conscious of a responsibility to the community; and its financial resources were unmatched. New York's prime weakness was its city government, headed by the Tammany dandy, Jimmy Walker. But Walker's peccadilloes were soon to be his undoing and there was as an outside resort a more competent and responsible administration in Albany.

In the first year of the depression the load fell almost entirely upon the established private agencies. The religious charities, especially the Catholic and Jewish agencies, sought to care for their own. The main program, however, was run by the Association for Improving the Condition of the Poor under William H. Matthews, a tireless and cheerful friend of the needy. AICP had pioneered with work relief during the depressions of 1914–15 and 1921–22 and so instituted a similar program in 1929–30. After arrangements with the city, AICP hired unemployed workers to make improvements in the public parks under the supervision of the regular staff. As of the year ending September 30, 1930, $200,000 had been spent in wages to employ 1564 men for varying periods. This outlay barely scratched the surface of the relief problem, and the AICP was without further resources.

Mounting unemployment and the anticipation of winter made a bigger program imperative. In August 1930, therefore, the Charity Organization Society drew up an emergency plan for work relief. The city estimated the number of men it could use on municipal projects, and nonprofit organizations — churches, settlements, educational institutions — indicated their work opportunities. The assumption was that the emergency would last six months. The program would be administered jointly by the AICP and COS through an Emergency Work Bureau headed by Matthews.

The central problem was money. In September, Seward Prosser of the Bankers Trust Company agreed to head an Emergency Employment Committee of financiers and industrialists to raise funds. When the Prosser Committee launched its drive on October 15, the announced goal was about $4 million — $150,000 a week to provide jobs for 10,000 men at the rate of $3 a day for a five-day week. It became clear almost at once that the sights were too low.

On November 5, Prosser raised them to $6 million — $200,000 a week to provide 13,500 jobs for thirty weeks. New York, he declared, was experiencing "a community disaster" with some 300,000 jobless. Matthew Woll of the AFL protested the $3 wage rate. Early in December it was raised to $5 a day for a three-day week. By this time it was obvious that the funds would be insufficient. On December 4, for example, 158 men were in line at five o'clock in the morning at the Work Bureau and when the doors opened at eight the queue extended for two blocks. The Prosser Committee therefore lifted its goal once again, to $8 million. The campaign was a success: the Committee raised $8,520,000, mainly in large gifts. The Rockefellers contributed $1 million, Edward S. Harkness $500,000, and the Milbank Memorial Fund $250,000 from its capital resources.

The Emergency Work Bureau program was efficiently conducted. Each case was carefully screened to establish need and to avoid duplication. The program provided a substantial volume of employment for five months, from December 1930 to April 1931. In all, 37,531 persons received work relief, with a peak of 26,039 in January. Slightly over half were assigned to governmental projects — constructing roads, surfacing playgrounds, building fences and water fountains, clearing vacant lots, renovating hospitals, and so on. The remainder were employed in nonprofit institutions, chiefly in renovation and repair. A relatively small number of women who were family breadwinners were engaged, mainly in sewing rooms to produce garments for the needy. The administrative and operating expenses came to only $382,000, of which 56 per cent went in wages to people otherwise unemployed.

This program, however, gave relief to only a small fraction of the city's jobless. In the winter of 1930–31 it was necessary to improvise emergency feeding for thousands of New Yorkers who might otherwise have starved. The bread line, that most degrading and offensive form of relief, burgeoned all over the city. In January 1931 there were eighty-two lines serving 85,000 meals a day. Many — notably those run by the Salvation Army, the churches, and the missions — were designed to help the needy. Some, however, were set up by publicity seekers. Racketeers moved in on the philanthropic rich, setting up soup kitchens in swanky neighborhoods and pocketing a large part of the funds. Bowery bums never had it so good; they toured the bread lines, putting away ten or twelve meals a day. The respectably unemployed were either reluctant or refused to ask for food on the streets.

In the winter of 1930–31, the streets of Manhattan became a battleground in the struggle for survival. Beggars appeared in large numbers, asking, "Brother, can you spare a dime?" That absurd symbol of the depression, the apple, made its entrance. Thread-bare jobless men stood on street corners peddling the fruit in frigid weather as the offices emptied. The apple became a minor issue of public policy. When the Bureau of the Census classified apple sellers as employed (with some reason), the enemies of the Hoover Administration joyfully trotted out their big guns. The President himself stubbornly argued that the peddlers demonstrated sound American enterprise in launching these ventures. Oregon and Washington growers had shrewdly devised a method of unloading their crop at high prices. "Many persons," Hoover later wrote, "left their jobs for the more profitable one of selling apples." The hit song of a 1931 Broadway musical, entitled "When Yuba Plays the Tuba Down in Cuba," developed this theme:

> *Any sap can sell an apple*
> *But this chap would rather grapple*
> *With his oompa, oompa, oompa.*
> *He prefers it to a boopa, doopa, doopa.*

The bread lines, the soup kitchens, the street beggars, and the apple sellers gave the City of New York a black eye. The world's richest city was losing its reputation — and not just in America. In the spring of 1931, the natives of the Cameroons in West Africa sent over $3.77 for the relief of "the starving."

The inadequacies of the Prosser program, both as to size and duration, and public revulsion against the scenes on the streets made the city's intervention imperative. It began in a characteristically haphazard way. The police in the fall of 1930 made a count of the families in need. The city then "suggested" to its 125,000 employees that they donate 1 per cent of their earnings to a relief fund. The money was used by the police to purchase huge quantities of food which were doled out in the precincts especially at Thanksgiving and Christmas. More important was the emergency lunch program for school children established by the Board of Education and financed by teachers and school employees. Thousands of children were fed each day in the schools with hot balanced meals, cooked and served by women on relief. "Depression's children . . . are learning to look to the public-school system," Frances Warfield wrote, "not only for the three 'R's but for food, medical attention, and, if necessary, three 'C's: clothing, coal, and cash — just a little cash; enough, say, to fend off the landlord a while."

The big question was what would happen when the Prosser funds ran out in the spring of 1931. In the preceding November the Welfare Council created a coordinating committee of prominent citizens headed by Al Smith to plan a program. One of its first acts was to denounce the proliferation of bread lines and street begging. On January 6, 1931, Prosser warned the mayor that his committee was incapable of meeting the need and asked the city to appropriate $10 million for relief. Walker was noncommittal. At the end of the month Smith announced "a crisis" in relief. The mayor still did nothing. On February 27, a mass meeting staged by social workers at Town Hall demanded an appropriation of at least $10 million to be spent on work relief at the rate of $2 million a month. The city's Corporation Counsel, Arthur Hilly, responded that the charter forbade such an expenditure. By this time, the Prosser fund was virtually exhausted; there could be no further delay. On March 31, the state legislature passed an enabling act to allow the city to borrow for relief, and Governor Roosevelt promptly signed it. On April 10, a first installment of $2 million became available. The City of New York was now, willy-nilly, in the business of unemployment relief.

The program was administered by existing municipal departments, and the unemployed were registered in public buildings. To qualify, a needy person must have been a legal resident and voter for at least two years. No effort was made to avoid duplication. Men given work were considered city employees on part time and received the standard rate for common labor, $5.50 a day. At first they got three days a week (earnings of $71.50 a month), but it was soon cut to two ($44 a month). In the spring and summer of 1931, the program provided work relief for approximately 15,500 people at a cost of $1,250,000 per month. The program was riddled with inefficiency and political favoritism. Much of the work done was of no value. Some of the participants received help from other sources. The Seabury investigation revealed serious irregularities: employed persons accepting relief (one family had a weekly income of $115), the ignoring of the residence requirement, and preference for enrolled Democrats.

New York's relief programs provided a certain amount of wry humor. There was, for example, the story of the woman fired because of slack business whose final paycheck was short $1.52 — "deducted for the unemployed." And there was the society matron with a big place in Westchester who let fourteen of her twenty-two servants go so that she could contribute their wages to the relief fund. Finally, there was the volunteer lady who feared that the amount given in relief by her agency was insufficient to support a family. "It's all right, my dear," she was told, "statistics prove that three people can live quite satisfactorily on fifteen dollars a week — without food, of course."

These jokes were not really very funny because it was not possible to laugh long at misery. The prospect of another winter of depression, as 1931 drew to its close, left New Yorkers grim. The number of jobless grew larger and hope dimmed for an early improvement. Private charity, even with the emergency help of leading financiers, was inadequate and exhausted. The city, reluctantly driven to action, had proved itself inept and corrupt.[3]

But the New York relief program was masterfully organized in contrast with the chaos that ruled Chicago. That city entered the depression bankrupt — financially and morally. Its archaic tax structure had collapsed in the twenties. In order to meet day-to-day expenses, administrative units had been compelled to issue tax anticipation warrants that the banks accepted; by the time of the crash the combined obligations exceeded $125 million. Reassessment, undertaken in 1927, had not been completed by 1930. As a result, many property owners had not paid taxes for three years. In late 1929, the banks announced that they would accept no more warrants. Chicago was flat broke, heavily in debt and without credit. Policemen and firemen were discharged; schoolteachers received no salaries; the County Hospital and the public welfare stations had not paid their 1929 bills; mothers' pension checks were not sent out. The mayor, Big Bill Thompson, was incompetent and corrupt. His chief claim to fame was the political threat to punch King George V in the snoot. Organized crime, operating with the connivance of the Thompson regime, ruled Cook County as no American metropolis has been controlled before or since. The boss of Chicago was not the mayor but Al Capone. The city's leading citizens and newspapers were mainly without a sense of social responsibility.

Into this unsavory gumbo was poured the misery of mass unemployment. Joblessness was serious even before the crash and became acute thereafter. In the first year of the depression private charities on insignificant budgets struggled helplessly with the immense relief load. The schoolteachers, despite the fact that they were seldom paid, financed an emergency lunch program. As the winter of 1930–31 approached, outside help became indispensable. The city, obviously, was without resources. Hence in October 1930 Governor Louis L. Emmerson of Illinois established a Commission on Unemployment and Relief. "We are afraid, confidentially," he informed a top official of the Hoover Administration, "that the situation will be greater than we can cope with. . . ." The main function of his commission was to raise $5 million from private sources for relief in Chicago. The drive was barely successful. Direct relief absorbed $4 million. The remainder was set aside to expand a work-relief program that the United Charities had launched in the summer of 1930 on a $60,000 donation by an individual. About 8000 persons found employment in governmental and nonprofit agencies, none earning more than $50 a month.

Chicago, as the nation's transportation hub, had a severe transiency problem. Throngs of homeless men, joined by boys and women as the depression wore on, descended upon the city. In the fall of 1930, a shanty town appeared at the foot of Randolph Street. Its citizens called it Hooverville and its thoroughfares Prosperity Road, Hard Times Avenue, and Easy Street. When food ran low, "Mayor" Donovan appointed a committee to visit the hotels for leavings. "There is not a garbage-dump in Chicago," Edmund Wilson observed, "which is not diligently haunted by the hungry." The relief agencies improvised means to deal with the flood of transients, putting them up in asylums, poorhouses, and veterans' homes, or, best of all, getting them out of town. The Oak Forest poorhouse in 1931 lodged them in the corridors and was compelled to turn away 19,000.

By the fall of 1931, Chicago was desperate. On October 15, according to the Illinois Department of Labor, 624,000 persons were out of work in the city. The private charities were incapable of handling the load and the municipality was incompetent to do anything. The only hope was outside aid — from the state or the federal government.[4]

Philadelphia provided the most imaginative and effective of the municipal relief programs in the early years of the depression. The city had not spent public funds on relief since 1879, thereby making the burden of the private agencies notably heavy. Perhaps as a consequence community responsibility was highly developed. Both the University of Pennsylvania and Swarthmore College sponsored research programs on unemployment, and the entire press, and especially J. David Stern's *Record*, vigorously supported unemployment relief. Perhaps most important was the quality of leadership: two distinguished social workers, Jacob Billikopf, executive director of the Federation of Jewish Charities as well as impartial chairman in the New York men's clothing industry, and Karl de Schweinitz, secretary of the Community Council; a remarkable banker, Horatio Gates Lloyd, partner in Drexel & Company, the local branch of the House of Morgan; and to a lesser extent the Republican mayor, Harry A. Mackey.

Philadelphia's unemployment problem was unusually severe, the rate exceeding that in all major cities except Detroit and Cleveland. This was because several of its industries, especially in the textile trades, suffered sharp declines before the crash. By the fall of 1930, therefore, the need was acute. Billikopf and de Schweinitz sparked a mass meeting of leading citizens at the Bellevue-Stratford Hotel on November 7, 1930, which resulted in the creation of the Committee for Unemployment Relief. The social workers persuaded Lloyd to accept the chairmanship, a job to which he was to devote his full time at a salary of a dollar a year. De Schweinitz became the secretary. Drexel & Company made a whole floor of its building available as office space (the irony of relief for the jobless emanating from the nation's leading banking house aroused no comment). The Lloyd Committee raised almost $4 million at once in private donations and was responsible for the disbursement of over $14 million by the time of its demise in the summer of 1932.

The program was highly diversified. Between November 14, 1930, and July 15, 1931, direct relief was granted to 33,000 families through the facilities of nine established agencies. In early 1931, the Committee helped disburse, in addition to its own funds, $400,000 of city money for family relief. A large work-relief program was created in public and nonprofit agencies. A total of 15,515 heads of families found jobs on these projects, most of them at the rate of $4 a day. The Committee directed special attention to projects employing white-collar people: a study of the city's traffic problem by 650 unemployed men of various skills, a survey of colonial landmarks by jobless architects and draftsmen, Braille typesetting by unemployed typographers, concerts given by out-of-work musicians, and so on. The Baldwin Locomotive Works donated a building that was converted into a shelter for homeless men where 11,993 persons received lodging, supper, and breakfast between November 1930 and June 30, 1931. Mayor Mackey, disguised as a hobo, periodically visited the shelter to inspect its facilities. The Philadelphia Loan Fund was set up to aid families in straitened but not desperate circumstances. By May 1931 the Fund had issued loans either without interest or at very low rates to 563 families, ranging in amount from $18 to $175. Emergency school breakfasts, prepared and served by women on work relief, were given 10,000 children in private and parochial schools. A committee collected discarded clothing and arranged for its repair and distribution to the needy.

Despite its drive and ingenuity, the Lloyd Committee fought a losing battle. The number of jobless continuously outgrew its resources. Hence Billikopf, de Schweinitz, and even Lloyd became insistent champions of public relief. In late 1931, Philadelphia had 250,000 out of work. "We have unemployment in every third house," J. Prentice Murphy, executive director of the Philadelphia Children's Bureau, told the Senate Subcommittee on Manufactures.

"It is almost like the visitation of death to the households of the Egyptians at the time of the escape of the Jews from Egypt."[5]

Detroit suffered the most acute relief crisis of any major American city. Severe unemployment in the auto industry antedated the crash and mounted sharply afterward, giving the motor city the doubtful distinction of possessing the highest jobless rate in the nation. The Ford payroll slumped from 128,000 in March 1929 to 37,000 in August 1931. In contrast with a "normal" relief registration of 17,000, the city had 211,000 applications on hand in February 1931. By spring, they were coming in at the rate of 600 a day. On the basis of reduced demand for their services, the utilities estimated that 150,000 people moved out of Detroit in 1931. Civic responsibility was virtually nonexistent. Henry Ford's views on relief received wide publicity and set the tone. Senator Couzens' offer in late 1929 to donate $1 million for relief if other citizens would raise $9 million went begging. As late as January 1932, private groups had raised a mere $700,000, including $200,000 from Couzens. The press, excepting the Hearst paper, had little sympathy for the jobless. The bankers insisted upon a lowering of the relief standard to bare survival as a condition for loans to the city. The Department of Public Welfare at the outset of the depression was both inefficient and corrupt.

Detroit, as a consequence of these conditions, could do little more than mass-disaster relief. There was no time to distinguish the differential needs of families and no money for relatively costly work relief. In the municipal campaign of 1930, Frank Murphy won election as mayor on a platform of aid to the unemployed. A liberal Democrat, a devout Catholic, and a warm and sympathetic human being, Murphy's main preoccupation as mayor was the fulfillment of this pledge.

With a virtual absence of private resources, the city had no alternative but the assumption of public responsibility for relief. Murphy at once set about the reorganization of the Department of Public Welfare. He established the Mayor's Emergency Committee under the chairmanship of G. Hall Roosevelt to register the unemployed, help them find what little work was available, and screen out those in greatest need. He created a Homeless Men's Bureau, which by April 1931 was providing lodging or meals to over 10,000 persons.

The load of the Department of Public Welfare mounted steadily from monthly expenditures of $116,000 in February 1929 to $1,582,000 in the same month of 1931. By April 1931 the Department was supporting 45,464 families. The standards, under banker pressure, were terribly low. In late 1931, Public Welfare gave two adults $3.60 a week for food with an added allowance for each child. The city was seldom able to provide for all of the needy. A study of 900 families dropped from the rolls in 1931 revealed that their average income per person from all sources was $1.56 a week.

When Mayor Murphy appeared before the Senate Manufactures Subcommittee on January 7, 1932, he admitted that Detroit was staggering under its relief burden. Tax income was declining and the city's capacity to borrow was narrowing. Though he was a strong advocate of local responsibility, Murphy reluctantly declared "that there ought to be Federal help, as at present the assistance we are able to render is inadequate. . . ." [6]

New York, Chicago, Philadelphia, and Detroit attacked their relief problems in the early years of the depression with varying methods and uneven achievements. The thread that ran through all four experiences was the breakdown of private and municipal resources in face of the magnitude of the crisis. In this they were typical of all American cities. Many communities, particularly the smaller ones, did nothing at all. A survey of fifty-nine cities in New York State in the winter of 1930–31, for example, revealed that most were without definite programs, that few of their welfare commissioners felt competent to deal with the task, and that only a handful based relief upon actual need. Some towns substituted hokum for action. The "Grand Rapids Plan," put over by an advertising man, utilized the press and radio to sell "the basic soundness and greatness of the United States." Folks would not "think straight" until "panic" was removed from their minds. "A relaxed and determined mind is necessary to constructive thought." A full stomach, apparently, had no relationship to a happy mental state.

By the fall of 1931, municipal relief — private and public — was bankrupt in virtually every city of the United States. *Fortune* generalized the crisis in this fashion:

The theory was that private charitable organizations and semi-public welfare groups, established to care for the old and the sick and the indigent, were capable of caring for the casuals of a world-wide economic disaster. And the theory in application meant that social agencies manned for the service of a few hundred families, and city shelters set up to house and feed a handful of homeless men, were compelled by the brutal necessities of hunger to care for hundreds of thousands of families and whole armies of the displaced and the jobless. And to depend for their resources upon the contributions of communities no longer able to contribute, and upon the irresolution and vacillation of state Legislatures and municipal assemblies long since in the red on their annual budgets. The result was the picture now presented in city after city ... heterogeneous groups of official and unofficial relief agencies struggling under the earnest and untrained leadership of the local men of affairs against an inertia of misery and suffering and want they are powerless to overcome.[7]


## 3

The federal government could hardly stand by in a state of complete inaction as this disaster unfolded. Hoover had held off for a year following the crash for fear that the creation of a federal agency to deal with unemployment and relief would "magnify" the emergency in the public mind. The dreary prospect of the winter of 1930–31 and the demand for a special session of Congress, however, made some overture necessary. Consequently, in October 1930 he called Mrs. William Brown Meloney, an editor of the New York *Herald Tribune*, and told her that he had decided to create an emergency committee. He asked her to suggest the names of a prominent man for chairman, an outstanding woman, and a public relations expert. Mrs. Meloney recommended Colonel Arthur Woods, Dr. Lillian Gilbreth, the industrial engineer, and Edward L. Bernays, an advertising man. The first two were to serve; Bernays participated only in the organizational stage. His main contribution was the agency's name: President's Emergency

Committee for Employment (PECE). He urged against the word *un*employment.

The President appointed Woods chairman of PECE on October 21, 1930. He was a good choice. Attractive and engaging, Woods had a background in both business and social service. A Harvard graduate and an intermittent businessman, Woods had taught at Groton, been a reporter, the police commissioner of New York during the Mitchell reform administration, a colonel in World War I, had been responsible for finding employment for discharged soldiers after the Armistice, and secretary of President Harding's 1921 Conference on Unemployment. In the twenties he had been associated with the Rockefellers — in charge of developing Rockefeller Center, a director of the Rockefeller Foundation and the General Education Board, and involved in the Williamsburg restoration. His key assistants at PECE were the vice-chairman, Fred C. Croxton of the Ohio Department of Industrial Relations, and the secretary, Edward Eyre Hunt, long associated with Hoover. The members of the Committee, numbering thirty, were about equally divided between businessmen and experts on unemployment. The latter included the labor economists Joseph H. Willits, Bryce M. Stewart, Leo Wolman, and W. Jett Lauck, as well as Porter R. Lee, director of the New York School of Social Work.

Hoover knew precisely what PECE was to do or, rather, not do. The agency, he announced at its public launching on October 30, was to encourage local responsibility for unemployment relief, which meant that the United States government's role would be minimal. "The federal government," Hunt wrote, "can supply moral leadership for coordinated action, and ... the action itself emerges out of a feeling of local responsibility and local initiative." Woods conceived of PECE as a "booster engine" to help the train up "a stiff grade." There should be no inference that "there was anything wrong with the existing motive power." Its services would be needed only for "a brief emergency period." This last notion was of the utmost importance. Woods himself took the chairmanship for only a few months and the other Committee members expected to be home shortly. The President opposed an appeal to Congress for either legislation or an appropriation. PECE funds, an insignificant $157,000 for almost a year, were supplied by the Department of Commerce. The assumption was plain: the emergency would be over in 1931, and even if it were not, no PECE would be around to deal with it.

The function of PECE, then, was not to do things itself but to stimulate others to do them. Its energies went into propaganda and prodding. By these means the Committee sought to spread good cheer, to increase the total volume of employment, to decrease the number of persons seeking jobs, to spread the existing employment over a larger number of workers, and to secure relief for the victims of unemployment.

Although the Committee was hardly as prolific in optimism as the White House, much of its effort was devoted to lifting the spirit. Woods appeared frequently on radio and at press conferences usually to report that the situation was in hand. His favorite technique was to telephone the governors of the forty-eight states or the mayors of a large number of cities and then issue a cheerful general press release. No one seems to have been convinced. PECE could not escape the fact that unemployment was growing worse rather than better. A PECE member with business connections, for example, reported after a visit to Wall Street that he uncovered nothing but "Stygian gloom." There was little confidence that the Committee would change "the direction of business from downward to upward." PECE's public relations campaign was frustrated in unexpected quarters. Postmaster General W. E. Brown refused to stamp envelopes with "Help the Man Who Wants to Work" because the dies were too expensive.

The Committee spent a small part of its energies in seeking to create jobs, mainly in federal construction. On November 21, 1930, Woods urged the President to support a $600 million federal-state highway program, a federal public works expenditure of $100 million, and the establishment of a Federal Reconstruction Board with an appropriation of $50 million for loans to the states for works. Hoover, who talked about increasing governmental building, rejected these proposals because he felt that the government's construction program was already at the limits of "financial prudence." "All right-thinking people," Howard Brubaker observed in the *New Yorker,* "will stand behind the President in his two new policies: rigid economy . . . and a colossal building program. . . . We might have them on alternate days." As a consequence of Hoover's decision, PECE's public works activities were confined to speeding up projects already committed, a useful but hardly significant function. In addition, Woods went on the radio to urge universities, hospitals, and other nonprofit institutions to take advantage of low building costs by expanding their facilities. Finally, the Committee tried to persuade private citizens to make work by broadcasting pamphlets with such titles as "Suggestions for Possible Repairs and Improvement in the Home and Its Equipment" and "Spruce Up Your Garden." A plan to start a "Buy Now" campaign never got started because economists thought it either irrelevant or objectionable. It is, of course, impossible to know how many jobs PECE created, but it is certain that their number was only a tiny fraction of the jobless total.[8]

PECE participated in a limited way in the Hoover Administration's program to curtail the supply of labor by eliminating aliens — foreign and resident — from the labor force, as well as by other means. In September 1930, the President imposed a virtual embargo against those seeking to enter the United States by invoking the "likely to become a public charge" provision of the immigration statute. In the succeeding five months only 10,000 visas were issued to residents of twenty-one nations with combined quotas of 74,233. The embargo was imposed with special severity against Canada and Mexico. In February 1931 only 3147 immigrants entered the United States, the smallest monthly figure since the inception of records in 1820. Secretary of Labor Doak, responsible for the Immigration and Naturalization Service, launched a vigorous deportation campaign against aliens who had entered the country illegally, many of whom he described as "Reds." The methods of Doak's agents, characterized by Senator Wagner as "dragnet," left civil libertarians aghast. In 1931 Doak shipped an estimated 20,000 persons out of the country. The labor movement cheered him on. In January 1931 Green urged Congress to raise the appropriation for the border patrol in order to protect American jobs. Violence was inevitable. In California, Filipino field hands were beaten, shot, and barred from employment in the agricultural valleys. PECE assisted in this program. The Committee's representative in Texas arranged with the southwestern railroads to move over 25,000 alien Mexicans to the border. In the summer of 1931 it mobilized educational and other organizations to urge young people to return to school in September. To its credit, PECE refused to yield before the pressure to discriminate against employed married women in the labor market. This policy, Hunt declared, was not "sound from a business point of view or desirable from a social point of view."[9]

Much the most important of PECE's labor-market policies was to spread the diminishing amount of employment over more workers. Hoover had laid down the line in the autumn of 1929 by urging industry to "so distribute employment as to give work to the maximum number of employees." The Committee vigorously pushed work-sharing, arguing with businessmen that it kept workers off relief, helped maintain hourly wage rates, increased employee loyalty to the firm, and resulted in no significant rise in unit costs. Industries with regular schedules were told how to cut weekly or daily hours; continuous-operation plants were shown how to alternate shifts or gangs to maximize the number of jobs; retailers were advised on scheduling for the long days and weeks that many stores remained open.

The policy had a great effect. In July 1931 Croxton announced that one third of the workers in a sample of firms studied by PECE were on part time. Myron C. Taylor took to the radio to state that United States Steel, operating at only 38 per cent of capacity in December 1930, had as many employees as it had had in the same month of 1929. This company's average weekly hours declined from 46.2 in 1929 to 34.4 in 1931. Numerous large corporations adopted the same policy: American Telephone and Telegraph, Bethlehem Steel, Du Pont, General Electric, General Motors, International Harvester, Standard Oil of New Jersey, Westinghouse. Average weekly hours declined between 1929 and 1931 from 44.2 to 40.5 in manufacturing, from 44.8 to 41.1 on the railroads, and from 38.4 to 28.3 in bituminous coal.

PECE's enthusiasm for work-spreading was alloyed with a certain concern for its cost. The Committee's pamphlet *Emergency and Permanent Policies of Spreading Work in Industrial Employment* admitted: "The policy of spreading work shifts a part of the loss in earnings to those employees who would have been retained on full time." R. A. Stevenson, director of the University of Minnesota's Employment Stabilization Research Institute, more bluntly described work-sharing as a device by which "industry [is] asking American labor to bear the major cost of unemployment relief." In specific cases he cited, workers were compelled to give up half their incomes. "No such request has been made of those in managerial positions or of capital." The contributions of workers, Stevenson concluded, were "entirely out of proportion to their responsibilities in the present emergency." [10]

PECE's most immediate problem was relief for the unemployed, and it was here that its policy of local responsibility was put to a searching test. In the cities there were governmental and private authorities, no matter how inept or corrupt, to shoulder the obligation; in nonurban areas such agencies were either weak or non-existent. A relief crisis of national magnitude emerged in the southern Appalachian coal fields in the winter of 1930–31. The full story of the collapse of coal will be told in due course. Here it is necessary only to call upon one witness to testify as to the terrible price in human misery that was paid in the bituminous fields. Fred A. Krafft, Director of Industrial Relations for the Consolidation Coal Company with offices in Fairmont, West Virginia, made a careful investigation of conditions, particularly in the Monongahela Valley. They constituted, he wrote on April 11, 1931, "destitution," the result of "unemployment . . . in the mines of this region." This situation existed "not only . . . among the lower laboring classes, but likewise prevails among persons who have never known the meaning of destitution or the . . . degradation of seeking relief." Even a casual survey of the district would reveal "many families . . . who lack food, shelter and clothing." Many children were unable to attend school during the winter months "because of a lack of stockings, shoes and heavy clothing." In some fields, notably Harlan and Hazard in Kentucky, miners were working for "starvation wages, as low as $1.75 to $2.00 per day."

The relief crisis was aggravated by the great drought that had parched the Southwest and the Mississippi and Ohio Valleys in the summer of 1930, causing severe losses to farmers in those regions. Congress had appropriated $45 million for agricultural relief and the Red Cross had raised $10 million to aid the stricken farmers. A number of the coal fields — especially those in West Virginia, Kentucky, and southern Illinois — were in areas affected by the drought.

PECE could hardly escape the double-barreled crisis of coal and drought. Its relief expert, Porter Lee, concluded after careful study that national action was required and that the only organization that could supply it was the American Red Cross. It had readily assumed responsibility for aiding the victims of drought. Lee, however, could get nowhere in persuading ARC to help the miners and their families. The Red Cross argued that its sole obligation was to persons who suffered from a natural disaster, or, in the words of its chairman, John Barton Payne, "a temporary condition brought about by some uncontrollable act or acts." The misery in the coal camps was man-made and so beyond its jurisdiction.

PECE brushed this argument aside. In early February 1931 Croxton visited the coal fields. He reported on February 9 that "the people in the mining regions simply cannot exist under the present conditions." An official of a coal company told him that the situation was "breeding anarchy in West Virginia." PECE concurred with Lee: immediate help was indispensable and the Red Cross alone could provide it. Colonel Woods visited Payne the same day and was told that "the coal mining problem . . . is not the job of the Red Cross." On February 11, at Woods's insistence, he and Payne met with the President at the White House. Hoover urged Judge Payne "very quietly and unobtrusively . . . to relieve the distress." According to Woods's impression, "Payne agreed that the Red Cross would do this." The colonel then went to West Virginia for a two-day personal inspection of the mining districts. On February 14 he wrote Payne that he had found "desperate suffering" and the most pressing need for "immediate help." He certified six counties — Boone, Logan, Harrison, Monongalia, Marion, and Kanawha — in which there were conditions of "desperate distress." They were, he pointed out, in the drought area and had suffered from that natural disaster.

Judge Payne was determined to confine the commitment he

had given the President and Colonel Woods within narrow limits. The word went out to Red Cross chapters in West Virginia now dispensing relief to drought victims that miners should also receive help, provided they lived on "some acreage." Since few of the miners were farmers, most could not qualify. In the Monongahela Valley the relief load, such as it was, was carried by the County Relief Board, the Family Welfare Society, and the Salvation Army. The local Red Cross chapter granted no relief at all to miners. The local newspapers as well as those in New York, Baltimore, and Washington carried statements by ARC officials minimizing the seriousness of conditions in West Virginia. "From a community standpoint," Krafft wrote on April 11, "we are frank to state that, as a result of the indifference of the local Red Cross chapter . . . the citizens of this community will not in the future subscribe to the activities of this organization as they have generously done in the past."

PECE also sought to get assistance for the miners from the congressional appropriation for drought relief. On February 17, 1931, Woods wrote Secretary of Agriculture Arthur Hyde to ask that the Department distribute seed packets to miners farming less than an acre and make loans for the purchase of seed to those working an acre or more. Hyde replied on February 25 that, since it was "extremely doubtful" the loans would be repaid, PECE should instead ask the Red Cross to distribute free seed packets, a suggestion failing to stir Woods. Again, he went to the White House and persuaded Hoover to direct Hyde to work out a small loan program to place seed potatoes and garden seed in the hands of miners. Hoover's instructions were not carried out. Dr. C. W. Warburton, secretary of the Agriculture Department's Federal Drought Relief Committee, vigorously opposed the plan. He wrote Woods on April 7 that under the law this distribution could be made only on a loan basis. In order to obtain a $1.50 packet, a miner would have to make formal application and execute a note and mortgage on his crop. This would make "a prime morsel for newspaper photographers" and leave the Administration "ridiculed from one end of the country to the other." He carried his views to the President, who readily understood the position and ordered Warburton "to drop the project entirely."

PECE had come to bat twice for the destitute miners and had struck out both times. On the third try it reached first base on a scratch hit. PECE invited the American Friends Service Committee to assume responsibility for relief in the coal camps. This Quaker organization agreed to do so, provided that $200,000 could be raised. Late in May the President offered to approach the Red Cross for a transfer of this sum. On June 1, Judge Payne flatly turned Hoover down. PECE refused to give up. A month later Croxton arranged for Clarence Pickett, head of AFSC, and himself to meet with the ARC officials. Payne told them that the Red Cross would not indirectly expend money which it would be improper to disburse directly. The condition in the coal fields had not arisen "by reason of an Act of God" and so was not "an emergency." He also had "a well-prepared lecture on the value of self-help." PECE and the Friends then succeeded in raising the money privately, apparently from the Rockefellers. In August 1931, at long last, a modest relief program for destitute miners and their families began, directed mainly to feeding children.[11]


4


By the fall of 1931, President Hoover's theory of local responsibility for unemployment relief was in ruins. Private institutions were virtually defenseless; the municipalities were submerged under the weight of the relief load; the President's Committee, as planned, had been dismantled and Woods had returned to New York in disgust. Hoover, who had assumed that the PECE would no longer be needed, now faced more severe unemployment in the winter of 1931–32. He would be compelled to improvise still another emergency federal agency: the President's Organization on Unemployment Relief (the Gifford Committee).

Hoover's theory had failed in practice because it assumed the impossible, that a national problem could be managed with local means. On all sides voices were raised in the demand for direct federal responsibility for relief. Among them were the social workers. Heretofore few people had bothered to listen to them. When in June 1931 the American Association of Public Welfare Officials strongly endorsed federal relief, they found a large and receptive audience. No group knew as much firsthand about the plight of the unemployed as the social workers.

Further, the idea was gaining currency that local relief combined with work-sharing was a tax-dodging scheme designed to protect the rich by transferring the burden of unemployment relief to the poor. "We have the dole in America," Sumner H. Slichter wrote. "But the real recipients . . . are not the men who stand for hours before the Salvation Army soup stations . . . [they] are the great industries of America." "I am completely satisfied," Governor Gifford Pinchot of Pennsylvania wrote his brother on November 17, 1931, "that the moving impulse behind Hoover's whole handling of the unemployment situation has been his desire to protect the big fellows from additional taxation, just as you said."[12]

Hoover's personal popularity could not withstand the bankruptcy of his relief policy. At this time Babe Ruth held out for his usual $80,000 salary from the Yankees. A friend, cognizant of the depression, remonstrated, "That's more money than President Hoover gets." "So what," Ruth replied, "I had a better season than he did." And Hoover still had the winter of 1931–32 before him.

CHAPTER 8

# Collapse

In 1931 an obscure twenty-five-year-old Czech mathematician at the University of Vienna named Kurt Gödel published a paper in a German scientific journal with the forbidding title "On Formally Undecidable Propositions of *Principia Mathematica* and Related Systems." "Gödel's proof," as the conclusions came to be known, demolished the axiomatic method, the foundation of mathematics since the Greeks. Gödel demonstrated that arithmetic could not be brought into order because the axioms upon which it was based were irreconcilable. Even that most precise of the sciences, mathematics, was now in a state of disarray.

The publication of Gödel's paper could not have been more symbolically timed: collapse was in the air. In 1931, central Europe lay prostrate, ripe for fascism. The economic rot spread swiftly westward; the failure of the banking systems of Austria and Germany was followed by Britain's dramatic abandonment of the gold standard on September 21, 1931. In the United States an economic decline that for two years had been little different from earlier depressions became in the fall of 1931 the Great Depression. Concern gave way to despair; gray turned black.

On the day the Bank of England stopped the redemption of pounds in gold, Thomas Wolfe wrote his mother in North Carolina:

The trouble in England will affect the whole world, and we may soon be in as serious a condition ourselves — and perhaps we will not meet it as well as they have. No one seems to be doing anything about it, everyone is standing around with his mouth open as if he expected the gates of heaven to open the next moment and rain milk and honey all over him. People talk about "the pendulum swinging backward" and "conditions are bound to change" — This is foolish talk: conditions are not *bound* to change unless something is done to change them, and at present it seems that any change will be for the worse. . . . I think we are at the end of a period.

A few weeks later President Hoover met secretly with thirty of America's captains of finance. To avoid notice, the conference was held at the Massachusetts Avenue apartment of Secretary Mellon rather than at the White House. Looking down from the walls upon the grim bankers were the art treasures that would one day form the nucleus of the collection of the National Gallery. The President was overwhelmed with gloom and the fear of impending disaster. He had himself written out a long memorandum analyzing the situation, which he read to the assemblage. He carefully described the imminent danger to the American banking system as a consequence of the events in Europe. A large number of banks had already closed their doors in the Midwest, as well as in Pennsylvania and New York, and the failures were soon to reach into New England. Although he probably did not do so, he might as readily have set forth the terrible economic and social price that American labor was to pay.[1]

1

The Hoover Administration's policy of wage maintenance had already collapsed. "Some banks and some bankers," the outspoken Commissioner of Labor Statistics, Ethelbert Stewart, declared in the spring of 1931, "are hell-bent to get wages back to the 1913 level." James A. Farrell, president of United States Steel, was equally concerned. "We are living in a fool's paradise," he told the American Iron & Steel Institute in May, "if we think that every steel manufacturer in the U.S. has maintained . . . the current rates of wages; it has not been done." In July 1931 wages in the building trades in many cities began to fall. At the same time U.S. Steel cut its dividend rate from $7 to $4 and announced a reduction in the salaries of its executive and white-collar people.

Secretary of Commerce Lamont, known to be close to the steel industry, began talking publicly in July about the desirability of lower wages. In September the news was released: United States Steel would reduce wage rates 10 per cent effective October 1, 1931.

Given the historic pattern of wage change in the steel industry, Big Steel's action was certain to be followed by all the other companies, both in amount and in timing. Even more important, it shattered the wage line in American industry generally. General Motors, U.S. Rubber, the textile industry, and the Pittsburgh Coal Company quickly followed the example. A few weeks later wage maintenance could be declared officially dead when Henry Ford, the nation's champion of high wages, abandoned the $7 day. Ford, in fact, went beyond steel's 10 per cent; he cut the wages of men earning between $8 and $9.60 to between $6 and $6.40. In the following few months wage-cutting became the order of the day. A prominent manufacturer, according to the *New Yorker*, not only reduced his employees' wages 10 per cent but also sent notices to his two divorced wives to whom he paid alimony: "Owing to business conditions, I regret, etc." The City of Toledo chopped the salaries of its employees 25 per cent. The Philadelphia *Public Ledger*, the *New York Times*, and the New York *Evening Post* bit off 10 per cent. The Chamber of Commerce of the United States cut the same amount. In the spring of 1932 building tradesmen in New York City and Chicago suffered 25 per cent reductions. Hoover's thumb was no longer plugging the hole in the wage dike.

The reductions in the heavy industries were made unilaterally by the great corporations in the absence of collective bargaining. In a handful of cases the unions were sufficiently strong either to prevent or to delay the cuts. In anthracite coal, for example, one of the few residual fields of United Mine Workers' strength, wage rates suffered no reduction despite a proposal by the operators for a 35 per cent cut in August 1932. John L. Lewis remained unflinchingly faithful to the Hoover wage-maintenance policy. More interesting was what occurred on the railways.

In the first two years of the depression the carriers had sustained a devastating loss of business. Of the 1,700,000 men they had employed in 1929, 500,000 were jobless and another 500,000 were on part time. In early 1931 the top executives of the great eastern trunk lines met in Philadelphia: General W. W. Atterbury of the Pennsylvania, P. E. Crowley of the New York Central, J. J. Bernet of the Chesapeake and Ohio, and Daniel Willard of the Baltimore & Ohio. They discussed the alternatives of higher rates or lower wages. The former was rejected as self-defeating, leaving no choice but a wage reduction. Willard held out the hope of achieving it by peaceful negotiations. He was the only one present who had any standing with labor. Willard had long accepted collective bargaining, and the B & O shops had provided the trial area for one of the notable labor-management cooperation plans of the twenties. It was common knowledge that when an eastbound freight car arrived in the Pittsburgh yards without route assignment, the railway clerks would "just slip it to Uncle Dan." The time had come for Willard to test his good will with labor.

In September 1931, Willard proposed a 10 per cent reduction, the anticipated figure for steel. On October 12, the four executives met with the heads of the operating unions — Alvanley Johnston of the Locomotive Engineers, D. B. Robertson of the Firemen, S. C. Berry of the Conductors, and A. F. Whitney of the Trainmen — at the Biltmore Hotel in New York. Willard made his proposition and the labor men agreed to explore it. In November representatives of eighty railroads, after heated debate between Willard and the great western roads, which wanted a deeper cut and its unilateral imposition, voted to designate a negotiating committee of nine and to serve notice of a 15 per cent reduction. On January 15, 1932, this committee met with a similar one representing both the operating and nonoperating crafts at the Palmer House in Chicago, surrounded by 1500 union general chairmen. Weeks were consumed in exhausting public speeches for the record. The committees met in the interstices for real bargaining. The unions, while talking about achieving the six-hour day, actually sought to confine the wage cut to 10 per cent. Willard joined them in this objective. The problem was that his committee had no representation from the antiunion roads and so he did not know whether he could deliver the Union Pacific, the Burlington, and the Southern Pacific, which insisted upon 15 per cent. On January 31, just as the committee was about to disintegrate, agreement was reached: wage rates would be reduced 10 per cent, effective February 1, 1932, for a period of one year; on February 1, 1933, they would revert to the pre-cut level.

Willard, Robertson, and the other negotiators were hailed as statesmen for working out this difficult problem. The unions, according to Wall Streeters, had struck the better bargain: they had preserved existing rates four months longer than steel; they had negotiated 10 per cent at a time when 15 per cent had come to prevail; and they had won automatic restoration in 1933.[2] What no one noticed contemporaneously was that the railroad industry for the first time in its history had engaged in nation-wide collective bargaining. Even more remarkable, this had occurred with far from universal union organization. In fact, a precedent of industry-wide bargaining had been set which was to prove the major accomplishment of the 1931–32 negotiations.

2

"Being a proletarian in good standing," Heywood Broun remarked laconically, "is no bed of roses." The shrinkage of employment between the fall of 1931 and the spring of 1933 was beyond doubt the saddest proletarian episode in American history. Joblessness in the first two years of the depression, though grave, was hardly disastrous. In fact, according to the estimates of the Committee on Economic Security, there was a modest seasonal improvement in the warm months of 1931: unemployment declined from 8,334,000 in February to 7,971,000 in July. Thereafter the mounting flood of joblessness was irresistible. In October 1931 the figure stood at 9,138,000 and by December had climbed to 10,814,000. The year 1932 was an unmitigated calamity. January found unemployment at almost 11.5 million; 12 million was reached in March, 13 million in June, and 13,587,000 in December. The statistics for the first three months of 1933, when the banking system teetered and then collapsed, were almost beyond belief: 14,492,000 in January, 14,597,000 in February, and 15,071,000 in March. On the day that Hoover left the presidency, March 4,

1933, one out of every three wage and salary earners in the United States was totally without work and there is no way of knowing what proportion of the others were on part time.

Some communities and industries suffered almost total devastation, as though they had been visited by natural disaster. By early 1932, coal-rich Williamson County, Illinois, provided almost no employment. In the town of Coello with a population of 1350, Mauritz A. Hallgren amazingly reported, only two persons had jobs. In Benton at least 2000 children had not tasted milk for a year. Donora, Pennsylvania, in March 1932 had 277 persons employed out of a population of 13,900. At the Edgar Thomsen Works of United States Steel at Braddock, Pennsylvania, in January 1932 there were 424 full-time employees out of a "normal" force of 5235. While 3292 others were listed as part-time, only 800 of them found work on a given day. At the height of the season in the men's clothing industry in January 1932, according to Sidney Hillman of the Clothing Workers, only 10 per cent of the New York membership was employed. Of the 108,000 wage and salary earners in the congressional district including Birmingham, Alabama, Representative George Huddleston reported, 25,000 were totally jobless on January 5, 1932, and 60,000 to 75,000 others were on short time. When the city advertised for 750 laborers to do "the hard, dirty work of digging" a canal at $2 for a ten-hour day, there were over 12,000 applicants.

Unemployment, of course, affected individual industries differently. The Committee on Economic Security calculated an index of employment by various industry groups with the 1929 monthly average considered as equal to 100. In March 1933 the index for building stood at 18.7, for forestry and fishing at 31.1, for mines and quarries other than coal at 32.5, for manufacturing at 58.2, and for coal at 64.4. Other industries were less affected. The index for wholesale and retail trade fell only to 72 by March 1933, for telephone and telegraph to 73.2, and for banking and insurance to 79.4. That is, unemployment was most severe in construction, the extractive industries, and manufacturing. While the depression took a toll in all sectors of the economy, the heavy industries suffered far more joblessness than the light.[3]

Little is known about the volume of unemployment in relation to

other economic and social factors. A study of the jobless in
Minneapolis, St. Paul, and Duluth revealed that small firms proportionately had fewer layoffs than large. There are numerous indications that the very young and older workers sustained more severe unemployment than those in the middle years of life. A man
over forty-five who lost his job found it virtually impossible to obtain another. Women were subject to conflicting forces. Since they
were employed in the industries or jobs which suffered the least
unemployment, they maintained a higher retention rate than men.
At the same time, married women with working husbands were
under pressure to retire from the labor force. The City of
Syracuse, for example, fired 170 women in December 1931 for this
reason. Married women, Teamster Dan Tobin editorialized, have
no business working. Negroes suffered devastating losses. The
Urban League in 1931 reported that while Negroes constituted only
17 per cent of Baltimore's population, they provided 34 per cent
of the people on relief; similar ratios prevailed in Akron, Des
Moines, Houston, and St. Louis.[4]

The oppressive weight of unemployment distorted the labor
market. Wage earners whose ability and seniority justified promotion to better jobs found the jobs nonexistent. On the railroads,
for example, the fireman and trainman had no opportunity to rise
to engineer and conductor. In addition, there was a widespread
but immeasurable downgrading throughout the labor force. As work
crews were reduced in size, the highly skilled bumped down into
low-skill jobs. Some employers fired high-wage employees and
replaced them from the pool of the jobless with workers at lower
rates. The study of unemployment in Minnesota cities revealed
that a majority of those who had lost jobs and then found new
ones came on at a lower occupational level. The case of the graduate engineer who became an office boy was by no means unusual.
A survey of people terminated by a New Haven rubber factory
indicated that in the third year following the layoff the average
annual earnings of those formerly skilled were $34 less than those
who had been unskilled and $98 below those formerly semiskilled.
Massive unemployment, of course, dried up voluntary turnover.
In the Minnesota study only two of the 500 people interviewed left
their jobs because of dissatisfaction with working conditions. The

Bureau of Labor Statistics' quit rate for manufacturing declined precipitously: in February 1933 only 0.49 workers per 100 in American factories quit work for reasons other than discharge or layoff. The individual wage earner's sole bargaining weapon — the voluntary quit — had virtually ceased to exist; unemployment assured the employer that his employee would love his work.

Unemployment severely strained the American wage system. Unfortunately, it is not possible to chart the movement of wages with precision because of the absence of monthly data. The annual statistics are necessarily crude: the figures for the year 1931 include both the periods of wage maintenance and of its collapse, and those for 1933 both the wage trough and the revival with NRA. Hence it is necessary to keep these shortcomings in mind in dealing with annual data.

The average hourly earnings of production workers in manufacturing, according to the Bureau of Labor Statistics, declined from 51.5 cents in 1931 to 44.2 cents in 1933, or 14.2 per cent. In bituminous coal for the same years the decrease was from 64.7 cents to 50.1 cents, or 22.6 per cent; on the railroads it was from 65.1 cents to 59.5 cents, or 8.6 per cent. Average weekly earnings between 1931 and 1933 followed a similar downward course: in manufacturing from $20.87 to $16.73 (19.8 per cent), in coal from $17.69 to $14.47 (18.2 per cent), and on the railways from $26.76 to $23.09 (13.7 per cent). Real wages did not fall as rapidly as money earnings at this time because prices declined. The BLS Cost of Living Index (1913 = 100) decreased from 153.9 in June 1931 to 129.8 in June 1933, or 15.7 per cent.

The wage averages conceal the extremely low rates that appeared in growing numbers in 1932 and 1933. While they were in the minority, they were by no means unusual. Briggs Manufacturing Company in Detroit paid men 10 cents and women 4 cents per hour ("If poison doesn't work," auto workers chanted, "try Briggs"). A study of 355 female department store clerks in Chicago revealed that 294 received less than 25 cents an hour, with over half under 15 cents, one fourth under 10 cents, and 24 under 5 cents. A rate of $1.50 a day for a coal miner in the nonunion fields was cited. The labor rate in Birmingham, Alabama, was about the same figure. When Bibbs Manufacturing slashed wages, Edward **F.**

McGrady told the Senate Manufactures Subcommittee, the president of the company informed his textile workers that they should be able to get along on 2 cents a meal. The Pennsylvania Department of Labor uncovered rates of 5 cents an hour in sawmills, 6 cents in brick and tile manufacturing, and 7.5 cents in construction. The State Commissioner of Labor reported that sweatshops in Connecticut paid girls between 60 cents and $1.10 for a fifty-five-hour week. The average daily rate for farm labor without board in the United States in 1933 was $1.11.

The distribution of wage decline by industry group followed that of unemployment. Per capita weekly earnings for the years 1931–32, according to Leo Wolman, fell 22.3 per cent in bituminous coal, 19.2 per cent in manufacturing, 19.0 per cent in metal mining, 12.1 per cent on the railways, 11.2 per cent in trade, 7.6 per cent in anthracite, and 6.3 per cent in public utilities. Once again, employees in the heavy industries bore the brunt of the decline, except where they were represented by unions strong enough to slow the pace of wage reduction. The wages of unorganized workers fell far more rapidly than did those of the unionized during the depression. By 1933, H. M. Levinson concluded, the differential between workers in the two groups, whose wages had been approximately equal in 1914, was at least 30 per cent in favor of the organized, much of it the result of the unequal rate of decline in the years immediately preceding 1933.

There is some evidence that wage-cutting in the later years of the depression had a greater impact upon high than upon low rates, with the result that the extraordinarily wide differentials between the skilled and the unskilled that prevailed in 1929 were narrowed by 1933. The data are so skimpy that they merely suggest rather than confirm this conclusion. Between 1930 and 1932, according to BLS, the average hourly earnings of top and bottom classifications in various industries declined as follows: in boots and shoes, turn sewers' earnings decreased 29.1 per cent in comparison to 21 per cent for female table workers; in textile dyeing and finishing, machine engravers fell off 19.5 per cent and female plaiters dropped 14.6 per cent; in hosiery, footers' earnings declined 47.4 per cent as winders' actually rose 7.1 per cent; in men's clothing, cutters fell 19.2 per cent as female examiners went down 16.1 per cent; in motor vehicles, hammermen's earnings declined 20.4 per cent in comparison to a drop of 4.7 per cent for female laborers; in rayon mills, spinning bathmen fell 31.6 per cent, but female truckers increased 9 per cent. In all these cases, of course, the cents-per-hour decline for the top job far exceeded that for the bottom job. The automobile hammermen's earnings, for example, dropped from an average of $1.005 in 1930 to 80 cents in 1932, a loss of 20.5 cents; the female laborers' earnings declined from 38.2 cents to 36.4 cents, or 1.8 cents.[5]

3

In November 1932 the California Unemployment Commission, made up of distinguished citizens chosen by Governor James Rolph, issued an exhaustive report on joblessness in the Golden State. The Commission's findings on the social price paid by the victims of unemployment justify quotation at length.

This study of the human cost of unemployment reveals that a new class of poor and dependents is rapidly rising among the ranks of young, sturdy, ambitious laborers, artisans, mechanics, and professionals, who until recently maintained a relatively high standard of living and were the stable self-respecting citizens and taxpayers of this State. Unemployment and loss of income have ravaged numerous homes. It has broken the spirits of their members, undermined their health, robbed them of self-respect, destroyed their efficiency and employability. Loss of income has created standards of living of which the country cannot be proud. Many households have been dissolved; little children parcelled out to friends, relatives, or charitable homes; husbands and wives, parents and children separated, temporarily or permanently. Homes in which life savings were invested and hopes bound up have been lost never to be recovered. Men, young and old, have taken to the road. They sleep each night in a new flophouse. Day after day the country over, they stand in the breadlines for food which carries with it the suggestion "move-on," "We don't want you." In spite of the unpalatable stew and the comfortless flophouses, the army of homeless grows alarmingly. Existing accommodations fail to shelter the homeless; jails must be opened to lodge honest jobhunters. Destitution reaches the women and children. New itinerant types develop: "women vagrants" and "juvenile transients." There are no satisfactory methods of dealing with these thousands adrift. Precarious ways of existing, questionable methods of "getting by" rapidly develop. The law must step in and brand as criminals those who have neither desire nor inclination to violate accepted standards of society.

Numerous houses remain physically intact, but morally shattered. There is no security, no foothold, no future to sustain them. Savings are depleted, and debts mount with no prospect of repayment. Economic make-shifts are adopted. Woman and child labor further undermine the stability of the home. The number of applicants for charitable aid increases seriously. There is not enough money to do the job well and adequately. Food rations are pared down, rents go unpaid, families are evicted. They must uproot their households frequently. Physical privations undermine body and heart. The peace and harmony of the home vanish. The effect upon children differs, but it is invariably detrimental.

Idleness destroys not only purchasing power, lowering the standards of living, but also destroys efficiency and finally breaks the spirit. The once industrious and resourceful worker becomes pauperized, loses faith in himself and society.

The Great Depression was an eruption that wrought profound changes in the social structure of the American labor force — in the movement of population, in the character of the family, in the birth rate, in the welfare of children, in health, and in morale.

The physical movement of people, historically a response to economic opportunity, was drastically changed by the removal of that opportunity. As a consequence of unemployment and Hoover's restrictive policy, immigration into the United States virtually ceased. In contrast with an annual average of over 300,000 between 1925 and 1929, the number of immigrants declined to 97,139 in 1931, 35,576 in 1932, and 23,068 in 1933. There is evidence that a declining share of even these few persons intended to enter the labor force; the proportion of males, which stood at over 55 per cent in the late twenties, fell steadily after 1929 to a low of 39 per cent in 1932. Emigration from the United States revealed only a modest increase from about 250,000 in 1929 to approximately 290,000 in 1931–32. Since the depression was world-wide, there was little point in fleeing unemployment in the New World in order to find it in the Old.

Within the United States the immense movement of population from farm to city that had occurred in the preceding decade was significantly slowed. The average annual number of persons who left the land in the twenties was well over 2 million. This figure declined to 1,762,000 in 1931, 1,219,000 in 1932, and 1,433,000 in 1933. The reverse movement from city to farm rose at the outset of the depression and fell thereafter. In contrast with a shift of 1,604,000 people to the farm in 1929, 1,740,000 went back in 1930 and 1,683,000 in 1931; the number dropped to 1,544,000 in 1932 and to 951,000 in 1933. The first impulse of the unemployed who had recently migrated to the city was to return to the farm. This feeling soon wore off. They missed the bright lights and, as public relief gradually became established, the higher city allowances. A good many compromised by settling on small farms on the outskirts of cities, where they could engage in agriculture and at the same time be available for industrial employment as well as qualify for urban relief. The Labor Department experimented tentatively and confidentially with a back-to-the-farm movement in 1931. Thirty-two South Carolina families who had migrated in the twenties from the hills to the mill towns, only to run into unemployment later on, were relocated on farms in the state. Although the results appear to have been satisfactory, the program was not expanded. Since agriculture was as depressed as industry, back-to-the-land despite its bucolic appeal was no solution to joblessness.[6]

A far more dramatic and significant aspect of migration was the appearance of the depression transient who simply wandered, the jobless, rootless worker, increasingly accompanied by his family. The transient was the worker adrift in a sea of unemployment, sailing aimlessly without home port or destination. He had lost his job or his farm and had no hope of finding another. The migrant was on the margin of organized society, in a vague sense its disturbing responsibility but not really a part of it. In February 1932 a jobless San Franciscan, after being evicted from his home for nonpayment of rent, deserted his wife and children for the road. He declared that he would shift for himself, but that society must assume the obligation to support the family. His wife agreed. The transient was in an ironic sense the hero of the depression epic, the symbol of a floundering America. He was Dos Passos' Vag in *U.S.A.* and Steinbeck's Tom Joad in *The Grapes of Wrath*, the stark, beaten, weathered face staring out of the pages of scores of books of photographs of the thirties. A song popular with the transients, "You Wonder Why I'm a Hobo," went like this:

*You wonder why I'm a hobo and why I sleep in the ditch.*
*Well, it ain't because I'm lazy; no, I just don't want to be rich.*
*Now I could eat from dishes, it's just a matter of choice;*
*But when I eat from an old tin can, there ain't no dishes to wash.*

*Now I could be a banker, if ever I wanted to be,*
*But the very thought of an iron cage is too suggestive to me.*
*Now I could be a broker, without the slightest excuse,*
*But look at 1929, and tell me what's the use.*

The hobo was nothing new in American society. His way of life — Hobohemia — was well known: Skid Row, the cheap saloon, the Bowery flophouse, and Jeff Davis, a self-crowned King of the Hobos. But time was running out; by 1929 growing mechanization had reduced his numbers and distorted the pattern of his existence. The Great Depression changed everything by driving hundreds of thousands of new people onto the road. The hobo and the transient differed basically in outlook. To the perpetual vagrant, work was repulsive; he rejected it as a matter of principle. To the depression migrant, work was the *summum bonum*; he hoped desperately to find a job.

No one, of course, ever made a reliable census of transients; it would be like counting birds of passage. A common estimate was that their number reached a million by early 1933. In the year ending with September 1932, the Chicago Clearing House registered 50,000. The Southern Pacific Railroad reported that it ejected a staggering 683,457 from its trains in 1932. The California Highway Patrol in the spring of 1932 counted at each station an average of 150 boys per week hitchhiking into the state. A remarkable aspect of the transients, upon which all observers commented, was their youth. By the end of 1932, Newton D. Baker estimated that 200,000 boys were wandering. Many older sons in families on relief left home so that the younger children would have more to eat. As the depression ground on, there was a marked increase in the number of women migrants. The Women's Bureau in mid-1933 counted almost 10,000 and estimated that they were only one sixth of the total, an increase of 90 per cent over 1932. Almost none of these females was over thirty years of age. Among all transients there was an unusually large number of college graduates, of unemployed doctors, pharmacists, lawyers, and teachers.

The migrants left home for one central reason: economic crisis. In some cases they sought work elsewhere; in others they simply fled from its absence where they were. For the former the venture was pointless. Since most of the transients came from the industrial cities, they were deserting the most likely areas of economic opportunity. But this was not a rational movement of population; it was, rather, what the National Resources Committee called it, "a migration of despair." In fact, few of the transients knew where they were going. "Means of locomotion vary," *Fortune* observed, "but the objective is always the same — somewhere else." When Morris Markey asked an eastern girl in a decrepit car on the Redwood Highway south of Seattle where she was going, she snapped: "Going? Just going."

The only meaningful direction to the flow was an inclination to the South. The weather can be cruel on the road; it is better to be hot than cold. When Frank Bane of the American Association of Public Welfare Officials gave a state-by-state summary of the relief problem to the Senate Manufactures Subcommittee in January 1932, he pointed to critical transiency situations in Florida, Texas, New Mexico, Arizona, Nevada, and Southern California.

No one wanted the transients. The states and cities, overburdened with the relief of their own, refused to accept the responsibility for others. In the smaller communities the migrants were simply told to get out of town. Some of the large cities had temporary shelters — the Hotel de Bum — where the vagabond received a night's lodging and a meal or two. He was expected to move on the next day. California was unique among the states in establishing labor camps for migrants — twenty-eight in forestry and two for highways. Men who volunteered worked six hours a day building firebreaks and roads mainly in the mountain areas. In return they received food, clothing, shelter, medical care, and tobacco — no money. The Army and Navy supplied surplus equipment. Supervision was by the State Forestry and Highway Divisions. The capacity of the camps was only 3352 men, a tiny fragment of the state's transient population. Mainly, the migrants were shunted back and forth between the communities that sought to be rid of them, the cruel policy of "passing on." Atlanta went a step farther: unwanted nonresidents were put in chain gangs. The railroads and the towns waged constant warfare, the former ejecting them from trains and the latter forcing them to leave town, usually by rail.

The transients devised an ingenious solution to the dilemma of unwantedness — the urban jungle. "Anyone who wants actually to see civilization creaking," the *New Yorker* reported in February 1932, "will do well to visit the corner of West and Spring Streets. . . . There is a whole village of shacks and huts there, made of packing boxes, barrel staves, pieces of corrugated iron, and whatever else the junkman doesn't want, and the people who live there do so because the New York Central hasn't got around to driving them off." Practically every city in the country had its jungle, an improvised community that existed on the edge of society. It differed from the city in many respects but above all in this: transients were welcome. In Oklahoma City there was a town for vagrants in the river bottom. Oakland had its "Sewer-Pipe City" at the foot of 15th Avenue. A kindly manufacturer of sewer pipe invited several hundred transients to live in his unsold products. Joseph Mitchell wrote a famous story about the Hollinan couple, an unemployed New York carpenter and a hotel maid. Dispossessed from their apartment in December 1932, they set up housekeeping in a cave in Central Park, where they lived for a year. The police, aware of their household, did not disturb them. The publicity induced a flood of contributions, including $25 from the novelist Robert Nathan, whose *One More Spring* was about derelicts who lived in the park.

The conditions of life among transients, both on the road and in the jungles, were bad. Feeding was irregular and inadequate; there was only sporadic shelter against the elements; clothing soon wore out and was hard to replace; it was impossible to keep clean; medical care was unavailable except in emergencies. The California Unemployment Commission described a jungle in that state which on June 8, 1932, was home for 185 single men and 86 families with 150 children: "Sanitation is ... bad; grounds filthy; no garbage collection; open improvised toilets, inadequate in number. Only one water faucet within half a mile of camping site; undoubtedly much water used for domestic purposes is taken from the Putah Creek." Venereal disease was endemic among transients. With hundreds of thousands of boys available, sexual perversion flourished. The education of children ceased. When an eastern traveler on a transcontinental train that stopped for water in inland California expressed surprise at the transient conditions in the neighborhood, the proprietor of a roadside stand bitterly commented: "Man, you don't know you are alive. Spend a week at this spot and I'll show you some things about these United States that will make you sick, or maybe afraid. Something is wrong. . . ." [7]

Men became transients because the depression uprooted their families. "In our society," E. Wight Bakke observed, "the family, not the individual, is the economic unit." The pressures upon this institution were severe: unemployment, poverty, social disgrace, loss of home, and overcrowding. To these forces families responded in two diametrically opposed ways. Those which were well integrated became more unified in face of the crisis. Those which were already under tension split apart. There is, of course, no way of knowing what proportion each constituted of the total.

There is, however, abundant evidence that the number of families that exhibited some manifestations of breakdown was very large. There were numerous criminal acts arising out of family deterioration: stealing, assault, even murder. There was a marked increase in prostitution, as the Lynds noted in Middletown, particularly on the part of married women eager to supplement the family income. Sexual promiscuity flourished in general. Social intercourse, because of the cost, declined. Drinking and drunkenness, despite the Eighteenth Amendment, increased. Families who lost their homes or were evicted from their flats often parceled out children to relatives or friends. Desertions were common. "My husband went North about three months ago," declared a California woman in 1932, "to try his luck. The first month he wrote pretty regularly.... For five weeks we have had no word from him.... Don't know where he is or what he is up to."

A family phenomenon upon which many sociologists commented was the denigration of the father. "The part of the breadwinner ... is the residual economic role," Bakke wrote, "without which self-respect is difficult in a culture which places ... economic responsibility upon the family." The jobless worker was not "a good provider"; he no longer played the leading role in the family drama. The father who washed dishes and made beds lost status in the eyes of his wife and children. Women, particularly in the early years of the depression, refused to believe that jobs were not to be had; something must be wrong with the man. "Have you anybody you can send around ... to tell my wife you have no job to give me?" an unemployed Philadelphian asked a social worker. "She thinks I don't want to work."

The number of marriages declined sharply. Young people who planned to wed were compelled to postpone the date. The marriage rate per thousand of population in the United States dropped from 10.1 in 1929 to 9.2 in 1930, 8.6 in 1931, and 7.9 in 1932. The birth rate, in face of this slowed pace of family formation and the burdensome cost of raising children, inevitably declined. The average annual number of births per thousand of population dropped from about 20 in the late twenties to 18.9 in 1930, 18 in 1931, 17.4 in 1932, and 16.6 in 1933. Falling reproductivity at this time produced what later was to become the famous "depression generation," marked for its small size and undesirable impact upon the labor force.[8]

The child who exhibited the good judgment to remain unborn made out better than many who embarked upon life during the depression. "The load of suffering," the Chicago social worker,

Sophonisba Breckinridge, wrote on October 17, 1932, "falls so definitely on the children." They were "cold and hungry and lacking security and developing physical conditions sure to bring on tuberculosis, and other maladies, and mental attitudes sure to bring on delinquency." She had just learned that the doctors and social workers at Chicago's Children's Memorial Hospital were "terribly upset because of the death of a child which they all said was due to the inadequate food ration given the family by the Unemployment Relief Service."

The effects of transiency and family deterioration upon children have already been noted. Equally serious was the re-emergence of the sweatshop, particularly in New England, the Middle Atlantic states, and the textile South. By early 1933 some 200,000 children and women were employed under shocking and illegal conditions in Pennsylvania. Governor Pinchot's investigating commission uncovered sweatshops all over the state: wages of under $4 a week, girls forced to humiliate themselves to hold jobs, an Allentown employer who checked off 33 cents from each child's pay to reimburse himself for a $100 fine for failure to carry workmen's compensation, work weeks of fifty to ninety hours. These conditions appeared in the men's clothing, shirt, pajama, silk, hosiery, cigar, and coal industries. But this was outside the law; within the zone of legality child labor continued to decline under long-term forces and the rate was accelerated by unemployment. The number of work certificates issued to young people dropped off sharply; school enrollments for children in the mid-teens rose; some cities, like New York, launched "stay-in-school" campaigns.

On May 16, 1932, Secretary of the Interior Ray Lyman Wilbur delivered a famous speech on child welfare to the National Conference of Social Work. "Our children," Wilbur declaimed, "are apt to profit, rather than suffer, from what is going on." He argued that prosperity made parents neglectful. "With adversity the home takes its normal place." Children, the Secretary contended, receive "better and more suitable food than in past good times." His audience, social workers with firsthand acquaintance with actual conditions, was outraged.

Wilbur might have been sobered had he read the report on the health of West Virginia miners' children written by Dr. Ruth Fox in September 1931. She found their average weight 12 per cent below standard. A steady diet of pinto beans, potatoes, and sow belly had caused low resistance to infectious diseases. None had drunk milk since weaning. There were no shoes and no schooling in the winter. In the town of Gallagher typhoid and dysentery were epidemic because the water source was polluted by mine outhouses. None of the families could afford ice or proper screening. Child mortality, Dr. Fox ominously concluded, was very high.[9]

Reports like that of Dr. Fox led the Hoover Administration to make health an important political issue. On January 2, 1932, the White House issued a statement by Surgeon General Hugh S. Cumming: "Despite the economic depression ... during the past year we have every reason to be thankful that in the matter of the most important wealth of the people, their health, the country has never been as prosperous in its history as during the year 1931." In the presidential campaign of 1932, Hoover stressed this point repeatedly. In accepting the Republican nomination on August 11, for instance, the President remarked that "the national averages of infant mortality, general mortality, and sickness ... are less today than in times of prosperity."

To support this position the Administration relied primarily upon the fact that fewer people died. The death rate, responding to long-term forces, declined per thousand from 11.9 in 1929 to 11.3 in 1930, 11.1 in 1931, 10.9 in 1932, and 10.7 in 1933. While this was cheering, it could hardly serve as substantiation for the conclusion that health improved during the depression. For one thing, these were averages. It was small comfort to the person who starved that he was exceptional. More important, poverty typically impaired rather than destroyed health. In his study of 400 Philadelphia families dropped from relief rolls in 1932, Clague found that they did not perish. By foraging like stray cats they somehow managed to stay alive.

There is, of course, an indirect relationship between income and health. While money of itself cannot prevent or cure disease, it can buy the things that reduce its incidence — good food, adequate housing, warm clothing, and sufficient medical, hospital, and public health services. The fact that a huge segment of the American population sustained a drastic cut in income inevitably reflected itself in poor health. The basic problem was malnutrition and the diseases it caused. "You eat just as much loafing as you do working," Will Rogers observed ironically. "In fact, more; you got more time." A 1931 survey of rural areas in Pennsylvania revealed an average rise of 25 per cent in undernourishment among children; examinations in fourth-class school districts showed that 216,000 out of 800,000 pupils suffered from malnutrition; new patients at tuberculosis clinics had nearly doubled since 1929. The medical department of the Ford Motor Company found that workers were catching infections because they were inadequately fed. The Milbank Memorial Fund in cooperation with the United States Public Health Service studied the health of 7500 families in eight cities. The rate of illness in 1932 was nearly 40 per cent higher for families with per capita annual incomes of less than $150 than for those with incomes of $425 or more. The highest sickness rate occurred among those whose incomes had suffered a sharp decline since 1929. Families of the unemployed had 27 per cent more illness than those with part-time workers and 66 per cent more than those with full-time wage earners.

Most dramatic were the cases of actual starvation. In 1931, New York City hospitals reported the following numbers: Bellevue, 59; Kings County, 33; Harlem, 2; Gouverneur, 1. A four-year-old boy, Narcisson Sandoval, died of starvation in Oakland. Ignatz Wlosinski perished from the same cause in a barn near Troy, New York. The sensational New York *Evening Graphic* ran a series on cases of starvation in 1932. Albert H. Wiggin, chairman of the board of the Chase National Bank, when asked by Senator La Follette whether he thought "the capacity for human suffering is unlimited," replied, "I think so."[10]

The most serious social impact of the Great Depression was upon the morale of the American people. The depression of the mind was more severe than that of the economy. The year 1929 became the frontier between one world and the next. Alfred Kazin remarked, "Society was no longer a comfortable abstraction, but a series of afflictions." The future, once so rosy, ceased to exist. The official plea for good cheer rang hollow. When Mrs. Hoover in 1932 asked folks to "just be friendly and neighborly with all those who just happened to have bad luck," she was greeted with derision. The President begged comedians to make people laugh, but the jokes were largely at his own expense. (Straight man: "Business is improving." Comedian: "Is Hoover dead?")

The evidence of the breakdown in morale was abundant. "I'm afraid," Charles Schwab of Bethlehem Steel said, "every man is afraid." The unemployed were drained of their vitality. Leisure became a misery. Young people grew aimless and apathetic, accepting the idea that they would never find jobs. The self-reliant lost their self-reliance. Fear and inactivity were the enemies of mental stability. "I cannot stand it any longer," a jobless Pennsylvanian wrote Governor Pinchot. A group of forty experienced stenographers called back to work in 1933 after at least a year of unemployment found that they could not face their employers for dictation without breaking down emotionally. Psychiatrists reported a deterioration in mental health. The suicide rate rose from 14 per 100,000 of population in 1929 to 15.7 in 1930, 16.8 in 1931, and 17.4 in 1932.

There were some beneficiaries of this attrition of morale. The churches that specialized in personal solace noted an increase in attendance. The fortunetellers in South Bend, Indiana, enjoyed a boom in 1932. Some newspapers specialized in hard-luck stories on the theory that folks who were having a tough time liked to read about others who were worse off. Billy Minsky devised a formula for the male half of the population: continuous burlesque. "Give the people something else to think about," Billy pronounced. "No man plots or even thinks when he attends my shows." Patrons would enter his Central Theatre at 47th and Broadway in Manhattan when the doors opened in the morning and not re-emerge until 1 A.M. of the following day, when they closed.

Millions of Americans were to bear the scars of this experience for the whole of their lives. They were the creatures of the Great Depression — the insecure who yearned for security, the believers in the business system of the twenties who no longer believed. The patron saint of the world that had died, Calvin Coolidge, became utterly discouraged. "I can see nothing to give ground for hope," the former President confided to a friend.[11]

*

## 4

On a transatlantic liner en route to Europe in the spring of 1932, Louis Adamic met a midwestern manufacturer and his son. "He and I got tired of the Depression," the businessman told Adamic, "of answering 'phone calls from people in need of help which we couldn't render, of seeing our well-to-do friends go broke, of feeling our purse-strings tighten." They decided to "make a trip on a comfortable nice boat and forget all about business and troubles for a while. . . . We left the old kit-bag back home." The kit-bag, the difference between the former payroll of 280 and the current one of 27, consisted of some 250 jobless workers. They could not run away.[12]

In *The Green Pastures*, Marc Connelly's play that enlivened Broadway during the depression, the Angel Gabriel remarked, "Everything nailed down is comin' loose." So it seemed. Between the fall of 1931 and the spring of 1933, economic and social burdens were imposed upon workers without equal in American history. At the same time the minority among them who were members of trade unions witnessed the disintegration of their organizations.

## CHAPTER 9

# Unionism at Low Tide

FOLLOWING HIS ELECTION to the Senate from Pennsylvania in November 1930, James J. Davis announced his resignation as Secretary of Labor. A bitter contest ensued over the succession.

The American Federation of Labor had traditionally regarded the Department of Labor as its own and the Secretary as its voice in the Cabinet. Gompers had played the decisive role in the creation of the Department on March 4, 1913. No one from outside the AFL had ever been Secretary of Labor. William B. Wilson, who occupied the post in the Wilson Administration, was a member of the Mine Workers; Davis, who served under Harding, Coolidge, and Hoover, was a member of the Iron, Steel and Tin Workers. "The A.F. of L. is . . . the American labor movement. . . . The officers and members of this organization believe that the Secretary of Labor, sitting in the President's cabinet, should be a man who understands the American labor movement, its problems and the thought and mind of American labor," William Green declared.

Shortly after the Davis announcement, Green called at the White House to ask the President to name a man from the Federation. He suggested five prominent leaders: William L. Hutcheson of the Carpenters, John L. Lewis of the Miners, Matthew Woll of the Photo-Engravers, John P. Frey of the Metal Trades, and John R. Alpine of the Plumbers. Green urged Hoover "to maintain the precedent set by your predecessors."

The President, however, chose to break with tradition. He appointed William N. Doak of the independent Brotherhood of Railroad Trainmen as Secretary of Labor. In Hoover's judgment the AFL could be ignored even on an issue of moment.[1]

✿

1

Union membership was unable to withstand staggering unemployment and severe wage-cutting. The labor movement, according to Leo Wolman, lost 469,600 members, declining in number from 3,442,600 in 1929 to 2,973,000 in 1933. Actually, this loss would have been greater but for the fact that "so much had already been surrendered since 1920." Important organizations like the Miners, the Ladies' Garment Workers, and the Textile Workers had been decimated prior to the crash. The unions suffering most during the depression were those that had remained strong in 1929, principally the building trades and the transportation and communication organizations. The construction unions fell in size from 919,000 in 1929 to 582,700 in 1933, a loss of 336,300. The transportation and communication group declined from 892,200 in 1929 to 609,300 in 1933, a drop of 282,900. Their combined loss was 619,200, or more than one third of their membership in 1929.

These statistics hardly reveal the devastation inflicted upon individual unions. The Amalgamated Clothing Workers, which had 177,000 members in 1920, received per capita payments from only 7000 in the low month of 1932. The Ladies' Garment Workers, with 105,400 in 1920, fell to 40,000 in 1932, many of whom paid no dues. The Oil Workers in early 1933 had 300 members, hardly more than the Long Beach, California, local. Membership in the shop crafts at the Baltimore & Ohio was sustained only by the active intercession of the railroad. The trials of the union that suffered most, the United Mine Workers, will be set forth in the next chapter.

Unions sought with diminishing success to retain what they had; organization of the unorganized was hopeless. The Teamsters stood helplessly aside as the new over-the-road trucking industry emerged; the drivers, many of them "gypsies," could not be brought into the ranks. When an exceptional union did undertake an organizational campaign, it faced almost certain defeat. In the fall of 1931, for example, the Hosiery Workers called an organizational strike against the Berkshire Knitting Mills of Reading,

Pennsylvania, the largest hosiery producer in the United States with 7000 employees. The conditions, considering the times, were relatively favorable: the Socialist administration of Reading allowed the union to import 3500 pickets from New Jersey and to conduct mass picketing. Nevertheless, the Hosiery Workers, *Fortune* declared, sustained "as humiliating a defeat as union labor has ever suffered."

The decline in income that accompanied falling membership subjected the internal machinery of the labor movement to severe strain. Officers' salaries were cut; organizers were laid off; benefit and strike funds were exhausted; conventions were deferred; newspapers were reduced in size, published infrequently, or eliminated entirely.

In the fall of 1931, for example, the executive board of the Bricklayers exempted unemployed members from the per capita tax to the international for the months of November and December 1931 and January 1932. The board did this in anticipation of a revival of construction in the spring of 1932. The action proved disastrous. Building did not improve and employed members refused to pay dues because their jobless brothers were exonerated. Some locals paid the per capita out of reserves, which were soon wiped out. Neither the international nor the locals could afford to hold their scheduled national convention in 1932. The executive board introduced a waiver-note system for jobless bricklayers. An unemployed member was allowed to remain in good standing without paying dues by signing a promissory note and by waiving his rights to relief and mortuary benefits.

The Clothing Workers in 1932 cut the salaries of its officers and staff by 50 per cent and dropped most publications. The Chicago Joint Board had already laid off eight organizers at the close of 1930. The Hotel and Restaurant Employees curtailed its organization staff from twenty to one and held no convention in 1931. San Francisco Waiters Local 30, probably the strongest and wealthiest in the international, found itself without reserves in 1932. The Hosiery Workers at the end of 1931 was forced to abandon its Philadelphia unemployment insurance plan because of lack of funds. The International Ladies' Garment Workers, which entered the depression in debt, had its very existence threatened by the collapse of the International-Madison Bank in the fall of 1931. The ILGWU was unable to meet payments on outstanding bonds and instituted a rigorous economy program, including the suspension of *Justice* for five months in 1932–33. On January 19, 1932, President Benjamin Schlesinger begged New York's lieutenant governor, Herbert Lehman, for a loan of $10,000, which Lehman was unable to grant. The International Typographical Union found its pension and mortuary funds in jeopardy because of the devaluation of the state and municipal bonds in which the monies were invested. By the end of 1932, the ITU strike fund was exhausted. The International Brotherhood of Electrical Workers cut officers' salaries 25 per cent in 1931 and 50 per cent in 1932, strove desperately to preserve pension, death, and other benefit plans, and deferred several conventions. Despite savings of $18,000 a month in the cost of operating the international, the IBEW was still $10,000 a month short at the end of 1932. The AFL was also forced to retrench. The southern textile drive was liquidated largely for this reason; organizers were compelled to take two-month vacations without pay in the summer of 1932; when, finally, the Federation came out for unemployment insurance, Green invited a group of distinguished experts to serve as advisers *without* pay.[2]

The Great Depression undermined the labor movement's experiments in respectability, undertaken, as we have seen, with high hopes in the twenties. Labor-management cooperation virtually disappeared; the labor banks collapsed; and the productivity-wage theory became irrelevant.

In the shops of the Baltimore & Ohio the union-management program to improve efficiency was submerged by unemployment. The maintenance-of-equipment payroll dropped from 17,237 in 1929 to 8751 in 1933. Hence the unions sought to extend rather than to save labor. Further, the carrier was financially incapable of investing in labor-saving machinery. The number of suggestions from employees fell from 1659 in 1929 to 534 in 1933. Hard times, in fact, provoked irritability rather than cooperativeness. In the Cleveland ladies' garment industry the production-standards scheme collapsed at the end of 1931. Fierce competition and mounting unemployment persuaded the employers that they could save on costs by abolishing these standards and by shifting to piecework. The union was helpless to strike. The manufacturers therefore dissolved their association and eliminated the standards. The depression wrecked the cooperative venture at the Naumkeag Steam Cotton Company. The plan had been designed to make Pequot sheeting competitive by stretching out high-wage labor. "The very much higher wage rate on the Naumkeag than in any other cotton mill in the country," its chief official wrote in 1932, "has risen up to smite me." The workers, suspicious at the outset, lost patience in November 1931 when the company insisted upon a wage cut. In the following January the research staff was dismembered, the technician was fired, and wages were cut. A second pay reduction on July 3, 1932, resulted in a strike, the very opposite of the original "cooperative" intention.[3]

The labor banking movement collapsed. At its peak in 1926, there had been thirty-five banks with resources of over $126 million. By 1929 the number had fallen to eighteen with resources of just under $79 million. In 1931 only seven labor banks remained, with resources of less than $31 million. By 1933 the two Amalgamated banks operated by the Clothing Workers in New York and Chicago were the sole survivors. They managed to keep afloat only by pursuing policies of extreme conservatism. As early as 1930 they began selling securities for cash even at a loss, and by March 1933 had 99 per cent of their holdings in either cash or United States bonds. The Amalgamated banks managed to withstand runs in late 1930, 1932, and early 1933. The mere fact of survival was a heroic achievement.[4]

The AFL's productivity-wage policy was soon forgotten. It presupposed, of course, a rising volume of output in which labor would share through higher wages. In an economy of falling production, widespread unemployment, and lower wages this theory became meaningless.

As if its economic and internal problems were not enough, the labor movement in the early thirties became infested with racketeering. While corruption had a long history in the building trades, in trucking, among motion picture operators, and in the live poultry and fresh fish industries, the wholesale shift of organized crime into union rackets in Chicago, New York, Detroit, Cleveland, and Jersey City was a new phenomenon. The golden era of the Eighteenth Amendment came to an end in 1929; few could any longer afford bootleg liquor. Yet the overhead costs of the mobs remained high; it was hardly safe to lay off gunmen with salaries of $100 to $500 a week. The syndicates therefore turned to the unions as the way out of their financial troubles.

The Chicago experience was typical. Al Capone had had only slight experience with industrial racketeering in the twenties, and that mainly out of a desire to help friends. After 1929, however, Capone's overhead costs forced him into a new business. He summoned one of Chicago's most influential labor leaders, informed him that the mob would take over his unions and through them the trade associations, and offered to allow him to retain nominal control. The unionist accepted.

In the bootleg wars in Cook County, Capone had learned that transportation was the key to grand strategy. He quickly captured the coal teamsters, the machinery movers, the laundry drivers, the oil wagon drivers, the freight drivers, the tire vulcanizers, and the garage workers. This victory was won at a great cost in blood. Petty racketeers already entrenched and rival mobs seeking the same objective engaged in pitched battles with Capone's gunmen. The "honor roll" of the dead was long: Wakefield, Delre, and Special of the bakery drivers murdered in a South Wells Street barroom; "Red" Barker, a racketeer in the coal teamsters, shot dead; three West Side gangsters killed by detectives in the offices of the vulcanizers' union; Pat Berrell, vice-president of the Teamsters, and his friend, Willie Marks, a gunman in "Bugs" Moran's mob, murdered while on vacation in Wisconsin; Harry Berger, general organizer for the truck union, assassinated; Mulcahy and Ruberry of Capone's plumbers' union murdered as they were about to call a strike, and Courchane of the rival organization mowed down by machine gunners; and so on.

Frank J. Loesch of the Chicago Crime Commission declared in 1932 that "fully two-thirds of the unions in Chicago are controlled by or pay tribute directly to Al Capone's terroristic organizations." At least the following industries and trades were gangster-dominated: laundry, cleaning, linen supply, soft drinks, barbers, bakers, coal, kosher meat, building materials, paving, excavating, flour, tobacco, ice, beauty culture, roofing material, municipal trucking, sanitation, garages, dairy products, wrecking, long-distance hauling, circular distribution, ice cream, storage, garbage removal, machinery moving, railway express, florists, janitors, window washers, oil drivers, electrotyping, and motion picture operators.

The Capone formula, though without his genius for organization and scale, was applied in other cities. Louis "Lepke" Buchalter and Charlie "Gurrah" Shapiro, who had supplied strike thugs to both unions and employers in the late twenties, seized control of New York's painting, flour trucking, baking, fur, and motion picture industries during the depression. "Dutch" Schultz set up a union and trade-association racket in the restaurant industry. Detroit's Purple Gang muscled into cleaning and dyeing, coal, and the building trades. In Cleveland the "association" made a racket out of undertaking. Jersey City was dominated by the amazing Theodore Brandle — businessman, banker, politician, employer-association mogul, as well as business agent of Local 45 of the Iron Workers and president of the Hudson County Building Trades Council. His leading lieutenant was Joey Fay of the Operating Engineers and his main confederate was Mayor Frank Hague of Jersey City. Their principal interest was construction, including such satellite activities as bonding. The motion picture operators' union, according to Norman Thomas, was "one of the most nefarious rackets I have ever heard of." Its particular star was Sam Kaplan, boss of Local 306 in New York and president of the Kaplan Supply Company, which specialized in the sale of projection equipment at outrageously high prices to theaters with which Local 306 bargained.

The American Federation of Labor did virtually nothing either to prevent the racket invasion or to throw out gangsters, once established. The reasons were simple enough: the affected internationals were among the most powerful in the Federation; there were constitutional limits to the AFL's jurisdiction over subordinate bodies; and Green had no stomach for a showdown. In the summer of 1932, after both Brandle and Kaplan had been exposed in the press and caught up by the law, Green finally, with the express sanction of the Executive Council, wrote to Presidents P. J.

Morrin of the Iron Workers and W. C. Elliott of the International Alliance of Theatrical Stage Employees to call their attention to the charges. Morrin ignored the Federation by offering Brandle his full support. Elliott did not remove Kaplan from office until forced to do so by the courts.

The unaffiliated Amalgamated Clothing Workers, by contrast, successfully resisted infiltration. The problem arose in largely autonomous New York Cutters Local 4, headed by Philip Orlofsky, who both stole union funds and served as agent for "Lepke" and "Gurrah" in a shakedown racket. The top leaders of the Amalgamated, in cooperation with some of the manufacturers, determined to drive the gangsters out. The international called in the books of Local 4 in May 1931 and uncovered gross irregularities. At a mass meeting in June, Hillman openly declared war. Strikes at gangster-dominated shops and a demonstration before City Hall followed. On August 24, Hillman personally filed charges against Orlofsky and his henchmen, and, after trial before the executive board, they were expelled from the union. They refused to yield physical possession of the local's office. Hillman's cohorts with police protection seized the offices on August 29. "Lepke" and "Gurrah" had been driven out of the men's clothing industry.[5]

## 2

The depression crippled unions as collective-bargaining instruments. This was evident in what happened to the strike, labor's principal bargaining weapon. "I have a queer guilty feeling just now," Sherwood Anderson wrote Edmund Wilson from the textile South in 1931, "about taking any part in pulling people out on strike. We go and stir them up. Out they come and presently get licked."

Very few strikes were called in the United States — 637 in 1930, 810 in 1931, and 841 in 1932. Although this volume was only moderately lower than the annual average for the preceding five-year period — 914 — it was far below any other years of the twentieth century. More significant was the fact that the strike in the early thirties became an essentially defensive instrument.

The proportion called to resist a wage decrease rose from 14 per cent in 1929 to 25.7 in 1930, 42.4 in 1931, and 50.6 in 1932. Instead of serving as a tool for improving the welfare of workers, the strike became an act of desperation. The percentage of stoppages that failed climbed to 44.5 in 1930, 46.8 in 1931, and 51.9 in 1932.

The policy of the businesslike and relatively powerful International Brotherhood of Teamsters is instructive. The executive board in February 1931 notified the locals that strikes should not be used to improve wages and hours. A year later President Dan Tobin urged the locals to prevent jobless members, even if in good standing, from voting in strike calls. Their ballots were inclined to reflect the view, Tobin wrote, "that the more misery obtains the quicker will relief come." In April 1932 the executive board announced that it would not sanction a strike for higher wages. "When sending in your wage scale for approval, understand it will not be approved if it contains any changes over wages and working conditions of last year." Under this policy, members who walked out without the authorization of the general president and the local joint council were denied strike benefits. The international revoked the charter of Cincinnati Taxi Drivers Local 818 and denounced its leadership for calling a strike in defiance of this policy. In fact, the only sanctioned stoppages were in resistance to wage cuts, such as those of Boston Truck Drivers Local 25 and the Oakland Milk Wagon Drivers.

Most of the notable strikes of the time were both defensive and unsuccessful. This was certainly the case with the many that occurred in the coal industry, to be dealt with shortly. The strike-lockout of Hotel and Restaurant Employees Locals 106, 107, and 167 and the Cleveland Hotels Association in 1930–31 was of the same character. In July 1930, the association announced that it was terminating the agreements and that henceforth workers would be employed under yellow-dog contracts. A bitter walkout ensued that dragged on for a full year, exhausted the defense funds of both the locals and the international, and ended with re-employment of the workers under neither yellow-dog nor union contracts. In the summer of 1932 some 12,000 unorganized seamless hosiery, full-fashioned hosiery, cotton mill, and furniture workers in the North Carolina Piedmont struck spontaneously against wage cuts. Excepting the hosiery walkout at High Point, where Governor O. Max Gardner's intervention resulted in the restoration of the wage scale, these stoppages were in the typical pattern of southern defeat. The northern textile industry was the scene of a series of desperate and often violent strikes over wage reductions: at the American Woolen mills in Lawrence, Massachusetts, in 1931, among silk workers at Allentown, Pennsylvania, in 1931, at the silk mills in Paterson, New Jersey, in 1931–32. The United Textile Workers had nothing to do with the conduct of these stoppages; the union that took over was the Communist-dominated National Textile Workers.[6]

The reluctance of established trade unions to assume responsibility for desperation strikes gave the radicals — notably the Communists and to a lesser extent the Industrial Workers of the World — an opportunity to exert leadership. The Communist Party viewed the depression and especially wage-cutting as the chance to radicalize the working masses of the United States and to form revolutionary cadres in the mines and factories. With these objectives, the party had no interest in settling workers' grievances and opposed the intercession of "reformist" mediators. The Communist Trade Union Unity League's National Miners' Union conducted hopeless coal strikes in Pennsylvania, Ohio, and Kentucky; its National Textile Workers ran the already mentioned northern textile stoppages; its agricultural union staged a desperation strike among Mexican field laborers in the Imperial Valley of California in 1930; its Tobacco Workers Industrial Union conducted a violent strike of Latin cigar makers in Tampa, Florida, in 1932; and its Auto Workers Union struck the shops of Briggs Manufacturing and Motor Products in Detroit early in 1933. At the same time the IWW assumed control over strikes of coal miners in Kentucky and of construction workers at Boulder Dam in Nevada.[7]

The depression eroded that vital economic function of the trade union — the maintenance of wage rates in the face of falling business activity. Labor organizations fought a hopeless rear-guard action; declining rates in the nonunion sector of the economy combined with a falling cost of living proved irresistible. In partly unionized industries, like coal, shipping, textiles, and hosiery, competition compelled the organized employers to follow the downward movement of wages in the unorganized mines and factories. In 1931, for example, President Samuel Pursglove of the unionized Pittsburgh Terminal Coal Corporation wrote John L. Lewis that his scale was 5 to 7 cents higher than that of his unorganized neighbors. "I do not think that the Directors of this company are going to stand for this much longer," Pursglove warned. "The only thing for us to do is to put our own house in order and go along the same as the rest of the operators." In several cases unions voluntarily reduced wages in order to keep friendly employers afloat. In 1931, for example, UMW miners offered the Rocky Mountain Fuel Company half their wages for five payroll periods (two and one-half months) as an interest-free loan with no fixed date for repayment. In 1932, when Hart, Schaffner & Marx contemplated liquidation (Hillman wept when he heard the news), the 4000 employees who were members of the Amalgamated Clothing Workers extended a wage cut to the firm for a year as a loan. In several industries unions accepted wage reductions in order to undermine rival organizations. This dangerous policy was pursued by the Hosiery Workers as well as by the Mine Workers in northern West Virginia, Pennsylvania, and Illinois.

Company unions, of course, suffered at least as severe wage-cutting as trade unions. In the Pacific Northwest in 1932 the lumber industry operated at 20 per cent of capacity, half the labor force was totally unemployed, and the remainder was mainly on part time. The minimum wage of the company-dominated Loyal Legion of Loggers and Lumbermen (the 4L) was lowered again and again, to $2.60 per day in the spring of 1932. The competition of non-4L mills, paying as little as $1.50, forced the complete suspension of the wage scale in November.[8]

Unemployment and the inadequacy of public relief forced trade unions to come to the assistance of their needy members. As of January 2, 1932, Green estimated that AFL affiliates alone had contributed $52 million. He listed the Printing Pressmen for $2,300,-000, the Carpenters for $5 million, the Electrical Workers for $2,841,948, the Bricklayers for $700,000, the Operating Engineers for $150,000, the Plumbers for $1,150,000, the Mine Workers for $4 million, the Typographical Union for $4,500,000, and the Machinists for $8,310,620. Some thirty Philadelphia locals gave their out-of-work members more assistance than the city provided. The Amalgamated Clothing Workers' New York Unemployment Insurance Fund donated $100,000 to relief early in 1930. The responsibility appears to have fallen primarily upon the locals rather than the internationals. Typographical Local 6 in New York taxed each employed member either 8 per cent of his earnings or a day's wages for the relief of jobless printers. By early 1932, this local had raised $3 million. The Hebrew Butchers of New York gave one day's pay a month to relief. Clothing Workers' members in Chicago assessed themselves $8 per person. San Francisco Teamsters Local 85 levied a tax of a dollar a month upon each member who worked three or more days a week. Perhaps the most heart-warming program was that of the San Francisco Hotel and Restaurant Employees. A rank-and-file committee of Waiters Local 30 in 1932 persuaded Business Agent Hugo Ernst to petition the city to turn over to the union the money being expended for relief of their members. Mayor Rossi reluctantly agreed. Locals 30, 44, and 110 then established "soup-barns" in their headquarters at which 500 persons received three warm meals a day. The plain food was superbly cooked by some of the top chefs in the nation and was elegantly served by San Francisco's noted waiters.[9]

3

The most significant long-term effect of the Great Depression upon the labor movement was to cause it to re-examine its basic philosophy of voluntarism, the concept of the self-reliant trade union that did not depend upon the state. Massive unemployment, declining wage rates, falling membership, and hopeless strikes demonstrated that history had outsped Gompers. The notion that the state was the enemy of the worker may have made some sense in 1912; it seemed absurd in 1932. Where else was the worker to turn for help? Certainly not to the trade union, which was itself bordering on collapse.

At the outset the leaders of the AFL seriously underestimated the severity of the depression. They counted on an early upturn of business, embraced the Hoover wage-maintenance policy as though it would solve their problems, repeated worn slogans, and asserted little leadership on behalf of the people they represented. A good illustration is the paper on unemployment delivered by Matthew Woll to the American Academy of Political and Social Science in December 1930. Labor, Woll argued, must not be treated as a commodity and there must be a mutual recognition of rights in industry. "It is the opinion of labor that the adoption of ... two policies, higher wages and shorter hours ... would increase opportunities for employment, leaving a wholly minor or secondary role for all other unemployment remedies. ..." The state must not be allowed to deal with joblessness; that would be "a resort fraught with the direst of consequences ... prey to abuse and chicanery." "Industry," Woll concluded, "must work it out within itself."

In the context of the times this voluntaristic outlook invited criticism. Liberal writers like Louis Adamic, Louis Stanley, and J. B. S. Hardman wrote devastating attacks on the AFL philosophy. Tobin, on reading the Adamic article in *Harper's,* observed, "It is awful and somewhat true." Green was outraged. "I would with perfect propriety," he demanded of Tobin, "inquire as to what part of the article denouncing the American Federation of Labor ... is in your opinion true?" *Amour-propre* could hardly still the outcry. Unions not affiliated with the Federation joined the attack. The Amalgamated Clothing Workers, which had never had any use for voluntarism, took the AFL to task. The Communists, of course, maintained a steady barrage of denunciation against the outlook of the AFL "fakers." More important was mounting criticism within the Federation itself. In May 1931, President George Berry of the Printing Pressmen wrote that "our capitalistic system requires a radical reorganization ... to meet the changing situation of the day." A few months later Tobin admitted that he was changing his mind on public relief, or, as he preferred to call it, the dole. Somehow people would have to be got off the streets. Early in 1932, President J. C. Shanessy of the Barbers union denounced the AFL economic program as indefinite and inadequate, "a reiteration of the platitudinal orations and beseechments we have heard so often."[10]

The decisive test of voluntarism was fought out over the issue of unemployment insurance. The lines, though slow in forming, were to be sharply drawn: rigorous adherents of the traditional voluntary philosophy opposed to growing numbers of workers and union leaders seeking government-sponsored unemployment insurance. The former looked backwards to Gompers; the latter faced the current crisis. Before the House Labor Committee in 1916 Gompers had denounced unemployment insurance as "socialist." He would rather see workers suffer "than give up one jot of the freedom ... to strive and struggle for their own emancipation through their own efforts." The state and the trade union could not complement each other; they could only compete. As late as the 1929 AFL convention, the Executive Council reaffirmed this position: there was no demonstrated need for unemployment insurance.

The joblessness that followed the crash strengthened the opposition. In 1930 the California Federation of Labor unanimously voted to urge the AFL to back a state-supervised unemployment insurance system to which the employer, the employee, and the public would contribute. At the Federation's Boston convention in October, the Newport, Rhode Island, Central Labor Union, the Textile Workers, and the Teachers introduced resolutions favoring the reform. The Executive Council, dominated by the voluntarists, proposed quiet burial: study by the Council of insurance and other plans "for the relief of members out of work." The Resolutions Committee, with Woll as chairman and Victor Olander of the Seamen as secretary, reported in favor of the Council recommendation.

The debate that followed was quite sharp. The issue, as Olander defined it, was whether the Federation shall "hew to the line in demanding a greater freedom for the working people of America, or whether liberty shall be sacrificed ... to enable the workers to obtain a small measure of unemployment relief under government supervision and control." Insurance in his word was a "dole." The AFL traditionally had opposed alien registration; under unemployment insurance citizens would be compelled to register. Olander found "industrial passports" repugnant. America was a great land with immense resources. "Are we prepared to admit defeat," he inquired, "in our efforts to so increase the consuming power of our people that it will meet their great productive capacity?" As the need for immigration restriction demonstrated, conditions here were superior to those in Europe. If the United States followed the European model of unemployment insurance, however, it would make the damaging admission that foreigners have "found a way of making life for the working people better over there than it is here." Unemployment insurance would impair mobility by making it difficult for workers to quit their jobs. Finally, and perhaps most important, Olander argued that it would "prevent the workers from joining in movements to increase wages and improve working conditions because of fears that they might thus sacrifice their eligibility to unemployment insurance."

Henry Ohl of the Wisconsin Federation replied that the scheme need not be a dole if the state did not contribute; nor did he wish the worker to do so. The financial obligation for unemployment "should be placed at the door of those who are responsible . . . industry." T. A. Slavens of the Newport Central Labor Union declared that employers should set aside part of the gains of rising productivity for "the payment of wages to the unemployed." They must recognize that "they have a social service to perform, one which must take precedence over the making of profits." Max Zaritsky of the Cap Makers observed that millions of jobless workers were looking to the Federation for leadership on this issue. Those who were hungry could not eat rugged individualism. Unemployment compensation, Zaritsky argued, was superior to charity.

Green himself participated in the debate. Slavens, he felt, was unrealistic in believing that industry would assume the whole cost. Even in Britain, where the labor movement was stronger, the worker was forced to contribute. Unemployment insurance, Green feared, would weaken the trade unions. The employment exchange would say to the organized workman: "Go work in this non-union mass production industry where I found you a job or lose your insurance." Let the Executive Council study the question, Green urged, and perhaps it would find a solution. The report of the Resolutions Committee carried easily.[11]

The pressure for unemployment insurance mounted with joblessness in the year that followed the Boston convention. Senator Wagner, busy drafting a bill, wrote Green in January 1931 to ask the Federation's support. Shortly afterward Senator Couzens urged the AFL to reverse itself. The *International Teamster* published as its lead article in the February issue a vigorous attack on the AFL for its views on unemployment compensation. Since Tobin personally edited this paper, there could be little doubt that he was changing his own mind. In July, Major Berry of the Pressmen threw his support to the reform.[12]

When the delegates convened at Vancouver early in October 1931, a major battle was certain. The California Federation, the Seattle Central Labor Council, the Teachers, and the Flint Glass Workers introduced resolutions in favor of unemployment insurance. The Executive Council, anticipating a fight, comprehensively reviewed foreign experiences, particularly the British and German, and vigorously restated the voluntaristic philosophy. These European plans, the Council observed, filled merely temporary needs. Under them employers felt no responsibility for their employees. "Unemployment insurance may be a crutch that permanently weakens industry and keeps it from solving a problem whose solution is essential." In both Britain and Germany the labor movements were strong and faced no concerted efforts by employers to destroy them, "in striking contrast to the situation in the United States." Insurance had not made relief unnecessary during periods of severe joblessness. Hence, the Council concluded, "Compulsory unemployment insurance ... would be unsuited to our economic and political requirements. ... American working people want work. ... They abhor charity. ... They must not and will not become the victims of a paternalistic policy."

The Resolutions Committee, still controlled by Woll and Olander, dutifully expressed "emphatic approval of the declaration of the Executive Council." The debate that followed, however, was spirited.

The proponents argued that something must be done immediately. Workers, both those with and without jobs, demanded that the AFL reverse itself on unemployment insurance. Unless the Federation did so, it would have no right to speak on their behalf. W. D. Mahon, president of the Street Railway Employees, warned that unemployment was too big for the labor movement to tackle on its own; government intercession was necessary. The alleged deficiencies of the British and German systems were brushed aside. We have "brains enough in our Executive Council," declared J. A. Duncan of the Seattle Central Labor Council, "to work out a system of unemployment insurance that will thoroughly safeguard the working people of the United States." The proponents, however, were conspicuously silent about the details of the system they urged. Finally, the old argument about industry's responsibility for unemployment was reiterated.

The voluntarists also repeated themselves. Olander rang the changes on liberty and self-help. "Our duty," Green declaimed, "is plain, and that is, first of all, to protect the movement that we love and represent." They did, however, advance several new arguments. Frey contended that compulsory unemployment insurance was unconstitutional "because there is no such power vested in the Federal Government." Nor could it be arranged by federal grants-in-aid to the states. "There is a serious question as to a single state constitution that would permit of doing that." Charles P. Howard, president of the Typographical Union, pointed to the failure of the proponents to bring forth a definite plan. This, he felt, was because there were "insuperable obstacles" in the way of devising a system that was both administratively workable and acceptable to trade unionists. Finally, Green observed that the basic affirmative argument — the urgent need to do something for the jobless — confused unemployment insurance with relief. "The one force pulls at our heads and the other at our hearts." Relief, Green argued, would give immediate assistance to the hungry; unemployment insurance would not.

The 1931 convention was marked by a sharp accretion in the strength of the antivoluntarists. Tobin and Mahon, both powerful international presidents who had been nurtured by Gompers, changed sides. There was, furthermore, evidence of defection within the United Mine Workers. While the voluntarists still carried the voice vote, their margin had uncomfortably narrowed. An experienced observer estimated that 11,000 to 12,000 of the 30,000 convention votes were now in favor of unemployment insurance. Green, at last in doubt, told the convention that "we are travelling rapidly" toward unemployment insurance, but "the time has not yet arrived." [13]

The winter of 1931–32, which broke so many things, broke the back of voluntarism in the American labor movement. In the face of staggering joblessness, union leaders could no longer tell their followers that they opposed unemployment insurance. At its convention late in January 1932, the United Mine Workers swung around. After comprehensively reviewing the problem, John L. Lewis, Philip Murray, and Thomas Kennedy urged "laws compelling the establishment of unemployment reserves." Organized labor had proved itself incapable of stabilizing employment. "Let the power of the state be directed to this end. . . . Labor should speak with a collective voice." In February the New York State Federation of Labor openly endorsed unemployment insurance. Rank-and-file pressure forced the leaders to shift.

Ironically, the AFL was even subject to pressure by employers. In the spring of 1932, Gerard Swope of General Electric met with Green and Woll to urge them to support unemployment compensation. Swope was especially anxious that they accept a system to which the employee as well as the employer made contributions. He found that "their opposition was largely based upon prejudice and their denouncement of the British system." Swope, nevertheless, was optimistic that they would soon change their views.[14]

On April 11 Green wrote to Frank Duffy, secretary of the Carpenters and a member of the Federation's Executive Council: "If we can formulate some constructive plan through the creation of reserves out of which benefits could be paid to the unemployed without endangering the standing, efficiency and propriety of our labor movement I am quite willing to subscribe to such a plan." The Council, at its meeting scheduled for late July, would have the "obligation" to consider unemployment insurance.

The Executive Council on July 22 in Atlantic City succumbed to the inevitable. The motivation was simple: "Industry," in Green's words, "must either provide employment or accept unemployment insurance legislation. . . . Instead of providing work for the unemployed, the number out of work has steadily increased." The Council directed Green to draw up a plan embodying two "very vital principles": (1) a scheme providing for federal rather than state legislation and (2) "a plan which will safeguard ... in every possible way the exercise of the right of a workman to belong to and to maintain membership in a labor union." Green was to present a bill to the next meeting of the Council on October 18 in Washington and, if approved, it would be submitted to the Federation's November convention in Cincinnati.

Green conscientiously set about his task. He corresponded with authorities on social insurance, including John B. Andrews, William M. Leiserson, and Edwin E. Witte, as well as with such legal experts as Professors Francis Sayre, Felix Frankfurter, and Herman Oliphant, along with labor attorney Donald Richberg. Green arranged a meeting in Washington early in October that was attended by many of these advisers. Here Sayre was primarily responsible for drafting a report. The lawyers apparently confirmed Frey's constitutional reservations at least in so far as a federal system was concerned. This "vital principle" was consequently discarded.[15]

The Council adopted Green's report at its meeting in late October and submitted it to the convention on November 21, 1932. The fact that 11 million people were out of work, the Executive Council declared, made it "absolutely necessary" to enact legislation creating "an unemployment insurance plan which will provide for the payment of weekly benefits to working men and women." The responsibility rested squarely upon industry. "If industrial management fails to provide work, it must be compelled to assume the burden of supplying relief." While a uniform federal statute was to be preferred, decisions holding that the regulation of manufacturing was within the province of the states cast doubt upon its constitutionality. Hence the Council advocated unemployment insurance legislation for the separate states supplemented by federal statutes covering employees in interstate commerce as well as in the District of Columbia and the territories. Marked local variations made it unwise to submit a model bill.

The Council did, however, urge the following standards in framing the state bills. Union members should not be obligated to accept work contrary to the rules of their organizations. The legislation should stimulate regular employment as well as provide for out-of-work benefits. The system should be "compulsory by law." No contributions should be made by wage earners; "the whole should be paid by management as part of the cost of production." The rate should be not less than 3 per cent of payroll. The Council took no position as between the plant reserves system recently enacted in Wisconsin and the insurance plan then under consideration in Ohio. Private insurance companies were to be precluded from this field. Funds should be invested exclusively in federal, state, and municipal bonds. No person should forfeit his right to benefits if he refused to accept employment because of a strike, or if the wages offered were less favorable than those prevailing for similar work in the locality, or if acceptance of employment would abridge his right to join or retain membership in a labor organization. Coverage should be "as wide as possible," extending even to persons on part time. The amount of benefits would vary with local conditions. The state commissions charged with administration should be supplemented by advisory committees with equal representation from labor and management. Unemployment insurance and employment exchanges should be merged into a unified administrative structure.

The Resolutions Committee, still controlled by Woll and Olander, reported the Council's recommendation favorably but, in deference to a firm minority, gave no reasons. The debate that followed was perfunctory, little more than the repetition of old arguments. The main purpose was to afford unreconstructed voluntarists a platform from which to sing their swan song. "Your responsibility here," Furuseth, the Seamen's leader, thundered, "is frightful. I will not share that responsibility with you." "If you feed lions cooked meat," Frey argued, "they are not going to roar. . . . You have to hold raw meat under their noses and then they will roar." Howard feared that "a great fundamental question" would be resolved on the basis of "sympathy rather than upon judgment." The convention, nevertheless, adopted the report by "overwhelming vote."

November 30, 1932, was a turning point in the history of the American labor movement: the American Federation of Labor, by endorsing unemployment insurance, turned its back upon voluntarism. "We have been irresistibly forced to take new positions," Green remarked on that day, "to pursue a flexible policy and to adjust ourselves to the changed order." In this attitude Green was closer to Gompers than the die-hards. Gompers was pragmatic rather than doctrinaire. "The wisdom of voluntarism ... must be tested by experience rather than theory alone," Father Higgins has pointed out. The searing experience of the Great Depression found the philosophy wanting.[16]

It would not be quite right to describe voluntarism as dead. Convictions deeply held by strong men through most of their lives do not disappear overnight. "In addition to going among the unorganized and preaching the simple, direct gospel of trade unionism," Frey wrote on December 8, 1932, "we will also be insurance peddlers." As an official of the Illinois Federation of Labor, Olander early in 1933 dutifully carried the unemployment insurance bill to Springfield in one hand while holding his nose with the other. Voluntarism was still alive, just barely.

Voluntarism was eclipsed by a new mood — militancy. Union leaders who had striven for respectability in the twenties became strident spokesmen for urban discontent in 1932. "I say to you gentlemen, advisedly," Edward F. McGrady, legislative representative for the AFL, told the Senate Manufactures Subcommittee during the spring, "that if something is not done ... the doors of revolt in this country are going to be thrown open." In May, A. F. Whitney and D. B. Robertson of the railroad brotherhoods warned Hoover at the White House that "unless something is done to provide employment and relieve distress among the families of the unemployed ... we will refuse to take the responsibility for the disorder which is sure to arise." In August one of the labor movement's severest critics, J. B. S. Hardman, published an article entitled "Labor on the Warpath?" The situation, he wrote, is not "revolutionary," rather "miserable." "But labor has seemingly become aware of this fact in a rather intelligent way, and this is of primary and revolutionary importance." "There are rather definite indications," H. M. Douty wrote in November, "that this depression marks the end of an era in the history of American trade unionism. ... A narrow labor philosophy formulated in the eighties loses its validity and its appeal." He noted especially the ferment within the railway organizations — "something fresh is stirring." On December 12, 1932, even John Frey, who could hardly be accused of threatening to overthrow the established order, declared with bitterness: "We have been so 'good' that we have almost become no good, and unless we ... insist upon being heard in the nation's councils ... we might as well fold up our tent and continue to receive with thanks what industry may be willing to give us." [17]

4

This militancy was confined to words: union leaders delivered stirring speeches, wrote firm letters, issued stern warnings, and in their conventions adopted emphatic resolutions. They accomplished little, however, because the labor movement was by now so weak. Symptomatic of this debility was the fate of recurrent union proposals for labor-management conferences to deal with important issues.

Immediately following the crash Frey urged the Administration to call a private weekend meeting of industrialists and unionists. His agenda included such misty items as limitation of output, communication between employer and employee, government commissions, and AFL opposition to the class struggle. Frey's real purpose, as he confided to President James Wilson of the Pattern Makers, was "the beginning of the establishing of a relationship which should permit us to once more do business with the big corporations employing metal trades workers." He dealt mainly with the Department of Commerce and had meetings in January 1930 with Secretary Robert Lamont, his assistant, Julius Klein, and White House adjutant Edward Eyre Hunt. Frey talked hopefully about sitting down with such tycoons as Owen D. Young and Gerard Swope of General Electric, Walter C. Teagle of Jersey Standard, Alfred P. Sloan of General Motors, Myron C. Taylor of United States Steel, and Alexander Legge of International Harvester. The only one who evinced any interest at all was Young, and it would not be an exaggeration to describe it as slight. Throughout 1930 and 1931, Frey continued to write to officials of the Administration and the AFL. If a meeting was ever held, it has been lost to history; certainly neither Frey's ostensible nor his real objectives were achieved.

The AFL itself repeatedly urged the President to call "a national economic conference" of representative groups. Organized labor, of course, would be invited "as a producing partner in industry and as a major social group." The purpose, stated in the most general language, was to coordinate economic knowledge and initiate national planning of economic life. Whether the Federation took this proposal seriously is doubtful. It was greeted with deafening silence by both the White House and industry.[18]

Far more concrete and serious was the proposal of the United Mine Workers for a labor-management conference to deal with the collapse of coal. The union, it will be recalled, had for some time urged a program to allow producers to set output quotas and fix prices as well as to guarantee to miners the rights of self-organization and collective bargaining. Lewis, emboldened in the summer of 1931 by the resumption of bargaining by a major Pennsylvania producer, felt the time ripe for an overture. On June 11 he asked Hoover, to whom he had given enthusiastic political support, to convene the operators and miners to develop this program under presidential sponsorship. On June 30, to his bitter disappointment, the President replied that he had referred the matter to the Secretaries of Commerce and Labor "to advise me as to the present attitude of those directly concerned in the industry." Administration policy, according to the union, had been made by the Secretary of the Treasury. The Mellons controlled the Pittsburgh Coal Company, the nation's largest, and its management had vowed never to sit at the same table with officials of the United Mine Workers.

The Lewis proposal degenerated into a burlesque. On July 9, Lamont met with fifteen operators from thirteen companies to discuss the question of whether there ought to be a discussion. If any small flame of hope still burned, the Secretary extinguished it quickly. He announced in advance that he expected no "big things" and at the conclusion that no decisions had been reached and, in fact, that there had been no such endeavor. To compound the absurdity, fifty supporters of the National Miners' Union picketed the meeting with banners reading, "Down with Hoover's Strike-Breaking Conference." The Washington police took the signs away.

Doak met with the UMW officials on July 13 and Lamont

joined them the following day. Lewis urged that Hoover proceed on his own initiative and pointed out that the handful of operators at the earlier meeting was hardly representative. To meet the second point, Lamont and Doak late in July took a straw poll of coal companies to determine their willingness to confer. Of the 160 queried, 101 were opposed or failed to reply, 21 questioned its utility but were willing to attend, and 38 were in favor. On August 31, Doak wrote Lewis that, in view of these results, the Administration saw no purpose in pursuing the proposal any further.[19]

This frustration suffered by the United Mine Workers was hardly unique. The disastrous plight of that organization amid the wreckage of the coal industry was the decisive trade-union experience of the Great Depression.

## CHAPTER 10

# Catastrophe in Coal

THE TROUBLES IN COAL were singing troubles. The mournful songs the miners and their womenfolk sang echo down the years.

Aunt Molly Jackson of Straight Creek, Kentucky, a midwife and minstrel, was the author of "Dreadful Memories." "In 19 and 31," Aunt Molly later recalled, "the Kentucky coal miners was asked to dig coal for 33 cents a ton." From this amount the operator deducted the costs of carbide for lighting, of coalite for blasting, of sharpening picks and augers, and of the company doctor. But when the miners were blacklisted for joining the union on March 5, 1931, the doctor refused to come unless paid in advance. There was no money. "So I had to nurse all the little children till the last breath left them.... Thirty-seven babies died in my arms in the last three months of 1931. Their little stomach busted open." Aunt Molly's nerves were "so stirred up" that she wrote this song:

> *Dreadful memories! How they linger;*
> *How they pain my precious soul.*
> *Little children, sick and hungry,*
> *Sick and hungry, weak and cold.*

A blues song that described the conditions in Harlan County, Kentucky, went like this:

> *This minin town I live in*
> *    is a sad an a lonely place,*
> *For pity and starvation*
> *    is pictured on every face,*
> *Everybody hongry and ragged,*

*no slippers on their feet,*
*All goin round place to place*
*bummin for a little food to eat.*

The plight of the union was a recurrent theme, for example, in "Harlan County Blues":

*"You didn't have to be drunk," they said,*
*"To get throwed in the can;*
*The only thing you needed be*
*Was just a union man."*

The most famous of the coal songs and one of the most popular of American labor songs was written during a bloody strike in Kentucky in 1931. Sam Reece was a union organizer. At a time of violence a band of armed deputies, searching for Reece, ransacked his cabin. Several days later Mrs. Reece, who had faced the deputies alone, tore a sheet off a wall calendar and wrote "Which Side Are You On?" to the tune of an old Baptist hymn, "Lay the Lily Low":

*Come all you good workers,*
*Good news to you I'll tell,*
*Of how the good old union*
*Has come in here to dwell.*

REFRAIN: *Which side are you on?*
*Which side are you on?*

*Oh workers, can you stand it?*
*Oh tell me how you can.*
*Will you be a lousy scab*
*Or will you be a man?*

*My daddy was a miner,*
*He is now in the air and sun*
*He'll be with you fellow workers*
*Until the battle's won.*[1]

1

The coal industry of the United States collapsed during the Great Depression. The output of bituminous fell from 535 million tons in 1929 to 468 in 1930, 382 in 1931, and 310 million in 1932. Production had not sunk so low since 1904. A southern mine, for which an offer of $750,000 had been refused in 1927, was sold to the junkman for $4000 in 1932. The average price of coal per ton at the mine dropped from $1.78 in 1929 to $1.31 in 1932. The performance of anthracite was only a little better. Production slumped from 74 million tons in 1929 to 49 million in 1932 and the price per ton from $5.22 to $4.17.

The structure of the bituminous industry was totally inadequate to meet the crisis. Capacity vastly exceeded demand; the business units were all small and much too numerous; the horizon of the typical operator was fixed at the line of his own property. The consumers of bituminous — mainly large steel, railroad, and utility corporations — played one operator against the other in fixing prices. Further, prices failed to adjust output to demand. In the mines capital investment was large and depreciation unusually rapid, accelerating with time. Hence the operator often lost less money by maintaining high output even if he had to sell his coal below cost. To describe the price market as disorderly would be an understatement; it was a classic illustration of cutthroat competition.

Since labor constituted about two thirds of mine costs, the operator passed on his falling prices in lower wages. Survival depended upon wiping out union wage scales and with them the union itself. Average hourly earnings in bituminous fell from 68 cents in 1929 to 50 cents in 1932. These averages merely hint at the wage collapse that occurred, particularly in the Southern Appalachian fields. By early 1933, 32 per cent of the mines of the United States paid less than $2.50 per day in contrast with the Jacksonville scale of the twenties of $7.50. Reinhold Niebuhr told the Senate Manufactures Subcommittee in May 1932 that miners he had talked with in Pineville, Kentucky, received 30 cents a ton, were compensated for seven to eight tons daily, and averaged a day and a half of work a week. Very few earned as much as $5 weekly, and one third of the 4500 miners in the district were totally unemployed.

A common method of cutting wages where miners were paid by the car or the ton was the falsification of weights. Where there was collective bargaining, protection was afforded by the contract specifying that the car should be "plumb level full at the tipple" and that there should be a checkweighman. In the nonunion fields, and especially in the South, the operator decided when the car was full, and there was no one to check. "Just across the Harlan County line," M. P. Levy, a visitor from New York, observed in the fall of 1931, "I . . . talked for an hour with a weighman and was amazed to see that he noted down the weights of cars without even looking at the scale. . . . When I finished talking to him, I went over to the weighing machine . . . and saw that it did not register at all." The miners told him that they were credited with ten tons when they loaded twenty. Two brothers operated a mine in eastern Kentucky. One got converted at a revival. "Richard," he asked the other, "why can't you join the church like me?" "But if I join," returned Richard, "who's going to weigh the coal?" The general practice in the South was that the loaded car received a "hump." In the McDowell County, West Virginia, mines the brakeman placed his elbow on top of the car and the miners loaded to the tips of his extended fingers. Some operators hung chains from the drift mouth; if the load failed to reach them, the miner was docked half a car. In the early thirties the extra loads were called "Hoover humps."

The operators cut wages with impunity because of the enormous oversupply of labor. In the Alabama, Virginia, Kentucky, and southern West Virginia camps George Korson heard the miners talk with fear about "the barefootman": "There's a barefoot, hungry man outside waiting for your job." Even in the twenties there had been severe unemployment. By 1932, the miner who worked a short week was fortunate. Average weekly hours in bituminous declined from 38.4 in 1929 to 27.2 in 1932. The average number of days worked annually dropped from 219 in 1929 to 146 in 1932, the lowest figure ever recorded. And the men did not leave the mining camps: "Once a miner, always a miner." [2]

The routine field reports of officials of the United Mine Workers to headquarters reveal the extent of the disaster at the local level. A typical account was that of James Mark, president of District 2 in central Pennsylvania, to Vice-President Philip Murray on November 13, 1931. The recent strikes at the Buffalo & Susquehanna Coal Company and the Helvetia Coal Company had petered out in failure. The men at New Mine and Yatesboro as well as at Margaret returned to work because of injunctions and evictions. When the strike was over, "the company immediately issued a number of eviction notices at New Mine." At Yatesboro and Margaret the operators refused to rehire 150 miners and had just evicted sixteen families. "We are powerless ... and the men tell us they haven't got a cent in their pockets." When the men at Shamut Coal Company asked for a checkweighman, the employer ordered them to quit UMW and set up a company union. The miners refused, leading to the discharge of the union president and a strike. "Last week the company started to operate ... and succeeded in getting 30 men to return to work, claiming that was all they needed as they only had orders for 50 tons per day. Served eviction notices on 9 families." Conditions among the people at Brandy Camp and Elbon were bad. "Many of them haven't enough to eat." The miners at Gipsy were on strike against a wage reduction. The Empire Coal Company at Barnesboro had issued "a proposition where their men load 100 tons of coal they will be paid for 90 tons." At Hastings, where 250 men had just joined the union, "the situation ... is in somewhat of a muddle." [3]

Economic collapse spelled poverty in the coal fields, want on a scale and of an intensity rarely if ever witnessed in the United States. "In all my experiences," Van Bittner wrote from West Virginia in 1930, "I have never seen anything to compare with these conditions." A social worker who in 1931 toured coal-rich Franklin County, Illinois, uncovered numerous cases of starvation. Hundreds of children had not had a balanced meal in two years. James Myers of the Federal Council of Churches, who visited the mining camps of Kentucky and West Virginia in late 1931, reported "alarming need." Frank Bane of the American Association of Public Welfare Officials on December 29, 1931, gave the Senate

Manufactures Subcommittee a state-by-state summary of unemployment. The coal states were severely disabled: Arkansas' coal areas were "hard pressed"; Williamson and Franklin Counties, Illinois, revealed "actual destitution"; "the most serious conditions" in Kansas were in the Pittsburgh field; the soft coal regions of Kentucky presented "most serious problems"; the situation in the bituminous counties of Pennsylvania was "deplorable"; in Tennessee the mining area revealed "bad conditions"; the position of Virginia's coal district was "depressed" and "serious"; West Virginia was "especially distressing." "I am deeply impressed," Governor Gifford Pinchot declared on March 18, 1932, "with the pitiable condition of the miners and their families in nearly every part of the soft coal region in Pennsylvania." Morris Markey, visiting Fairmont, West Virginia, in 1932, remarked on "the melancholy air of poverty . . . that hushed air of rural poverty which is so much more deeply affecting than the worst city slum." A miner told Markey: "You don't go singing no 'Star Spangled Banner' when you got hungry women and young 'uns sitting in the cabin." [4]

Hunger stalked the mining camps. Early in 1932 a teacher asked a miner's little girl if she were sick. "No," the child replied, "I'm all right, only I'm hungry." When the teacher suggested that she go home to get something to eat, she replied, "It won't do any good . . . because this is sister's day to eat." Entering West Virginia in 1931, the Quakers weighed the children in the schools and automatically chose for feeding those who were at least 10 per cent underweight. Governor and Mrs. Pinchot themselves financed six milk stations in Pennsylvania's bituminous districts. The miner's menu was a national disgrace: "miner's strawberries" (beans — for variety white beans one day and red the next); "bulldog gravy" (flour, water, and a little grease); a "water sandwich" for the miner's lunch pail (stale bread soaked in lard and water). In season the families with gardens enjoyed fresh vegetables. Meat, milk, and fruit were seldom available. Although miners had a great craving for beef, they almost never tasted it; on the rare occasions when they did, it seemed to come from the cow that had entered the ark with Noah. Daniel Willard's advice — steal before you starve — was taken. Malcolm Ross reported from the Blue Ridge, "Petty thievery is now common. . . . Calves are being butchered in lonely woods. Chickens disappear in the night. Company store windows are smashed. . . . Delegations of miners . . . offer storekeepers the choice between handing out free food or having it taken by violence." A conservative southern politician had a solution: "Let them starve to death, the quicker the better." [5]

Malnutrition bred disease. The incidence of tuberculosis rose markedly. Most disturbing was "flux," bleeding dysentery of the stomach and entrails, the terrible ailment that caused the death of the children Aunt Molly Jackson tended. Medical services were seriously inadequate. Franklin County, Illinois, for example, found itself incapable of paying the county doctor in 1931. In the company towns the miners complained about the doctors. As employees of the operators, they often discriminated against the families of union miners and testified against the men in compensation cases. Even when kindly as individuals, they were powerless to deal with the basic problem of malnutrition.

The miners purchased virtually no new clothing. Wives mended old clothes and families sometimes acquired hand-me-downs. In a Kentucky village in November 1931, when the cold had already set in, not a single child had shoes, and very few possessed underwear. The men regularly worked without underclothes in the cold and damp below ground. Children with no shoes, of course, were unable to attend school in the winter.

Housing, a serious problem in the twenties, deteriorated markedly during the depression. Since the mine would someday give out and the miner was considered a transient, the operator had little incentive either to build or to maintain proper housing. In Kentucky in 1931 a group of writers (the Dreiser Committee) discovered "tumble-down and decaying shacks in various states of decrepitude and disrepair." They were built of flimsy board, had never known paint, were papered with newspapers, were full of gaping holes, and were "criminally unfit for habitation by man or beasts." John Dos Passos visited an injured miner, the floor of whose house had rotted away. When the writer leaned against the wall, "it gave way with his weight, not at all to the surprise of the miner." Company houses were occupied under leases that terminated automatically with loss of employment. The company was protected in its rights to deduct rent from wages and to remove furniture and belongings at will. Hence eviction was a powerful weapon in the war against the union.[6]

Especially grating grievances were the company store and the payment of wages in scrip. A number of Kentucky operators confided to Louis Stark of the *New York Times* that they made more money by keeping store than by selling coal. Prices were considerably higher in what the miners called the "pluck-me" than in the independent store. Stark found that a sack of flour that went for $1 outside cost $1.40 at the commissary. B. A. Scott of the West Virginia Mine Workers claimed in 1931 that prices were 40 to 60 per cent higher. A variety of pressures forced the miners to buy from the company stores. Sometimes it was simply a condition of employment. "If you trade at Piggly Wiggly's," the superintendent of a mine at Kitts, Kentucky, told the men at the drift mouth, "you can get your job at Piggly Wiggly's." Further, the miner, who had little cash, needed credit for day-to-day expenses, and independent merchants considered him a poor risk in hard times. Finally, there was scrip — crude coins of aluminum or cardboard honored only at company stores, called variously by the men "chicken-feed," "stickers," "flickers," and "drag." With scrip the operator had the dual advantages of conducting his business without money and of maximizing his commissary sales. It was invariably discounted, generally at 25 per cent. A sign at the movie house in Cedar Grove, West Virginia, in 1931 read as follows:

## ADMISSION

| Children | Adults |
|---|---|
| 15 cents | 30 cents |
| Scrip 20 cents | Scrip 40 cents |

Although some of the states had regulatory legislation (West Virginia required that scrip be honored at par and Kentucky forbade its use for regular wage payments), the laws were universally ignored or evaded.[7]

The miners' most serious grievance was the deprivation of their civil liberties. "What's the use of going to law," a Kentucky coal digger told Stark in 1931, "ain't no justice for us in Harlan courts." The reporter estimated that 90 per cent of the men in the industry wanted to join the union. In most fields the operators denied them this right and in some, especially in the South, did so with the aid of the authorities by abrogating fundamental constitutional rights. As Howard Eavenson of the Harlan County Coal Operators Association told the Senate Manufactures Subcommittee in 1932, "The only answer is to buy machine guns." The miners in many fields did not enjoy free speech or freedom of assembly; they had assurance neither of due process nor of equal protection of the laws; if they or their friends entered a hostile town, they were subjected to unlawful search and seizure. To these legal deprivations must be added the economic discrimination already noted.[8]

Under these economic and legal disabilities the United Mine Workers' organization disintegrated. In fact, the international union had virtually no history during the Great Depression. Its fragments did. To recount those histories it is necessary to deal separately with Illinois, Kentucky, West Virginia, the Pennsylvania-Ohio-Indiana vestiges of the Central Competitive Field, and anthracite.

2

The bitter conflict between the international officers of the United Mine Workers and the officials of District 12, Illinois, as was pointed out in Chapter 2, had its origins in the twenties. The basic issue was district autonomy. Lewis, anxious to concentrate power in the international, set out to undermine the districts. He met formidable opposition in District 12. Illinois remained the only important area in which bituminous miners were well organized. Hence District 12 contributed a growing share of the international's revenues for which it received little in return. At conventions the district found itself outvoted by delegates from paper organizations in states in which the UMW had collapsed. The main service the international could perform for District 12 — organization of the unorganized — was beyond realization; Illinois coal was increasingly undersold within its own markets by bituminous from the nonunion fields. The breakdown of national bargaining in the late twenties shifted control over the contract and the wage scale from the international to District 12 in 1928. Lewis could not long tolerate this condition. To these basic policy issues was added a clash of personalities. The opposition leaders — Frank Farrington, Alex Howat, John Walker, Harry Fishwick, Oscar Ameringer, Adolph Germer, John Brophy, and Powers Hapgood — were strong, and in some cases colorful personalities. John L. Lewis resolved that these men should find careers outside the United Mine Workers of America. They yearned as insistently for his departure.

Characteristically, Lewis struck the first blow on June 8, 1929, by revoking the charter and replacing the officials of Subdistrict 9 in Franklin County. He based this action upon well-founded charges that the officers had engaged in fraudulent real estate transactions and had embezzled strike funds. The subdistrict leaders refused to stand trial at UMW headquarters in Indianapolis, filed a libel suit against the international, and sought an injunction, only temporarily granted, to restrain Lewis from executing his order. Meantime, the district officers annoyed Lewis by refusing to support his brother Denny's reappointment as Illinois Director of Mines. He reciprocated on September 20 by informing District 12 that a section of its constitution was invalid because of a conflict with that of the UMW. "The International Executive Board, by constitutional mandate," he warned, "is the supreme authority and directing agency of our organization." The district executive board on October 5 defied the charter revocation, parceled out Subdistrict 9 among adjoining subdistricts, and refused to disavow the libel suit. On October 15, 1929, Lewis responded by revoking the charter of District 12. He charged insubordination stemming from the Franklin County conflict, the libel suit, alleged dissipation of funds, and attacks by the *Illinois Miner* upon the international officers. He appointed a new slate of provisional officers. The battle began.[9]

The officers of District 12 retaliated with both court action and a bold attempt to take over the international. They immediately obtained a temporary injunction restraining Lewis from carrying out the revocation order. It was confirmed by the Circuit Court of Sangamon County, Illinois, in January 1930. Judge N. L. Jones ruled that Lewis had violated the UMW constitution by removing district officers without trial by the district executive board. Heartened by this action, the leaders of District 12 joined with anti-Lewis elements from other parts of the country at a "state of the union" meeting in Chicago. Calling themselves the "organization committee," they declared that the constitution of the United Mine Workers had lapsed on March 31, 1929. On February 15, 1930, therefore, they issued the call for an international convention to meet at Springfield, Illinois, on March 10 to reconstitute the union. The signers were bitter enemies of Lewis: the officers of District 12, headed by Fishwick; Howat and August Dorchy, the leaders of Kansas District 14; Walker, former miner and now president of the Illinois Federation of Labor; John Brophy, who had headed the "Save-the-Union" movement in 1926 and was presently a salesman for the Hapgoods' Columbia Conserve Company; Germer, at one time secretary of the Socialist Party and currently a real estate agent. Farrington, though sympathetic, did not sign because both honest trade unionists and liberals objected to him. The mastermind of the operation was the brilliant socialist publisher of the *Illinois Miner*, Oscar Ameringer, better known by his *nom de plume*, Adam Coaldigger. In the fine art of character assassination, a form much appreciated by miners, Ameringer was a match for Lewis, though hardly his superior. A friend of Adam's, visiting Lewis at the "miners' boarding house," the Hotel Stratford Avon in Philadelphia, described John L. as "the only man I ever knew who can strut sitting down ... a turkey gobbler with spreading tail feathers, full of ... gobble, gobble."[10]

Lewis, a stickler for legal niceties when the occasion demanded, called a convention for the same day in Indianapolis. Thus began "the race for the name." Somehow each faction became persuaded that the first to hold its convention would thereby gain the legal right to call itself the United Mine Workers of America.

The rebels won the race. At Springfield 450 delegates adopted those parts of their proposed constitution dealing with name and jurisdiction at 11:21 A.M. on March 10, exactly forty minutes before the Indianapolis convention extended the UMW constitution. Each faction now had a paper basis for claiming to be the UMW. The Springfield delegates were mainly from Illinois, with a sprinkling from other states. Among the latter was a tough West Virginian, Frank Keeney, of whom we shall hear more in due course.

The Springfield convention quickly degenerated into democratic license. Fishwick, who began as temporary chairman, was hooted from the platform and Howat was installed in his place. The delegates insisted that committees should be elected rather than appointed (who, it was asked, would count the votes in the race for teller?). The salary of president, reflecting the hatred for Lewis that bound the convention together, was chopped from $12,000 to $5000. Two days were consumed in debate over the seating of Farrington, publicizing anew his outrageous personal contract with the Peabody Coal Company while serving as president of District 12. His Illinois friends won him a seat and thereby gave Lewis an issue.

The economic program of the Reorganized (as the rebel group came to be called) would have done nothing to improve the condition of the coal miner. It consisted primarily of charges that Lewis was personally responsible for the ills of the industry. The delegates had no wage policy. Their resolution vacuously called for scales negotiated "on the sound competitive basis so ably announced . . . by John Mitchell." To deal with unemployment, the convention urged lawmakers to consider legislation "to the end that every man who is willing to work . . . shall have provided for he and his that which will furnish proper food, clothes, and shelter."

The real struggle at Springfield was over the slate of officers. The signers of the call had agreed that Walker, who had ability, should be president and that Howat, who was popular, should be vice-president. Kingmaker Ameringer upset the plan by throwing his support and that of the *Illinois Miner* behind Howat for the top office. It has been alleged that Ameringer's motives were not entirely pure. His shop in which the paper was printed was outside Illinois. Howat is supposed to have agreed to the continuation of this arrangement, which Walker insisted upon ending. The election of the alcoholic and irresponsible Howat was to prove disastrous. Walker in consolation was made secretary. A sharp contest developed over the vice-presidency between Germer and Hapgood, with the "progressives" behind the latter. Germer won 299 to 95 and, in view of Howat's incompetence, was to be the Reorganized's workhorse.

Finally, the Springfield convention adopted a unity formula that was forwarded to President Green of the AFL. It proposed a joint convention of the rival groups. Only delegates from locals in good standing would be seated; those from provisional districts would be disqualified. The credentials committee would be chosen by the Federation's Executive Council. Former Secretary of Labor William B. Wilson would be temporary chairman and Green would be secretary. The books of both the UMW and District 12 would be audited and those responsible for irregularities would resign.[11]

Lewis had no interest in peace. The absence of his enemies gave him complete control over the Indianapolis assemblage. "Some of the delegations over there," Adam Coaldigger observed, "didn't leave enough membership behind them to constitute one whole man. . . . Six delegates from . . . old Kentucky are voicing the sentiments of one-half of one per cent of a coal digger." Nevertheless, the convention included a large group from southern Illinois. The delegates authorized Lewis to revoke the charter of District 14, thereby unseating Howat and his Kansas followers. Twenty leaders of the Reorganized, including Howat, Walker, Germer, and Fishwick, were ordered to appear before the executive board to show cause why they should not be expelled from membership. Most important in the long run, the convention adopted a constitutional amendment empowering the president at his discretion and without limit as to time to revoke the charters of and establish provisional governments for districts, subdistricts, and local unions. By this means the United Mine Workers became a constitutional dictatorship. In the war against the "rum and rumpies" Lewis played his trump card: William Green. The president of the AFL addressed the Indianapolis convention, pledged Federation support for Lewis, and denounced the rebels for the crime of dual unionism.[12]

The chief victim was Walker. Even before the conventions the UMW had asked Green to remove him as president of the Illinois Federation. Since the two old miners were friends, this was to prove painful. On March 6, Green demanded an explanation of Walker's participation in the Springfield convention call. Walker replied that he had acted as a mine union member rather than as an official of the state federation. Since the UMW constitution had lapsed, it was the duty of members to rehabilitate the organization. "John Mitchell said that it was not treason to fight to take control of a union from such men as control our old union." Lewis had corrupted the UMW and had lost 370,000 members. He had ruled with "a contemptible campaign of lies and character assassination." Green refused to accept this explanation and on March 20 insisted upon Walker's resignation. The Executive Council confirmed this decision. On April 9, Walker submitted his resignation in a bitter nine-page letter. The pursuit, however, was not over. Late in the summer Green instructed Olander that no one from the Reorganized was to be seated at the Illinois Federation convention. He notified Walker in October that he would not be allowed to attend the AFL convention.[13]

Each faction enthusiastically expelled the leaders of the other. Howat, Walker, Fishwick & Co., ordered to stand trial before the UMW board, refused to appear and were tossed out *in absentia.* Howat retaliated by ordering Lewis to appear before his board on charges of dual unionism, which Lewis, of course, ignored. The Panama, Illinois, local, in which Lewis had got his start, returned his union card with the notification that he was unfit to be a member of the United Mine Workers.

The Reorganized started with 65 per cent of the Illinois membership and Howat's personal following in Kansas. Lewis held everything else in bituminous and all of anthracite. Most important, he had a firm foothold in Illinois: all thirty-nine locals in Franklin County excepting that of Royalton, half of Williamson County, the Peoria subdistrict, and a scattering elsewhere.

He struck first at Howat in Kansas by revoking the District 14 charter on March 26 and by naming a provisional government. Three days later the Southwestern Coal Operators Association, which had had distasteful strike experiences with Howat, announced recognition of the new district officers and checked off dues to them. Miners reluctantly signed "loyalty oaths" to Lewis (the principle of the yellow-dog contract had its uses in an interunion rivalry). The president of the Reorganized could not even deliver the men in his own district.

The rebels sought halfheartedly to organize outside Illinois.

Germer made brief forays into Indiana, Ohio, and West Virginia. They achieved nothing. Howat invaded Missouri, spreading, in the words of the local UMW man, "false Gospal and Slanderious attacks on the National Officers."

More important, Lewis took the offensive on the Reorganized's home ground, sopping up its limited resources of manpower and money. Twelve hundred men at the Crescent mines near Peoria struck during the spring of 1930 in loyalty to Lewis. Frank J. Hayes and Philip Murray made intensive speaking tours in the southern part of the state. Lewis men in Franklin County went on several "educational crusades" into enemy territory, sometimes with violent results. The most notorious took place in Royalton on April 18, 1930. Germer was scheduled to address the only local in the county loyal to the Reorganized. Ray Edmundson brought three hundred miners from West Frankfort and Zeigler to break up the meeting. The town of Royalton became a battlefield. When the shooting ended, five miners were wounded and Barney Davie, a "crusader," lay dead. Riots were narrowly averted in Zeigler and Du Quoin. "All that spring," McAlister Coleman has said, "there was civil war . . . in Southern Illinois. Germer . . . was brass-knuckled on the streets of a Lewis-held camp. . . . Through twisting alleyways in the small towns, out along the new hard roads, union man hunted union man in feudist fury."

The Reorganized could not win by standing still and it had lost the initiative. By the summer of 1930 it was clear that Lewis had the upper hand. Howat's drunkenness had become an open scandal. On August 7, Fishwick announced that he would not run for re-election as president of District 12. He was to be succeeded by Walker.[14]

The death blow was struck by Judge Harry Edwards of the Lee County Circuit Court at Dixon, Illinois, in late February 1931. His decree, in effect, restored the status that existed prior to October 15, 1929. The Lewis order of that date, revoking the charter of District 12, was rescinded. The officers the district had elected in 1928 remained in office until April 1, 1931, and the provisional government was thrown out. District 12 was still a lawful segment of the United Mine Workers. The UMW was the Lewis organization; its constitution had continued in force after March

31, 1929, it was decreed, as had its officers. The constitution adopted and the officers elected by the Springfield convention were not those of the United Mine Workers. The Reorganized, therefore, was legally dead.[15]

For a year there was an uneasy truce in Illinois. The miners of that district and Lewis eyed each other suspiciously across no man's land. Each waited for the excuse to pull the trigger. It came with the expiration of the contract between District 12 and the Illinois Coal Operators Association on April 1, 1932.

The producers, determined to undermine the wage scale, demanded a 30 per cent cut in the currently astronomical $6.10 daily base rate. Walker refused. In the absence of a contract a walkout of 50,000 miners commenced on April 1. After three months of attrition Walker recognized that he would have to make concessions. On July 8, he initialed an agreement providing for a $5 day and a reduction in the rate for those working above ground from $8.04 to $5.70. Walker had grievously underestimated the militancy of his membership. On July 16, the miners of Illinois rejected the contract in referendum by a margin of 4 to 1 and continued their strike. Walker was persuaded that his usefulness was at an end. Convinced that a wage cut was inevitable, he was incapable of putting it into effect. Hence he appealed to the international, inviting Lewis to take over the Illinois negotiations.

This was the opportunity that Lewis had awaited for twelve years: control over the collective bargaining of District 12 and so ultimately over the government of the district itself. He was determined to seize it — by persuasion if possible, by force and fraud if necessary. It is a curious irony of history that Walker, who had fought Lewis so passionately and at such great personal sacrifice, should have opened this door for him.

Late in July, with the friendly intervention of Governor Emmerson, Lewis renegotiated the agreement. While there were a few minor improvements, the wage rates were identical — $5 below ground and $5.70 above. On August 2, Lewis called upon the Illinois miners to ratify. "The agreement, distasteful as it may be, represents every concession that, at this time, can be wrung from the impoverished coal companies in a stricken and almost expiring industry." If the men rejected the contract, he warned, they would jeopardize the existence of their union and pave the way for the entry of Kentucky and West Virginia rates into Illinois. His plea fell on deaf ears.

The referendum took place on August 8. The miners, anticipating fraud, took precautions. Voting in the locals was by secret ballot, and the men insisted that watchers should be present in Springfield at the tallying. The first returns from about 100 locals showed a heavy majority for repudiation. The official tellers, Orlie Blackman and George Gee, deposited the uncounted ballots in a vault at the Ridgeley-Farmers Bank overnight. The following morning Blackman and Gee collected the tallies and began walking down the street. Marquis Childs has described what next occurred on that morning of August 10:

> After a block or two they encountered a car in which Fox Hughes, a district official, was riding. One of the tellers spoke to Hughes and then beckoned to the other teller, who came up to the car and tossed the bundle into it. A few minutes later the two tellers appeared at the union offices and announced that they had been robbed of the ballots.

Lewis, conveniently ignoring the fact that duplicate tallies were available at the locals, immediately proclaimed a state of emergency within District 12. Because of the alleged stealing of the ballots he would have to act in the best interests of the union. That same day, August 10, he pronounced the agreement ratified and signed with the producers. The contract rate for coal diggers in Illinois was now $5. Would the miners work for it?

During the remainder of August this question was answered on the battlefield: there was warfare in the mine fields of Illinois. The men spontaneously conducted mass meetings to protest the scale and the fraudulent referendum. Thousands of miners swore that they would not return to work under the Lewis agreement; at Benld on August 14 a meeting of 10,000 repudiated the $5 wage. The rebels launched crusades culminating in massive picketing against the mines in which work had resumed. At Taylorville on August 15, 8000 people, armed with shotguns, pistols, and farm implements, picketed the four big mines of the Peabody Coal

Company. On August 22 the inevitable armed clash occurred at the Langley mine near Zeigler in Franklin County: one killed and six injured. The strikers warned that a huge force would descend upon that county to stop all operations. Sheriff Browning Robinson replied that he was ready. The march of 10,000 to 15,000 miners was stopped by 300 armed deputies in the darkness of August 24 on the county line near Mulkeytown. The deputies routed the unarmed invaders, and about 150 people were injured. The governor called out the National Guard. Lewis announced that twenty rebel leaders had been expelled from the union.

In the retreat from the Battle of Mulkeytown on the night of August 24, fifty leaders of the defeated forces met at the Gillespie city hall. They were especially embittered by the cooperation between the police and the United Mine Workers against them. Their cause within the union seemed hopeless. Hence they voted to send out a call to all mine locals in Illinois to meet in Gillespie on September 1 to form a new union.[16]

Two hundred and seventy-two delegates convened at Gillespie on September 1. This was a rank-and-file movement. The leaders of national reputation who had dominated the Springfield convention of the Reorganized were conspicuously absent. Only the coal diggers of Illinois knew the men who met at Gillespie. The delegates voted unanimously to found a new union, the Progressive Miners of America. They condemned the Lewis contract and pledged the restoration of the $6.10 scale. The organization scheduled its first constitutional convention in Gillespie for October 3. The delegates invited the coal operators to meet with them concurrently in a wage conference at Edwardsville.

The operators held the fate of PMA in their hands. The large companies, with mines concentrated in the southern part of the state, dominated the Illinois Coal Operators Association. The smaller firms, clustering in central Illinois, resented their inferior status. Hence operators from the vicinities of Peoria, Springfield, and Belleville came to Edwardsville. They were to provide the nucleus for a rival employers' association, the Coal Producers Association of Illinois. These operators agreed to recognize and bargain with the Progressives. Most important, they consented to the check-off of union dues. The CPAI, however, was adamant on the wage scale, insisting upon the $5 rate of the Lewis agreement. The PMA leaders were forced to accept the wage reduction as the price of survival. They did not dare submit this contract to the membership for ratification, simply putting it into effect. Ironically, a union that came into being because of rank-and-file opposition to a wage cut and dictatorial leadership found itself in its first important act accepting the reduction as well as autocratic methods. A condition of wage dependency, from which PMA was never to escape, had been established.

The contract of October 8 insured the existence of the Progressives. By the end of 1932, about 18,000 of the 50,000 working miners in Illinois were covered by this agreement, and another 1200 worked for operators who checked off PMA dues but refused to sign because they retained membership in the Illinois Coal Operators Association.

On December 22, the UMW and the ICOA extended the $5 wage for two years. Lewis drew a fine distinction between a new contract and the extension of an old one: the latter did not require ratification. He exacted a heavy price for this wage concession — the union shop. Henceforth the PMA had no means of invading the territory held by the UMW in Illinois.

Feeling between the rivals was, of course, acrimonious. It was manifested mainly in propaganda. PMA shouted "Down with Lewis!" and the UMW declaimed that the Progressives were dominated by Communists. While some strikes for recognition occurred in the winter of 1932–33, they were relatively minor and had lost the violence of the earlier struggles. The public, nevertheless, was aroused. The new Democratic governor, Henry Horner, sought without success to bring the two organizations together. The Illinois legislature instituted an investigation which resulted merely in another report.

In February 1933 Lewis achieved his aim of absolute control over District 12. Ravaged by the depression, exhausted by the fight with PMA, and $225,000 in debt, the district executive board invited Lewis to establish a provisional government in Illinois. The international assumed the financial obligation, and Lewis named William J. Sneed provisional president to succeed Walker. He thereby snuffed out autonomy in the most important bituminous

district in the nation and eliminated the last of his important enemies. All that remained was the annoying sore of the Progressive
Miners.[17]

3

If the theme in Illinois was division, in Kentucky it was despair.
By the spring of 1931 the Harlan coal field, comprising the eastern
counties of Harlan, Bell, Knox, Hazard, and Breathitt, had collapsed. The miners had suffered a drastic curtailment of both
wage rates and employment. The result was destitution in the
camps. A Harlan miner wrote:

> We are half fed because we can'nt feed ourselves and family's
> with what we make. And we can'nt go to a Cut rate Store and
> buy food because most all the company forbids such tradeing.
> If you got the cash. But now we have no cash. And the com-
> panies keeps their food stuffs at high prices at all time. So
> you can not clear enough to go anywhere. And if you do go
> some where and buy food you are subjects to be canned. . . .
> We have been eating wild green. . . . Such as Polk salad.
> Violet tops, wild onions. forget me not wild lettuce and such
> weeds as cows eat as a cow wont eat a poison weeds. . . .
> Our family are in bad shake childrens need milk women need
> nurishments food shoes and dresses — that we cannot get. and
> there at least 10,000 hungry people in Harlan County daily. I
> know because I am one off them. . . . I would leave Harlan
> County if I had only $6 to send my wife and boy to Bristol, Va.
> and I could walk away — But I can't clear a dollar per month that
> why I am here. that why hundreds are here.[18]

There was only the dim memory of a union in the Harlan field.
The United Mine Workers, which had organized the region during World War I, was destroyed locally in the early twenties.
District 19, with jurisdiction over Harlan and Bell Counties, was
a "paper" organization headed by William Turnblazer. Harlan had
the reputation, richly deserved, of being "the toughest spot to
unionize" in the United States. A Harlan operator put it suc-

cinctly: "We can't do business if they have unions." The mining companies and the public officials they controlled had no intention of yielding this distinction to another locality.

In February 1931, the Harlan employers cut wages 10 per cent. While this was merely the latest in a long series of reductions, the reaction was unique. "We starve while we work; we might as well strike while we starve." The UMW staged a meeting at Pineville, the Harlan county seat, on March 1 at which Philip Murray exhorted 2000 miners to join up. Many did. The Black Mountain Company retaliated by firing 175 of its men and the Black Star Company discharged 35. Evictions from company houses followed. Another meeting was held at La Follette three weeks later, addressed by Turnblazer and Congressman J. Will Taylor. They denounced the discriminatory discharges and evictions and urged the men to sign. Turnblazer promised that the UMW would provide food and money for a strike. Over 11,000 miners streamed into the union, and the mines shut down. Violence, endemic in the Kentucky mountains, soon appeared. The strikers, failing to receive food from the union, looted stores and gardens. Deputized mine guards physically assaulted the striking miners.

Near the town of Evarts on May 4 several carloads of deputies, carrying rifles and machine guns, engaged in pitched battle with about a score of armed miners. The Battle of Evarts lasted thirty minutes and at its end four men (three deputies and one miner) lay dead. An obscure strike in a remote mountain region suddenly erupted into nation-wide prominence. Harlan County entered the national consciousness, like the name of the state in which it was situated, as "a dark and bloody ground."

Governor Flem D. Sampson was urged to send troops into Harlan. His agents first entered into an agreement with Turnblazer: the UMW would welcome the soldiers; food would be supplied; mine guards would be disarmed and their commissions as deputies revoked. The National Guard, 400 strong, arrived on May 6. The agreement was immediately repudiated. Union leaders were arrested, scabs, many of them Negroes, were imported, and mine guards retained their arms and commissions. In fact, on May 11, Sheriff J. H. Blair announced that he knew of no agreement and had no intention of relieving deputies. On May 16, Blair conducted a raid upon the offices of the UMW local in Evarts and uncovered evidence of IWW activity. Some of the members were Wobblies and they had applied for a charter in the Industrial Workers of the World. This allowed the enemies of the union to invoke Kentucky's criminal syndicalism law by claiming a conspiracy to overthrow the government. Further, twenty-eight UMW members were charged with first-degree murder for the death of a mine guard at the Battle of Evarts.

At this point the United Mine Workers quit. Turnblazer told the men that their strike was a "wildcat" and that they should return to work. The UMW gave no reason, then or later, for the sharp reversal of policy. This failure gave apparent substance to the charge, repeatedly leveled by its enemies, that the union had "sold out" its Kentucky members. Whatever the merits of the accusation, there was abundant evidence that the cause was hopeless: the operators were relentless, the apparatus of the state was on their side, food and funds were virtually nonexistent, and economic conditions were desperate. The strike of the mountaineer coal diggers, which slowly petered out, was not a collective bargaining dispute: it was a revolt born of desperation and doomed to defeat.

Recognizing this, the Communist Party filled the vacuum UMW left. The attractions were irresistible: Here, in fact, was the class war with capitalism Marx had predicted, with the state joined against the workers. The "reformist" trade union was bankrupt. In their present mood the miners, innocent of unionism and collective bargaining, to say nothing of political polemics, were readily manipulable. The Harlan murder trial before a prejudiced judge whose wife was a member of the Coal Operators Association (the people of Harlan, Judge David Crockett Jones declared, don't need "anyone from Russia or any warped twisted individuals from New York to tell us how to run our government") might be exploited as another Mooney-Billings or Sacco-Vanzetti case. The party, sensitive to the charge of foreign influence, would speak for an impeccably "American" constituency: the Kentucky mountain folk were indubitably Anglo-Saxon, their pioneer ancestors had followed Daniel Boone through the Cumberland Gap, they spoke Elizabethan English, did square dances, and sang old English ballads. American writers and intellectuals, by 1931 moving into the Communist Party and its environs in large numbers, could be counted on to dramatize the Harlan spectacle and to evoke national and even international sympathy. The party considered Harlan, Malcolm Ross observed, as "one of those powder boxes where a well placed fuse can blow a hole in the Capitalist System."

Dan Brooks, organizer for the leftist National Miners' Union, arrived in Harlan on June 19 and was soon followed by Jessie Wakefield of the International Labor Defense, who took over legal and relief activities. Many of the miners were eager for any outside assistance regardless of source. The local union held a secret meeting on July 2 which voted to send delegates to the NMU convention in Pittsburgh in mid-July. The organization then came into the open. A picnic attended by 2000 miners and their families was staged on July 26 and was followed by a state convention of 500 delegates at Wallins Creek on August 2.

Behind the NMU marched the writers and intellectuals, those estimable tourists Judge Jones called "snake doctors from New York." Early in November the Dreiser Committee made a widely publicized voyage to Harlan County. Theodore Dreiser was chairman of the National Committee for the Defense of Political Prisoners. In open telegrams he invited a number of prominent citizens — senators, businessmen, publishers, college presidents — to join the trip. Almost all refused. His group consisted mainly of writers — John Dos Passos, Sherwood Anderson, Charles Rumford Walker, and Bruce Crawford, among others. Their results were published in a book, *Harlan Miners Speak*. Early in 1932 a committee of New York writers, including Waldo Frank, Edmund Wilson, Malcolm Cowley, and Mary Heaton Vorse, descended upon Harlan with several truckloads of food and clothing. They were followed by a delegation of pastors and several groups of students. Finally, in May 1932, a committee of prominent attorneys made the trip under the sponsorship of the American Civil Liberties Union. It seemed that a writer or intellectual who failed to reach Harlan in 1931–32 was hardly worth his salt. The attendant publicity gave the county's name a certain stench in the national nostrils and helped to launch an investigation by the Senate Manufactures Subcommittee in the spring of 1932.

Any disposition the operators may have had to abide by the rules evaporated with the arrival of the Communist union in the summer of 1931. They were no longer merely defending low wages, union-busting, and evictions; they now guarded the American Way of Life. This required the suppression of civil liberties by terror in Harlan and Bell Counties. According to Herbert Abel, the operators conducted

> . . . a systematic unrelenting campaign. The forces of the coal guards roam the countryside at night, terrorizing the inhabitants. Meetings are broken up with tear-gas bombs, raids are conducted almost every night with their consequent toll of deaths, houses are broken into and property confiscated, the mails are tampered with, the slightest resistance is met with the force of guns.

Scores of people were arrested for criminal syndicalism. Visitors were made unwelcome. The Harlan County attorney notified Arthur Garfield Hays that his "godless, self-appointed, nondescript, iconoclastic minority of grandiloquent egotists" would be treated like "mad dogs." Outsiders were beaten, ridden out of the county, and subjected to seizure of property. The operators called in a notorious gunman, Bill Randolph ("He's killed three or four men," one of his defenders admitted). Relief was denied to strikers. Herndon Evans, editor of the Pineville *Sun* and chairman of the local Red Cross, admitted that he checked with the employer to determine whether applicants were on strike. "We tell the men on strike that they'd better go back to work, even if there is water in the mines and conditions aren't what we'd like to have them."

The campaign was a spectacular success. By the end of 1931, the National Miners' Union was smashed and the Harlan and Bell operators had achieved control over their workers. At this point the union performed an act of irresponsibility to its few remaining loyal members: NMU called a general strike for January 1, 1932. It proved a disaster. The union disappeared from Kentucky and its members were hounded out of the mines.[19]

4

Destitution among the miners of West Virginia was even greater than in Kentucky. By early 1931 one third of the state's 112,000 diggers were wholly jobless and another third worked only one or two days a week. Returning from a tour of the camps in April, Fred Croxton of the President's Emergency Committee called "conditions so bad they almost were unbelievable." Seven months later Louis Stark, after a swing through several coal areas, declared that the situation in West Virginia was the worst in the nation. There was no union, the United Mine Workers having disintegrated in 1924. The Hitchman doctrine — the yellow-dog contract enforced by the labor injunction — won very wide acceptance in that state.

The emergence of depression unionism was largely the work of a single man — Frank Keeney. From a family that had lived in the hills for generations and a West Virginian by birth, Keeney had a natural bond with the state's miners. "Who are you," he asked them, "you dirty despised people who can't walk into Charleston because you'd give them a disease? That's what they say. . . . It's no disgrace to dig coal. Coal makes civilization possible. . . . Quit hanging your heads." At one time Keeney had been a Socialist as well as president of the West Virginia district of UMW. In 1920 he had been the hero of a strike that became a civil war. Four years later he fell out with Lewis over the Jacksonville wage scale, and no one disagreed with Lewis amicably. In the late twenties Keeney became a businessman, first the proprietor of an orange-drink stand and later a speculator in gas and oil. His heart remained with the men in the pits. Edmund Wilson, who visited him in 1931, wrote this description:

> Frank Keeney is a short man, with a square face and stub-toed shoes. He has a straight black bang on his forehead, eyes like fragments of blue bottle-glass, a face as deep-seamed as if the battles of the miners had left their slashes there, and two solid-gold teeth. It has been said of him that he can talk to operators as if they were his own miners, and that he talks to miners like the captain of a ship.

Keeney's lieutenant, Brant Scott, had lost a leg in a mine accident for which he received no compensation. He got about on a cork substitute held by a leather harness of his own devising. Scott had served with Keeney in the Socialist Party and in the mine wars of a decade earlier.

In 1930, Keeney decided to leave business and go back to the miners. He and Scott were delegates to the Reorganized convention in Springfield. They returned to West Virginia to open a local branch of the new union. When the Reorganized collapsed early in 1931, they determined to go ahead on their own, forming the West Virginia Mine Workers Union. Keeney received $100,000 from northern liberals and a cadre of dedicated organizers from A. J. Muste's Brookwood Labor College. In outlook the union stood midway between the Communist National Miners' Union and the more conservative United Mine Workers.

WVMWU made rapid progress in organizing. By the late spring of 1931, it was estimated to have enrolled between 18,000 and 23,000 members. Keeney effectively dramatized the plight of his people, notably in a hunger march of 300 miners and their families upon Charleston on May 20 to ask Governor William G. Conley for relief. The chief executive received them and listened to the plea that they were out of work and had nothing to eat. "Whatever conditions may be now," Conley replied, "we have the best government on earth." He read them the state's constitution to explain that he lacked authority to help; the legislature had appropriated nothing for relief and he was forbidden to divert funds from other purposes. "But," the governor concluded munificently, "I am going to turn over $10 of my own money to your presiding officer." That ten-dollar bill was to achieve a certain notoriety in West Virginia's politics.

Keeney needed to solidify his growing organization by negotiating a collective bargaining agreement with the West Virginia operators. Given their unalterable opposition to unions, he knew this could not be achieved peaceably. There would have to be a strike and the times were hardly propitious. Keeney's strategy was to shut the mines in the peak month, July, when the operators would normally be filling orders for Great Lakes bunker coal. The risk was that these orders would be transferred to other bituminous districts, which is what actually happened.

The strike was called in the Kanawha field on July 6, 1931. Keeney's rivals sought to undercut him. William Z. Foster, boss of the Communist Party, and Frank Borech, secretary of the National Miners' Union, came to West Virginia to induce the miners of that state to join the NMU walkout then under way in Ohio and Pennsylvania. The United Mine Workers denounced the WVMWU stoppage as "unwarranted and untimely."

Keeney had little trouble persuading the men to go out. They detested the operators, especially for cheating them at the scales and at the company stores. His great problem was to keep 8000 miners housed and fed during a long struggle. The operators evicted strikers *en masse*; James Myers reported 106 families thrown out of their houses one morning at a single camp. Evictions were sometimes accompanied by physical brutality. The union shouldered the burden of establishing tent colonies for these families. Food was more critical. Keeney had a warehouse in Charleston from which trucks carried beans, flour, and coffee over the mountains to the "cricks" and "hollers." The supply would not last long, and the Red Cross had cut off assistance to strikers. By mid-August the resources of the West Virginia Mine Workers Union were at an end. The operators had found "barefootmen" among the ranks of the jobless, and their families now occupied the company houses. Keeney called off his hopeless strike and his union disintegrated.

Meantime, the UMW capitalized on the militancy that Keeney had stirred up. In May the miners at Scotts Run in the northern part of the state had struck spontaneously against a wage cut. Van Bittner, the Lewis man in the district, assumed leadership. He negotiated an agreement with forty operators providing for a checkweighman, the eight-hour day, pay for "dead" work, and a grievance procedure. Bittner paid dearly for these gains in low wages. His rate was only 30 cents a ton in contrast with local nonunion scales of 38 to 43 cents. Bittner argued that his wage was honest, while the others should be discounted by false weights. This was only partly correct. The Rockefellers' Consolidation Coal Company had checkweighmen and paid an actual 39 cents. Bittner's position became hopeless in September when the organized operators forced him to accept a 25 per cent cut. On October 1, when the union rate dropped to 22.5 cents, Consolidation was 74 per cent higher. The UMW, in fact, was helpless to defend its members. The only weapon the operators would respect was a strike, which the union was incapable of winning. Frank Keeney's prostrate form lay before it.[20]

## 5

The Central Competitive Field, at one time the heart of collective bargaining in bituminous coal, slid into chaos. The union, the interstate agreement, and the wage structure had broken up in the twenties in Indiana, Ohio, and Pennsylvania. Disintegration increased in pace after the crash and lapped over into the anthracite industry in northeastern Pennsylvania. It was marked by bitter union rivalries and an extraordinary incidence of violence.

In Indiana the mines still organized by District 11 of the UMW paid a basic wage of $6.10 a day under the contract that expired on March 31, 1932. The operators insisted upon a 25 per cent wage cut; the union refused and called a strike. A number of the operators decided to continue production with nonunion miners, and the UMW determined to shut them down. On April 6, Governor H. G. Leslie notified William Mitch, head of District 11, that he would not hesitate to call out state troopers. The warning went unheeded. UMW pickets in July besieged twenty scabs for two days in the Hoosier mine at Dugger. Only the intervention of the National Guard allowed their release. A few weeks later 4000 pickets held 70 nonunion men prisoner in a washhouse at the Dixie Bee mine in Vigo County. On August 2, one miner was killed and eight others injured. Leslie shipped in 1000 guardsmen and a wing of aircraft to lay down a tear-gas barrage. The Dixie Bee reopened. On September 10, 1932, District 11 caved in and accepted a reduction in rate from $6.10 to $4.75, almost the full 25 per cent the operators had offered in March.[21]

In Ohio the story was both more complicated and more violent. Economic conditions in the fields were worse. Early in 1931, Hugh Fullerton reported in the Columbus *Dispatch*, many Ohio miners were paid only 25 cents a ton to take coal from the earth. In Columbus a man who moved a ton from the sidewalk to the cellar received 50 cents. Fullerton dwelt especially upon the suffering of the children.

The National Miners' Union in 1931 sought to organize both eastern Ohio and western Pennsylvania. The demands appeared reasonable enough: moderately higher wages, the eight-hour day, checkweighmen, and union recognition. But the Communist apparatus was much in evidence: Foster and Wagenknecht spoke in the fields, and copies of the *Daily Worker* with bloodthirsty headlines deluged the camps. In June, since the operators refused to bargain, NMU struck. Hundreds of armed miners descended upon the New Lafferty mine in St. Clairsville to force a shutdown. Eighteen of them were incarcerated, and on June 11, 2000 people unsuccessfully attacked the jail. At some mines the pickets were joined by mothers with babes in arms. In Belmont County three of these women and their seven children landed in jail. In this area a pitched battle took place on June 18 between strikers and mine guards in which eight were injured. Two days later William Simon of the NMU met death by a bullet on a picket line at Martins Ferry. This desperation strike soon collapsed, and by the end of the summer NMU was only a memory in the Ohio coal fields.

In November, Governor George White sought to establish stability by calling a conference of Ohio operators and the UMW. The employers refused to deal with the union. Early in 1932, in fact, they cut wages. At the Hanna Coal Company the base rate fell from $4.30 to $3.20 a day; the Ohio-Pennsylvania Company lopped off 15 per cent; many of the mines dropped the wage to $3.00. The men objected bitterly and the UMW was emboldened to call strikes against the reductions. Seven thousand miners went out in the Hocking Valley and Sunday Creek fields in March. The next month President Lee Hall of District 6 asked for a general strike. The men gradually shut down the Ohio mines, as well as some in northern West Virginia. Where work continued, there was the usual violence. On April 5, nonunion miners in Muskingum County, Ohio, were stoned. On April 14, at the Somers mine in Harrison County one man was killed and thirty were injured. The governor sent in the National Guard. On the following day at Cadiz another miner met death. On April 20, a tremendous explosion occurred outside Cadiz.

Secretary of Labor Doak invited the operators and the UMW

to Washington to work out a settlement. The employers refused to come. In May, Governor White proposed a formula: the end of the strike, a daily rate of $3.28, checkweighmen, arbitration of local grievances, payment in currency, and *no* union recognition. By September the UMW, obviously beaten, swallowed hard and accepted these terms. Most of the operators went along. The Ohio Collieries Company of Hollister, however, refused, leading to further armed conflict. Result: two dead.[22]

Pennsylvania was the major battleground of the old Central Competitive Field. Conditions in the mining camps were very bad and relief was grossly inadequate. The UMW was in eclipse, and the NMU found its main support in western Pennsylvania.

In 1931 the left-wing union presented demands for higher wages, checkweighmen, and union recognition, which the operators rejected. In early June the NMU called a strike that took effect within a seventy-five-mile district from southwestern Washington County to New Kensington. It was to prove unusually violent. On June 8 serious rioting occurred near Pittsburgh, resulting in the death of two miners and the beating of a state trooper by a mob. At Ellsworth a marching column of strikers and the coal and iron police fought at the barricades on the highway.

On June 13, the Pittsburgh Terminal Company, the second-largest in the state, announced a wage agreement with the United Mine Workers. This company, which had repudiated collective bargaining in 1927, was willing to grant a small increase, risking the chicken pox from UMW in order to avoid the smallpox from NMU. The negotiations proceeded in the executive mansion in Harrisburg with the blessing of Governor Pinchot. The NMU howled in outrage. Borech led a protest delegation to the capitol on June 18 to denounce the contract and Pinchot. He warned the governor that NMU would destroy the agreement.

On June 16, Judge H. H. Rowand issued an extraordinarily sweeping injunction which forbade the NMU to picket or even gather about the Consolidated Coal Company mine at Wildwood. The union replied with a demonstration of 7000 miners and their families before the Washington County courthouse. An armed clash took place in Wildwood on June 21 in which one man was killed and twelve were injured. Forty-two miners were arrested, and deportation proceedings were instituted against the twenty of them who were aliens. Wildwood experienced further violence in July with sporadic bombing of boarding places of nonunion miners and sniping at them on their way to work. Only one person was injured.

At Arnold City on June 23, a storekeeper was killed and four men were injured in a battle between miners and mine guards. Six girls were arrested at Castle Shannon for throwing mud at Pittsburgh Terminal's company houses. On June 29 three truckloads of NMU pickets were chased out of Ellsworth by deputies armed with clubs and tear gas. On June 30 the union staged a hunger march of 8000 singing miners through downtown Pittsburgh. There was no trouble; a cordon of police armed with gas and riot clubs lined the route.

On July 19 in Canonsburg, a UMW meeting erupted into a riot in which the speakers were routed and 100 people were injured. UMW organizers began to use armed bodyguards. A remarkable incident occurred on July 26. P. T. Fagan, president of District 1 of UMW, was at home in Pittsburgh. Two men entered. One announced that he had been sent to kill Fagan. The UMW man, who was armed, fired first and killed his would-be assailant. The other man escaped.

Late in the summer of 1931, the New Republic totted up an incomplete list of Pennsylvania casualties: three miners killed, fifty-five hospitalized, over 2000 gassed, injured, or wounded. Despite the cost, the NMU had accomplished nothing. The combination of the operators, the UMW, and the government had proved too weighty. As if this were not enough, the Comintern denounced the National Miners' Union for its conduct of the strike. Its eleven-point resolution boiled down to one — defeat.[23]

The troubles in soft coal in western Pennsylvania had a counterpart in hard coal in the eastern part of the state. While the UMW maintained its membership and contracts more effectively in anthracite than in bituminous, the depression brought many problems.

Early in 1931, 20,000 miners at the Glen Alden Coal Company in Wilkes-Barre went out in a wildcat strike. Lewis denounced the act as a violation of "the joint wage agreement, and the pledge made by the officers of your union to the anthracite operators." The men drifted back to work. On September 22 they came out in a second wildcat at Glen Alden. The UMW again disavowed the walkout, and Murray was sent to Wilkes-Barre to persuade the men to return to work. He did not get them back until October 9.

During the winter of 1931–32, the disaffection among the hard coal miners turned against the union. An insurgent faction centered in Luzerne and Lackawanna Counties emerged under the leadership of John Maloney. Defeated earlier in a race for president of District 1, Maloney charged that he had been "counted out" and sought to take over the district with his rump movement. His apparent objective was to gain control over the two other anthracite districts, 7 and 9, in order to create a hard coal union. His slogan was "equalization of work." The operators had shut down their less economic mines, throwing employees in these operations wholly out of work. Maloney demanded that employment in the working mines should be spread over all the men. This had a natural appeal to the idle, who, unfortunately for Maloney, were hardly effective strikers. Nevertheless, in March 1932 he called an outlaw strike in District 1 over this issue. The UMW, of course, denounced the stoppage and ordered the men to work. Armed clashes between the factions took place on March 19. A week later at Exeter there was a sharp interchange between pickets and working miners. Eight men were injured and twelve cars were demolished. The power of the operators and Lewis was too much for Maloney. By the end of March, his strike had collapsed and with it his insurgent movement.[24]

# 6

By the winter of 1932–33, the coal industry was in a state of complete demoralization. Its condition called to mind the old western Pennsylvania story about the final day of a worked-out mine: The last grizzled miner placed the last lump of coal on the last worn-out pit car. He threw his battered broom and his rusty pick and shovel atop the load and guessed at its weight. With the help of his faithful but ancient dog harnessed to the car (the mine mule had died), he laboriously dragged the load to the tottering old tipple and dumped it into the last railroad car below on the rusty siding. The tipple at that moment collapsed. The pit car dropped in a heap and fell to pieces. The old dog died. Since the grizzled old miner didn't know what else to do, he went on strike.[25]

## CHAPTER 11

# The Anti-Injunction Movement

THE PLIGHT of the coal miner was to lead indirectly to the first of the great labor laws of the thirties, the Norris–La Guardia Act. The initiative for this legislation came primarily from one man, Senator George W. Norris of Nebraska. It is a curiosity that Norris represented a predominantly rural state and had only a handful of union members among his constituents. His interest in the linked problems of the yellow-dog contract and the injunction was aroused by the devastation they had inflicted upon the miners.

### 1

Norris, born on a farm in northern Ohio in 1861, lived intimately in his youth with poverty and personal tragedy. His family just managed to survive. "There on that farm," he wrote later, "I lost all fear of poverty. I learned to live most simply, and I learned to get a great joy out of work." He slept in an unheated loft and viewed the stars in the night sky through cracks between the shingles. He could not afford ice cream until his twenty-first birthday. His education — in the common schools of Ohio, Baldwin University, and the Northern Indiana Normal School — was gained at the price of great personal and family sacrifice.

Death pursued the Norris family. George's father died when he was three, leaving a stern and devoted widow with a large brood. His older brother lost his life in the same year, 1864, marching with Sherman through Georgia. A sister died the next year. After he moved to the Beaver Valley of Nebraska, his wife failed to survive a childbirth, leaving him with three little girls.

In 1906, when he was serving in the House of Representatives, his second wife lost twins at their birth and almost gave her own life. From poverty and tragedy George Norris learned compassion. He viewed himself as a spokesman for the common man. Wholly without desire for material goods, Norris distrusted the wealthy. "No man can stick his legs under the tables of the idle rich every night," he declared, "and be fit to sit in judgment on those who toil." Hence he dedicated himself to "the unceasing struggle ... to protect the helpless, the weak, and the poor from exploitation by the strong." Mainly, as he saw it, this was to do battle against "the greed and avarice of individuals and groups for wealth; the injection of privilege, favoritism, and discrimination in national policy."

George Norris was a Republican. His mother had been a Republican; the neighbors were Republican; Ohio was Republican. Elder Long had told his mother, when George was a boy, that a Democrat could not get into heaven. Norris then believed that the party of Lincoln was the sole repository of good; the Democrats had a monopoly over evil. In 1896 he supported McKinley over his fellow-Nebraskan, Bryan.

His mature political education began with his election to the House of Representatives in 1902. He learned that machines controlled both parties and that privilege spoke with a loud voice in his own. In 1910, Norris led the insurgents in the House who unhorsed Speaker Joe Cannon. He was now a tough-minded, astute, and determined political maverick. The voters of Nebraska, in 1912, sent Norris to the Senate, a seat he was to hold for thirty years. He was a political independent wearing no party's collar.

Norris was out of sorts in the twenties, a period he called "the era of reaction." Big business was in control. He had little use for Harding or Coolidge and detested Hoover. The Teapot Dome oil scandals, unearthed by his good friend, Democratic Senator Tom Walsh of Montana, disgusted him.

In 1926 Norris became disturbed over the results of the Republican primary in Pennsylvania. William S. Vare, boss of the corrupt Philadelphia machine, had defeated Governor Pinchot in the race for the Senate nomination. Norris characterized Vare's methods as "disreputable, illegal, and disgraceful." The Nebraskan stumped Pennsylvania on behalf of the Democratic candidate, William B. Wilson, former mine-union official and Secretary of Labor. In the course of this campaign the senator learned at first hand about the conditions of the miners. Scheduled to address a meeting in a coal town, Norris discovered that no notice had appeared in the newspapers. The operators had imposed a conspiracy of silence. In another coal town he met the victim of a mine disaster. All his limbs and his collarbone had been broken, his spinal cord had been injured, his head had been twisted out of shape, and the exposed areas of his skin had been seared black. This man told him of the hardships of the miners — the poverty, the company stores, the assault upon the union. He drove the Nebraskan to a nearby cemetery where they found an old tombstone amid the tumbled weeds. Upon it was this epitaph:

*For 40 years beneath the sod, with pick and spade I did my task,*
*The coal king's slave, but now, thank God, I'm free at last.*

"I was impressed greatly by the experience of this day," Norris later wrote. He determined to assist the coal miners. His interest turned to two of their most pressing problems, the yellow-dog contract and the labor injunction. His position as chairman of the Senate Judiciary Committee was to prove strategic.[1]


2

"Indeed," Felix Frankfurter and Nathan Greene wrote in 1928, "the use of the injunction in labor legislation furnishes the most striking instance, barring the history of the due process clause, of the luxurious development of American legal doctrine." Morris Ernst of the American Civil Liberties Union told a subcommittee of the Senate Judiciary Committee in the same year that he had uncovered injunctions that forbade persons to pray on the roadside or to sing in groups, that required pickets to be American citizens or to speak the English language, and that denied the rights of free assembly and communication. Most significant from the standpoint of unionization, the injunction was employed to enforce the yellow-dog contract under the Hitchman doctrine. The law of the injunction and the yellow-dog contract has been set forth at length in Chapter 4.[2]

An inevitable reaction set in during the twenties. Distinguished members of the bar, like George Wharton Pepper and Newton D. Baker, warned the judges that their orders invited disrespect for the law and the courts. Serious study of the problem was undertaken at the universities, notably the law schools. The American Federation of Labor, now persuaded that the Hitchman doctrine was a threat to its existence, made the injunction–yellow-dog issue its foremost legislative objective.

John P. Frey of the Metal Trades Department published a book in 1923 entitled *Labor Injunction: An Exposition of Government by Judicial Conscience and Its Menace*. The following year Frey conferred about legislation with Dean Roscoe Pound of the Harvard Law School. Pound advised a brief statute to be enacted by the states simply declaring yellow-dog contracts void as contrary to public policy. "I see no valid reason ... why the courts should not be bound to accept that declaration," Pound stated. Frey carried on the discussion with Professors Francis B. Sayre of Harvard and Joseph P. Chamberlain and Herman Oliphant of Columbia. Chamberlain and Oliphant drafted a bill along the lines of Pound's suggestion which Frey in 1925 had introduced in the legislature of his home state, Ohio. It gained little attention. That year the same measure was placed in the legislative hopper in Illinois and met the same fate. By 1927, however, it had become the highest priority item on the agenda of the Illinois Federation of Labor. Wisconsin in 1929 became the first state to enact the "Ohio bill." It was maneuvered through the legislature by adding a provision that contracts obligating farmers not to join cooperative associations would be unenforceable.

In 1928 the AFL did what it could to make the injunction a major issue in the presidential campaign. Early in the year Governor Alfred E. Smith of New York, the leading Democratic candidate, threw his weight behind a measure sponsored by the New York Federation of Labor. Known as the Byrne-Lefkowitz bill, it would have forbidden injunctions during a strike except after a hearing with representation by both sides. This measure made no progress in Albany. Smith, however, went on to win the presidential nomination. His party's platform denounced the spread of the injunction and proposed legislation to curb its use in labor disputes. In his campaign Smith reiterated this pledge. The Republican platform merely deplored the injunction abuse. While Hoover referred to this in several campaign speeches, he made no legislative proposal. His landslide victory hardly demonstrated a major concern about the issue.[3]

Though barely noticed in the presidential campaign, an attempt to enact a federal anti-injunction statute was under way. On December 12, 1927, Senator Henrik Shipstead of Minnesota had introduced S. 1482, which read as follows: "Equity courts shall have jurisdiction to protect property when there is no remedy at law; for the purpose of determining such jurisdiction, nothing shall be held to be property unless it is tangible and transferable, and all laws and parts of laws inconsistent herewith are hereby repealed."

Shipstead had little interest in the bill that bore his name. He introduced it as a favor to its author, his friend Andrew Furuseth, president of the International Seamen's Union. That grizzled, self-educated, and obstinate sailor had devoted a quarter century to delving into the history of chancery. He had concluded that the equity courts issued injunctions on a strained definition of property. If intangible property rights were excluded by definition, Furuseth argued, there could be no labor-injunction problem. This idea had been advanced originally by Thomas S. Spelling, a writer on equity, and had been picked up early in the century by Gompers and Furuseth. It had found its way into the stillborn Pearre anti-injunction bill of 1908 and lay behind the ill-fated concept of the Clayton Act that labor is not a commodity. In the twenties Furuseth, whose mind changed slowly if at all, persuaded Shipstead to make another try.

S. 1482 was referred to a subcommittee of the Senate Judiciary Committee. Norris was its chairman and he chose Senators Tom Walsh of Montana and John J. Blaine of Wisconsin as his associates. It would have been hard to select any other men in the 70th Congress as competent as these three to deal with this issue.

Hearings opened on February 8 and continued till March 22, 1928. Norris was present at every session and his colleagues were almost as constant. They must have found the testimony frustrating. Except for Furuseth and Winter S. Martin, a Seattle attorney who helped the seafarer draft the language, no one seemed to favor the Shipstead bill. A conference of 125 AFL and railway brotherhood leaders on February 7 had uncovered sharp disagreement. Donald Richberg, counsel to the brotherhoods, had warned that the measure might cause more injunctions and would protect the yellow-dog contract as transferable property. An outraged Furuseth replied at length, leading John L. Lewis to complain, "The gentleman doesn't seem to have any terminal facilities."

At the hearings William Green denounced the injunction but never quite endorsed S. 1482. Frey was more interested in his own Ohio bill. Joseph Padway, counsel to the Wisconsin Federation, bluntly warned that vagueness of language would allow the courts to defeat the bill's intent. Attorneys for the United Mine Workers declared the measure irrelevant to their problems. Alex J. Groesbeck, who had represented the Street Railway Employees in an important Indianapolis injunction proceeding, flatly stated that it would be ineffective. Morris Ernst of the American Civil Liberties Union was delightfully eclectic; he urged the subcommittee to try everything. The American Patent Law Association held that S. 1482 would undermine the law of patents, trade marks, and copyrights. The National Association of Manufacturers, the American Bar Association, the League for Industrial Rights, and the Association of Railway Executives opposed any legislative tampering with either the injunction or the yellow-dog contract.

Norris' annoyance over this state of affairs was unrestrained. Although Walsh and Blaine were less blunt, they agreed that the Furuseth measure would not do. At an executive session on February 18, the senators decided upon a drastic overhaul. Shipstead assured them that he would offer no objection.[4] The subcommittee's dilemma was summarized neatly by Frankfurter and Greene:

> With indomitable tenacity, Mr. Furuseth has persisted in his own conception of legal history and in the espousal of a reform deemed by him the correct legal tradition. There is much that is gallant in the picture of this self-taught seaman challenging

with power and skill an entire learned profession. For, almost without exception, the informed opinion of lawyers, even of those most sympathetic with Mr. Furuseth's aims, regards his proposal as an attempt to throw out the baby with the bath. The Shipstead bill condemns many well-settled and beneficent exercises of equitable jurisdiction that do not touch even remotely the interests of labor.[5]

## 3

At the conclusion of the hearings the subcommittee called in expert advisers to draft a new bill. Early in May 1928, Frankfurter, Richberg, Oliphant, Sayre, and Edwin E. Witte (chief of the Wisconsin Legislative Reference Library) were invited to Washington. Their collective knowledge about the labor injunction was unmatched in the United States, and several among them were legislative draftsmen of high skill. Norris turned over the quarters of the Judiciary Committee. "They locked themselves in," the Nebraskan wrote, "and for forty-eight hours gave their undivided attention ... to every court decision.... They reviewed the decisions of the United States Supreme Court with the most scrupulous care, aware that . . . the constitutionality of the law would be subjected to challenge immediately." The result of these deliberations was a wholly new measure that Norris introduced on May 29, 1928, as a substitute for the Shipstead bill. It was to serve as the basis for the ultimate legislation.

Section 1 would deny jurisdiction to federal courts to issue injunctions in cases growing out of labor disputes unless the procedure and order complied with the definitions and limitations contained in the Act and the injunction conformed with the declaration of public policy. The Supreme Court on many occasions had sustained the power of Congress to define the jurisdiction of the federal courts.

Section 2 would set forth a new public policy for the United States:

Whereas under prevailing economic conditions, developed with the aid of governmental authority for owners of property to organize in the corporate and other forms of ownership association, the individual unorganized worker is commonly helpless to exercise actual liberty of contract and to protect his freedom of labor, and thereby to obtain acceptable terms and conditions of employment, wherefore it is necessary that he have full freedom of association, self-organization, and designation of representatives of his own choosing, to negotiate the terms and conditions of his employment, and that he shall be free from the interference, restraint, or coercion of employers of labor, or their agents, in the designation of such representatives or in self-organization or in other concerted activities for the purpose of collective bargaining or other mutual aid or protection; therefore, the following definitions of, and limitations upon, the jurisdiction and authority of the courts of the United States are hereby enacted.

Authority for this declaration was found in Chief Justice Taft's opinion in the American Steel Foundries case and, more important, in Section 2 of the Railway Labor Act of 1926.

Section 3 would make the yellow-dog contract unenforceable in the federal courts. Such an "undertaking or promise" was contrary to the public policy set forth in Section 2 and would afford no basis for legal or equitable relief. The draftsmen did not declare the yellow-dog contract unlawful *per se* because that would have flown in the face of Supreme Court decisions in the Adair and Coppage cases. Two recent holdings by New York courts, however, in the Interborough Rapid Transit and Exchange Bakery cases, revealed a reluctance in one state, at least, to enforce antiunion pledges.

Section 4 would deny federal courts jurisdiction to issue an injunction in a case growing out of a labor dispute which prohibited persons from doing singly or in concert any of the following acts: (a) refusing to perform work or to remain in a relation of employment; (b) becoming or remaining a member of a labor or employer organization; (c) paying or withholding strike benefits; (d) by lawful means aiding a person involved in a labor dispute who is being proceeded against or is prosecuting a lawsuit; (e) giving publicity to a labor dispute by advertising, speaking, patrolling, or any other method not accompanied by force or violence;

(f) assembling peaceably to promote an interest in a labor dispute; (g) advising any person of an intention to perform any of these specified acts; (h) agreeing with other persons to do or not to do any of these acts; and (i) advising, urging, or causing to be performed without force or violence any of the acts heretofore specified. All of these activities had been prohibited by the courts in numerous recent injunction proceedings.

Section 5 would deny jurisdiction to the federal courts to issue restraining orders "upon the ground that any of the persons participating and interested in a labor dispute constitute or are engaged in an unlawful combination or conspiracy because of the doing in concert of the acts enumerated in section 4. . . ." The notorious orders issued by Judge James H. Wilkerson in 1923 in the shop-crafts strike and by Judge John J. Parker in 1927 in the Red Jacket case had invoked the conspiracy theory.

Section 6 would absolve officers and members of labor organizations as well as the organizations themselves of liability for the unlawful acts of individuals except upon clear proof of participation in, authorization of, or ratification of such acts. This was a restatement of the law of agency to ban injunctions like Wilkerson's, which had held union officials responsible for acts of pickets that the officers had warned against.

Section 7 would drastically overhaul the procedure for the issuance of injunctions by the federal courts:

No court of the United States shall have jurisdiction to issue an injunction in any case involving or growing out of a labor dispute . . . except after hearing the testimony of witnesses in open court (with opportunity for cross-examination) in support of the allegations of a complaint made under oath, and except after finding of fact by the court, to the effect —

(a) That unlawful acts have been committed and will be continued unless restrained;

(b) That substantial and irreparable injury to complainant's property will follow;

(c) That as to each item of relief sought greater injury will be inflicted upon complainant by the denial of relief than will be inflicted upon defendants by the granting of relief;

(d) That complainant has no adequate remedy at law; and

(e) That the public officers charged with the duty to protect complainant's property are unable or unwilling to furnish adequate protection.

Such hearing shall be held after due and personal notice thereof has been given, in such manner as the court shall direct, to all known persons against whom relief is sought, and also to those public officers charged with the duty to protect complainant's property.

A proviso would permit the issuance of a temporary restraining order upon an allegation of "substantial and irreparable injury to complainant's property." It could be effective for no more than five days, and the complainant would be required to file a bond sufficient to compensate those enjoined for loss and court costs. In Section 7 the draftsmen sought to excise the cancerous mass of procedural abuse that the courts had spread with the labor injunction.

Section 7a would deny injunctive relief to a complainant who had himself failed to comply with the law in a labor dispute or who had failed "to make every reasonable effort to settle such dispute." This was in part an application of the "clean hands" doctrine. Section 7b would forbid the court to issue an injunction unless it had first made findings of fact. Section 7c would provide for appeal of injunction cases to the circuit courts with the greatest possible expedition.

Section 8 would authorize jury trials for persons charged with criminal contempt of an injunction issued by a federal court. Section 9 consisted of the definitions; Section 10 provided for separability; and Section 11 would repeal all laws in conflict with this one.[6]

Although the subcommittee accepted the Norris bill, the full Judiciary Committee took no action and Congress adjourned for the 1928 presidential campaign. Before the legislature could act, of course, the American Federation of Labor must take a position, and the Federation was to consume a year and a half in making up its collective mind.

At the New Orleans convention in November 1928, Furuseth's influence was still in the ascendant. The Federation withheld its support from the Norris bill and referred the matter to the Executive Council. The Council designated a committee, with Woll as chairman and including Frey and Olander, to study the various proposals and recommend legislation. The Woll committee reported in June 1929, urging acceptance of the Norris bill as the basis for a statute. The committee, however, proposed numerous amendments, several of consequence. On August 16, at its Atlantic City meeting, the Executive Council accepted the Woll report.

The Council submitted a revised bill to the Toronto AFL convention of October 1929. The significant deviations from the Norris measure were the following. The policy declaration of Section 2 would be amended to allow workers full freedom of "trade union organization" association. Section 3 would make the yellow-dog contract not merely contrary to public policy and unenforceable but also "wholly void." To the acts specified in Section 4 for which federal courts would be denied jurisdiction to issue injunctions would be added:

> (aa) Ceasing, failing or refusing to work upon, handle or use any product or material made or produced, in whole or in part, by non-union or by a rival labor union, irrespective of whether such material has been shipped in interstate commerce;
> (aaa) Ceasing or refusing to patronize or employ any person participating and/or interested in a labor dispute, or any other person whatsoever, regardless of whether he stands in the relation of employer and employe or is participating and/or interested in a labor dispute.
> (j) Nor shall any of the acts described in this section be considered or held to be unlawful acts.

In several places in Section 4 the word "violence" would be qualified by the adjective "physical" and references to "by all lawful means" and "peaceably" would be omitted. Paragraph (c) of Section 7, requiring a showing of greater injury to the complainant than to the defendant, would be dropped. Section 7b would be expanded to forbid blanket injunctions. A new Section 8a would be inserted to nullify retroactively outstanding injunctions that would have contravened the Act had it been in existence.

"It seems to me most essential," Frey declared in opening floor debate, "that not only should our position be unanimous, but so vigorous that there can be no possible mistake on the part of any member of Congress." Furuseth did not listen. "This is a crucial moment," he thundered, "and this convention ... is up against something that will determine, perhaps forever ... the possibility ... of the labor movement continuing." The seaman drew a forbidding historical parallel with the Richmond convention of the Knights of Labor, which, he declared, led to that organization's downfall. This point was lost on the delegates since, as Woll admitted, they had never heard of the Knights' Richmond convention!

Furuseth protested most vigorously because the bill gave the courts some equity jurisdiction over labor disputes. Equity power "is the most absolute and irresponsible power that the world has ever known." The equity judge set aside statutory law and the Constitution itself. Equity was "the antithesis of government by law." Furuseth pleaded with the convention to return the report to the Executive Council.

Woll opened his defense by granting what must have been evident to all who heard the debate, namely, that none of the speakers fully grasped "this highly intricate, vexing and complex problem." No statute, he argued, could remove the equity jurisdiction of the courts because that authority had been conferred by the Constitution. The Shipstead bill would have eradicated the injunction in many areas not affecting labor in which it served a useful function. The revised bill, Woll contended, will "enable us to secure some relief." He urged the convention to adopt the report unanimously, and "go out, undivided and not dismembered and dissociated."

Tom Kennedy, secretary of the Mine Workers, observed wryly that "this injunction matter has harvested quite a crop of barristers." The UMW attorneys had advised him that the Norris bill would afford substantial relief to his union. It would be necessary to take the gamble on constitutionality with any legislation. Nothing more could be asked. Hence the job of the Federation was not to debate the wisdom of the measure but to put it over. During the last session of Congress disunity within the labor movement was "the laughing-stock of Washington." Labor must not allow that to occur again.

The motion to adopt the Executive Council report carried. In fact, Furuseth alone voted in the negative. The AFL and Norris were now more or less in tandem.[7]

The immediate problem was the reconciliation of differences between the two drafts. Norris circulated the AFL amendments to the experts; their reaction was hardly enthusiastic. Frankfurter, Oliphant, and Witte in a long joint memorandum declared that the new Sections 4(j) and 8a raised grave constitutional doubts. The omission of "lawful" from Section 4 served no purpose and the insertion of "physical" appeared to sanction some forms of violence. The proposed paragraphs (aa) and (aaa) of Section 4 would merely insure bitter opposition in Congress and provoke judicial resistance. Richberg was less obstinate. He was willing to accept the additions to Section 4 — (aa), (aaa), and (j). Nor did he raise objection to the word "physical." The amendment to the declaration of policy, however, would gain no advantage. Richberg felt that the retroactive feature of 8a was of doubtful legality.

The revised bill that Norris brought in on May 19, 1930, though differing somewhat from the 1928 measure, contained none of the significant AFL amendments. The major changes were organizational, but a new Section 12 would permit a defendant in a contempt of court proceeding to challenge the character and conduct of the sitting judge in order to get a substitute.[8]

By the spring of 1930, the form of anti-injunction legislation was complete. Organized labor had given its substantial endorsement. The contest now shifted from the legislative drafting room to the political arena. Here Norris and the AFL were weak, but they were to get help from a most surprising source — the President of the United States.

4

On February 3, 1930, Hoover nominated Charles Evans Hughes to succeed Taft as Chief Justice of the United States, thereby touching off the explosive Supreme Court controversy that was to resound for most of a decade. The appointment on its face was without flaw. Excepting perhaps the President himself, Hughes was the most distinguished Republican in the nation and was by common consent an extraordinarily gifted lawyer. He had been a progressive governor of New York, a member of the Supreme Court until his resignation to run for President in 1916, and a brilliant Secretary of State in the Harding Administration, from whose scandals he had been wholly dissociated. Since 1925, Hughes had practiced law in New York with unusual financial success. His nomination compelled family sacrifice. Charles Evans Hughes, Jr., who as Solicitor General represented the government before the court, had resigned to smooth the way for his father.

The immediate reaction to the appointment was favorable to an excess. The press acclaimed it with virtual unanimity. The bar was ecstatic. Such noted liberal jurists as Justice Louis D. Brandeis and Judge Benjamin N. Cardozo expressed keen pleasure. Labor, Green told the AFL Executive Council, "would stand a fair chance with Hughes." "There is no objection to the confirmation of Mr. Hughes," Norris declared. "I think it will be unanimously voted by the Judiciary Committee."

Hughes, whose political ear was well-tuned, had been apprehensive. "I don't want a fight over the nomination," he warned the President. "I don't want any trouble over it." Hoover offered confident assurances. The Judiciary Committee, however, was not unanimous, recommending confirmation 10 to 2. Norris had changed his mind and was now among the dissenters. On February 8 the Nebraskan ominously handed the press without comment a list of fifty-four cases in which Hughes had appeared before the Supreme Court since 1925, almost all as the representative of great corporations. On February 10 Norris took the Senate floor to lead "the Hughes Rebellion."

The Senate insurgents had decided to exploit the Hughes appointment, which they were helpless to stop, as the occasion for a great public debate over the role of the Supreme Court. In the United States, Norris declared, there were three legislative bodies: the House, with over 400 members, the Senate, with 96, and "another . . . called the Supreme Court, of nine men; and they are more powerful than all the others put together." On critical questions the justices were guided by their social predilections. Where, then, did Hughes stand? "No man in public life," Norris charged, "so exemplifies the influence of powerful combinations in the political and financial world as does Mr. Hughes." A man who had lived a "one-sided life" in the service of "powerful industry" should not be the "supreme and final arbitrator" over "the men who toil and the men who suffer."

"We . . . are filling the jury box," Senator Robert M. La Follette, Jr., of Wisconsin concurred, "which ultimately will decide the issue between organized greed and the rights of the masses." "Under the Fourteenth Amendment," Senator William E. Borah of Idaho declared, "the Supreme Court becomes really the economic dictator in the United States." The insurgents raked over the cases Hughes had presented to the court on behalf of large corporations. They pointed at his resignation from the bench to run for political office. They looked suspiciously at his fortune. Not since Taney's appointment a century earlier had a Supreme Court nomination raised such a furor. The vote itself was anticlimactic: Hughes was confirmed 52 to 26.[9]

"Mr. Hughes," Frank R. Kent wrote, "will be a better Chief Justice for the experience." He had hardly taken his seat when the court heard the first of the great labor cases of the decade — *Texas & New Orleans Railroad Co. v. Brotherhood of Railway & Steamship Clerks*. It will be recalled from Chapter 4 that the lower federal courts had ordered the disestablishment of the company union created by T & NO as a violation of Section 2 of the Railway Labor Act and had upheld the constitutionality of that statute. The declaration of policy of the Norris bill was a restatement of this provision of the 1926 law. The stakes, indeed, were high.[10]

Hughes himself wrote the opinion for a unanimous court (Justice McReynolds did not participate). Section 2 of the statute said, "Representatives . . . shall be designated . . . without interference, influence, or coercion, exercised by either party over the self-organization or designation of representatives by the other." The object of Congress in the legislation was to encourage industrial peace on the interstate railways. "Freedom of choice in the selection of

representatives on each side of the dispute is the essential foundation of the statutory scheme," Hughes declared. Hence Congress
prohibited certain types of behavior embraced by the language
"without interference, influence, or coercion." The words "interference" and "coercion" were well understood in the law.
"Influence" in this context meant pressure designed to defeat self-
organization. The acts of the T & NO — establishment of and financial assistance to the company union as well as discrimination against
union members and officers — were interdicted by Section 2.
Hence the injunction issued by the district court was appropriate.

The Supreme Court entertained "no doubt of the constitutional
authority of Congress to enact the legislation." The power to
regulate commerce encompassed the power to enact legislation
for its protection and advancement, including diminution of labor
disputes that might impede the agencies of interstate transportation. Railway employees had long enjoyed the legal right
to organize for the object of collective bargaining. Congress could
legislate to safeguard this right under the commerce clause. "Collective action would be a mockery if representation were made
futile by interferences with freedom of choice." Hughes distinguished the earlier decisions in the Adair and Coppage cases.

The T & NO ruling, Edward Berman observed contemporaneously, was "one of the most important rendered in a labor case in
many years" and "a great victory for organized labor." Its promise
was that the court would henceforth cast a friendlier eye upon
"state and federal legislation designed to protect workers from the
coercive activities of anti-union employers." Norris, whatever
qualms he may now have felt over his position on the Hughes confirmation, looked upon the Chief Justice's opinion in T & NO as an
omen for the future of his bill.[11]

Even more important in the emerging history of anti-injunction
legislation was Hoover's nomination of Judge John J. Parker to the
Supreme Court on March 21, 1930. The insurgent senators,
somewhat to their surprise, had found the attack upon Hughes
popular with the country. The President now hung for them a
far more vulnerable target. Parker was a technically proficient,
if undistinguished, circuit court judge. He was, as well, a southern
Republican. In 1920 he had run for governor of North Carolina

and had made a campaign remark that the Negroes of that state considered slighting. Of larger significance, he had handed down the Red Jacket decision in 1927, perhaps the most hated labor injunction of its era. The United Mine Workers were enjoined from "trespassing upon the properties" or "inciting, inducing, or persuading the employees of the plaintiffs to break their contract of employment." The plaintiffs were 316 coal companies with some 40,000 employees in southern West Virginia and the contracts were yellow dogs. If Hoover had set out deliberately to inflame the Senate, to say nothing of the National Association for the Advancement of Colored People and the American Federation of Labor, he could have chosen no better means than the Parker appointment.

The attack on the jurist was not personal. It could not be, because Parker was a man of high character. "Lowell Mellett has asked me to tell you," the newspaperman Ray Tucker wrote Norris, "that despite a pretty careful ... scrutiny of Judge Parker's record, he cannot find sufficient material ... for going after him." The insurgents, therefore, concentrated upon the issues that the appointment lifted into the limelight.

Parker denied that he had advocated in 1920 that Negroes should not be permitted the suffrage. Walter White of the NAACP sent Norris affidavits from a number of North Carolina Negroes who alleged that they had heard him make such a statement. A. Philip Randolph, president of the Brotherhood of Sleeping Car Porters, urged Senator Wagner to vote against confirmation on both the racial and labor issues.[12]

The main task of the supporters of the nomination was to explain away the Red Jacket decision. Parker himself set out the line by arguing that he had been bound by the Hitchman doctrine. "I followed the law laid down by the Supreme Court. . . . It is, of course, the duty of the judges of the lower Federal courts to follow the decisions of the Supreme Court." The backers of Parker did not defend the yellow-dog contract as such. In fact, they denounced it almost as vigorously as his opponents. They urged the eradication of the yellow dog by legislation rather than by blocking Parker's confirmation. This line of reasoning was not without a certain appeal to Norris.

The AFL mobilized a formidable campaign against Parker. Green on March 26 had successfully urged this upon the Executive Council. The international unions and other subsidiary bodies were exhorted to intervene with their senators, and a flood of letters and telegrams ensued. Notable among them was the following communication from Lewis, whose union had been the object of the Red Jacket decision:

The eminent lawyers of the United States Senate will scarcely be influenced by the opinion of a layman affecting fine legal equations involved in the Hitchman decision, yellow dog contracts and the Red Jacket injunction case. The human factors, however, deserve consideration.

Admittedly, the mine worker is unfortunately placed in the domestic economy of the nation; intermittently employed in an over-developed and intensely competitive industry, his annual earnings are most meager and his bodily wants are unsatisfied; constantly beset by the ghastly horror of underground work, his numbers are daily decimated by falling earth, breaking equipment, rush of water, noxious and explosive gases, occupational diseases and economic neglect; living most often in isolated camps, devoid of modern sanitary and living conveniences, and lacking social, educational and spiritual advantages, his children are denied the inspirational outlook upon life which is given to the sons and daughters of other men; recognizing the value of mutual association with his fellow mine workers and having the desire of a normal man to improve his lot, he is yet prevented by judicial decree, in large areas, from collectively bargaining for his labor and denied the right as an employee to join the trade union of his choice.

If these things be true, and none can gainsay them, then why, from all that long list of eminent legal minds comprising our federal judiciary, was it necessary for the President to appoint, and why is it necessary for the Senate to confirm the elevation to the Supreme Bench of Parker, the Judge, who in the Red Jacket injunction suit, delivered fifty thousand (50,000) free Americans into indentured servitude? Why lay another lash across the tortured shoulders of the struggling mine workers, by placing in a position of vastly increased power a man who regards them as industrial bondmen? Why should any consideration of politics or statecraft impel any Senator to vote for the confirmation of a man who would operate American industry with bonded men-servants?

On April 11, Green, sensing victory, requested the President to withdraw Parker's name. Hoover indignantly refused. The AFL, he argued, had been misled and was doing a grave injustice to a distinguished jurist. Green replied on April 16 that one would have to go back to Dred Scott to find a parallel with the Hitchman decision. In the Red Jacket case Parker had revealed no lack of sympathy for the Hitchman doctrine. Hence the labor movement was persuaded that he actually approved of the yellow-dog contract and would carry this philosophy onto the supreme bench. Furthermore, since the facts in Red Jacket differed from those of Hitchman, the judge could have distinguished if he had wished.

On May 7, 1930, the Senate rejected Parker by a vote of 41 to 39. For the first time in thirty-six years a presidential appointment to the Supreme Court had been turned down. Frankfurter congratulated Norris for his role in preventing confirmation: "I regard the result as extremely wholesome and for the best interests of the Supreme Court." Joel Seidman wrote, "The Senate ... was in reality passing judgment, not on him [Parker], but upon the yellow-dog contract." The public and Congress, in fact, had been quite unfamiliar with it prior to the Parker affair. The debate had served an educational purpose and had aroused revulsion for the device.[13]

Senator Norris had already capitalized on this wave of public indignation. On April 26, when Parker's defeat appeared inevitable, the Judiciary subcommittee reported the anti-injunction bill favorably. Within the full Committee, dominated by conservative Republicans, the maneuvering was adroit. At an early stage a poll revealed a 7 to 7 vote on the measure itself, which would have allowed Norris to bring the bill onto the Senate floor. On May 28, to his dismay, the Judiciary Committee voted 8 to 4 to submit the measure to Attorney General Mitchell for an advisory opinion on constitutionality. Mitchell quite properly declined. On June 9, therefore, the Judiciary Committee reported adversely on the merits 10 to 7. The Norris bill was returned to its pigeonhole for the remainder of the 71st Congress.[14]

5

Because of the political composition of the Congress as well as legislative obstacles in the Senate, Norris was unable to bring his bill out for a year and a half. During this time, however, there were important political developments and the anti-injunction movement made significant gains. In the elections of November 1930, the Democrats reduced a Republican majority in the Senate from eleven seats to one and won a House lead of five in contrast with a previous deficit of one hundred. In the campaign the AFL had made the Norris bill and the Parker appointment the prime tests of its support. A consequence of the elections was the reconstitution of the membership of the Senate Judiciary Committee. Further, as a result of the depression, politicians in both parties were shifting leftward. In the latter part of 1930, the National Committee on Labor Injunctions was formed under the sponsorship of the American Civil Liberties Union. Richberg and Alexander Fleischer, a Philadelphia civil libertarian, had suggested its creation. The chairman was Charles F. Amidon, former federal judge and author of the remarkable decision in the Brosseau case during the railway-shop strike of 1922. The Committee's membership was a glittering roster of American liberalism exclusive of the labor movement — distinguished writers, educators, journalists, and churchmen. Fleischer was the workhorse. The Committee's purposes were to back the Norris measure, draft a model state bill based upon it, and lobby in the state capitols. Nor was this the only source of help. On January 11, 1931, the National Civic Federation's commission on industrial inquiry, under James W. Gerard, former ambassador to Germany, came out against the Hitchman doctrine, denounced the issuance of injunctions *ex parte*, and supported the Norris bill.

The anti-injunction movement made more rapid progress in the states than in the federal government. On April 9, 1930, Governor

Roosevelt signed New York's anti-injunction law, which required notice to the defendant before a restraining order might issue. At the time no one knew whether or not the courts would construe the language so as to abolish *ex parte* proceedings. In February 1931 the National Committee on Labor Injunctions presented its model state bill. Nathan Greene, Frankfurter's collaborator, drafted the measure on the pattern of the Norris bill.

Wisconsin, under the leadership of Governor Philip La Follette, pioneered in enacting a "little Norris–La Guardia Act" even before the federal government had acted. In July 1931, this state adopted what the *Nation* called "the most progressive piece of labor legislation in the country." Reform was in the wind. At approximately the same time Pennsylvania imposed restrictions upon the issuance of injunctions, Ohio enacted the "Ohio bill," and Arizona, Colorado, and Oregon sought to outlaw the yellow-dog contract.

At the federal level the AFL made a final effort in the latter part of 1931 to gain acceptance of its amendments. The Woll committee was reconstituted and the Vancouver convention formally endorsed the Norris bill as amended by this committee. Witte and Frankfurter dutifully wrote memoranda pointing out the old reasons for rejecting the amendments. Norris informed the AFL that he would not accept them. In December 1931 the Federation at long last conceded, giving its unqualified support to the Norris bill as drafted by the experts. Furuseth of course continued to bark at everyone's heels. He wrote a pamphlet bitterly denouncing the measure, and neither Green nor Norris had any success in persuading him to remain quiet.[15]

If a further obstacle remained in Norris' way, Hoover removed it on January 12, 1932, by naming Judge James H. Wilkerson of Chicago to the 7th Circuit Court of Appeals. While the most detested injunction of the time was Red Jacket, the most noxious "injunction judge" was Wilkerson, who had issued the notorious shop-crafts order. His only distinction, if it could be called that, was that he had recently sentenced Al Capone after a jury had convicted the gangster of income tax evasion. Wilkerson's record, Professor Sumner H. Slichter wrote, "is probably the most outrageous of any judge in the country." The labor movement

objected violently to the nomination, with the railway brotherhoods raising the shrillest cry. The opposition within the Senate
Judiciary Committee was so formidable that Wilkerson eventually
asked the President to withdraw his name.[16]

On January 27, 1932, at the height of the outcry over Wilkerson, the Senate Judiciary Committee reported the Norris bill
favorably by a vote of 11 to 5. Shortly thereafter the AFL called
a conference of 109 union leaders in Washington to urge passage of
the legislation. Norris, after nearly four years of patient waiting,
presented the anti-injunction bill to the Senate on February 23.

The debate was anticlimactic in that the opposition was defeat-
ist, divided, and incompetent. Norris, Blaine, Walsh, and Wagner
delivered set speeches justifying the legislation for the conventional
reasons. Senator Felix Hebert of Rhode Island was the "opposition" leader. His strategy, if it may be called that, was to announce his objection on principle to the yellow-dog contract and
then to offer a series of crippling amendments to the bill. The
Senate rejected them by large majorities; for example, 47 to 18
and 53 to 16. A diverting footnote was dropped by the reading of
a letter from the American Bar Association, opposing any limitation
on injunctions. The ABA, apparently, was under the impression
that the Senate was debating the long dead Shipstead bill! This
gave Shipstead the opportunity, perhaps in deference to Furuseth,
to offer his old bill as a substitute. The Senate turned it down 72
to 6.

The only significant disagreement was between supporters of the
bill. Montana's Walsh introduced an amendment to Section 7(a)
to allow the federal courts to issue injunctions restraining threatened
as well as actual violence. The AFL opposed this change, and
Green to no avail had urged Walsh not to offer his amendment.
Norris concurred, fearing that the language would afford judges
the opportunity to issue sweeping injunctions. Walsh would not be
put off, however, and eventually Norris conceded. Norris did
persuade Walsh to confine orders granted to restrain threatened
violence only to the persons or associations actually making the
threats, so as to prevent the courts from invoking the conspiracy
doctrine against unions for the derelictions of their members. The
senators agreed on a new Section 7(a) to read as follows:

That unlawful acts have been threatened and will be committed unless restrained or have been committed and will be continued unless restrained, but no injunction or temporary restraining order shall be issued on account of any threat or unlawful act excepting against the person or persons, association, or organization making the threat or committing the unlawful act or actually authorizing or ratifying the same after actual knowledge thereof.

On March 1, the Senate passed the Norris bill by the staggering margin of 75 to 5. All the Democrats and a large majority of the Republicans, including Hebert, voted for it.[17]

Meantime, Norris had given a copy of the bill to Representative Fiorello H. La Guardia of New York. This liberal Republican, who had had no prior connection with anti-injunction legislation, introduced the Norris bill in the House and thereby won the right to place his name on the measure.

House debate took place on March 8, a week after the Senate's action, and was dismal. The representatives had little familiarity with or interest in the injunction problem. Much of the discussion turned on an irrelevancy — whether the AFL was for or against Communism. Many of those who knew that the AFL was opposed to Communists gave this as their reason for supporting the bill. The high point of the "debate" was a speech by James Beck, the Pennsylvania Republican who had been Solicitor General under Daugherty at the time the Wilkerson injunction was secured. Beck, unlike Hebert, was a forthright advocate of the injunction and the yellow-dog contract. Passage of the bill, he declaimed, would constitute "a long march toward Moscow." He and his colleagues put forward a series of amendments that were overwhelmingly defeated. At the end of the day the House passed the Norris–La Guardia bill 362 to 14, an astonishing majority in the eyes of its supporters.[18]

It was now up to the President. What Hoover's views were at the time it is impossible to say. Many Republicans, Hoover among them, were later to claim credit for the Norris–La Guardia Act. As this chapter has demonstrated, neither the President nor his Administration had had anything to do with the genesis of the statute. Norris, in fact, was persuaded that Hoover opposed the bill and secretly worked to block its passage. The business and legal organizations against Norris–La Guardia certainly looked with greater hope for a presidential veto than for an unfavorable vote in either house. If Hoover, in fact, had wanted to veto, the immense majorities in the Senate and House assured him that he would be overridden.

Hoover solved this dilemma on March 23, 1932, by signing the Norris–La Guardia Act and at the same time releasing an opinion by Attorney General Mitchell that was obviously intended to influence the courts. The provisions of the bill, Mitchell wrote, "are of such a controversial nature that they are not susceptible of final decision by the executive branch of the Government. . . . These questions . . . can only be set at rest by judicial decision." He did not believe that Congress intended to exempt racketeering, extortion, or violence from injunctions. More important, antitrust suits to enjoin conspiracies, in Mitchell's opinion, would still be permissible.[19]

# 6

The publication of the Mitchell memorandum by the White House incensed Norris. He issued a statement immediately after enactment in which he described the opinion as a peg on which corporations would hang lawsuits to invalidate the statute. He also argued that Hoover signed only because he knew that a veto would be overridden. In the 1932 presidential campaign, in which Norris took the stump for Roosevelt, he went further. At Cleveland on October 19 the Nebraskan charged that Secretary of Labor Doak had offered Richberg a federal judgeship for sabotaging the Norris–La Guardia Act. In the face of Doak's denial, Norris repeated the charge on the following day at Saginaw, Michigan, and Richberg affirmed it as "absolutely accurate."

If Hoover and Mitchell, in fact, counted on the courts to hold the statute unconstitutional, they were to be thwarted. The draftsmen had exercised notable care to avoid this eventuality. The Supreme Court did not disappoint them in handing down *Lauf* v. *E. G. Shinner & Co.* in 1938. "There can be no question of the power of Congress," Justice Owen J. Roberts wrote, "thus to define and limit the jurisdiction of the inferior courts of the United States."[20]

The Norris–La Guardia Act was a great forward stride in labor legislation; it meant the eventual extinction of the yellow-dog contract. It would, as Witte wrote contemporaneously, "make injunctions in labor disputes infrequent and put an end to the most serious abuses."[21]

Despite the historic importance of the event, the enactment of the law evoked little notice. The *New York Times* of March 24, 1932, buried the story on page 37 in the financial section. The *American Labor Legislation Review* for June carried only a few lines. The *American Federationist* of April ran a short story that little more than summarized the statute. Although Norris–La Guardia was labor's greatest legislative victory and easily its most impressive achievement at this time, the mood of the labor movement was less than exultant. This was because the law was a lone bright star in an otherwise dark sky. Only the day before the House voted, there had been a bloody riot at the Ford plant in Dearborn, Michigan, a manifestation of labor's unrest at the time.

CHAPTER 12

# Rumblings of Discontent

THE DEPRESSION, Frederick Lewis Allen has said, was hard to see with the naked eye. Except for standing in bread lines, which they were not long required to do, the jobless stayed off the streets. They huddled at home, seeking to keep body and spirit warm.

The unemployed had plenty of time to think. Were they thinking about a basic change in the economic system that had dealt with them so harshly? A growing number of Americans asked themselves this question — conservatives with fear and radicals with hope. Would the jobless organize themselves as the shock troops of revolution? Would left-wing political groups, notably the Communists, do it for them?

Observers, like Diogenes looking for an honest man, trooped across the American landscape in 1931–32 in search of revolution. They failed to find it, but they uncovered much else: self-help programs within and without the law; unrest, frequently under Communist leadership, erupting into violence; and rootless veterans in quest of government handouts.

1

In the summer of 1931 the jobless of Seattle formed the Unemployed Citizens' League, the first self-help organization in the United States. The initiative came from Hulet M. Wells and Carl Brannin of the Seattle Labor College, an offshoot of A. J. Muste's Brookwood Labor College. The League enjoyed an immediate and extraordinary growth. By the end of 1931 it had 12,000 members; a year later there were 80,000 in the state of Washington.

At the outset the League had three objectives: self-help, relief, and employment. It was later to add a fourth — political action. Members throughout the city were organized into twenty-two locals, each of which had a commissary. Each local elected five representatives to sit on the central body, which met weekly. Headquarters were downtown in what had formerly been the High Hatters' Club, an exclusive cabaret that had not survived the depression. There were no dues and the UCL's employees were unpaid. John F. Cronin, an unemployed contractor, was president and Charles W. Gilbreath, a jobless trucker, general manager.

In the warm months of 1931 the League emphasized self-help, becoming, in Tom Jones Parry's phrase, "the republic of the penniless." The fishermen's union arranged for the use of idle fishing boats; farmers in Yakima County allowed the jobless to dig potatoes and pick unmarketable pears and apples; owners of scrub-timber lands permitted the League to cut trees. Trucks and gasoline were borrowed. In return for food and fuel, women mended clothing, carpenters rebuilt furniture, barbers cut hair, cobblers repaired shoes, and physicians tended the sick. An advanced economic society based on money had reverted to barter.

Winter, by ending the harvest season, wrecked self-help. The League turned to the city for assistance. The city council, fearful of the organization's growing political power, voted an emergency relief appropriation of $462,000. The commissaries of the Unemployed Citizens' League became Seattle's relief machinery. The operation was conducted quite efficiently and at the remarkably low overhead cost of less than 1 per cent.

At the time of the municipal election in March 1932, it was estimated that a third of Seattle's 144,000 voters were members of UCL. Its support had become a prize that politicians sought. The League's slate, headed by John F. Dore, won with the largest plurality in the city's history. In the campaign Dore said he favored taking huge fortunes away "from those who stole them from the American workers." After becoming mayor, he took the administration of relief away from UCL and threatened the use of machine guns against demonstrations by the unemployed. The jobless called him "revolving" Dore.

Similar leagues sprang up in many parts of the state of Washington. Representatives of almost ninety organizations met at Tacoma on May 30, 1932, to form the United Producers' League. It hoped to persuade the farmers to join with the urban jobless.

During the winter of 1932–33 both UCL and UPL went into decline. Self-help was unseasonable; relief was now a public obligation; employment was unattainable at the municipal level; and political action had paid bitter rewards. In February 1933 the Communists seized control of UCL on the eve of its collapse.[1]

Self-help gained widest acceptance in California. By early 1933 there were ninety units with 25,000 participating families in Los Angeles County, seventeen groups in Orange County, and forty units with 5000 families in Alameda County. The concentration in Southern California was due mainly to the mild climate and the availability of agricultural surpluses.

In June 1932, when only one tenth of the state's jobless were on relief, the unemployed in Los Angeles began to group themselves into self-help cooperatives. Their organizations were informal and highly democratic. As they multiplied they founded exchanges, usually abandoned stores, to coordinate the units. The main function, as in Seattle, was barter. Members traded off their labor for food. They were fortunate in the fact that many truck farmers in Los Angeles were Japanese who considered acceptance of charity a family disgrace.

In July 1932 these units federated into the Unemployed Cooperative Relief Association. UCRA successfully pressured the county board of supervisors to provide gasoline for trucks. The county fathers reasoned, apparently, that this was cheaper than relief. Demands on the Red Cross for help aroused antagonism, that agency fearing competition for donations. UCRA also took over a warehouse for inter-unit exchange.

The Los Angeles movement, unlike Seattle's, experimented with scrip, forming the Los Angeles Cooperative Exchange for this purpose. When a member had a commodity to offer, the Exchange bought it from him at a fair valuation, paying in scrip. If he had a service to offer, he listed it at the Exchange, which then tried to find someone who needed it. If successful, LACE paid him in scrip at an agreed-upon rate. He could then use his earnings to purchase commodities.

This system was in continuous trouble. The Exchange did not control the amount of "currency" in circulation, thereby debasing its value. No security, of course, was afforded; when LACE went out of existence, holders of its scrip held worthless paper. In California scrip was illegal for payment of wages, and the Exchange served as an employment agency without a license. Labor unions were quick to point out these defects.

During the winter of 1932–33 the amount of food available declined, leading to internal bickering within UCRA and radicalization of the membership. In the early months of 1933 the Communists penetrated the Los Angeles movement with some success. Further, the policy of trading labor for food gave way to "chiseling," that is, taking food without work. Conservative elements in the county, fearful of these developments, increased the food supply to UCRA in the spring of 1933, thereby dampening left-wing influence.[2]

Following the West Coast lead, self-help spread to other parts of the nation. By the end of 1932, there were 330 organizations in 37 states with a nominal membership in excess of 300,000. At this stage, when relief was grossly inadequate, their main purpose was barter.

One of the more interesting was the Mormon movement founded in Salt Lake City in 1931, the Natural Development Association. To meet the urgent needs of its members, NDA engaged in barter. It also advocated "Natural Government," a reformist system proposed by Benjamin B. Stringham. NDA spread over the state of Utah and into Mormon communities in neighboring states. By early 1933, it had fourteen branches with an estimated 2000 active members.

A less solemn form of self-help was the Harlem rent party. This institution originated in the twenties but really caught on during the depression. Negro jazz musicians played in private apartments in order to collect the month's rent. They were fed for their services. A number of the musicians — James P. Johnson, Willie (The Lion) Smith, and Fats Waller — were to become famous. Willie has described the parties: "A hundred people would crowd into one seven-room flat until the walls bulged. Food! Hog maws (pickled pig bladders) and chitt'lins with vinegar — you never ate nothing until you ate 'em. Beer and gin. When we played the shouts, everyone danced."

A movement with a fundamentally different outlook from the barter organizations was the Dayton Association of Cooperative Production Units, which tried to overhaul society in accordance with the views of Ralph Borsodi. A Utopian, Borsodi sought to turn the clock back on the factory and the city, urging a return to the land. A group of cooperating families would raise their own foods and fibers and fabricate them by handicraft methods. Like Gandhi, Borsodi attached a mystical significance to textile devices that antedated the Industrial Revolution. In the Borsodian system the main function of the unit was production for use; barter was merely an incident.

In 1932 the Dayton, Ohio, Council of Social Agencies engaged Borsodi to plan a series of production homesteads for the city's unemployed. Dr. Elizabeth Nutting took the lead in executing his program. Compromise with Borsodi's philosophy was necessary. A unit would usually acquire an abandoned house or store as headquarters. Sewing machines, shoemaking equipment, bakery ovens, and other devices were installed. Those who worked on these machines distributed their surplus to other members in accordance with need. Each family built its own house and outbuildings on the homestead and grew its own crop. The unit, however, owned the land and improvements, leasing them to the member. By the spring of 1933, DACPU operated ten units, comprising 800 families and 4000 persons. The Borsodian philosophy of production rather than barter was to have its widest influence in the New Deal era.[3]

A people not long removed from the land yearned nostalgically for escape from the misery of the city. To many the Great Depression seemed to prove that industrialism was both impractical and evil. Borsodi was the most coherent of the back-to-the-landers. Millions of individual city dwellers simply picked up and returned to the farm. Twelve southern agrarian writers in *I'll Take My Stand,* published in 1930, denounced urban industrialism and called upon the South to re-create a civilization based upon "the culture of the soil . . . the best and most sensitive of vocations." Such diverse Americans as Henry Ford, Eleanor Roosevelt, and Bernarr Macfadden (publisher of *Physical Culture* and *Liberty*) dreamed of a return to the land, of a soybean-spinning-wheel civilization. The Department of Labor in 1931 assisted thirty-two South Carolina mill families to relocate on farms in the state. General Pelham D. Glassford, after achieving fame as chief of the Washington police during the Bonus Army incident, turned his energies in 1932 to the problem of resettling jobless families on the farm. He was especially interested in the Bankhead bill, which would have made the Soldiers' Adjusted Compensation Certificates immediately payable for the purchase of small farms in communities created for veterans by the government.[4]

Back-to-the-land was a flight from reality. The agricultural depression was, if anything, more severe than the industrial. It was economic nonsense to increase the agricultural population and output at a time when both were in heavy surplus. The city and the farm were in the same economic yoke; they would suffer and recover in tandem.

Self-help could take the form of an embryonic trade unionism, as in the North Carolina revolt in the summer of 1932. On the morning of July 18, a few hundred unorganized stocking-boarders struck spontaneously at six hosiery mills in High Point against a wage cut (the rate for men's half hose was reduced from $2 to $1.50 a hundred pairs), their second of the year. Economic calamity had converted the Piedmont into a tinder box, awaiting this struck match. By the end of the day the 1600 workers at the Adams-Millis Corporation had quit, and other hosiery mills were similarly affected. Bands of workers roamed the countryside, spreading the word. By the evening of the second day, over a hundred factories in this hosiery and furniture center were closed, and the general strike had spread to Kernersville, Jamestown, Lexington, and Thomasville. On July 20, twenty-five workers forced their way into the Rialto movie house in High Point without paying admission, declaring that they were out of work and entitled to entertainment. When the police drove them out, the town's electricity was shut off. The men said that they had wrecked a motor in the Diamond Hosiery mill "to teach the big fellows that we hain't going to stand for no more bad treatment."

"This outburst at High Point and Thomasville," Governor O. Max Gardner wrote a friend on July 21, "was almost spontaneous and spread like the plague. It only confirms my general feeling that the spirit of revolt is widespread." A wage dispute had "engulfed the community." North Carolina's own operatives had sparked the outburst; Communists had had nothing to do with it. "This thing," Gardner continued, "burst forth from nervous tension of the people who have lost and lost and many of whom are now engaged in the battle for the bare necessities of life." The governor rose to the crisis. He maneuvered the disputants into an arbitration and himself served as chairman of a tripartite board that awarded restoration of the High Point wage cut. The strikes gradually petered out and by October 16, 1932, all the men with jobs were back at work.[5]

The Rialto movie incident in High Point revealed the thin line that separated legal from illegal self-help. Desperate workers repeatedly took the law into their own hands. Most of these incidents are lost to history; the press in many communities refused to publish the news in fear of stimulating similar action.

Eleven hundred men standing in a Salvation Army bread line on March 19, 1930, near the Bowery Hotel in Manhattan descended upon two trucks delivering baked goods to the hotel. Jelly rolls, cookies, rolls, and bread were flung into the street, with the hungry jobless chasing after them. Joseph Drusin of Indiana Township, Pennsylvania, in November 1930 stole a loaf of bread from a neighbor for his four starving children. When caught, Drusin went to the cellar and hung himself. Three hundred unemployed men in July 1931 marched on the storekeepers of Henryetta, Oklahoma, to demand food. They insisted that they were not begging; they threatened force if necessary. Violence was avoided only by the unusual tact of several leading citizens. By 1932 organized looting of food was a nation-wide phenomenon. Helen Hall, a Philadelphia social worker, told a Senate committee that many families sent their children out to steal from wholesale markets, to snatch milk for babies, to lift articles from pushcarts to exchange for food. A New York reporter told Louis Adamic that bands of thirty to forty men would descend upon a market to demand food. The chain stores as a matter of policy refrained from calling the police in order to keep the incidents out of the papers. In Detroit the jobless smashed shop windows at night to loot, children snatched bundles as customers left markets, men simply walked out of chain stores without paying for groceries. Clayton Fountain, a jobless auto worker, swiped milk bottles from porches in swank Rosedale Park and stole field corn from farmers at night which he peddled from door to door in Detroit at 15 cents a dozen ears. In Mississippi whites organized a systematic campaign of brutality to drive Negroes out of their jobs as locomotive firemen on the Illinois Central. By mid-1933, seven had been murdered, seven wounded, and one flogged.[6]

The most remarkable illustration of illegal self-help was the creation of an entire industry in northeastern Pennsylvania — anthracite bootlegging. Jobless miners in broad daylight dug coal on company lands by primitive methods and sold it in the open market. Bootlegging was carried on in brazen disregard of private property. It was, in fact, stealing, but it had the approval of both the constituted authorities and of public opinion.

William Keating, a coal bootlegger, composed a ballad in 1932 about his industry. Keating called it "My Wee Coal Hole."

*While the woes of unemployment were increasing,*
*While the price of foodstuff swelled the grocer's till,*
*For to fix 'gainst next winter's chill breeze,*
*Lest our poor families do freeze,*
*We dug a wee coal hole on God's hill.*

*But our terrible toil was wasted; we worked in vain,*
*Two Cossack-mannered coal and iron cops came.*
*On next winter's cold nights,*
*We'll have no anthracite,*
*'Cause the cops caved in our wee coal hole.*

*My mule-driving record proves at Oak Hill mine,*
*I'm unfairly unemployed for four years' time.*
*To no soup house I'll be led,*
*Because I'll dig my family's bread,*
*Or by cops be killed, in my wee coal hole.*

*Right demands I keep my family fed and warm,*
*God put coal 'neath these hills; here I was born.*
*So call it bootleg or what,*

*I'll have coal in my cot,*
*While there's coal in Good God's coal vein.*

In the early days of anthracite it had been customary for
miners to pick coal from the culm dumps for their own household heating. Improved equipment introduced in the twenties
virtually eliminated these "pickings." When the depression struck,
therefore, the miners began to dig below the surface for household
coal. In Centralia, where the legitimate industry shut down in 1929,
the men sold the coal they mined. During the winter of 1930–31,
county poor boards in the anthracite towns instructed the unemployed to dig their own fuel.

Bootlegging methods were rudimentary. Of necessity the miners
operated near the surface because equipment was limited to pick,
shovel, dynamite, lamp, pail, and hoisting rope. Hours were long.
Safety precautions were nonexistent. Adamic wrote:

> Imagine a hole in the ground, barely wide enough for a man
> to let himself down in, usually vertical, sometimes cut into
> living rock, anywhere from twenty to a hundred feet deep,
> with just sufficient room at the bottom for a miner to sit or
> kneel and work his pick and shovel and sticks of dynamite. . . .
> It took two, three, or four men from two weeks to two months
> to sink a hole and reach the outcrop, after which they usually
> struck coal. Working mainly on hunches, they very often found
> no coal, and all the terrific labor was in vain. When they found
> it, two, three, or four men produced about as many tons a day,
> hoisting the stuff to the top of the hole with rope and buckets,
> then breaking it, often by hand with hammers or chunk against
> chunk, and cleaning and sorting it also by hand, unless they
> had a primitive breaker and shaker either at the hole or behind
> their houses in town. The work was back-breaking and extremely
> hazardous. Most holes were inadequately timbered and cave-ins
> were frequent, trapping or crushing the men below.

In 1931 anthracite bootlegging was a petty affair. Perhaps a half-
million tons were dug and they were sold only in nearby communities. In 1932 illegal output trebled. About a thousand boot-

leggers acquired trucks and peddled anthracite in the large cities of the eastern seaboard. They offered coal at a price $1 to $3 below the prevailing scale. By 1933 bootlegging had become an important industry in northeastern Pennsylvania — $30 to $35 million. In the following year, when Adamic visited the region, employment was 15,000 to 20,000 and vehicles numbered 3500 to 5000. The anthracite towns — Centralia, Shamokin, Mt. Carmel, Shenandoah — now depended upon bootlegging for survival.

The companies from whose properties this coal was stolen were helpless to suppress bootlegging. When a hole was dynamited, three appeared in its place; local courts were disinclined to sentence bootleggers; wardens released them from jail. The illegal industry had the solid backing of the community. Public opinion, rather than considering the men thieves, esteemed them as heroes for facing the hazards of their trade. Storekeepers depended upon bootlegging; the newspapers winked; the police shrugged; parish priests in a predominantly Catholic community argued that the Eighth Commandment had no bearing; Governor Pinchot's sympathies were with the miners.[7]

2

"With the present breakdown," Edmund Wilson wrote in 1931, "we have come to the end of something." The depression "may be nothing less than one of the turning-points in our history, our first real crisis since the Civil War." Capitalism, he felt, had run its course. For Wilson, as for thousands of other American intellectuals, the Marxist prognosis was coming to pass. The capitalist system had exposed its inner contradictions; the rich were getting richer and the poor poorer; the class struggle was emerging. For the two Marxist parties in the United States, the Socialists and the Communists, economic collapse was an unrivaled opportunity and they viewed the capture of the jobless as a great prize.

The Socialists were the first in the field. The party's national executive committee in May 1929 had urged the creation of unemployed councils in every city to agitate for relief and public works. Except for Chicago, the Socialists had no success in this organizational undertaking, which was, in fact, barely tried. Karl Borders, secretary of the Socialists' League for Industrial Democracy in Chicago, established that city's Workers' Committee on Unemployment. At the outset it consisted mainly of teachers, lawyers, social workers, and preachers. Some workers joined later. The committee enjoyed a fair success in dramatizing the plight of the jobless and in raising relief standards despite the bitter competition of a rival Communist council. More typical was the situation in Detroit. Here the Socialist Party was one of a large number of ineffective radical splinter groups, was torn by internal dissension, and had no significant contact with workers or influence upon their welfare.

A German Social-Democrat who visited Detroit in 1932 observed, "There are too many school teachers coming into the [Socialist] party to do it any good." This was the Socialist dilemma: the appeal to the middle class rather than to labor, employed or unemployed. Norman Thomas, the party's presidential candidate in 1928 and 1932, could fill Carnegie Hall with middle-class intellectuals; he could not reach workers in the factories or on relief.[8]

The Socialists, in effect, defaulted to the Communists, who alone were ready to get out on the streets to organize the jobless for revolution. This, it must be remembered, was the "third period" of international Communism. Stalin had moved sharply to the left in order to undercut Trotsky and his followers. He ordered Communist parties all over the world to adopt ultrarevolutionary tactics. The Communist Party of the United States had as one of its main goals the organization of the unemployed into a cadre of revolution.[9]

On February 11, 1930, Communist speakers incited 3000 unemployed men to storm the Cleveland city hall. They dispersed only after the police threatened to spray them with water from fire hoses. Four days later the Council of Unemployed in Philadelphia led a demonstration of 250 persons to City Hall demanding an interview with Mayor Mackey. The police drove them off. A week later 1200 jobless men and women marched upon the seat of municipal government in Chicago. Mounted police armed with nightsticks dispersed them as thousands watched from the windows of Loop office buildings. Their leader, Steve Nelson, was arrested. On February 26 a crowd of 3000 was repulsed with tear gas before the Los Angeles city hall. The following week the New York police broke up an unemployed demonstration at City Hall with brutal tactics.

March 6, the Communists announced, was International Unemployment Day. Demonstrations were staged in virtually every major city of the United States. There was a wild riot of 10,000 in Cleveland. A display in front of the White House was broken up by tear gas. New York City experienced its worst street riot in generations. William Z. Foster addressed a crowd of 35,000 in Union Square, exhorting his hearers to march on City Hall. Police Commissioner Grover Whalen refused permission, offering instead his own car to escort Foster and a small committee to the mayor. Foster, far more interested in broken heads than in conversing with Jimmy Walker, indignantly refused. The beatings began.

These Communist demonstrations in early 1930 failed to produce the revolution in America. They did, however, have two important results that the party could hardly have anticipated or enjoyed. Bleeding heads converted unemployment from a little-noticed to a page-one problem in every important city in the United States. No one could any longer afford to ignore it. Non-Communist forces seeking relief and employment were strengthened.

These riots also led to the inception of congressional investigations of un-American activities. On March 6, the very day of the Union Square demonstration, Republican Representative Hamilton Fish of New York, with the backing of the AFL, introduced a resolution to create a special five-man House committee to investigate Communist activities. He argued that Communism was a threat to the internal security of the United States and that many of its leaders were aliens who should be deported. (While we are in the deporting business, Representative Green of Florida observed, we should deport everyone not of white blood.) Some congressmen, notably La Guardia, contended that the way to defeat Communism was by restoring full employment. Fish cited Whalen as authority for the charge that the Soviet government was behind the riots. La Guardia refused to believe that revolution was imminent because Reds in New York had stuck needles "into the fleshy part of Grover Whalen's anatomy." The House, nevertheless, adopted the resolution by a vote of 210 to 18, and Speaker Nicholas Longworth named Fish chairman. Before the year was out, Foster was called before the committee. The House Committee on Un-American Activities, though not yet known by that name, was on its way.[10]

Encouraged by the notoriety they achieved in the street riots, the Communists on July 4, 1930, held a conference in Chicago to establish the National Council of the Unemployed, of which Marcel Scherer was named secretary. It would create subsidiary councils in the cities to organize the jobless, especially the Negro, and to stage demonstrations over evictions for nonpayment of rent. Its overt goal was unemployment insurance.

These councils of the unemployed were set up in many cities, achieving greatest strength in Chicago and Pittsburgh. Eviction cases, as the Communists calculated, readily aroused public sympathy. In Detroit a Polish family under Communist prodding resisted dispossession and had to be thrown out by an army of over one hundred policemen. In the same city two families that held on to the premises by shooting the landlord were later acquitted of murder by sympathetic juries.

Since the persons evicted were frequently Negroes, the Communists could often pursue two tactics at once. In Chicago they organized the "black bugs," an amorphous battalion of jobless Negro Reds. When a family was evicted in the Black Belt, a long procession of seedy colored people would march through the streets to the house and reinstall the family with its belongings. Horace Cayton described such an incident, one in which a woman with religious zeal thanked God for the Communists. The response of the "black bugs" was more in the manner of a revival meeting than a soviet about to seize power. These demonstrations were followed by street meetings at which soapbox orators preached the Communist line, with heavy emphasis on the Scottsboro case. This inevitably led to police intervention, swinging billies, and bleeding heads. An eviction riot in August 1931 resulted in the death of three Negroes at the hands of the police. Mayor Anton Cermak thereupon ordered landlords to stop evictions.[11]

The 13th plenum of the Communist Party, USA, in 1931 adopted a resolution on work among the unemployed. The comrades, the party bigwigs admonished, had been lax. They were ordered to step up organizational activities during the fall, which were to culminate in a massive National Hunger March on Washington at the end of the year. This resolution was printed at least as early as October, and the Communist intention was known to anyone who had taken the trouble to read their publications. Nevertheless, the Secret Service put itself on the front pages on November 29 by "uncovering" a Communist plot to descend upon the nation's capital. "Riot Threat Is Bared in March on Capital," the Washington *Post* headlined. "Red Columns to Converge Here." The Secret Service, after six weeks of investigation, revealed "the most portentous nation-wide organization of professional agitators" to subvert the government. The "master plan" called for the convergence on Washington of three columns from the Midwest and East, consisting of 1144 trucks and 92 auxiliary vehicles, on December 7, the day Congress convened. Most suspicious in the eyes of the Secret Service had been the recent arrival of a number of telegrams at the White House demanding that Hoover release Tom Mooney from San Quentin!

An advance guard of fourteen Reds led by Herbert Benjamin demonstrated in front of the White House late in November. Park policeman Jack Rabbitt arrested them for unlawful parading. They were fined $100.

In the first week of December official Washington stewed over how to receive the approaching main body. The *Post*, considering it "a conspiracy against the United States," demanded "the annihilation of communism in the United States." "The law," it editorialized, "should smite." The Baltimore *Sun*, with a statesmanlike thirty-five miles separating its editor from the battlefield, cautioned moderation: "Without nightsticks." On December 2, Vice-President Curtis, Speaker Longworth, Senators Frazier, Thomas, Black, Costigan, and Wheeler, Representative Kvale, District Commissioner Crosby, Park Police Chief Montgomery, Colonel Starling of the White House police, Captain Gnash of the Capitol police, and high officials of the metropolitan police met to map a plan. The White House and Curtis were nervous and demanded rigorous precautions. Representative Fish and Senator Oddie of Nevada (the latter had introduced a bill to restrict trade with Russia) allegedly asked for police guards at their homes to protect their children. (Fish later denied that he had made such a request and publicly demanded that the cops be withdrawn. The former Harvard football player feared no one.) General Glassford, chief of the metropolitan police, took a milder view. The marchers, he declared, were "simply tourists . . . heralded by publicity." So long as they behaved themselves, they should be allowed to enjoy the lawful rights of American citizens. He would arrange to feed and house them.

Meantime, the Communists had gathered their forces in the Midwest and East and the trucks had begun to roll toward Washington. The number anticipated by the Secret Service had shrunk. Instead of 1144 trucks, there were actually 71. The press, ever vigilant, infiltrated the marchers with reporters dressed as bums, who later wrote "inside" stories for their papers. They dealt mainly with complaints about the food and accommodations. The Communists, convinced that they were performing a needed national service, demanded handouts at each town. In Cumberland they were bitter over having to sleep on the cold, hard floor of the ice rink. In Baltimore they denounced hot oatmeal with sugar and milk for breakfast.

On the afternoon of December 6, this "army" reached the District of Columbia line. The planned heroic entry was delayed by a "strike" of the truck drivers. They demanded payment for hauling the Reds before the journey was completed. Most got it. In fact, there were 1570 "marchers" who rode into the city singing the "Internationale." They were heavily outnumbered by curious watchers as well as by the police. Glassford alone had 1400 cops on duty and could call upon several hundred detectives and the various auxiliary forces. It did not seem necessary to call out the Army. The invaders were quartered in the Marine barracks near the Old Presbyterian Church and in the Salvation Army Hotel. As usual, the food was not up to Communist standards, despite the fact that some of it was prepared by the chef of the Mayflower Hotel and was served on plates supplied by the Washington Hotel. The marchers, upon leaving the commissary of the Central Union Mission, shouted, "Down with Hoover and his beans!" In their spare time many read the newspapers, obviously relishing the publicity they received. Some needed relaxation from their grim purpose. Two colored youths produced a pair of dice. "They conducted their game in an alley," the *Herald* reported, "and had plenty of customers."

At a meeting at the Washington Auditorium that evening the Reds denounced Hoover, Curtis, Wall Street, the AFL, the American Legion, the Socialist Party, and the food; they also demanded unemployment insurance and freedom for Mooney and Billings. "When I left the hall to catch a train," John Dos Passos wrote, "the Brigadier General [Glassford] was sitting in the audience in mufti, placidly smoking his pipe, while Weinstone thundered a *Daily Worker* editorial into the mike." Downstairs a dance marathon was going on, already in its ninetieth hour. "A young man in a white sweater, bearing the letters National Products Company had keeled over onto his platinum-blond partner's neck. She was ... trying to revive him with an occasional pecking kiss." "Anyway," Dos Passos concluded, "the jazz age is dead."

On December 7, the Communists marched on Capitol Hill. Glassford, mounted on his trusty blue motorcycle, whizzed by to insure that there was no incident. The marchers demanded admission to the floor of both Senate and House and were politely turned away. "Comrades and fellow workers," William F. Dunne cried, "the Congress of the United States ... has refused to hear the proposals of the unemployed councils brought to it through the hunger marchers." "We demand unemployment insurance," his followers chanted back. Their written petition, however, was received.

That afternoon a smaller contingent paraded in front of the White House. Since Hoover would not receive them, they yelled their demands at him through a megaphone. They would have had to be in good voice to have been heard, assuming that the President was at home.

On December 8, the marchers, shivering in the bitter cold, left town. They jammed into forty-five trucks; the remaining drivers had already departed because they had not been paid. The National Hunger March had been a flop. Instead of an army, the Communists had mobilized a corporal's guard. Glassford had outsmarted them. They left with no bleeding martyrs. In fact, the only arrest to occur out of the incident was of one William Boughan, a spectator on Pennsylvania Avenue, who laughed so loudly at the marchers that the police took him in for disorderly conduct. The judge admonished Boughan henceforth to express his views more quietly. It seemed appropriate that this visit should have coincided with a conference held in Washington on "the noise evil." "Needless sounds," a psychiatrist warned, "are afflicting the nerves of urban dwellers to the point of actual deterioration." [12]

The "hungry" were not through with Washington. An army of approximately 12,000 Pennsylvanians led by Father James R. Cox arrived in 2243 trucks and cars on January 7, 1932. Cox was a Pittsburgh priest, a war veteran, and a noted radio orator. Known at home as "The Mayor of Shantytown," Cox had interested himself in the unemployed and had sought to undercut the Communist jobless movement in Pittsburgh. He denounced Andrew Mellon over the radio. Shortly before departing for Washington, he had assembled 60,000 people in Pitt Stadium on a cold day to hear an attack on the government and the bankers for failing to provide relief. Cox also threatened to form a third party of the jobless. His financial sponsors were the Independent Merchants of Allegheny County, who were conducting an anti-chain-store campaign in Pittsburgh.

Cox received the red-carpet treatment from official Washington. His followers marched to the Capitol with American flags flying, singing "The Star-Spangled Banner." One of his followers, E. R. Brown, got his picture in the papers by dressing up as Uncle Sam. The priest presented a petition to Pennsylvania's Senator James J. Davis and Representative Clyde Kelly calling for public works, federal relief, and a soak-the-rich tax program. Cox later gave the same demands to the President at the White House. Hoover appeared cordial, swallowed hard, and promised to give these matters "our undivided attention." The priest then led his followers to Arlington to lay a wreath on the Tomb of the Unknown Soldier. Father Cox, it seemed, had stolen the Red thunder.[13]

In striking contrast with the failure of the Communists in Washington was their success in the Ford Hunger March in Dearborn, Michigan, on March 7, 1932. The Detroit area, of course, was seething with labor unrest and much of it was directed at Henry Ford. Late in February the party announced a plan for a demonstration, and on the night of March 6, Foster himself came to town to assure the final arrangements.

The following morning, a cold day with a biting wind, a crowd of approximately 3000 formed in downtown Detroit and paraded under police escort without incident to the Dearborn line. Under Mayor Frank Murphy's policy, anyone could obtain a permit for an orderly demonstration. The leadership of the parade was Communist; most of the marchers were unemployed workmen. In all probability some had formerly worked at Ford. The ostensible purpose was to advance down Miller Road to the River Rouge and present the following demands to the management: jobs for the jobless, payment of 50 per cent of wages, the seven-hour day, the end of the speed-up, rest periods, no discrimination against Negroes, free medical care at the Ford Hospital, free coal, liquidation of Harry Bennett's Service Department, company assumption of home mortgages and back taxes, and winter relief of $50 per family.

A few hundred feet from the town line the parade halted. Alfred Goetz, a Communist, instructed the crowd to avoid violence. No one was armed. A force of thirty to forty Dearborn policemen blocked Miller Road and warned the marchers not to come on. These policemen were hardly free agents. Clyde M. Ford, the mayor of Dearborn, was a distant cousin of Henry's and owned a Ford agency; Carl Brooks, the chief of police, was a former Ford detective on Bennett's payroll.

The marchers defiantly announced that they would proceed down Miller Road. The police replied with tear gas, most of which was blown away by the swirling wind. Some of the demonstrators returned the fire with stones and lumps of frozen dirt. No one seems to have been hurt. The outnumbered police slowly retreated toward the factory. At the first intersection firemen were frantically working to hitch their hoses to hydrants before the demonstration arrived. They failed and joined the police withdrawal. The stand was made at the employment gate with its steel footbridge thirty feet above the roadway. Here firemen sprayed icy water from overhead and policemen pumped tear gas from the bridge and the street into the advancing crowd. There was also sporadic shooting by the police. Joe York, a marcher, was killed.

The demonstrators then withdrew to an adjoining field, where a speaker told them that Ford had given his answer to their demands. A car with several passengers, including Bennett, emerged from the factory gate and proceeded toward the crowd. "I actually thought," he later recalled, "[that] I was going to pull off a big thing and stop the whole riot by myself." Bennett stepped from the car and was immediately struck in the head by a flying chunk of slag which knocked him unconscious.

The police then opened point-blank fire on the demonstrators with pistols and a machine gun. Three marchers — Joe Bussel, Joe De Blasio, and Coleman Lenz — were killed and at least fifty others were seriously wounded. John Collins, a photographer for the *New York Times*, received a bullet in the hand. The remainder of the crowd fled.

The shortsightedness of the Ford Motor Company and the Dearborn police had given the Communists what they wanted: publicity and martyrs. They quickly capitalized on this success. On March 12, the bodies of the dead were laid out in state in Ferry Hall beneath a huge red banner bearing a likeness of Lenin and the slogan, "Ford Gave Bullets for Bread." A band played the Russian funeral march of the 1905 revolution. A cortege of 10,000 persons moved solemnly down Woodward Avenue from the Institute of Arts to Grand Circus Park, where a crowd of 30,000 had gathered. They listened to speeches by Red orators, and the band played the "Internationale." The procession then marched five miles to the Woodmere Cemetery, where the four bodies cloaked in red were laid in a common grave — within sight of Ford's River Rouge factory.[14]

Despite momentary successes — the street demonstrations in 1930 and the Dearborn riot of 1932 — the Communist program among the unemployed was a failure. Its principal achievement was to raise relief standards in some communities and to hasten the coming of federal relief. This could hardly have been a major objective, if it did not actually defeat the party's purpose.

The real aim — organization of the jobless for revolution — did not come to pass. In fact, the unemployed had much shorter-term goals: relief and jobs. Their obsession with survival made them bad material for revolution. The special appeal to the Negro fell on deaf ears. "It's bad enough to be black," the saying went, "without being red too." The unemployed council movement had little foundation. Its leadership came from the hard-core Communist who shunted back and forth between party, Trade Union Unity League, and council as the line dictated. There were few permanent followers. The party's membership in 1932 was barely 12,000, a gain of only 4000 over 1930. Foster polled a mere 103,000 votes in his campaign for the presidency in 1932. In the eyes of its recently deposed secretary, Jay Lovestone, the American party in its jobless demonstrations was more concerned with impressing Moscow than with overthrowing the government in Washington. Moscow was not impressed. In a resolution published in January 1933, the Executive Committee of the Communist International denounced the CP, USA, for "isolation . . . from the decisive masses of the American proletariat" and branded its work among the unemployed as "largely neglected." [15]

### 3

"Our vegetable garden is coming along well . . . and we are less worried about revolution than we used to be," the *New Yorker* editorialized on June 25, 1932. While it would be fine to be a good rebel, "it has always seemed to us difficult to be a rebel in this country, where there is nothing to rebel against except one's own stupidity." America's ills were melancholia and hypochondria, not revolution. "People are in a sad, but not a rebellious mood."

The writers who toured the nation in search of revolution confirmed this conclusion. Louis Adamic and Benjamin Stolberg agreed that the American proletariat was physically and spiritually exhausted. "I have a definite feeling," Adamic wrote on December 15, 1931, "that millions of them, now that they are unemployed, are licked." One reason, he felt, was that the foreign-born feared to expose themselves. Theodore Dreiser, himself an outspoken Communist, admitted in 1932 that "the workers do not regard Communism as their cause." Sherwood Anderson was amazed by the absence of bitterness. He discerned a "breaking down of the moral fiber of the American man." Anderson picked up hitchhikers on the highway who apologized for being down and out. They accepted the whole responsibility themselves. The only exception he could find was the coal miners. "There is something distinct and real separating them now from the defeated factory hands of the cities. They are not defeated men." [16]

Melancholia and defeat had overwhelmed not only the jobless but also those who sought to infuse spirit into them. Workers on the way down were in no mood to improve, far less to reorganize, society. At this time the spirit of revolt was far more evident in agriculture than in labor. American farmers — "the last bastion of individualism" — readily organized to express their grievances by violent means. By contrast, the self-help organizations of the urban jobless were pathetically inadequate and transitory. The Socialists had got nowhere. The Communists, despite the expenditure of considerable energies, had little to show for their efforts beyond yellowing newspaper headlines. Melancholia and defeat were, as well, the hallmarks of the most notable venture of the jobless during the Great Depression — the Bonus Army.

## CHAPTER 13

# The Bonus Army

In 1924 Congress had passed the bonus bill for war veterans over the veto of President Coolidge. Each veteran received an adjusted service certificate, based upon the number of days he spent in service, which became payable in twenty years. As with a twenty-year-endowment insurance policy, approximately 60 per cent of the maturity value would result from deferral of payment. That is, an ex-serviceman entitled to a benefit of $400 in 1925 would receive $1000 in 1945. This scheme was a neat compromise of the two pressures at work in the twenties: the bonus to satisfy the veterans' lobby and postponement in deference to those who opposed large federal outlays. The sponsors, however, failed to anticipate a severe depression and the impact it would have upon this program.

Massive unemployment after 1929, affecting veterans severely, led to agitation for current payment of the bonus. For many jobless ex-servicemen the adjusted service certificate was their only asset. But it put no food on the table when it was desperately needed. Early in 1932, Representative Wright Patman of Texas introduced a bill providing for immediate payment at full maturity value of the soldiers' adjusted service certificates. The Patman bill, in effect, called for federal relief on a discriminatory basis. The prospects of its passage were remote. Strong opposition existed in Congress, especially the Senate, and Hoover was certain to veto.

1

The Patman bill set in motion a remarkable display of jobless transiency. Thousands of unemployed veterans left home to journey to Washington. Many deserted their families; others brought wives and children with them. They rode the rods, or hitchhiked, or traveled by jalopy.

No one had anticipated the Bonus Army, least of all those who enlisted. What caused these men to join up?

A coal miner from Morgantown, West Virginia, who had served in the Rainbow Division, had not worked for a year and a half and had been supported by his parents. He and a few other fellows got together and talked about the bonus. "The next thing they know they are on the way in any sort of transportation they can get." A sheet-metal worker from Columbus, Georgia, formerly an infantryman with the 1st Division, had not had a job in three years. Several veterans in Columbus "just got started," picking up others as they went along. A Philadelphia truck driver who had served in the 15th Engineers had been out of work for two years. His wife supported the children. There seemed no reason to stay home. A Pole from Chicago, at one time with the 39th Division, had been jobless for three years. His wife was dead and his mother looked after the children in Indiana. He slept in flophouses, usually with other veterans. One day they got to talking about the bonus and "the next thing he knew he was on his way." The Bresnahans — husband, wife, and three-year-old boy — spent three months on freight trains in a trek across the country from California. "The railroad guys was good to us," providing milk for the child and smuggling them into boxcars. Abraham Lincoln's cousin, Charles Frederick Lincoln of Massachusetts and California, had enlisted in 1918 but had not got to France. He was a sign painter and song writer who had not worked for eight months and was almost penniless. He hoped to support his wife and five children with the bonus. Chief Running Wolf, a jobless Mescalero Indian from New Mexico, had served in the AEF. The chief showed up in full regalia, including bow and arrow. He liked to shoot three milk cans named Hoover, Dawes, and Mellon off a stump at twenty-five paces.

Of such people was the motley Bonus Army composed. They were "a fair cross section" of America, wrote Thomas R. Henry in the Washington *Star:*

> They are truck drivers and blacksmiths, steel workers and coal miners, stenographers and common laborers. They are black

and white. Some talk fluently of their woes. Some hardly can muster enough English to tell where they came from and why. The soft Georgia drawl mingles with the characteristic patois of the New York sidewalks.

What started it all? What common impulse moved these men almost simultaneously in Harlem and Salt Lake City, on the Texas plains and in the Chicago flop houses? What impelled colored street laborer and bow-legged cowboy to leave everything familiar behind them and start out together on the open road?

Curiously enough, little can be gained from conversations with the men. The East Sider and the fellow "who used to have a good racket" in Miami tell stories that are almost indistinguishable except that both talk in the characteristic speech of their sections. Both are vague. It is obvious that this strange social phenomenon is something that transcends the individual. But nearly all have one thing in common — a curious melancholy, a sense of the futility of individual struggle, a consciousness of being in the grip of cruel, incomprehensible forces. Their presence here is a supreme escape gesture. . . .

There is one common element. The men have been out of work for a long time. They have been "just getting by somehow." Few can tell a connected story of how they have been "getting by." In most cases, it is fair to assume, they have survived going without. Somehow or other — none know just how — this impulse struck them to come to Washington. It seemed to be on the lips of many men, gathered in American Legion, or V.F.W. club rooms, simultaneously. They read the stories in the newspapers. The next thing they knew they were on their way to Washington.

After talking with many men from all parts of the country — not the leaders, but the rank and file — we are as far as ever from any logical localization of the widespread intangible, subconscious forces that have shoved this growing host of dusty, weary, melancholy men on the District of Columbia. Perhaps a psycho-analyst might explain it.

They are in a struggle which is too severe for them. They have come to the point where they recognize the futility of fighting adverse fate any longer. They are fixating on a symbol — the symbol of the security and plenty of happier days. This symbol happens to be Uncle Sam and the war period with its military relief from responsibility. It is becoming analogous to the infancy period of the psychotic. This bonus march might well be described as a flight from reality — a flight from hunger, from the cries of the starving children, from the humiliation of accepting money from worn, querulous women, from the harsh rebuffs of prospective employers. It is very like the peace of infancy there in the warm June sunshine of the Anacostia field.

Perhaps this may explain the orderliness — the way in which these very diverse elements of the American population have fallen into a semi-military organization, without leaders in authority. Orderliness is a part of the symbol of security to whose protection they have fled from the mysterious, heartless forces that are crushing them in the outside world.

Henry's observations were shared. Mauritz A. Hallgren, who visited the bonus marchers in July, found "every one of them . . . thoroughly whipped by his individual circumstances." They lived in an atmosphere of "hopelessness, of utter despair, though not of desperation." He could find no sign of "revolt, no fire, not even smoldering resentment." They displayed their patriotism with a heavy hand. "That army," the New Yorker observed, "was something more than a lobby: it was the expression of men's desire to huddle together when their courage was gone." The trip to Washington was "a change of scene, a temporary escape from the aimlessness of idleness." "To go among them," wrote Mark Sullivan, "was to recognize instantly their complete harmlessness. A child or a lost pocketbook would be safer among them than among any average cross-section of a city population." [1]

The bonus march began in Oregon in mid-May when 300 veterans set out for the nation's capital. Their leader was Walter W. Waters, a thirty-four-year-old cannery worker from Portland, who had been out of work for eighteen months. Born in Oregon and raised in Idaho, Waters had served on the Mexican border and as a sergeant with the 146th Field Artillery in numerous battles in France. He was an attractive leader — tall, handsome, with a shock of thick blond hair pushed back from his brow. Waters affected whipcord breeches, riding boots, khaki shirt, and walking stick.

A good speaker, he swayed audiences with furious flag waving. Perhaps his most notable talent was for political infighting.

The Waters group rode the rods and lived on handouts across the continent. On May 21, in East St. Louis, officials of the Baltimore & Ohio forbade his men to board an eastbound freight. When they uncoupled cars and soaped rails, the Illinois National Guard was called out and packed them off in trucks. The "Battle of the B & O" hit the front pages of the nation's press. The Oregon contingent mockingly referred to itself as the "Bonus Expeditionary Force," a name that quickly caught on. The remainder of the trip was well covered by the newspapers and prompted others to join the trek to Washington. The Oregon group arrived on May 29. "We are going to stay," Waters announced, "until the veterans' bill is passed."

In the next fortnight a flood tide of ex-servicemen flowed into the city. Two hundred inmates of the National Soldiers' Home in Johnson City, Tennessee, set out in four rented boxcars. Seven hundred came down from Philadelphia. At least 600 left New Orleans. A caravan of 131 cars voyaged from Los Angeles. Muncie, Indiana, contributed 610. Three hundred left Cleveland. Thirty men departed by truck from Pineville, Kentucky. Some 465 set out from Utah, 500 from Chicago, 250 from Oklahoma, 200 from Texas and California, 100 from Lexington, Kentucky, 500 from Boston, 500 from Denver, 25 from Des Moines, 200 from Kansas City, 250 from San Francisco, and so on and on. The Texas crowd brought along a goat named Hoover.

Just how many men came to Washington has never been determined. The BEF leaders claimed 80,000, an obvious exaggeration. A crude census of cantonments late in July produced a figure of 23,000. General Glassford estimated a peak number of 22,000.[2]

## 2

The sudden arrival of thousands of penniless, homeless men caught the city of Washington completely unprepared. The burden of providing for them and of keeping them in order fell upon the metropolitan police and so primarily upon its major and superintendent, Pelham D. Glassford.

Born in New Mexico, the son of an army officer, Glassford's early years were spent on western military posts and in Washington, where he studied art. He entered the military academy at seventeen and graduated with the class of 1904. Here he came to know Douglas MacArthur, whom he esteemed highly. Glassford then taught painting at West Point and saw service in the Philippines, in Hawaii, and on the Mexican border. During the war he commanded the 103d Field Artillery at the Marne, at Château-Thierry, at St.-Mihiel. He found time to sketch the 103d's insignia: a scared dachshund in flight with an artillery shell in his behind. On October 18, 1918, Glassford was promoted to brigadier general at the age of thirty-four. He was wounded, decorated for gallantry in action, and came home with a Distinguished Service Medal.

Life in the peacetime army in the twenties bored Glassford. He piled up annual leave and took off months to travel through the West by motorcycle or flivver. He worked briefly as a reporter for Hearst's San Francisco *Examiner;* his style was a crisp, precise military prose. He did odd jobs with a circus: painting ballyhoo signs, pinch-hitting for the barker, keeping the electrical circuits working.

Glassford painted constantly — screens, murals, water colors. When he was stationed in Washington, his works became fashionable and hung in hundreds of homes and buildings. His ridiculous house in Georgetown, known as the "Borneo Embassy," was "a combination of Bohemia and military discipline."

Glassford was an adolescent girl's romantic conception of the army officer: six feet three, slender as a reed, handsome, intelligent, frank, gallant, charming. His zest for life was unquenchable (always the blue motorcycle). He appeared totally without fear. His circle of friends was enormous and his capacity for wangling help from them for good causes was almost limitless. They called him "Happy." Beyond a rudimentary patriotism, Glassford had no commitments to class, to political party, to ideology, to personal ambition. In the committed world of 1932, his was an unusually free spirit.

At forty-seven, bored with the Army, Glassford retired. He went to Arizona to help run the family fruit ranch. Two weeks later his father died. In the latter part of 1931, he returned to Washington to help prepare for the Armistice Day Jubilee. The District of Columbia police department, wracked with scandal, was being reorganized. The District commissioners were searching for a new chief; no one in the ranks seemed capable of "selling the force to the public." His old friend, Commissioner Herbert B. Crosby, offered Glassford the job. He accepted because it promised "plenty of fun and action." The money could not have been an attraction. Glassford received a net increase in income of $3363 per annum, giving up a military pension of $3920 against a salary of $7313.

Glassford was innocent of police work. When a reporter asked him about his experience, the chief brightened and replied, "Well, I've been arrested. Once for driving through a red light and once for speeding on a motorcycle." Characteristically, he threw himself into the work, reading books on criminology, attending lectures on abnormal psychology, learning to be "just a cop." His first major challenge was the Communist hunger march, which instinct led him to manage superbly. He now faced a far graver crisis.[3]

Glassford's immediate problems were to provide shelter, food, and medical care for the men, to raise money, and to maintain discipline. When the BEF formally organized itself on May 31, Waters became commander-in-chief and Glassford secretary-treasurer. The latter was now in position to keep a firm hand on the organization's affairs from the standpoint of the public interest.

For a few days the Salvation Army and the Volunteers of America tended the men, but their facilities were soon overwhelmed. A number of other locations were made available. Most important, by far, was the Anacostia camp between the 11th Street bridge and Bolling Field. Two smaller ones were Camps Simms (for rest and recuperation) and Meigs. Finally, Glassford secured permission to use several old vacant buildings in the square area bounded by 3d and 4th Streets, N.W., and Missouri and Pennsylvania Avenues in order to house approximately 600 men.

The buildings were federal property within the jurisdiction of the Treasury Department. The plan was to tear them down at an unspecified future date in order to make way for public buildings and parks that would be part of the Federal Triangle. On June 10,

1932, Ferry K. Heath, Assistant Secretary of the Treasury, wrote Glassford as follows:

> The department has no objection to the temporary use of the property.... However, the property in question is now under contract to be wrecked, and it will be necessary to grant the contractor, Rhine & Company, an extension of time under his contract, and it is consequently requested that the occupancy of the property be not extended beyond the actual need therefor. The contractor has been communicated with and it is the understanding with him that you may occupy the premises just as soon as you desire.

In fact, the area contained four structures. The old National Guard Armory on the east side of the square could be torn down because it stood alone. The three buildings to the west could not be demolished, according to Rhine & Company, until possession could be taken of Lee's Undertaking Establishment. One of the structures shared a retaining wall with the undertaker and the others would have to be dynamited onto his property. Lee had obtained a court injunction forbidding the seizure of his property. In Rhine's view, this restraining order would remain in effect at least until October.[4]

The Anacostia camp, which housed the great majority of the veterans, had to be built from scratch. Glassford desperately sought military tentage and bed sacks. He appealed to his old friend MacArthur, Army chief of staff, to no avail. The War Department said it needed the supplies and, in any case, feared they might be destroyed. The National Guard was forbidden by regulation to turn anything over. The commandant of the Marine Corps had nothing to spare. Hence the Anacostia camp was constructed by the BEF itself out of whatever materials could be begged or borrowed. At Anacostia Flats, wrote John Dos Passos, "the men are sleeping in little lean-tos built out of old newspapers, cardboard boxes, packing crates, bits of tin or tarpaper roofing, every kind of cockeyed makeshift shelter from the rain scraped together out of the city dump."

Feeding 22,000 men was a formidable undertaking. Glassford

put a local food broker in charge of the commissary on the second floor of a garage at 473 C Street, N.W. The chief then wheedled bakers, coffee concerns, and meat wholesalers into making deliveries — on a philanthropic basis where possible.

Medical care was a serious problem because of the wretched conditions at Anacostia. The medical troop of the 6th Marine Reserve Brigade held sick call twice daily on Indiana Avenue, but was soon swamped. With the cooperation of the District of Columbia medical and dental societies, a large dispensary that included a fifty-bed hospital was set up on John Marshall Place. The fear that Anacostia would breed epidemic, constantly iterated by the press, never came to pass.

All these undertakings required money. Glassford persuaded Clark Griffith, owner of the Washington baseball team, to turn over the Senators' park for an athletic benefit. Jimmy Lake, proprietor of the Gayety burlesque house, was equally cooperative. The police chief dunned the American Legion and the Veterans of Foreign Wars for funds. A large number of business concerns and private individuals sent in contributions, some substantial. On July 25, for example, General Henry Reilly phoned: "Mrs. P wants to know from General Glassford HOW MUCH MONEY GENERAL GLASSFORD WANTS." "I am very glad to send you the enclosed check for $500," wrote newspaper publisher Eleanor "Cissie" Patterson on July 27. Father Charles E. Coughlin, the Detroit radio priest, contributed a well-publicized $5000. Glassford himself was an important contributor.

The maintenance of order proved less of a problem than was anticipated. The BEF quickly organized itself under army discipline. It created a military police force of over 300 men commanded by a hard-boiled Bowery tout named Eddie Atwell. This force kept order in the camps and billets, helped direct traffic, imposed an embargo on liquor and firearms, and quarantined the Communists. According to the records of the metropolitan police, the number of crimes committed in the District of Columbia actually diminished during the time the Bonus Army was in town. Atwell was bitterly anti-Communist and Glassford had to restrain him in the use of force. At one point the chief accused him of dumping seven Reds into the river. "Sure I did," Atwell admitted, "they needed a bath."

Glassford repeatedly issued press statements intended to discourage more veterans from coming to Washington. To the same end, he urged congressional leaders to expedite a decision on the Patman bill. He negotiated with the railroads for low-cost fares to move the men out of town. Correctly sensing the mood of the BEF, he had little confidence that any of these measures would be effective.[5]

The Communists, like everyone else, had been caught unprepared by the swiftness with which the BEF had emerged. Nevertheless, it seemed to them a heaven (Marxist style)-sent opportunity. Here was an enormous mass of disaffected jobless workers in the nation's capital. If the Communist Party could seize control over the Bonus Army, it might have a ready-made revolutionary engine.

About the first of June the party opened a front organization, the Workers Ex-Servicemen's League, at 905 Eye Street, N.W. The boss was Emanuel Levin, editor of the *Daily Worker* and Communist candidate for the California assembly in 1928. Levin was not a veteran. The John Reed Club of Washington at a meeting on June 1 offered its cooperation (two police agents were present).

The WESL announced a "monster demonstration" (the language of the throwaway) for June 8. Glassford persuaded the BEF to stage a parade on Pennsylvania Avenue the preceding evening. Eight thousand veterans marched before a crowd of 100,000 spectators. These numbers so overshadowed the Communists that they called off the "monster" rally. Later they obtained a police permit to hold a parade over the same route. When only 160 people showed up, they gave up.

On June 10, the Communists were reinforced by a small contingent from Detroit led by John Pace. He had the reputation of being "an energetic field commander," had participated in the Dearborn riot, and was a veteran. So heartened was the WESL by this accretion of strength, that 200 men mounted an assault on Anacostia that evening. It was not a success. "Husky buddies from the Texas plains vied with lanky New Englanders," reported the Washington *Herald*, "for the privilege of 'going to work' on the Communists." A hurry call was put in for the police. When Glassford arrived, "the Communist group was huddled in a corner of the camp, trembling with fear as the veterans started toward them." The chief persuaded the BEF to desist, marched the Reds out, and bivouacked them in a vacant lot.

By mid-June it was obvious that the Communist venture had failed. On June 9, a knowledgeable Washington reporter sent the following message to Glassford:

I have absolutely authentic information. . . . I have a friend who is a leader of the Communist Party here and he told me that the communists tried in every way possible to put communists in the Bonus Army and to convert veterans, but they failed. This communist leader told me that they could not do a thing with the veterans.

Much of Glassford's time, in fact, was devoted to listening to Communist complaints and rescuing them from disaster. Since he was the only person who would give them a hearing, they were constantly on his doorstep. He arranged to get them shelter and food over the strong opposition of the BEF. He had to restrain Atwell's police from beating them up. He granted them permits for street meetings and parades. He tried to keep them out of jail. The Communists, instead of seizing the BEF and staging a revolution, barely survived by police sufferance.[6]

The ostensible purpose of the Bonus Army was to persuade Congress to pass the Patman bill. This endeavor enjoyed an initial success. By June 4, the requisite number of signatures — 145 — was obtained to force a vote in the House of Representatives. The House on June 15 passed Patman's bill 209 to 176. Trouble lay ahead in the upper chamber. The Senate Finance Committee recommended against the bill on June 16 by a vote of 14 to 2. The next day, while 12,000 restless but orderly veterans waited outside the Capitol, the Senate rejected the bonus bill by the overwhelming margin of 62 to 18. The marchers sang "America" and dispersed.

The antibonus forces sighed with relief and waited hopefully for the BEF to go home. A handful left town, but the great majority remained. "They can take me out of Washington," Waters declared, "but only feet first." "The B.E.F.," Thomas R. Henry wrote, "seems to have settled down for a nice, long visit." Foraging parties canvassed the city's junk piles for rusty iron, roofing tin, old auto bodies, and discarded beds with which to build "permanent" homes. Wives and children arrived in greater number. The press reported from Arizona that a contingent of 3000 Californians was on its way. A New Jersey outfit planted flowers. "No use going back home," a veteran told Henry, "because there's nothing to do and nothing to eat. They've got to feed me here."

Hoover, who was anxious to get the BEF out of Washington, had introduced in Congress a bill authorizing the expenditure of $100,000 to convey the men back home. The Veterans Bureau would advance a veteran his railroad fare and subsistence (at 75 cents a day). Money would be turned over as an interest-free loan, deductible from the bonus when paid. The Hoover bill became law early in July. Within a few weeks some 6000 men received loans. Some used the money to pay for the trip; others — probably most — stayed in Washington and spent the money as they pleased.[7]


### 3

In the month following the defeat of the Patman bill, the tension mounted in Washington. The District of Columbia commissioners, especially Crosby, became sharply critical of Glassford's conduct. They argued that he, in effect, invited more veterans to come to town. On June 27, Crosby accused Glassford of dereliction of duty by failing to enforce an ordinance forbidding the occupancy of buildings that were not equipped with sewers. He urged the chief to eject the men from these buildings. Glassford replied that this would almost certainly create a riot and so make necessary the calling out of the National Guard or the Army. "It was . . . apparent," Glassford noted in his diary, "that he advocated, without assuming any responsibility therefor, the use of force." On July 9 and 11, Crosby repeated the charge of failure to uphold the oath of office on the sewer issue. On the latter date, Glassford told the commissioners that he considered the use of force "dangerous . . . to the Police, the Community and the welfare of the District." He strongly urged them to go out to the billets and talk to the men. They refused.

On July 12, the recently arrived California contingent — 250 men rather than 3000 — announced that it would camp on the Capitol grounds. Vice-President Curtis would not grant them permission. Glassford, therefore, ordered these men to sleep elsewhere. On the following day Curtis, now joined by Speaker John N. Garner, reaffirmed this position. They placed the responsibility for enforcement of their directive upon the metropolitan police and urged Glassford to avoid violence. The California group agreed not to camp, but insisted on walking in file through the Capitol grounds, which no law nor regulation prohibited. This parading went on for several days and nights, attracted large crowds, and got heavy press notice. Despite several tense moments, violence was avoided.

The Capitol incident led to a conference on July 14 in General MacArthur's office attended by a number of high Army officers, Admiral H. V. Butler, commandant of the Navy Yard with some marines at his disposal, Crosby, and Glassford. MacArthur, Glassford recorded in his diary, "was highly complimentary in his statement of the manner in which the [Bonus Army] situation had been handled." He also stated flatly that "the Army would not be used unless directed by the President." Curtis had notified the conference that he now wished the Capitol grounds completely cleared, while still insisting on the avoidance of force. Glassford warned that this would "greatly aggravate the situation." He finally got a compromise requiring the clearing of only the plaza in front of the Capitol. This was accomplished by the police without incident. The parading continued but at some distance from the building.

On July 15 the Communists, 165 strong, arrived at the Capitol with a petition. The police forbade them to parade on the grounds. They read their petition on the steps of the Library of Congress.

On July 16 orders were issued for the security of the White House. Crosby wrote them on the back of an envelope for Glassford at 9:40 P.M. The metropolitan police would be responsible for Pennsylvania Avenue and all approaches except from the south. The park police would be responsible for East and West Executive Avenues and the southern approach. No parading whatsoever was to be permitted about the White House. Force, to be avoided if possible, was to be used if needed "to prevent the congregation and parading of unauthorized groups." "In the event of a call for

Federal troops responsibility shall pass to the commander thereof." [8]

The Hoover Administration now determined upon a drastic change of policy, namely eviction of the BEF, first from the buildings in the Pennsylvania Avenue square and later from all the encampments, including Anacostia, within the District of Columbia. If the veterans would not leave voluntarily, the government would drive them out. As a consequence of this decision, Glassford lost control over the situation.

On July 20, Heath revoked the Treasury's permission to use the buildings on Pennsylvania Avenue. "It is now imperative that the contractor be permitted to complete his work." He asked Glassford to "take immediate steps to vacate the building . . . and the area therebetween." On July 21 the district commissioners handed Glassford an order to secure the evacuation of these structures by midnight, July 22, of all other buildings by midnight, July 24, and of Anacostia, Camp Meigs, and Camp Simms by noon, August 4.

This change of policy, the chief felt, would inevitably lead to "persecution and forcible ejection." "I tried to convince the Commissioners of the great danger inherent in this sudden and drastic change of policy. They were determined. They appeared unwilling to argue this point." It did seem to him that several sections of the order might be illegal. He, therefore, referred it to the corporation counsel, who concurred. This led to frantic conferences and a stay of execution by the commissioners of their order.

Meantime, Glassford notified Waters that the BEF would soon have to evacuate the Pennsylvania Avenue buildings. He recommended that the veterans take advantage of the federal loans to go home. Waters replied that his first obligation was to his men. They were determined to remain in the District of Columbia. Unless the government found other shelter, he would not evacuate them into the open.

The legal complications were worked out by July 26, when Heath announced that demolition would begin the next day. The contractor, however, refused to proceed because of a concern over workmen's compensation. On July 27, Hoover conferred with Secretary of the Treasury Mills, Secretary of War Hurley, Attorney General Mitchell, General MacArthur, Heath, and a Treasury lawyer. Finally, at 4 P.M. that afternoon the commissioners received a letter from the Treasury announcing that the destruction of the old National Guard Armory would commence at 10 A.M. the following day. Treasury agents would appear at that time to repossess the property. Heath asked for police protection. The commissioners immediately ordered Glassford "to render all protection necessary to the Treasury Department in securing the repossession of these premises."[9]

July 28, 1932, was a clear, warm Washington summer day. It was to prove memorable.

At 9:30 A.M., Glassford explained the commissioners' order to a detail of almost 100 police officers. He had already dispatched an agent to Waters to secure his cooperation. Waters came to the Pennsylvania Avenue encampment, which housed about 1100 veterans, and sought to persuade its commander to move 200 of his men immediately to Camp Bartlett, a private facility in the outskirts of the District of Columbia. He was told that they would not go. At 9:45 Waters addressed the men: "We do not intend to move until they provide us with proper shelter. . . . However if the Army comes they will move us and you can depend on that." The men voted by acclamation to remain.

At 10:15 the police detail formed a circle about the old armory. Twenty minutes later the Treasury officials arrived and with police assistance evacuated the building. This work was accomplished quickly and with only minor incident.

Meantime, a crowd had gathered, including many members of the BEF from other camps. At noon a Communist delegation, about thirty-five in number, tried to force its way into the building. Glassford blocked the way. A man named Bernard McCoy tore the chief's badge from his shirt and struck him. A melee with flying bricks followed. No one was seriously injured. Three or four men were arrested and the remaining assailants disappeared into the crowd. This disturbance lasted five minutes.

Glassford then left the scene to report to the District commissioners. He told them that the first building had been evacuated and repossessed by the Treasury without serious incident. The police, in his judgment, could hold the present line. He strongly recommended against a further evacuation that day because of the strong feeling among the veterans. Glassford opposed a call for federal aid. If, however, the commissioners rejected his advice and insisted upon an immediate extension of the evacuated area, troops would be needed. The commissioners told him to hold what he had. They did not instruct him to extend the evacuated area; nor did they notify him that they were asking the President to call out the Army.

At 2:15 P.M. an argument between two bonus marchers occurred in the building nearest 4½ Street. A large crowd gathered. When police entered to quiet the disturbance, a group of veterans attacked them. In the resulting fight three officers were injured, one marcher was killed, and another was wounded. As the disturbance subsided, a newspaperman informed Glassford that troops were on the way.[10]

The District commissioners, in fact, had already dispatched the following letter to the President, which was immediately published:

It is the opinion of the major and superintendent of police, in which the commissioners concur, that it will be impossible for the Police Department to maintain law and order except by the free use of firearms, which will make the situation a dangerous one; it is believed, however, that the presence of Federal troops in some number will obviate the seriousness of the situation and result in far less violence and bloodshed.

The Commissioners of the District of Columbia, therefore, request that they be given the assistance of Federal troops in maintaining law and order in the District of Columbia.

Hoover immediately ordered the War Department to send in the Army. He also sent a reply to the commissioners which was released to the press. "In response to your information that the police of the District were overwhelmed by an organized attack of several thousand men, and were unable to maintain law and order, I complied with your request for aid from the Army to the police." Since martial law was not declared, the civil authorities retained responsibility for the maintenance of order. They must find the "instigators of this attack" and bring them to justice. The majority of the veterans had already gone home. "Subversive influences," the President wrote, "obtained the control of the men remaining in the District, a large part of whom were not veterans, secured repudiation of their respective leaders and inaugurated and organized this attack." They were encouraged by "lax enforcement" of ordinances and laws by the police. Henceforth enforcement must be strict. "There is no group, no matter what its origins, that can be allowed either to violate the laws of this city or intimidate the Government."[11]

The armed forces that gathered in the vicinity of the White House consisted of four troops of cavalry, four companies of infantry, a mounted machine gun squadron, and six whippet tanks. MacArthur himself was in command. At his side was his aide, Major Dwight D. Eisenhower, and one of his officers was the dashing George S. Patton, Jr. The operation was delayed an hour while an orderly rushed across the Potomac to Fort Myer for MacArthur's tunic, service stripes, sharpshooter medal, and English whipcord breeches.

He then led the troops in dramatic display down Pennsylvania Avenue before a huge crowd, arriving at the troubled area at 4:45 P.M. "We are going to break the back of the B.E.F.," MacArthur told Glassford. The soldiers, using tear gas, quickly cleared the old buildings and set them on fire. By 7:15, all the encampments within the city had been evacuated and burned.

MacArthur then sent his forces across the Anacostia bridge. Thousands of veterans, their wives, and children fled before the advancing soldiers. The troops attacked with tear gas and set fire to a number of huts. There was virtually no resistance. The veterans then spread the conflagration. By morning Anacostia was a smoldering ruin.

The military operation was carried out swiftly and efficiently. Total casualties, including those in the earlier police fracas, were two veterans shot to death, an eleven-week baby in grave condition (he later died), an eight-year-old boy partially blinded by gas, two policemen with fractured skulls, a bystander shot through the shoulder, a veteran's ear severed by cavalry saber, a veteran stabbed in the hip by a bayonet, more than a dozen persons injured by bricks and clubs, and over 1000 gassed. Property damage of value was slight, perhaps the most important loss being twenty old sycamores and elms seared by flames near the Pennsylvania Avenue encampment.

The veterans, of course, were driven out of the District of Columbia. Many went to Johnstown, Pennsylvania, at the invitation of Mayor Eddie McCloskey, where their conditions were even more wretched than they had been in Washington. The others simply melted away into the sea of joblessness. Glassford, hopelessly deadlocked with the commissioners, resigned on October 20, 1932.

During the Battle of Anacostia, President Hoover sat in the Lincoln study at the White House with the California capitalist, Henry M. Robinson, and the assistant attorney general, Seth Richardson. From the window they observed the crimson glow in the southeast. "The glow gradually spread until the whole sky over Anacostia was red." Shortly thereafter the President retired. On the following day the press was informed that "the President was pleased."[12]

4

It is probable that no act of Hoover's proved so unpopular as his decision to drive out the BEF. The public reaction to the use of armed force against jobless veterans, regardless of the merits of their bonus claim, was shock and dismay. The reporter Thomas L. Stokes, who witnessed the burning of Anacostia, wrote:

This, I said to myself, may be the end of this country as we know it. The United States Army turned on to American citizens — just fellows like myself, down on their luck, dispirited, hopeless. My mood was one of despair. It was an experience that stands apart from all others in my life. So all the misery and suffering had finally come to this — soldiers marching with their guns against American citizens. I had nothing but bitter feelings toward Herbert Hoover that night.[13]

In October 1932, Amos Pinchot, the Pennsylvania governor's brother, published a satiric playlet entitled *General Goober at the Battle of Anacostia*. Boardman Robinson did a tomato-face caricature of Hoover in Army uniform and campaign hat for the cover. Pinchot dedicated his cruel farce to the President. The playlet takes place in the Blue House. As the sounds of battle are heard from Anacostia, General Goober asks Pompey, a Negro retainer left over from the Chester A. Arthur Administration, for his Sam Browne belt. It was left at Rapidan when the President reviewed the Boy Scouts. "My God, man, you don't expect me to fight without a Sam Browne belt? This is war!" "Dis sure am war," Pompey returns. "But it ain't de kind ob war you-all kin win with Sam Browne belts nor tank wagons neither. What dis war needs is lunch wagons, an' de ham sandwich division, an' de po'k an' beans brigade. An' de beer wagon. Don't fo'git about dat wagon, suh." [14]

## CHAPTER 14

# Relief: The Emergence of a National Policy

PRESIDENT HOOVER misgauged the Bonus Army. He viewed it as a potential insurrection; in fact, it was a manifestation of transient joblessness. The answer, as Pompey observed, was not the bayonet but the ham sandwich. The Bonus Expeditionary Force would never have come into existence if there had been an adequate relief program in the summer of 1932. But the nation had no program; it was still fumbling its way toward one.

Hoover's policy of local responsibility for unemployment relief, as pointed out in Chapter 7, had broken down by the fall of 1931. Private charitable agencies and many municipalities were incapable of handling their loads. The President's Emergency Committee for Employment had disintegrated. Yet the burden of relief for the jobless and their families grew steadily heavier.

The times were ripe for radical change, for a bold policy that would mark a sharp break with the past. This required leadership and the White House supplied none. Hoover was the servant rather than the master of events. Hence responsibility shifted to the governors' mansions, notably the Victorian edifice in Albany, and to the Congress.

1

By June 1931, Governor Franklin D. Roosevelt was persuaded that New York State faced a relief crisis. This conviction was reinforced in midsummer by a joint report of the State Board of Social Welfare and the State Charities Aid Association, which pointed out that private resources were exhausted and that the municipalities were overloaded. A tough winter lay ahead. William Hodson, director of the Welfare Council of New York City, urged Roosevelt to call the legislature into special session. This the governor did on August 25. "The ... responsibility of the State," he told the Republican legislature, "undoubtedly applies when . . . economic conditions render large numbers of men and women incapable of supporting either themselves or their families. . . . To these unfortunate citizens aid must be extended by government — not as a matter of charity but as a matter of social duty."

In the Wicks bill Roosevelt proposed the creation of a new agency of three unpaid members, the Temporary Emergency Relief Administration. It would be given $20 million to distribute among the counties and cities in accordance with local need and the initiative they displayed in tapping their own resources. TERA would sponsor both home and work relief programs. Actual administration would be in the hands of local agencies operating in conformity with state standards. Funds would be raised by a 50 per cent increase in income taxes. The Republicans proposed two changes: administration by the Department of Social Welfare, whose head was a member of their party, and unlimited matching of local and state funds. Roosevelt opposed the first because, he argued, it would inject politics into relief and the second because it would commit the state to unspecified outlays. The legislature backed down, and on September 23 the governor signed the law in the form he had proposed.

Within the week he named the members of TERA: Jesse Isidor Straus, president of R. H. Macy & Company, as chairman; Philip J. Wickser, a Buffalo insurance man and banker, who was a Republican; and John Sullivan, president of the State Federation of Labor. Though all were to prove devoted public servants, none could spare much time. The choice of an executive director, therefore, was critical. Straus, on the advice of Lieutenant Governor Lehman, offered the job to William Hodson. The Welfare Council would not release him. Hodson suggested the director of the New York Tuberculosis and Health Association. On October 7, 1931, Harry L. Hopkins was invited to become the executive director of TERA; he began work the next day. When Straus and Wickser resigned the following spring, Hopkins succeeded as chairman. He was to make his mark with TERA.

The son of a harnessmaker, Hopkins was born in Sioux City, spent most of his youth in Iowa, and attended Grinnell College. Upon graduation in 1912, he considered entering the newspaper business in Bozeman, Montana. But the college had a request for a student to act as counselor at the Christadora House summer camp for underprivileged New York children. He leapt at the opportunity to get to New York. Though Hopkins had been familiar with the rural poor, he was wholly unprepared for the products of immigrant poverty in the urban slums. That summer the boys from the East Side made him a champion of the underprivileged. In the fall he became a social worker, starting his apprenticeship at Christadora House. His obvious abilities led to rapid advancement. In 1921 he became director of the health division of the Milbank Memorial Fund and in 1924 executive director of the Tuberculosis Association. Prior to TERA his only meeting with Roosevelt was a quick handshake at the 1928 Democratic convention.

Hopkins was an exceedingly complex human being. He was passionately devoted to improving the welfare of the poor and at the same time loved night clubs and fashionable society. He read Keats and played the horses. He was cadaverous, intense, a chain smoker, a black-coffee drinker, seldom changed his shirt, and was in continuous bad health (after his death, the Hopkins "papers" delivered to the Roosevelt Library contained enough vials of pills to stock a small pharmacy). Hopkins divided people into two classes — the "talkers" and the "doers." He placed himself in the latter category. This was no false pride. "It is next to impossible," *Fortune* observed, "for Mr. Hopkins to do nothing." In the art of sheer free-wheeling accomplishment few could match Harry Hopkins.

Under his driving leadership, TERA quickly became the outstanding relief organization in the nation and the model for other states and the federal government. It provided assistance to every tenth family in the state. This necessitated the raising of funds, mainly by bond issues, far beyond the original $20 million appropriation. By January 1933 TERA had expended over $83 million, and by the end of 1935 the total had risen to almost $933 million. The agency placed heavy emphasis on work relief which, though expensive, maintained the self-esteem of the recipient and improved the state. Hopkins insisted that the local administrative agencies employ professional people. "Social workers," he said, "are at the bat." TERA's reputation, despite the enormous sums it handled, remained untarnished by either corruption or political favoritism. New York, because of the success of this program, was among the last of the states to ask for federal aid.[1]

Other states fell into line behind New York. The New Jersey legislature in special session established an emergency relief administration on October 13, 1931, with an appropriation of $10 million. Rhode Island took similar action the next month, setting aside $2.5 million. Governor Philip La Follette called the Wisconsin legislature into special session in November, but he did not get a relief program until the following February. Early in 1932, Oklahoma, New Hampshire, Maryland, California, and Ohio joined the procession. By March 4, 1933, the majority of the states had created emergency relief administrations.

The problems in Illinois and Pennsylvania were especially acute. Local funds in Cook County were exhausted by the end of January 1932. The anticipated crisis had been repeatedly called to the attention of the Illinois legislature, which, because of downstate dominance, did nothing. On February 1, when the governor called a third special session, the legislature could no longer ignore the emergency in Chicago. The result was the Illinois Emergency Relief Commission with an appropriation of $20 million.

In August 1931 a committee of prominent citizens and social workers reported to Governor Pinchot that Pennsylvania faced a relief crisis. They found staggering unemployment, the exhaustion of both private and public local funds, administrative disorganization outside the big cities, and catastrophe in the coal fields. The constitution of Pennsylvania declared, "No appropriations . . . shall be made for charitable . . . purposes, to any persons or community. . . ." Further, it forbade the state to create a debt for any but specified purposes, not including relief. The attorney general ruled that the legislature had no authority to appropriate money for unemployment relief. Hence, when Pinchot called the legislature into special session in November, he merely asked for improved facilities for the regular departments of welfare, health, and labor. Funds for relief would have to be raised privately. The pressure was so great, however, that the legislature appropriated $10 million directly for relief, justifying this action under the general welfare clause of the constitution. The Pennsylvania Supreme Court was eventually to bless this unusual constitutional theory.[2]

2

In 1931 influential political voices — mainly those of progressive Republicans — were heard calling for federal action. On May 21 Senator La Follette asked the President to convene a special session of Congress to enact a relief program. On August 4, Senator Couzens joined in the appeal. A week later Senator Blaine urged a special session. Governor Pinchot maintained a steady drumbeat on behalf of federal relief.

Hoover, obviously, could not allow winter to come without making some gesture. The President's Emergency Committee for Employment could not be resurrected. It was simpler to create a new agency: the President's Organization on Unemployment Relief, or the Gifford Committee. Hoover made no bones about his objective; he sought to stave off "a socialistic dole."

On August 19, 1931, he named Walter S. Gifford, president of the American Telephone and Telegraph Company, chairman of POUR, along with sixty-one prominent persons as an advisory committee. The business orientation of the agency was clear cut: the economists and social workers who had displayed their independence on the Woods Committee were not retained. Gifford did appoint a representative in each state to serve as a liaison between POUR and the local relief agencies.

At the outset Gifford stressed the fact that POUR would not be a centralized, national organization. It would proceed on the assumption that relief programs were local and state responsibilities. "This organization will in no way disturb those activities." POUR would merely "coordinate" them. Its main venture was a campaign under the direction of Owen D. Young of General Electric in the fall of 1931 to support the fund-raising drives of local charitable agencies. Conducted with high-powered advertising, this "mobilization" enjoyed some success. It had a comic side as well. One ad showed Gifford and Young urging a girl with beautiful eyes to forgive her husband for having contributed so liberally to relief. The model was the hatcheck girl at Tony's speakeasy in Manhattan's east fifties!

This was POUR's difficulty: it was hard to take seriously. Despite its name, the organization made no effort to deal with the economic problem of unemployment and almost none to extend relief to the jobless. It became the butt of depression jokes: "Mr. Gifford's committee of sixty Big Names has now passed sixty-five and we have a tip that it will go to par before the month is over. Then, Mr. Unemployed, goodbye."

POUR's most notable claim to fame was the shocking ignorance its chairman, presumably the best-informed man in the nation on relief, revealed before the Senate Subcommittee on Manufactures under the withering cross-examination of Senators Costigan and La Follette in January 1932. They had just introduced the first of the major federal relief bills. Costigan, in fact, had written Gifford on November 3, 1931, to inquire into relief needs, the capacity of existing agencies, and the resources of communities without organized campaigns. Gifford replied blandly that with "a very few exceptions, each community . . . in which there is an unemployment problem requiring organized effort, has an organization setup to care for the unemployed situation this coming winter." The exceptions would be cared for "in the immediate future." Costigan would not be put off. He wrote again for details and again received no satisfaction. Gifford was called before the Subcommittee on January 8, 1932.

He asserted flatly that local and state programs adequately met relief needs. He opposed federal action as both unnecessary and dangerous; it would undermine local responsibility and so worsen the lot of the unemployed. Under cross-examination, however, Gifford admitted that he did not know how many persons needed relief, how many were on relief, or what the standards were. A typical colloquy was the following:

Senator Costigan. Do you know or does anyone else whom you can turn to know what the relief needs are in the smaller cities of the country which have no community chest organizations?

Mr. Gifford. No; I do not know.

Senator Costigan. Do you know what the relief needs are in the rural districts of the United States?

Mr. Gifford. No.

Senator Costigan. Your committee has not assembled information of that sort?

Mr. Gifford. That is correct.

Senator Costigan. Did you turn to the Red Cross for information?

Mr. Gifford. Yes; we have some reports from the Red Cross.

Senator Costigan. Did they supply you with any definite information as to the needs of the country as a whole?

Mr. Gifford. No.

Senator Costigan. Did you, from any other source, acquire information which would enable you specifically to advise us how many people in the United States at this hour are on the verge of starvation?

Mr. Gifford. I have no such information.

After the telephone man left the witness chair, no one could any longer pay attention to POUR as a relief organization. On July 5, 1932, Hoover sent a message to Congress noting that it had failed to include an appropriation for the Gifford Committee in the deficiency bill. He asked for $120,000. Congress ignored his request. POUR died quietly and its passing went unlamented except by Hoover.[3]

### 3

Between the summer of 1931 and the spring of 1932 the American social work profession, formerly divided, united itself behind federal relief. This development was to have an important effect upon the molding of both public opinion and public policy. Social workers knew more firsthand about the conditions among the unemployed than anyone else, and their disinterestedness was hardly open to challenge. They now found their reports and opinions both newsworthy and the subject of interest in legislative halls. The rise of Hopkins in New York was symptomatic.

The National Conference of Social Work meeting in Minneapolis in June 1931 was the last stand of local relief. Several voices were heard urging federal intervention. "We are rapidly approaching the point," declared Jacob Billikopf of the Philadelphia Federation of Jewish Charities, "where the national government will be compelled to step in and do something commensurate with the need." Father John A. Ryan of the National Catholic Welfare Council categorically demanded action from Washington. But this view did not dominate the Conference. The outgoing president, Dr. Richard Cabot of Boston, spoke of professional standards. His successor, C. M. Bookman, director of the Cincinnati Community Chest, reaffirmed local responsibility. "I do not believe it will be necessary to make or take national or state grants for direct relief. However, I should not hesitate to sanction them if no other way can be found to feed the hungry."

By the time of the Philadelphia meeting in May 1932, no other way had been found and the Conference turned into a ringing declaration for federal relief. "It is time for plain speaking," Bookman stated in his presidential address. No one could afford any longer to be frightened by the word "dole." The nation was staggering under an immense burden of unemployment without plan or program. Private agencies were overwhelmed. "This country should never again face such an emergency with such inadequate machinery." Bookman urged government — local, state, and federal — to shoulder the load. Governor Pinchot told the social workers, "The welfare of the working people . . . cannot be left to the occasional benevolence of the wealthy." It was a "solemn responsibility of society as a whole . . . a national responsibility and a national duty." Senator Costigan echoed this philosophy. Clarence A. Dykstra, the city manager of Cincinnati, called for a national approach to the unemployment problem. Frank Bane, director of the American Association of Public Welfare Officials, described federal relief as "inevitable." William Hodson voiced the hope that even Hoover would see the light. The American social work profession was now firmly committed to federal relief.[4]

In October 1931 a group of leading members of the profession, headed by Linton B. Swift, director of the Family Welfare Association, formed themselves into the Social Work Conference on Federal Action on Unemployment. Their purpose was to set forth principles of a federal statute. Both Costigan and La Follette sought their advice. When Congress convened in December, each of the senators introduced a relief bill based upon these principles.

The Costigan measure would have appropriated $375 million for federal grants to the states for unemployment relief, one third during the current fiscal year and two thirds in the following year. Excepting sums needed for administration, 40 per cent of the funds would be allocated among the states on the basis of population and 60 per cent on the basis of need. The Children's Bureau would administer the program under the supervision of a federal board for unemployment relief, consisting of the chief of the Children's Bureau, the director of Agricultural Extension, and the head of the Vocational Rehabilitation Service. La Follette's bill was similar. The main differences were that $250 million would be made immediately available and the members of the board would be named by the President. Both measures were referred to the Subcommittee on Manufactures, of which La Follette was chairman.

The hearings held by this body between December 28, 1931, and January 9, 1932, were of great importance. They provided the first comprehensive and detailed study of unemployment during the Great Depression. Most of the witnesses were social workers who presented a vivid, firsthand account of destitution. They came from all parts of the nation and revealed in detail the relief loads, standards, needs, and resources of the towns, counties, and states. Their testimony was confirmed by labor leaders and local government officials. In effect, the hearings constituted a powerful brief for federal relief.

In the latter part of January, La Follette and Costigan combined their bills and won a favorable report from the Manufactures Subcommittee. Debate opened on February 1. Each of the sponsors made a long, fact-crammed, impassioned speech for federal relief. The Administration Republicans, of course, strongly opposed the measure. Senator Simeon Fess of Ohio, chairman of the Republican National Committee and spokesman for the White House, denounced the La Follette–Costigan bill for "opening the floodgates" of the Treasury and for creating a "dole." Federal relief would undermine local responsibility.

Even more serious was Democratic opposition. On February 3, Senators Hugo Black of Alabama, Tom Walsh of Montana, and Robert J. Bulkley of Ohio introduced a substitute. It would appropriate $375 million for roads and an equal amount for direct loans to the states for unemployment relief. After three years these loans would either be repaid or the amounts would be deducted from future federal highway grants. There would be no national board to administer the program or to set standards for the states. The Democratic rationale was that Hoover would be less likely to veto a bill substituting loans for grants and avoiding the creation of a federal "bureaucracy." The Democrats, facing a presidential election, must have been concerned as well with the potential political implications of a large relief fund. The differences between the measures were narrowed on February 11, when the Senate adopted a series of amendments to the La Follette–Costigan bill to add a $375 million highway appropriation and to restrict the powers of the federal relief board. On February 15, the Senate rejected the Democratic substitute by a vote of 48 to 31. The majority consisted of a bloc of conservative Republicans and progressives. The next day the La Follette–Costigan bill was dealt the same fate by a margin of 48 to 35. The alliances were reconstituted. Here the majority was composed of Administration Republicans and conservative Democrats and the minority of progressives and liberal Democrats.[5]

Federal relief had lost a battle but not a war. In fact, the sentiment for a national program continued to grow during the spring of 1932. This was because the relief situation worsened markedly. Politicians of both major parties, with a presidential campaign in the offing, could hardly ignore the signs.

On April 15 *Survey* published the reports of welfare experts in thirty-seven large cities: "Fitted together they make a sorry picture for a proud country to contemplate. . . . The industrial cities of the Middle West and the large cities of Pennsylvania are in desperate plight. . . . Complete breakdown is imminent." The Subcommittee on Manufactures resumed hearings on May 9. Walter West of the American Association of Social Workers described the situation as "desperate." J. Prentice Murphy of the Seybert Institution called for "extraordinary measures of relief." H. L. Lurie of the Boston Jewish Charities found "distress growing daily more desperate . . . uncertainty and . . . increasing fears that the communities will be unable for the rest of the year to continue the meager relief which is being offered." "Pennsylvania," its secretary of welfare, Helen Tyson, warned, "is facing an economic and social crisis so acute, so devastating in its effect on family life, as to beggar description." On June 1, the mayors of twenty-eight large cities admitted that they had lost control and demanded federal help.

The unpublished field reports flowing into the Gifford Committee at this time fully confirmed the crisis. In February large industrialists were worried. They had already spread the work as thin as it would go; there would have to be big spring layoffs. New York City in March was found in a "critical situation." Private funds were nearing exhaustion and Tammany, worried about the Walker scandals, had lost interest in relief. The need in Pennsylvania was "very heavy" in sixteen counties and parts of eleven others and was "acute" in Philadelphia, Pittsburgh, and the coal regions. The Russian Orthodox Church, with a large following in the steel and coal communities, begged the federal government to help. The community chest of Waterloo, Iowa, was wiped out by the failure of the Pioneer National Bank. In the early summer the Quaker relief program in the coal fields halted for lack of funds.

There were "ominous mutterings" in the Southern Appalachian camps. A West Virginia editor told the Red Cross that almost every man in his county had a rifle. Clarence Pickett of the Friends wrote POUR of a dangerous possibility of rioting. Crowds were increasingly aggressive. At Hazard, Kentucky, the police were unable to maintain control at the Red Cross food warehouse. "The Negro is not laughing and he is not dancing," Roy Wilkins of the NAACP warned. "The leaders of our organization," Edward F. McGrady of the AFL told the Manufactures Subcommittee, "have been preaching patience. . . . But I say to you gentlemen, advisedly, that if something is not done and starvation is going to continue and perhaps increase the doors of revolt in this country are going to be thrown open." When Mayor Cermak of Chicago appeared before the House Banking and Currency Committee on June 21, he said the federal government had a basic choice: relief or troops.

The Chicago relief crisis broke the back of opposition in Congress and the White House. The $20 million appropriation for the Illinois Emergency Relief Commission was to run out in the early summer, and the state legislature refused to vote more. There were three quarters of a million persons out of work in Cook County. The city's 14,000 schoolteachers had been paid in only five of the preceding thirteen months. They now faced a payless summer vacation. Many, of course, had been driven onto relief and that source was about to dry up. On June 2, Chicago's leading industrialists, bankers, and civic leaders appealed to President Hoover for federal relief. The list included the chief executives of Armour, Wilson, Cudahy, International Harvester, the Santa Fe Railroad, Marshall Field, Colgate-Palmolive-Peet, Inland Steel, Bendix, U. S. Gypsum, A. B. Dick, Illinois Bell Telephone, the First National Bank, the *Daily News*, and the *American*. These were voices Hoover could not ignore.[6]

On February 17, 1932, the day following the rejection of the La Follette–Costigan bill, Senator Wagner had introduced a new relief measure that combined its administrative features with the loan provisions of the Democratic substitute. Wagner's bill lay in its pigeonhole for almost three months.

On May 11, the Democratic leader of the Senate, Joseph T. Robinson of Arkansas, declared himself for federal relief. He proposed a bond issue of $2.3 billion: $300 million to finance advances to the states for relief and $2 billion for construction loans to the states and cities for self-liquidating projects. Robinson spoke for a group of influential conservative Democrats. The proposal had been devised by J. Cheever Cowdin, a Wall Street investment banker, and had the support of Al Smith, Owen D. Young, Bernard Baruch, and Silas Strawn.

On the following day Robinson and his Republican counterpart,

Senator James E. Watson of Indiana, met with the President. The result was a historic White House press statement that was to lead to a new relief policy for the United States. Responsibility for relief, Hoover declared, "belongs to private organizations, local communities, and the states. That fundamental policy is not to be changed." But he immediately qualified it by endorsing federal loans to the states for unemployment relief out of a Reconstruction Finance Corporation fund of $250 or $300 million. He also proposed an increase in RFC borrowing capacity for self-liquidating loans to both governmental instrumentalities and private enterprises.

The Senate Democrats promptly set up a legislative drafting committee, consisting of Wagner as chairman, Robinson, Walsh of Montana, Pittman, and Bulkley. On May 20, the Wagner committee agreed on a bill providing for $300 million in relief loans, $1.5 billion for self-liquidating projects, and $500 million for public works. The House Democrats also came forward with a bill. Speaker John Nance Garner, then campaigning for the presidential nomination, proposed a $1 billion bond issue for public works, a $1 billion increase in RFC capitalization for loans to private corporations, and a $100 million grant to the President for distribution to the needy.

On May 31, Hoover appeared personally before the Senate to denounce the public works feature of the Wagner bill in the name of a balanced budget. However, he did endorse the $300 million RFC authorization for loans to the states for unemployment relief.

The Senate Banking and Currency Committee held hearings in early June, at which Secretary of the Treasury Ogden Mills was the main witness. His testimony left no doubt that the Administration had embraced federal relief with something less than passion. This appropriation would be "an emergency fund" to loan to a state that had "exhausted" its own resources and "actually needs funds for the relief of destitution." Senator Blaine observed wryly that in going this far the Secretary demonstrated that he could "rise above principle." The federal government, Mills warned, must fix definite tests to determine the exhaustion of a state's resources and not rely upon the word of the governor. "I know of no conceivable reason why great, rich States like New York and Pennsylvania should receive a grant from the Federal treasury." Mills, of course, strongly opposed the $500 million public works appropriation. "The fundamental objection . . . is that it unbalances the Budget." His views found a certain support. "Your statements about the Wagner bill . . . will, I believe," wrote Albert Shaw, editor of *Review of Reviews*, "stand out permanently as classical gems in the documentary history of American public finance."

On June 7, the House, after a brief, bitter debate, enacted the Garner bill by a margin of 216 to 182. The Senate passed the Wagner bill by a vote of 72 to 8 on June 10, with only a handful of extreme conservatives in the minority. Hoover was dissatisfied with both measures. He denounced the House version as "porkbarrel" and as making "the United States Government . . . the most gigantic banking and pawnbroking business in all history." He attacked the Wagner bill for allocating relief to the states on the basis of population rather than need and for fostering "non-productive" public works.

The conference report of July 1 on the legislation, now known as the Wagner-Garner bill, made little more than a gesture toward conciliating the President. The conferees agreed on a $2.1 billion program: $1.5 billion for loans to public instrumentalities, private enterprises, and individuals; $300 million directly for public works; $200 million for relief loans to the states based on population, and $100 million for such loans based on need. The House enacted this bill on July 7 by a vote of 202 to 157, and the Senate followed two days later with a margin of 43 to 31. Wagner, anticipating a frosty reception from the White House, had begun work on a substitute even before the Senate voted. Hoover on July 11 issued a stinging veto message. Wagner's revision was then adopted by the House on July 14 by a vote of 296 to 46 and by the Senate two days later by voice vote. Hoover signed the law on July 21, 1932.

Title 1 of the Emergency Relief and Construction Act of 1932 established an RFC fund of $300 million for loans to the states "to be used in furnishing relief and work relief to needy and distressed people and in relieving the hardship resulting from unemployment." Not more than 15 per cent of this amount might be allocated to any one state. Loans would be put out at 3 per cent interest and would be repayable from federal highway grants beginning in 1935. The governor would petition the RFC for a loan, certifying that both public and private resources were inadequate to meet the state's relief needs. ERCA also appropriated $322,224,000 from the Treasury for direct public works. Finally, the Act greatly expanded the capitalization of RFC for self-liquidating loans.

In the development of both federal relief and federal public works July 21, 1932, was a historic day. But the President made no ceremony of the signing, and Congress simply adjourned. Tempers at both ends of Pennsylvania Avenue, lacerated by the presidential conventions, the Bonus Army, and the heat of the Washington summer, had been shredded. The legislative process had degenerated into an exercise in snarling. The participants were too exhausted to recognize the significance of what they had done.[7]

## 4

The RFC was immediately inundated by a flood of requests from the states for relief funds. On July 18, three days before Hoover signed the bill, the board of directors granted a hearing to an Illinois delegation. Relief stations in Cook County would close on July 22 and in the remainder of the state on July 31. Illinois could not borrow because there was no market for its notes. On July 19, Governor Pinchot of Pennsylvania requested $45 million, the 15 per cent maximum under the still not enacted bill. Before the end of July, in fact, RFC had received applications totaling $171.5 million, and those from only thirteen states.

Under the urging of Mills, the RFC engaged Fred Croxton from collapsing POUR to head its emergency relief division. He set up a small regionalized field staff to report on conditions in the states and to assist the governors in preparing their petitions.

The RFC, given the composition of its board of directors, administered relief as a banking rather than a welfare program. It was run, the Corporation's president, Charles A. Miller, declared, "on a business basis." "I have a very high regard for social workers, but God forbid, they should have the purse strings." Policies reflected this outlook. Except for Illinois, the RFC was slow in putting out its emergency funds. The $300 million authorized by the statute were expected to last for two years. The Corporation insisted that the governor make a conclusive showing of the exhaustion of private and public resources within the state before applying for federal funds. It granted far less than the governors asked for. Finally, RFC loans were for only thirty days; the state had to return each month for another infusion of federal money.

The experiences of Illinois and Pennsylvania illustrate the effects of these policies. The crisis in Chicago, of course, demanded immediate action, and an advance of $3 million was made to Illinois within a week of the signing of the Act. In mid-August the state requested $26,279,475 to cover the remainder of the year. The RFC granted $6 million, along with the caution that no further funds would be available unless the state raised some money on its own. The governor called a special session and the legislature did nothing. On September 23, Mayor Cermak appeared before the directors of RFC to ask for $9,050,000. The previous loan would be used up the next day and the relief stations would close. He repeated a now familiar argument. "I want this Commission to know and the Governor to know that the stations should not be closed till after the Militia has been called." The RFC granted $5 million. In October there was another loan of $6,303,-150, in November one of $4,935,072, in December of $7,255,000, and so on. By March 1933, only eight months after the inception of the program, Illinois reached the statutory maximum of $45 million.

Mills, probably the most influential member of RFC's board, was on record against any loan to Pennsylvania. Governor Pinchot, however, demanded $45 million. On August 2, 1932, the governor told the board that Pennsylvania had 1,250,000 persons out of work and 800,000 on part time, with about 1 million dependent on public relief. Private resources had dried up and the state could hardly raise the money to meet the need. Chairman Atlee Pomerene told Pinchot that the RFC could grant Pennsylvania no funds until its tax system was overhauled. Miller read the governor a lecture on local responsibility. Mills demanded to know why Pennsylvania did not raise more money by taxation.

Pinchot left Washington with something besides money. The RFC insisted upon a comprehensive report on the relief-tax situation in the state. He responded with a large report. The RFC found it insufficient and could hardly be charged with indefiniteness in its further demands. Pinchot was asked for a certification by the attorney general that each of the state's sixty-seven counties had exhausted its legal resources for fund raising, a statement on whether the privilege to borrow on delinquent taxes applied to counties of all classes, and a report for each month of 1931 and 1932 for every county on the number of families on relief, nonfamilies on relief, private funds spent, local funds spent, state funds spent, national funds spent, and other funds spent on relief.

Pinchot was incensed. The delay this would cause, he wrote Pomerene on September 8, was "cruel and unnecessary." In fact, it was impossible to obtain all this information in the form requested, and it would take weeks to gather the little that was available. "Our people are not in favor of splitting hairs while children starve." He charged that Congress wrote no red-tape requirements into the statute and that the RFC had no authority to overhaul a state's tax structure as the price of a loan. "I am not asking for a gift but for an advance. I am not asking for this advance as a favor. I am asking for it as the unquestionable right of Pennsylvania under the law of Congress."

Senator Wagner, certainly an authority on the legislative intent, confirmed Pinchot's view of the law. The governor need only certify as to need and the inadequacy of the state's resources. The RFC, Wagner wrote Pinchot, had no authority to initiate an independent investigation or to oversee the administration of relief within a state.

Finally, on September 23, the Corporation made a $2.5 million loan to Pennsylvania. The RFC required that this money should be spent only in the three counties for which the governor had submitted complete reports. Two days later he turned in data for the remaining sixty-four counties, bitingly observing that they were not worth the paper they were written on. They were based on either inaccurate or nonexistent records. On October 4, Pennsylvania received $3,342,183. November brought $5,462,265. The Keystone State was finally on the monthly relief list.

The RFC's policies evoked sharp criticism, especially among social workers. Sophonisba Breckinridge of the School of Social Service Administration of the University of Chicago wrote Pomerene on October 2 of "the bitterness engendered" by the difference between the RFC's treatment of banks and of the jobless. "That at the present moment the grants made should be so limited in amount that the standard of relief already recognized as cruelly, stupidly, and anti-socially inadequate, should have to be reduced is to me inexplicable if not incredible."

The social workers determined to take the lead in formulating new legislation. In the latter part of November they met in Chicago under the chairmanship of Louis T. Brownlow of the Public Administration Clearing House in a conference on the maintenance of welfare standards. They adopted a set of principles that, in effect, condemned the RFC policies and laid the groundwork for a new program. The conference endorsed federal relief, urged grants rather than loans to the states, recommended the development of public agencies to administer relief, and urged the employment of professionally trained social workers.

The RFC policies also produced disaffection among the Democrats and progressive Republicans in Congress. Wagner complained constantly about delay and indifference. He dusted off his old relief bill. La Follette and Costigan dug back into their files as well. With Hoover's defeat in the November elections and the imminent exhaustion of RFC relief funds, it seemed certain that the new Roosevelt Administration would face a relief crisis. Hearings were held by the Senate Manufactures Subcommittee in January and by the Senate Banking and Currency Committee in February 1933. The now familiar parade of social workers and economists appeared to describe the terrible plight of the jobless and to urge a big federal program. While no one knew exactly where the new President stood, his record in Albany suggested that federal unemployment relief might soon be confirmed as the settled policy of the United States.[8]

5

Public relief was the product of labor's suffering during the Great Depression. In the summer of 1932 the concept of private responsibility for unemployment relief officially died, although it lingered in the minds of some. The states, with New York in the forefront, led the way and the federal government followed. Despite the fumbling, inevitable in a democracy, one of labor's most pressing problems was at last being confronted. Institutions were being adapted to social needs. This same impulse was evident in other labor areas — the hours of work, old age pensions, and unemployment insurance.

CHAPTER 15

# The Halting Progress of Reform

PUBLIC RELIEF, though necessary, was an expedient. Even its stanchest supporters recognized it as only a temporary solution for most of those out of work. For the long run, American workers needed permanent protection against the occupational hazards of an industrial society.

Hence mass unemployment stirred the impulse to reform. Americans in growing numbers questioned the organization of economic society, probing for structural weaknesses and exploring potential remedies. The European experience with social legislation received careful scrutiny. In the summer of 1931, for example, Frances Perkins, New York's Industrial Commissioner, visited England for six weeks to study unemployment insurance, as the basis for a report to Governor Roosevelt. Reform organizations won a prominence they had not theretofore enjoyed. John B. Andrews' American Association for Labor Legislation and Abraham Epstein's American Association for Old Age Security suddenly found themselves influential. Labor economists, who had worked for years in academic obscurity, discovered an awakened public interest in their researches. Governors and legislatures now called upon them for advice at the policy level. A notable cluster of these experts was at the University of Wisconsin. The leader of the "Wisconsin school" was the great institutional economist Professor John R. Commons, and among his followers were Arthur Altmeyer, Paul A. Raushenbush, Elizabeth Brandeis, and Edwin E. Witte. Other prominent scholars were Professors Paul H. Douglas of the University of Chicago, William M. Leiserson of the University of Toledo, and Alvin H. Hansen and Roland A. Stevenson of the University of Minnesota. Those active outside academic circles included Bryce M. Stewart and Murray W. Latimer of the Rocke-fellers' Industrial Relations Counselors, Leo Wolman of the Amal-gamated Clothing Workers, and the Ohio actuary, I. M. Rubinow. These experts helped pave the road to reform.

1

In 1929 the hours of work in American industry were long. Only 19 per cent of the wage earners in manufacturing were scheduled for fewer than 48 hours per week; 26.5 per cent were at 48; 31.1 per cent were scheduled between 49 and 54; 15 per cent between 55 and 59; and 7.4 per cent worked a schedule of 60 hours or longer. At this time workers in virtually all the industrialized na-tions of Europe and Australasia enjoyed the eight-hour day. The Soviet Union introduced the seven-hour principle in 1927. A shortening of the work week in American industry was to be ex-pected even if there had been no depression. Unemployment added a note of urgency.

Shorter hours had been a basic goal of the American labor move-ment from its inception. The union doggerel ran:

> *Whether you work by the piece,*
> *Or work by the day,*
> *The longer the hours,*
> *The shorter the pay.*

Historically, the unions had advanced three arguments to support this aim: workers needed leisure to improve themselves cultur-ally and as citizens; long hours impaired health; and, as produc-tivity advanced, available work should be divided among all wage earners with no reduction in hourly wage rates in order to increase employment and raise the standard of living. In the context of the Great Depression the economic argument crowded out the others.

At the outset the labor movement reaffirmed its historic faith in shorter hours. In May 1930 the Railway Employees Depart-ment of the AFL, representing the nonoperating crafts, urged the forty-hour week as the solution to joblessness. In November, the train-service brotherhoods launched a campaign for the six-hour day. At the same time the AFL Metal Trades Department endorsed the five-hour day. The demand for shorter hours was a central theme of the Federation's Boston convention of October 1930. "We have arrived at the period in the history of our nation and of our industrial progress," President Green said, "when the institution of the five day week in all industries outside of the service industries should be immediately inaugurated." The Executive Council called for a reduction in hours per day and endorsed the five-day week in order to reduce unemployment. The metal trades' extreme proposal for the five-hour day was seriously considered, and the convention voted to refer it to the Executive Council for "immediate and thorough consideration."

The unions, already weak in 1929 and staggering under the depression's unemployment, lacked the strength to enforce the demand for shorter hours in collective bargaining. Strikes for this purpose were hopeless. Slight gains were made in government. The City of Pittsburgh, for example, in 1932 imposed the thirty-hour week upon its contractors and subcontractors. At the same time the Government Printing Office instituted the five-day week. The railway unions, though unable to achieve actual gains, persuaded Congress to direct the Interstate Commerce Commission to investigate the feasibility of the six-hour day in railroad transportation. In 1932 the ICC reported that it was operationally practicable but would result in a substantial rise in costs.

A handful of nonunion firms reduced hours unilaterally. The Snow King Baking Powder Company went on five days in 1929; the Standard Oil Company of New Jersey adopted the forty-hour week in 1930; the Kellogg Company instituted the six-hour day in 1930, as did the India Tire and Rubber Company and the Owens-Illinois Glass Company in 1932; and several of the automobile manufacturers cut scheduled hours. These instances were exceptional. A Bureau of Labor Statistics survey in 1932 revealed that only 5.4 per cent of 44,025 establishments had adopted the five-day week for all or part of their employees.[1]

A few unions, especially in the needle and printing trades, adopted work-sharing. This, of course, differed from a reduction in scheduled hours. The shrinking number of actual working hours was spread over a larger number of people, with no advance in hourly wage rates. A consequence was lower earnings for the employed. Work-sharing was an expedient rather than a reform. The part-time schedule was temporary; if employment picked up, the shop would return to the old schedule. For these and other reasons many unions opposed share-the-work. The International Brotherhood of Electrical Workers, for example, denounced it as a device "to make the poor keep the poor." President A. F. Whitney of the Railroad Trainmen wrote Green that "the reduction of all working men to an equal state of poverty is not the solution that should be sought by the representatives of labor. . . . This is communism in its worst form — equal sharing of poverty."

Nevertheless, some unions espoused share-the-work. The Amalgamated Clothing Workers had a long-standing policy of equal division of work in periods of seasonal unemployment. This practice was continued during the depression, supplemented in New York City by a rule forbidding working members to take overtime so long as some were jobless. The printers' unions in many cities voted that each employed member should yield a certain number of working hours per week to the idle. President Charles Howard of the Typographical Union defended this policy on the ground that it was preferable to assessing the employed for the relief of the jobless. Early in 1932, the Printing Pressmen of New York City and their employers agreed to a work-spreading program to give some employment to 1200 jobless union members.[2]

Share-the-work, of course, won enthusiastic support among many employers. The National Association of Manufacturers and numerous large corporations embraced the program. Both the Woods and Gifford committees urged industry to adopt work-sharing. By the early fall of 1931, American Telephone and Telegraph had put salaried employees on the five-day week, thereby reducing incomes by one eleventh; Bethlehem Steel had severely curtailed the hours of both blue- and white-collar people; General Electric was on short time; Goodyear required salaried employees to take two weeks off without pay; International Harvester and Jersey Standard cut hours; United States Rubber reduced salaries one eleventh by eliminating the sixth day; at Westinghouse most wage earners were on part time, and salaried employees had Friday and Saturday off without remuneration, lost their paid vacations, and were given two- to four-week holidays without compensation. The movement grew as employment shrank. A survey by the Commerce Department in early 1933 suggested that four fifths of the nation's employers had adopted work-sharing and that one fourth of those employed owed their part-time jobs to it.

Share-the-work, in fact, became a low-key employer crusade and gained a prophet. He was L. C. Walker, proprietor of the Shaw-Walker Company and other enterprises as well as vice-chairman of the Share-the-Work Movement. The nation's problem, as he saw it, stemmed from the great advances in technology that displaced labor. Full employment would not return for many years, if ever. There were alternatives: share-the-work or public relief. Walker reasoned, "If we have not enough work to keep everybody working full time, the next best thing is to keep everybody employed part time." In his view, share-the-work provided economic security, removed the fear of loss of job, and gave workers an incentive to spend rather than save. Walker denied that work-spreading shifted the burden of relief to the wage earners. Employed workers, he argued, paid the bulk of taxes. Their choice was between supporting the jobless by part-time employment or by public relief. Since industry was inherently more efficient than government, the cost to employed wage earners would be less if they shared jobs than if they paid the taxes to finance the "dole."

The White House accepted this economic doctrine. On August 26, 1932, Hoover convened in Washington a national conference of banking and industrial leaders from the twelve Federal Reserve districts. "It is doubtful," the President told them, "whether any action we could take at this time would so greatly accelerate our progress, serve the welfare of our unemployed millions, or so quickly give us as a nation the benefit of widespread spending power as further spread of equitable plans of sharing the available work." He named Walter C. Teagle, president of Jersey Standard, as chairman of his share-the-work committee.

Teagle announced the goal of putting a million men back to work. The committee's slogan was "Job security by job sharing." The oilman took to the radio to explain the economics of his plan: A company employed eight men at $125 a month, making a total wage bill of $1000. The workers spent $800 and saved $200. If hours were cut 10 per cent, the individual's monthly earnings would decline to $112.50. A ninth man could then join them at $100 a month. The payroll would remain at $1000, but now only $100 would be saved instead of $200. It sounded more persuasive if one did not think about it.

Whether the Teagle Committee effectively encouraged work-spreading or merely blessed an existing tendency of employers it is not possible to say. The Committee did announce the names of several cooperating firms: General Motors, Socony-Vacuum, Metropolitan Life.

Share-the-work, with both its economics and its equity suspect, received severe criticism. Ernest G. Draper, an executive of Hills Brothers, pointed out two defects: most workers had nothing but hardship to share since they were already at the subsistence level; work-spreading could not create jobs because it did not increase purchasing power. Professor Sumner H. Slichter described sharing as a device to impose an unfair burden on those fortunate enough to have jobs. Professor R. A. Stevenson supplied a graphic illustration:

> Mr. S. is a factory operative who is about 57 years of age and has a family of three grown children. He had been thrifty, had followed the advice of civic leaders in saving enough to purchase a home and had a little margin left. He was put on the spread-work program . . . receiving less than fifty per cent of his regular wages. This has not been enough for him to maintain even a decent standard of living. He has exhausted his savings, and now . . . finds it necessary to place a mortgage on his home in order to secure the necessary food and clothing for himself and wife. The spread-work program is compelling him to contribute over fifty per cent of his income and to dissipate his life savings in order to share with others the job which he would hold on a full-time basis otherwise.

The *New Republic* in October 1932 suggested that Teagle share the presidency of Standard Oil with an independent oil operator and that Hoover and Roosevelt share the White House! [3]

Although Green allowed his name to be used by the Teagle

Committee and was severely criticized within the labor movement for doing so, both he and the AFL were fundamentally interested in the traditional goal of shorter hours. On July 24, 1931, in fact, Green had urged Hoover to call a White House conference of representatives of industry and labor to establish the five-day week and a shorter workday. The President did not even bother to reply. He referred the letter to Gifford, who in turn passed it on to Harry A. Wheeler, chairman of the Committee on Employment Plans of the President's Organization on Unemployment Relief. Almost two months elapsed before Wheeler acknowledged Green's missive by asking for clarification of a minor point. Thus the Federation's proposal was allowed to sink into the bureaucratic sands.

A year later Green tried again. This time he called upon the President personally. He wrote the AFL Executive Council on July 29, 1932, that he came away from the White House with the impression that Hoover was sympathetic and would call a labor-management conference on hours of work in the near future. Whether this was external deception or self-delusion is not known. Green's expectation came to nothing. The President's only response was the Teagle Committee and share-the-work.

The AFL convention that gathered in Cincinnati at the end of November 1932 faced a fundamental policy decision on hours of work. Gompers had taught that the state should regulate the hours of women and children only; men should bargain for themselves through trade unions. His successors had faithfully adhered to this voluntaristic philosophy. But it had not proved itself. Hours were onerously and, from an economic viewpoint, absurdly long; the decisive segments of American industry were beyond the Federation's reach; even in the organized sector the AFL was powerless to strike; and President Hoover had refused to cooperate by calling a joint conference of industry and labor on hours. If somehow the Gompers ideological legacy could be waved away, a route remained open — legislation. Its prospect had recently brightened. In the presidential election a few weeks earlier the voters had repudiated Hoover and the Republican Party. On March 4, 1933, there would be a new occupant of the White House and a new, Democratic Congress.

In this setting Green opened the Cincinnati convention by calling for a reformed work schedule — the five-day week and the six-hour day. "It would ... electrify this whole economic situation," he declared, "if this great reform ... was accepted and applied immediately." The Committee on the Shorter Workday reported "with all the earnestness possible ... the overwhelming importance of an immediate reduction in the hours of labor as a condition absolutely essential to the restoration and maintenance of prosperity." Technology had displaced labor, leaving millions of workers jobless and so unable to consume. "One must marvel at the sheer absurdity of the whole situation." Hours must go down and wages go up if production and consumption were to come into balance. Conditions "compel a great forward movement." The Committee called for the five-day week and the six-hour day with no reduction in weekly wages.

The response from the floor was enthusiastic. President W. D. Mahon of the Street Railway Employees spoke glowingly of the report. His only fear was that it "will go out to the world as another one of our declarations and there it will end." He urged bringing it forcefully to public attention. President Howard of the Typographical Union echoed these views. Green then made an impassioned speech for the five-day week that brought the delegates to their feet in warm applause. Finally, the convention unanimously adopted a resolution favoring shorter hours that included this significant language: "That we instruct our Executive Council to take all necessary steps toward having proper legislation ... presented to the incoming session of congress...." Although neither the Committee nor the delegates on the floor had discussed legislation or voluntarism, the convention had voted decisively to seek the aid of the state in regulating the hours of work for men. Gompers had been gently reversed.[4]

On December 21, 1932, less than three weeks after the close of the Cincinnati convention, Senator Hugo L. Black of Alabama introduced the thirty-hour bill in the dying 72d Congress. This measure would have denied the channels of interstate and foreign commerce to articles produced in establishments "in which any person was employed or permitted to work more than five days in any week or more than six hours in any day." The Black bill was remarkably simple. More important, according to the sober Brookings Institution economists Harold G. Moulton and Maurice Leven, "no legislative proposal has ever been advanced which is more revolutionary in its economic and social implications." Even a year or two earlier no one would have taken the bill seriously. At this time — with 14 million wage earners jobless, the banking system on the edge of collapse, and congressmen proposing that the government deny patents to inventions that displaced labor — the thirty-hour bill was earnestly debated. Moreover, there was an excellent chance that the 73d Congress would enact it.

Hearings opened before Senator Norris' friendly subcommittee of the Senate Judiciary Committee on January 5, 1933. Green, the first witness, argued that the compulsory thirty-hour week was indispensable to the recovery of the nation's prostrate economy. He predicted that it would create 6.5 million jobs. Vice-President Philip Murray of the United Mine Workers agreed. He was concerned, however, about the absence of a floor under wages. If workers organized, unions would protect their wages. Hence he suggested an amendment to guarantee the right to organize and to outlaw the yellow-dog contract, which, he said, persisted despite the Norris–La Guardia Act. The bill also won the support of the Textile Workers, the Hosiery Workers, several railway unions, and a handful of textile, hosiery, and furniture employers.

Most of industry, of course, vigorously opposed the Black bill. James A. Emery, general counsel of the National Association of Manufacturers, attacked it both as bad economics and as unconstitutional. With respect to the latter he lavished special attention upon the child labor case. In *Hammer* v. *Dagenhart*, as noted in Chapter 4, the Supreme Court in 1918 had struck down the federal law regulating the number of hours children might work as exceeding the power of Congress under the commerce clause. Emery concluded that Congress had no more authority to legislate over the hours of "any person" than it had over the hours of children. In fact, the bill's supporters agreed with Emery. Black himself was much disturbed by *Hammer* v. *Dagenhart*. Henry Warrum, counsel for the Mine Workers, admitted that the measure was currently unconstitutional. He hoped that the Supreme Court would reverse itself. The tribunal had divided narrowly by five to four in 1918 and there had been changes in its membership in the intervening fourteen years.[5]

There was no hope of enacting the thirty-hour bill in the expiring 72d Congress. Hence the Judiciary Committee withheld its report until after the new legislature convened on March 4, 1933.

## 2

The year 1929 marked a turning point in the history of the old age pension movement in the United States. The number of old people had recently risen sharply. According to the census of 1920 there were 4,933,000 persons aged sixty-five and over; by 1930 the number had increased to 6,639,000. Their proportion of the population advanced from 4.7 per cent in 1920 to 5.4 per cent in 1930. At the same time the shift from self-employment in agriculture to working for an employer in industry, the speed of modern machinery, and discrimination by employers combined to shrink the employment opportunities for older workers. Many who left the labor force lacked the means to finance retirement. For those over sixty-five in 1930, I. M. Rubinow estimated that 1.9 million held no property, 2.4 million had no earnings, and 1.2 million had neither. These numbers must have increased substantially as the depression deepened. The traditional methods of supporting the aged — care by children and almshouses — were unsatisfactory. Many people of advanced years had no children, or their children refused to help. County almshouses were a national disgrace. Some mixed the aged indiscriminately with the insane and the incurably diseased. Far too many were firetraps and filthy, the products of public neglect. The almshouse, furthermore, was a very expensive device.

In the twenties, as we observed in Chapter 4, interest in the problems of the aged grew. The American Association for Labor Legislation and the Fraternal Order of Eagles lobbied in the states for pension laws. In 1926–27, Abraham Epstein, an authority on social insurance who had advised the Eagles, founded the American Association for Old Age Security, which soon became a center of information and activity. In 1929 the American Federation of Labor at its Toronto convention reversed Gompers and endorsed government pensions. In the same year California enacted the first mandatory pension statute. The states that had acted earlier had adopted the county-option system: the state left the decision to accept or reject pensions to the county and the latter was required to carry the burdens of administration and cost. As a result, few counties adopted pension systems and the number of beneficiaries was infinitesimal. The California law, however, obligated the counties to establish programs and the state paid half their cost. The consequence was a sharp increase in the number of pensioners. Further, a precedent was set that no state could henceforth ignore.

Employers, who opposed most reforms in the labor area, were divided on old age pensions. The National Association of Manufacturers was reliably negative. The insurance companies vigorously opposed public intrusion into what they considered a private preserve. But many employers, some prominent, worked actively for pensions. Gerard Swope, president of General Electric, was an eager advocate. Alfred I. du Pont of the chemical dynasty led the pension movement in Delaware and was vice-president of Epstein's organization. Both the Hearst and Scripps-Howard newspaper chains supported public pension systems. Industrial Relations Counselors, Inc., sponsored Murray W. Latimer's massive study, *Industrial Pension Systems*.

Latimer revealed that in 1929 there were 397 companies, mainly large ones, with pension plans that covered 3,745,418 employees. This latter figure was a little less than 15 per cent of the wage and salary earners in industry and commerce. The systems clustered in the railroad, public utility, steel, oil, and chemical industries. By and large, he found, they were inadequately financed, were actuarially unsound, failed to provide legal safeguards with respect to funds or the rights of employees, and lacked definite administrative procedures for carrying out their terms. Further, most of the plans were defective in requiring excessive continuous service and in establishing an abnormally high retirement age, usually seventy. Many systems discriminated, paying out disproportionately more to executives than to wage earners. These defects became painfully evident in the early depression years. To meet their pension obligations, companies tapped current revenues because reserves were inadequate. A number of plans were abandoned; pensions, especially on the railroads, were cut; workers eligible for retirement were retained in employment to reduce costs. Latimer held out no hope that these voluntary plans would solve the problems of the aged. Even if the defects he had uncovered were remedied, the plans could operate successfully only in those few large firms with a stable labor force and a business that was relatively insensitive to the cycle. "The movement," he wrote, "is unlikely ever to embrace more than a minor fraction of the whole. . . . Voluntary provision of complete old age security by industry, under a business economy in which the criterion of success . . . is profits, inevitably involves inescapable contradictions."[6]

An increasing number of Americans agreed with Latimer: only government could establish an inclusive system of old age pensions. Hence the public pension movement grew steadily during the Great Depression, making modest legislative gains.

Early in 1930, Senator Clarence C. Dill of Washington and Representative William P. Connery, Jr., of Massachusetts introduced a federal old age pension bill drafted by the American Association for Old Age Security. It sought to stimulate state action by offering federal grants-in-aid equal to one third of the cost of pensions. Persons over sixty-two would be eligible for benefits ranging from $4 to $8 a week. The House Committee on Labor held hearings on the Dill-Connery bill in February, the first congressional investigation ever conducted on this issue. The list of supporters was impressive: Representatives Hamilton Fish, James Mead, and William Sirovich of New York, Rabbi Stephen S. Wise (the noted leader of liberal Judaism), the American Association for Labor Legislation, the Association for Old Age Security, the AFL, and the railroad brotherhoods (Doak was their spokesman). The NAM provided the only significant opposition. James A. Emery simply argued that federal pensions were unconstitutional. The sponsors hardly expected favorable action from the 71st Congress; with the hearings they were preparing the ground for the future.

Meantime, the movement made gains in the states. In his campaign for the governorship of New York in 1928, Franklin D.

Roosevelt had endorsed old age pensions. In February 1929 he called upon the legislature to create a commission to investigate and draft a bill to deal with security for the aged. He proposed a pension system based upon the insurance principle to which urban workers would contribute, as well as an overhaul of rural almshouses. The legislature set up the New York State Commission on Old Age Security with Senator Seabury Mastick as chairman. The American Association for Labor Legislation and the Eagles had converted Mastick into an enthusiastic pension advocate. The Commission consisted of three senators, two assemblymen, and six prominent citizens. At the hearings in the fall of 1929 the witnesses, except those representing insurance companies, were overwhelmingly in favor of pensions. Their testimony received a good press. The Commission reported in March 1930, recommending state-wide pensions but without the contributory feature Roosevelt had urged. Mastick then introduced bills that passed both houses unanimously and were signed by the governor with some reluctance on April 10. Following the California lead, the legislation created a mandatory system with financing shared equally by state and county. The pensionable age was seventy and a person must have resided ten years in the state to qualify. The Department of Social Welfare supervised the system, and the Board of Charities was empowered to condemn and close county almshouses, of which the Commission had taken an exceedingly dim view.

In 1930 politicians began to exploit the pension issue. Roosevelt, in a speech to the Governors' Conference in Salt Lake City on June 30, an important stop on his road to the presidential nomination, strongly urged old age benefits. Although the press gave greater prominence to his endorsement of unemployment insurance, Roosevelt had already linked the two into the system that Epstein was later to call "social security." In anticipation of the 1930 elections, the Democratic Party in New Jersey, Rhode Island, New Hampshire, Delaware, Nebraska, and Idaho and the Republican Party in Michigan, Maryland, Texas, and Pennsylvania supported state legislation. The number of newspapers that lent their editorial backing to the pension movement grew constantly.

Massachusetts enacted a mandatory pension law in 1930. The state supplied one third of the funds, and the localities the remainder. The pensionable age was seventy and the residence requirement was twenty years. In 1931 more than 100 bills were introduced into the state legislatures. Delaware, New Jersey, Idaho, and New Hampshire enacted mandatory laws. The state provided 100 per cent of the financing in Delaware and 75 per cent in New Jersey. West Virginia passed a county-option statute. Wisconsin and Colorado converted their voluntary systems to a mandatory base. The year 1932 witnessed a slowing of the state movement. The courts held the Colorado law unconstitutional. The only gain was in Missouri where the voters by referendum amended the constitution to empower the legislature to enact a pension law.

The results of this activity began to be evident. In 1928 only 1221 aged persons received public pensions, in the amount of $222,559. By 1932 the number of beneficiaries had risen to 102,537 and the money disbursed to $22,616,004. New York, however, accounted for more than half the number of pensioners and the money benefits. The new state programs demonstrated conclusively that the cost of supporting an aged person was substantially lower on a pension than in an almshouse.

In 1932 there was limited advance at the federal level. The Dill-Connery bill was reintroduced. The House Labor Committee unanimously recommended passage and the Senate Committee on Pensions reported favorably. Hoover had no sympathy for the proposed legislation. In 1931, in fact, he had named several officials of the Metropolitan Life Insurance Company as a government committee to visit Europe to study foreign experience with social insurance. Epstein was incensed. It was as though the President had appointed "Al Capone and a commission of bootleggers to report on the workings of the prohibition law." The Dill-Connery bill failed to come to a vote in either house before the expiration of the 72d Congress.[7]

## 3

The reform issue that stirred greatest interest was unemployment insurance. For workers it related directly to their prime concern with joblessness. Employers feared it more than shorter hours and pensions. To the labor movement it was decisive in the ideological controversy over voluntarism. Left-wingers made it their number one political issue.

At the beginning of the Great Depression there was no American experience with public unemployment insurance. This was in sharp contrast with all other important industrial nations as well as with many small countries. Great Britain, for example, enacted the National Insurance Act in 1911. It was a compulsory scheme, with approximately equal contributions from worker, employer, and government. In 1929 it covered all wage earners except farm workers, domestic servants, and public employees, a total of almost 12 million. An out-of-work man received a benefit of 17 shillings a week and a woman got 15 shillings.

Experimentation in the United States was restricted to voluntary plans. Insurance companies considered unemployment an uninsurable risk and refused to write policies. Between 1916 and 1929, fourteen employers with twenty-nine establishments unilaterally introduced jobless insurance or employment guarantees. The mortality of these plans was high. By 1929 only eight survived, with a coverage of 5500 workers. More than half this number were under Procter & Gamble's guaranteed work plan, which was not true unemployment insurance. Union payment of out-of-work benefits began in 1831 but never became widespread. At the time of the crash some forty-five locals, thirty of which were in the printing trades, and three tiny internationals paid benefits. Much the most important systems were created by collective bargaining. The wallpaper industry plan, which began in 1894, promised forty weeks of employment a year. The agreement between the Cleveland Garment Manufacturers and the Ladies' Garment Workers guaranteed forty-one weeks of work. The Chicago Men's Clothing Association and the Amalgamated Clothing Workers in 1923 created the first genuine insurance scheme. The clothing markets in Rochester and New York City followed in 1928. The lace, millinery, straw hat, and cleaning and dyeing industries experimented with similar arrangements. These negotiated plans covered 63,000 workers.

The voluntary principle made some progress during the depression. In June 1930, Swope announced the General Electric unemployment program. Some 4500 employees in the twelve lamp works were guaranteed fifty weeks of employment; 45,000 people in twelve apparatus plants were placed under unemployment insurance. The system was contributory; benefits were half of earnings but not to exceed $20 a week for twelve weeks. The GE plan was the most carefully thought out company scheme and much the largest. Governor Roosevelt cheered Swope on enthusiastically from the sidelines.

In 1930, as well, five firms with 300 workers in Fond du Lac, Wisconsin, followed the GE example. In February 1931 fourteen companies in Rochester, New York, announced a plan covering 28,000 employees. Marion Folsom of Eastman Kodak was the architect of this arrangement. Hills Brothers, J. I. Case, and the Minnesota Mining and Manufacturing Company also experimented with private insurance in 1931–32.

Despite this progress, voluntary unemployment insurance was no substitute for a public system. Employer, union, and negotiated plans combined never covered as much as 1 per cent of the labor force. The depression exacted a heavy toll. Many of the older schemes, which were inherently defective, were abandoned. In 1932 even General Electric was forced by economic circumstance to convert from unemployment insurance to a relief-in-kind system. The Rochester plan did not actually take effect during the Great Depression. Persons seriously concerned with insuring the economic risk of unemployment, Swope among them, became convinced that private action was no solution. Swope, in fact, went so far as to argue with Green and Woll in order to overcome their prejudice, but they were not persuaded.[8]

In 1930 the American Association for Labor Legislation considered the time ripe to press for a public system. Early in the year John B. Andrews of AALL tried to persuade Senator Wagner to add an unemployment insurance bill to the program outlined in Chapter 6. The senator refused on the ground that opponents of his statistical, public works, and employment exchange measures would use the "entering wedge" argument against those less controversial matters. "It is ... inadvisable," Wagner wrote, "to frighten away possible support by the introduction of other legislation which they are not yet ready to follow."

It seemed more fruitful to begin at the state level. Andrews obtained the advice of a distinguished group of authorities in drafting a model state bill. They included Stewart, Douglas, Commons, Frances Perkins, Sir William Beveridge, the British social insurance expert, Sidney Hillman and Leo Wolman of the Amalgamated Clothing Workers, Morris E. Leeds, the Philadelphia industrialist, Ernest G. Draper of Hills Brothers, and Professor Joseph P. Chamberlain of the Columbia Law School.

On December 21, 1930, the Association announced "An American Plan for Unemployment Reserve Funds." The organization had lavished as much care on the title as a young mother in naming her first child. The suspect phrase "unemployment insurance" was nowhere in evidence. In fact, the scheme was not insurance, a matter of concern to insurance advocates like Douglas. The name "American Plan," obviously, was stolen from the antiunion crusade of the early twenties. Noel Sargent of the National Association of Manufacturers wrote rather sternly to Andrews in protest. The Labor Legislation Association wished to remove any suspicion that the origins of the bill were foreign; or, as Andrews wrote Governor Roosevelt, "It is developed out of *American* experience."

"An American Plan" was based upon the principles of limited liability, segregation of funds by industry, and self-administration by the industry. The employer would contribute 1.5 per cent of his payroll to an industry reserve fund. The employee would not contribute. The maximum benefit was $10 a week for no more than thirteen weeks. To qualify, the worker must have been employed for at least twenty-six weeks in the preceding two years. Strikers were not eligible for benefits. The employer who stabilized employment would receive a refund from the reserve.

During 1931 this model bill was introduced into the legislatures of eighteen states. None acted favorably. In most the sentiment against any form of unemployment benefits was still too great. In the three states in which prospects were brightest — New York, Ohio, and Wisconsin — An American Plan was not acceptable. Governor Roosevelt was committed to the contributory and insurance principles; key Ohio figures — Leiserson and Rubinow — concurred about insurance; and Wisconsin had its own peculiar tradition arising out of Commons' work.[9]

## 4

The New York governor was the first major political figure in the nation to commit himself to unemployment insurance. Roosevelt's address to the governors at Salt Lake City on June 30, 1930, dealt with joblessness: "Some form of insurance seems to be the only answer. Unemployment insurance we shall come to in this country just as certainly as we have come to workmen's compensation for industrial injury." He would sidestep two pitfalls: the handout that encouraged idleness and the underwriting of joblessness out of current governmental revenues. "It is clear to me, first," the governor said, "that unemployment insurance must be placed on an actuarial basis, and secondly, that contribution must be made by the workers themselves." He expected the system to be self-supporting.

Roosevelt carried the fight to the enemy. He urged upon the New York Federation of Labor a state system of unemployment insurance. Some might call him "Bolshevistic," but he was speaking "as part of a humanitarian movement." He told the Life Underwriters Association that the time had come to enact jobless insurance, and that it could be placed on an actuarial basis.

On November 14, 1930, Roosevelt's Committee for the Stabilization of Industry reported that unemployment insurance deserved "patient, full and fair-minded investigation." The governor, under Miss Perkins' urging, decided to seize this opportunity to call an eastern regional interstate conference on unemployment to meet in Albany. Roosevelt, concerned lest the other governors consider his leadership a diminution of their status, had Miss Perkins sound them out through their labor commissioners. Six were receptive. Miss Perkins engaged Paul Douglas to prepare an agenda and work materials for the conference. Roosevelt and Douglas hit it off at once and the governor quickly digested the ideas and facts the professor presented. Roosevelt issued invitations to the chief executives of Massachusetts, Rhode Island, Connecticut, New Jersey, Pennsylvania, and Ohio to meet for three days in the New York capital in January 1931. The agenda covered employment exchanges, public works, standardization of labor laws, workmen's compensation, taxation, and "the study of unemployment insurance in its broad aspects."

Governors Joseph B. Ely, Norman S. Case, Wilbur L. Cross, Morgan F. Larson, Gifford Pinchot, and George White assembled in Albany under Roosevelt's leadership on January 23, 1931. Jobless insurance became the key issue at once. Leiserson told the governors that it was a logical extension of workmen's compensation, that it was a reserve for labor analogous to a money reserve for capital, and that, unlike relief, which was a subsidy to industry, it was a direct charge upon business. Douglas urged an insurance system with contributions by employees. Chamberlain argued that legislation could be drafted to meet the constitutional test. James D. Craig of the Metropolitan Life Insurance Company said that seasonal unemployment might be placed on an actuarial basis, but was doubtful about other forms of joblessness. The conference served to focus the growing public interest in unemployment insurance. Roosevelt, according to Miss Perkins, achieved a brilliant personal and political success.

The conference voted to create the Interstate Commission on Unemployment Insurance, a body of technical experts, to explore the problem exhaustively. On May 29, 1931, the governors announced their representatives: Wolman for New York, A. Lincoln Filene for Massachusetts, Leiserson for Ohio, Labor Commissioner Charles R. Blunt for New Jersey, Professor C. A. Kulp for Pennsylvania, Professor Eliot D. Smith for Connecticut, and Labor Commissioner Daniel McLaughlin for Rhode Island.[10]

Meantime, controversy developed in Albany over the issue. On March 3, Senator Mastick and Assemblyman Irwin Steingut introduced the model bill of the Association for Labor Legislation. It achieved the remarkable effect of uniting the National Association of Manufacturers and the State Federation of Labor in opposition. Roosevelt, of course, objected to it. Hence, on March 25, he sent a message to the legislature urging creation of a small state commission to investigate unemployment insurance, consisting mainly of two or three legislators and experts named by the governor. The Republican legislature was in no mood to heed his advice. It established the Joint Legislative (Marcy) Committee on Unemployment with a majority of legislative members. The

Republicans then proceeded to pass the Dunmore bill, which would have given private insurance companies preference in writing unemployment insurance. The underwriters and the NAM sponsored the measure. While the New York Federation of Labor opposed it, the AFL was silent. When Andrews urged Green to denounce it, he was rewarded with a sermon on voluntarism and the iniquities of public unemployment insurance. On April 14, Roosevelt vetoed the Dunmore bill. "It would be inconsistent now to provide for one form of unemployment insurance and thus discriminate against other proposals. . . ." If the bill were enacted, the governor reasoned, private companies could claim that they had pre-empted the field and there was no longer room for a public system.

The Marcy Committee did not even hold hearings until November 1931. In the interval Roosevelt sent Miss Perkins to England and received her report on October 23. She was persuaded that jobless insurance was adaptable to the American environment and urged creation of an interstate insurance authority to administer a common fund on behalf of the participating states. Miss Perkins concluded:

> Unemployment insurance is not in any sense a cure for unemployment, but . . . it is a technique of extending a well-known principle, to offer some protection for the individual against the hazard of unemployment, which as an individual, he can in no way foresee or prevent. It arises out of the economic organization of society, in which he must work. It will ease the burden of the individual in the face of this industrial hazard, and it will immensely relieve the community of the cost of poor relief and charity in periods of unemployment. For while it cannot meet the total cost of unemployment relief, it will meet a very significant portion of that cost, even in a period of great depression, such as the one in which we are now.

Although the Republicans in control of the Marcy Committee dutifully listened to expert testimony, they had no intention of reporting a bill. Time, the Committee said, was needed for study. Early in 1932, Mastick and Steingut reintroduced their measure, certain that it had no chance of passage.

On February 15, 1932, the Interstate Commission on Unemployment Insurance issued its report to the governors. The Rhode Island representative had dropped out; though Leiserson disagreed quite fundamentally, he signed the report in the interest of unanimity. "Our proposals," the experts wrote, "are extremely modest." They recommended: compulsory state-wide systems of unemployment reserves; employer contributions of 2 per cent of payroll with no contributions by employees; individual employer reserves; a maximum benefit of half of earnings or $10 a week, whichever was lower, for no more than ten weeks in any year; a limitation of the employer's liability to the amount of his own reserve; a decline in the employer's contribution rate to 1 per cent when the reserve per employee reached $50 and to zero when it was $75; and state custody, investment, and disbursement of the fund.

Though Roosevelt could hardly have been pleased with this report, he warmly congratulated the authors and transmitted it to the legislature with the hope that it would lead to a law. He got nowhere. The Marcy Committee had corked the jobless insurance bottle to allow its contents to age.

In the summer of 1932, the Democratic National Convention endorsed state unemployment insurance. Roosevelt, in his presidential campaign in October, reaffirmed his support. The successful Democratic candidate for governor of New York, Herbert H. Lehman, had believed in jobless insurance for years. The AFL at its Cincinnati convention in the fall dramatically reversed itself on the issue, and the New York Federation seemed to trot obediently behind.

When the legislature convened in Albany in January 1933, therefore, it seemed that New York at last would take action. The Marcy Committee, doubtless sensing these pressures, announced that it would report a bill. But governor-elect Lehman, to Andrews' horror, declared that it was impractical to launch an insurance scheme at the moment when joblessness was at the highest level in history. The State Federation of Labor brought in the Byrne bill, which would have paid benefits to strikers. This was certain to stiffen the opposition of employers and alienate many long-time supporters of jobless insurance. The press said that labor's objective was to frustrate legislation. The Marcy Committee could not fail to seize the opportunity. On February 19, 1933, the Committee reversed itself; this was not the time to enact jobless insurance. Despite three years of arduous effort, Governor Roosevelt left Albany empty-handed.[11]

## 5

The achievement of Ohio was equally dismal. That state, however, made a notable contribution in the area of ideas, significant for the future development of jobless insurance.

The Ohio movement began in the summer of 1930 with the formation of the Cleveland Committee for Unemployment Insurance under the chairmanship of Rabbi Abba Hillel Silver. The Committee drafted a bill that Senator James A. Reynolds introduced into the Ohio legislature. He then held hearings that attracted considerable publicity. Although Reynolds failed to pry the measure out of committee, he did get a joint resolution establishing the eleven-member Ohio Commission on Unemployment Insurance "to investigate the practicability and advisability of setting up unemployment reserves or insurance funds . . . and to recommend what form of legislation, if any, may be wise or suitable. . . ."

Governor George White was an irresolute supporter of jobless insurance. He had, of course, participated in Roosevelt's Albany conference and had named Leiserson to the technical commission. But he had no ambition to make Ohio the pioneer state. The fact that its employers and farmers opposed unemployment insurance more bitterly than those in New York and Wisconsin may have restrained him. White did, however, appoint capable people to the Ohio Commission, notably Leiserson as chairman, Miss Elizabeth S. Magee as secretary, and Rubinow as member. Douglas later characterized its massive two-volume report, published at the end of 1932, as "by all odds the best American study of the question which had been made." Henceforth no discussion of jobless insurance could afford to ignore the "Ohio plan."

"We find," the Commission reported, "that unemployment insurance is not only desirable and practical, but that the state cannot safely face the employment insecurity of the future without preparing for it by a compulsory system of insurance." Insurance, as the experience with workmen's compensation demonstrated, was the soundest and cheapest way to deal with the hazard. Company reserves were more costly and an insufficient incentive to the employer to stabilize production. Moreover, even perfect regularization of employment would not eliminate unemployment.

Since an insurance system in a democratic society should be self-supporting and preserve the worker's self-respect, the plan must be contributory. The Commission recommended contributions by employer and employee respectively of 2 and 1 per cent, the heavier burden falling upon industry because it was responsible for joblessness. On condition that business recovered, the payment of premiums would begin January 1, 1934. The Commission bowed modestly to the popular company-reserve principle by proposing graduated contribution rates by employers from 1 to 3.5 per cent commencing January 1, 1937, by which date there would be accumulated experience with the steadiness of employment of individual companies. The insurance fund would meet administrative expenses, including those of the existing state-city employment offices.

The combined contribution of 3 per cent would finance a benefit of 50 per cent of earnings not exceeding $15 a week for sixteen weeks. The waiting period was three weeks. To qualify, the insured must have worked twenty-six weeks in the preceding year or forty weeks in the preceding two years. Strikers would be ineligible for benefits. All wage and salary earners with annual incomes of $2000 or less would be covered excepting farmers, farm laborers, domestic servants, teachers, government employees, casual laborers, and those in establishments with fewer than three employees.

A Commission on Unemployment Insurance of three members named by the governor would administer the insurance system and the employment exchanges. The Commission would invest its funds exclusively in securities of the United States and Ohio and in school-district bonds within the state.

The Leiserson Commission made an actuarial estimate of what would have happened if this scheme had been put into effect a decade earlier. The reserve in 1929 would have totaled $104 million. This sum combined with current income would have permitted a distribution of $180 million during the first two depression years. The reserve would have run out in 1932. At that time the state could have applied to the Reconstruction Finance Corporation for a loan, as private insurance companies had done.

The Ohio report had no immediate legislative effect. The press in the state, excepting the Scripps-Howard papers, buried the story. The Ohio Chamber of Commerce launched an abusive attack upon Rubinow as a Russian Bolshevik and a fake actuary. "I committed the crime," Rubinow wrote Andrews, "of having been born in Russia (my only defense being Mother couldn't help it)." He was not a member of the Actuarial Society of America because its membership was confined to life insurance actuaries and he did not practice in that field. He was, however, the founder and past president of the Casualty Actuarial Society.

Governor White ended the hope for legislation in January 1933 by announcing that the time was unripe for so ambitious a program, and recommended another study commission to report in two years! When Douglas wrote Rubinow about a dog-tax analogy to unemployment insurance, Rubinow replied that he was looking for a dog that would go to Columbus and bite Governor White.[12]

6

John R. Commons was the decisive influence in Wisconsin. He had written the state's workmen's compensation law, enacted in 1911, and his student, Arthur Altmeyer, was secretary of the administrative agency, the Wisconsin Industrial Commission. The statute's major feature was experience rating, the employer's contribution rate varying directly with the accident record in his plant. This was naturally an incentive to reduce the number of accidents. After World War I, Commons applied the same principle to unemployment. The goal, again, was prevention rather than relief, to induce the employer to stabilize employment by offering him a financial incentive by a flexible contribution rate. Hence Commons rejected the European precedent based on contributions by employee and state as well as by employer. The idea was both original and ingenious. It was also, as Commons wrote, "extraordinarily an individualistic and capitalistic scheme," adapted to the American mood of the twenties.

In 1921 Senator Henry Huber introduced the Commons bill into the Wisconsin legislature. That maverick within the AFL, the Wisconsin Federation of Labor, was the main backer. Nevertheless, the bill met defeat in 1921 and in each succeeding session of the legislature during the decade. In 1931, Paul Raushenbush, a student of Commons' and an economist at the state university, redrafted the old measure. Major changes were individual company reserves rather than a state-wide fund and a limit on the employer's liability by linking his contribution to the length of time the employee had worked for him. Assemblyman Harold M. Groves, also a Commons student, introduced the bill. The Legislative Interim Committee on Unemployment held hearings all over the state during the summer and fall.

The support was impressive: the State Federation of Labor, organized farmers (who preferred that industry rather than property taxpayers support the unemployed), several religious denominations, and experts. Andrews, himself a former student of Commons', set up an effective publicity organization. The jobless insurance issue here, as in other states, produced strange bedfellows. The Communist Party and the Wisconsin Manufacturers Association joined to fight the Groves bill. When the employer representative testified before the Interim Committee, he referred jokingly to the Communist who preceded him as "my colleague in opposition." The Committee reported the bill favorably by a margin of 5 to 2. The Wisconsin Manufacturers Association then voted to engage an expert to draft a plan for voluntary unemployment compensation, thus admitting the soundness of the jobless reserve principle.

Governor Philip F. La Follette called the legislature into special session in November 1931 to enact the Groves bill, which he called "the soundest and fairest plan yet suggested anywhere." The governor capitalized on the opening provided by the Manufacturers Association. Employers would receive the opportunity to set up voluntary plans. "If by July 1, 1933," the bill read, "the employers of not less than two hundred thousand employees have voluntarily established systems of unemployment reserves ...

then the compulsory system . . . shall not take effect; otherwise, it shall take effect July 1, 1933." This maneuver broke the back of the opposition. The only amendment in the legislature was to reduce the quota from 200,000 to 175,000 employees. The Assembly, dominated by Progressives, passed the Groves bill 63 to 15; the Senate, where a close contest had been anticipated, concurred 20 to 10. La Follette signed the law on January 28, 1932. Wisconsin was the pioneer in enacting the first unemployment reserve, if not insurance, statute in the United States.

If employers failed to set up voluntary plans, the Groves Act would establish a compulsory system of company reserves. At the outset the employer would contribute 2 per cent of his payroll to his fund; when the reserve per employee passed $55, his rate dropped to 1 per cent; at $75 he no longer needed to contribute. The worker's benefit was 50 per cent of the weekly wage with a $10 maximum and a $5 minimum. The duration fluctuated with his length of service with the individual employer but might not exceed ten weeks a year. The law did not cover workers with incomes of more than $1500 a year, persons who had resided in the state less than two years or worked there less than forty weeks, farm laborers, domestic servants, reliefers, teachers, government employees, part-time workers, employees in the railroad and logging industries, the physically handicapped, strikers, and workers in firms with fewer than ten employees. The Industrial Commission administered the system with funds provided by a separate contribution by employers of not over 0.2 per cent of their payrolls.

The sponsors of the Groves Act were overjoyed by its passage. Their exultation was soon dampened by the difficulties of putting the Act into operation and the storm of controversy it provoked. The law was scheduled to take effect a year and a half after passage, July 1, 1933. Since business conditions were bad at that time, the date was pushed forward another year. In 1934, because the federal social security law was under consideration, Wisconsin again delayed. The statute did not actually begin operation until July 1, 1936. Hence it afforded no relief in the unemployment crisis out of which it arose.

Proponents of the insurance principle and the Ohio plan vigorously attacked the Wisconsin act. They included such authorities as Rubinow, Douglas, Leiserson, and Epstein. Walter A. Morton wrote the most incisive critique. He argued that the prevention and the relief of joblessness were irreconcilable goals. The law would not significantly reduce unemployment because it gave the employer too little inducement to stabilize production. Further, the employer acting alone could not deal with the most serious forms of joblessness. "The unemployed," Morton reasoned, "cannot be taken care of by reserves accumulated by themselves, or by their employers. . . . Unemployment relief can be provided only by dividing the burden among all on the theory of social responsibility, not by raising the rate on the employer on the erroneous theory of individual responsibility." Morton himself was an economist on the faculty of the University of Wisconsin.[13]

## 7

Unemployment was a national rather than a state problem. Senator Wagner wrote, "The reasons . . . are inherent in our economic organization. State boundaries are not economic barriers. . . . The stabilization of industry . . . must be national. . . ." Yet few supporters of jobless insurance at this time advocated a federal system.

"None of us," Miss Perkins later wrote, "thought in terms of a federal law." Encouraged by Roosevelt's Albany conference, she favored the regional interstate authority approach. In fact, she urged Roosevelt to persuade Governors La Follette and O. Max Gardner of North Carolina to lead similar regional movements in the Midwest and the South. Nothing came of the suggestion.

Beyond hostility in Congress and the White House, there were good reasons for avoiding federal action. The first was that the Constitution seemed an insurmountable barrier. Professor Felix Frankfurter wrote in 1932 that a law national in scope for workers in industries other than interstate transportation was "clearly unattainable." "There can be no constitutional federal legislation as to employees engaged in manufacture, construction, and the like activities." He had no faith in "legal hocus-pocus." "If I speak dogmatically, it is because the Supreme Court decisions leave no escape." The second impediment, thanks to Hoover's veto of the

Wagner bill, was the absence of a national employment service. The European experience demonstrated that unemployment insurance and employment exchanges were inextricably linked. Finally, many supporters of jobless insurance felt that local experimentation should be encouraged in this new area. These voices, not unnaturally, were heard most loudly in Wisconsin.

Despite this discouraging outlook, Wagner probed the prospects for federal action. On December 27, 1930, he introduced two bills. One would have authorized federal grants-in-aid of one third of cost to states that set up unemployment compensation funds. The 72d Congress gave no consideration to this proposal. The other was less controversial, to create a special committee to study jobless insurance. The Senate adopted this resolution on February 28, 1931.

By Senate custom the sponsor of such a motion automatically became chairman of the investigating committee without regard to the party that controlled the upper house. Vice-President Curtis assumed the custom would be honored, and Wagner began to organize the hearings. The Administration, however, defied the tradition, in Robert S. Allen's words, "to rob Wagner of his committee." Hoover summoned Felix Hebert of Rhode Island and Otis F. Glenn of Illinois to the White House. They were, according to Allen, two of "the most servile and reactionary Administration followers in the Senate." As the committee majority, they were ordered to deprive the New Yorker of the position. They promptly voted Hebert into the chairmanship. This Rhode Islander had been a lobbyist for insurance companies in his home state for years and, in fact, had continued to represent them after taking his Senate seat. He was, as Glenn said, "an expert on insurance," and that fact cast a shadow over the activities of the Hebert Committee.

In the summer of 1931, Hebert junketed to Europe for the stated purpose of studying jobless insurance. He returned directly to Hoover's summer camp at Rapidan, Virginia. Hebert then announced: "I am firmly convinced as a result of my study of unemployment insurance in Europe that the institution of such a system in the United States would be the first step toward a national dole." Senator Fess, the Republican National Chairman, said that the President wanted to deal with unemployment without resort to this "dole."

These conclusions, of course, preceded the hearings, and their announcement must have been intended to throw cold water on the testimony. When the hearings began in October, Wagner brought in a number of expert witnesses — E. A. Filene, Sumner Slichter, Jacob Billikopf, Miss Perkins, Leiserson, Swope, Epstein, and Wolman. They outshone the adverse witnesses. Hebert and Glenn, therefore, voted suddenly to terminate the hearings on November 13, 1931.

In its report of June 30, 1932, the majority of the Hebert Committee opposed federal unemployment insurance as impracticable and undesirable. Hebert and Glenn observed that a direct federal system was unconstitutional and that grants-in-aid were of dubious validity. They also disapproved of state compulsory systems, though admitting that they might come to pass ultimately. The ideal solution was plant reserves voluntarily established by the employer. To this end, Hebert and Glenn recommended that the tax law be changed to permit the employer to deduct contributions for unemployment reserves as a cost of doing business. They also urged the states to authorize private insurance companies to enter the jobless insurance field.

Wagner dissented from the report. He argued that unemployment insurance was no more a "dole" than life insurance. He urged the states to enact compulsory systems. The federal government should encourage such laws by establishing a nation-wide employment service and by allowing employers to deduct contributions from their income taxes. "To advocate insurance with sincerity," Wagner concluded, "is to advocate compulsory insurance." He was not yet ready to propose a federal system.[14]


# 8

The energies expended upon reform during the first years of the Great Depression produced few tangible results. Inertia and reaction were still too deeply seated in the places of power in the White House, in the Congress, in the state legislatures, in industry, in the press, and, for a while, in the labor movement.

There had been almost no gains in the daily and weekly hours of work. The public pension movement had won a modest acceptance. A handful of states, of which California and New York were most important, had established mandatory systems. But the great majority of old people remained uncovered and there was little prospect for federal legislation. Only Wisconsin had passed an unemployment "insurance" law, which would not take effect for several years and which many authorities viewed with skepticism.

The principal advance was in that intangible area called public education. A growing number of Americans had come to believe in the desirability of legislation to reduce the hours of work, to give the aged pensions, and to provide insurance against the risk of joblessness. The American Federation of Labor's internal struggle over voluntarism was symptomatic of this shift in opinion. The Federation endorsed state intervention on pensions in 1929, and on hours of work for men and unemployment insurance in 1932.

The process of public education was slow and tortured. The investigating commission was the main device for its achievement. To the impatient reformer this seemed an invention of the devil to cause delay and to provoke controversy. "I [am] sick of investigating commissions," Rubinow wrote Andrews in 1931. "A warm, judicious supporter of our proposal [unemployment insurance] told me consolingly that after all we could not expect any action on so important a measure sprung on the public. With this I agreed. After all, we have only discussed this matter for twenty years, and what is twenty years in comparison with eternity?" [15]

Rubinow's impatience was understandable. He stood too close to the goals he cherished. But in a democratic society a reform needs time to prepare the public for acceptance. This time was provided in the early years of the Great Depression. All over America citizens were at last confronting the proposals that reformers had been urging for so long. One such citizen was the governor of New York. This was the period of his education in the problems revolving about the great hub issue of unemployment. He talked with experts, trade unionists, and businessmen, read the reports of the investigating commissions, and sent his agents about the country and the world to acquire information and ideas. When Roosevelt assumed the presidency on March 4, 1933, he was ready to put this knowledge and these ideas to the test of experience.

# Epilogue: What Next?

IN 1932, ROGER W. BABSON, the business consultant, got out a letter of advice to the jobless entitled "How to Get Work When There Is No Work!" The sign "No Help Wanted" is always a lie. "Anyone who can be of real help can always get employment."

If you apply for a job, Babson counseled, don't talk about your troubles. The prospective employer has ten to every one of yours. "Be an optimist on business and life in general." If you can't think yourself into a job, work yourself into one. "Insist on working even without pay."

Unemployment, he said, is not an affliction but an opportunity. This is the time to build yourself up physically, mentally, and spiritually. "Breathe deeply, drink much water, exercise sufficiently, chew your food, and get a lot of sleep." Don't waste time reading the newspapers or listening to the radio. Rather, go to the public library and read about the industry to which you wish to return. "Remember that you have as much time as President Hoover and Henry Ford. The difference between you and them is how you use this time." [1]

The future, according to Babson, beckoned. But no one believed him.

1

American workers were in a vulnerable position as the 1920's drew to a close, more so than in any earlier era in the nation's history. This was largely because they were now decisively removed from the land. They had become dependent upon wage income for the support of their families. "Any considerable and sustained interruption in their money income," President Hoover's Committee on Social Trends pointed out, "exposes them to hardships which they were in a better position to mitigate when they were members of an agricultural or rural community."

Workers had not won a fair share of the decade's prosperity. The gains of advancing technology and rising productivity had gone mainly into profits rather than into real wages. Industry, in fact, paid off many workers in technological unemployment. Joblessness was an irritant that refused to go away. The worker who lost his job found it hard to find another, especially if he was over forty. The disorganization in the labor market made his task no easier. The distribution of income and wealth was inequitable and grew more distorted. Only the rich saved; those with modest incomes could not. Wage differentials were too wide and were spreading. Hours of work were uneconomically and onerously long. Wage earners enjoyed almost no fringe benefits.

Trade unions, whose function was to protect workers in the labor market, were weak. "The [American] Federation [of Labor]," *Fortune* said, "has been suffering from pernicious anaemia, sociological myopia, and hardening of the arteries. . . ." The membership of the AFL declined markedly after 1920. Those who remained members were only a fragment of the labor force, concentrated mainly in the traditional crafts. The great industries of the nation were predominantly nonunion. The Federation made almost no effort to organize the workers in these industries, missing even the opportunity afforded by the Piedmont revolt. The quality of union leadership deteriorated and there were few infusions of new blood. Hence the unions had little power to promote the welfare of wage earners in collective bargaining or to protect their rights within the plant by grievance procedures.

The Great Depression, therefore, struck American workers with the force of a tidal wave. For them it was primarily a massive experience in joblessness. Unemployment passed 4 million in January 1930, 5 million by September, 10 million at the end of 1931, and 15 million in March 1933. In all probability more persons were on short time.

The experience of the nation's largest manufacturing company, United States Steel, is illustrative. In 1929 the Corporation had

224,980 full-time employees. Their number fell to 211,055 in 1930, 53,619 in 1931, 18,938 in 1932, and zero on April 1, 1933. All who remained were part-time and they were only half as numerous as those employed full time in 1929.

Unemployment on this scale affected every aspect of the worker's life. It fell with unusual severity upon those over forty-five and those just entering the labor force, upon women, upon Negroes, and upon aliens. It distorted the job structure. Those whose ability and seniority merited promotion found that better jobs did not exist. Skilled workmen bumped down into unskilled jobs. Voluntary turnover dried up. The great weight of joblessness pressed wages down, in numerous cases to startlingly low levels.

This economic catastrophe had severe social consequences. The physical movement of population changed drastically. Immigration practically ceased; the shift from farm to city slowed down. In their stead came transiency, perhaps the saddest tale in the saga of the Great Depression. Transiency developed because poverty tore many families apart. The breakdown of this institution was evident in other ways: criminal acts, prostitution, drunkenness, desertion, the denigration of the husband-father. The marriage rate declined sharply and the birth rate followed inevitably. Unemployment also took its toll in health.

Joblessness sapped the little remaining strength of the labor movement. Union membership and dues fell off, forcing the organizations to curtail their activities. Racketeers took the occasion to penetrate the unions on a hitherto unknown scale. The unions were incapable of calling strikes except in desperation. Thus they were powerless to improve the wages and working conditions of their members and had little ability even to hold the line on wages. That once mightiest of the unions, the United Mine Workers of America, disintegrated.

Government offered little help to the worker in this hour of need. The traditional private relief system was unable to cope with the immense load. The cities and states were slow to assume responsibility. President Hoover opposed federal relief until driven to it by the force of circumstances. He seemed against all the proposals to deal with unemployment — public works, employment statistics, the modernization of the employment service, and unemployment insurance. The only labor legislation he signed, and then with obvious reluctance, was the Norris–La Guardia Act, labor's sole legislative achievement of the period.[2]

2

American workers expressed their reaction to these events in the 1932 presidential election — with a vengeance. Roosevelt polled 22,809,638 votes to Hoover's 15,758,901, a plurality of 7,050,737. In the electoral college the New York governor captured 42 states with 472 votes, leaving the President only 6 states with but 59 votes. Roosevelt swept in a Democratic Congress. In the 73d Congress the Senate would have 59 Democrats, 36 Republicans, and 1 Farmer-Laborite, the House 313 Democrats, 117 Republicans, and 5 Farmer-Laborites. Despite the depression, the left-wing parties made a poor showing. Norman Thomas, the Socialist presidential candidate, polled only 885,458 votes, and William Z. Foster, the Communist, got a mere 103,152.

Seldom, if ever, in American history had there been so dramatic a reversal in so short a time. Hoover's immense triumph over Smith in 1928 — by 6.5 million votes — had been wiped out; Roosevelt had achieved an even wider margin only four years later.

Paul Y. Anderson had predicted a Roosevelt victory because "the country is wet, broke, and disgusted." Roosevelt's landslide was largely due to those who were wettest, brokest, and most disgusted: urban workers and coal miners. In 1932 they deserted the Republican Party. This shift had begun in 1928, as pointed out in Chapter 1, when Al Smith made a notable appeal to city workers who were ethnically of the "new" immigration and by religion either Catholic or Jewish. Since these voters concentrated in large metropolitan centers, Smith had relaxed the traditional Republican grip on the cities outside the South. Roosevelt shattered it four years later. The labor vote, because of its great size and strategic location in the big states, now made the Democratic Party the majority party and established a new pattern that was to dominate American politics for almost a generation. The table on the opposite page reveals the percentage of the major party vote for President garnered by the Democrats in 1932 in the principal cities of the United States in contrast with 1928.

# DEMOCRATIC PER CENT OF MAJOR PARTY VOTE

| City | 1928 | 1932 |
|---|---|---|
| *Northeast* | | |
| Jersey City | 60.5% | 73.4% |
| New York | 62.1 | 71.4 |
| Boston | 67.3 | 69.1 |
| Baltimore | 48.3 | 67.0 |
| Providence | 53.1 | 58.4 |
| Pittsburgh | 42.7 | 55.5 |
| New Haven | 50.5 | 52.4 |
| Hartford | 46.4 | 49.9 |
| Buffalo | 46.6 | 48.2 |
| Newark | 41.3 | 47.0 |
| Philadelphia | 39.7 | 44.0 |
| *Midwest* | | |
| Milwaukee | 57.4 | 75.7 |
| Kansas City | 43.3 | 67.5 |
| St. Louis | 52.2 | 64.7 |
| Detroit | 37.1 | 59.4 |
| Chicago | 46.9 | 57.1 |
| Minneapolis | 39.2 | 56.7 |
| Cleveland | 46.1 | 52.8 |
| Indianapolis | 40.1 | 52.1 |
| Cincinnati | 42.7 | 50.9 |
| *West* | | |
| San Francisco | 50.2 | 67.3 |
| Seattle | 32.6 | 63.2 |
| Portland | 37.4 | 62.6 |
| Salt Lake City | 49.8 | 59.8 |
| Los Angeles | 29.0 | 59.7 |
| Denver | 35.9 | 55.1 |
| Oakland | 33.9 | 54.4 |
| *South* | | |
| New Orleans | 79.5 | 94.0 |
| Atlanta | 59.8 | 90.7 |
| Birmingham | 48.1 | 87.2 |
| Memphis | 60.1 | 85.8 |
| Houston | 44.2 | 84.5 |
| Dallas | 39.0 | 80.7 |
| Richmond | 48.7 | 72.3 |
| Miami | 39.0 | 65.8 |
| Louisville | 39.7 | 51.9 |

The Republican candidate, Harding, had carried all twenty-seven of the nonsouthern cities in 1920. Smith in 1928 won over eight and made gains in sixteen others; but he lost six of the nine southern communities. Roosevelt in 1932 captured thirty-two of the thirty-six cities; he lost only Hartford, Buffalo, Newark, and Philadelphia, all in the Northeast. He swept every major metropolitan center in the Midwest, the West, and the South. His average gain for all thirty-six cities over 1928 was a formidable 17.2 per cent. The average in the Northeast was 7.1 per cent, in the Midwest 14.7, in the West 21.9, and in the South 28.3 per cent.

The same swing was evident in the nonurban coal mining counties of Pennsylvania, Illinois, Indiana, West Virginia, Kentucky, and Alabama. Hoover had swept up the miner's vote in all six of these states in 1928, winning in thirty-six of the forty-five counties. Roosevelt reversed the outcome in 1932, capturing thirty-nine of the counties. In the ten predominantly coal counties of Pennsylvania the Democratic share of the two-party vote mounted from 44.7 per cent in 1928 to 54.2 per cent in 1932. In the five Illinois counties the gain was from 48.7 to 64.1 per cent. Smith had won 45.3 per cent of the vote in the two Indiana bituminous counties; Roosevelt got 60.6 per cent. In West Virginia's sixteen leading coal counties the Democratic vote advanced from 42.8 per cent in 1928 to 54.4 per cent in 1932. In Kentucky's ten main coal counties the corresponding figures were 40.7 and 58.3. In Alabama's two coal counties the Democratic vote leapt from 49.2 per cent in 1928 to 85.4 per cent in 1932.

"Unemployment," a Republican committeeman in Chicago declared, "was by far the most important factor in the 1932 election." Labor voted overwhelmingly against joblessness and Hoover's failure to deal with it. Workers who had voted for Smith in 1928 cast their ballots for Roosevelt in 1932; many who had voted for Hoover four years earlier switched to Roosevelt; and a great number who had not voted at all in 1928 came out to support Roosevelt in 1932. The forty-three urban communities of Michigan had gone overwhelmingly Republican in 1928; Hoover won 63 per cent of the Detroit vote. In 1932, Roosevelt carried twenty-eight of these towns, including all the large cities — Detroit, Grand Rapids, Flint, Saginaw, Lansing, Pontiac, Dearborn, and Jackson.

The foreign-born, concentrated in urban areas, gave Roosevelt enormous majorities. In a Polish section of Chicago, where unemployment was unusually severe, his margin was 20 per cent above that in the city as a whole. The Negroes, traditionally the most loyal Republican bloc in the nation, broke from that party. In some Michigan cities as many as 50 per cent of the Negroes cast Democratic ballots. "The 1932 election will be a historic one for Negroes," Walter White reported to the National Association for the Advancement of Colored People. "The era of their blind allegiance to the Republican party is definitely ended."

The labor protest vote went to Roosevelt rather than to the Socialist or the Communist. In Philadelphia Thomas received a proportionately smaller vote in the working-class districts than in the middle-class 42d ward. In the riverfront wards, where unemployment was heaviest, Thomas polled only 166 of 23,000 votes. The political editor of the Atlanta *Journal* said that Atlanta's entire labor vote was cast for Roosevelt. Labor leader John Frey was astonished by the poor Socialist performance.

The labor unions as organizations made virtually no contribution to Roosevelt's victory. Although Green was a Democrat and approved of the Democratic candidate, he maintained an official silence. The Executive Council of the Federation reaffirmed its traditional nonpartisan political policy and, in fact, denounced both the Democratic and Republican platforms. The United Mine Workers adopted the same policy. Speaking for himself, John L. Lewis endorsed Hoover. Big Bill Hutcheson was chairman of the Republican labor committee, and Woll, an ardent protectionist, even endorsed Senator Reed Smoot, the author of the Smoot-Hawley tariff, who had consistently voted against labor. The needle-trades unions and the Hosiery Workers were for Thomas. The only consequential labor leaders who worked for Roosevelt were Dan Tobin of the Teamsters and George L. Berry of the Printing Pressmen. Both were so obviously seeking personal gain that they could have had little effect upon the outcome. Berry was embittered when Roosevelt, trying to placate the Smith faction with the appointment of a Boston Irish-Catholic, named Tobin to head the Democratic labor committee. Neither Tobin nor Berry made any secret of the fact that he desperately wanted to become Secretary of Labor.

Hence Roosevelt owed the labor movement nothing for his victory. In fact, he made little appeal to organized labor in his campaign, devoting far more attention to the farm and progressive Republican votes. When an official of the United Mine Workers complained about the absence of a collective-bargaining plank in the Democratic platform, Roosevelt called it an oversight and promised to deal with the subject in a campaign speech. He never did.[3]

## 3

In the election American workers, like the American people as a whole, voted for presidential leadership. "Currents . . . are moving swiftly and with power," Governor O. Max Gardner of North Carolina had written Roosevelt a few months earlier, "sweeping people and laws before them. . . . What this Nation needs is a strong man, with a sense of social justice . . . to guide this flood of righteous indignation. . . . The American people are against things as they are. . . . The camp fires of the past are being abandoned."

In Washington, Saturday, March 4, 1933, was cold, overcast, windy, and dreary. Fifteen million Americans had lost their jobs; the banking system had collapsed; only thirty-three days before, Adolf Hitler had seized power in Germany. "The American experiment in self-government," Arthur M. Schlesinger, Jr., has written, "was now facing what was, excepting the Civil War, its greatest test."

On the steps of the Capitol, Franklin Delano Roosevelt took the oath of office in a clear, ringing voice from Chief Justice Hughes. The new President faced an immense throng before the rotunda and millions more at their radio sets. "The only thing we have to fear is fear itself." The money changers had fled from their high seats in the temple. "Our greatest primary task is to put people to work." Roosevelt would "assume unhesitatingly the leadership of this great army of our people" and would ask Congress for laws to revive the stricken nation. If the legislature failed to give them, "I shall ask the Congress for the one remaining instrument to meet the crisis — broad Executive power to wage a war against the emergency."

March 4, 1933, was a watershed. On that day an era ended and a new one began. When the inaugural parade was over, Morris Markey reported, "Mr. Hoover was weeping as his train drew out of the station toward obscurity." No one knew what the future held in store. But it was a certainty that the new Roosevelt Administration and the American people must wrestle with the decisive labor issues of the twenties and the early years of the Great Depression.[4]

# NOTES

# ABBREVIATIONS

# INDEX

# *Notes*

To SPARE the reader, I have grouped the notes by chapter here at the back of the volume.

A number of manuscript collections have been cited. The Franklin D. Roosevelt Library at Hyde Park, New York, contains the papers of Roosevelt, both as Governor and as President, as well as those of Morris L. Cooke and Herbert H. Lehman. The Manuscript Division of the Library of Congress has the Otto S. Beyer, James J. Davis, John Frey, Ogden Mills, George W. Norris, and Gifford Pinchot collections. The National Archives possesses those of the Committee on Economic Security, the Federal Employment Stabilization Board, the Labor Department, the President's Emergency Committee for Employment, and the President's Organization on Unemployment Relief. The School of Industrial and Labor Relations Library at Cornell University contains a microfilm of the William Green Papers and the collections of John B. Andrews and I. M. Rubinow. The Robert F. Wagner Papers are at Georgetown University. Those of Fiorello H. La Guardia are in the Archives of the City of New York. Some of the United Mine Workers Papers were in the possession of the old CIO and have been transferred to the Industrial Union Department of the AFL-CIO. The Pelham D. Glassford collection is at the Institute of Industrial Relations Library of the University of California, Los Angeles. The Harry Lang, Edwin E. Witte, and Arthur H. Young Papers are privately held.

❊

The notes have been consolidated wherever possible, and the following short references have been given:

Louis Adamic, *My America, 1928–1938* (New York: Harper, 1938), cited as Adamic, *My America*.

American Federation of Labor, *Proceedings*, cited as AFL, *Proceedings*, with the year date in parentheses.

Bureau of the Census, *Historical Statistics of the United States, 1789–*

*1945* (Washington: Government Printing Office, 1949), cited as *Historical Statistics.*

Conference on Unemployment, *Recent Economic Changes in the United States* (New York: McGraw-Hill, 1929), cited as *Recent Economic Changes.*

Felix Frankfurter and Nathan Greene, *The Labor Injunction* (New York: Macmillan, 1930), cited as Frankfurter and Greene, *Labor Injunction.*

Herbert Hoover, *State Papers and Other Public Writings of* . . . , William Starr Myers, ed. (New York: Doubleday, Doran, 1934), cited as Hoover, *State Papers.*

Don D. Lescohier, *Working Conditions,* and Elizabeth Brandeis, *Labor Legislation,* volume 3 of *History of Labor in the United States, 1896–1932,* John R. Commons and Associates, eds. (New York: Macmillan, 1935), cited as Lescohier and Brandeis, *History of Labor.*

Robert S. and Helen Merrell Lynd, *Middletown: A Study in Contemporary American Culture* (New York: Harcourt, Brace, 1929), cited as Lynds, *Middletown.*

William Starr Myers and Walter H. Newton, *The Hoover Administration: A Documented Narrative* (New York: Scribner, 1936), cited as Myers and Newton, *Hoover Administration.*

Selig Perlman and Philip Taft, *Labor Movements,* volume 4 of *History of Labor in the United States, 1896–1932,* John R. Commons and Associates, eds. (New York: Macmillan, 1935), cited as Perlman and Taft, *History of Labor.*

President's Research Committee on Social Trends, *Recent Social Trends in the United States* (New York: McGraw-Hill, 1933), cited as *Recent Social Trends.*

Arthur M. Schlesinger, Jr., *The Crisis of the Old Order, 1919–1933* (Boston: Houghton Mifflin, 1957), cited as Schlesinger, *Crisis.*

Sumner H. Slichter, *Union Policies and Industrial Management* (Washington: Brookings Institution, 1941), cited as Slichter, *Union Policies.*

In addition to a few well-known abbreviated references to unions, the abbreviations listed below by initials are used for organizations or periodicals:

| | |
|---|---|
| AER | *American Economic Review* |
| ALLR | *American Labor Legislation Review* |
| BLS | Bureau of Labor Statistics |
| CR | *Congressional Record* |

JASA   *Journal of the American Statistical Association*
JPE   *Journal of Political Economy*
MLR   *Monthly Labor Review*
NICB   National Industrial Conference Board
PECE   President's Emergency Committee for Employment
POUR   President's Organization on Unemployment Relief
PSQ   *Political Science Quarterly*
QJE   *Quarterly Journal of Economics*
UMWJ   *United Mine Workers Journal*

✲

PROLOGUE *(Pages 1–43)*

1. Claudius T. Murchison, "Southern Textile Manufacturing," *Annals*, 153 (Jan. 1931), 30, 33–42; George Sinclair Mitchell, *Textile Unionism and the South* (Chapel Hill: University of North Carolina Press, 1931), vi; Sinclair Lewis, *Cheap and Contented Labor* (Philadelphia: Women's Trade Union League, 1929), 14; Liston Pope, *Millhands and Preachers* (New Haven: Yale University Press, 1942), 189–91; AFL, *Proceedings* (1929), 274; W. J. Cash, *The Mind of the South* (Garden City: Doubleday, 1954), 345; *Working Conditions of the Textile Industry in North Carolina, South Carolina, and Tennessee*, Hearings on S. Res. 49, Senate Committee on Manufactures, 71 Cong., 1 sess. (1929), 54.

2. Clarence Heer, *Income and Wages in the South* (Chapel Hill: University of North Carolina Press, 1930), 12; Jennings J. Rhyne, *Some Southern Cotton Mill Workers and Their Villages* (Chapel Hill: University of North Carolina Press, 1930), 83, 97–98; Harry Mortimer Douty, "The North Carolina Industrial Worker, 1880–1930" (unpublished Ph.D. dissertation, University of North Carolina, 1936), 60; Fielding Burke, *Call Home the Heart* (New York: Longmans, Green, 1932), 11; Paul Blanshard, "Communism in the Southern Cotton Mills," *Nation*, 128 (Apr. 24, 1929), 500; Edgerton is quoted in Broadus Mitchell and George Sinclair Mitchell, *The Industrial Revolution in the South* (Baltimore: Johns Hopkins University Press, 1930), 37; Wheeling is quoted in Senate Hearings, *Working Conditions*, 25; Marjorie A. Potwin, *Cotton Mill People of the Piedmont* (New York: Columbia University Press, 1927), 16; Pope, *Millhands*, 86.

3. Tom Tippett, *When Southern Labor Stirs* (New York: Cape and Smith, 1931), 29; the mill manager is quoted in Lois MacDonald, *Southern Mill Hills* (New York: Hillman, 1928), 44; Rhyne, *Cotton Mill Workers*, 102, 125, 136–37; Lewis, *Cheap . . . Labor*, 18–19; Pope, *Millhands*, 68, 160, 163.

4. "Cotton Mill Colic" is quoted in Tippett, *Southern Labor*, 251; *Working Conditions in the Textile Industry in North Carolina, South Carolina, and Tennessee*, Senate Report No. 28, pt. 2, Minority Rep. of the Committee on Manufactures, 71 Cong., 1 sess. (1929), 4, 5; Abraham Berglund, George T. Starnes, and Frank T. DeVyver, *Labor in the Industrial South* (Charlottesville: University of Virginia Press, 1930), 74, 98–99, 124, 127; Lewis, *Cheap . . . Labor*, 17–18.

5. Sen. Min. Rep., *Working Conditions*, 2, 4–5; *AFL Weekly News Service*, Mar. 9, 1929; the South Carolina report was republished in Senate Hearings, *Working Conditions*, 7–14.

6. Berglund, *et al.*, *Labor*, 74, 98–99; A. F. Hinrichs, "Historical Review of Wage Rates and Wage Differentials in the Cotton-Textile Industry," *MLR*, 40 (May 1935), 1173; Sen. Min. Rep., *Working Conditions*, 4–5; Heer, *Income and Wages*, 30; *Business Week* is quoted in Samuel Yellen, *American Labor Struggles* (New York: Harcourt, Brace, 1936), 293.

7. Robert R. R. Brooks, "The United Textile Workers of America" (unpublished Ph.D. dissertation, Yale University, 1935), 114, 182, 260–69, 275. See also Mitchell, *Textile Unionism*, 3, 57, 65; Jean Carol Trepp, "Union-Management Co-operation and the Southern Organizing Campaign," *JPE*, 41 (Oct. 1933), 607, 612; Lewis L. Lorwin, *The American Federation of Labor* (Washington: Brookings, 1933), 260; Albert Weisbord, "Passaic — New Bedford — North Carolina," *Communist*, 8 (June 1929), 319–20.

8. The millhand is quoted by Lois MacDonald in "Normalcy in the Carolinas," *New Republic*, 61 (Jan. 29, 1930), 269; Douty, "The North Carolina Industrial Worker," 300–303; AFL, *Proceedings* (1928), 55–56, 290; Mitchell, *Textile Unionism*, 63–64.

9. The Bowen statement is in AFL, *Proceedings* (1929), 276; Sherwood Anderson, "Elizabethton, Tennessee," *Nation*, 128 (May 1, 1929), 527; Duane McCracken, *Strike Injunctions in the New South* (Chapel Hill: University of North Carolina Press, 1931), 100–102; *New York Times*, Apr. 5, 1929, p. 10; Paul J. Aymon, "Rayon Workers Strike, Elizabethton," *American Federationist*, 36 (May 1929), 547–48; Tippett, *Southern Labor*, 60–61.

10. *Time*, Nov. 23, 1936, p. 15. See also Bruce Minton and John Stuart, *Men Who Lead Labor* (New York: Modern Age, 1937), 56–63; Paul Y. Anderson, "So They Found the Body," *Nation*, 138 (Feb. 21, 1934), 220.

11. *New York Times*, Apr. 5, p. 10, Apr. 6, p. 29, Apr. 8, p. 4, May 11, p. 10, May 26, p. 1, May 27, p. 14, June 2, 1929, p. 6; George Fort Milton, "The South Fights the Unions," *New Republic*, 59 (July 10, 1929), 202–3; Senate Hearings, *Working Conditions*, 44, 48; McCracken, *Strike Injunctions*, 94–95; *To Investigate Communist Activities in the United States*, Hearings before Special House Committee, 71 Cong., 2 sess. (1930), pt. 6, vol. 1, p. 56; Lehman to

Mothwurf, Apr. 18, John Sullivan and John O'Hanlon to Lehman, May 1, Lehman to D. C. Dunlop, May 2, Dunlop to Lehman, May 6, Lehman to Mothwurf, May 24, Green to Lehman, Sept. 26, Lehman to Green, Oct. 7, 1929, Lehman Papers; Green to Lehman, May 7, Lehman to Green, May 9, Green to Horton, May 9, 1929, Green Papers. On September 5, 1930, long after the strike was over, the Court of Appeals set aside the convictions on the ground that the agreement of March 21–22 settled all issues in dispute and rendered the injunction unnecessary. The Supreme Court of Tennessee denied *certiorari* on January 30, 1931. McCracken, *Strike Injunctions*, 104.

12. Quoted in Robin Hood, "The Loray Mill Strike" (unpublished M.A. dissertation, University of North Carolina, 1932), 33–34. This study and the equally exhaustive and objective work by Liston Pope (*Millhands*) provide the basis for this account of the Gastonia strike and no further citations will be made to either. See also Fred E. Beal, *Proletarian Journey* (New York: Hillman-Curl, 1937), 17–109, 140; *New York Times*, Apr. 7, 1929, p. 26; Blanshard, "Communism in . . . Cotton Mills," 501.

13. The events of the night of June 7, 1929, have been the subject of bitter controversy. The account is based upon the careful study by Robin Hood.

14. Judge Frank Carter of North Carolina, after joining the defense, resigned in disgust over ILD tactics. The ACLU felt that the lack of a distinguished attorney from the state jeopardized the defendants' case. *New York Times*, Aug. 2, 1929, p. 38. See also Nell Battle Lewis, "Tar Heel Justice," *Nation*, 129 (Sept. 11, 1929), 273.

15. *New York Times*, Sept. 11, pp. 1, 5, Sept. 16, p. 1, Sept. 17, p. 23, Oct. 21, 1929, p. 24; Margaret Larkin, "Ella May's Songs," *Nation*, 129 (Oct. 9, 1929), 382. See also "The Gastonia Strikers' Case," *Harvard Law Review*, 44 (May 1931), 1124.

16. *Time*, May 31, 1948, p. 19; Beal to Lucy and Harry Lang, May 11, 1941, Green to J. Melville Broughton, Dec. 6, 1941, Lang Papers.

17. The Kiwanis Club is quoted in Sinclair Lewis, *Cheap . . . Labor*, 30–31. The best account of the strike is in Tippett, *Southern Labor*, 109–55, to which no further references will be made. See also letter to the editor, *New Republic*, 60 (Sept. 18, 1929), 126; *New York Times*, Oct. 3, p. 1, Oct. 5, pp. 1, 8, Nov. 9, 1929, p. 2; Benjamin Stolberg, "Madness in Marion," *Nation*, 129 (Oct. 23, 1929), 462; Mitchell and Mitchell, *Industrial Revolution*, 207; Lewis, *Cheap . . . Labor*, 10, 16–17.

18. The Brandon striker is quoted in Paul Blanshard, "One-Hundred Per Cent Americans on Strike," *Nation*, 128 (May 8, 1929), 554; *New York Times*, July 14, 1929, p. 1; Green to Googe, May 3, 1929, Green Papers.

19. *AFL Weekly News Service*, July 20, 1929; Tippett, *Southern Labor*, 134–35, 173–76, 182–92; George Sinclair Mitchell, "Organization

of Labor in the South," *Annals,* 153 (Jan. 1931), 185; AFL, *Proceedings* (1929), 60, 265–83; AFL, *Proceedings* (1930), 85–87, 276–79; *Textile Worker,* Nov. 1929, p. 506; Trepp, "Union-Management Co-operation," 619, 621; Green to Frank Duffy, May 14, Green to W. L. Hutcheson, May 15, 1929, Green to Brown, May 16, Green to Paul Smith, May 28, 1930, Green Papers.

20. Louis Stanley, "Danville: Labor's Southern Outpost," *Nation,* 132 (Jan. 21, 1931), 69–70; Tippett, *Southern Labor,* 210–13; Jonathan Mitchell, "Here Comes Gorman!" *New Republic,* 80 (Oct. 3, 1934), 204; *Time,* Sept. 10, 1934, p. 12; McCracken, *Strike Injunctions,* 116–20; Green to McMahon, Sept. 2, 1930, Green Papers; Fitzgerald is quoted in Tippett, *Southern Labor,* 227, 244, 265.

21. Weimar Jones, "Southern Labor and the Law," *Nation,* 131 (July 2, 1930), 16; *New York Times,* Aug. 10, 1929, p. 22; Tippett, *Southern Labor,* 156–59; *Textile Worker,* Nov. 1930, p. 501.

CHAPTER 1 (*Pages 47–82*)

1. The basic data appear in *Historical Statistics,* 29, 31; National Resources Committee, *The Problems of a Changing Population* (Washington: 1938), 88; Harry Jerome, *Mechanization in Industry* (New York: National Bureau of Economic Research, 1934), 122–25; Edward E. Lewis, *The Mobility of the Negro* (New York: Columbia University Press, 1931), 131–32; National Urban League, *Negro Membership in American Labor Unions* (New York: National Urban League, 1930), 8; John A. and Alan Lomax, comps., *American Ballads and Folk Songs* (New York: Macmillan, 1934), xxx; *Recent Social Trends,* vol. 2, p. 806.

2. Preston William Slosson, *The Great Crusade and After, 1914–1928* (New York: Macmillan, 1930), 299–301; *Historical Statistics,* 33; "The U.S. Steel Corporation: III," *Fortune,* 13 (May 1936), 136; H. B. Butler, *Industrial Relations in the United States* (Geneva: International Labor Office, 1927), 14; Sumner H. Slichter, "The Current Labor Policies of American Industries," *QJE,* 43 (May 1929), 393.

3. *The Daily Mail Trade Union Mission to the United States* (London: Daily Mail, [1927]), 81, 84. See also Parliament of the Commonwealth of Australia, *Report of the Industrial Delegation . . .* (Canberra: 1927), 16–17, and André Siegfried, *America Comes of Age* (New York: Harcourt, Brace, 1927), 149; Edward Bliss Reed, ed., *The Commonwealth Fund Fellows and Their Impressions of America* (New York: Commonwealth Fund, 1932), 90. The American employer is quoted in D. D. Lescohier, *What Is the Effect and Extent of Technical Changes on Employment Security?* (American Management Association, Personnel Series No. 1, 1930), 12.

4. Jerome, *Mechanization, passim.*

5. *Historical Statistics,* 71–72; David Weintraub, "Unemployment and Increasing Productivity," in National Resources Committee, *Technological Trends and National Policy* (Washington: 1937), 77; Frederick C. Mills, *Economic Tendencies in the United States* (New York: National Bureau of Economic Research, 1932), 243–51; *Daily Mail,* 21; Simon Kuznets, *National Income and Its Composition, 1919–1938* (New York: National Bureau of Economic Research, 1941), vol. 1, pp. 216–17; Maurice Leven, Harold G. Moulton, and Clark Warburton, *America's Capacity to Consume* (Washington: Brookings, 1934), 28.

6. *Historical Statistics,* 64–65; *Daily Mail,* 83; Lynds, *Middletown,* 1–2, 13, 33, 187; *Recent Social Trends,* vol. 1, pp. 305, 713, 730–31, vol. 2, pp. 777–79, 810–11; National Resources Committee, *Technological Trends,* 194–97; Ewan Clague and W. J. Couper, "The Readjustment of Workers Displaced by Plant Shutdowns," *QJE,* 45 (Feb. 1931), 326; Isador Lubin, *The Absorption of the Unemployed by American Industry* (Washington: Brookings, 1929), 18; "Age Limits in Industry in Maryland and California," *MLR,* 32 (Feb. 1931), 39; *Hearings before Committee on Education and Labor,* Senate, 70 Cong., 2 sess. (1928–29), xv.

7. Lynds, *Middletown,* 48, 68; Herman Feldman, *Racial Factors in American Industry* (New York: Harper, 1931), ch. 2; John Greenway, *American Folksongs of Protest* (Philadelphia: University of Pennsylvania Press, 1953), 113.

8. Hugh Grant Adam, *An Australian Looks at America* (London: Allen and Unwin, 1928), 23, 80; "British Report on Industrial Conditions in the United States," *MLR,* 24 (June 1927), 1199; Edwin G. Nourse and Associates, *America's Capacity to Produce* (Washington: Brookings, 1934), 416; Weintraub, "Unemployment," 70; *Recent Economic Changes,* vol. 2, pp. 469–78, 876; "Unemployment Survey of Philadelphia," *MLR,* 30 (Feb. 1930), 227; Fred C. Croxton and Frederick E. Croxton, "Unemployment in Buffalo, N.Y., in 1929 . . . ," *MLR,* 30 (Feb. 1930), 236; Lynds, *Middletown,* 56–59; Clague and Couper, "Readjustment of Workers," 309–46; Robert J. Myers, "Occupational Readjustment of Displaced Skilled Workmen," *JPE,* 37 (Aug. 1929), 473–89; Clinch Calkins, *Some Folks Won't Work* (New York: Harcourt, Brace, 1930), 18–20; Senate *Hearings,* 84; *Recent Social Trends,* vol. 1, p. 309, vol. 2, p. 808; Jerome, *Mechanization,* 367–82; George Korson, *Coal Dust on the Fiddle* (Philadelphia: University of Pennsylvania Press, 1943), 141–42.

9. Elizabeth Faulkner Baker, *Displacement of Men by Machines* (New York: Columbia University Press, 1933), 28 ff.; Jerome, *Mechanization,* 393 ff.; W. S. Woytinsky, *Three Aspects of Labor Dynamics* (Washington: Social Science Research Council, 1942), 29–33; Slichter, "Current Labor Policies," 429–31.

10. Lynds, *Middletown*, 63; Calkins, *Some Folks*, 20–21; on the abortive Swarthmore project there is an extensive correspondence between Brandeis and Cooke and Douglas and Cooke, dealing mainly with raising money and convincing Douglas to leave the University of Chicago, Cooke Papers; Senate *Hearings*, vii–xv.

11. Leven, *et al.*, *America's Capacity*, 54–56, 93, 103–4; "Cost of Living of Federal Employees in Five Cities," *MLR*, 29 (Aug. 1929), 315; Paul H. Douglas, *Wages and the Family* (Chicago: University of Chicago Press, 1925), 5–6; Steffens to Jo Davidson, Feb. 18, 1929, in *Letters of Lincoln Steffens*, Ella Winter and Granville Hicks, eds. (New York: Harcourt, Brace, 1938), vol. 2, p. 830; Paul H. Douglas, *Real Wages in the United States, 1890–1926* (Boston: Houghton Mifflin, 1930), 391; Paul H. Douglas and Florence Tye Jennison, *The Movement of Money and Real Earnings in the United States, 1926–28* (Chicago: University of Chicago Press, 1930), 27. Wages in 1929 differed little from 1928 figures. Annual earnings in manufacturing rose to $1341 in 1929 from $1325 in 1928. Since the cost of living also advanced, by one point, real wages rose by a fraction of 1 per cent. Paul H. Douglas and Charles J. Coe, "Earnings," *American Journal of Sociology*, 35 (May, 1930), 935–39; *Recent Economic Changes*, vol. 1, pp. 60–67, 325; *Recent Social Trends*, vol. 2, pp. 827, 858–89, 915–26; Siegfried, *America Comes of Age*, 159. See also *Daily Mail*, 23. Some of the British made the admission more cautiously, while an Australian stated flatly that real wages were higher in his country. *Report of the Delegation Appointed to Study Industrial Conditions in . . . the United States*, Cmd. 2833 (Mar. 1927), 33; Adam, *An Australian*, 46.

12. Adam, *An Australian*, 37; Douglas, *Real Wages*, 96, 101, 135, 152, 189–90, 205–11; Douglas and Jennison, *Movement of Money*, 36, 38, 177, 179; NICB, *Wages in the United States, 1914–1929* (New York: NICB, 1930), 36, 39–42; *Historical Statistics*, 68–70; United States Steel Corporation, *Annual Report, 1955*, 30; Butler, *Industrial Relations*, 14, 25; Allan Nevins and F. E. Hill, *Ford: Expansion and Challenge, 1915–1933* (New York: Scribner, 1957), 330; A. F. Hinrichs, "Historical Review of Wage Rates and Wage Differentials in the Cotton-Textile Industry," *MLR*, 40 (May 1935), 1173; Abraham Berglund, George T. Starnes, and Frank T. DeVyver, *Labor in the Industrial South* (Charlottesville: University of Virginia Press, 1930), 74; *Recent Economic Changes*, vol. 2, pp. 437–39; BLS, Bull. No. 513, *Wages and Hours of Labor in the Iron and Steel Industry, 1929* (1930), 35, 37, 91, 92; BLS, No. 522, *Wages and Hours of Labor in Foundries and Machine Shops, 1929* (1930), 2–3; BLS, No. 526, *Wages and Hours of Labor in the Furniture Industry, 1910 to 1929* (1931), 2, 3; BLS, No. 535, *Wages and Hours of Labor in the Slaughtering and Meat-packing Industry, 1929* (1931), 5, 6, 11–12, 14–15, 22–23, 29; BLS, No. 532, *Wages and Hours of Labor in the*

*Cigarette Manufacturing Industry, 1930* (1931), 2; BLS, No. 539, *Wages and Hours of Labor in Cotton-Goods Manufacturing, 1910 to 1930* (1931), 4, 5 ,7; Parliament of . . . Australia, *Report*, 41; Harold M. Levinson, *Unionism, Wage Trends, and Income Distribution, 1914–1947* (Ann Arbor: University of Michigan Press, 1951), 42; Mills, *Economic Tendencies*, 477.

13. NICB, *Wages* . . . *1914–1929*, 201; Butler, *Industrial Relations*, 37; Douglas, *Real Wages*, 590; Kuznets, *National Income*, 332–33, 352–53; U.S. Steel Corp., *Annual Report, 1955*, 30–31; Charles P. Taft, 2d, to Martin Egan, June 7, 1934, Record Group No. 25, National Archives; Mills, *Economic Tendencies*, 404.

14. Douglas, *Real Wages*, 112–16, 208; Solomon Fabricant, *Employment in Manufacturing, 1899–1939* (New York: National Bureau of Economic Research, 1942), 234; Lazare Teper, *Hours of Labor* (Baltimore: Johns Hopkins University Press, 1932), 35; BLS, Bull. No. 513, *Wages and Hours*, 4; "Hours of Labor and the 7-Day Week in the Iron and Steel Industry," *MLR*, 30 (June 1930), 184–85; Marion Cotter Cahill, *Shorter Hours: A Study of the Movement Since the Civil War* (New York: Columbia University Press, 1932), *passim;* "Extent of the Five-Day Week in Manufacturing," *MLR*, 30 (Feb. 1930), 368; Lynds, *Middletown*, 54; Adam, *An Australian*, 117–18.

15. BLS, Bull. No. 491, *Handbook of Labor Statistics* (1929), 749–53; *Report of the Delegation*, 35; Adam, *An Australian*, 81.

16. Perlman and Taft, *History of Labor*, 328–29; Slichter, "Current Labor Policies," 411–12; Lynds, *Middletown*, 70; Adam, *An Australian*, 53–54; the Ford worker is cited in Edmund Wilson, *The American Jitters* (New York: Scribner, 1932), 52; the iron discipline imposed in the Ford plants is set forth in Nevins and Hill, *Ford*, 514–18; BLS, Bull. No. 491, *Handbook of Labor*, 490–91; Thomas Kennedy, *Effective Labor Arbitration* (Philadelphia: University of Pennsylvania Press, 1948), 20–25; Herbert Lehman to Herman Gardner, Oct. 1, 1929, Lehman Papers.

17. Vaughn Davis Bornet, "Labor and Politics in 1928" (unpublished Ph.D. dissertation, Stanford University, 1951), 437; the Hoover campaign card, White, and the St. Paul *Pioneer-Press* are cited in Roy V. Peel and Thomas C. Donnelly, *The 1928 Campaign: An Analysis* (New York: Smith, 1931), 86, 99, 121; Samuel Lubell, *The Future of American Politics* (2d ed., rev.; Garden City: Doubleday, 1956), 29–43; Richard Hofstadter, *The Age of Reform* (New York: Knopf, 1955), 280–300.

18. This table and the data on mining areas that follow are based upon an analysis of the election statistics in Edgar Eugene Robinson, *The Presidential Vote 1896–1932*, (Palo Alto: Stanford University Press, 1934). Robinson's figures are actually by counties but have been arranged by cities because the counties are not as familiar.

19. Peel and Donnelly, *1928 Campaign*, 171.

20. Lynds, *Middletown*, 75; Lewis L. Lorwin, *The American Federation of Labor* (Washington: Brookings, 1933), 239; Siegfried, *America Comes of Age*, 165; Douglas, *Real Wages*, 572-74.
21. See Tillman M. Sogge, "Industrial Classes in the United States in 1930," *JASA*, 28 (June 1933), 199-203; Lynds, *Middletown*, 23-24.

CHAPTER 2 (*Pages 83-143*)

1. Hugh Grant Adam, *An Australian Looks at America* (London: Allen and Unwin, 1928), 6-10; Berry to Spencer Miller, Jr., Nov. 19, 1929, Green Papers; Earl W. Shimmons, "The Twilight of the A. F. of L.," *American Mercury*, 16 (Mar. 1929), 295.
2. Leo Wolman, *Ebb and Flow in Trade Unionism* (New York: National Bureau of Economic Research, 1936), *passim;* Schlesinger to Lehman, Jan. 19, 1932, Lehman Papers; Harry Lang, "*62*": *Biography of a Union* (New York: Underwear . . . Workers, Local 62, ILGWU, 1940), 191-92; Vernon H. Jensen, *Heritage of Conflict* (Ithaca: Cornell University Press, 1950), 465; *Brewery, Flour, Cereal, and Soft Drink Workers' Journal*, Mar. 9, 1929, p. 1; Matthew Josephson, *Union House, Union Bar* (New York: Random House, 1956), 129, 165; Hyman Weintraub, *Andrew Furuseth: Emancipator of the Seamen* (Berkeley: University of California Press, 1959), 159; C. L. Christenson, *Collective Bargaining in Chicago: 1929-30* (Chicago: University of Chicago Press, 1933), chs. 1, 9. The pattern of organization in Middletown in 1929 paralleled that in Chicago. Of 13,000 in working-class occupations, 900 were union members, 7 per cent. The AFL Central Labor Union had 16 affiliated locals: 7 building trades, 2 metal trades, 2 railway trades, and 1 each of printing trades, motion picture operators, musicians, letter carriers, barbers. The city's great glass and automotive plants were unorganized and the town was notorious as an open-shop center. Robert S. and Helen Merrell Lynd, *Middletown in Transition* (New York: Harcourt, Brace, 1937), 27, 41-42.
3. Irving Bernstein, "The Growth of American Unions," *AER*, 44 (June 1954), 301-18; William Allen White, *A Puritan in Babylon* (New York: Macmillan, 1938), 335. Myron W. Watkins argues that trustification was decisive in the defeat of unionism, but this is going too far. See his "Trustification and Economic Theory," 21, *AER*, supp. (Mar. 1931), 59-61.
4. H. M. Douty, "The Trend of Industrial Disputes, 1922-1930," *JASA*, 27 (June 1932), 170-72; John I. Griffin, *Strikes: A Study in Quantitative Economics* (New York: Columbia University Press, 1939), 91; Sumner H. Slichter, "The Current Labor Policies of American Industries," 43 (May 1929), 429.
5. Clifton Fadiman, "Clerihews," *New Yorker*, May 5, 1956, p. 37.

Unless otherwise noted, this section is drawn from Louis S. Reed, *The Labor Philosophy of Samuel Gompers* (New York: Columbia University Press, 1930). John R. Commons, "Karl Marx and Samuel Gompers," *PSQ* 41 (June 1926), 285; the machinist quip is from B. A. Botkin and A. F. Harlow, eds., *A Treasury of Railroad Folklore* (New York: Crown, 1953), 293; George E. Barnett, "The Causes of Jurisdictional Disputes in American Trade Unions," *Harvard Business Review*, 9 (July 1931), 401; Gompers on Socialism is cited in John P. Frey to W. A. Appleton, July 5, 1932, Frey Papers.

6. Max D. Danish, *William Green: A Pictorial Biography* (New York: Inter-Allied, 1952), 13 ff.; Charles A. Madison, *American Labor Leaders* (New York: Harper, 1950), 108–35; Raymond Clapper, "Labor's Chief: William Green," *Review of Reviews*, 88 (Nov. 1933), 21. In 1929 Green said privately of industrial unionism, "If the rubber workers and the auto workers ever organize it will be on an industrial basis." Harold Roberts, *The Rubber Workers* (New York: Harper, 1944), 87; UMW, *John L. Lewis and the International Union, United Mine Workers of America* (Washington United Mine Workers, 1952), 122, 214; Benjamin Stolberg, "William Green's Convention," *Nation*, 123 (Nov. 3, 1926), 449; *Proceedings of the 34th Constitutional Convention of the United Mine Workers of America, 1936*, vol. 1, p. 299.

7. The first Green quotation is cited in Paul F. Gemmill, *Present-Day Labor Relations* (New York: Wiley, 1929), 20; William Green, "Recent Trend in the Organized Labor Movement," *Annals*, 149 (May 1930), 190; Jean T. McKelvey, *AFL Attitudes toward Production, 1900–1932* (Ithaca: Cornell University Press, 1952), 91. The railway experience is summarized in Louis Aubrey Wood, *Union-Management Cooperation on the Railroads* (New Haven: Yale University Press, 1931), and Slichter, *Union Policies*, chs. 15, 16. Slichter deals with the other plans in chs. 14, 17, 18. Richmond C. Nyman, *Union-Management Cooperation in the "Stretch Out"* (New Haven: Yale University Press, 1934); Mary Van Kleeck, *Miners and Management* (New York: Russell Sage, 1934), Green to Tom Kennedy, May 23, 1929, Green Papers; Gladys Palmer, "Job Conscious Unionism in the Chicago Men's Clothing Industry," *AER*, 20 (Mar. 1930), 35–36; Wharton is quoted in R. W. Bruère to Morris L. Cooke, Jan. 22, 1929, Cooke Papers.

8. McKelvey, *AFL*, chs. 4, 5; Milton J. Nadworny, *Scientific Management and the Unions, 1900–32* (Cambridge: Harvard University Press, 1955), chs. 7, 8.

9. AFL, *Proceedings* (1925), 271; McKelvey, *AFL*, 97.

10. *Recent Social Trends*, vol. 2, pp. 837–38; J. B. S. Hardman, ed., *American Labor Dynamics* (New York: Harcourt, Brace, 1928), ch. 28; Earl D. Strong, *The Amalgamated Clothing Workers of America* (Grinnell, Iowa: Herald-Register, 1940), 247–49; **AFL,**

*Proceedings* (1927), 228–31; H. B. Butler, *Industrial Relations in the United States* (Geneva: International Labor Office, 1927), 50.

11. Vaughn Davis Bornet, "Labor and Politics in 1928" (unpublished Ph.D. dissertation, Stanford University, 1951), chs, 3, 7, 20.

12. AFL, *Proceedings* (1925), 286–87; AFL, *Proceedings* (1928), 86–87, 310, 314–39; Kerchen is quoted in Marius Hansome, *World Workers' Educational Movements: Their Social Significance* (New York: Columbia University Press, 1931), 199, 237.

13. Frey to Mary White Ovington, May 8, 1929, Mary Van Kleeck to Frey, Jan. 15, 1929, Frey Papers; Sterling Spero and Abram L. Harris, *The Black Worker* (New York: Columbia University Press, 1931), 461; National Urban League, *Negro Membership in American Labor Unions* (New York: National Urban League, 1930), 2, 33–34, 101–3; *A Bill to Amend the Judicial Code . . .* , Hearings on S. 1482, Senate Subcommittee of the Committee on the Judiciary, 70 Cong., 1 sess. (1928), 604.

14. Maxwell C. Raddock, *Portrait of an American Labor Leader: William L. Hutcheson* (New York: American Institute of Social Science, 1955), 8. This dubious biography is the source for Hutcheson's early background, which may be more reliable than the later material. See also "Boss Carpenter," *Fortune*, 33 (Apr. 1946), 121, 125; Robert A. Christie, *Empire in Wood* (Ithaca: Cornell University Press, 1956), 15, 17–18, 253, 266, ch. 16; William Haber, *Industrial Relations in the Building Industry* (Cambridge: Harvard University Press, 1930), 180–90; Herbert Harris, *American Labor* (New Haven: Yale University Press, 1938), 170; Lewis is quoted in Raddock, *Portrait*, 81.

15. The Welsh notice is cited in Ness Edwards, *The History of the South Wales Miners* (London: Labour Publishing Co., 1926), 30; Saul Alinsky, *John L. Lewis* (New York: Putnam, 1949), 15, 55, 354–56, 365, 367; "John Llewellyn Lewis," *Fortune*, 14 (Oct. 1936), 97, 154, 159; C. L. Sulzberger, *Sit Down with John L. Lewis* (New York: Random House, 1938), 5, 15, 17, 31–32, 34–35; James A. Wechsler, *Labor Baron: A Portrait of John L. Lewis* (New York: Morrow, 1944), 6; Charles A. Madison, *American Labor Leaders* (New York: Harper, 1950), 182; UMW, *Lewis and the International*, 41, 239, 244, 250; John L. Lewis, *The Miners' Fight for American Standards* (Indianapolis: Bell, 1925), 70; Mitchell is cited in George Korson, *Minstrels of the Mine Patch* (Philadelphia: University of Pennsylvania Press, 1938), 216.

16. McAlister Coleman, *Men and Coal* (New York: Farrar & Rinehart, 1943), 137; Walton R. Hamilton and Helen R. Wright, *The Case of Bituminous Coal* (New York: Macmillan, 1926), 166, 212. The authors quote W. S. Gilbert: "Here's a pretty mess." The statistics are drawn mainly from Bituminous Coal Institute, *Bituminous Coal, Facts and Figures, 1948* (Washington: 1948). Edmond M. Beame,

"The Jacksonville Agreement: Quest for Stability in Coal," *Industrial and Labor Relations Review*, 8 (Jan. 1955), 197; *Conditions in the Coal Fields of Pennsylvania, West Virginia, and Ohio*, Hearings on S. Res. 105, Senate Committee on Interstate Commerce, 70 Cong., 1 sess. (1928), 408, 860–63, 938, 995, 1322–23, 1846.

17. This section is based mainly upon Edward Dean Wickersham, "Opposition to the International Officers of the United Mine Workers of America: 1919–1933" (unpublished Ph.D. dissertation, Cornell University, 1951); Fannie Hurst's remarks are in Senate Hearings, *Conditions*, 987. See also *To Investigate Communist Activities in the United States*, Hearings before Special House Committee, 71 Cong., 2 sess. (1930), pt. 4, vol. 3, p. 73.

18. V. I. Lenin, *"Left-Wing" Communism: An Infantile Disorder* (republished New York: International, 1934), 36–38; Benjamin Stolberg, *Tailor's Progress* (Garden City: Doubleday, Doran, 1944), 115, 138; Matthew Josephson, *Sidney Hillman* (Garden City: Doubleday, 1952), 274–81; Donald B. Robinson, *Spotlight on a Union* (New York: Dial, 1948), 175–97; Philip S. Foner, *The Fur and Leather Workers Union* (Newark: Nordan, 1950), 105–319; Perlman and Taft, *History of Labor*, 543–46, 557–58; William Isaacs, *Contemporary Marxian Political Movements in the United States, 1917–1939* (New York: New York University Press, 1942), 16; William Z. Foster, "The T.U.U.L. Convention," *Communist*, Sept. 1929, p. 528; House Hearings, *Communist Activities*, pt. 1, vol. 4, p. 368, pt. 3, vol. 2, p. 3.

19. John S. Gambs, *The Decline of the I.W.W.* (New York: Columbia University Press, 1932), 204–5. See also Fred Thompson, *The I.W.W.: Its First Fifty Years* (Chicago: IWW, 1955), ch. 11; *Industrial Worker*, Feb. 16, 1929, p. 1.

20. Leiserson to Morris L. Cooke, Mar. 28, 1929, Cooke Papers; William Green to Paul Smith, June 17, 1929, Green Papers.

CHAPTER 3 (*Pages 144–189*)

1. Hugh Grant Adam, *An Australian Looks at America* (London: Allen and Unwin, 1928), 85; J. Alfred Spender, "Through English Eyes," in *America through British Eyes*, Allan Nevins, comp. (New York: Oxford, 1948), 421; Cyrus S. Ching, *Review and Reflection* (New York: Forbes, 1953), 29.

2. Sam A. Lewisohn, *The New Leadership in Industry* (New York: Dutton, 1926), 226; the iron superintendent is quoted in Morris Markey, *This Country of Yours* (Boston: Little, Brown, 1932), 6; *Recent Social Trends*, vol. 1, pp. xii–xiii.

3. Raymond B. Fosdick, *John D. Rockefeller, Jr.* (New York: Harper, 1956), 74; Ching, *Review*, 28–29; Edgerton is cited in J. W. Prothro,

*Dollar Decade: Business Ideas in the 1920's* (Baton Rouge: Louisiana State University Press, 1954), 151, 154; Adam, *An Australian,* 33, 54; H. B. Butler, *Industrial Relations in the United States* (Geneva: International Labor Office, 1927), 61; "Republic Steel," *Fortune,* 12 (Dec. 1935), 77; Perlman and Taft, *History of Labor,* 489–514; *New York Times,* Oct. 23, 1921, p. 10; "Employer Interference with Lawful Union Activity," *Columbia Law Review,* 37 (May 1937), 817; Burns is cited in Edwin E. Witte, *The Government in Labor Disputes* (New York: McGraw-Hill, 1932), 188; interview with Arthur H. Young, July 28, 1956; *Violations of Free Speech and Rights of Labor,* Senate Report No. 46, 75 Cong., 1 sess. (1937), pt. 3, pp. 9, 17, 26–28, 45–69, hereafter cited as *La Follette Committee Report* or *Hearings; La Follette Committee Hearings,* 177–78; "Employer Interference," 840; *La Follette Committee Report,* "Strikebreaking Services," Jan. 26, 1939; "Strikebreaking," *Fortune,* 11 (Jan. 1935), 57–61, 89; *La Follette Committee Report,* "Private Police Systems," pt. 2, pp. 3–4, 6, 11; Frederick Woltman and William L. Nunn, "Cossacks," *American Mercury,* 15 (Dec. 1928), 402, 406; "The U.S. Steel Corporation: III," *Fortune,* 13 (May 1936), 136, 138, 142; *La Follette Committee Report,* "Industrial Munitions," pt. 3, *passim;* Clarence E. Bonnett, *Employers' Associations in the United States* (New York: Macmillan, 1922), 550; *La Follette Committee Report,* "Employers' Associations and Collective Bargaining in California," pt. 2, pp. 91–106; *La Follette Committee Report,* "Labor Policies of Employers' Associations. National Metal Trades Association," pt. 4, pp. 1–48; *La Follette Committee Report,* "Labor Policies of Employers' Associations. The National Association of Manufacturers," pt. 3, pp. 1–42; NICB, *Collective Bargaining through Employee Representation* (New York: NICB, 1933), 6–10, 16; "The Pennsylvania Railroad: II," *Fortune,* 13 (June 1936), 148; BLS, Bull. No. 634, *Characteristics of Company Unions, 1935* (1937), 199.

4. The Ludlow strikers are cited in Ben M. Selekman and Mary Van Kleeck, *Employes' Representation in Coal Mines* (New York: Russell Sage, 1924), 10; the history of the Ludlow massacre is recounted in Barron B. Beshoar, *Out of the Depths* (Denver: Colorado Labor Historical Committee, 1942); Fosdick, *Rockefeller,* 149; "Formal Statement read by J. D. Rockefeller, Jr., before the United States Commission on Industrial Relations," *Survey,* 33 (Feb. 6, 1915), 525. A more critical estimate of King is in H. S. Ferns and B. Ostry, *The Age of Mackenzie King* (London: Heinemann, 1955), ch. 7.

5. "Rockefeller, Jr., Discovers Colorado," *Literary Digest,* 51 (Oct. 23, 1915), 928; the text of the plan is in John D. Rockefeller, Jr., *The Colorado Industrial Plan* (New York: The author, 1916), 63–94; John A. Fitch, "The Rockefeller Plan," *Survey,* 35 (Nov. 6, 1915), 147; Lescohier and Brandeis, *History of Labor,* 341; Clarence J.

Hicks, *My Life in Industrial Relations* (New York: Harper, 1941), 44–52; Selekman and Van Kleeck, *Employes' Representation, passim;* Fosdick, *Rockefeller,* 165; Mary Van Kleeck, *Miners and Management* (New York: Russell Sage, 1934), 324–25.

6. Rockefeller, *Colorado Industrial Plan, passim;* the executives' manifesto is cited in Arthur H. Young, "The Function of Industrial Relations," Sept. 5, 1927, Young Papers; *Recent Economic Changes,* vol. 2, p. 496; Paul H. Giddens, *Standard Oil Company (Indiana)* (New York: Appleton-Century-Crofts, 1955), 334; "Thirty Years of Labor Peace," *Fortune,* 34 (Nov. 1946), 206. The Jersey program is set forth in George Sweet Gibb and Evelyn H. Knowlton, *History of Standard Oil Company (New Jersey): The Resurgent Years, 1911–1927* (New York: Harper, 1956), ch. 18, and Anthony Alvanos, "Standard Oil Company (New Jersey): A Study of Its Board of Directors and Employee Relations Policy Development" (unpublished M.B.A. dissertation, New York University, 1955). Hicks, *My Life,* ch. 8, p. 81; Fosdick, *Rockefeller,* ch. 9, p. 187; interview with Arthur H. Young, July 28, 1956.

7. Otto S. Beyer, *et al., Wertheim Lectures on Industrial Relations, 1928* (Cambridge: Harvard University Press, 1929), 154–60; Perlman and Taft, *History of Labor,* 581; Arthur H. Young, "Some Facts and Factors Which Measure the Success of Employe Representation," Aug. 29, 1924, Young Papers; NICB, *Collective Bargaining,* 6–10, 16–17; BLS, Bull. No. 634 *Characteristics;* Adam, *An Australian,* 49; Gibb and Knowlton, *Standard Oil,* 591–92; Herbert Feis, *Labor Relations: A Study Made in the Procter & Gamble Company* (New York: Adelphi, 1928), 29; Butler, *Industrial Relations,* 92; Arthur H. Young, "The Obligations of Employer and Workers in Successful Production," May 6, 1924, Young Papers.

8. Lewisohn, *New Leadership,* 98; Sumner H. Slichter, "The Current Labor Policies of American Industries," *QJE,* 43 (May 1929), 393–95; Adam, *An Australian,* 20, 102; Beyer, *et al., Wertheim Lectures,* 125–26; "American Workingman," *Fortune,* 4 (Aug. 1931), 54; Lescohier and Brandeis, *History of Labor,* ch. 17; NICB, *Industrial Relations in Small Plants* (New York: NICB, 1929), 20.

9. Arthur H. Young, "Constructive Management Policies," Apr. 16, 1923, Young Papers; "The U.S. Steel Corporation: III," *Fortune,* 13 (May 1936), 141; Slichter, "Current Labor Policies," 411; Arthur H. Young, "How Industrial Accidents Are Being Prevented," Nov. 23, 1922, "The Dollar Side of Safety," Apr. 23, 1923, Young Papers; Beyer, *et al., Wertheim Lectures,* 143.

10. *New York Times,* Oct. 22, 1921; *Recent Economic Changes,* vol. 2, p. 523; "American Workingman," 54, 131; George Soule, *Prosperity Decade* (New York: Rinehart, 1947), 220; Keith Sward, *The Legend of Henry Ford* (New York: Rinehart, 1948), 201–4. Allan Nevins and Frank Ernest Hill paint a rosier picture of Ford, but they do not

contradict these statements in *Ford: Expansion and Challenge, 1915–1933* (New York: Scribner, 1957), ch. 20.

11. P. Sargent Florence, *Economics of Fatigue and Unrest* (New York: Holt, 1924); Prothro, *Dollar Decade*, 6–12; Arthur H. Young, "The Five-Day Week," May 26, 1927, Young Papers.

12. Murray Webb Latimer, *Industrial Pension Systems* (New York: Industrial Relations Counselors, 1932), vol. 2, p. 902; "Presbyterian Copper," *Fortune*, 6 (July 1932), 48; J. David House, *What the Employer Thinks* (Cambridge: Harvard University Press, 1927), 103; Adam, *An Australian*, 21; Slichter, "Current Labor Policies," 408–10; Robert F. Foerster and Else H. Dietl, *Employee Stock Ownership in the United States* (Princeton: Princeton University Press, 1927); NICB, *Employee Stock Purchase Plans and the Stock Market Crisis of 1929* (New York: NICB, 1930); *Recent Social Trends*, vol. 2, p. 845; Raskob is cited in Joe Alex Morris, *What A Year!* (New York: Harper, 1956), 285.

13. Insull is quoted in Schlesinger, *Crisis*, 120; Young is quoted in "American Workingman," 66; Bryce M. Stewart, *Unemployment Benefits in the United States* (New York: Industrial Relations Counselors, 1930), 95, 537–54; Feis, *Labor Relations*, 96–98; *Hearings before Committee on Education and Labor*, Senate, 70 Cong., 2 sess. (1928–29), xi; Arthur H. Young, "The Employer and Unemployment," May 27, 1929, Young Papers; "Obsolete Men," *Fortune*, 6 (Dec. 1932), 94.

14. NICB, *Industrial Relations*, 57; Ordway Tead, *New Tactics in Social Conflict* (New York: Vanguard, 1926), 124; Slichter, "Current Labor Policies," 433–34; "The Benevolent St. Joe," *Fortune*, 15 (June 1937), 98; Beyer, *et al.*, *Wertheim Lectures*, 138–39.

15. Edison is quoted in Morris, *What a Year!* 289; Henry F. May, "Shifting Perspectives on the 1920's," *Mississippi Valley Historical Review*, 43 (Dec. 1956), 425.

CHAPTER 4 (*Pages 190–243*)

1. Frankfurter and Greene, *Labor Injunction*, 52; Donald Richberg, *Tents of the Mighty* (New York: Willett, Clark & Colby, 1930), 162; Henry F. Pringle, *The Life and Times of William Howard Taft* (New York: Farrar & Rinehart, 1939), vol. 2, pp. 967, 1030.

2. *American Steel Foundries* v. *Tri-City Central Trades Council*, 257 U.S. 184, 209 (1921). General statements of the law of labor relations at the end of the twenties are found in Edwin E. Witte, *The Government in Labor Disputes* (New York: McGraw-Hill, 1932), and E. S. Oakes, *The Law of Organized Labor and Industrial Conflicts* (Rochester, N.Y.: Lawyers Co-operative, 1927). *Dorchy* v. *Kansas*, 272 U.S. 306, 311 (1926); *Duplex Printing Press Co.* v.

*Deering,* 254 U.S. 443, 474 (1921); *Bedford Cut Stone Co.* v. *Journeymen Stone Cutters,* 274 U.S. 37, 55 (1927); *Truax* v. *Corrigan,* 257 U.S. 312, 344 (1921); *Loewe* v. *Lawlor,* 208 U.S. 274 (1908); *Gompers* v. *Bucks Stove & Range Co.,* 221 U.S. 418 (1911).

3. Frankfurter and Greene, *Labor Injunction,* 52, 80, 81. In addition to this study, the enormous contemporary literature on the injunction notably included Witte, *Government,* chs. 5, 6; C. O. Swayzee, *Contempt of Court in Labor Injunction Cases* (New York: Columbia University Press, 1935); Duane McCracken, *Strike Injunctions in the New South* (Chapel Hill: University of North Carolina Press, 1931); P. F. Brissenden and C. O. Swayzee, "The Use of the Labor Injunction in the New York Needle Trades," *PSQ,* 44 (Dec. 1929), 548–68, and 45 (Mar. 1930), 87–111; Homer F. Carey and Herman Oliphant, "The Present Status of the Hitchman Case," *Columbia Law Review,* 29 (Apr. 1929), 441. See also *Hitchman Coal & Coke Co.* v. *Mitchell,* 172 Fed. 963 (D.C. W. Va. 1909); 202 Fed. 512 (D.C. W. Va. 1912); 214 Fed. 685 (4th Cir. 1914); 245 U.S. 229 (1917); *Coppage* v. *Kansas,* 236 U.S. 1, 27 (1915); Walter Wheeler Cook, "Privileges of Labor Unions in the Struggle for Life," *Yale Law Journal,* 27 (Apr. 1918), 798; John H. Walker to Green, Apr. 12, 1930, Green Papers; George Wharton Pepper, "Injunctions in Labor Disputes," *Proceedings of the American Bar Association* (1924), 176, 179; *Great Northern Ry.* v. *Brosseau,* 286 Fed. 414, 416 (D.C. N. Dak. 1923); Francis B. Sayre, "Labor and the Courts," *Yale Law Journal,* 39 (Mar. 1930), 682.

4. *United Mine Workers* v. *Coronado Coal Co.,* 259 U.S. 344, 385–91 (1922); Witte, *Government,* ch. 7.

5. Irving Bernstein, *The New Deal Collective Bargaining Policy* (Berkeley: University of California Press, 1950), 9–14; William M. Leiserson, *Right and Wrong in Labor Relations* (Berkeley: University of California Press, 1938), 24–27.

6. 26 Stat. 209 (1890). The argument for inclusion of unions under the Sherman Act is in Alpheus T. Mason, *Organized Labor and the Law* (Durham: Duke University Press, 1925), ch. 7; that for exemption is in Edward Berman, *Labor and the Sherman Act* (New York: Harper, 1930). 38 Stat. 730 (1914); Dallas L. Jones, "The Enigma of the Clayton Act," *Industrial and Labor Relations Review,* 10 (Jan. 1957), 201–21; Frankfurter and Greene, *Labor Injunction,* 145; Berman, *Labor,* 129–30, 145, App. B; G. W. Terborgh, "The Application of the Sherman Law to Trade-Union Activities," *JPE,* 37 (Apr. 1929), 204, n. 6; Witte, *Government,* 69–70; *Coronado Coal Co.* v. *United Mine Workers,* 268 U.S. 295 (1925); *United Mine Workers* v. *Red Jacket Consolidated Coal & Coke Co.,* 18 F. (2d) 839 (4th Cir. 1927); *cert. denied,* 275 U.S. 536 (1927); Schlesinger, *Crisis,* 51; *United States* v. *Brims,* 272 U.S. 549 (1926); *Industrial Assn. of San Francisco* v. *United States,* 268 U.S. 64

(1925); Alpheus T. Mason, *Harlan Fiske Stone* (New York: Viking, 1956), 255–60; Frankfurter and Greene, *Labor Injunction*, 197; Terborgh, "Application of the Sherman Law," 207; Sayre, "Labor and the Courts," 690; Witte, *Government*, 74.

7. H. D. Wolf, *The Railroad Labor Board* (Chicago: University of Chicago Press, 1927), ch. 16; C. O. Fisher, "The New Railway Labor Act," *AER*, 17 (Mar. 1927), 177–87; Donald R. Richberg, *My Hero* (New York: Putnam, 1954), 125 ff.; Philip Taft, *The AF of L from the Death of Gompers to the Merger* (New York: Harper, 1959), 67–71; 44 Stat. 568 (1926); *Brotherhood of Railway & Steamship Clerks* v. *Texas & New Orleans Railroad Co.*, 24 F. (2d) 426 (1928); 25 F. (2d) 873 (1928); 33 F. (2d) 13 (5th Cir. 1929); William H. Spencer, "The National Railroad Adjustment Board," *Journal of Business*, 11 (Apr. 1938), 11–12.

8. 37 Stat. 738 (1913); Howard S. Kaltenborn, *Governmental Adjustment of Labor Disputes* (Chicago: Foundation, 1943), 14–15; Harry A. Millis and Royal E. Montgomery, *Organized Labor* (New York: McGraw-Hill, 1945), 727–30; Witte, *Government*, 251–55; Ting Tsz Ko, *Governmental Methods of Adjusting Labor Disputes* (New York: Columbia University Press, 1926), ch. 2.

9. E. F. Dowell, *A History of Criminal Syndicalism Legislation in the United States* (Baltimore: Johns Hopkins Press, 1939); *Whitney* v. *California*, 274 U.S. 357 (1927).

10. Social legislation in the twenties is described in Lescohier and Brandeis, *History of Labor*; Harry A. Millis and Royal E. Montgomery, *The Economics of Labor* (New York: McGraw-Hill, 1938), vols. 1, 2; and John R. Commons and John B. Andrews, *Principles of Labor Legislation* (4th rev. ed.; New York: Harper, 1936). Workmen's compensation, which developed in the early twentieth century, was not an important issue in either the twenties or thirties and so will not be discussed.

11. *Muller* v. *Oregon*, 208 U.S. 412, 422 (1908); Alpheus T. Mason, *Brandeis: A Free Man's Life* (New York: Viking, 1946), 248–52; *Atkin* v. *Kansas*, 191 U.S. 207, 224 (1903); *Wilson* v. *New*, 243 U.S. 332 (1917); *Holden* v. *Hardy*, 169 U.S. 366 (1898); *Lochner* v. *New York*, 198 U.S. 45 (1905); *Bunting* v. *Oregon*, 243 U.S. 426 (1917).

12. *Stettler* v. *O'Hara*, 243 U.S. 629 (1917); Thomas Reed Powell, "The Judiciality of Minimum-Wage Legislation," *Harvard Law Review*, 37 (Mar. 1924), 566, 572; J. F. Paschal, *Mr. Justice Sutherland: A Man against the State* (Princeton: Princeton University Press, 1951), 124–25, 236–41; *Adkins* v. *Children's Hospital*, 261 U.S. 525 (1923); *Murphy* v. *Sardell*, 269 U.S. 530 (1925); *Topeka Laundry Co.* v. *Court of Industrial Relations*, 119 Kan. 12 (1925); *Donham* v. *West-Nelson Mfg. Co.*, 273 U.S. 657 (1927).

13. Gardner Jackson, "Harvard — School for Scrubwomen" and "Harvard

'Explains,'" *Nation*, 130 (Jan. 29, Feb. 19, 1930), 118–19, 212–13; *New York Times*, Mar. 17, May 8, 15, 1930; *Collected Edition of Heywood Broun*, Heywood Hale Broun, comp. (New York: Harcourt, Brace, 1941), 233; Powell, "Judiciality," 545; NICB, *Minimum Wage Legislation in Massachusetts* (New York: NICB, 1927), ch. 6.

14. *Hammer v. Dagenhart*, 247 U.S. 251 (1918); *Bailey* v. *Drexel Furniture Co.*, 259 U.S. 20, 38 (1922).

15. *Adams* v. *Tanner*, 244 U.S. 590 (1917); *Ribnik* v. *McBride*, 277 U.S. 350 (1928); Paul H. Douglas, "Connecting Men and Jobs," *Survey*, 45 (Dec. 1, 1930), 253; George H. Trafton, "The Wagner Bill and the Hoover Veto," *ALLR*, 21 (Mar. 1931), 86.

16. The Illinois law is cited in Lescohier and Brandeis, *History of Labor*, 224–25. See also Josephine Chapin Brown, *Public Relief, 1929–1939* (New York: Holt, 1940), 3–59.

17. Pringle, *Taft*, vol. 2. pp. 967, 1044; William Allen White, *A Puritan in Babylon* (New York: Macmillan, 1938), 366; Mason, *Stone*, 263.

CHAPTER 5 (*Pages 247–261*)

1. Herbert Hoover, *The New Day* (Palo Alto: Stanford University Press, 1928), 16.

2. *New York Times*, Aug. 11, 1955, p. 12; Thomas L. Stokes, *Chip Off My Shoulder* (Princeton: Princeton University Press, 1940), 234–35; Donald R. Richberg, *My Hero* (New York: Putnam, 1954), 149; Willmott Lewis is quoted in the *New York Times*, Nov. 7, 1930, p. 5; Richard Hofstadter, *The American Political Tradition* (New York: Knopf, 1948), 283. Hoover's philosophy is set forth in his *Principles of Mining: Valuation, Organization and Administration* (New York: Hill, 1909), 167–68; Hoover, *American Individualism* (New York: Doubleday, Page, 1923), 7–9; Hoover, *New Day, passim.*

3. Department of Commerce, *Survey of Current Business, 1931 Annual Supplement* (Washington: 1931), 3, 13, 81; John Kenneth Galbraith, *The Great Crash, 1929* (Boston: Houghton Mifflin, 1955); Professor Ripley is quoted in William Allen White, *A Puritan in Babylon* (New York: Macmillan, 1938), 337–38; Myers and Newton, *Hoover Administration*, 26–27, 136–37; Schlesinger, *Crisis*, 163; *New York Times*, Nov. 22, 1929, p. 1; William Green to international unions, Nov. 27, 1929, to J. H. Walker, Jan. 3, 1930, Green Papers; Hoover, *State Papers*, vol. 1, pp. 137, 184; John Frey to W. A. Appleton, Dec. 2, 1929, Frey Papers.

4. Anne Page, *Employment and Unemployment, 1929 to 1935*, Office of National Recovery Administration, Division of Review, No. 45, pt. B (Washington: 1936), 12; James Couzens, "Long Wages,"

*Survey*, 64 (Apr. 1, 1930), 8; Beulah Amidon, "Toledo: A City the Auto Ran Over," *Survey*, 63 (Mar. 1, 1930), 672; Samuel M. Levin, "The Ford Unemployment Policy," *ALLR*, 22 (June 1932), 101–7; Helen Hall, "When Detroit's Out of Gear," *Survey*, 64 (Apr. 1, 1930), 51–52; Porter R. Lee to Arthur Woods, Nov. 4, 1930, PECE Papers; McMahon is cited in Adamic, *My America*, 263; Gardner Jackson, "Women Workers in Massachusetts," *Nation*, 131 (Dec. 3, 1930), 608; Gertrude Springer, "Up from Bankruptcy," *Survey*, 66 (July 1, 1931), 361; J. Frederic Dewhurst and Robert R. Nathan, *Social and Economic Character of Unemployment in Philadelphia, April, 1930*, BLS, Bull. No. 555 (1932), 1–2, 3–5; "Employment Survey of Metropolitan Life Insurance Company," *MLR*, 32 (Mar. 1931), 573–74; Page, *Employment*, 24, 34; Ewan Clague and Webster Powell, *Ten Thousand Out of Work* (Philadelphia: University of Pennsylvania Press, 1933), 77–78.

5. *New York Times*, Feb. 9, p. 1, Feb. 29, p. 29, Mar. 17, 1930, p. 22; Davis Address to Kiwanis Club of Harrisburg, Pa., Feb. 3, 1930, Davis to S. S. Fontaine, Mar. 28, 1930, Davis Papers; Daniel Fusfeld, *The Economic Thought of Franklin D. Roosevelt and the Origins of the New Deal* (New York: Columbia University Press, 1956), 166, 170; Frankfurter to Roosevelt, Apr. 18, 1930, Roosevelt Papers; Steffens to Yvonne Davidson, Dec. 18, 1930, in *The Letters of Lincoln Steffens*, Ella Winter and Granville Hicks, eds. (New York: Harcourt, Brace, 1938), vol. 2, p. 885; Gardner to B. B. Gossett, Feb. 1, 1930, *Public Papers and Letters of Oliver Max Gardner*, D. L. Corbitt, ed. (Raleigh, N.C.: Council of State of N.C., 1937), 584; *New York Times*, Apr. 6, 1956, p. 12; Stuart Chase, "The Nemesis of American Business," *Harper's*, 161 (July 1930), 129; Green to Ben Tillett, Aug. 22, 1930, Green Papers; Cooke to Joseph Willitts, Oct. 3, 1930, Cooke Papers.

6. BLS, Bull. No. 540, *Union Scales of Wages and Hours of Labor, May 15, 1930* (1931), 4; J. M. Hunter, *Wage Trends in Prosperity and Depression Prior to NRA*, Office of National Recovery Administration, Division of Review, No. 45, pt. C (Washington: 1936); Hunt to Arthur Woods, Oct. 31, 1930, PECE Papers; Alfred L. Bernheim, "Are Wages Going Down?" *Nation*, 131 (Nov. 5, 1930), 489–91; Leo Wolman, "Wages and the Recovery of Business," *Proceedings of the Academy of Political Science*, 14 (June 1931), 105–6; *Historical Statistics*, 67, 68; Leo Wolman, *Wages During the Depression*, National Bureau of Economic Research, Bull. No. 46 (1933), 2.

CHAPTER 6  (*Pages 262–286*)

1. Unfortunately, there is no biography of Wagner. This sketch is based upon various articles in the *New York Times;* Philip Ham-

burger, "The Mayor," *New Yorker,* Jan. 26, 1957, pp. 39–61, Feb. 2, 1957, pp. 39–67; *Time,* July 11, 1932, p. 4; *Newsweek,* Feb. 2, 1935, p. 21; Frances Perkins, *The Roosevelt I Knew* (New York: Viking, 1946), 22–23; P. F. Brissenden and C. O. Swayzee, "The Use of the Labor Injunction in the New York Needle Trades," *PSQ,* 44 (Dec. 1929), 559–62; *Schlesinger* v. *Quinto,* 192 N.Y. Supp. 564 (Sup. Ct. 1922); Robert F. Wagner, "Sound Policy to Break the Bread Lines," *Independent,* 120 (Apr. 14, 1928), 353–54; Oswald Garrison Villard, "Pillars of Government," *Forum and Century,* 96 (Sept. 1936), 124–28.

2. Van Kleeck to Simon H. Rifkind, Jan. 18, Rifkind to Paul U. Kellogg, Jan. 19, Bryce M. Stewart to Rifkind, Mar. 4, 1929, Supplementary Memorandum *in re* Census Amendment, n.d., Wagner Papers; Perkins, *Roosevelt,* 95–96; Myers and Newton, *Hoover Administration,* 36; Herbert Hoover, *Memoirs . . . The Great Depression . . .* (New York: Macmillan, 1952), 48–49; Charles E. Persons, "Census Reports on Unemployment in April, 1930," *Annals,* 154 (Mar. 1931), 12–16; Robert R. Nathan, "Estimates of Unemployment in the United States," *International Labour Review,* 33 (Jan. 1936), 63; Paul A. Samuelson and Russell A. Nixon, "Estimates of Unemployment in the United States," *Review of Economic Statistics,* 22 (Aug. 1940), 108–9; *New York Times,* Jan. 21, p. 1, Jan. 23, p. 11, April 29, p. 2, June 19, p. 27, July 2, 1930, p. 4; 46 Stat. 1019 (1930); BLS, Bull. No. 542, *Report of the Advisory Committee on Employment Statistics* (1931); Aryness Joy, "Recent Progress in Employment Statistics," *JASA,* 29 (Dec. 1934), 358–59; *Unemployment in the United States,* Hearings before the House Committee on the Judiciary, 71 Cong., 2 sess. (1930), 164.

3. Arthur D. Gayer, *Public Works in Prosperity and Depression* (New York: National Bureau of Economic Research, 1935); House Hearings, *Unemployment,* 1–4; *A Bill to Provide for the Advance Planning . . . of Public Works . . . ,* Hearings on S. 3059, Senate Subcommittee of the Committee on Commerce, 71 Cong., 2 sess. (1930); *CR,* vol. 72, pt. 7, pp. 7796–7803, pt. 11, pp. 12238–53, vol. 74, pt. 3, p. 2763, pt. 4, pp. 3813–17; Andrews to La Guardia, June 19, 1930, La Guardia Papers; *New York Times,* June 20, p. 24, Oct. 4, 1930, p. 6; Buttenheim to R. P. Lamont, Oct. 23, Arthur Woods to Hoover, Nov. 21, Mallery to Woods, Dec. 12, Hunt, *et al.,* to Woods, Dec. 12, 1930, PECE Papers; Buttenheim to Wagner, Jan. 3, 1931, Wagner Papers; Hoover, *State Papers,* vol. 1, pp. 432–33; 46 Stat. 1084–87 (1931); Myers and Newton, *Hoover Administration,* 66; Mills to E. C. Stokes, May 13, 1932, Mills Papers; D. H. Sawyer, "Municipal Construction as Unemployment Relief," *Annals,* 162 (July 1932), 134; Sawyer to Julius Klein, July 24, 1931, J. S. Taylor Draft Statement, June 9, 1930, Report, FESB, July 1, 1932, Federal Employment Stabilization Board Papers.

4. The text of S. 3060 is in House Hearings, *Unemployment,* 4–7; A

*Bill to Provide for . . . a National Employment System . . .*, Hearings on S. 3060, Senate Subcommittee of the Committee on Commerce, 71 Cong., 2 sess. (1930); Wagner to J. B. Andrews, Apr. 3, 1930, Wagner Papers; *CR*, vol. 72, pt. 8, pp. 8740–49, vol. 74, pt. 6, pp. 5764–65; Cooke to Andrews, June 21, Andrews to Florence Kelley, Oct. 10, 1930, Andrews Papers; *New York Times*, Apr. 11, p. 19, June 29, 1930, p. 18.

5. Woods to Hoover, Nov. 21, B. M. Stewart to Woods, Dec. 19, Hunt to Woods, Dec. 23, Committee Meeting, Dec. 26, 1930, Willits to Woods, Jan. 31, Willits to Doak, Feb. 11, 1931, PECE Papers; E. P. Hayes, *Activities of the President's Emergency Committee for Employment, 1930–1931* (Concord, N.H.: Rumford, 1936), 141; Wagner to Doak, Feb. 6, Andrews to Wagner, Feb. 13, 1931, Wagner Papers. Hoover named Doak Secretary of Labor over vigorous AFL opposition. Green to Hoover, Nov. 24, Dec. 4, 1930, Green Papers; *New York Times*, Feb. 20, p. 1, Feb. 21, 1931, p. 13; *CR*, vol. 74, pt. 6, pp. 5752–77. The Labor Department Papers contain a great number of letters imploring Hoover to sign; Wagner to Hoover, Mar. 7, 1931, Wagner Papers; Gilbreth to Woods, Mar. 6, 1931, Analysis of the President's Statement . . . , Mar. 9, 1931, PECE Papers.

6. The veto message is in Hoover, *State Papers*, vol. 1, pp. 530–31; Lescohier and Brandeis, *History of Labor*, 209–10; Slichter to Andrews, Mar. 16, 1931, Andrews Papers; Analysis of the President's Statement . . . , Mar. 9, 1931, PECE Papers; Hoover, *State Papers*, vol. 1, p. 47.

7. Hoover, *State Papers*, vol. 1, pp. 532–33; Gladys L. Palmer, "The History and Functioning of the United States Employment Service," Nov. 1934, pp. 15–17, Committee on Economic Security Papers; *New York Times*, Sept. 2, 1931, p. 3; Hall to Doak, May 2, 1931, Wagner Papers; Rooksbery to Andrews, Aug. 12, 1931, as well as numerous letters to Andrews from state officials at approximately this date, Andrews Papers; R. C. Atkinson, L. C. Odencrantz, and Ben Deming, *Public Employment Service in the United States* (Chicago: Public Administration Service, 1938), 21; the Legion official is cited in Abraham Epstein, *Insecurity: A Challenge to America* (New York: Random House, 1938), 281–82.


CHAPTER 7  *(Pages 287–311)*

1. Hoover, *State Papers*, vol. 1, pp. 470, 496.
2. Ewan Clague and Webster Powell, *Ten Thousand Out of Work* (Philadelphia: University of Pennsylvania Press, 1933), 79, 98–103, 111, 115; *Unemployment Relief*, Hearings on S. 262, Senate Subcommittee on Manufactures, 72 Cong., 1 sess. (1931–32), 18–19; Helen Hall, "Rents," *Survey*, 68 (Apr. 1, 1932), 42–44; Samuel M. Levin,

"The Ford Unemployment Policy," *ALLR*, 22 (June 1932), 107; *New York Times*, May 3, 1931, p. 5; Allan Nevins and Frank Ernest Hill, *Ford: Expansion and Challenge, 1915–1933* (New York: Scribner, 1957), 493; Gerard Swope, "Management Cooperation with Workers for Economic Welfare," *Annals*, 154 (Mar. 1931), 135–37; "Relief Measures of Special Conference Committee Companies," Oct. 7, 1931, PECE Papers; "Can Prices, Production and Employment Be Effectively Regulated?" *Proceedings of the Academy of Political Science*, 14 (Jan. 1932), 14–17; "No One Has Starved," *Fortune*, 6 (Sept. 1932), 19.

3. New York's relief program in the early depression years is treated in Adamic, *My America*, 294–97; Lillian Brandt, *An Impressionistic View of the Winter of 1930–31 in New York City* (New York: Welfare Council, 1932); Joanna C. Colcord, *Emergency Work Relief* (New York: Russell Sage, 1932), 136–60; Gertrude Springer, "The Job Line," *Survey*, 65 (Feb. 1, 1931), 496 ff.; Frances Warfield, "Emergency Lunches," *New Yorker*, Apr. 30, 1932, pp. 32 ff.; and the *New York Times*; Hoover's observations on apples are in *Memoirs of Herbert Hoover: The Great Depression . . .* (New York: Macmillan, 1952), 195; "When Yuba Plays the Tuba" is from *Third Little Show* (New York: Harms, 1931). The *New Yorker*, especially Howard Brubaker's column, is rich in relief jokes.

4. Karl Borders, "Cashless Chicago," *Survey*, 53 (Feb. 15, 1930), 567 ff.; Colcord, *Emergency Work Relief*, 64–74; Senate Hearings, *Unemployment Relief*, 28–42, 256–70; Edmund Wilson, *Travels in Two Democracies* (New York: Harcourt, Brace, 1936), 24–30; *New York Times*, Nov. 12, 1930, p. 12; Emmerson to Arthur Woods, Nov. 6, 1930, PECE Papers.

5. Jacob Billikopf, "What Have We Learned about Unemployment?" *Proceedings of the National Conference on Social Work* (Chicago: University of Chicago Press, 1931), 25–50; Colcord, *Emergency Work Relief*, 166–81; Committee for Unemployment Relief, *Unemployment Relief in Philadelphia* (Philadelphia: 1933); Community Council of Philadelphia, *A Cooperative Study of School Breakfasts* (Philadelphia: 1932); Community Council of Philadelphia, *Personal Loans in Unemployment Relief* (Philadelphia: 1933); Karl de Schweinitz, "Philadelphia Takes Heart," *Survey*, 66 (May 15, 1931), 217–19; Senate Hearings, *Unemployment Relief*, 52.

6. Beulah Amidon, "Detroit Does Something About It," *Survey*, 65 (Feb. 15, 1931), 540–42; Helen Hall, "When Detroit's Out of Gear," *Survey*, 64 (Apr. 1, 1930), 9 ff.; Mauritz A. Hallgren, "Detroit's Liberal Mayor," *Nation*, 132 (May 13, 1931), 526–28; William J. Norton, "The Relief Crisis in Detroit," *Social Service Review*, 7 (Mar. 1933), 1–10; Senate Hearings, *Unemployment Relief*, 282–83; Pierce Williams Report, Jan. 9, 1931, POUR Papers.

7. Bernard Bellush, *Franklin D. Roosevelt as Governor of New York*

(New York: Columbia University Press, 1955), 134–36; Senator Arthur H. Vandenberg to Arthur Woods, Oct. 25, 1930, PECE Papers; "No One Has Starved," 19.

8. Formation of Committee: Interview with E. P. Hayes and E. L. Bernays, Feb. 26, Hunt to Alice Dickson, Feb. 9, Preliminary Report of the PECE, n.d., Hoover to Senator W. L. Jones, June 11, 1931, Hayes to Woods, Dec. 29, W. E. Brown to Woods, Nov. 29, Woods to Hoover, Nov. 21, 1930, PECE Papers; William Hard, "Our Doctor of Unemployment," *Review of Reviews*, 82 (Dec. 1930), 42–43; Myers and Newton, *Hoover Administration*, 53; E. P. Hayes, *Activities of the President's Emergency Committee for Employment* (Concord, N.H.: Rumford, 1936), 3, 38–95; *New Yorker*, Aug. 15, 1931, p. 15.

9. Niles Carpenter, "The New American Immigration Policy and the Labor Market," *QJE*, 45 (Feb. 1931), 720; Gardner Jackson, "Doak the Deportation Chief," *Nation*, 132 (Mar. 18, 1931), 295–96; Green to members of Congress, Jan. 30, 1931, Green Papers; Woods to R. P. Lamont, Jan. 28, 1931, Hunt to Laurence Richey, Nov. 29, 1930, PECE Papers.

10. Hayes, *Activities*, 1, 2, 67–68; Myron C. Taylor, *Spreading Work to Avoid Lay-Offs*, Jan. 27, 1931; Wage and Salary Retrenchment in Special Conference Committee Companies Memorandum, Sept. 23, 1931, PECE Papers; *Historical Statistics*, 67–68; Stevenson to W. S. Gifford, Nov. 11, 1931, POUR Papers.

11. Krafft to Woods, Apr. 11, Lee to Woods, Jan. 14, Payne to Woods, Feb. 9, Confidential Report, Feb. 9, Payne to Woods, Feb. 9, Memorandum of conversation with President Hoover and Judge Payne, Feb. 16, Woods to Payne, Feb. 14, Conferences with Red Cross Officials, Feb. 21, 24, Hyde to Woods, Feb. 25, Committee Meeting, Mar. 21, Warburton to Woods, Apr. 7, Croxton memorandum, May 28, Payne to Hoover, June 1, Croxton memorandum, June 2, Pickett to Croxton, June 9, Croxton memorandum, July 2, Pickett to Payne, July 3, Pickett to Croxton, Aug. 5, 1931, PECE Papers.

12. Sumner H. Slichter, "Doles for Employers," *New Republic*, 65 (Dec. 31, 1930), 183; Gifford Pinchot to Amos Pinchot, Nov. 17, 1931, Pinchot Papers.


CHAPTER 8 (*Pages 312–333*)


1. Ernest Nagel and James R. Newman, "Gödel's Proof," *Scientific American*, 194 (June 1956), 71–86; Thomas Wolfe to Julia Elizabeth Wolfe, Sept. 21, 1931, *Thomas Wolfe's Letters to His Mother*, J. K. Terry, ed. (New York: Scribner, 1943), 210–11. The full story of what took place at Mellon's apartment must remain shrouded in some mystery until the Hoover archives are opened. It is briefly

described in Thomas L. Stokes, *Chip Off My Shoulder* (Princeton: Princeton University Press, 1940), 283–84.

2. "The Diminishing Wage," *Nation*, 133 (Oct. 7, 1931), 351; "Supplementary: Steel," *Fortune*, 4 (July 1931), 114; *New York Times*, July 30, p. 3, Sept. 25, 1931, p. 19; "Wage Cut," *Fortune*, 5 (Apr. 1932), 57–59, 120–25.

3. "It Seems to Heywood Broun," *Nation*, 130 (Mar. 26, 1930), 353; Anne Page, *Employment and Unemployment, 1929 to 1935*, Office of National Recovery Administration, Division of Review, No. 45, pt. B (Washington: 1936), 12, 22; Mauritz A. Hallgren, "Bloody Williamson is Hungry," *Nation*, 134 (Apr. 20, 1932), 457–58; "No One Has Starved," *Fortune*, 6 (Sept. 1932), 24; William Hard, "Ingots and Doles," *Survey*, 67 (Jan. 15, 1932), 454; *Unemployment Relief*, Hearings before the Senate Subcommittee on Manufactures, 72 Cong., 1 sess. (1931–32), 42, 27.

4. A. H. Hansen, M. G. Murray, R. A. Stevenson, and B. M. Stewart, *A Program for Unemployment Insurance and Relief in the United States* (Minneapolis: University of Minnesota Press, 1934), 34; J. A. Bloodworth, *Social Consequences of Prolonged Unemployment*, University of Minnesota, Employment Stabilization Research Institute, Bull. No. 5 (1933), 16; Wladimir Woytinsky, *The Social Consequences of the Economic Depression* (Geneva: International Labor Office, 1936), 147; "The President Violates the Law," *Nation*, 133 (Dec. 30, 1931), 712; "Negroes Out of Work," *Nation*, 132 (Apr. 22, 1931), 442; *International Teamster*, Mar. 1931, p. 3.

5. Bloodworth, *Social Consequences*, 16; Ewan Clague and W. J. Couper, *After the Shutdown* (New Haven: Yale University Press, 1934), 110–11; BLS, Bull. No. 616, *Handbook of Labor Statistics* (1936); *Historical Statistics*, 67, 68, 70; Clarence J. Enzler, *Some Social Aspects of the Depression* (Washington: Catholic University Press, 1939), 15; Senate Hearings, *Unemployment Relief*, 19, 25, 27, 148–49; Schlesinger, *Crisis*, 249; Leo Wolman, *Wages During the Depression*, National Bureau of Economic Research, Bull. No. 46 (1933), 2; Harold M. Levinson, *Unionism, Wage Trends, and Income Distribution, 1914–1947* (Ann Arbor: University of Michigan Press, 1951), 44–45.

6. *Report and Recommendations of the California State Unemployment Commission* (Sacramento: State Printing Office, 1932), 145–46; *Historical Statistics*, 31, 33, 37, 38; National Resources Committee, *The Problems of a Changing Population* (Washington: 1938), 9, 85; H. L. Kerwin to T. F. McMahon, Feb. 26, C. L. Richardson to Kerwin, Aug. 17, 1931, Labor Department Papers.

7. The San Francisco desertion is reported in the *New York Times*, Feb. 13, 1932, p. 30; the hobo song is in B. A. Botkin and Alvin F. Harlow, *A Treasury of Railroad Folklore* (New York: Crown, 1953), 461; Morris Markey's road experiences appear in *This Country of*

*Yours* (Boston: Little, Brown, 1932), 135, 200-2; the Bane report is in Senate Hearings, *Unemployment Relief*, 106-9; S. Rexford Black deals with the transient camps in *California State Labor Camps* (San Francisco: California State Unemployment Commission, 1932); the Hollinan story is in *The Roosevelt Era*, Milton Crane, ed., (New York: Boni and Gaer, 1947), 32-35; the trackside remark is in J. Prentice Murphy, "America on the March," *Survey*, 22 (Mar. 1933), 147 ff. Some other items in the immense literature of transiency are Nels Anderson, *Men on the Move* (Chicago: University of Chicago Press, 1940); Children's Bureau, *Memorandum on the Transient Boy* (Washington, 1932); "No One Has Starved," *Fortune*, 6 (Sept. 1932), 28; "200,000 Wandering Boys," *Fortune*, 7 (Feb. 1933), 47; John Kazarian, "The Starvation Army," *Nation*, 136 (Apr. 12, 19, 26, 1933), 396, 443, 472; A. Wayne McMillen, "An Army of Boys on the Loose," *Survey*, 68 (Sept. 1, 1932), 389-93; James Munsey, "Oakland's 'Sewer-Pipe City,'" *Nation*, 136 (Jan. 25, 1933), 93; National Resources Committee, *The Problems of a Changing Population* (Washington: 1938), 88; *New Yorker*, Feb. 27, 1932, p. 10; Karl Pretshold, "How We Solved It in Oklahoma City," *Nation*, 133 (Oct. 7, 1931), 359-61; and the Report of the California Unemployment Commission.

8. Adamic, *My America*, 283-93; E. Wight Bakke, *The Unemployed Worker* (New Haven: Yale University Press, 1940), 17, 115; Ruth S. Cavan and Katherine S. Rauck, *The Family and the Depression* (Chicago: University of Chicago Press, 1938); *Historical Statistics*, 46, 49; Robert S. and Helen Merrell Lynd, *Middletown in Transition* (New York: Harcourt, Brace, 1937), 149, 163, 544; *Report of California Unemployment Commission*, 115; Samuel A. Stouffer and Paul F. Lazarsfeld, *Research Memorandum on the Family in the Depression* (New York: Social Science Research Council, 1937); Senate Hearings, *Unemployment Relief*, 75.

9. Breckinridge to F. C. Croxton, Oct. 17, 1932, POUR Papers; "Child Labor in the United States in 1932," *MLR*, 37 (Dec. 1933), 1361-73; P. C. French, "Children on Strike," *Nation*, 136 (May 31, 1933), 611-12; "Sweatshop Conditions," *MLR*, 36 (Mar. 1933), 500-502; Ray Lyman Wilbur, "Children in National Emergencies," *Proceedings of the National Conference of Social Work* (Chicago: University of Chicago Press, 1933), 27-30; Fox to Editor, *Nation*, 133 (Sept. 9, 1931), 257-58.

10. Ewan Clague, "When Relief Stops, What Do They Eat?" *Survey*, 68 (Nov. 15, 1932), 583-85; Senate Hearings, *Unemployment Relief*, 116-23; F. H. La Guardia to Howard Swain, June 14, 1932, La Guardia Papers; Hoover, *State Papers*, vol. 2, pp. 101, 256, 283-84, 345; *Nation*, 134 (Apr. 27, 1932), 479, 135 (Dec. 14, 1932), 579; Allan Nevins and F. E. Hill, *Ford: Expansion and Challenge, 1915-1933* (New York: Scribner, 1957), 587; Will Rogers, "Bacon and

Beans and Limousines," *Survey*, 67 (Nov. 15, 1931), 185; Mary Ross, "Health Inventory: 1934," *Survey*, 23 (Jan. 1934), 15–17, 38–40; Edgar Sydenstricker, "Sickness and the New Poor: Income and Health for 7500 Families, 1929–1933," *Survey*, 23 (Apr. 1934), 160–62, 208.

11. Adamic, *My America*, 111; Jane Addams, "Social Consequences of Depression," *Survey*, 67 (Jan. 1, 1932), 370–71; Frederick Lewis Allen, *The Big Change* (New York: Harper, 1952), 147–49; Enzler, *Social Aspects*, 55; John Kenneth Galbraith, *The Great Crash, 1929* (Boston: Houghton Mifflin, 1954), 134; Alfred Kazin, *On Native Grounds* (New York: Reynal & Hitchcock, 1942), 363–66; Alva Johnston, "A Tour of Minskyville," *New Yorker*, May 28, 1932, p. 37; Schlesinger, *Crisis*, 244–45; William Allen White, *A Puritan in Babylon* (New York: Macmillan, 1938), 427.

12. Adamic, *My America*, 114–15.

CHAPTER 9  (*Pages 334–357*)

1. John Lombardi, *Labor's Voice in the Cabinet* (New York: Columbia University Press, 1942); *AFL Weekly News Service*, Dec. 6, 1930; Green to Hoover, Nov. 24, 1930, Green Papers.

2. Leo Wolman, *Ebb and Flow in Trade Unionism* (New York: National Bureau of Economic Research, 1936), 34, 41; Matthew Josephson, *Sidney Hillman* (Garden City: Doubleday, 1952), 343, 348; Benjamin Stolberg, *Tailor's Progress* (Garden City: Doubleday, 1944), 152; Harvey O'Connor, *History of the Oil Workers International Union* (Denver: Oil Workers, 1950), 26–27; Memorandum of conference between Emerson and McGee, Aug. 29, 1931, Beyer Papers; *International Teamster*, Mar. 1931, pp. 15–16; "Berkshire Knitting Mills," *Fortune*, 5 (Jan. 1932), 54, 59; Harry C. Bates, *Bricklayers' Century of Craftsmanship* (Washington: Bricklayers, 1955), 227–28; *Advance*, Dec. 19, 1930, p. 4; Matthew Josephson, *Union House, Union Bar* (New York: Random House, 1956), 186–89; *Hosiery Worker*, Dec. 31, 1931, p. 1; *Justice*, Oct. 1931, p. 1, Jan., p. 2, June 1932, p. 1; Schlesinger to Lehman, Jan. 19, Lehman to Schlesinger, Jan. 21, 1932, Lehman Papers; *Typographical Journal*, Apr., p. 367, June 1932, p. 650, Jan. 1933, p. 3; *Journal of Electrical Workers*, Mar., p. 120, May, p. 230, Dec. 1931, p. 622, Sept. 1932, p. 430, Jan., p. 12, Aug. 1933, p. 310; Green to George Googe, Jan. 12, Green to Googe, May 21, Green to Frankfurter, *et al.*, Sept. 1932, Green Papers.

3. Slichter, *Union Policies*, 497–502, 430–32, 544–54; Richard C. Nyman, *Union-Management Cooperation in the "Stretch Out"* (New Haven: Yale University Press, 1934); J. Foster Smith to Morris L. Cooke, June 6, 1932, Cooke Papers.

4. *Recent Social Trends,* vol. 2, pp. 837–38; Josephson, *Hillman,* 348–49, 358.

5. Harold Seidman, *Labor Czars: A History of Labor Racketeering* (New York: Liveright, 1938); Malcolm Johnson, *Crime on the Labor Front* (New York: McGraw-Hill, 1950); Sidney Lens, *Left, Right and Center* (Hinsdale, Ill.: Regnery, 1949), ch. 14; Thomas to Lehman, Nov. 5, 1931, Lehman Papers; Green to Morrin, July 27, Green to Elliott, Aug. 29, Elliott to Green, Sept. 3, 1932, Green Papers; Josephson, *Hillman,* 327–39.

6. Anderson to Wilson, July 1931, *Letters of Sherwood Anderson,* H. M. Jones and W. B. Rideout, eds. (Boston: Little, Brown, 1953), 249; John I. Griffin, *Strikes: A Study in Quantitative Economics* (New York: Columbia University Press, 1939), 39, 77, 91; *International Teamster,* Mar. 1931, p. 2, Feb., p. 15, Apr., pp. 1, 9, May, pp. 6–9, Aug. 1932, pp. 14–15; Josephson, *Union House,* 181–86; H. M. Douty, "Labor Unrest in North Carolina, 1932," *Social Forces,* 2 (May 1933), 579–88; *Textile Worker,* Apr., p. 41, May, p. 67, Aug., p. 235, Sept. 1931, p. 300.

7. William Z. Foster, "The Coal Strike," *Communist,* 11 (July 1931), 595–99; "Lessons of the Strike Struggles in the U.S.A.," *Communist,* 11 (May 1932), 402–13; Jack Stachel, "Struggle for Elementary Needs," *Communist,* 12 (Jan. 1933), 18–32; Conrad Seiler, "Cantaloupes and Communists," *Nation,* 131 (Sept. 3, 1930), 243–44; Anita Brenner, "Tampa's Reign of Terror," *Nation,* 135 (Dec. 7, 1931), 555–57; Samuel Romer, "The Detroit Strike," *Nation,* 136 (Feb. 15, 1933), 167–68; *Industrial Worker,* June 6, p. 1, Aug. 15, 1931, p. 1.

8. Pursglove to Lewis, Dec. 1931, United Mine Workers Papers; Mary Van Kleeck, *Miners and Management* (New York: Russell Sage, 1934), 114–15; Josephson, *Hillman,* 348; David J. Saposs, "Labor," *American Journal of Sociology,* 37 (May 1932), 893; Vernon H. Jensen, *Lumber and Labor* (New York: Farrar & Rinehart, 1945), 151–52.

9. *AFL Weekly News Service,* Jan. 2, 1932; "Unions and Their Unemployed," *American Federationist,* 39 (June 1932), 640–51; *Advance,* Mar. 14, p. 6, Oct. 31, 1930, p. 1; "Unions Take Hold," *Survey,* 48 (Apr. 15, 1932), 86; *International Teamster,* Aug. 1932, p. 13; Josephson, *Union House,* 188–89.

10. Matthew Woll, "The Economic Policy Proposed by American Labor," *Annals,* 154 (Mar. 1931), 85–88; Green to Tobin, Jan. 11, Green to Representatives, Mar. 17, 1932, Green Papers; *Advance,* Oct. 10, 1930, p. 1; *American Pressman,* May 1931, p. 27; *International Teamster,* Aug. 1931, pp. 10–12.

11. G. G. Higgins, *Voluntarism in Organized Labor in the United States, 1930–1940* (Washington: Catholic University Press, 1944), 59–60; *Seamen's Journal,* Oct. 1930, p. 407; AFL, *Proceedings* (1930), 23–24, 63, 137, 158, 163–64, 305, 309–19.

12. Green to Wagner, Jan. 19, Green to Couzens, July 1, 1931, Green Papers; *International Teamster*, Feb. 1931, pp. 1–2; *American Pressman*, July 1931, pp. 25–27.

13. AFL, *Proceedings* (1931), 79, 148–64, 178, 182, 207, 233, 368–98; Louis Stark, "Labor on Relief and Insurance," *Survey*, 67 (Nov. 15, 1931), 187.

14. The UMW report appears in AFL, *Proceedings* (1932), 127–35; John B. Andrews to George M. Harrison, Feb. 25, Andrews memorandum, June 14, 1932, Andrews Papers; "Editorial Notes," *New Republic*, 71 (Aug. 3, 1932), 298–99; Green to Frank Duffy, July 22, 1932, Green Papers.

15. Green to Duffy, Apr. 11, 1932, Green Papers; *AFL Weekly News Service*, July 30, 1932; Green to Andrews, Aug. 12, 1932, Andrews Papers. The Green Papers contain a voluminous correspondence with the authorities named, as well as many others, in September and October 1932.

16. AFL, *Proceedings* (1932), 39–44, 325–60; Higgins, *Voluntarism*, 30.

17. Frey to Appleton, Dec. 8, Frey to C. B. Ross, Dec. 12, 1932, Frey Papers; Olander to Andrews, Feb. 23, 1933, Andrews Papers; the McGrady and Whitney-Robertson remarks are cited in Schlesinger, *Crisis*, 176, 185; J. B. S. Hardman, "Labor on the Warpath?" *New Republic*, 72 (Aug. 31, 1932), 61–63; H. M. Douty, "Ferment in the Railroad Unions," *Nation*, 135 (Nov. 30, 1932), 526–27.

18. Klein to Frey, Dec. 9, 1929, Frey to Appleton, Jan. 10, Frey to O'Connell, Jan. 10, Lamont to Frey, Jan. 11, Frey to Wilson, Jan. 31, Lamont to Frey, Mar. 27, 1930, Frey to Wilson, Aug. 20, 1931, Frey Papers; AFL, *Proceedings* (1932), 81–82, 37.

19. *New York Times*, July 1, p. 11, July 3, p. 33, July 5, II, p. 1, July 10, p. 13, July 11, p. 25, July 15, p. 5, July 24, p. 33, Sept. 1, p. 40, Oct. 16, 1931, p. 8; *UMWJ*, June 15, 1931, p. 5; *AFL Weekly News Service*, July 4, 1931.

CHAPTER 10 (*Pages 358–390*)

1. John Greenway, *American Folksongs of Protest* (Philadelphia: University of Pennsylvania Press, 1953), 169–71, 273–74; George Korson, *Coal Dust on the Fiddle* (Philadelphia: University of Pennsylvania Press, 1943), 316; John Dos Passos, "Harlan: Working under the Gun," *New Republic*, 69 (Dec. 2, 1931), 62–67.

2. *Historical Statistics*, 68, 142–43; Homer L. Morris, *The Plight of the Bituminous Coal Miner* (Philadelphia: University of Pennsylvania Press, 1934), 1–34; *Conditions in the Coal Fields of Harlan and Bell Counties, Kentucky*, Hearings on S. Res. 178, Senate Subcommittee on Manufactures, 72 Cong., 1 sess. (1932), 29, 94; Malcolm Ross, *Machine Age in the Hills* (New York: Macmillan, 1933), 58; Korson, *Coal Dust*, 175, 177–78, 182–83.

3. Mark to Murray, Nov. 13, 1931, CIO files, United Mine Workers Papers.

4. Bittner to Murray, June 27, 1930, CIO files, United Mine Workers Papers; Wilma Walker, "Distress in a Southern Illinois County," *Social Service Review,* 5 (Dec. 1931), 581; *Unemployment Relief, Hearings before the Senate Subcommittee on Manufactures,* 72 Cong., 1 sess. (1931–32), 106–9, 348; Pinchot statement, Mar. 18, 1932, Pinchot Papers; Morris Markey, *This Country of Yours* (Boston: Little, Brown, 1932), 19, 32.

5. Morris, *Plight,* 107; Senate Hearings, *Unemployment Relief,* 59, 214; Korson, *Coal Dust,* 68–71; Ross, *Machine Age,* 34, 60.

6. Senate Hearings, *Conditions,* 17, 33–34; Theodore Dreiser, *et al., Harlan Miners Speak* (New York: Harcourt, Brace, 1932), 83, 86–87; Walker, "Distress," 576; Morris, *Plight,* 90; Ross, *Machine Age,* 88; *New York Times,* Sept. 30, p. 3, Nov. 27, 1931, p. 25.

7. *New York Times,* Apr. 3, p. 14, Sept. 28, p. 1, Sept. 30, 1931, p. 3; Senate Hearings, *Conditions,* 17–18; Grace Abbott, "Improvement in Rural Public Relief: The Lesson of the Coal Mining Communities," *Social Service Review,* 6 (June 1932), 214; Korson, *Coal Dust,* 72–73; Edmund Wilson, *The American Jitters* (New York: Scribner, 1932), 151; Helen G. Norton, "Feudalism in West Virginia," *Nation,* 133 (Aug. 12, 1931), 155.

8. *New York Times,* Sept. 29, p. 3, Nov. 30, 1931, p. 6; Senate Hearings, *Conditions,* 19–21, 56–61, 211; Sherwood Anderson, *Puzzled America* (New York: Scribner, 1935), 6–7; Dreiser, *et al., Harlan Miners,* 88; Arthur Garfield Hays, "The Right to Get Shot," *Nation,* 134 (June 1, 1932), 619.

9. The best work on the first phase of the Illinois revolution is Edward Dean Wickersham, "Opposition to the International Officers of the United Mine Workers of America, 1919–1933" (unpublished Ph.D. dissertation, Cornell University, 1951), ch. 6, to which no further reference will be made. See also Louis Stanley, "The Miners' Rebellion," *Nation,* 130 (Mar. 26, 1930), 356; Lewis to Fishwick, *et al.,* Sept. 20, 1929, CIO files, United Mine Workers Papers.

10. *Illinois Miner,* Feb. 22, 1930, p. 4.

11. Stanley, "Miners' Rebellion," 356–57; *New York Times,* Mar. 11, p. 18, Mar. 13, p. 2, Mar. 14, p. 23, Mar. 16, 1930, p. 18; *Illinois Miner,* Mar. 22, 1930, p. 1; R. Lee Guard to Green, Mar. 15, 1930, Green Papers. Ameringer's autobiography, *If You Don't Weaken* (New York: Holt, 1940), is remarkably silent on the Springfield convention.

12. *Illinois Miner,* Mar. 22, 1930, p. 4; United Mine Workers files, 1930; *UMWJ,* Apr. 1, 1930, pp. 4–5; *Nation,* 130 (Apr. 9, 1930), 411.

13. Green to Tom Kennedy, Mar. 3, Green to Walker, Mar. 6, Walker to Green, Mar. 8, Green to Walker, Mar. 20, Green to Executive Council, Apr. 1, Walker to Green, Apr. 9, Walker to Green, Apr. 12, Green to Executive Council, Apr. 14, Green to Olander, Aug. 5,

Green to Walker, Oct. 13, 1930, Green Papers. Farrington, desperate for work in the summer of 1931, begged for a job with the AFL. For obvious reasons Green could not help him. Green to Hutcheson, June 9, Green to T. A. Rickert, July 3, 1931, Green Papers.

14. *New York Times*, Mar. 21, p. 16, Mar. 23, p. 4, Mar. 25, p. 1, Mar. 27, p. 16, Apr. 1, p. 15, Apr. 13, p. 26, Apr. 19, 1930, p. 36; *Illinois Miner*, Apr. 5, 1930, p. 1; *UMWJ*, Apr. 1, 1930, p. 5; James Ferns to Murray, July 23, 1930, CIO files, United Mine Workers Papers; McAlister Coleman, *Men and Coal* (New York: Farrar & Rinehart, 1943), 141.

15. The text of the decree is in *UMWJ*, Mar. 15, 1931, p. 8.

16. Harriet Hudson, *The Progressive Mine Workers of America: A Study in Rival Unionism* (Urbana: University of Illinois, 1952), ch. 2; Marquis W. Childs, "The Illinois Mine Battle," *New Republic*, 72 (Sept. 14, 1932), 121–23; *UMWJ*, Aug. 15, 1932, pp. 8–9; *New York Times*, Apr. 1, p. 38, July 9, p. 11, July 13, p. 3, July 18, p. 30, Aug. 11, p. 22, Aug 13, p. 26, Aug. 16, p. 12, Aug. 19, p. 19, Aug. 23, p. 12, Aug. 25, p. 1, Aug. 26, p. 6, Aug. 27, p. 8, Aug. 28, 1932, p. 26.

17. Hudson, *Progressive Mine Workers*, 21–41; *New York Times*, Oct. 11, p. 30, Dec. 23, 1932, p. 34; *UMWJ*, Oct. 15, 1932, p. 3, Jan. 1, p. 7, Feb. 15, pp. 7, 10, March 1, pp. 4, 7, March 15, 1933, p. 13; *Progressive Miner*, Sept. 16, p. 1, Sept. 23, p. 1, Oct. 7, 1932, p. 1.

18. Kentucky miner to Arthur Garfield Hays, n.d., *Nation*, 134 (June 8, 1932), 651.

19. The most balanced work on Harlan is Charles Rumford Walker's chapter, "Organizing a Union in Kentucky," in Dreiser, *et al.*, *Harlan Miners*, 38–49. The rest of the book contains much valuable information. See also Ross, *Machine Age*, 171–78; the testimony in Senate Hearings, *Conditions*; Louis Stark's series in the *New York Times*, Sept. 28, p. 1, Sept. 29, p. 3, Sept. 30, p. 3, Oct. 2, p. 12, Oct. 3, 1931, p. 19; S. D. Spero and J. B. Aronoff, "War in the Kentucky Mountains," *American Mercury*, 25 (Feb. 1932), 226–33; Herbert Abel, "Gun-Rule in Kentucky," *Nation*, 133 (Sept. 23, 1931), 306–7; Oakley Johnson, "Starvation and the 'Reds' in Kentucky," *Nation*, 134 (Feb. 3, 1932), 140–42; Arthur Garfield Hays, "The Right to Get Shot," *Nation*, 134 (June 1, 1932), 619; J. C. Byars, Jr., "Harlan County: Act of God?" *Nation*, 134 (June 15, 1932), 672–74; Tess Huff to editor, *Nation*, 135 (July 13, 1932), 37; Dos Passos, "Harlan," 62–67. An interesting exercise in Communist breast-beating over the collapse of the NMU strike is Jack Stachel, "Lessons of Two Recent Strikes," *Communist*, 11 (June 1932), 527–36.

20. Edmund Wilson published two articles on West Virginia in the *New Republic* in July 1931, which are reprinted as "Frank Keeney's Coal Diggers" in *The American Earthquake* (Garden City: Doubleday, 1958), 310–27; Stark dealt with the strife in West Virginia in the *New York Times*, Nov. 27, p. 25, Nov. 28, p. 15, Nov. 29, p. 3,

Nov. 30, 1931, p. 6. See also Ross, *Machine Age*, 156–63; James Myers, "Close-ups in the Coal Fields," *New Republic*, 68 (Sept. 16, 1931), 118–20; Helen G. Norton, "Feudalism in West Virginia," *Nation*, 133 (Aug. 12, 1931), 154–55; *New York Times*, Apr. 3, p. 14, Apr. 4, p. 36, May 21, p. 24, June 15, p. 2, July 7, p. 17, Aug. 18, 1931, p. 4.

21. *New York Times*, Apr. 6, p. 12, July 22, p. 6, July 23, p. 21, Aug. 4, p. 2, Aug. 23, p. 12, Sept. 11, 1932, p. 5.

22. Mauritz A. Hallgren, "Danger Ahead in the Coal Strike," *Nation*, 133 (Aug. 5, 1931), 131–33; *UMWJ*, Mar. 1, p. 3, Nov. 15, 1931, p. 3, Apr. 15, p. 3, May 1, p. 3, Oct. 1, 1932, p. 10; *New York Times*, June 13, p. 2, June 14, p. 19, June 19, 1931, p. 3, Mar. 22, p. 15, Mar. 24, p. 3, Apr. 1, p. 38, Apr. 6, p. 12, Apr. 15, p. 15, Apr.16, p. 34, Apr. 21, p. 26, May 22, p. 6, Sept. 19, p. 2, Sept. 27, 1932, p. 46.

23. Frank Butler, "Pennsylvania's Bloody Mine War," *Nation*, 133 (July 8, 1931), 38; "The Struggle in Coal," *New Republic*, 67 (Aug. 5, 1931), 301–2; "Lessons of the Strike Struggles in the U.S.A.," *Communist*, 11 (May 1932), 402–13; *UMWJ*, July 1, p. 3, Aug. 1, 1931, p. 3; *New York Times*, June 9, p. 21, June 14, p. 19, June 17, p. 4, June 19, p. 3, June 24, p. 2, June 30, p. 2, July 1, p. 11, July 24, p. 33, July 27, 1931, p. 34. According to UMW, NMU was behind the attempt to murder Fagan. JOL to Henry Allai, Sept. 2, 1931, CIO files, United Mine Workers Papers.

24. *New York Times*, Apr. 2, p. 22, Sept. 24, p. 2, Sept. 29, p. 3, Oct. 10, 1931, p. 5, Mar. 21, p. 1, Mar. 25, p. 5, Mar. 27, p. 12, Mar. 30, p. 8, Apr. 1, 1932, p. 38.

25. Korson, *Coal Dust*, 392.


CHAPTER 11 *(Pages 391–415)*

1. George W. Norris, *Fighting Liberal: The Autobiography of George W. Norris* (New York: Macmillan, 1945), 1–38, 59–68, 234–44, 402; Alfred Lief, *Democracy's Norris* (New York: Stackpole, 1939); Schlesinger, *Crisis*, 122–24.

2. Felix Frankfurter and Nathan Greene, "The Use of the Injunction in American Legal Controversies," *Law Quarterly Review*, 44 (Apr. 1928), 164; *Limiting Scope of Injunctions in Labor Disputes*, Hearings on S. 1482, Senate Committee on the Judiciary, 70 Cong., 1 sess. (1928), 158; the discussion of the law is at pp. 194–202.

3. Pound to Frey, Oct. 29, 1924, Frey to Daniel Callahan, Aug. 22, 1929, Frey Papers; *Reminiscences of John P. Frey*, Oral History Research Project, Columbia University, vol. 3, pp. 443–47; Eugene Staley, *History of the Illinois Federation of Labor* (Chicago: Univer-

sity of Chicago Press, 1930), 472–73; Cornelius Cochrane, " 'Yellow Dog' Abolished in Wisconsin," *ALLR*, 19 (Sept. 1929), 315–16; Vaughn Davis Bornet, "Labor and Politics in 1928" (unpublished Ph.D. dissertation, Stanford University, 1951), 103, 135–39, 148–49, 195–203; Marie Elizabeth Lynch, *Labor and Tariff Issues in the Major Party Platforms* (Washington: Catholic University Press, 1953), 19–20.

4. Edwin E. Witte to Roger N. Baldwin, Dec. 24, 1931, Witte Papers; Senate Hearings, *Limiting Scope, passim; New York Times*, Feb. 8, p. 27, Feb. 19, 1928, p. 15.

5. Frankfurter and Greene, *Labor Injunction*, 207.

6. Norris, *Fighting Liberal*, 312–13. The text of the original Norris bill appears in Frankfurter and Greene, *Labor Injunction*, 279–88. The intent of the draftsmen is set forth in Donald Richberg, "Outline of Explanation of Bill Drafted to Limit and Define the Jurisdiction of the Federal Courts in Labor Cases," May 1928, and E. E. Witte, "Memorandum in Support of the Several Provisions and Clauses of the Tentative Bill to Define and Limit the Jurisdiction of the Federal Courts, Based Mainly upon Injunctions Issued by the Federal Courts in Labor Cases Since 1920," May 1928, Witte Papers. The case citations are *American Steel Foundries* v. *Tri-City Central Trades Council*, 257 U.S. 184 (1921); *Adair* v. *United States*, 208 U.S. 161 (1908); *Coppage* v. *Kansas*, 236 U.S. 1 (1915); *Interborough Rapid Transit Co.* v. *Lavin*, 247 N. Y. 65 (1928); *Exchange Bakery & Restaurant* v. *Rifkin*, 245 N. Y. 260 (1927); *United States* v. *Railway Employes Dept., A.F.L.*, 286 Fed. 228 (N.D. Ill. 1923); *United Mine Workers* v. *Red Jacket Consolidated Coal & Coke Co.*, 18 F. (2d) 839 (4th Cir. 1927). The Norris subcommittee held hearings on December 18–19, 1928, at which proponents of the labor injunction and Furuseth attacked the new bill. Senate Hearings, *Limiting Scope*, 733 ff.

7. AFL, *Proceedings* (1928), 109–14, 250–53; Woll to Norris, June 13, 1929, Norris Papers; *New York Times*, Aug. 17, 1929, p. 15; AFL, *Proceedings* (1929), 194–98, 317–33, 340–52.

8. Frankfurter, Oliphant, and Witte Observations of Proposed AFL Amendments, n.d., Richberg memorandum, n.d., Norris Papers; the text of the 1930 bill appears in Duane McCracken, *Strike Injunctions in the New South* (Chapel Hill: University of North Carolina Press, 1931), 146–55.

9. Alpheus T. Mason, *Harlan Fiske Stone* (New York: Viking, 1956), 297–99; Merlo J. Pusey, *Charles Evans Hughes* (New York: Macmillan, 1951), vol. 2, pp. 648–62; Philip Taft, *The AF of L from the Death of Gompers to the Merger* (New York: Harper, 1959), 21.

10. The Kent remark is from Lief, *Democracy's Norris*, 344; the earlier discussion of T & NO is on p. 218.

11. *Texas & New Orleans Railroad Co.* v. *Brotherhood of Railway &*

*Steamship Clerks,* 281 U.S. 548 (1930); Edward Berman, "The Supreme Court Interprets the Railway Labor Act," *AER,* 20 (Dec., 1930), 638–39.

12. Tucker to Norris, n.d., White to Norris, May 2, 1930, Norris Papers; Randolph to Wagner, Apr. 24, 1930, Wagner Papers. Parker defended himself against both charges on April 24 in a letter to Senator Overman of North Carolina published in *CR,* vol. 72, pt. 7, p. 7793.

13. Green to Executive Council, Mar. 26, Green to international presidents, Mar. 28, 1930, Green Papers; Lewis to Wagner, Apr. 19, 1930, Wagner Papers; Green to Hoover, Apr. 11, Hoover to Green, Apr. 14, Green to Hoover, Apr. 16, 1930, Green Papers; Frankfurter to Norris, May 9, 1930, Norris Papers; Joel Seidman, *The Yellow-Dog Contract* (Baltimore: Johns Hopkins University Press, 1932), 36.

14. Witte to writer, Oct. 7, 1954; *New York Times,* Apr. 27, p. 1, May 29, p. 2, June 10, 1930, p. 6.

15. Norris to Roger Baldwin, Dec. 15, Fleischer to Norris, June 19, 1930, National Committee on Labor Injunctions to Norris, Jan. 31, 1931, Norris Papers; *New York Times,* Jan. 5, p. 2, Jan. 12, p. 13, Feb. 15, 1931, p. 16; Paul Donovan, "Legislation Affecting Labor Injunctions," *American Bar Association Journal,* 16 (Sept. 1930), 561–63; "A Triumph for Labor," *Nation,* 133 (July 22, 1931), 81; Norris to Frankfurter, Mar. 27, Fleischer to Norris, Oct. 21, Furuseth to Norris, Dec. 2, Frankfurter to Baldwin, Dec. 9, Norris to Baldwin, Dec. 12, Baldwin to Norris, Dec. 14, 1931, Norris to Furuseth, Jan. 9, 1932, Norris Papers; Green to Olander, Dec. 14, 1931, Green Papers.

16. *New York Times,* Jan. 13, p. 25, Jan. 14, p. 34, Mar. 18, p. 6, May 3, p. 4, May 7, p. 22, June 28, p. 18, Dec. 7, 1932, p. 17; Slichter to Frey, Jan. 13, 1932, Frey Papers. The Wilkerson appointment had several interesting aspects. The Hoover Administration's authorized historians point with pride to the fact that Hoover, in Harding's Cabinet during the railway strike, had "vigorously stated his opposition to the policy of Attorney General Daugherty in using the injunctive power of the Federal courts for the purpose of breaking strikes." Yet, they do not explain why the President turned about later and conferred a great honor upon the very judge whose injunction he had opposed. Myers and Newton, *Hoover Administration,* 491–92. Wilkerson's nomination was made at the moment when Holmes resigned from the Supreme Court. The designation of his successor was, of course, far more important than filling the vacancy on the 7th circuit. The loss of Holmes diminished the "liberal" minority by one third. The AFL was most anxious that a jurist of similar viewpoint should be named. Green on January 15 urged Hoover to appoint Judge Kenyon of Iowa, or, in the alternative, Judge Cardozo of New York, Judge Hutcheson of Texas (author of the T & NO decision), or Senator Walsh of Montana.

Frey, at least, would have been willing to "swallow" Wilkerson in return for a Cardozo or Kenyon. Green to Hoover, Jan. 15, 1932, Green Papers; Frey to Slichter, Jan. 15, 1932, Frey Papers. From the AFL standpoint the result was much better: Wilkerson was defeated and Hoover named Cardozo, by common consent the most gifted state court judge in America and a worthy successor to Holmes.

17. *New York Times*, Jan. 28, p. 2, Feb. 5, 1932, p. 39; *CR*, vol. 75, pt. 4, pp. 4502–4630, pt. 5, pp. 4677–5019; Green to Norris, Feb. 29, 1932, Norris Papers.

18. Since the Senate and House bills differed slightly, the House on March 17 adopted the Senate version. *CR*, vol. 75, pt. 5, pp. 5462–5511, pt. 6, pp. 6014–17, 6334–37.

19. Baldwin to Norris, Mar. 22, 1932, Norris Papers; Hoover, *State Papers*, vol. 1, pp. 145–46.

20. Lief, *Democracy's Norris*, 387; *New York Times*, Oct. 19, p. 11, Oct. 20, p. 14, Oct. 21, 1932, p. 10; *Lauf v. E. G. Shinner & Co.*, 303 U.S. 323, 330 (1938).

21. Edwin E. Witte, "The Federal Anti-Injunction Act," *Minnesota Law Review*, 16 (May 1932), 647.

CHAPTER 12 (*Pages 416–436*)

1. The basic study of self-help is Clark Kerr's 4-volume "Productive Enterprises of the Unemployed, 1931–38" (unpublished Ph.D. dissertation, University of California, 1939); pp. 1188–1268 deal with Washington. See also Robert C. Hill, "Seattle's Jobless Enter Politics," *Nation*, 134 (June 29, 1934), 718–20; George R. Leighton, *Five Cities* (New York: Harper, 1939), 319–22; Tom Jones Parry, "The Republic of the Penniless," *Atlantic*, 150 (Oct. 1932), 449–57; Hulet M. Wells, "They Organize in Seattle," *Survey*, 67 (Mar. 15, 1932), 665–67.

2. Kerr, "Productive Enterprises," 70–124, 303–26, 327–72; Malcolm Ross, "The Spread of Barter," *Nation*, 136 (Mar. 1, 1933), 228.

3. Kerr, "*Productive Enterprises*," 1057–1116; Rudi Blesh and Harriet Janis, *They All Played Ragtime* (New York: Knopf, 1950), 194–95; Ralph Borsodi, *Flight from the City* (New York: Harper, 1933); Ralph Borsodi, "Dayton, Ohio, Makes Social History," *Nation*, 136 (Apr. 19, 1933), 447–48.

4. Twelve Southerners, *I'll Take My Stand* (New York: Harper, 1930); H. L. Kerwin to T. F. McMahon, Feb. 26, 1931, C. L. Richardson to Kerwin, Aug. 17, 1931, Labor Department Papers; "Land Scheme" file, 1932, Glassford Papers.

5. H. M. Douty, "Labor Unrest in North Carolina, 1932," *Social Forces*,

11 (May 1933), 579–88; Gardner to B. B. Gossett, July 21, 1932, *Public Papers and Letters of Oliver Max Gardner*, D. L. Corbitt, ed. (Raleigh N.C.: Council of State of N.C., 1937), 620–21; A. J. Muste, "Southern Labor Stirs," *Nation*, 135 (Aug. 10, 1932), 121–22.

6. *New York Times*, Mar. 20, p. 20, Nov. 13, 1930, p. 16, Jan. 11, 1933, p. 6; Adamic, *My America*, 309; *Nation*, 133 (July 29, 1931), 98; Mauritz A. Hallgren, "Grave Danger in Detroit," *Nation*, 135 (Aug. 3, 1932), 99; Clayton W. Fountain, *Union Guy* (New York: Viking, 1949), 36–37; Hilton Butler, "Murder for the Job," *Nation*, 137 (July 12, 1933), 44.

7. Adamic, *My America*, 316–24; George Korson, *Minstrels of the Mine Patch* (Philadelphia: University of Pennsylvania Press, 1938), 270, 278–80.

8. Edmund Wilson, *The Shores of Light* (New York: Farrar, Straus & Young 1952), 524–25; Edmund Wilson, *The American Jitters* (New York: Scribner, 1932), ch. 28; Karl Borders, "The Unemployed Strike Out for Themselves," *Survey*, 67 (Mar. 15, 1932), 663–65; Edmund Wilson, "Hull House in 1932," *New Republic*, 73 (Jan. 25, 1933), 287–90; Hallgren, *Grave Danger*, 101; David A. Shannon, *The Socialist Party of America* (New York: Macmillan, 1955), 204–26.

9. Daniel Bell, "Marxian Socialism in the United States," in D. G. Egbert and Stow Persons, eds., *Socialism and American Life* (Princeton: Princeton University Press, 1952), 350–52.

10. *New York Times*, Feb. 12, p. 4, Feb. 15, p. 8, Feb. 22, p. 2, Feb. 27, p. 25, Mar. 2, p. 1, Mar. 6, pp. 1, 9, Mar. 7, p. 1, May 10, p. 5, May 23, p. 1, May 29, p. 6, June 14, 1930, p. 36; Adamic, *My America*, 93–95.

11. *To Investigate Communist Activities in the United States*, Hearings before Special House Committee, 71 Cong., 2 sess. (1930), pt. 4, vol. 3, pp. 86–88; Adamic, *My America*, 69; *Nation*, 133 (Aug. 19, 1931), 170; Horace R. Cayton, "The Black Bugs," *Nation*, 133 (Sept. 9, 1931), 255–56.

12. The Glassford Papers contain a large number of clippings that supplied most of the material for this section. See also "Resolution on Work Among the Unemployed," *Communist*, 10 (Oct. 1931), 838–48; *New York Times*, Nov. 29, 1931, p. 1; John Dos Passos, "Red Day on Capitol Hill," *New Republic*, 69 (Dec. 23, 1931), 153–55.

13. Glassford Papers; *New York Times*, Jan. 7, 1932, p. 1; Felix Morrow to editor, *Nation*, 134 (Feb. 3, 1932), 144; Mauritz A. Hallgren, "Panic in the Steel Towns," *Nation*, 134 (Mar. 30, 1932), 364.

14. Keith Sward, *The Legend of Henry Ford* (New York: Rinehart, 1948), ch. 18; Oakley Johnson, "After the Dearborn Massacre," *New Republic*, 70 (Mar. 30, 1932), 172–74; Maurice Sugar, "Bullets —

Not Food — for Ford Workers," *Nation*, 134 (Mar. 23, 1932), 333–35; Harry Bennett, *We Never Called Him Henry* (New York: Fawcett, 1951), 90–94; *New York Times*, March 8, 1932, p. 1; Fred Croxton to Rowland Haynes, Mar. 14, 1932, POUR Papers. It is curious that the presumably definitive work — Allan Nevins and F. E. Hill, *Ford: Expansion and Challenge, 1915–1933* (New York: Scribner, 1957) — contains no reference to the Dearborn riot.

15. C. R. Walker, "Relief and Revolution," *Forum and Century*, 88 (Sept. 1932), 155–58; Frederick Lewis Allen, *The Big Change* (New York: Harper, 1952), 180; Bell, "Marxian Socialism," 353; Adamic, *My America*, p. 95; "Forward in the Line of the 12th Plenum of the E.C.C.I." *Communist*, 12 (Jan. 1933), 9, 10–11.

16. "Talk of the Town," *New Yorker*, June 25, 1932, p. 5; Adamic, *My America*, 72, 298, 302; Dreiser to Dallas McKown, June 9, 1932, *Letters of Theodore Dreiser*, R. H. Elias, ed. (Philadelphia: University of Pennsylvania Press, 1959), vol. 2, p. 588; Sherwood Anderson, *Puzzled America* (New York: Scribner, 1935), ix, 17, 46, 164.

CHAPTER 13 (*Pages 437–455*)

1. *Washington Star*, June 6, July 27, 1932; *Washington Daily News*, Mar. 13, 1933; Mauritz A. Hallgren, "The Bonus Army Scares Mr. Hoover," *Nation*, 135 (July 27, 1932), 71–72; "Talk of the Town," *New Yorker*, July 2, 1932, p. 5.

2. Walde memorandum, n.d., Registration Figures, n.d., Glassford Papers; Schlesinger, *Crisis*, 256–57; the Glassford Papers contain an immense number of press clippings that chart the progress of the BEF; interview with Glassford, May 3, 1955.

3. Fleta Campbell Springer, "Glassford and the Siege of Washington," *Harper's*, 165 (Nov. 1932), 641–43; "The Glassford They Remember," *Providence Journal*, Aug. 7, 1932.

4. Heath to Glassford, June 10, 1932, Information Reference to Buildings and Grounds in the Area Bounded by Pennsylvania Avenue . . . , July 31, 1932, Glassford Papers.

5. John Dos Passos, "The Veterans Come Home to Roost," *New Republic*, 71 (June 29, 1932), 177; Glassford memoranda, June 2, 10, 11, 21, Police Department memorandum, July 25, Eleanor Patterson to Glassford, July 27, 1932, Communists memorandum, n.d., Glassford Papers.

6. Communists memorandum, n.d., WESL throwaways, Walde memorandum, n.d., Police memoranda, June 2, July 2, 7, 8, 19, 20, 23, J. Edgar Hoover to Glassford, June 6, Reck to Glassford, June 9, Alan G. Straight to H. W. Moran, June 1, 1932, Glassford Papers; *Washington Herald*, June 10, 1932.

7. This section is based upon the clippings in the Glassford collection;

the Henry article appeared in the *Washington Star*, June 19, 1932.

8. Glassford diary, June 27–July 16, Crosby memorandum, July 16, 1932, Glassford Papers.

9. Heath to Crosby, July 20, Heath to Glassford, July 20, Glassford memorandum, July 21, Glassford to Seymour Lowman, July 22, Circumstances Leading Up to the Use of Federal Forces against the Bonus Army, July 31, 1932, Glassford Papers; *Washington Times*, July 27, 1932; Paul Y. Anderson, "Tear-Gas, Bayonets, and Votes," *Nation*, 135 (Aug. 17, 1932), 138.

10. Report of Private J. O. Patton, July 29, Glassford memorandum, July 29, Circumstances Leading Up to . . . , July 31, Aldace Walker memorandum, Sept. 10, 1932, Glassford Papers.

11. *Washington Star*, July 29, 1932.

12. Schlesinger, *Crisis*, 262–63; Anderson, "Tear-Gas," 138; Glassford memorandum, n.d., "Seen from a White House Window," July 29, 1932, Glassford Papers; *Washington Star*, July 29, Aug. 4, 1932; J. Prentice Murphy, "America on the March," *Survey*, 22 (Mar. 1933), 149–50.

13. Thomas L. Stokes, *Chip Off My Shoulder* (Princeton: Princeton University Press, 1940), 303–4.

14. Amos Pinchot, *General Goober at the Battle of Anacostia* (New York: Privately published, 1932).


CHAPTER 14 (*Pages 456–474*)

1. Frank Freidel, *Franklin D. Roosevelt: The Triumph* (Boston: Little, Brown, 1956), ch. 15; Robert E. Sherwood, *Roosevelt and Hopkins* (New York: Harper, 1948), 5, 14–37; Straus to Lehman, Oct. 7, 1931, Hopkins to Roosevelt, Jan. 11, 1932, Roosevelt as Governor Papers; "Harry Hopkins," *Fortune*, 12 (July 1935), 129; Alexander L. Radomski, *Work Relief in New York State, 1931–1935* (New York: King's Crown, 1947); Gertrude Springer, "The Lever of State Relief," *Survey*, 67 (Jan. 15, 1932), 407–10; Bernard Bellush, *Franklin D. Roosevelt as Governor of New York* (New York: Columbia University Press, 1955), ch. 7; Daniel Fusfeld, *The Economic Thought of Franklin D. Roosevelt and the Origins of the New Deal* (New York: Columbia University Press, 1956), ch. 12.

2. Josephine C. Brown, *Public Relief, 1929–1939* (New York: Holt, 1940), 94–97; Rowland Haynes, *State Legislation for Unemployment Relief* (Washington: POUR, 1932); Frank Z. Glick, "The Illinois Emergency Relief Commission," *Social Service Review*, 7 (Mar. 1933), 23–49; Pinchot to Walter S. Gifford, Sept. 4, 1931, POUR Papers.

3. *New York Times*, May 22, p. 17, Aug. 5, p. 20, Aug. 8, p. 1, Aug. 20, p. 1, Aug. 21, 1931, p. 1; "The President's Organization on

Unemployment Relief," *MLR*, 33 (Nov. 1931), 38–39; *New Yorker*, Sept. 12, p. 24, Nov. 21, 1931, pp. 11–12; Costigan to Gifford, Nov. 3, Gifford to Costigan, Nov. 9, Costigan to Gifford, Nov. 12, 1931, POUR Papers; *Unemployment Relief*, Hearings on S. 262 before the Senate Subcommittee on Manufactures, 72 Cong., 1 sess. (1931–32), p. 330; Hoover, *State Papers*, vol. 2, pp. 220–21.

4. Brown, *Public Relief*, 79–83; Gertrude Springer, "The Fighting Spirit in Hard Times," *Survey*, 68 (June 15, 1932), 260–71; *Proceedings of the National Conference of Social Work, May, 1932* (Chicago: University of Chicago Press, 1933), 3–23, 65–80, 91–95.

5. *CR*, vol. 72, pt. 3, pp. 3068 ff., pt. 4, pp. 3503 ff.

6. "How the Cities Stand," *Survey*, 68 (Apr. 15, 1932), 71; *Federal Cooperation in Unemployment Relief*, Hearings on S. 4592, Senate Subcommittee on Manufactures, 72 Cong., 1 sess. (1932), pts. 1, 2; *New York Times*, June 2, p. 1, June 3, p. 10, June 22, 1932, p. 2; W. J. Barrett to Fred Croxton, Feb. 17, Croxton to H. C. Couch, Feb. 26, Rowland Haynes to Croxton, Mar. 21 (two letters), Rev. John Semanitzky to Hoover, Mar. 22, Frank W. Connor to Croxton, Apr. 7, Haynes to Croxton, Apr. 19, Haynes to Croxton, May 4, Pickett to Croxton, May 17, Mary Kelsey to Bernard Waring, June 5, Waring report, July 6, 1932, POUR Papers.

7. *New York Times*, Feb. 18, p. 12, May 12, p. 1, May 13, p. 1, May 14, p. 1, May 17, p. 12, May 20, p. 1, May 21, p. 2, May 26, p. 1, May 27, p. 1, May 28, p. 1, May 29, p. 1, June 7, p. 1, June 8, p. 1, June 11, p. 1, July 2, p. 1, July 7, p. 1, July 8, p. 1, July 10, p. 1, July 12, p. 1, July 13, p. 1, July 14, p. 1, July 17, p. 1, July 22, 1932, p. 1; Hoover, *State Papers*, vol. 2, pp. 187–88, 202–3, 216, 223–26, 229–33; *Federal Loans to Aid Unemployment*, Hearings on S. 4632, Senate Banking and Currency Committee, 72 Cong., 1 sess. (1932), 9–42; Shaw to Mills, June 3, 1932, Mills Papers; Bascom Timmons, *Garner of Texas* (New York: Harper, 1948), 150–51; 47 Stat. 709 (1932).

8. Minutes of the Board of Directors of the Reconstruction Finance Corporation, July 18, 20, 22, Aug. 2, Pinchot to Pomerene, Sept. 8, 23, R. W. Kelso Confidential Report, Sept. 8, Breckinridge to Pomerene, Oct. 2, Pomerene to Pinchot, Nov. 7, 1932, POUR Papers; Wagner to Pinchot, Sept. 26, 1932, Wagner Papers; *New York Times*, July 19, p. 27, July 31, p. 8, Aug. 16, p. 2, Sept. 4, p. 8, Sept. 24, p. 19, Sept. 26, p. 2, Oct. 10, p. 11, Dec. 7, p. 1, Dec. 20, 1932, p. 2, Jan. 1, 1933, p. 11; *Federal Aid for Unemployment Relief*, Hearings on S. 5125, Senate Subcommittee on Manufactures, 72 Cong., 2 sess. (1933); *Further Unemployment Relief through the RFC*, Hearings on S. 5336, Senate Committee on Banking and Currency, 72 Cong., 2 sess. (1933), 11.

CHAPTER 15 (*Pages 475–504*)

1. Harry A. Millis and Royal E. Montgomery, *Labor's Progress and Some Basic Labor Problems* (New York: McGraw-Hill, 1938), 473, 478, 486–88; *Labor*, May 13, p. 1, Nov. 25, 1930, p. 1; AFL, *Proceedings* (1930), 3, 60, 262–67; H. B. Rust to Walter S. Gifford, Apr. 19, 1932, POUR Papers; Otto Beyer to B. M. Jewel, Apr. 21, 1932, Beyer Papers.

2. *Journal of Electrical Workers and Operators*, Nov. 1932, p. 540; Whitney to Green, Nov. 8, 1932, Green Papers; *Advance*, Jan. 31, 1930, p. 6; Matthew Josephson, *Sidney Hillman* (Garden City: Doubleday, 1952), 341–43; James J. Davis to Fiorello H. La Guardia, Oct. 6, 1930, La Guardia Papers; *Typographical Journal*, Jan. 1932, p. 14; "Unemployment Relief," *MLR*, 34 (May 1932), 1046–47.

3. "Wage and Salary Retrenchment in Special Conference Committee Companies," Sept. 23, 1931, POUR Papers; L. C. Walker, "The Share-the-Work Movement," *Annals*, 165 (Jan. 1933), 13–19; Hoover, *State Papers*, vol 2, pp. 272–73; *New York Times*, Aug. 27, p. 1, Sept. 1, p. 1, Sept. 26, p. 14, Sept. 30, pp. 1, 3, Oct. 14, p. 3, Oct. 30, 1932, p. 5, Jan. 15, 1933, p. 2; Sumner H. Slichter, "Unemployment Relief by Business," *New Republic*, 69 (Dec. 30, 1931), 181–84; Stevenson to Gifford, Nov. 11, 1931, POUR Papers; "Editorial Notes," *New Republic*, 72 (Oct. 12, 1932), 216–17.

4. Green to Executive Council, July 29, Green to Matthew Woll, Oct. 17, Whitney to Green, Nov. 8, 1932, Green Papers; Green to Hoover, July 24, Wheeler to Green, Sept. 18, Green to Wheeler, Sept. 22, 1931, POUR Papers; AFL, *Proceedings* (1932), 5–6, 284–96.

5. *CR*, vol. 77, pt. 6, p. 5901; Moulton and Leven are quoted in Peter Masiko, Jr., "Recent Wage and Hour Legislation — An Economic Analysis" (unpublished Ph.D. dissertation, University of Illinois, 1939), 28; W. G. Schoenwetter to E. F. Andrews, Sept. 29, 1931, Roosevelt Papers; *Thirty-Hour Work Week*, Hearings before a Senate Subcommittee of the Committee on the Judiciary, 72 Cong., 2 sess. (1933); *Hammer v. Dagenhart*, 247 U.S. 251 (1918).

6. The background of the pension movement is treated in Abraham Epstein, *Insecurity: A Challenge to America* (New York: Smith and Haas, 1933), pt. 7; I. M. Rubinow, *The Quest for Security* (New York: Holt, 1934), book 4; Paul H. Douglas, *Social Security in the United States* (New York: Whittlesey House, 1936), ch. 1; Harry A. Millis and Royal E. Montgomery, *Labor's Risks and Social Insurance* (New York: McGraw-Hill, 1938), ch. 8; Murray W. Latimer, *Industrial Pension Systems* (New York: Industrial Relations Counselors, 1932), especially vol. 2, ch. 19.

7. Douglas, *Social Security*, 9–11; *Old-Age Pensions*, Hearings before the House Committee on Labor, 71 Cong., 2 sess. (1930); Frank Freidel, *Franklin D. Roosevelt: The Triumph* (Boston: Little, Brown,

1956), 41, 53, 100; Daniel Fusfeld, *The Economic Thought of Franklin D. Roosevelt and the Origins of the New Deal* (New York: Columbia University Press, 1956), 158–61; Andrews to Henry R. Seager, Apr. 29, 1929, Andrews Papers; "New York Commission Recommends Old Age Security," *ALLR*, 20 (Mar. 1930), 73–82; *Bulletin of the American Association for Old Age Security* (became *Old Age Security Herald* in Jan. 1930), Apr., p. 1, Oct. 1929, p. 1, Jan., pp. 1, 4, Mar., pp. 1, 4, Apr. 1930, pp. 1, 3, May 1931, p. 2; Millis and Montgomery, *Labor's Risks*, 380–82; Lescohier and Brandeis, *History of Labor*, 614–16; Epstein, *Insecurity*, 533.

8. Millis and Montgomery, *Labor's Risks*, ch. 3; Lescohier and Brandeis, *History of Labor*, ch. 13; David Loth, *Swope of G.E.* (New York: Simon and Schuster, 1958), 197–98, 202–6; Roosevelt to Swope, July 1, 1930, Roosevelt Papers; "Can Prices, Production and Employment Be Effectively Regulated?" *Proceedings of the Academy of Political Science*, 14 (Jan. 1932), 11–21; BLS, Bull. No. 544, *Unemployment-Benefit Plans in the United States and Unemployment Insurance in Foreign Countries* (1931); Memorandum of Andrews-Swope conference, June 14, 1932, Andrews Papers.

9. Andrews to Wagner, May 17, Wagner to Andrews, May 28, 1930, Wagner Papers; "An American Plan for Unemployment Reserve Funds," American Association for Labor Legislation, Dec. 1930; Douglas to Andrews, n. d., Sargent to Andrews, Dec. 22, 1930, Andrews to Roosevelt, Jan. 1, 1931, Andrews Papers; Leo Wolman, "Unemployment Insurance for the United States," *ALLR*, 21 (Mar. 1931), 21; Leonard P. Adams, "An Analysis of the Recent Legislative Proposals for Unemployment Insurance in the United States" (unpublished Ph.D. dissertation, Cornell University, 1935), 129–30.

10. *New York Times*, July 1, p. 22, Aug. 28, p. 1, Nov. 18, 1930, p. 1, Jan. 24, p. 1, Jan. 26, p. 1, Mar. 7, 1931, p. 34; Frances Perkins, *The Roosevelt I Knew* (New York: Viking, 1946), 102–7; Press Release, May 29, 1931, Roosevelt Papers. An anonymous correspondent, perhaps Ralph Easley of the National Civic Federation, wrote Roosevelt to denounce Douglas as a "red sympathizer." The governor referred the letter to Miss Perkins, who defended Douglas as a recognized authority on unemployment. Anonymous memorandum on Paul Howard Douglas, Dec. 12, 1930, Perkins to Roosevelt, Jan. 6, 1931, Roosevelt Papers.

11. *New York Times*, Mar. 3, p. 23, Mar. 7, p. 34, Mar. 19, p. 2, Mar. 26, p. 20, Apr. 15, 1931, p. 16, Oct. 14, p. 1, Dec. 2, 1932, p. 1, Jan. 29, p. 1, Feb. 20, p. 4, Feb. 21, 1933, p. 21; Andrews to Green, Jan. 8, Green to Andrews, Jan. 9, Andrews to Roosevelt, Apr. 6, 1931, Andrews to Howard Cullman, Oct. 27, 1932, Lehman to Mrs. V. G. Simkhovich, Feb. 16, 1933, Andrews Papers; "Roosevelt on Unemployment Insurance," *ALLR*, 21 (June 1931), 219; Perkins Report, Oct. 23, 1931, Report of the Interstate Commission on Unemployment Insurance, Feb. 15, 1932, Roosevelt Release, Feb. 15, 1932,

Roosevelt Papers; Frances Perkins, "Unemployment Insurance," *Survey*, 67 (Nov. 1, 1931), 117–19.

12. *Report of the Ohio Commission on Unemployment Insurance* (Columbus: 1932); William E. Leiserson, "Ohio's Answer to Unemployment," *Survey*, 58 (Dec. 1, 1932), 643 ff.; I. M. Rubinow, "The Movement toward Unemployment Insurance in Ohio," *Social Service Review*, 7 (June 1933), 186–224; Elizabeth S. Magee, "Ohio Takes Stock," *Proceedings of the National Conference of Social Work* (Chicago: University of Chicago Press, 1933), 285–93; *New York Times*, Dec. 4, 1932, p. 5; Rubinow to Andrews, Dec. 13, 16, 1932, Douglas to Rubinow, Jan. 6, Rubinow to Douglas, Jan. 13, 1933, Rubinow Papers.

13. Roger S. Hoar, *Wisconsin Unemployment Insurance* (South Milwaukee: Stuart, 1934); Charles A. Myers, "Employment Stabilization and the Wisconsin Act" (unpublished Ph.D. dissertation, University of Chicago, 1939); Lescohier and Brandeis, *History of Labor*, 616–20; Paul A. Raushenbush, "The Wisconsin Idea: Unemployment Reserves," *Annals*, 170 (Nov. 1933), 65–75; Paul A. Raushenbush, "The Wisconsin Unemployment Compensation Law," *Proceedings of the National Conference of Social Work* (Chicago: University of Chicago Press, 1933), 275–84; Harold M. Groves, "Compensation for Idle Labor in Wisconsin," *ALLR*, 22 (Mar. 1932), 7; John R. Commons, "The Groves Unemployment Reserves Law," *ALLR*, 22 (Mar. 1932), 8–10; Witte to Andrews, Jan. 16, 1932, Andrews Papers. Morton's attack is "The Aims of Unemployment Insurance with Especial Reference to the Wisconsin Act," *AER*, 23 (Sept. 1933), 396–412. Groves and Miss Brandeis replied in "Wisconsin Unemployment Reserves Act," *AER*, 24 (Mar. 1934), 38–52.

14. Robert F. Wagner, "Rock-Bottom Responsibility," *Survey*, 68 (June 1, 1932), 256; Frankfurter is quoted in Philip Taft, *The A. F. of L. from the Death of Gompers to the Merger* (New York: Harper, 1959), 36; Perkins, *Roosevelt*, 101–2; Perkins to Roosevelt, Dec. 13, 1930, Roosevelt Papers; *New York Times*, Dec. 28, 1930, p. 1, Mar. 1, p. 2, Mar. 19, p. 4, Mar. 21, p. 33, Mar. 23, p. 40, Mar. 24, p. 56, Mar. 26, p. 6, Aug. 11, p. 2, Oct. 20, p. 1, Nov. 7, p. 4, Nov. 14, 1931, p. 3; Robert S. Allen, "Business Talks," *Nation*, 133 (Nov. 25, 1931), 564; *Report of the Select Committee to Investigate Unemployment Insurance*, Senate Report No. 964 (June 30, 1932), 72 Cong., 1 sess.

15. Rubinow to Andrews, Mar. 25, 1931, Andrews Papers.

EPILOGUE (*Pages 505–513*)

1. *Nation*, 135 (Aug. 17, 1932), 145.
2. *Recent Social Trends*, vol. 2, p. 806; "The American Federation of

Labor," *Fortune*, 8 (Dec. 1933), 80; United States Steel Corporation memorandum, n.d., Roosevelt Papers.

3. Paul Y. Anderson, "Buying California for Hoover," *Nation*, 135 (Oct. 26, 1932), 393; the table and the data on mining areas are based upon Edgar Eugene Robinson, *The Presidential Vote, 1896–1932* (Palo Alto: Stanford University Press, 1934); Roy V. Peel and Thomas C. Donnelly, *The 1932 Campaign* (New York: Farrar & Rinehart, 1935), 231; Edward H. Litchfield, *Voting Behavior in a Metropolitan Community* (Ann Arbor: University of Michigan Press, 1941); Samuel J. Eldersveld, *Michigan Politics in Transition* (Ann Arbor: University of Michigan Press, 1942); Harold F. Gosnell and Norman N. Gill, "An Analysis of the 1932 Presidential Vote in Chicago," *American Political Science Review*, 29 (Dec. 1935), 967–84; *Nation*, 135 (Nov. 23, 1932), 487; *AFL Weekly News Service*, July 23, Aug. 13, Sept. 24, Oct. 1, 1932; *UMWJ*, July 1, 1932, p. 6; *Advance*, Nov. 1932, p. 6; *Justice*, June 1932, p. 7; Green to Woll, July 29, Green to Berry, Aug. 16, Sept. 6, 1932, Green Papers; Frey to C. B. Ross, Oct. 12, Dec. 19, 1932, Frey to W. A. Appleton, Jan. 3, 1933, Frey Papers; Frank Freidel, *Franklin D. Roosevelt: The Triumph* (Boston: Little, Brown, 1956), 358.

4. Gardner to Roosevelt, July 22, 1932, *Public Papers and Letters of Oliver Max Gardner*, D. L. Corbitt, ed. (Raleigh, N.C.: Council of State of N. C., 1937), 622–23; Schlesinger, *Crisis*, 484; *Public Papers and Addresses of Franklin D. Roosevelt*, Samuel I. Rosenman, ed. (New York: Random House, 1938–50), vol. 2, pp. 11–16; Morris Markey, "Washington Weekend," in *The Roosevelt Era*, Milton Crane, ed. (New York: Boni and Gaer, 1947), 5.

# Abbreviations Used in This Book

| | |
|---|---|
| AALL | American Association for Labor Legislation |
| ACLU | American Civil Liberties Union |
| AFL | American Federation of Labor |
| AFSC | American Friends Service Committee |
| AICP | Association for Improving the Condition of the Poor |
| AMA | American Management Association |
| ARC | American Red Cross |
| B & O | Baltimore & Ohio Railroad Company |
| BEF | Bonus Expeditionary Force |
| BLS | Bureau of Labor Statistics |
| BRT | Brotherhood of Railroad Trainmen |
| CF & I | Colorado Fuel & Iron Corporation |
| COS | Charity Organization Society |
| CP | Communist Party |
| CPAI | Coal Producers Association of Illinois |
| CP, USA | Communist Party, United States of America |
| DACPU | Dayton Association of Cooperative Production Units |
| ERCA | Emergency Relief and Construction Act |
| FESB | Federal Employment Stabilization Board |
| 4L | Loyal Legion of Loggers and Lumbermen |
| GE | General Electric Company |
| IAM | International Association of Machinists |
| IBEW | International Brotherhood of Electrical Workers |
| ICOA | Illinois Coal Operators Association |
| ILD | International Labor Defense |
| ILGWU | International Ladies' Garment Workers' Union |
| IRC | Industrial Relations Counselors, Inc. |
| ITU | International Typographical Union |
| IWW | Industrial Workers of the World |
| LACE | Los Angeles Cooperative Exchange |
| NAACP | National Association for the Advancement of Colored People |
| NAM | National Association of Manufacturers |
| NDA | Natural Development Association |
| NICB | National Industrial Conference Board |

| NMTA | National Metal Trades Association |
| NMU | National Miners' Union |
| NTW | National Textile Workers Union |
| PECE | President's Emergency Committee for Employment |
| PMA | Progressive Miners of America |
| POUR | President's Organization on Unemployment Relief |
| RFC | Reconstruction Finance Corporation |
| T & NO | Texas & New Orleans Railroad Company |
| TERA | Temporary Emergency Relief Administration |
| TUEL | Trade Union Educational League |
| TUUL | Trade Union Unity League |
| UCL | Unemployed Citizens' League |
| UCRA | Unemployed Cooperative Relief Association |
| UMW | United Mine Workers of America |
| UPL | United Producers League |
| USES | United States Employment Service |
| UTW | United Textile Workers of America |
| WESL | Workers Ex-Servicemen's League |
| WVMWU | West Virginia Mine Workers Union |
| YCL | Young Communist League |

# Index

Abel, Herbert, 381
Abelson, Paul, 74
*Adair* v. *United States*, 199, 398, 406
Adam, H. G., 83, 144, 175, 183
Adamic, Louis, 256, 333, 346, 422, 424, 435
Aderholt, O. F., 24, 26
Adkins, Oscar F., 30–31, 32
*Adkins* v. *Children's Hospital*, 227–232
Agriculture, urban-rural movements, 47–50, 323
Alinsky, Saul, 121
Allen, Frederick Lewis, 416
Allen, Robert S., 502
Alpine, John R., 284–285, 334
Altmeyer, Arthur, 475, 498
American Association for Labor Legislation, 226, 238, 276, 283–284, 475, 484, 486, 487, 490, 491, 493
American Association for Old Age Security, 238, 475, 484, 486
American Association of Public Welfare Officials, 310–311
American Bar Association, 396, 412
American Civil Liberties Union, 25, 27, 28, 380, 410
American Farm Bureau Federation, 237
American Federation of Labor: southern textile organizing campaign, 11–12, 13–20, 29–32, 33–40, 41; on hours, 72; condition in 1920's, 83–86, 142–143; and union-management cooperation, 97–103; conservatism of, 103–104; and 1928 election, 104; and workers' education, 105–106; and Negroes, 107–108; and Communists, 136–139, 141; on judicial policies affecting labor, 194, 207, 215; and Railway Labor

Act, 216; and criminal syndicalism laws, 222; on regulation of hours, 224; on minimum wages, 226; on old age pensions, 238, 484–485, 486, 504; on employment exchanges bill, 275; unsuccessfully urges appointment of AFL official as Secretary of Labor, 334; and racketeering, 338–341; decline of voluntarism, 345–355; movement for national economic conference, 356; anti-injunction campaign, 394–397, 400–403, 407–413, 415; and Bonus Army, 431; supports shorter hours and work-sharing, 476–478, 481–483; and unemployment insurance, 495, 504; general decline, 506; and 1932 election, 511
American Friends Service Committee, 310
American Institute of Architects, 115, 116
American Legion, 431
American Management Association, 171, 176
American Patent Law Association, 396
American Plan, 88, 146 ff., 155, 171; company-union device, 156–157; legality of employer tactics, 205–206
"American Plan for Unemployment Reserve Funds," 491
American Statistical Association, 267
*American Steel Foundries* v. *Tri-City Central Trades Council*, 191, 193–194, 210, 398
American Telephone and Telegraph Co., 168, 306, 478
American Woolen mills, 343
Ameringer, Oscar, 367–370

# ABOUT HAYMARKET BOOKS

Haymarket Books is a nonprofit, progressive book distributor and publisher, a project of the Center for Economic Research and Social Change. We believe that activists need to take ideas, history, and politics into the many struggles for social justice today. Learning the lessons of past victories, as well as defeats, can arm a new generation of fighters for a better world. As Karl Marx said, "The philosophers have merely interpreted the world; the point, however, is to change it."

We take inspiration and courage from our namesakes, the Haymarket Martyrs, who gave their lives fighting for a better world. Their 1886 struggle for the eight-hour day reminds workers around the world that ordinary people can organize and struggle for their own liberation.

For more information and to shop our complete catalog of titles, visit us online at www.haymarketbooks.org.

## ALSO FROM HAYMARKET BOOKS

*The Bending Cross*
A Biography of Eugene Victor Debs • Ray Ginger, introduction by Mike Davis

*The Labor Wars*
From the Molly Maguires to the Sit Downs • Sidney Lens

*Live Working or Die Fighting*
How the Working Class Went Global • Paul Mason

*Revolution in Seattle*
A Memoir • Harvey O'Connor

*Sin Patrón*
Stories from Argentina's Worker-Run Factories • edited by lavaca collective, foreword by Naomi Klein and Avi Lewis

*Subterranean Fire*
A History of Working-Class Radicalism in the United States • Sharon Smith

*The Turbulent Years*
A History of the American Worker, 1933-1941 • Irving Bernstein, introduction by Frances Fox Piven